# Handbook of Parenting

### *Second Edition*

### Volume 1
### Children and Parenting

Edited by

## Marc H. Bornstein

*National Institute of Child Health and Human Development*

Psychology Press
Taylor & Francis Group

New York   Hove

This edition published 2012 by Psychology Press
27 Church Road, Hove, East Sussex, BN32FA
Simultaneously published in the USA and Canada by Psychology Press
711 Third Avenue, New York, NY 10017

Editor:                              Bill Webber
Editorial Assistant:                 Erica Kica
Cover Design:                        Kathryn Houghtaling Lacey
Textbook Production Manager:         Paul Smolenski
Full-Service Compositor:             TechBooks

This book was typeset in 10/11.5 pt. Times, Italic, Bold, Bold Italic.
The heads were typeset in Helvetica, Italic, Bold, Bold Italic.

**Library of Congress Cataloging-in-Publication Data**

Handbook of parenting / edited by Marc H. Bornstein.—2nd ed.
    p.   cm.
    Includes bibliographical references and indexes.
    Contents: v. 1. Children and parenting—v. 2. Biology and ecology of parenting—v. 3. Being
and becoming a parent—v. 4. Social conditions and applied parenting—v. 5. practical issues
in parenting.


    1. Parenting.   2. Parents.   I. Bornstein, Marc H.

HQ755.8.H357   2002
649'.1—dc21                                                    2001058458
First issued in paperback 2012
*Psychology Press is an imprint of the Taylor & Francis Group, an informa business*

ISBN13: 978-0-415-64822-6 (PBK)
ISBN13: 978-0-805-83778-0 (HBK)

10  9  8  7  6  5  4  3  2

For *Marian* and *Harold Sackrowitz*

# Contents of Volume 1: Children and Parenting

# Preface

This new edition of the *Handbook of Parenting* appears at a time that is momentous in the history of parenting. The family generally, and parenting specifically, are today in a greater state of flux, question, and redefinition than perhaps ever before. We are witnessing the emergence of striking permutations on the theme of parenting: blended families, lesbian and gay parents, teen versus fifties first-time moms and dads. One cannot but be awed on the biological front by technology that now renders postmenopausal women capable of childbearing and with the possibility of designing babies. Similarly, on the sociological front, single parenthood is a modern-day fact of life, adult–child dependency is on the rise, and parents are ever less certain of their roles, even in the face of rising environmental and institutional demands that they take increasing responsibility for their offspring. The *Handbook of Parenting* is concerned with all facets of parenting.

Despite the fact that most people become parents and everyone who has ever lived has had parents, parenting remains a most mystifying subject. Who is ultimately responsible for parenting? Does parenting come naturally, or must we learn how to parent? How do parents conceive of parenting? Of childhood? What does it mean to parent a preterm baby, twins, or a child with a disability? To be a younger or an older parent, or one who is divorced, disabled, or drug abusing? What do theories in psychology (psychoanalysis, personality theory, and behavior genetics, for example) contribute to our understanding of parenting? What are the goals parents have for themselves? For their children? What are the functions of parents' beliefs? Of parents' behaviors? What accounts for parents' believing or behaving in similar ways? What accounts for all the attitudes and actions of parents that differ? How do children influence their parents? How do personality, knowledge, and world view affect parenting? How do social status, culture, and history shape parenthood? How can parents effectively relate to schools, daycare, their children's pediatricians?

These are some of the questions addressed in this second edition of the *Handbook of Parenting* . . . for this is a book on *how to parent* as much as it is one on *what being a parent is all about.*

Put succinctly, parents create people. It is the entrusted and abiding task of parents to prepare their offspring for the physical, psychosocial, and economic conditions in which they will eventually fare and, it is hoped, flourish. Amidst the many influences on child development, parents are the "final common pathway" to children's development and stature, adjustment and success. Human social inquiry—at least since Athenian interest in Spartan childrearing practices—has always, as a matter of course, included reports of parenting. Yet Freud opined that childrearing is one of three "impossible professions"—the other two being governing nations and psychoanalysis. And one encounters as many views as the number of people one asks about the relative merits of being an at-home or a working mother, about whether daycare, family care, or parent care is best for a child, about whether good parenting reflects intuition or experience.

The *Handbook of Parenting* concerns itself with different types of parents—mothers and fathers, single, adolescent, and adoptive parents; with basic characteristics of parenting—behaviors, knowledge, beliefs, and expectations about parenting; with forces that shape parenting—employment, social status, culture, environment, and history; with problems faced by parents—handicaps, marital difficulties, drug addiction; and with practical concerns of parenting—how to promote children's health, foster social adjustment and cognitive competence, and interact with school, legal, and public officials. Contributors to the *Handbook of Parenting* have worked in different ways toward understanding all these diverse aspects of parenting, and all look to the most recent research and thinking in the field to shed light on many topics every parent wonders about.

Parenthood is a job whose primary object of attention and action is the child. But parenting also has consequences for parents. Parenthood is giving and responsibility, but parenting has its own intrinsic pleasures, privileges, and profits as well as frustrations, fears, and failures. Parenthood can enhance psychological development, self-confidence, and sense of well-being, and parenthood also affords opportunities to confront new challenges and to test and display diverse competencies. Parents can derive considerable and continuing pleasure in their relationships and activities with their children. But parenting is also fraught with small and large stresses and disappointments. The transition to parenting is formidable; the onrush of new stages of parenthood is relentless. In the final analysis, however, parents receive a great deal "in kind" for the hard work of parenting—they are often recipients of unconditional love, they gain skills, and they even pretend to immortality. This edition of the *Handbook of Parenting* presents the many positives that accompany parenting and offers solutions for the many challenges.

The *Handbook of Parenting* encompasses the broad themes of who are parents, whom parents parent, the scope of parenting and its many effects, the determinants of parenting, and the nature, structure, and meaning of parenthood for parents. This second edition of the *Handbook of Parenting* is divided into five volumes, each with two parts:

Volume 1 concerns CHILDREN AND PARENTING. Parenthood is, perhaps first and foremost, a functional status in the life cycle: Parents issue as well as protect, care for, and represent their progeny. But human development is too subtle, dynamic, and intricate to admit that parental caregiving alone determines the developmental course and outcome of ontogeny. Volume 1 of the *Handbook of Parenting* begins with chapters concerned with how children influence parenting. The origins of parenting are, of course, complex, but certain factors are of obvious importance. First, children affect parenting: Notable are their more obvious characteristics, like age or developmental stage; but more subtle ones, like gender, physical state, temperament, mental ability, and other individual-differences factors, are also instrumental. The chapters in Part I, on Parenting Children and Older People, discuss the unique rewards and special demands of parenting children of different ages—infants, toddlers, youngsters in middle childhood, and adolescents—as well as the modern notion of parent–child relationships in adulthood and later years. The chapters in Part II, on Parenting Children of Varying Status, discuss the common matters of parenting siblings and girls versus boys as well as more unique situations of parenting twins, adopted and foster children, and children with special needs, such as those born preterm, with mental retardation, or aggressive and withdrawn disorders.

Volume 2 concerns the BIOLOGY AND ECOLOGY OF PARENTING. For parenting to be understood as a whole, psychophysiological and sociological determinants of parenting need to be brought into the picture. Volume 2 of the *Handbook* relates parenting to its biological roots and sets parenting within its ecological framework. Some aspects of parenting are influenced by the biological makeup of human beings, and the chapters in Part I, on the Biology of Parenting, examine the evolution of parenting, hormonal and psychobiological determinants of parenting in nonhumans and in human beings, parenting in primates, and intuitive universals in human parenting. A deep understanding of what it means to parent also depends on the ecologies in which parenting takes place. Beyond the nuclear family, parents are embedded in, influence, and are themselves affected by larger social systems. The chapters in Part II, on the Social Ecology of Parenting, examine employment status and parenting, the socioeconomic, cultural, environmental, and historical contexts of parenting, and provide an overarching developmental contextual perspective on parenting.

Volume 3 concerns BEING AND BECOMING A PARENT. A large cast of characters is responsible for parenting, each has her or his own customs and agenda, and the psychological makeups and social interests of those individuals are revealing of what parenting is. Chapters in Part I, on The Parent, show how rich and multifaceted is the constellation of children's caregivers. Considered successively are mothers, fathers, coparenting, single parenthood, grandparenthood, adolescent parenthood, nonparental caregiving, sibling caregivers, parenting in divorced and remarried families, lesbian and gay parents, and the role of contemporary reproductive technologies in parenting. Parenting also draws on transient and enduring physical, personality, and intellectual characteristics of the individual. The chapters in Part II, on Becoming and Being a Parent, consider the transition to parenting, stages of parental development, personality and parenting, parents' knowledge of, beliefs in, cognitions about, attributions for, and attitudes toward childrearing, as well as relations between psychoanalysis and parenthood. Such parental cognitions serve many functions: They generate and shape parental behaviors, mediate the effectiveness of parenting, and help to organize parenting.

Volume 4 concerns SOCIAL CONDITIONS AND APPLIED PARENTING. Parenting is not uniform in all communities, groups, or cultures; rather, parenting is subject to wide variation. Volume 4 of the *Handbook* describes socially defined groups of parents and social conditions that promote variation in parenting. The chapters in Part I, on Social Conditions of Parenting, include ethnic and minority parenting in general and parenting among Latino, African American, and Asian populations, in particular, as well as parents in poverty and parenting and social networks. Parents are ordinarily the most consistent and caring people in the lives of children. In everyday life, however, parenting does not always go right or well. Information, education, and support programs can remedy these ills. The chapters in Part II, on Applied Issues in Parenting, explore parenting competence, maternal deprivation, marital relationships and conflict, parenting with a sensory or physical disability, parental psychopathology, substance-abusing parents, parental child maltreatment, and parent education.

Volume 5 concerns PRACTICAL ISSUES IN PARENTING. Parents meet the biological, physical, and health requirements of children. Parents interact with children socially. Parents stimulate children to engage and understand the environment and to enter the world of learning. Parents provision, organize, and arrange children's home and local environments and the media to which children are exposed. Parents also manage child development vis-à-vis childcare, school, the worlds of medicine and law, as well as other social institutions through their active citizenship. Volume 5 of the *Handbook* describes the nuts and bolts of parenting as well as the promotion of positive parenting practices. The chapters in Part I, on Practical Parenting, review the ethics of parenting, parenting and attachment, child compliance, the development of children's self-regulation, children's prosocial and moral development, socialization and children's values, maximizing children's cognitive abilities, parenting talented children, play in parent–child interactions, everyday stresses and parenting, parents and children's peer relationships, and health promotion. Such caregiving principles and practices have direct effects on children. Parents indirectly influence children as well, for example, through their relationships with each other and their local or larger community. The chapters in Part II, on Parents and Social Institutions, explore parents and their children's childcare, schools, media, and doctors and delve into relations between parenthood and the law and public policy.

Each chapter in the second edition of the *Handbook of Parenting* addresses a different but central topic in parenting; each is rooted in current thinking and theory as well as in classical and modern research in that topic; each has been written to be read and absorbed in a single sitting. Each chapter in this new *Handbook* follows a standard organization, including an introduction to the chapter as a whole, followed by historical considerations of the topic, a discussion of central issues and theory, a review of classical and modern research, forecasts of future directions of theory and research, and a set of conclusions. Of course, each chapter considers the contributors' own convictions and research, but contributions to this new edition of the *Handbook of Parenting* present all major points of view and central lines of inquiry and interpret them broadly. The *Handbook of Parenting* is intended to be both comprehensive and state of the art. To assert that parenting is complex is to understate the obvious. As the expanded scope of this second edition of the *Handbook of Parenting* amply shows, parenting is naturally and closely allied with many other fields.

The *Handbook of Parenting* is concerned with child outcomes of parenting but also with the nature and dimensions of variations in parenting per se. Beyond an impressive range of information, readers will find *passim* critical discussions of typologies of parenting (e.g., authoritarian–autocratic, indulgent–permissive, indifferent–uninvolved, authoritative–reciprocal), theories of parenting (e.g., ecological, psychoanalytic, behavior genetic, ethological, behavioral, sociobiological), conditions of parenting (e.g., mother versus father, cross cultural, situation-by-age-by-style), recurrent themes in parenting studies (e.g., attachment, transaction, systems), and even aphorisms (e.g., "A child should have strict discipline in order to develop a fine, strong character," "The child is father to the man").

In the course of editing this new edition of the *Handbook*, I set about to extract central messages and critical perspectives expressed in each chapter, fully intending to construct a comprehensive Introduction to these volumes. In the end, I took away two significant impressions from my own efforts and the texts of my many collaborators in this work. First, my notes cumulated to a monograph on parenting . . . clearly inappropriate for an Introduction. Second, when all was written and done, I found the chorus of contributors to this new edition of the *Handbook* more eloquent and compelling than one lone voice could ever be. Each chapter in the *Handbook of Parenting* begins with an articulate and persuasive Introduction that lays out, in a clarity, expressiveness, and force (I frankly envy), the meanings and implications of that contribution and that perspective to parenting. In lieu of one Introduction, readers are urged to browse the many Introductions that will lead their way into the *Handbook of Parenting*.

Once upon a time, parenting was a seemingly simple thing: Mothers mothered; Fathers fathered. Today, parenting has many motives, many meanings, and many manifestations. Contemporary parenting is viewed as immensely time consuming and effortful. The perfect mother or father or family is a figment of past imagination. Modern society recognizes "subdivisions" of the call: genetic mother, gestational mother, biological mother, birth mother, social mother. For some, the individual sacrifices that mark parenting arise for the sole and selfish purpose of passing one's genes on to succeeding generations. For others, a second child is conceived to save the life of a first child. A multitude of factors influence the unrelenting advance of events and decisions that surround parenting—biopsychological, dyadic, contextual, historical. Recognizing this complexity is important to informing people's thinking about parenting, especially information-hungry parents themselves. This second edition of the *Handbook of Parenting* explores all these motives, meanings, and manifestations of parenting.

Each day more than three fourths of a million adults around the world experience the rewards and the challenges as well as the joys and the heartaches of becoming parents. The human race succeeds because of parenting. From the start, parenting is a "24/7" job. Parenting formally begins during or before pregnancy and can continue throughout the lifespan: Practically speaking for most, *once a parent, always a parent*. But parenting is a subject about which people hold strong opinions and about which too little solid information or considered reflection exists. Parenting has never come with a *Handbook* . . . until now.

## ACKNOWLEDGMENTS

I would like to express my sincere gratitude to the staffs at Lawrence Erlbaum Associates, Publishers, and TechBooks who perfectly parented production of the *Handbook of Parenting*: Victoria Danahy, Susan Detwiler, Sheila Johnston, Arthur M. Lizza, Paul Smolenski, and Christopher Thornton.

—Marc H. Bornstein

# Foreword

Edward Zigler
*Yale University*

Social scientists' interest in parenting has lagged far behind their attention to other aspects of human development. Early in the twentieth century, professional efforts were child focused, progressing from infant schools to nursery schools to child study centers to work like that of Arnold Gesell to chart the entire course of children's physical and social growth. Few professional people noticed parents, an exception being the U.S. Children's Bureau, which published handbooks devoted to the practical aspects of parenting such as feeding, toilet training, and the stern advice that mothers should not play with their infants so they learn regulation and self-sufficiency (Kessen, in press). By the second half of the century, researchers were immersed in discovering ways to increase children's intelligence. Yet the only notice parents (read: mothers) received in the scientific literature was blame for all types of psychopathology and other deviant child outcomes. Then, in 1965, the first Head Start centers opened their doors to economically disadvantaged preschool-age children and invited their mothers in to assume key roles in the children's preschool education. Years later, the importance of fathers in children's lives was discovered.

Eventually, attention to the critical roles parents play in every facet of child development became more and more common in a host of professional disciplines ranging from education to health care to social work. The literature blossomed so quickly that, when Marc Bornstein decided to synthesize it in 1996, the first edition of this *Handbook of Parenting* filled four thick volumes. The contents amazed and inspired workers, who for the first time realized the breadth of theory and research being conducted in fields far removed from their own. Yet even as readers began to familiarize themselves with this virtual knowledge base on parenting, critics of the view that parents have a profound influence on early development garnered publicity (Bruer, 1999; Harris, 1998). On the heels of and in symbolic rebuttal to such views, this second edition of the *Handbook* fills five thick volumes.

There are two major reasons why professional interest in parenting has gained such rapid momentum. One was the massive effort by a committee of the National Research Council and the Institute of Medicine to evaluate the entire science of early childhood development. The conclusions, published in a book titled *From Neurons to Neighborhoods* (Shonkoff and Phillips, 2000), focused on the importance of early experiences—particularly early relationships—in every type of developmental task. This authoritative work presented clear proof that early parent–child interactions relate to academic, behavioral, socioemotional, and most other outcomes. The scientists were careful to emphasize that human development is a continuous, lifelong process. Although the earliest years have prominence, all stages of growth are critical and are affected by what occurs within the child and in the child's environment. The committee underscored that, although there is ample scientific evidence that "early environments matter and nurturing relationships are essential," this knowledge has not been put to full use. "Society is changing and the needs of young children are not being addressed" (Shonkoff and Phillips, 2000, p. 4).

This leads to the second reason why expert interest in parenting is justified and well timed. Americans in general are pragmatic people who have developed a government expected to be responsive to societal needs. When they sense that something is missing, that there is a problem without a solution or a challenge without the supports to overcome it, they demand that the vacuum be filled and the solutions and supports be forthcoming. Policymakers turn to experts on the matter for knowledge and guides to action. Before that can happen, of course, the experts must have spent time constructing a knowledge set to the point at which it is ready to put to use.

These are truly hard times for parents. Their elemental role of rearing children has taken on many new dimensions, creating some distance between their family needs and supports provided by society. For one, today's parents face what may be unprecedented levels of social and economic stress. In just a few decades, the incidence of such major social problems as failing schools, homelessness, juvenile violence, weapons, and substance abuse has ballooned. Although poverty affects a smaller but still significant percentage of the population, its face has grown uglier and the gap between the haves and the have-nots has widened. In many communities, poverty and its accompanying stressors make it difficult for parents to create a decent life for themselves, much less protect their children from harm and plan for their futures. Such anxieties have an especially hard impact on households headed by single parents (usually a mother)—a now relatively common type of family structure (approximately 25% of all children and over 60% of African American children). In many cases the double disadvantage of poverty and single parenting is combined with extreme youth, as the number of father-absent teenage births remains extremely high compared with that of just a few generations ago. Teen mothers can be expected to lack adequate guidance, support, and preparation for parenthood, but in this they are not alone. With today's mobile lifestyle and changing family structures, most parents miss the cross-generational passing down of childrearing wisdom that once occurred within extended families.

Today's brands of economic stresses affect single- and two-parent families alike. Single parents no longer have welfare payments as an option and must be in the labor force (or at the very least preparing for it). Among married couples, both parents typically work outside the home to make ends meet. There are two added stresses on parents who have employment, which is the large majority of all parents: the stress of finding quality childcare they can afford and the stress of having too little time to spend with their children. To make matters worse, a large number of adults today are in the so-called "sandwich generation," caring for their elderly parents even as they struggle to rear their own children.

Parents living in the United States must tackle all of these challenges largely without the considerable social supports offered in other industrialized nations. Such supports include paid parental leave and government-subsidized childcare, health care, and higher education. Although America's policymakers have shown increased interest in supportive programming and some improvement in meeting family needs (e.g., passage of an unpaid parental leave law in the form of the Family and Medical Leave Act), parents are still largely on their own in the challenging and complex task of nurturing those who will take over the nation.

However, Americans do not like vacuums, and American parents today are demanding that something be done to help them be better parents. The *Handbook of Parenting* should prove invaluable in meeting this need for expert guidance. Of course, this is not a handbook in the sense of a manual, although the chapters describing what it is like, for example, to parent a child born prematurely or how to foster sound moral development, can offer valuable insights. Rather, the volumes that make up the *Handbook* offer a comprehensive account of the state of our scientific and social knowledge regarding virtually every facet of parenting, from a social history of the topic to its psychological, educational, medical, and legal aspects. The knowledge represented in these five volumes should help professionals to help parents and also to meet the critical need for increased family supports by enlightening our policymakers. This knowledge can immediately be put to use by such home visitation programs as Parents as Teachers and Healthy Families America. It will also provide the scholarly underpinnings of the myriad of family support programs that can now be found coast to coast.

At minimum, the stellar contributors assembled for the *Handbook of Parenting* succeed admirably in their effort to capture and describe the many aspects of parenting today. These volumes have an extraordinary scope in that the authors share with us an impressive breadth, as well as depth, of experience and learning. The writers are acknowledged experts in their individual fields, and they represent a remarkable diversity of perspective. This comprehensive approach is essential to reveal the social ecology of parenthood.

All of the forces that make up the larger sociopolitical world create the context in which parents must nurture, educate, and struggle to understand their children and themselves as parents. The *Handbook of Parenting* offers us a detailed roadmap to that context. It tells us a good deal about the needs, beliefs, troubles, wishes, and triumphs of the parents who inhabit our increasingly complex society. The contributors to this excellent compendium have provided a great resource for parents and for the clinicians, educators, and other professionals who strive to assist parents in carrying out their important work as guardians of the next generation. They have also provided policymakers with a solid base of knowledge to guide the construction of family-friendly social policies.

## REFERENCES

Bruer, J. T. (1999). *The myth of the first three years.* New York: Free Press.
Harris, J. R. (1998). *The nurture assumption: Why children turn out the way they do. Parents matter less than you think and peers matter more.* New York: Free Press.
Kessen, W. (in press). *Untitled Children's Bureau Book.* New Haven, CT: Yale University Press.
Shonkoff, J. P., and Phillips, D. A. (Eds.). (2000). *From neurons to neighborhoods. The science of early childhood development.* Washington, DC: National Academy Press.

# Foreword

## Jerome Kagan
### *Harvard University*

The replacement of experiential explanations of the emergence of universal dispositions or individual variation with biological ones has occurred rapidly and with much less resistance than I would have expected, given the implications of this substitution. The reasons for the shift in perspective are multiple.

On the one hand, thousands of hours of observations of parents interacting with children have not yielded conclusions with the effect sizes investigators expected. Almost 20 years ago, Maccoby and Martin, following a thorough examination of the evidence on family socialization, concluded, "In most cases, the relationships that have appeared are not large. . . . The implications are either that parental behaviors have no effect, or that the only effective aspects of parenting must vary greatly from one child to another within the same family." How can we explain such a pessimistic conclusion?

One reason is that most of the research was relatively unsophisticated. Some investigators asked a mother how she behaved with her child. Others based inferences on less than an hour of observation in a laboratory waiting room. Neither source of evidence was likely to yield robust insights. More important, many psychologists expected to find a relation between what parents did and particular child outcomes and failed to appreciate that the child is always interpreting the actions of parents. The effect of every experience, for example a father's prolonged absence or a divorce, depends on how the child interprets the event. Rarely is there a fixed consequence of any particular event, even a traumatic one.

Most scholars now recognize that parents affect children in subtle and complex ways that are not revealed by crude methods. The assumption that the family has power is supported by the chapters in this *Handbook*, as well as by the fact that the profiles of children from different class or ethnic groups, all of whom watch the same television programs and attend the same movies, can be dramatically different. For example, Mexican American children are more cooperative and less competitive than African American or European American children living in the same town or city. Japanese children in California work harder in school than Mexican American children from the same region.

Few social scientists would argue with the claim that the experiences associated with a family's social status have a profound influence on development. Well-educated parents are generally more convinced than less well-educated ones that their child can develop internal controls on temptation. Less well-educated parents are more likely to believe that much of the control lies in the outside environment. Middle-socioeconomic parents expect that their decisions and actions have consequences and therefore have faith in their ability to control life events and to guide their children, through their agency, to the ego ideal they hold. Economically less-advantaged parents are vulnerable to believing that they are victims of forces beyond their control. That is one reason why children from families divergent in social-status background develop very different phenotypes. Emmy Werner's elegant longitudinal study of Hawaiian children revealed that the social status of the child's family was the best predictor of asocial behavior, school drop-out rates, and the development of psychiatric symptoms.

The chapters in this *Handbook* document that parents affect their children through at least three different mechanisms. The most obvious, and the one easiest to measure, refers to the consequences of interactions with the child that can be recorded on film. A mother praises her 3-year-old toddler for eating properly or names an unfamiliar animal in a picture book. These mundane events, which often involve the rewarding of desirable actions and the punishment of undesirable ones, have a cumulative effect. That is why a consistent failure to discipline acts of disobedience or aggression is predictive of later asocial behavior.

These first-order effects have second-order consequences that often appear in later childhood and adolescence. An 8-year-old child with a more extensive vocabulary than her peers, because her parents encouraged language development during the preschool years, will master the tasks of the elementary school more easily and perceive herself as more competent than many of her peers. This belief will embolden the child to resist domination by others and motivate the initiation of challenging tasks.

An emotional identification with parents and one's social status and ethnic category represents the second, different way families affect children. Most 5-year-old children believe, unconsciously, that some of the attributes of their parents are part of their own repertoire, even though this belief has little objective foundation. A girl with a mother who is afraid of storms is tempted to assume that she, too, is afraid of this danger. By contrast, a girl with a relatively bold, fearless mother will come to the opposite conclusion.

The third form of family influence is more symbolic. Some parents tell and retell stories about relatives who were, or are, especially accomplished in some domain. Perhaps an uncle made an important discovery, performed a courageous act, or was a talented athlete, writer, or public official. The child feels pride on hearing these stories because of the implication that, because the child is biologically related to that family member, she or he, too, might possess some part of the admirable characteristics. George Homans, an influential Harvard sociologist, noted in a memoir written shortly before his death, that he coped with his childhood anxiety over poor school grades and unpopularity with peers by reminding himself that he could trace his pedigree to John Adams. Charles Darwin's description of his father glows with awe for his father's intelligence, sympathy, kindness, and good business sense. Darwin knew about the inheritance of psychological features because of his acquaintance with animal breeders and may have felt that, given his family's eminence, his talents were inevitable.

Direct interactions, identifications, and knowledge of the accomplishments of family members are three of the ways families affect children. The first mechanism has its most profound effect on cognitive development and character traits. The second and the third have a greater influence on children's confidence or doubt about their talents and therefore on expectations of future success or failure when a challenge is encountered.

However, the family represents only one component of a large constellation of conditions. A child's temperamental biases, size of community, peer friendships, school quality, chance events, and, always, the historical era in which the adolescent years are spent, share power with the family. The influence of the historical period is seen in Glen Elder's study of the cohort of Americans who were between 10 and 20 years of age during the economic depression in America from 1930 to the beginning of the Second World War. A large proportion of those adolescents, who are now in their seventh decade, saved more money than the generation before or after them and conducted their lives with a gnawing concern over financial loss.

The youth protests against the Vietnam War at the end of the 1960s affected a large numbers of privileged adolescents who turned against established authority. Some college students seized administration buildings and shared sexual partners in unheated communal homes during long winters. Some high school youth marched out of their classrooms to protest the war and got away with it.

It is heady for a 16-year-old teenager to defy the rules of authority and escape punishment. Such experiences erode a tendency to worry too much about coming to work at 10 in the morning instead of 9 and leaving at 4 instead of 5. A proportion of American middle-socioeconomic youth thumbed their noses at authority because they happened to be young adults during a brief period when many adults in American society were uncertain of the legitimacy of such actions.

It is more accurate therefore to describe the effects of the family by arguing that parental qualities contribute to a child's profile rather than claim that family conditions determine particular outcomes. Eleanor Maccoby has also argued that the contribution of parental practices to children's personality cannot be viewed in isolation. Put plainly, the consequences of growing up in a home in which both parents work from 8 to 6, five days a week, will depend on the child's temperamental vulnerability to uncertainty, the economic resources of the family, the values of the peers in the surrogate care context, and whether 10%, 50%, or 70% of the children in that community have working parents.

The values of this extraordinarily rich *Handbook* rest, in part, on its acknowledgment of the many factors that sculpt the child. The editor and the authors are entitled to our gratitude for the conscientiousness and wisdom they brought to their assignments.

# Contents of Volume 2:
# Biology and Ecology of Parenting

# PART II: SOCIAL ECOLOGY OF PARENTING

# Contents of Volume 3: Being and Becoming a Parent

# Contents of Volume 4:
# Social Conditions and Applied Parenting

## PART II: APPLIED ISSUES IN PARENTING

# Contents of Volume 5:
# Practical Issues in Parenting

# About the Authors in Volume 1

**MARC H. BORNSTEIN** is Senior Investigator and Head of Child and Family Research at the National Institute of Child Health and Human Development. He holds a B.A. from Columbia College and a Ph.D. from Yale University. Bornstein was a Guggenheim Foundation Fellow and received a RCDA from the NICHD, the Ford Cross-Cultural Research Award from the HRAF, the McCandless Young Scientist Award from the APA, the United States PHS Superior Service Award from the NIH, and the Arnold Gesell Prize from the Theodor Hellbrügge Foundation. Bornstein has held faculty positions at Princeton University and New York University as well as visiting academic appointments in Munich, London, Paris, New York, and Tokyo. Bornstein is Editor Emeritus of *Child Development* and Editor of *Parenting: Science and Practice*. He has contributed scientific papers in the areas of human experimental, methodological, comparative, developmental, cross-cultural, neuro-scientific, pediatric, and aesthetic psychology. Bornstein is coauthor of *Development in Infancy* (four editions) and general editor of *The Crosscurrents in Contemporary Psychology Series* (ten volumes) and the *Monographs in Parenting* (four volumes). He also edited the *Handbook of Parenting* (Vols. I–V, two editions), and he coedited *Developmental Psychology: An Advanced Textbook* (four editions) as well as a dozen other volumes. He is the author of several children's books and puzzles in *The Child's World* series.

\* \* \*

**DAVID M. BRODZINSKY** is Associate Professor in the Department of Psychology and Director of the Foster Care Counseling Project in the Graduate School of Applied and Professional Psychology at Rutgers University. He received his B.A. and Ph.D. from the State University of New York at Buffalo. Brodzinsky is past Vice-President of the Jean Piaget Society. His current research interests include the psychology of adoption and foster care, stress and coping in children, and divorce and child custody. He maintains a private practice in psychology, focusing on child and family therapy, as well as court-related evaluations associated with child custody, guardianship hearings, contested adoptions, and child abuse. Brodzinsky is the coauthor of *Being Adopted: The Lifelong Search for Self* and *Children's Adjustment to Adoption: Developmental and Clinical Issues* as well as coeditor of *The Psychology of Adoption* and *Adoption and Prenatal Alcohol and Drug Exposure: Research, Policy, and Practice*.

\* \* \*

**KIM B. BURGESS** is an Assistant Research Professor in the Department of Human Development, University of Maryland at College Park. Burgess received her Honors B.Sc. at the University of Victoria and Ph.D. from the University of Ottawa, Canada. She is on the Editorial Board of *Child Development*. Her research focuses on child psychological adjustment, peer relationships, and parent–child relationships.

\* \* \*

**W. ANDREW COLLINS** is Rodney S. Wallace Professor for the Advancement of Teaching and Learning and Morse-Alumni Distinguished Teaching Professor at the Institute of Child Development, University of Minnesota. He received his Ph.D. from Stanford University. Collins has served as Director of the Institute of Child Development, as Secretary of the Society for Research in Child Development, and as President of the Society for Research on Adolescence. Collins's interests are in the study of social processes and relationships in middle childhood and adolescence, and he has investigated developmental aspects of children's and adolescents' responses to television and parent–child and peer relationships during the transitions to adolescence and to young adulthood. He served as chair of the National Research Council's Panel on the Status of Basic Research on Middle Childhood (ages 6–12 years) and was editor of *Development During Middle Childhood: The Years from Six to Twelve*. Collins also coedited *Relationships as Developmental Contexts*.

\* \* \*

**BARBARA A. DIVITTO** is a Psychologist at the Neurodevelopmental Center, North Shore Children's Hospital, Salem, Massachusetts. She received her B.A. from Mount Holyoke College, M.A. from Tufts University, and Ph.D. from Brandeis University. She has worked at the Pediatric Rehabilitation Program, Jewish Memorial Hospital, Boston, and the Developmental Disabilities Unit of Massachusetts Mental Health Center, Boston, and has been co-director of education for the Boston Institute for the Development of Infants and Parents. Divitto's interests include socioemotional development, parent education in high-risk groups, and mood disorders in children. She is coauthor of *Born too Soon: Preterm Birth and Early Development*.

\* \* \*

**CAROLYN POPE EDWARDS** is Professor of Psychology and Family and Consumer Sciences at the University of Nebraska, Lincoln. She earned her doctorate in human development and bachelor's degree from Harvard University. She has been an invited Senior Fellow at the Norwegian Centre for Advanced Study in Oslo and Visiting Professor of psychology at the National Research Council in Rome and has held faculty positions at the University of Kentucky, University of Massachusetts–Amherst, and Vassar College. Edwards' interests center on social and moral development in cultural context and socialization processes within the family and childcare and educational settings. Her books include *Promoting Social and Moral Development of Young Children; Creative Ideas for the Classroom*; and *Children of Different Worlds: The Formation of Social Behavior*, along with the edited works, *Bambini: The Italian Approach to Infant-Toddler Care* and *The Hundred Languages of Children: The Reggio Emilia Approach to Early Childhood Education*.

\* \* \*

**DAVID J. EGGEBEEN** is an Associate Professor of Human Development and Senior Research Associate, Population Research Institute at the Pennsylvania State University. He received his B.A. from Calvin College and his M.A. and Ph.D. from the University of North Carolina–Chapel Hill. His research interests include the changing social demography of childhood, intergenerational support over the life course, and fatherhood.

\* \* \*

**WYNDOL FURMAN** is a Professor and Director of Clinical Training in the Department of Psychology at the University of Denver. He received a B.A. from Duke University, an M.A. from George Peabody College, and a Ph.D. from the University of Minnesota. He was a W. T. Grant Faculty Scholar and received the Provost's Award and the Distinguished Scholar Award from the University of Denver. His research interests have focused on children and adolescents' close relationships, including relationships with siblings, parents, friends, and romantic partners. Furman coedited *The Development of Romantic Relationships in Adolescence*.

\* \* \*

**SUSAN GOLDBERG** is a Research Scientist in the Research Institute at the Hospital for Sick Children, Toronto, and Professor of Psychiatry and Psychology at the University of Toronto. She completed her undergraduate work at Antioch College (A.B.), her graduate studies at Tufts University (M.S.) and University of

Massachusetts (Ph.D.), and taught at Brandeis University. Her research focuses on early parent–child relationships and how they are influenced by early diagnosed medical problems. She is coauthor of *Born too Soon: Preterm Birth and Early Development* and author of *Attachment and Development*.

\* \* \*

**JEFFREY HAUGAARD** is Associate Professor of Human Development and Stephen H. Weiss Presidential Fellow at Cornell University. He received his B.A. from the University of California at Santa Cruz, an M.A. from Santa Clara University, and Ph.D. from the University of Virginia. He was the Founding President of the Section on Child Maltreatment of the Division of Child, Youth, and Family Services of the American Psychological Association. He is an associate editor of *Law and Human Behavior* and is on the editorial boards of *Child Maltreatment* and *Adoption Quarterly*. He was a foster father for a boy who came from Viet Nam and continues in his expanded role of foster father, foster father-in-law, and foster grandfather. Haugaard is the author of *Problematic Behaviors During Adolescence* and *The Sexual Abuse of Children*.

\* \* \*

**CINDY HAZAN** is Associate Professor in the Department of Human Development at Cornell University. She received her education (B.A., M.A., and Ph.D.) at the University of Denver. She is a member of the American Psychological Society, International Society for the Study of Personal Relationships, the New York Academy of Sciences, is on the editorial board for *Personal Relationships*, and is a consulting editor for *Personality and Social Psychology Bulletin*. Her research interests include processes of attachment formation, pair bonding, and evolutionary models of human mating.

\* \* \*

**ROBERT M. HODAPP** is Professor in the Department of Education, Graduate School of Education and Information Studies, at the University of California, Los Angeles. Hodapp received his B.A. from Columbia College and Ph.D. from Boston University. His research interests concern developmental issues in children with mental retardation and the development of and parental reactions toward children with different genetic syndromes of mental retardation. He is on the editorial boards of the *American Journal on Mental Retardation*, *Mental Retardation*, and *Early Education and Development*. Hodapp is the author of *Development and Disabilities* and coauthor of *Genetics and Mental Retardation Syndromes*, and he coedited *Issues in the Developmental Approach to Mental Retardation* and the *Handbook of Mental Retardation and Development*.

\* \* \*

**RICHARD P. LANTHIER** is Assistant Professor of Human Development at The George Washington University in Washington, D.C. He received his Ph.D. from the University of Denver and previously held an appointment at Texas Tech University. Lanthier's current research interests revolve around social relationships and personality across the lifespan.

\* \* \*

**CAMPBELL LEAPER** is Professor in the Department of Psychology and Associate Dean of Social Sciences at the University of California at Santa Cruz. He was educated at Boston University (B.A.) and UCLA (Ph.D.). Leaper was a NIMH research fellow at Harvard Medical School. He is a member of the American Psychological Association, the American Psychological Society, the Society for Research in Child Development, the Society for Research on Adolescence, the International Society for the Study of Behavioral Development, the International Society for the Study of Personal Relationships, and the Society for Personality and Social Psychology. He is currently on the editorial board of *Developmental Psychology* and *Sex Roles*. His research focuses on the origins and consequences of gender inequities across the lifespan, how gender is defined and maintained, and contextual influences on gender development. Leaper edited *Childhood Gender Segregation: Causes and Consequences*.

\* \* \*

**WEN–LI LIU** is in the interdisciplinary doctoral program in Human Resources and Family Sciences at the University of Nebraska-Lincoln. She earned her bachelor's degree in biology from Beijing Teacher's College, her master's degree in education from Beijing Normal University, and her master's degree in family and consumer sciences from the University of Nebraska-Lincoln. Her interests center on sex education and early childhood education, including parents' knowledge, attitudes, and practices around sex education for adolescents. Liu coauthored *Sexual Behavior in Modern China—Report on the Nationwide Survey of 20,000 Men and Women*.

\* \* \*

**HUGH LYTTON** is Professor Emeritus of Educational Psychology, University of Calgary, Canada. Lytton received his training in school and clinical child psychology at the Tavistock Clinic, London, and his Ph.D. at the University of London, England. After service in the Armed Forces during World War II, his career spanned school teaching and professional (child clinical and school) psychology in England and Scotland. He then taught at the Universities of Exeter, England, and Calgary, Canada. He is a Fellow of the British Psychological Society and of the Canadian Psychological Association. His research interests—mainly in the areas of developmental and educational psychology—have focused on bidirectional effects in parent–child relationships and on issues surrounding the origins of moral and antisocial behavior in genetic–biological substrates and in interactions within the family and the social environment. Lytton's books include *Creativity and Education*, *Parent–Child Interaction: The Socialization Process Observed in Twin and Singleton Families*, and *Social Development: History, Theory and Research*.

\* \* \*

**STEPHANIE D. MADSEN** is a graduate student at the Institute of Child Development at the University of Minnesota. She received her B.A. from Carleton College and her M.A. from the University of Minnesota. Madsen is engaged in research on the parental influence on adolescent romantic relationships and the salience of adolescent romantic experiences for relationships in young adulthood.

\* \* \*

**ELLEN E. PINDERHUGHES** is Research Assistant Professor in the Department of Psychology and Human Development at Peabody College, Vanderbilt University. She received her B.A. from the University of Colorado at Colorado Springs and her Ph.D. from Yale University. Her research focuses on child and family adjustment in special-needs adoptions, cultural and contextual influences on parenting, and prevention of conduct problems in adolescence.

\* \* \*

**SAMUEL P. PUTNAM** is Assistant Professor at Bowdoin College. He received his B.S. from the University of Iowa and completed his Ph.D. at the Pennsylvania State University. He was a postdoctoral research associate at the University of Oregon. His research interests include approach/withdrawal behavior in infants and young children, relations between emotional behavior and autonomic nervous system activity, and interactions between parenting and temperament in the development of normal and problem behaviors.

\* \* \*

**MARY K. ROTHBART** is a Distinguished Professor of Psychology at the University of Oregon and Senior Fellow at the Sackler Institute for Developmental Psychobiology, Weill Medical College of Cornell University, New York. Her undergraduate work was completed at Reed College and her graduate studies at Stanford University. She is the current recipient of a Senior Scientist Award and MERIT Research Award from the National Institutes of Health. Her work on temperament has included the development of measures involving parent report (the Infant Behavior Questionnaire, Supplement to the Toddler Behavior Assessment Questionnaire, Children's Behavior Questionnaire) and self-report (the Early Adolescent Temperament Questionnaire, Adult Temperament Questionnaire), standardized laboratory observations (the Laboratory Temperament Assessment Battery), and home observations. She studies the early development of attention in relation to temperamental self-regulation.

She has coedited *Temperament in Childhood* and is coauthor of *Early Development of Attention: Themes and Variations.*

\* \* \*

**KENNETH H. RUBIN** is Director and Professor, Center for Children, Relationships, and Culture in the Department of Human Development, University of Maryland. He received his B.A. from McGill University, Canada, and his M.S. and Ph.D. from the Pennsylvania State University. Rubin is a Fellow of the Canadian and American Psychological Associations and has been a recipient of both a Killam Research Fellowship (Canada Council) and an Ontario Mental Health Senior Research Fellowship. He has been an Associate Editor of *Child Development* and is currently President of the International Society for the Study of Behavioral Development. Rubin's research interests include the study of children's peer and family relationships and their social and emotional development.

\* \* \*

**ANN V. SANSON** is an Associate Professor in Psychology at the University of Melbourne and Principal Research Fellow at the Australian Institute of Family Studies. She completed a B.A. at the University of Western Australia and a Ph.D. at La Trobe University. She studies temperament in children from infancy to 18 years of age, and her research interests revolve around the interplay of intrinsic child characteristics and family and contextual factors in the development of good and poor psychosocial adjustment. She is a Fellow of the Australian Psychological Society and has held various positions in the Society, including Vice President and Director of Social Issues, and is a member of the Committee for the Psychological Study of Peace of the International Union of Psychological Science.

\* \* \*

**JENNIFER S. SILK** is a doctoral candidate in clinical psychology in the Department of Psychology at Temple University. She received her B.A. from the University of Virginia and earned an M.A. from Temple University. Her research interests include the study of developmental psychopathology, affect regulation among children and adolescents, family interactions, and adolescent development.

\* \* \*

**LAURENCE STEINBERG** is the Distinguished University Professor and Laura H. Carnell Professor of Psychology at Temple University. He taught previously at the University of California, Irvine, and at the University of Wisconsin—Madison. Steinberg was educated at Vassar College and at Cornell University, where he received his Ph.D. He is a Fellow of the American Psychological Association and the immediate Past-President of the Society for Research on Adolescence. Steinberg is the author or coauthor of *You and Your Adolescent: A Parent's Guide for Ages 10 to 20; Adolescence; When Teenagers Work: The Psychological and Social Costs of Adolescent Employment; Crossing Paths: How Your Child's Adolescence Triggers Your Own Crisis; Studying Minority Adolescents: Conceptual, Methodological, and Theoretical Issues; Beyond the Classroom;* and *Why School Reform Has Failed and What Parents Need to Do.*

\* \* \*

**AMY SUSMAN-STILLMAN** is Program Coordinator at the Irving B. Harris Training Center for Infant and Toddler Development at the University of Minnesota. She received her Ph.D. from the Institute of Child Development at the University of Minnesota. Susman-Stillman is interested in understanding ecological influences on social and emotional development in early and middle childhood and in adolescence. Her interests also extend to the application of developmental science, particularly linking research findings with practice and public policy. Susman-Stillman has served on SRCD's Committee on Child Development, Public Policy and

Public Information and has engaged in policy education for the Children, Youth and Family Consortium at the University of Minnesota. She is currently serving on the editorial board of the Michigan State University Series on Children, Youth, and Families.

*   *   *

**STEVEN H. ZARIT** is Professor of Human Development and Assistant Director of the Gerontology Center at the Pennsylvania State University and Adjunct Professor, Institute of Gerontology, University College of Health Sciences in Jönköping, Sweden. He received his B.A. from the University of Michigan, his A.M. from the University of Pennsylvania, and his Ph.D. from the University of Chicago. He is a Fellow of the American Psychological Association and the Gerontological Society of America, former member and chair of the Committee on Aging of the APA, and a member of the National Advisory Board of the Alzheimer's Association. His research interests include stresses and interventions for family caregivers of older people and functional competency of the oldest-old population. He is coauthor of *Mental Disorders in Older Adults: Principles of Assessment and Treatment.*

*   *   *

# Handbook of Parenting

**Volume 1
Children and Parenting**

# PART I

## PARENTING CHILDREN AND OLDER PEOPLE

# 1

# Parenting Infants

Marc H. Bornstein
*National Institute of Child Health and Human Development*

*New parents around the world use similar-sounding familial kin terms, such as /ma/, /pa/, and /da/. Why? The linguistic theorist Jakobson (1971) once proposed the romantic view that parents adopt as names for themselves the sounds that infants initially produce. Jakobson (1969) claimed that, when infants first begin to speak, their articulations are limited to a set of sounds that follow a universal pattern of development based on the anatomical structure of the oral cavity and vocal tract and on ease of motor control (Kent, 1984). In this view, certain sound combinations—consonants articulated at the lips (/m/ and /p/) or teeth (/d/), and vowels articulated at the back of the oral cavity (/a/)—have primacy because their production maximizes contrasts. Thus infants' earliest sound combinations consist of front consonants with back vowels. Significantly, of four logically possible combinations, the front-consonant–back-vowel pairs (pa/, /da/, and /ma) are used as parental kin terms in nearly 60% of more than 1,000 of the world's languages, many more than would be expected by chance (Murdock, 1959). It seems that parents of infants have adopted as generic labels for themselves their infants' earliest vocal productions.*

## INTRODUCTION

Nothing stirs the emotions or rivets the attention of adults more than the birth of a child. By their very coming into existence, infants forever alter the sleeping, eating, and working habits of their parents; they change who parents are and how parents define themselves. Infants unthinkingly keep parents up late into the night or cause them to abandon late nights to accommodate early waking; they unknowingly require parents to give up a rewarding career to care for them or to take a second job to support them; they unwittingly lead parents to make new friends of others in similar situations and sometimes cause parents to abandon or lose old friends who are not parents. Yes, parents may even take for themselves the names that infants uncannily bestow. Parenting an infant is a "24/7" job, whether by the parent herself or himself or by a surrogate caregiver who is on call. That is because the human infant is totally dependent on parents for survival. Unlike the newborn colt which is on its feet within minutes of birth or the newborn chick which forages on its own more or less immediately after being hatched, the newborn human cannot walk, talk, or even ingest food without the aid of a competent caregiver. In a given year, approximately 4 million new babies are born in the United

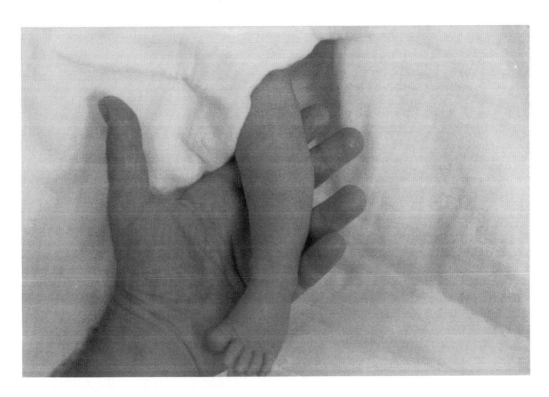

States, and worldwide each day approximately three fourths of a million adults experience the joys and heartaches and challenges and rewards of becoming new parents (Population Reference Bureau, 2000). The wonder is that every day 11,000 babies are born in the United States (National Center for Health Statistics, 2000), a number equivalent to the population of a small town—and yet each one is unique and special.

Infancy defines the period of life between birth and the emergence of language approximately $1\frac{1}{2}$ to 2 years into childhood. Our generic terms "infant" and "baby" both have their origins in language-related concepts. The word infant derives from the Latin *in + fans*, translated literally as "nonspeaker," and the word baby shares a Middle English root with "babble" (another front-consonant—back-vowel combination). Our *newborn* and *infant* are for the Chagga of Tanganyika *mnangu* (the "incomplete one") and *mkoku* ("one who fills lap"). For us, children are infants until they talk, and become toddlers when they walk; but for the Alor of the Lesser Sundra Islands, the first stage of infancy lasts from birth to the first smile, and the second stage from the smile to the time when the child can sit alone or begins to crawl (Mead and Newton, 1967, in Fogel, 1984).

Infancy encompasses only a small fraction of the average person's life expectancy, but it is a period highly attended to and invested in by parents all over the world. Parenting responsibilities are greatest during infancy, when the child is most dependent on caregiving and the child's ability to cope alone is almost nonexistent. Not by chance, infants' physiognomic structures are especially attractive to adults; infants engender feelings of responsibility and solicitude. Infants are also fun to observe, to talk to, and to play with; infants do not know how to be agonistic, deceiving, or malicious, but infants make undeniable demands. Furthermore, infancy is a period of rapid development in practically all spheres of human expression and function, and people are perennially fascinated by the dramatic ways in which the helpless and disorganized human newborn transforms into the competent and curious and frustrating and frustrated child.

Reciprocally, infants may profit most from parental care. Infancy is the phase of the life cycle when adult caregiving is not only at its most intense, but is thought to exert significant influence.

Infants are believed to be particularly susceptible and responsive to external events. The sheer amount of interaction between parent and child is greatest in infancy; parents spend more than twice as much time with their infants as they do with their children in middle childhood (Hill and Stafford, 1980). In effect, parents and caregivers are responsible for determining most, if not all, of infants' earliest experiences. It is the evolutionary and continuing task of parents to prepare their children for the physical, economic, and psychosocial situations in which they are to develop (Benedict, 1938; Bornstein, 1991; LeVine, 1988). Parents everywhere appear highly motivated to carry out this task, and infants are reciprocally sensitive to their parents. From a very early age, they appear to recognize and prefer the sights, sounds, and smells of their caregivers (Bornstein and Arterberry, 1999) and over the course of the first year develop deep and lifelong attachments to them (Cummings and Cummings, in Vol. 5 of this *Handbook*).

At their best, parent and infant activities are characterized by intricate patterns of synchronous interactions and sensitive *mutual* understandings (Bornstein, 1989a; Bornstein and Tamis-LeMonda, 1990; Sroufe and Fleeson, 1986; Stern, 1985), or, as Winnicott (1965, p. 39) put it, "There is no such thing as an infant." One study submitted 2- to 4-month-old infants' sensitivities in interacting to tests (Murray and Trevarthen, 1985). Infants first viewed real-time images of their mothers interacting with them by means of closed-circuit television, and during this period infants were seen to react with normal interest and pleasure. Immediately afterward, infants watched the videotaped recording of the same interaction; this time the infants exhibited signs of distress. The infants' negative reactions were considered to arise out of the lack of synchrony with their mothers that the babies suddenly experienced. Even months-old infants are sensitive to the presence or the absence of appropriate parenting interactions.

In this chapter, the salient features of parenting infants are presented. First, a brief history of interest in parenting infants is provided, followed by a discussion of the theoretical significance attached to parenting infants. Next, characteristics of infants and infant development that are especially meaningful for parenting are described, including developmental changes in state, stature, and physical abilities, perceiving, thinking, acquiring language, expressing emotions, and interacting socially. Then the main part of the chapter reviews principles of parenting infants, including direct and indirect effects, parenting beliefs and behaviors, stylistic differences between mothers and fathers, and probable mechanisms of action of these parenting principles. Next, forces that shape parenting during infancy are outlined, including biology, personality, infant effects, and various social, socioeconomic, and cultural determinants. Finally, nonparental (i.e., sibling, familial, and nonfamilial) infant caregiving is briefly discussed.

## A GLANCE AT THE HISTORY OF PARENTING INFANTS

Infancy is an easily definable stage of life, based on biological and mental data as well as on social convention. Infants do not speak, whereas young and old people do; infants creep and crawl, whereas young and old people walk and run. Harkness and Super (1983, p. 223) suggested that "a primary function of culture in shaping human experience is the division of the continuum of human development into meaningful segments, or 'stages. . . .' All cultures . . . recognize infancy as a stage of human development." Infancy had already achieved that recognition in pre-Classical times; when the Romans depicted periods in the career of a typical man on "biographical" sarcophagi, they included infancy. Indeed, artists everywhere and throughout the ages have represented infancy as typically a first age or early stage in the lifespan (Bornstein and Kertes, in preparation). Iconographically, infants symbolize origins and beginnings.

Informal interest and concerns for parenting infants have been motivated in large measure by perennial questions about the roles of heredity and experience in the course of child development. Speculation on the subject dates back centuries to ancient Egypt, the Code of Hammurabi, and the pre-Socratic philosophers (French, in Vol. 2 of this *Handbook*). Plato (*ca.* 355 B.C.) theorized about the significance of infancy; Henri IV of France had the physician Jean Héroard (1868) carefully document experiences of the Dauphin Louis from the time of his birth in 1601; and Charles Darwin (1877) and Sigmund Freud (e.g., 1949) both initiated scientific observations of infants and theoretical speculations about the role of infancy in development and in culture.

The formal study of parenting infants had its beginnings in attempts by philosopher, educator, or scientist parents to do systematically what parents around the world do naturally everyday—observe their babies. The first-ever studies of children were diary descriptions of infants in their natural settings written by their own parents—"baby biographies" (Darwin, 1877; Hall, 1891; Preyer, 1882; Rousseau, 1762; Taine, 1877; Tiedemann, 1787; see Jaeger, 1985; Prochner and Doyon, 1997; Wallace, Franklin, and Keegan, 1994). Darwin, who developed evolutionary theory in 1859 with the *Origin of Species*, published observations he had made in the early 1840s on the first months of life of his firstborn son, William Erasmus, nicknamed "Doddy." Darwin's (1877) "Biographical Sketch of an Infant" gave great impetus to infancy studies (Dixon and Lerner, 1999). In succeeding years, baby biographies grew in popularity around the world—whether they were scientific documents, parents' personal records, or illustrations of educational practices—and they still appear today (e.g., Brazelton, 1969; Church, 1966; Mendelson, 1990; Stern, 1990). Perhaps the most influential of the modern baby biographers, however, was Piaget (e.g., 1952), whose writings and theorizing refer chiefly to observations of his own young children.

These systematic historical observations of infancy had many salutary effects, heightening awareness in parents and provoking formal studies of how to guide infant development. Historians and sociologists of family life have documented evolving patterns of primary infant care (Colón with Colón, 1999). Because of high rates of infant mortality, parents in early times may have cared for but resisted emotional investment in the very young (Dye and Smith, 1986; Slater, 1977–1978), a point of view that persists where especially dire circumstances reign (e.g., Scheper-Hughes, 1989). One historian theorized that parents have generally improved in their orientation to and treatment of infants because parents have, through successive generations, improved in their ability to identify and empathize with the special qualities of early childhood (deMause, 1975). Today, advice on parenting infants can be found in professional compendia that provide comprehensive treatments of prenatal and perinatal development, such as *Effective Care in Pregnancy and Childbirth* (Chalmers, Enkin, and Keirse, 1989), in classic how-to books, such as *Dr. Spock's Baby and Child Care* (Spock, Parker, Parker, and Scotland, 1998) and *Your Baby and Child* (Leach, 1997), as well as in numerous popular periodicals that overflow drugstore magazine racks.

## THE THEORETICAL SIGNIFICANCE ATTACHED TO PARENTING DURING INFANCY

From the perspective of formal studies of parenting, infancy attracts attention in part because a provocative debate rages around the significance of events occurring in infancy to later development. Proponents from one viewpoint contend that infancy is not particularly influential because the experiences and the habits of infancy have little (if any) long-term significance on the life course. Others argue contrariwise that experiences and habits developed in infancy are of crucial lifelong significance; that is, the social orientations, personality styles, and intellectual predilections established at the start fix or, at least, contribute to enduring patterns. Either the invisible foundation and frame of the edifice are always and forever critical to the structure, or, once erected, what really matters to a building is upkeep and renovation. Theoreticians and researchers alike have been surprisingly hard pressed to confirm or to refute the significance of the child's earliest experiences to the course and the eventual outcome of development.

Prominently, psychoanalysis espoused the significance of early experience (Cohler and Paul, in Vol. 3 of this *Handbook*). Thus Freud (1949) theorized that child development is characterized by critical phases during which certain experiences take on unusual significance. Infancy defines the "oral phase," during which experiences and activities centered on the mouth, notably feeding, assume particular salience for personality. According to Freud, if the baby's needs for oral gratification are overindulged or underindulged, the baby will grow into an adult who continually seeks oral gratification. Overlapping the end of infancy, according to Freud, the oral phase is succeeded by the "anal phase." During this period, parent–infant interactions center on toilet training, with long-term personality consequences likely involving stubbornness and obsessiveness. Erik Erikson (1950) portrayed infant experiences provided by parents somewhat differently, but also asserted that experiences in infancy can exert telling long-term influences. From oral sensory experiences, Erikson suggested, infants develop basic trust or mistrust in others, and whether infants develop basic trust has implications for the way they negotiate the next muscular anal stage of development, in which the key issue is establishing autonomy or shame. More modern proponents of psychodynamic schools of thinking continue to see infancy as critical for the basic differentiation of self (e.g., Ainsworth, Blehar, Waters, and Wall, 1978; Bowlby, 1969; Greenspan and Greenspan, 1985; Mahler, Pine, and Bergman, 1975; Stern, 1985).

Like psychoanalysts, behaviorists and learning theorists also stressed the significance of infant experiences on the balance of the life course (e.g., Dollard and Miller, 1950; Watson, 1924/1970). Behaviorists eschew the idea that infancy should be set apart; but for them as well, an organism's earliest experiences are crucial because they are first, have no competing propensities to replace, and thus yield easy and rapid learning. Moreover, early behavior patterns lay the foundation for later ones. Students of the constructivist school of development, beginning with Piaget (1952), have likewise theorized that capacities of later life build on development early in life and that infants actively participate in their own development.

The exceptional place of infancy has also been emphasized by other theorists, including embryologists and ethologists (e.g., Bowlby, 1969; Lorenz, 1935/1970; Spemann, 1938; Tinbergen, 1951). In the view of those who study developmental physiology and animal behavior, the immature nervous system is in an especially plastic state, and during "sensitive periods" structural developments and behavioral tendencies are maximally susceptible to influence by specific types of experience (see Bornstein, 1989b). The sensitive period concept typically assigns great weight to infant experiences because it holds that experiences that occur within its boundaries are likely to have long-lasting influence and that, once that period had passed, the same experience will no longer exert the same formative influence. Demonstrations of sensitive periods in lower animals (such as imprinting, as in the "ugly duckling") accord biological and scientific credibility to the potency of experience in infancy in general, and the notion has been painted into many portraits of human infant growth and development. Indeed, *neoteny* (the prolongation of infancy), which is especially characteristic of human beings, is thought to have special adaptive significance (Gould, 1985) insofar as it allows for enhanced parental influence and prolonged learning (Bjorklund and Pellegrini, 2000). The notion of special sensitivity in infancy was seized on by Bowlby (1969), who contended that their state of immaturity renders infants dependent on the care and protection of parents and that infancy is an evolutionarily conditioned period for the development of attachment bonds to primary caregivers. The internal working models of caregiving and caregiver–infant relationships articulated in infancy generalize to other relationships lifelong.

Not all developmental theoreticians espouse the view that the experiences of infancy are formative. Some have, in equally compelling arguments, suggested that experiences in infancy are peripheral or ephemeral, in the sense that they exert little or no enduring effect on the balance of development. These individuals attribute the engine and controls of development instead to biology and maturation and to the influences of later experience. The embryologist Waddington (1962) contended that, based on principles of growth such as "canalization," early experiences, if influential, are not determinative (see, too, McCall, 1981). Infancy may be a period of plasticity and adaptability to transient conditions, but those effects may not persist or they may be altered or supplanted by subsequent conditions that are more consequential (Kagan, 2000; Lewis, 1997).

Infancy is the first phase of extrauterine life, and the characteristics we develop and acquire then may be formative and fundamental in the sense that they endure or (at least) constitute building blocks that later developments or experiences use or modify. Infancy is only one phase in the life-span, however, and so development is also shaped by experiences after infancy. Parenting the infant does not fix the route or the terminus of development, but it makes sense that effects have causes and that the start exerts an impact on the end. Because of this, parenting is central to infancy and to the long-term development of children. Therefore, we are motivated to know the meaning and the importance of infancy for later life out of the desire to improve the lives of infants and for what infancy tells us about parents. Indeed, social anthropological inquiry has almost always included reports of infant life and adults' first efforts at parenting (Bornstein, 1980, 1991; Harkness and Super, in Vol. 2 of this *Handbook*). Parents are fundamentally invested in infants: their survival, their socialization, and their education.

## IMPLICATIONS FOR PARENTING OF CHARACTERISTICS PECULIAR TO INFANCY AND INFANT DEVELOPMENT

For parents and professionals alike, the pervasiveness, rapidity, and clarity of changes in infancy engender both fascination and action. The most remarkable of these domains of change involve the growing complexity of the nervous system; alterations in the shape and capacity of the body; the sharpening of sensory and perceptual capacities; increases in the abilities to make sense of, understand, and master objects in the world; the acquisition of communication; the emergence of characteristic personal and social styles; and the formation of specific social bonds. Each of these domains of infant development fundamentally influences parenting. Parenting is also thoroughly affected by the dynamic in which these developments occur.

### Developing Domains in Infancy

During infancy, children transform from immature beings unable to move their limbs in a coordinated manner to children who control complicated sequences of muscle contractions and flections in order to walk, reach, or grasp, and from children who can only babble or cry to children who make needs and desires abundantly clear in language and other ways. During infancy, children first make sense of and understand objects in the world, first express and read basic human emotions, first develop individual personalities and social styles, and form first social bonds. Parents escort their infants through all these dramatic "firsts." Not surprisingly, all of these developmental dynamics are closely tracked by parents, all shape parenting, and all are, in turn, shaped by parents. In this section, some significant developments in infancy that influence and are influenced by parenting are briefly reviewed.

*State.* Infants vary in how soon they establish a predictable schedule of behavioral states (Thoman, 1990), and their regularity or lack thereof has critical implications for infantcare and development as well as for parental well-being. State determines how infants present themselves; and much of what infants learn about people, their own abilities, and the object world is acquired during periods of quiet alertness and attentiveness. Therefore infant state influences adult behavior: It has been estimated that mothers lose an average of 350 hours of sleep during their infant's first year (Dement and Vaughan, 1999) primarily because of the multiple awakenings of their infant (Michelsson, Rinne, and Paajanen, 1990; Osterholm, Lindeke, and Amidon, 1983) and that mothers experience negative effects of sleep deprivation without being fully aware of it (Coren, 1997). Adults soothe distressed babies instead of trying to play with them, and infants who are temperamentally fretful elicit different patterns of interaction than do infants who cry only infrequently (Putnam, Sanson, and Rothbart, in Vol. 1 of this *Handbook*). The amount of time infants spend in different states determines the fundamental circumstances under which they are with their parents: Babies are usually with their mothers when awake and alone when asleep. At the same time, infant state is modifiable: Cole (1999) documented cultural conditioning of infants' biological entrainment to the day–night cycle. Among the Kipsigis, a tribe of the Kenyan desert, infants sleep with their mothers at night and are permitted to nurse on demand. During the day, they are strapped to their mothers' backs, accompanying them on daily rounds of farming, household chores, and social activities. These babies often nap while their mothers go about their work, and so they do not begin to sleep through the night until many months later than do U.S. American infants (see too Kawasaki, Nugent, Miyashita, Miyahara, and Brazelton, 1994). State organization and getting "on schedule" are subject to parent-mediated experiential influences (Ingersoll and Thoman, 1999).

*Physical stature and psychomotor abilities.*   Infancy is a time of great physical and nervous system development. Growth through the first 2 postnatal years is manifest even on casual observation because of its magnitude and scope. On average, newborns measure approximately 49–50 cm and weigh approximately 3.4–3.5 kg. In the year after birth, babies grow half their birth length and their weight approximately triples (National Center for Health Statistics, 2001). These physical changes are paralleled by signal advances in motor skills. Consider the eagerness with which parents await their child's first step. This achievement signifies an important stage in infant independence, permitting new means of exploring the environment and of determining when and how much time infants spend near their parents. By walking, the baby asserts individuality, maturity, and self-mindedness. These changes, in turn, affect the ways in which parents treat the child: How parents organize the baby's physical environment and even how they speak to the walking, as opposed to the crawling, baby differ substantially.

Psychomotor growth too reflects the influence of parenting practices: Dennis and Dennis (1940) suggested that relative locomotor delay in Hopi Native Americans reflected Hopi babies' traditional early constriction on a cradleboard; Mead and MacGregor (1951) proposed that the manner in which Balinese mothers habitually carry their infants promoted the emergence of unique motor patterns; and Ainsworth (1967) attributed advanced Ganda infant motor abilities to a nurturing climate of physical freedom. Antecedent to behaviors, parental expectations also play an influential role. For example, Jamaican mothers living in England expect their infants to sit and to walk relatively early, whereas Indian mothers living in the same city expect their infants to crawl relatively late: Infants in each subculture develop in accordance with their mothers' expected timetables of growth (Hopkins and Westra, 1990).

*Perceiving and thinking.*   During infancy, the capacities to take in information through the major sensory channels, to make sense of the environment, and to attribute meaning to information improve dramatically. Although it is not always apparent, there is no question that infants have an active mental life. Infants are constantly learning and developing new ideas and do so in many different ways (see Bornstein and Lamb, 1992). Infants actively scan the environment, pick up, encode, and process information, and aggregate over their experiences (Bornstein and Arterberry, 1999). Newborns are equipped to hear, to orient to, and to distinguish sounds, and babies seem especially primed to perceive and to appreciate sound in the dynamic form and range of adult speech (Trehub and Hsing-Wu, 1977). Newborns also identify particular speakers—notably mother—right after birth (DeCasper and Spence, 1986), apparently on the basis of prenatal exposure to the maternal voice. By their preference reactions, newborns also give good evidence that they possess a developed sense of smell (Steiner, 1979), and babies soon suck presumptively at the smell of their mothers, and reciprocally, mothers recognize the scent of their babies with only 1 or 2 days' experience (Porter, 1991; Porter and Levy, 1995; Porter and Winberg, 1999).

By 4 or 5 months of age, infants discriminate among facial expressions associated with different emotions (Nelson, 1987) and even distinguish variations in some emotional expressions (Kuchuk, Vibbert, and Bornstein, 1986). How parents look to infants will meaningfully supplement what they have to say to them; indeed, as infants do not yet understand speech, looks may be more telling. Looking is not solely a source of information acquisition, of course; gaze is also a basic means in social exchange. Eye-to-eye contact between infant and caregiver is rewarding to both and sets in motion routines and rhythms of social interaction and play.

As a consequence of infants' information-processing skills (Bornstein, 1989c), parents' displays and infants' imitations provide a particularly efficient mechanism for infants' acquiring information of all sorts ... just by listening and watching. How early infants imitate and what they can imitate are disputed research issues (Nadel and Butterworth, 1999), but the significance of observational learning from infancy is not.

Infancy culminates with the development of representational thinking and language. In the first year, for example, play with objects is predominantly characterized by sensorimotor manipulation (mouthing and fingering) whose goal appears to be the extraction of information about objects. In the second year, object play takes on an increasingly symbolic quality as infants enact activities performed by self, others, and objects in simple pretense situations, for example pretending to drink from empty teacups or to talk on toy telephones (Bornstein and O'Reilly, 1993). Maternal play influences infant play (Bornstein, Haynes, O'Reilly, and Painter, 1999; Tamis-LeMonda, Užgiris, and Bornstein, in Vol. 5 of this *Handbook*), and cross-cultural comparisons confirm that, where parents emphasize particular types of play, infants tend to engage in those same types of play (Bornstein, Haynes, Pascual, Painter, and Galperín, 1999; Farver, 1993; Tamis-LeMonda, Bornstein, Cyphers, Toda, and Ogino, 1992).

*Speaking and understanding.* Early in life, infants communicate by means of emotional expressions like smiling and crying. However, babies quickly display the capacity to organize speech sounds, as indicated by babbling. In remarkably short order, the infant's repertoire of communicative tokens expands to include gestures and a growing range of social signals that eventuate in spoken language. The comprehension of speech combined with the generation of meaningful utterances rank among the major cognitive achievements of the infancy period, but the motivation to acquire language is social and is born in interaction, usually with parents (Bloom, 1998). For example, episodes of "joint attention" are believed to provide a fundamental framework for the acquisition of language (Bornstein, 1985; Moore and Dunham, 1995). That is, the acquisition of first language reflects the child's early and rich exposure to the parent-provided target language environment as much as it does competencies that are a part of the child. Language learning is active, but always is embedded in the larger context of adult–infant social communication. Parent-provided experiences swiftly and surely channel early speech development toward the adult target language. In the space of approximately 2 years, infants master the rudiments of language without explicit instruction and without noticeable effort, but they always speak the language to which they have been exposed.

*Emotional expressivity and temperament.* Emotional expressions are evidence of how babies respond to events, and new parents pay special attention to infants' emotions in their efforts to manage and modify them (Grolnick and Farkas, in Vol. 5 of this *Handbook*). The advent of emotional reactions—be they the first smiles or the earliest indications of stranger wariness—cue meaningful transitions for caregivers. Parents read them as indications of emerging individuality—as markers to what the child's behavioral style is like now and what it portends. From the first days of their infants' lives, mothers support their babies' experiences, as for example of joy by playing with facial expressions, vocalizations, and touch, and evoking gazing, smiling, and laughing from their infants (Stern, 1985). Reciprocally, by as soon as the second half of the first year of their infants' lives, parents' emotional expressions are meaningful to infants (Klinnert, Campos, Sorce, Emde, and Svejda, 1983; Nelson, 1987). Infants respond emotionally to the affective expressions they observe in other people as when, for example, their caregivers are depressed (Zahn-Waxler, Duggal, and Gruber, in Vol. 4 of this *Handbook*). Infants as young as 1 year old understand specific object or event referents of a communication (Churcher and Scaife, 1982), and they respond to emotional messages, showing signs of distress when witnessing angry interactions between family members (Cummings, Zahn-Waxler, and Radke-Yarrow, 1981).

Beyond emotional exchange, infants influence parenting by virtue of their individuality of temperament. Activity level, mood, soothability, and emotional intensity define dimensions of temperament by which parents typically characterize their infants. Just as parents and caregivers try to interpret, respond to, and manage infants' emotional states, they also devote considerable energy to identifying, adapting to, and channeling infants' temperament (Bornstein and Lamb, 1992; Putnam et al., in Vol. 1 of this *Handbook*). For one example, some infants appear better able to regulate their attention and emotions and so engage parents in more rewarding bouts of joint attention (Raver, 1996). For another, difficult babies have hunger cries that are higher pitched, and adults perceive them as more aversive and demanding (Lounsbury and Bates, 1982). Further to the point, mothers of irritable infants engage in less visual and physical contact and are less responsive and less involved with their babies (Van den Boom and Hoeksma, 1994), and maternal perceptions of infant difficultness predict their perceptions of aggressiveness and anxiety in children as they grow (Bates, Maslin, and Frankel, 1985).

Just as in other spheres of infant life, cultural variation shapes the interaction between infant emotional expression or temperament and parenting. No doubt there are temperament proclivities of the infant that transcend culture: Some smiles are more equal than others, and an infant's smile is unquestionably first among equals. Likewise, "difficult" babies are characterized by frequent and intense expressions of negative emotion, and they demand and receive different patterns of attention than do "easy" babies (Pettit and Bates, 1984). However, adults in different cultures surely socialize the emotional displays of their infants by responding in accordance with culture-specific requirements or interpretations of infants' expressions and emotions (Harkness and Super, 1985; Super and Harkness, 1986). For example, infants universally respond to separation from parents in characteristically negative ways (Ainsworth et al., 1978; LeVine and Miller, 1990), but mothers may perceive and interpret their reactions differently according to cultural values. European American and Puerto Rican mothers both prefer infants who display a balance of autonomy and dependence, but European American mothers attend to and place greater emphasis on the presence or absence of individualistic tendencies, whereas Puerto Rican mothers focus more on characteristics associated with a sociocentric orientation, that is, the child's ability to maintain proper conduct in a public place (Harwood, 1992; Harwood, Leyendecker, Carlson, Asencio, and Miller, in Vol. 4 of this *Handbook*). Thus the meaning of infant behavior for parents is a complex function of act and context (Bornstein, 1995). Although in some circumstances infant difficultness may be associated with long-term negative consequences (Putnam et al., in Vol. 1 of this *Handbook*), among Ethiopian infants otherwise dying of starvation, difficult temperament, which elicited adult attention and feeding, proved adaptive (DeVries and Sameroff, 1984).

*Social life.*    The infancy period sees the gradual dawning of social awareness, and over time babies assume increasing responsibility for initiating and maintaining social interactions (Green, Gustafson, and West, 1980). By 2 months of age, infants already engage in complex and responsive interactions with their mothers (termed protoconversations; Bateson, 1979). These interactions are characterized by mutual give-and-take exchanges in the form of coos, gazes, smiles, grunts, and sucks. On this basis, infants develop a sense of shared experience (termed intersubjectivity; Trevarthen, 1993). The development of emotional relationships with other people—mainly parents—constitutes one of the most important aspects of social development in infancy (Ainsworth et al., 1978; Bowlby,

1969). By the middle of the first year, the very social infant bears little resemblance to the seemingly asocial neonate. Infant–mother interactions have been referred to as the "cradle of social understanding" (Rochat and Striano, 1999) for how they presumably color later social relationships.

Once infants develop the capacity to recognize specific people, they begin to interact preferentially with, and gradually form enduring attachments to, the adults who have been consistently and reliably accessible during their first months in the world. Attachment formation is a product of the convergence of built-in tendencies on the part of infants and propensities of adults to respond in certain ways to infants' cues and needs (Ainsworth et al., 1978; Bowlby, 1969; Cummings and Cummings, in Vol. 5 of this *Handbook*). As discussed in the section on the principles of parenting infants, the ways in which parents interact with and respond to their babies vary depending on a variety of factors, including parents' gender, personalities, current social, emotional, and economic circumstances, life histories, and ideology and culture, as well as their infants' characteristics. The nature of parent–infant interactions provides a medium within which the chrysalis of the child's future life germinates and grows. The quality of parent–infant relationships shapes infants' relationships with others by multiple means: modeling the nature and course of interventions, affecting infants' willingness and ability to engage in interactions with others, as well as influencing what infants take away from those interactions.

The developmental changes that take place in individuals during the $2\frac{1}{2}$ years after their conception—the prenatal and the infancy periods—are more dramatic and thorough than any others in the lifespan. The body, the mind, and the ability to function meaningfully in and on the world all emerge and flourish with verve. That dynamism, in turn, engages the world, for infants do not grow and develop in a vacuum. Every facet of creation they touch as they grow and develop influences infants in return. These reciprocal relations in infancy ultimately cast parenting in a featured role.

### Developmental Change in Infancy

Development in infancy has strong stable components: Crying in 6-month-old infants and behavioral inhibition in 18-month-old toddlers may seem different, when in fact the underlying source construct of fear might be the same (Kagan, Snidman, Arcus, and Resnick, 1997). However, much of infancy is change, and all children change at their own rate (Kagan, 1971). Last week, Jonathan may have stayed in the spot where he was placed; this week he is creeping, and next month he will be scooting around faster than his mother can catch him. Another baby the same age may not begin to locomote for 2 more months. Understanding, anticipating, and responding to dynamic change in the context of individual variation present major challenges to parents of infants. Parents need to know about and be vigilant to all the complications and subtleties of infant development.

*Infancy is dynamic change.*    Infant development involves parallel and rapid growth in biological, psychological, and social spheres. Moreover, normal development may be nonlinear in nature, stalling sometimes, or even regressing temporarily (Bever, 1982; Harris, 1983; Strauss and Stavy, 1981). Infant growth well illustrates the "systems" perspective on development, in the sense that the organization of the whole changes as the infant matures and is exposed to new experiences, and changes take place at many levels at once (e.g., Gottlieb, Wahlsten, and Lickliter, 1998; Thelen and Smith, 1998). For example, the emergence of self-produced locomotion involves not only an advance in motor skills, but also affects visual–vestibular adaptation, visual attention, social referencing, and emotions (Bertenthal and Campos, 1990). Babies who can pull themselves up to standing position and walk (which occurs sometime between 11 and 15 months of age) engage the social and the object worlds in fundamentally new ways: The young infant was totally dependent on adults for stimulation; the older infant explores, self-stimulates, and self-educates. Likewise, achieving the ability to stand upright and walk alters the nature and the quality of parenting (e.g., Biringen, Emde, Campos, and Appelbaum, 1995). The Gusii of Kenya have the expression "lameness is up," meaning that, as

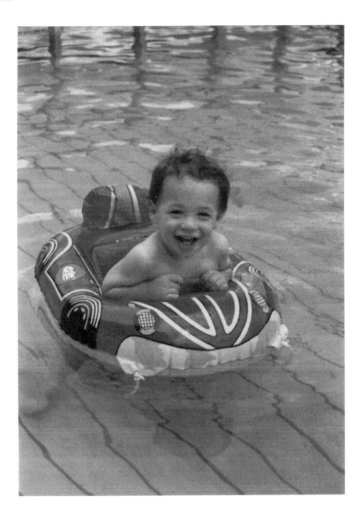

children become able to walk, they are liable to be hurt (LeVine, 1977). By the second year, infants initiate activities with parents more than 85% of the time (White, Kaban, Shapiro, and Attanucci, 1977). Standing infants seem more grown up to adults, who in turn treat them so. With each infant advance, parents' behaviors toward infants change; they must now be vigilant about a range of new, and possibly dangerous, circumstances. Much more than before, parents must communicate that infants need to regulate their own behavior.

*Infancy is individual variation.*    The notable developmental achievements that unfold during infancy are impressive (especially when infancy is viewed in terms of the small proportion of the entire lifespan that it is), but normal variability in the timing of infant achievements is equally compelling. Every infant is an original. Interest in the origins and expression of interinfant variability occupies a central position in thinking about infant development and parenting (e.g., Kagan, 1984). The ages at which individual infants might achieve a given developmental milestone typically vary enormously (some children say their first word at 9 months of age, others at 29 months of age), just as infants of a given age vary dramatically among themselves on nearly every index of development (at 1 year of age, some toddlers comprehend 10 words, others 75; some produce zero words, others nearly 30). Of course, when and how their infants talk or walk or what have you exercises a strong psychological impact on parents, even if it is temporary and the long-term significance of a given child's performance is meaningful in only extreme cases.

## Developing Infants

Parenting an infant is akin to trying to hit a moving target, with the ever-changing infant developing in fits and starts at her or his own pace. Amidst this spectrum of developmental issues and matters that parents must confront, infants themselves are mute but potent. The very young neither understand their parents' speech nor respond to them verbally. At the same time, they are also notoriously unco-operative and seem unmotivated to perform or conform. Still other pervasive infant characteristics vex parents or give them pause—depending on a parent's perspective or the moment: Infants possess limited attention spans and, in addition to lacking speech, have limited response repertoires; in their first months, they are also motorically incompetent or inept. Yet infants are consistent and voracious in their demands. Reciprocally, parents need to interpret aspects of infant function unambiguously and must accomplish this in spite of changes and fluctuations in infant state. Perhaps the major problem faced by parents of infants is that, at base, parents are constantly trying to divine what is "inside the baby's head"—what infants want, what they know, how they feel, what they will do next vis-à-vis the things and the people around them, and whether they understand and are affected by those same things and people. Thus parents of infants seem constantly in search of patterns, often even on the basis of single transient instances. New (usually inexperienced) parents have the job of disambiguating novel, complex, and rapidly emerging uncertain information, and at the same time they are called on to parent appropriately and effectively. Even if most face the formidable challenges of infancy with a degree of psychological naivete, parents do not meet these tests totally unprepared. Both biology and culture equip parents to respond, understand, and interpret infancy and its vicissitudes.

## PRINCIPLES OF PARENTING INFANTS

Infants do not and cannot grow up as solitary individuals; parenting constitutes the initial and all-encompassing ecology of infant development. Mothers and fathers guide the development of their infants by many direct and indirect means. Biological parents contribute to the genetic makeup of their infants. All parents shape their infants' experiences. Parents also influence their infants by virtue of each partner's influence on the other and their associations with larger social networks. Parents influence infant development both by their beliefs and by their behaviors. In this respect, similarities as well as differences in mothers' and fathers' attitudes and actions affect the nature and course of infant development, and they do so according to different mechanisms and following different models.

### Direct and Indirect Effects

Mothers and fathers contribute directly to the nature and the development of their infants by passing on their biological characteristics. Modern behavior genetics argues that a host of different characteristics of offspring—height and weight, intelligence and personality—reflects inheritance to a substantial degree (e.g., Plomin, 1999).

At the same time, all prominent theories of development put experience in the world as either the principal source of individual growth or as a major contributing component (Dixon and Lerner, 1999; Wachs, 2000). Studies of children with genetic backgrounds that differ from those of their nurturing families provide one means of evaluating the impacts of heredity and experience on infant development (e.g., Ho, 1987; Plomin, 1989; Plomin and DeFries, 1985). In (ideal) natural experiments of adoption, the child shares genes but not environment with biological parents, and the child shares environment but not genes with adoptive parents. Studies of 1-year-old infants, their biological parents, and their adoptive parents under these circumstances show that development of communicative competence and cognitive abilities relates to the general intelligence (IQ) of biological mothers and also to the behaviors of adoptive mothers (imitating and responding contingently to infant vocalization). These results point to direct roles for *both* genetics and experience in parenting infants (e.g., Hardy-Brown, 1983; Hardy-Brown and Plomin, 1985). Thus evidence for heritability effects neither negates nor diminishes equally compelling evidence for the direct effects of parenting (Collins, Maccoby, Steinberg, Hetherington, and Bornstein, 2000). To cite the most obvious example, genes contribute to making siblings alike, but (as we all recognize) siblings are normally very different from one another, and it is widely held that siblings' different experiences (the "nonshared environment") in growing up contribute to making them distinctive individuals (Dunn and Plomin, 1991). Even within the same family and home setting, parents (and other factors) help to create distinctive and effective environments for their children (Stoolmiller, 1999; Turkheimer and Waldron, 2000).

Empirical research attests to the short- and the long-term influences of parent-provided experiences in infant development. Mothers who speak more, prompt more, and respond more during the first year of their infants' lives have 6-month-old infants to 4-year-old children who score higher in standardized evaluations of language and cognition (e.g., Bornstein, 1985; Bornstein and Tamis-LeMonda, 1989; Bornstein, Tamis-LeMonda, and Haynes, 1999; Nicely, Tamis-LeMonda, and Bornstein, 1999). Even features of the parent-outfitted physical environment appear to influence infant development directly (Wachs and Chan, 1986): New toys and changing room decorations influence child language acquisition in and of themselves and independent of parental language.

Indirect effects are more subtle and less noticeable than direct effects, but perhaps no less meaningful. One primary type of indirect effect is marital support and communication. Conflicts and disagreements between parental partners increase with the birth of a first baby, marital satisfaction decreases from pregnancy to early childhood, and parents' attitudes about themselves and their marriages during this transition influence the quality of their interactions with their infants and, in turn, their infants' development (Cowan and Cowan, 1992). Effective coparenting bodes well for infant development (McHale, Khazan, Rotman, DeCourcey, and McConnell, in Vol. 3 of this *Handbook*), and mothers who report supportive relationships with "secondary parents" (lovers or grandparents) are more competent and sensitively responsive to their infants than are women who lack such relationships (Grych, in Vol. 4 of this *Handbook*).

In the extreme, conflict between spouses may reduce the availability of an important source of support in infantrearing, namely one's partner. Short of that, parents embroiled in marital conflict may have difficulty attending to the sometimes subtle signals infants use to communicate their needs. Infants in these homes may learn that their caregivers are unreliable sources of information or assistance in stressful situations. For example, year-old infants are less likely to look to their maritally dissatisfied fathers for information or clarification in the face of stress or ambiguity than are infants of maritally satisfied fathers (Parke, in Vol. 3 of this *Handbook*). In one study, the influence of the husband–wife relationship on mother–infant interaction in a feeding context was assessed (Pedersen, 1975). Ratings were made of the quality of mother–infant interaction during home observations when infants were 4 weeks of age. Feeding competence referred to the appropriateness of the mother in managing and pacing feeding without disrupting the baby and to her displays of sensitivity to the baby's needs for either stimulation of feeding or brief rest periods during the course of feeding. In addition, the husband–wife relationship was assessed by interview. Neonatal assessments (Brazelton, 1973) were also available. When fathers were more supportive of mothers, evaluating maternal skills more positively, mothers were more competent in feeding babies. (Of course, competent mothers could elicit more positive evaluations from their husbands.) The reverse held for marital discord. High tension and conflict in the marriage were associated with more inept feeding on the part of the mother. The marital relationship also predicted the status and the well-being of the infant as assessed by Brazelton scores. With an alert baby, the father evaluated the mother more positively; with a motorically mature baby, the marriage was characterized by less tension and conflict.

Research shows both direct and indirect effects of parenting on infants. In addition, both parents' beliefs and behaviors matter.

## Parenting Beliefs

When their infants are only 1 month of age, 99% of mothers believe that babies can express interest, 95% joy, 84% anger, 75% surprise, 58% fear, and 34% sadness (Johnson, Emde, Pennbrook,
Stenberg, and Davis, 1982). These judgments may reflect infants' expressive capacities, or contextual cues, or mothers' subjective inferences. In response to specific questions, mothers describe
infants' vocal and facial expressions, along with their gestures and arm movements, as the bases of
their judgments (Papoušek and Papoušek, in Vol. 2 of this *Handbook*). Because mothers commonly
respond differently to different emotional messages they perceive in their infants, they have frequent
opportunities to have their inferences fine-tuned or corrected, depending on how their babies respond
in turn. There is therefore good reason to invest confidence in maternal beliefs about infants.

Parents' beliefs—their ideas, knowledge, values, goals, and attitudes—hold a consistently pop-
ular place in the study of parent–infant relationships (e.g., Goodnow, in Vol. 3 of this *Handbook*;
Holden and Buck, in Vol. 3 of this *Handbook*; Sigel and McGillicuddy-De Lisi, in Vol. 3 of this
*Handbook*). Parental beliefs are conceived to serve many functions; they may generate and shape
parental behaviors, mediate the effectiveness of parenting, or help to organize parenting (Darling and
Steinberg, 1993; Maccoby and Martin, 1983; Murphey, 1992; Teti and Candelaria, in Vol. 4 of this
*Handbook*). Thus, how parents see themselves vis-à-vis infants generally can lead to their expressing
one or another kind of affect, thinking, or behavior in childrearing. Mothers who feel efficacious and
competent in their role as parents are more responsive (Parks and Smeriglio, 1986; Schellenbach,
Whitman, and Borkowski, 1992), more empathetic, less punitive, and more appropriate in their developmental expectations (East and Felice, 1996). How parents construe infancy in general functions
in the same way: Those who believe that they can or cannot affect infant personality or intelligence
modify their parenting accordingly. Mothers who feel effective vis-à-vis their infants are motivated to engage in further interactions that in turn provide them with additional opportunities to
understand and interact positively and appropriately with their infants (Teti, O'Connell, and Reiner,
1996). How parents see their own infants has its specific consequences too: Mothers who regard
their infants as being difficult are less likely to pay attention or respond to their infants' overtures,
and their inattentiveness and nonresponsiveness can then foster temperamental difficulties and cognitive shortcomings (Putnam et al., in Vol. 1 of this *Handbook*). In observing and understanding
infantrearing beliefs, we may come to better understand how and why parents behave in the ways
they do.

Significantly, parents in different cultures harbor different beliefs about their own parenting as
well as about their infants (e.g., Bornstein et al., 1995; Goodnow, in Vol. 3 of this *Handbook*). Parents
may then act on culturally defined beliefs as much or more than on what their senses tell them about
their babies. Parents in Samoa think of young children as having an angry and willful character, and,
independent of what children might actually say, parents consensually report that their children's
first word is *tae*—Samoan for "shit" (Ochs, 1988). Parents who believe that they can or cannot affect
their infants' temperament, intelligence, whathaveyou, tend to modify their parenting accordingly.
Parents in Mexico promote play in infants as a forum for the expression of interpersonal sensitivity,
whereas parents in the United States are prone to attach greater cognitive value to play (Farver, 1993).
The ways in which parents (choose to) interact with their infants appear to relate to parents' general
belief systems.

Are parents' beliefs about infants accurate? From their long-term, intimate experience with them,
parents surely know their own infants better than anyone else does. For that reason, parents (or
other close caregivers) have long been thought to provide valid reports about their infants (Thomas,
Chess, Birch, Hertzig, and Korn, 1963). However, parental report invites problems of bias owing,
for example, to parents' subjective viewpoint, personality disposition, unique experiences, and other
factors. One study compared maternal and observer ratings of manifest infant activity (reaching,
kicking, and other explicit motor behaviors) when infants were by themselves, when with mother, and
when with an observer (Bornstein, Gaughran, and Segu, 1991). Mother–observer assessments agreed,
but only moderately (see, too, Hagekull, Bohlin, and Lindhagen, 1984). Different observers have

different amounts of information about baby, and they also carry with them unique perspectives that have been shaped by different prior experiences; both information level and perspective influence judgments of infants.

Are parents' beliefs about their own behaviors accurate and valid? Some maternal behaviors correspond to maternal beliefs: for example, mothers' behaviors toward their infants and their beliefs about childrearing practices (Wachs and Camli, 1991) and mothers' infant caregiving competence and beliefs about their parenting effectiveness (Teti and Gelfand, 1991). Harwood, Miller, and Irizarry (1995) found that European American mothers underscore the importance of values such as independence, assertiveness, and creativity when asked to describe an ideal child, whereas Puerto Rican mothers underscore the importance of obedience and respect for others. In line with these values, U.S. mothers have been observed to foster independence in infants; for example, during naturalistic mother–infant interactions during feeding, U.S. mothers encourage their infants to feed themselves at 8 months of age. In contrast, Puerto Rican mothers hold their infants closely on their laps during mealtimes and take control of feeding them meals from start to finish. However, coordinate relations between parents' beliefs and behaviors have more often proven elusive (Miller, 1988), with many researchers finding no relations between mothers' activities with their infants and their professed parenting attitudes (e.g., Cote and Bornstein, 2000; McGillicuddy-DeLisi, 1992).

## Parenting Behaviors

More salient in the phenomenology of the infant are actual experiences that mother and father provide; behaviors are perhaps more direct expressions of parenting. Before children are old enough to enter formal or even informal social situations, like play groups and school, most of their worldly experience stems directly from interactions they have within the family. In that context (at least in Western cultures), their two adult caregiving figures are responsible for determining most, if not all, of their experiences. A small number of domains of parenting interactions have been identified as common "cores" of parental care (Bornstein, 1989a; LeVine, 1988). They have been studied for their variation, stability, continuity, and covariation, as well as for their correspondence with and prediction of infant development.

*Domains of parenting infants.* In infrahuman primates, the majority of maternal behaviors consist simply of biologically requisite feeding, grooming, protection, and the like (Bard, in Vol. 2 of this *Handbook*). The contents of parent–infant interactions are more dynamic, varied, and discretionary in human beings. Moreover, there is initially asymmetry in parent and child contributions to interactions and control: Postinfancy, children play more active and anticipatory roles in interaction, whereas initial responsibility for adaptation in child development lies unambiguously with the parent (Barnard and Solchany, in Vol. 3 of this *Handbook*).

Four superordinate categories of human parental caregiving (and reciprocally for the infant, experiences) have been identified: They are nurturant, social, didactic, and material. These categories apply to the infancy period and to normal caregiving. Not all forms of parenting or parenting domains appropriate for older children (for example, punishment) are accounted for in this taxonomy. Although these modes of caregiving are conceptually and operationally distinct, in practice, caregiver–infant interaction is intricate and multidimensional, and infant caregivers regularly engage in combinations of them. Together, however, these modes are perhaps universal, even if their instantiations or emphases (in terms of frequency or duration) vary across cultures. For their part, human infants are reared in, influenced by, and adapt to a social and physical ecology commonly characterized by this taxonomy and its elements.

(1) *Nurturant caregiving* meets the physical requirements of the infant. Infant mortality is a perennial parenting concern (LeVine, 1988; UNICEF, 1993), and parents centrally are responsible for promoting infants' wellness and preventing their illness from the moment of

conception—or even earlier. Parents in virtually all higher species nurture their very young, providing sustenance, protection, supervision, grooming, and the like. Parents shield infants from risks and stressors. Nurturance is prerequisite to infants' survival and well-being; recip-rocally, seeing a child to reproductive age enhances parents' probability of passing on their genes (Bjorklund, Yunger, and Pellegrini, in Vol. 2 of this *Handbook*).

(2) *Social caregiving* includes the variety of visual, verbal, affective, and physical behaviors parents use in engaging infants in interpersonal exchanges (kissing, tactile comforting, smil-ing, vocalizing, and playful face-to-face contact). Parental displays of warmth and physical expressions of affection toward their offspring peak in infancy. Social caregiving includes the regulation of infant affect as well as the management and monitoring of infant social relationships with others, including relatives, nonfamilial caregivers, and peers.

(3) *Didactic caregiving* consists of the variety of strategies parents use in stimulating infants to engage and understand the environment outside the dyad. Didactics include focusing the baby's attention on properties, objects, or events in the baby's surrounding; introducing, mediating, and interpreting the external world; describing and demonstrating; as well as provoking or providing opportunities to observe, to imitate, and to learn. Normally, didactics increase over the course of infancy.

(4) *Material caregiving* includes those ways in which parents provision and organize their infant's physical world. Adults are responsible for the number and variety of inanimate objects (toys, books) available to the infant, the level of ambient stimulation, the limits on physical freedom, and the overall physical dimensions of babies' experiences.

Four significant developmental characteristics distinguish these domains of parenting infants. The first has to do with variation among parents. Adults differ considerably in their caregiving behaviors, even when they come from the same culture and from socioeconomically homogeneous groups. For example, the language that parents use to address their infants varies enormously. One study reported that, even when from a relatively homogeneous group in terms of education and socioeconomic status (SES), some mothers talked to their 4-month-old infants during as little as 3% and some during as much as 97% of a home observation (Bornstein and Ruddy, 1984). Thus the range in amount of language that washes over babies is virtually as large as it can be. This is not to say that there are not also systematic group differences by SES or culture; there are (see the subsection on SES).

The second feature has to do with consistency in parenting infants. Stability connotes evidence of consistency in the relative ranks of individuals in a group over time and continuity evidence of consistency in the absolute level of group performance; the two are independent, but both add meaning to infants' experiences (Holden and Miller, 1999). One study examined activities of mothers toward their firstborn infants between the time babies were 2 and 5 months of age (Bornstein and Tamis-LeMonda, 1990). Two kinds of mothers' encouraging attention, two kinds of speech, and ma-ternal bids to social play in relation to infants' exploration and vocalization were recorded. Table 1.1 provides a conceptual summary of some findings, distinguishing activities that are stable and unstable as well as those that are continuous and discontinuous. Notable is the fact that every cell in the table is represented with a significant parenting activity. Some are stable and continuous as infants age (e.g., total maternal speech to baby). Others are stable and discontinuous, showing either a general developmental increase (e.g., didactic stimulation) or a decrease (e.g., the singsong tones of "child-directed" speech). Some activities are unstable and continuous (e.g., social play), whereas others are unstable and discontinuous, showing either a general developmental increase (e.g., the normal conversational tones of "adult-directed" speech) or a decrease (e.g., social stimulation). Maternal behavior toward firstborn and secondborn children when each child was 1 and 2 years of age shows similarly moderate to high stability in maternal affectionate verbal responsiveness and controlling behavior (Dunn, Plomin, and Daniels, 1985, 1986). Summarizing across a wide variety of samples, time intervals, and types of home assessments, Gottfried (1984) and Holden and Miller (1999)

TABLE 1.1
Developmental Stability and Continuity in Maternal Activities in Infancy

| Developmental Stability | Developmental Continuity | | |
|---|---|---|---|
| | | No | |
| | Yes | Increase | Decrease |
| Stable | Speech[a] | Didactic stimulation | Child-directed speech |
| Unstable | Social play | Adult-directed speech | Social stimulation |

[a]For example, across early infancy, mothers speak to their infants approximately the same amount in total (continuity), and those mothers who speak more when their infants are younger speak more when their infants are older, just as those mothers who speak less when their infants are younger speak less when their infants are older (stability).

determined that parent-provided experiences tend to be stable during infancy. Klein (1988) likewise found that Israeli mothers are stable in the amounts of learning experiences they provide in different situations of caregiving between middle infancy and toddlerhood.

Individual parents do not vary much in their activities from day to day, but parenting activities change over longer periods and in response to children's development. The ratio of positive to negative phrases that mothers make in reference to their infants increases across the first postpartum year, and there is a corresponding reduction in time devoted to caregiving activities (Fleming, Ruble, Flett, and Van Wagner, 1990). Sensitive parents also tailor their behaviors to match their infants' developmental progress (Adamson and Bakeman, 1984; Carew, 1980), for example by speaking more and providing more didactic experiences as infants age (Bornstein and Tamis-LeMonda, 1990; Bornstein, Tal, et al., 1992; Klein, 1988). Indeed, parents are sensitive to both infant age and, more especially, to infant capacity or performance (Bellinger, 1980): The mean length of mothers' utterances tends to match the mean length of utterances of their $1\frac{1}{2}$ to $3\frac{1}{2}$-year-old children (McLaughlin, White, McDevitt, and Raskin, 1983).

The fourth characteristic of these different categories of parenting has to do with their relative independence of these categories from one another. Classical authorities, including notably psycho-analysts and ethologists, once conceptualized maternal behavior as a more or less unitary construct—variously denoted as "good," "sensitive," "warm," or "adequate"—despite the wide range of activities mothers naturally engage in with infants (e.g., Ainsworth et al., 1978; Mahler et al., 1975; Rohner, 1985; Winnicott, 1957). In other words, the thinking was that parents behave in consistent ways across domains of interaction, time, and context. Alternatively, domains of parenting infants might constitute coherent, but distinctive, constructs (Bornstein, 1989a, 1995). Mothers who engage in more face-to-face play are not necessarily or automatically those who engage in didactics more, and this independence is characteristic of U.S. American as well as English, French, and Japanese mothers (Bornstein, Azuma, Tamis-LeMonda, and Ogino, 1990; Bornstein and Tamis-LeMonda, 1990; Bornstein, Tamis-LeMonda, Pêcheux, and Rahn, 1991; Bornstein, Toda, Azuma, Tamis-LeMonda, and Ogino, 1990; Dunn, 1977). In other words, individual mothers emphasize particular activities with their infants.

*Mutual responsiveness.* Infant caregiving is further differentiated by responsibility and lead. In Western industrialized cultures, parents are generally acknowledged to take principal responsibility for structuring their exchanges with babies: They engage infants in early game play (e.g., Hodapp, Goldfield, and Boyatzis, 1984) as well as in turn taking in verbal interchange (e.g., Vandell and Wilson, 1987). Frequently, then, thinking about parent–infant relationships highlights parents as agents of infant socialization with infants conceived of as passive recipients. To a considerable degree, however, parenting infants is a two-way street. Surely infants cry to be fed and changed, and when they wake they are ready to play. Thus parents' initiatives are proactive; often, however, they are reactive and thence interactive. Infants appear to be sensitive to contingencies between their own actions and the reactions of others, and such contingencies are a hallmark of responsive parenting (Gergely and Watson, 1999).

Responsiveness is a major component of parenting infants (Ainsworth et al., 1978; Bornstein, 1989d). Although responsiveness takes many guises, parents who respond promptly, reliably, and appropriately to their babies' signals give babies a good message from the start. They tell their children that they can trust their parents to be there for them. They give their children a sense of control and of self. A baby cries, a mother comes—the baby already feels she or he has an effect on the world. A baby whose parent has been unresponsive is frequently angry because the parent's inaccessibility may be painful and frustrating; furthermore, because of uncertainty about the parent's responsiveness, the infant may grow apprehensive and readily upset by stressful situations (Rubin and Burgess, in Vol. 1 of this *Handbook*).

Infants deliberately search for and use others' (parents') emotional (facial, vocal, gestural) expressions to help clarify and evaluate uncertain and novel events, a phenomenon called social referencing (Campos and Stenberg, 1981; Feinman, 1982; Feinman and Lewis, 1983). Between 9 and 12 months of age, infants look to mothers and fathers for emotional cues and are influenced by both positive and negative adult expressions (Dickstein and Parke, 1988; Hirshberg and Svejda, 1990). Indeed, in such situations infants may position themselves so they can keep their mother's face in view (Sorce and Emde, 1981). That negative qualities of caregivers' emotional expressions—distress, disgust, fear, anger—influence infant behavior seems sensible, given that the important message in a parent's emotional expressions is that the event is (or is not) dangerous or threatening to the baby. Infants not only play less with unusual toys when their mothers show disgust instead of pleasure, but when the same toys are presented a few minutes later infants show the same responses, even though mothers may no longer pose an emotional expression but are instead silent and neutral (Hornik, Risenhoover, and Gunnar, 1987). Infants are immediately and long-term affected by mothers' lapsing into a "still-face" (Cohn, Campbell, and Ross, 1991), and infants of depressed mothers show inferior social referencing skills, perhaps because their mothers provide less frequent or certain facial and vocal cues and fewer modeling responses (Field, 1995).

Responsiveness has been observed as a typical characteristic of parenting in mothers in different parts of the world (Bornstein, Tamis-Lemonda, et al., 1992). Some types of responsiveness are similar, and some vary relative to divergent cultural goals of parenting. Mothers in different cultures do not vary substantially in responding to infant vocal distress or nondistress. Responsiveness to distress, for example, is thought to have evolved an adaptive significance for eliciting and maintaining proximity and care (Bowlby, 1969). However, mothers respond variously in more discretionary interactions, as in determining which infant attentional behaviors to respond to and how to respond to them. In line with cultural expectations, Japanese mothers emphasize emotional exchange within the dyad in responsive interactions with their babies, whereas U.S. American mothers promote language and emphasize the material world outside the dyad (Bornstein, Tamis-Lemonda, et al., 1992).

*Parenting infants gone awry.*   Before we leave a consideration of how parents behave toward infants, some reality testing is in order. In everyday life, parenting infants does not always go well and right. Infanticide was practiced historically (French, in Vol. 2 of this *Handbook*), but thankfully it is very rare (although not unknown) today (Hrdy, 1999). Nonetheless, the local 10 o'clock news too often leads with a horrific telecast of some diabolical story about infant maltreatment or abandonment. Short of outright pathology, numerous other risks alter postnatal parenting and compromise the innocent infant (Carnegie Corporation of New York, 1994): More than one fourth of births in the United States are to unmarried mothers; more than one fourth of children under 3 years of age live below the federal poverty level; one in three victims of physical abuse is a baby; large numbers of women giving birth test positive for cocaine use at the time of delivery; fewer than one half of American 2-year-old children are fully immunized. Some parents are simply distressed and so supervise their infants less attentively and consequently know their infants less well (Crouter and Head, in Vol. 3 of this *Handbook*). Transient as well as ongoing pathology affects parenting. Depressed mothers demonstrate a style of interaction marked by intrusiveness, anger, irritation, and rough handling of their infants, a style to which infants respond with gaze aversion and avoidance (Field, 1995). Mothers who have abused drugs often fail simply to attend to elementary parenting responsibilities (Mayes and Bornstein, 1995; Mayes and Truman, in Vol. 4 of this *Handbook*). No matter if they are kissed publicly before every election as the ultimate demonstration of political caring, infants have always and in every society suffered physical and psychological neglect and abuse.

These descriptions of the characteristics of parenting beg the question: How do parental beliefs and behaviors develop? After brief interludes that compare maternal and paternal parenting and discuss mechanisms of parenting effects on infants, we return to explore the multiple forces that shape the parenting of infants.

## Mothers' and Fathers' Parenting of Infants

Mothers normally play the principal part in infant development (Barnard and Solchany, in Vol. 3 of this *Handbook*), even if historically fathers' social and legal claims and responsibilities on children were pre-eminent (French, in Vol. 2 of this *Handbook*). Cross-cultural surveys attest to the primacy of biological mothers' caregiving (e.g., Leiderman, Tulkin, and Rosenfeld, 1977), and theorists, researchers, and clinicians have often focused on mothering in recognition of this fact. Western industrialized nations have witnessed increases in the amount of time fathers spend with their children; in reality, however, fathers typically assume little or no responsibility for infantcare and rearing, and fathers are primarily helpers (Cabrera, Tamis-LeMonda, Bradley, Hofferth, and Lamb, 2000). On average, mothers spend between 65% and 80% more time than fathers do in direct one-to-one interaction with their infants (Parke, in Vol. 3 of this *Handbook*), and mothers spend more time with babies than do fathers whether in the United States (Kotelchuck, 1976), Britain (Jackson, 1987), Australia (Russell, 1983), or France or Belgium (Szalai, 1972). Mothers also interact with and take care of babies and toddlers more than fathers do (Belsky, Gilstrap, and Rovine, 1984; Collins and Russell, 1991; Greenbaum and Landau, 1982; Montemayor, 1982; Russell and Russell, 1987). Fathers may withdraw from their infants when they are unhappily married; mothers typically do not (e.g., Kerig, Cowan, and Cowan, 1993).

Fathers are neither inept nor uninterested in infant caregiving, however. When feeding infants, for example, both fathers and mothers respond to infants' cues, either with social bids or by adjusting the pace of the feeding (Parke and Sawin, 1980). Mothers and fathers alike touch and look more closely at an infant after the infant has vocalized, and both equally increase their rates of speech to baby following baby vocalization (Parke and Sawin, 1975).

Mothers and fathers interact with and care for infants in complementary ways; that is, they tend to divide the labor of caregiving and engage infants by emphasizing different types of interactions. When in face-to-face play with their $^1/_2$- to 6-month-old babies, for example, mothers tend to be rhythmic and containing, whereas fathers provide staccato bursts of both physical and social stimulation (Yogman, 1982). Mothers are more likely to hold their infants in the course of caregiving, whereas fathers are more likely to do so when playing with babies or in response to infants' requests to be held. When mother–infant and father–infant play were contrasted developmentally (Power, 1985), both mothers and fathers followed interactional rules of sharing attentional focus on a toy with baby; however, mothers tended to follow the baby's focus of interest, whereas fathers tended to establish the attentional focus themselves. In research involving both traditional American families (Belsky et al., 1984) and traditional and nontraditional (father as primary caregiver) Swedish families (Lamb, Frodi, Frodi, and Hwang, 1982), parental gender was found to exert a greater influence in these respects than, say, parental role or employment status: Mothers are more likely to kiss, hug, talk to, smile at, tend, and hold infants than fathers are, regardless of degree of involvement in caregiving. In general, then, mothers are associated with caregiving, whereas fathers are identified with playful interactions (Clarke-Stewart, 1980).

Mothers and fathers are both sensitive to infant language status, but, here too, they appear to play complementary roles with regard to the quality and the quantity of speech they direct to infants (Rondal, 1980). On the one hand, maternal and paternal speech to infants displays the same well-known simplification processes. On the other, mothers are more "in tune" with their infants' linguistic abilities: Maternal utterance length relates to child utterance length; paternal utterance length does not. Fathers' speech is lexically more diverse than mothers' speech, and it is also shorter, corrects children's speech less often, and places more verbal demands on the child; it thereby "pulls" for higher levels of performance (McLaughlin et al., 1983; Rondal, 1980). Despite the low quantity of interaction and variant style, however, infants become as attached to their fathers as they do to their mothers.

## Mechanisms of Parenting Effects on Infants

Parents' beliefs and behaviors influence infants and infant development by different paths. A common assumption in parenting is that the overall level of parental involvement or stimulation affects the infant's overall level of development (see Maccoby and Martin, 1983). An illustration of this simple model suggests that the development of language in infants is determined (at least to some degree) by the language infants hear (Hart and Risley, 1995, 1999). Indeed, mothers' single-word utterances are just those that appear earliest in their children's vocabularies (Chapman, 1981), and specific characteristics of maternal speech appear to play a big part in children's specific styles of speech as well (Bates, Bretherton, and Snyder, 1988).

*The nature of interactions.* Increasing evidence suggests, however, that sophisticated mechanisms need to be brought to bear to explain parenting effects (Collins et al., 2000). First, specific (rather than general) parental activities appear to relate concurrently and predictively to specific (rather than general) aspects of infant competence or performance, and, second, parent and infant mutually influence one another through time. The *specificity principle* states that specific parent-provided experiences at specific times exert specific effects over specific aspects of child development in specific ways (Bornstein, 1989a). Several such associations were observed in one illustrative longitudinal study of relationships between mothers and their 2- to 5-month-old infants (Bornstein and Tamis-LeMonda, 1990). For instance, mothers who encouraged their infants to attend to the mothers themselves had babies who later looked more at their mothers and less at the environment, whereas mothers who encouraged infant attention to the environment had babies who explored external properties, objects, and events more and their mothers less. Mothers' responses to their infants' communicative overtures are central to children's early acquisition of language, but exert less influence on the growth of motor abilities, play, or cognition broadly conceived (Tamis-LeMonda and Bornstein, 1994).

The *transactional principle* in development recognizes that the characteristics of individuals shape their experiences and reciprocally that experiences shape the characteristics of individuals through time (Sameroff, 1983). Biological endowment and experience mutually influence development from birth onward, and each life force affects the other as development proceeds to unfold through the lifespan (Lerner, 1997). By virtue of their unique characteristics and propensities—state of arousal, perceptual awareness, cognitive status, emotional expressiveness, and individuality of temperament—infants actively contribute, through their interactions with their parents, toward producing their own development. Infants influence which experiences they will be exposed to, and they interpret those experiences and so determine how those experiences will affect them (Scarr and McCartney, 1983). Infant and parent bring distinctive characteristics to, and each is believed to change as a result of, every interaction; both then enter the next round of interaction as different individuals. Thus infant temperament and maternal sensitivity operate in tandem to affect one another and eventually the attachment status of babies (Cassidy, 1994; Seifer, Schiller, Sameroff, Resnick, and Riordan, 1996). Vygotsky (1978) contended that, as a central feature of this transactional perspective, the more advanced or expert partner (usually the mother) will raise the level of performance or competence of the less advanced or expert partner (the infant), and the "dynamic systems perspective" posits that reciprocity between mother and infant specifically facilitates higher-level forms of interaction (Thelen and Smith, 1998). In essence, transactional goodness-of-fit models best explain the development of much in infant development. Thus Lea, who is an alert and responsive baby, invites her parents' stimulation; Lea's enthusiastic responses are rewarding to her parents, who engage her more, which in turn further enriches her life.

The specificity and the transactional principles together propel development from infancy onward. The working model of parenting infants and infant development is that specific experiences at specific times affect specific aspects of the infant growth in specific ways *and* that specific infant abilities and proclivities affect specific experiences and specific aspects of development.

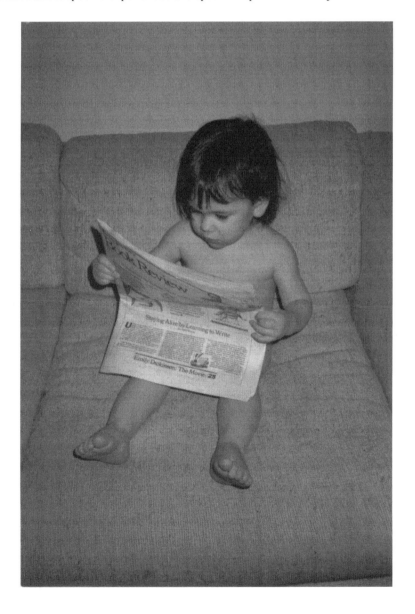

*Models of interaction effects.*    Parenting beliefs or behaviors affect development in infancy by means of different pathways (see Bornstein, 1989a; Bradley, Caldwell, and Rock, 1988). A parent-provided experience might influence the infant at a particular time point in a particular way, and the consequence for the infant endures, independent of later parenting and of any other contribution of the infant. Theoreticians and researchers have long supposed that the child's earliest experiences affect the course of later development (Plato, *ca.* 355 B.C.). This "early experience" model is consonant with a sensitive period interpretation of parenting effects (e.g., Bornstein, 1989b), and data derived from ethology, psychoanalysis, behaviorism, and neuropsychology support this model. Empirically, mothers encouraging their 2-month-old infants to attend to properties, objects, and events in the environment uniquely predicts infants' tactual exploration of objects at 5 months of age, that is, over and above stability in infant tactual exploration and any contemporaneous 5-month maternal stimulation (Bornstein and Tamis-LeMonda, 1990; see also Nicely et al., 1999).

In a second, "contemporary experience" model, parents exert unique influences over their infants at only a given point in development, overriding the effects of earlier experiences and independent of whatever individual differences infants carry forward. Empirical support for this model typically consists of failures of early intervention studies to show long-term effects and recovery of functioning from early deprivation (Clarke and Clarke, 1976; Lewis, 1997; Rutter and the English and Romanian Adoptees Study Team, 1998). Empirically, mothers' didactic encouragement of 5-month-old infants uniquely predicts infants' visual exploration of the environment at 5 months of age and does so more than mothers' didactic encouragement of 2-month-old infants (Bornstein and Tamis-LeMonda, 1990).

A third "cumulative/additive/stable environment" model combines the first two. That is, a parent-provided experience at any one time does not necessarily exceed threshold to affect the infant, but meaningful longitudinal relations are structured by similar parenting interactions that continually repeat and aggregate through time (e.g., Abelson, 1985; Olson, Bates, and Bayles, 1984). Empirically, maternal didactic stimulation when the infant is 2 and 5 months old has been shown to aggregate to predict unique variance in infant nondistress vocalization when the infant is 5 months old (Bornstein and Tamis-LeMonda, 1990; see also Olson et al., 1984).

Although longitudinal data in the first 6 months provide evidence for unique early, unique contemporary, and cumulative experiential effects between mothers and infants, for the most part it is typical for children to be reared in stable environments (Holden and Miller, 1999), so that cumulative experiences are very likely (Collins et al., 2000). Of course, there is nothing to prevent different models of parenting influence from operating simultaneously in different spheres of infant development. It would be equally shortsighted to assume that different kinds of parenting exert only independent and linear effects over infant development; such a stance fails to consider significant complex, conditional, and nonlinear effects of caregiving. Parenting of specific sorts might affect development monistically, but different behaviors certainly also often combine in conditional ways; parenting affects development over short or over long periods; parenting effects may be immediate, or they may need to aggregate; and some may be direct, others indirect.

## Summary

Parents influence their infants directly by means of their genes, beliefs, and behaviors as well as indirectly by means of their influences on one another and the multiple contexts in which they live. Out of the dynamic range and complexity of individual activities that constitute parenting infants, major domains of parent–infant interaction have been distinguished: They include nurturing, interacting socially, stimulating cognitively, and provisioning the environment. These domains are conceptually separable but fundamentally integral, and each is developmentally significant. The attitudes parents hold about their infants and the activities they engage them in are each meaningful to the development of babies. Mothers typically take more responsibility for and engage in infant caregiving more than do fathers, but fathers play complementary and signal roles. Parent-provided experiences affect infants by different mechanisms of action, but tend to follow principles of specificity and transaction.

## FORCES THAT SHAPE PARENTING INFANTS

A critical step on the path to fully understanding parenting is to evaluate forces that first shape it. The origins of individual variation in maternal and paternal infant caregiving—whether beliefs or behaviors—are extremely complex, but certain factors seem to be of paramount importance: (1) actual or perceived characteristics of infants, (2) biological determinants, (3) features of personality, and (4) contextual influences, including social situational factors, SES, and culture.

### Infant Effects

Subtle as well as not-so-subtle characteristics of infants influence parenting (and, on the transactional principle, infant development). So-called infant effects may be of different kinds. Some are universal and common to all infants; others will be unique to a particular infant or situation.

Some physical features of infancy probably affect parents everywhere in similar ways. By the conclusion of the first trimester, fetuses are felt to move *in utero* ("quickening"), and soon after (with support) fetuses may survive outside the womb ("viability"). These are significant markers in the life of the child *and* in the lives and psyches of the child's parents. After birth, the infant's nature as well as certain infant actions are likely to influence parenting. The newborn has a large head dominated by a disproportionately large forehead, widely spaced sizeable eyes, a small and snub nose, an exaggeratedly round face, and a small chin. The ethologist Konrad Lorenz (1935/1970) argued that these physiognomic features of "babyishness" provoke adults to express reflexively nurturant reactions toward babies—even across different species (Alley, 1981, 1983). Under ordinary conditions, specific infant behaviors elicit caregiving or other specific responses from parents (Bell and Harper, 1977; Bornstein, Tamis-LeMonda, et al., 1992). And from the moment of birth, babies exercise the several effective signals that are at their disposal: Crying will motivate adults to approach and soothe, and smiling will encourage adults to stay near.

Other structural characteristics of infants affect parenting and the quality of parent–infant interaction: Infant health status, gender, and age are three significant factors. Preterm infants, for example, often have difficulty regulating engagements with caregivers, as made evident by increased gaze aversion, decreased joint play, and lower levels of joint attention (Landry, 1995), and their mothers are reciprocally more active and directive (Goldberg and DiVitto, in Vol. 1 of this *Handbook*). Parental patterns of interaction with infant girls and boys are a second more complicated infant effect. On the one hand, there is evidence that parenting infant girls and boys is surprisingly similar (Leaper, in Vol. 1 of this *Handbook*; Lytton and Romney, 1991). On the other, nurseries for newborn infants provide color-coded blankets, diapers, and so forth; infant gifts, beginning with the baby shower, are carefully selected with gender in mind; and infants are uniformly dressed in gender-typed clothing (Shakin, Shakin, and Sternglanz, 1985). Gender organizes parents' initial descriptions, impressions, and expectations of their infants (Condry and Condry, 1976; Rubin, Provenzano, and Luria, 1974). Finally, infant development per se, a third structural infant effect, exerts pervasive control over parental behavior. For example, cross-cultural study shows that mothers of younger infants use more affect-laden speech but that, as infants achieve more sophisticated levels of motor exploration and cognitive comprehension, mothers increasingly orient, comment, and prepare their babies for the world outside the dyad by increasing amounts of their information-laden speech (Bornstein, Tamis-LeMonda, et al., 1992).

Other idiosyncratic characteristics of infants are no less stimulating to parents. Goldberg (1977) taxonomized the salient infant characteristics that affect parents: responsiveness, readability, and predictability. Responsiveness refers to the extent and the quality of infant reactivity to stimulation. Readability refers to the definitiveness of infant behavioral signals: An "easily read" infant is one who produces unambiguous cues that allow caregivers to recognize state quickly, interpret signals promptly, and thus respond contingently. Predictability refers to the degree to which infant behaviors can be anticipated reliably. Each baby possesses her or his unique profile of these characteristics.

Infant cognitive ability and temperament, actual or perceived, also influence adults and the effectiveness of adult ministrations. Trevarthen and Hubley (1978) noted that, once the infant begins to focus attention on interesting objects in the environment, the mother adjusts by starting to create "spectacles" for the child. Having a temperamentally easy baby or perceiving a baby as temperamentally easy (relatively happy, predictable, soothable, and sociable) enhances a mother's feelings that she is competent (Deutsch, Ruble, Fleming, Brooks-Gunn, and Stangor, 1988). More to the point, the same behavioral intervention may rapidly soothe one infant yet seem totally ineffective for another, leading parents of different infants to reach different conclusions about their competence as parents, despite similarities in their parenting (Putnam et al., in Vol. 1 of this *Handbook*).

## Biological Determinants of Parenting

Of course, forces within the parent shape parenting as well. Basic physiology is mobilized to support parenting (Corter and Fleming, in Vol. 2 of this *Handbook*; Rosenblatt, in Vol. 2 of this *Handbook*), and parenting cognitions and activities normally first arise around biological processes associated with pregnancy and parturition. However, prenatal biological events—parental age, diet, and stress, as well as other factors such as contraction of disease, exposure to environmental toxins, and even anesthetics—also affect postnatal parenting.

Papoušek and Papoušek (in Vol. 2 of this *Handbook*) developed the notion that some infant caregiving practices are biologically "wired" into human beings. Intuitive parenting, so-called, involves responses that are developmentally suited to the age and the abilities of the child and that often have the goal of enhancing adaptation and development. Parents regularly enact intuitive parenting programs in an unconscious fashion—such programs do not require the time and the effort typical of conscious decision making, and, being more rapid and efficient, they utilize less attentional reserve.

An example of intuitive parenting is the use of child-directed speech. Parents (as well as others) habitually and unconsciously modulate myriad aspects of their communication with infants to match infants' presumed or evaluated competencies. Special characteristics of such child-directed speech include prosodic features (higher pitch, greater range of frequencies, more varied and exaggerated intonation); simplicity features (shorter utterances, slower tempo, longer pauses between phrases, fewer embedded clauses, fewer auxiliaries); redundancy features (more repetition over shorter amounts of time, more immediate repetition); lexical features (special forms like "mama"); and content features (restriction of topics to the child's world) (Papoušek, Papoušek, and Bornstein, 1985). Cross-cultural developmental study attests that child-directed speech is (essentially) universal (Jacobson, Boersma, Fields, and Olson, 1983; Snow, 1977; but see Ratner and Pye, 1984). Indeed, parents find it difficult to resist or modify such intuitive behaviors, even when asked to do so (Trevarthen, 1979). Additional support for the premise that some interactions with infants are intuitive comes from observations that nonparents (males *and* females) who have little prior experience with infants modify their speech as the infants' own parents do when an infant is actually present and even when asked to imagine speaking to one (Jacobson et al., 1983). Children from 2 to 3 years of age also engage in such systematic language adjustments when speaking to their year-old siblings as opposed to their mothers (Dunn and Kendrick, 1982). When communicating with their infants, mothers with hearing and speech impediments modify their sign language the way hearing mothers use child-directed speech (Erting, Prezioso, and Hynes, 1994).

## Parental Personality

Parenting also reflects transient feelings as well as enduring personality traits (Belsky and Barends, in Vol. 3 of this *Handbook*; Lamb and Easterbrooks, 1981). Features of personality favorable to good parenting might include empathic awareness, predictability, nonintrusiveness, and emotional availability (Martin, 1989). Perceived self-efficacy is also likely to affect parenting because parents who feel competent are reinforced and thus motivated to engage in further interaction with their infants, which in turn provides them with additional opportunities to read their infants' signals fully, interpret them correctly, and respond appropriately; the more rewarding the interaction, the more motivated are parents to seek "quality" interaction again (Teti and Candelaria, in Vol. 4 of this *Handbook*).

Within the normal range, characteristics such as self-centeredness and adaptability will be especially pertinent to infant caregiving. Adult adaptability may be vital in the first few months when infants' activities appear unpredictable and disorganized, their cues less distinct and well differentiated, and infants themselves generally less "readable." Self-centeredness can lead to difficulties when adults fail to put infants' needs before their own (Dix, 1991). Middle-SES married women who are more preoccupied with themselves, as measured by physical and sexual concerns, show less effective parenting patterns in the postpartum year (Grossman, Eichler, and Winikoff, 1980). Self-absorbed, these mothers may not show sensitivity to their infants' needs (Cowan and Cowan, 1992), a situation that also seems prevalent among teen mothers (Osofsky, Hann, and Peebles, 1993).

Negative characteristics of personality, whether transient or permanent, are likely to affect parenting infants adversely. For example, depression might reflect an enduring psychological characteristic, or it might be fleeting, as in response to economic circumstances or even the birth of the baby (Zahn-Waxler, Duggal, and Gruber, in Vol. 4 of this *Handbook*). Depressed mothers fail to experience—and convey to their infants—much happiness with life. Such feelings no doubt diminish responsiveness or discoordinate interactions (Tronick and Gianino, 1986), and so depressed parenting may have short- as well as long-term consequences for infants (Lyons-Ruth, Zoll, Conell, and Grunebaum, 1986). Field (1984) observed that in face-to-face interactions infants of depressed mothers showed less positive and more negative facial affect, vocalized less, protested more, and seemed to make less effort to change or improve their lot than did infants of nondepressed mothers. Thus aspects of adult personality help to shape parenting.

Furthermore, through intergenerational transmission, by means of genetic or experiential pathways, purposefully or unintentionally one generation may psychologically influence the parenting beliefs and behaviors of the next (Van IJzendoorn, 1992). For example, a mother's experiences with her own mother may have long-range effects on her own personality and parenting (Smith and Drew, in Vol. 3 of this *Handbook*). Mothers who report having had secure and realistic perceptions of their attachments to their own mothers are themselves more likely to have securely attached infants (Cummings and Cummings, in Vol. 5 of this *Handbook*; Main, 1991).

A dynamic view suggests that personality factors that influence parenting are also molded by contemporary experiences. Thus infants as well as contextual settings help to shape parental beliefs and behaviors.

## Contexts of Parenting

Biology, personality, and perceptions of role responsibilities constitute factors that influence parenting from the start. However, societal factors condition and channel beliefs and behaviors of infants' parents as well. Family situation, social status, and culture, for example, encourage diverse patterns of parenting perceptions and practices. In some places, infants are reared in extended families in which care is provided by many relatives; in others, mothers and babies are isolated from almost all social contexts. In some groups, fathers are treated as irrelevant social objects; in others, fathers assume complex responsibilities for infants (Bornstein, 1991).

*Family situation.* Infant parenting is influenced by family configuration, level of parental stress, marital relationships, and parents' social networks, among other social-situational factors. For example, approximately one half of babies born in a given year are firstborn infants, and firstborn infants receive more attention and better care as infants than do laterborn infants (Sulloway, 1997). Mothers engage, respond, stimulate, talk, and express positive affection more to their firstborn babies than to their laterborn babies, even when firstborn and laterborn babies show no differences in their behavior, indicating that these maternal behaviors do not reflect infant effects (Belsky et al., 1984). However, mothers are also prone to rate their firstborn babies as difficult (Bates, 1987), which may derive from the fact that firstborn babies actually are more difficult babies or, alternatively, because first-time mothers are less at ease with their infants and thus tend to perceive them as more demanding. Relatedly, multiparas report higher self-efficacy than primiparas (Fish and Stifter, 1993). Among the more dramatic changes in family dynamics is the one that takes place when a second baby is born (Belsky, Rovine, and Fish, 1991; Mendelson, 1990; Stewart, 1990); consequently, the social and physical ecologies of firstborn and laterborn infants are thoroughly different (Dunn and Plomin, 1991). The births of later children alter the roles of each family member and forever affect the ways in which each interacts with all others. Parents of a secondborn infant are in many ways, therefore, not the same as parents of a firstborn infant.

Even though the absolute frequency of "daily hassles" reported by parents of infants is approximately the same as for children of other ages, parents of infants do not rate their intensity or salience as high (Crnic and Low, in Vol. 5 of this *Handbook*). Infancy may well represent a "honeymoon period" in which parents recognize the difficultness of parenting chores and choose not to make as stressful attributions about them. Parents also attribute greater willfulness to children's behavior once they make the transition out of infancy (Bugental and Happaney, in Vol. 3 of this *Handbook*).

Marital relationships and father involvement affect the quality of mother–child and father–child relationships and child outcomes (Gable, Crnic, and Belsky, 1994; Tamis-LeMonda and Cabrera, 1999), and how parents work together as a coparenting team may have far-reaching consequences for infants (Fincham, 1998).

The situations in which new mothers find themselves exert specific influences over parenting. A large number of new mothers in the United States have not finished high school, are not married, or are teenagers when their baby is born (Center for the Study of Social Policy, 2000). Nearly 70% of women on welfare are unmarried when they have their first child (Tamis-LeMonda and Cabrera, 1999). Having a baby is a major transition in a person's life, marked by dramatic changes in information seeking, self-definition, and role responsibility (Belsky, 1984; Cowan and Cowan, 1992). Teenage mothers are thought to have lower levels of ego strength, to be less mature emotionally and socially, and to lack a well-formed maternal self-definition, perhaps because they themselves are negotiating their own developmental issues and are unskilled on account of a dearth of life experience (Moore and Brooks-Gunn, in Vol. 1 of this *Handbook*). Many people appear to start their career as parents by being disadvantaged in some way.

Financial and social stresses adversely affect the general well-being and health of parents and demand attention and emotional energy from them (Magnuson and Duncan, in Vol. 4 of this *Handbook*). These circumstances, in turn, may reduce their attentiveness, patience, and tolerance toward children (Crnic and Low, in Vol. 5 of this *Handbook*). Emotional integration or isolation from potential support networks mitigates or exacerbates these effects in new parents (Cochran and Niego, in Vol. 4 of this *Handbook*). Social support consists of the people who are important in a parent's life, including a spouse or significant other, relatives, friends, and neighbors (Jennings, Stagg, and Connors, 1991). Social support can improve parenting satisfaction, affecting the availability of mothers to their infants as well as the quality of mother–infant interactions (Bradley and Whiteside-Mansell, 1997). Well-supported mothers are less restrictive and punitive with their infants than are less well-supported mothers, and frequency of contacts with significant others improves the quality of parent–infant relationships (Crnic, Greenberg, Ragozin, Robinson, and Basham, 1983; Powell, 1980) as well as the parents' sense of their own effectance and competence (Abernathy, 1973). Mothers report that community and friendship support are beneficial, but intimate support from husbands (those "indirect effects" mentioned in the subsection on direct and indirect effects) has the most general positive consequences for maternal competence (Crnic et al., 1983).

*Socioeconomic status.* SES influences parental behavior. Mothers in different SES groups behave similarly in certain ways; however, SES also orders the home environment and other behaviors of parents toward infants (Bornstein, Suwalsky, Hahn, and Haynes, 2001; Hoff, Laursen, and Tardif, in Vol. 2 of this *Handbook*). Low SES is considered a risk factor in children's development on account of its detrimental effect on the quality of mother–infant interaction (Dodge, Pettit, and Bates, 1994): Low SES adversely affects mothers' psychological functioning and promotes harsh or inconsistent disciplinary practices (Conger, McMarty, Yang, Lahey, and Kropp, 1984; McLoyd and Wilson, 1990; Simons, Whitbeck, Conger, and Wu, 1991). Low-SES compared with middle-SES parents typically provide infants with fewer opportunities for variety in daily stimulation, less appropriate play materials, and less total stimulation, for example (Gottfried, 1984).

Significantly, middle-SES mothers converse with their infants more, and in systematically more sophisticated ways, than do lower-SES mothers, even though young infants (presumably) understand little maternal speech (Hart and Risley, 1995; Hoff-Ginsberg, 1991). Such social status differences in maternal speech to infants are pervasive across cultures: In Israel, for example, upper-SES mothers talk, label, and ask "what" questions more often than do lower- or middle-SES mothers (Ninio, 1980). Higher-SES mothers' encouragement in language undoubtedly facilitates self-expression in children; higher-SES babies produce more sounds and later words than do lower-SES babies (Hart and Risley, 1995, 1999; Papoušek et al., 1985).

The lower-SES mother is likely to have been a poorer student, making it unlikely that she will turn to books readily as sources of information about pregnancy, infancy, and parenthood; among middle-SES women, reading material is primary (Furstenberg, Brooks-Gunn, and Chase-Lansdale, 1989; Hofferth and Hayes, 1987; Young, 1991). Middle-SES, more than lower-SES, parents also seek out and absorb expert advice about child development (Lightfoot and Valsiner, 1992). Indeed, social class and culture pervasively influence the complexity and the resourcefulness with which mothers view infant development (Palacios, 1990; Sameroff and Feil, 1985).

*Culture.* Cultural variation in beliefs and behaviors is always impressive, whether observed among different ethnic groups in one society or among different groups in different parts of the world. As illustrations throughout this chapter attest, cross-cultural comparisons show that virtually all aspects of parenting infants are informed by culture. An investigation of expected developmental timetables in new mothers from Australia versus Lebanon found that culture shaped mothers' expectations of children much more than other factors, such as their experiences in observing their own children, comparing them with other children, and receiving advice from friends and experts (Goodnow, Cashmore, Cotton, and Knight, 1984).

Culture influences parenting patterns and child development from very early in infancy through such factors as when and how parents care for infants, the extent to which parents permit infants freedom to explore, how nurturant or restrictive parents are, which behaviors parents emphasize, and so forth (Benedict, 1938; Bornstein, 1991; Erikson, 1950; Whiting, 1981). For example, Japan and the United States maintain reasonably similar levels of modernity and living standards and both are child centered, but the two differ dramatically in terms of history, culture, beliefs, and childrearing goals (e.g., Azuma, 1986; Bornstein, 1989e; Caudill, 1973). Japanese mothers expect early mastery of emotional maturity, self-control, and social courtesy in their offspring, whereas U.S. American mothers expect early mastery of verbal competence and self-actualization in theirs. American mothers promote autonomy and organize social interactions with their infants so as to foster physical and verbal assertiveness and independence, and they promote infants' interest in the external environment. Japanese mothers organize social interactions so as to consolidate and strengthen closeness and dependency within the dyad (e.g., Befu, 1986; Doi, 1973; Kojima, 1986), and they tend to indulge infants (Bornstein, Azuma, et al., 1990; Bornstein, Tal, and Tamis-LeMonda, 1991; Bornstein, Toda, et al., 1990). Japanese mothers encourage the incorporation of a partner in infant pretense play; by contrast, American mothers encourage exploration and function in play. For Americans, parent play with infants and the toys used during play are more frequently the topic or object of communication; for Japanese, the play setting serves to mediate dyadic communication and interaction (Tamis-LeMonda et al., 1992).

Mothers in different cultures show striking similarities in interacting with their infants as well. All must nurture and promote the physical growth of infants if their infants are to survive (Bornstein, 1989a, 1995; LeVine, 1988). Whether converging patterns in mothers reflect biological bases of caregiving, the historical convergence of parenting styles, or the increasing prevalence of a single childrearing pattern through migration or dissemination by mass media is difficult, if not impossible, to determine. In the end, different peoples (presumably) wish to promote similar general competencies in their young. Some do so in qualitatively and quantitatively similar ways. Others appear to do so differently, and of course, culture-specific patterns of childrearing can be expected to be adapted to each specific society's settings and needs (Lerner, 1989; Valsiner, 1987).

## Summary

Parenting stands at the confluence of many complex tributaries of influence; some arise within the individual, whereas others have external sources. Some reactions felt toward babies may be reflexive and universal; others are idiosyncratic and vary with personality. By virtue of their temperament and the quality and the contingency of their own responsiveness, infants have a major impact on how parents parent and how parents perceive themselves as parents. Family situation, social status, and culture loom large in shaping parenting and the ecology of infancy. The childrearing practices of one's own group may seem "natural" but may actually be rather unusual when compared with those of other groups. Social status differences color infantrearing practices, and cultural ideology also makes for meaningful differences in patterns of parenting beliefs and behaviors toward infants.

## NONPARENTAL CAREGIVERS AND INFANTS

Infant care by a biological parent is often supplemented. Siblings or other young children often care for infants, and in different cultures now and historically infants have been tended by nonparental careproviders—aunts and grandmothers, nurses and slaves, daycare workers and metaplot—whether in family daycare at home, daycare facilities, village centers, or fields. In short, many individuals—other than mother and father—"parent" infants.

## Siblings

In many cultures, especially non-Western nonindustrialized ones, infants are found in the care of an older sister or brother (Teti, 1992; Zukow-Goldring, in Vol. 3 of this *Handbook*). In such situations, siblings typically spend most of their infant-tending time involved in unskilled nurturant caregiving, thereby freeing adults for more rewarding economic activities (Werner, 1979). In Western and industrialized societies, by contrast, siblings are seldom entrusted with much responsibility for "parenting" infants per se and are themselves engaged in activities preparatory for maturity. Mothers are more likely to respond contingently to 6- and 9-month infants than are older siblings or peers (Vandell and Wilson, 1987).

Sibling orientation toward infants displays features of both adult–infant and peer–infant systems (Pepler, Corter, and Abramovitch, 1982). On the one hand, siblings and infants share common interests and have more similar behavioral repertoires than do adults and infants. On the other hand, sibling pairs resemble adult–infant pairs to the extent that they differ in experience and levels of both cognitive and social ability (Abramovitch, Corter, and Lando, 1979). Older siblings tend to "lead" interactions and engage in more dominant, assertive, and directing behaviors. Reciprocally, infants often take special note of what their older siblings do; they follow, imitate, and explore the toys recently abandoned by older children. Of course, this strategy maximizes infant learning from the older child. Older siblings spend at least some time teaching object-related and social skills to their younger siblings (including infants), and the amount of teaching increases with the age of the older child (Minnett, Vandell, and Santrock, 1983; Stewart, 1983). Older preschool-aged firstborn children create more "social" (e.g., game) and "intellectual" (e.g., language mastery) experiences for their infant siblings than do younger preschool-aged firstborn children (Teti, Bond, and Gibbs, 1986) and so may influence social and cognitive skills of infants through teaching and modeling (Zajonc, 1983). By the end of the first year, infants' positive emotional exchanges extend to peers. For example, Eckerman, Whatley, and Kutz (1975) found that play episodes of peers between the ages of 10 and 24 months contained behaviors indicating positive emotions. Toward the end of the first year children watch and imitate peers' actions with toys (Singer, 1995). One study revealed that 17- to 20-month-old children engage in more creative or unusual uses of objects during play with peers than during play with mothers (Rubenstein and Howes, 1976). Older sisters and brothers certainly also learn about themselves and about others as a result of their infant minding (Mendelson, 1990).

## Related and Unrelated Nonparental Infant Caregivers

Infants commonly encounter a social world that extends beyond the immediate family. In some societies, multiple-infant caregiving is natural (e.g., Bornstein et al., 1996; Morelli and Tronick, 1991). Today, the majority of infants in the United States are cared for on a regular basis by someone in addition to a parent (Clarke-Stewart and Allhusen, in Vol. 3 of this *Handbook*).

A common form of nonparental familial care involves relatives such as grandparents (Smith and Drew, in Vol. 3 of this *Handbook*). Parents with infants are very likely to receive support from their own parents (Eggebeen, 1992; Eggebeen and Hogan, 1990; Spitze and Logan, 1992). Maternal grandmothers are acknowledged to play an especially critical role in the life of infants of teen and ethnic minority mothers (McAdoo, in Vol. 4 of this *Handbook*; Moore and Brooks-Gunn, in Vol. 3 of this *Handbook*). Nonfamilial daycare providers constitute the other common participants in infant caregiving. Most provide infants with care in daycare centers; the next most provide infants with care in their own homes; and the fewest care for infants in the baby's home (Clarke-Stewart and Allhusen, in Vol. 3 of this *Handbook*).

It was once believed that only full-time mothers could provide infants with the care they needed in order to thrive: These beliefs were fostered by literature on the adverse effects of maternal deprivation (Bowlby, 1951; Rutter, in Vol. 4 of this *Handbook*). Theory maintained that infants become attached to those persons who have been associated over time with consistent, predictable, and appropriate responses to their signals as well as to their needs, and that attachment was critical to the development of a healthy and normal personality (Cummings and Cummings, in Vol. 5 of this *Handbook*). Since the 1960s, however, some social critics have argued that high-quality nonparental infant daycare is possible and that the normalcy of infants' emotional attachments to parents appears to depend, not on the quantity of time that parents spend with their infants, but on the quality of parents' interactions with them (Lamb, 1998).

## Summary

Siblings, grandparents, and various nonparents play salient roles in infantcare, offering degrees of nurturing, involvement, stimulation, and entertainment that vary depending on a variety of factors, including age, gender, age gap, quality of attachment, personality, and the like. Often infant caregivers behave in a complementary fashion to one another, dividing the full labor of infant caregiving among themselves by emphasizing one or another parenting responsibility and activity (Bornstein et al.,

1995). Still unclear, however, are the cumulative long-term implications of these diverse patterns of early "parenting" relationships for infant development.


## CONCLUSIONS

Because of the nature of the infant as well as the range, magnitude, and implications of developmental change early in life, infancy is intensely fascinating and undeniably appealing, but challenging and formidable in the extreme for parents. The popular belief that parent-provided experiences during infancy exert powerful influences on later behavior or personality has been fostered from many quarters. Nevertheless, human behavior is quite malleable, and plasticity remains a feature of adaptation in infancy and long after. Although not all infant experiences are critical for later development and single events are rarely formative, infant experiences doubtlessly can have long-lasting effects. Certainly, little and big consistencies of parenting aggregate over infancy to construct the person.

Parents intend much in their interactions with their infants: They promote their infants' mental development through the structures they create and the meanings they place on those structures, and they foster emotional understanding and development of self through the models they portray and the values they display. The complex of parent beliefs and behaviors with infants is divisible into domains, and parents tend to show consistency over time in certain of those domains. Some aspects of parenting are frequent or significant from the get-go, and wane after; others wax over the course of infancy. For new parents, the first years with an infant constitute a period of adjustment and transformation: Mothers typically assume primary responsibility for infantcare within the family, and mother–infant interactions are characterized by nurturant and verbal activities; father–infant interactions are dominated by play. As a result, infants' relationships with their two parents are distinctive from a very early age. The interactive and intersubjective aspects of parent and infant activities have telling consequences for the after-infancy development of the child. Researchers and theoreticians today do not ask *whether* parenting affects infant development, but *which* parent-provided experiences affect *what* aspects of development *when* and *how*, and they are interested also to learn the *ways* in which individual children are so affected, as well as the ways individual children affect their own development.

A full understanding of what it means to parent infants depends on the ecologies in which that parenting takes place. Within-family experiences appear to exert a major impact during the first years of life. Family composition, social class, and cultural variation exert salient influences on the ways in which infants are reared and what is expected of them as they grow. Infants also form relationships with siblings and grandparents as well as with other nonfamilial caregivers. Large numbers of infants have significant experiences outside the family—often through enrollment in alternative care settings—but the effects of out-of-home care vary depending on its type and quality, as well as on characteristics of infants and their families. These early relationships with mothers, fathers, siblings, and others all ensure that the parenting that the young infant experiences is rich and multifaceted.

Biology, personality, beliefs and intuitions, aspects of economic, social, and cultural circumstances, and quality of intimate relationships all play important roles in determining the nature of infant parenting. Of course, infants bring unique social styles and an active mental life to everyday interactions with adults that shape their caregiving experiences too. Infants alter the environment as they interact with it, and they interpret experiences and environment alike in their unique ways. Parent and infant convey distinctive characteristics to every interaction, and both are changed as a result. In other words, parent and infant actively coconstruct one another through time.

Infancy is a distinctive period, a major transition, and a formative phase in human development. Infants assume few responsibilities and are not at all self-reliant. Rather, parents have central roles to play in infants' physical survival, social growth, emotional maturation, and cognitive development. A better understanding of the nature of the human being is afforded by examination of parent–infant interaction and its consequences in this period of the dyad's initial accommodation—the unique and specific influences of parent on infant and of infant on parent. With the birth of a baby, a parent's life is forever altered. Those changes, in turn, shape the experiences of the infant and, with time, the person she or he becomes. Linked, parent and infant chart that course together. Infancy is a starting point of life for both infant *and* parent.

## REFERENCES

Abelson, R. (1985). A variance explanation paradox: When a little is a lot. *Psychological Bulletin, 97*, 129–133.

Abernathy, V. (1973). Social network and response to the maternal role. *International Journal of Sociology of the Family, 3*, 86–96.

Abramovitch, R., Corter, C., and Lando, B. (1979). Sibling interaction in the home. *Child Development, 50*, 997–1003.

Adamson, L. B., and Bakeman, R. (1984). Mothers' communicative acts: Changes during infancy. *Infant Behavior and Development, 7*, 467–478.

Ainsworth, M. (1967). *Infancy in Uganda*. Baltimore: Johns Hopkins University Press.

Ainsworth, M. D. S., Blehar, M. D., Waters, E., and Wall, S. (1978). *Patterns of attachment: A psychological study of the strange situation*. Hillsdale, NJ: Lawrence Erlbaum Associates.

Alley, T. R. (1981). Head shape and the perception of cuteness. *Developmental Psychology, 17*, 650–654.

Alley, T. R. (1983). Infantile head shape as an elicitor of adult protection. *Merrill-Palmer Quarterly, 29*, 411–427.

Azuma, H. (1986). Why study child development in Japan? In H. Stevenson, H. Azuma, and K. Hakuta (Eds.), *Child development and education in Japan* (pp. 3–12). New York: Freeman.

Bates, J. E. (1987). Temperament in infancy. In J. D. Osofsky (Ed.), *Handbook of infant development* (pp. 1101–1149). New York: Wiley.

Bates, E., Bretherton, I., and Snyder, L. (1988). *From first words to grammar*. New York: Cambridge University Press.

Bates, J. E., Maslin, C. A., and Frankel, K. A. (1985). Attachment security, mother–child interaction, and temperament as predictors of behavior problem ratings at age three years. In I. Bretherton and E. Waters (Eds.), Growing points of attachment theory and research. *Monographs of the Society for Research in Child Development, 50* (Serial No. 209).

Bateson, M. C. (1979). "The epigenesis of conversational interaction": A personal account of research development. In M. Bullowa (Ed.), *Before speech: The beginning of human communication* (pp. 63–77). New York: Cambridge University Press.

Befu, H. (1986). Social and cultural background for child development in Japan and the United States. In H. W. Stevenson, H. Azuma, and K. Hakuta (Eds.), *Child development and education in Japan* (pp. 13–27). San Francisco: Freeman.

Bell, R. Q., and Harper, L. (1977). *Child effects on adults*. Hillsdale, NJ: Lawrence Erlbaum Associates.

Bellinger, D. (1980). Consistency in the pattern of change in mother's speech: Some discriminant analyses. *Journal of Child Language, 7*, 469–487.

Belsky, J. (1984). The determinants of parenting: A process model. *Child Development, 55*, 83–96.

Belsky, J., Gilstrap, B., and Rovine, M. (1984). The Pennsylvania Infant and Family Development Project I: Stability and change in mother–infant and father–infant interaction in a family setting—1- to 3- to 9-months. *Child Development, 55*, 692–705.

Belsky, J., Rovine, M., and Fish, M. (1991). The developing family system. In M. Gunnar (Ed.), *Minnesota symposia on child psychology: Vol. 22. Systems and development* (pp. 119–166). Hillsdale, NJ: Lawrence Erlbaum Associates.

Benedict, R. (1938). Continuities and discontinuities in cultural conditioning. *Psychiatry, 1*, 161–167.

Bertenthal, B. I., and Campos, J. J. (1990). A systems approach to the organizing effects of self-produced locomotion during infancy. In C. Rovee-Collier (Ed.), *Advances in infancy research* (Vol. 6, pp. 1–60). Norwood, NJ: Ablex.

Bever, T. G. (1982). *Regressions in mental development*. Hillsdale, NJ: Lawrence Erlbaum Associates.

Biringen, Z., Emde, R. N., Campos, J. J., and Appelbaum, M. I. (1995). Affective reorganization in the infant, the mother, and the dyad: The role of upright locomotion and its timing. *Child Development, 66*, 499–514.

Bjorklund, D. F., and Pellegrini, A. (2000). Child development and evolutionary psychology. *Child Development, 72*, 1687–1708.

Bloom, L. (1998). Language acquisition in its developmental context. In W. Damon (Series Ed.), and D. Kuhn and R. S. Siegler (Vol. Eds.), *Handbook of child psychology: Vol. 2. Cognition, perception, and language* (5th ed., pp. 309–370). New York: Wiley.

Bornstein, M. H. (1980). Cross-cultural developmental psychology. In M. H. Bornstein (Ed.), *Comparative methods in psychology* (pp. 231–281). Hillsdale, NJ: Lawrence Erlbaum Associates.

Bornstein, M. H. (1985). How infant and mother jointly contribute to developing cognitive competence in the child. *Proceedings of the National Academy of Sciences (U.S.A.), 82*, 7470–7473.

Bornstein, M. H. (1989a). Between caretakers and their young: Two modes of interaction and their consequences for cognitive growth. In M. H. Bornstein and J. S. Bruner (Eds.), *Interaction in human development* (pp. 197–214). Hillsdale, NJ: Lawrence Erlbaum Associates.

Bornstein, M. H. (1989b). Sensitive periods in development: Structural characteristics and causal interpretations. *Psychological Bulletin, 105*, 179–197.

Bornstein, M. H. (1989c). Stability in early mental development: From attention and information processing in infancy to language and cognition in childhood. In M. H. Bornstein and N. A. Krasnegor (Eds.), *Stability and continuity in mental development: Behavioral and biological perspectives* (pp. 147–170). Hillsdale, NJ: Lawrence Erlbaum Associates.

Bornstein, M. H. (Ed.). (1989d). *Maternal responsiveness: Characteristics and consequences.* San Francisco: Jossey-Bass.

Bornstein, M. H. (1989e). Cross-cultural developmental comparisons: The case of Japanese–American infant and mother activities and interactions. What we know, what we need to know, and why we need to know. *Developmental Review, 9*, 171–204.

Bornstein, M. H. (1991). Approaches to parenting in culture. In M. H. Bornstein (Ed.), *Cultural approaches to parenting* (pp. 3–19). Hillsdale, NJ: Lawrence Erlbaum Associates.

Bornstein, M. H. (1995). Parenting infants. In M. H. Bornstein (Ed.), *Handbook of parenting* (Vol. 1, pp. 3–39). Mahwah, NJ: Lawrence Erlbaum Associates.

Bornstein, M. H., and Arterberry, M. E. (1999). Perceptual development. In M. H. Bornstein and M. E. Lamb (Eds.), *Developmental psychology: An advanced textbook* (4th ed., pp. 231–274). Mahwah, NJ: Lawrence Erlbaum Associates.

Bornstein, M. H., Azuma, H., Tamis-LeMonda, C. S., and Ogino, M. (1990). Mother and infant activity and interaction in Japan and in the United States: I. A comparative macroanalysis of naturalistic exchanges. *International Journal of Behavioral Development, 13*, 267–287.

Bornstein, M. H., Gaughran, J. M., and Seguí, I. (1991). Multimethod assessment of infant temperament: Mother questionnaire and mother and observer reports evaluated and compared at 5 months using the Infant Temperament Measure. *International Journal of Behavioral Development, 14*, 131–151.

Bornstein, M. H., Haynes, O. M., O'Reilly, A. W., and Painter, K. (1999). Solitary and collaborative pretense play in early childhood: Sources of individual variation in the development of representational competence. *Child Development, 67*, 2910–2929.

Bornstein, M. H., Haynes, O. M., Pascual, L., Painter, K. M., and Galperin, C. (1999). Play in two societies: Pervasiveness of process, specificity of structure. *Child Development, 70*, 317–331.

Bornstein, M. H., and Kertes, D. *Infancy as a stage of life: Revisiting Ariès and the art historical record.* Manuscript in preparation, National Institute of Child Health and Human Development, Bethesda, MD.

Bornstein, M. H., and Lamb, M. E. (1992). *Development in infancy: An introduction* (3rd ed.). New York: McGraw Hill.

Bornstein, M. H., and O'Reilly, A. W. (Eds.). (1993). *The role of play in the development of thought.* San Francisco: Jossey-Bass.

Bornstein, M. H., and Ruddy, M. (1984). Infant attention maternal stimulation: Prediction of cognitive linguistic development in singletons and twins. In H. Bouma and D. Bouwhuis (Eds.), *Attention and performance* (Vol. X, pp. 433–445). London: Lawrence Erlbaum Associates.

Bornstein, M. H., Suwalsky, J. T. D., Hahn, C.-S., and Haynes, O. M. *Socioeconomic status, maternal education, parenting, and infant development.* Manuscript in preparation, National Institute of Child Health and Human Development, Bethesda, MD.

Bornstein, M. H., Tal, J., Rahn, C., Galperín, C. Z., Pêcheux, M.-G., Lamour, M., Azuma, H., Toda, S., Ogino, M., and Tamis-LeMonda, C. S. (1992). Functional analysis of the contents of maternal speech to infants of 5 and 13 months in four cultures: Argentina, France, Japan, and the United States. *Developmental Psychology, 28*, 593–603.

Bornstein, M. H., Tal, J., and Tamis-LeMonda, C. S. (1991). Parenting in cross-cultural perspective: The United States, France, and Japan. In M. H. Bornstein (Ed.), *Cultural approaches to parenting* (pp. 69–90). Hillsdale, NJ: Lawrence Erlbaum Associates.

Bornstein, M. H., and Tamis-LeMonda, C. S. (1989). Maternal responsiveness and cognitive development in children. In M. H. Bornstein (Ed.). *Maternal responsiveness: Characteristics and consequences* (pp. 49–61). San Francisco: Jossey-Bass.

Bornstein, M. H., and Tamis-LeMonda, C. S. (1990). Activities and interactions of mothers and their firstborn infants in the first six months of life: Covariation, stability, continuity, correspondence, and prediction. *Child Development, 61*, 1206–1217.

Bornstein, M. H., Tamis-LeMonda, C. S., and Haynes, O. M. (1999). First words in the second year: Continuity, stability, and models of concurrent and predictive correspondence in vocabulary and verbal responsiveness across age and context. *Infant Behavior and Development, 22*, 65–85.

Bornstein, M. H., Tamis-LeMonda, C. S., Pascual, L., Haynes, O. M., Painter, K., Galperén, C., and Pêcheux, M.-G. (1996). Ideas about parenting in Argentina, France, and the United States. *International Journal of Behavioral Development, 19*, 347–367.

Bornstein, M. H., Tamis-LeMonda, C. S., Pêcheux, M. G., and Rahn, C. W. (1991). Mother and infant activity and interaction in France and in the United States: A comparative study. *International Journal of Behavioral Development, 14*, 21–43.

Bornstein, M. H., Tamis-LeMonda, C. S., Tal, J., Ludemann, P., Toda, S., Rahn, C. W., Pécheux, M.-G., Azuma, H., and Vardi, D. (1992). Maternal responsiveness to infants in three societies: The United States, France, and Japan. *Child Development*, *63*, 808–821.

Bornstein, M. H., Toda, S., Azuma, H., Tamis-LeMonda, C. S., and Ogino, M. (1990). Mother and infant activity and interaction in Japan and in the United States: II. A comparative microanalysis of naturalistic exchanges focused on the organization of infant attention. *International Journal of Behavioral Development*, *13*, 289–308.

Bowlby, J. (1951). *Maternal care and mental health*. Geneva: World Health Organization.

Bowlby, J. (1969). *Attachment and loss*. New York: Basic Books.

Bradley, R. H., Caldwell, B. M., and Rock, S. L. (1988). Home environment and school performance: A ten-year follow-up and examination of three models of environmental action. *Child Development*, *59*, 852–867.

Bradley, R. H., and Whiteside-Mansell, L. (1997). Children in poverty. In R. T. Ammerman and M. Hersen (Eds.), *Handbook of prevention and treatment with children and adolescents* (pp. 13–58). New York: Wiley.

Brazelton, T. B. (1969). *Infants and mothers: Differences in development*. New York: Dell.

Brazelton, T. B. (1973). *Neonatal behavioral assessment scale*. (Clinics in Developmental Medicine, No. 50.). Philadelphia: Lippincott.

Cabrera, N. J., Tamis-LeMonda, C. S., Bradley, R. H., Hofferth, S., and Lamb, M. E. (2000). Fatherhood in the twenty-first century. *Child Development*, *71*, 127–136.

Campos, J. J., and Stenberg, C. R. (1981). Perception, appraisal and emotion: The onset of social referencing. In M. E. Lamb and L. R. Sherrod (Eds.), *Infant social cognition: Empirical and theoretical considerations* (pp. 273–314). Hillsdale, NJ: Lawrence Erlbaum Associates.

Carew, J. V. (1980). Experience and the development of intelligence in young children at home and in daycare. *Monographs of the Society for Research in Child Development*, *45* (Serial No. 187).

Carnegie Corporation of New York (1994). *Starting points: Meeting the needs of our youngest children*. New York: Carnegie Corporation of New York.

Cassidy, J. (1994). Emotional regulation: Influences of attachment relationships. In N. A. Fox (Ed.), The development of emotion regulation: Biological and behavioral considerations. *Monographs of the Society for Research in Child Development*, *59* (Serial No. 240).

Caudill, W. (1973). The influence of social structure and culture on human behavior in modern Japan. *Journal of Nervous and Mental Disease*, *157*, 240–257.

Center for the Study of Social Policy. (2000). *2000 Kids count data online*. Baltimore: Annie E. Casey Foundation.

Chalmers, I., Enkin, M., and Keirse, M. J. N. C. (Eds.). (1989). *Effective care in pregnancy and childbirth*. New York: Oxford University Press.

Chapman, R. S. (1981). Cognitive development and language comprehension in 10- to 21-month-olds. In R. E. Stark (Ed.), *Language behavior in infancy and early childhood* (pp. 359–394). New York: Elsevier North Holland.

Church, J. (Ed.). (1966). *Three babies: Biographies of cognitive development*. New York: Vintage Books.

Churcher, J., and Scaife, M. (1982). How infants see the point. In G. Butterworth and P. Light (Eds.), *Social cognition* (pp. 110–136). Brighton, Sussex, England; Harvester.

Clarke, A. M., and Clarke, A. D. B. (Eds.). (1976). *Early experience: Myth and evidence*. New York: Free Press.

Clarke-Stewart, K. A. (1980). The father's contribution to children's cognitive and social development in early childhood. In F. A. Pedersen (Ed.), *The father–infant relationship: Observational studies in the family setting* (pp. 111–146). New York: Praeger Special Publications.

Cohn, J. E., Campbell, S. B., and Ross, S. (1991). Infant response in the still-face paradigm at 6 months predicts avoidant and secure attachment at 12 months. *Development and Psychopathology*, *3*, 367–376.

Cole, M. (1999). Culture in development. In M. H. Bornstein and M. E. Lamb (Eds.), *Developmental psychology: An advanced textbook* (4th ed., pp. 73–123). Mahwah, NJ: Lawrence Erlbaum Associates.

Collins, W. A., Maccoby, E. E., Steinberg, L., Hetherington, E. M., and Bornstein, M. H. (2000). Contemporary research on parenting: The case for nature *and* nurture. *American Psychologist*, *55*, 218–232.

Collins, W. A., and Russell, G. (1991). Mother–child and father–child relationships in middle childhood and adolescence: A developmental analysis. *Developmental Review*, *11*, 1–38.

Colón, A. R., with Colón, P. A. (1999). *Nurturing children. A history of pediatrics*. Westport, CT: Greenwood.

Condry, J., and Condry, S. (1976). Sex differences: A study of the eye of the beholder. *Child Development*, *47*, 812–819.

Conger, R. D., McMarty, J., Yang, R., Lahey, B., and Kropp, J. (1984). Perception of child, childrearing values, and emotional distress as mediating links between environmental stressors and observed maternal behavior. *Child Development*, *55*, 2234–2247.

Coren, S. (1997). *Sleep thieves: An eye-opening exploration into the science and mysteries of sleep*. New York: Free Press.

Cote, L. R., and Bornstein, M. H. (2000). Social and didactic parenting behaviors and beliefs among Japanese American and South American mothers of infants. *Infancy*, *1*, 363–374.

Cowan, C. P., and Cowan, P. A. (1992). *When partners become parents*. New York: Basic Books.

Crnic, K. A., Greenberg, M. T., Ragozin, A. S., Robinson, N. M., and Basham, R. B. (1983). Effects of stress and social support on mothers and premature and fullterm infants. *Child Development, 54*, 209–217.

Cummings, M. E., Zahn-Waxler, C., and Radke-Yarrow, M. (1981). Young children's responses to expressions of anger and affection by others in the family. *Child Development, 52*, 1274–1282.

Darling, N., and Steinberg, L. (1993). Parenting style as context: An integrative model. *Psychological Bulletin, 113*, 487–496.

Darwin, C. (1877). Biographical sketch of an infant. *Mind, 2*, 285–294.

DeCasper, A. J., and Spence, M. J. (1986). Prenatal maternal speech influences newborns' perception of speech sounds. *Infant Behavior and Development, 9*, 133–150.

deMause, L. (1975). The evolution of childhood. In L. deMause (Ed.), *The history of childhood* (pp. 1–73). New York: Harper.

Dement, W. C., and Vaughan, C. (1999). *The promise of sleep*. New York: Delacorte.

Dennis, W., and Dennis, M. G. (1940). The effect of cradling practices upon the onset of walking in Hopi children. *Journal of Genetic Psychology, 56*, 77–86.

Deutsch, F. M., Ruble, D. N., Fleming, A., Brooks-Gunn, J., and Stangor, C. (1988). Information-seeking and self-definition during the transition to motherhood. *Journal of Personality and Social Psychology, 55*, 420–431.

DeVries, M. W., and Sameroff, A. J. (1984). Culture and temperament: Influences on infant temperament in three East African societies. *American Journal of Orthopsychiatry, 54*, 83–96.

Dickstein, S., and Parke, R. D. (1988). Social referencing in infancy: A glance at fathers and marriage. *Child Development, 59*, 506–511.

Dix, T. (1991). The affective organization of parenting: Adaptive and maladaptive processes. *Psychological Bulletin, 110*, 3–25.

Dixon, R. A., and Lerner, R. M. (1999). History of systems in developmental psychology. In M. H. Bornstein and M. E. Lamb (Eds.), *Developmental psychology: An advanced textbook* (4th ed., pp. 3–45). Mahwah, NJ: Lawrence Erlbaum Associates.

Dodge, K. A., Pettit, G. S., and Bates, J. E. (1994). Socializing mediators of the relation between socioeconomic status and child conduct problems. *Child Development, 65*, 649–665.

Doi, T. (1973). *The anatomy of dependence* (J. Bester, Trans.). Tokyo: Kodansha International.

Dollard, J., and Miller, N. (1950). *Personality and psychotherapy*. New York: McGraw-Hill.

Dunn, J. B. (1977). Patterns of early interaction: Continuities and consequences. In H. R. Schaffer (Ed.), *Studies in mother–infant interaction* (pp. 438–456). London: Academic.

Dunn, J., and Kendrick, C. (1982). *Siblings: Love, envy, and understanding*. Cambridge, MA: Harvard University Press.

Dunn, J., and Plomin, R. (1991). *Separate lives: Why siblings are so different*. New York: Basic Books.

Dunn, J. F., Plomin, R., and Daniels, D. (1986). Consistency and change in mothers' behavior toward young siblings. *Child Development, 57*, 348–356.

Dunn, J. F., Plomin, R., and Nettles, M. (1985). Consistency of mother's behaviour toward infant siblings. *Developmental Psychology, 21*, 1188–1195.

Dye, N. S., and Smith, D. B. (1986). Mother love and infant death, 1750–1920. *Journal of American History, 73*, 329–353.

East, P. L., and Felice, M. E. (1996). *Adolescent pregnancy and parenting: Findings from a racially diverse sample*. Mahwah, NJ: Lawrence Erlbaum Associates.

Eckerman, C. O., Whatley, J. L., and Kutz, S. L. (1975). Growth of social play with peers during the second year of life. *Developmental Psychology, 11*, 42–49.

Eggebeen, D. J. (1992). Family structure and intergenerational exchanges. *Research on Aging, 14*, 427–447.

Eggebeen, D. J., and Hogan, D. P. (1990). Giving between generations in American families. *Human Nature, 1*, 211–232.

Erikson, E. (1950). *Childhood and society*. New York: Norton.

Erting, C. J., Prezioso, C., and Hynes, M. O. (1994). The interfactional context of deaf mother–infant communication. In V. Volterra and C. J. Erting (Eds.), *From gesture to language in hearing and deaf children* (pp. 97–106). Washington, DC: Gallaudet University Press.

Farver, J. M. (1993). Cultural differences in scaffolding pretend play: A comparison of American and Mexican mother–child and sibling–child pairs. In K. MacDonald (Ed.), *Parent-child play: Descriptions and implications* (pp. 349–366). Albany, NY: State University of New York Press.

Feinman, S. (1982). Social referencing in infancy. *Merrill-Palmer Quarterly, 28*, 445–470.

Feinman, S., and Lewis, M. (1983). Social referencing and second order effects in ten-month-old infants. *Child Development, 54*, 878–887.

Field, T. M. (1984). Early interactions between infants and their postpartum depressed mothers. *Infant Behavior and Development, 7*, 517–522.

Field, T. (1995). Psychologically depressed parents. In M. H. Bornstein (Ed.), *Handbook of parenting* (Vol. 4, pp. 85–99). Mahwah, NJ: Lawrence Erlbaum Associates.

Fincham, F. D. (1998). Child development and marital relations. *Child Development, 69*, 543–574.

Fish, M., and Stifter, C. A. (1993). Mother parity as a main and moderating influence on early mother–infant interaction. *Journal of Applied Developmental Psychology, 14*, 557–572.

Fleming, A. S., Ruble, D. N., Flett, G. L., and Van Wagner, V. (1990). Postpartum adjustment in first-time mothers: Changes in mood and mood content during the early postpartum months. *Developmental Psychology, 26*, 137–143.

Fogel, A. (1984). *Infancy: Infant, family, and society*. St. Paul, MN: West Publishing.

Freud, S. (1949). *An outline of psycho-analysis*. New York: Norton.

Furstenberg, F. F., Jr., Brooks-Gunn, J., and Chase-Lansdale, L. (1989). Teenaged pregnancy and child bearing. *American Psychologist, 44*, 313–320.

Gable, S., Crnic, K., and Belsky, J. (1994). Coparenting within the family system: Influences on children's development. *Family Relations, 43*, 380–386.

Gergely, G., and Watson, J. S. (1999). Early socio-emotional development: Contingency perception and the social-biofeedback model. In P. Rochat (Ed.), *Early social cognition: Understanding others in the first months of life* (pp. 101–136). Mahwah, NJ: Lawrence Erlbaum Associates.

Goldberg, S. (1977). Infant development and mother–infant interaction in urban Zambia. In P. H. Leiderman, S. R. Tulkin, and A. Rosenfeld (Eds.), *Culture and infancy: Variations in the human experience* (pp. 211–245). New York: Academic.

Goodnow, J. J., Cashmore, J., Cotton, S., and Knight, R. (1984). Mothers' developmental timetables in two cultural groups. *International Journal of Psychology, 19*, 193–205.

Gottfried, A. W. (Ed.). (1984). *Home environment and early cognitive development*. Orlando, FL: Academic.

Gottlieb, D., Wahlsten, D., and Lickliter, R. (1998). The significance of biology for human development: A developmental psychobiological systems view. In W. Damon (Series Ed.), R. M. Lerner (Vol. Ed.), *Handbook of child psychology: Vol. 1. Theoretical models of human development* (5th ed., pp. 233–273). New York: Wiley.

Gould, S. J. (1985). *Ontogeny and phylogeny*. Cambridge, MA: Belknap.

Green, J. A., Gustafson, G. E., and West, M. J. (1980). Effects of infant development on mother–infant interactions. *Child Development, 51*, 199–207.

Greenbaum, C. W., and Landau, R. (1982). The infants exposure to talk by familiar people: Mothers, fathers and siblings different environments. In M. Lewis and L. Rosenblum (Eds.), *The social network of the developing infant* (pp. 229–247). New York: Plenum.

Greenspan, S., and Greenspan, N. T. (1985). *First feelings*. New York: Viking.

Grossman, F. K., Eichler, L. W., and Winikoff, S. A. (1980). *Pregnancy, birth and parenthood*. San Francisco: Jossey-Bass.

Hagekull, B., Bohlin, G., and Lindhagen, K. (1984). Validity of parental reports. *Infant Behavior and Development, 7*, 77–92.

Hall, G. S. (1891). Notes on the study of infants. *Pedagogical Seminary, 1*, 127–138.

Hardy-Brown, K. (1983). Universals in individual differences: Disentangling two approaches to the study of language acquisition. *Developmental Psychology, 19*, 610–624.

Hardy-Brown, K., and Plomin, R. (1985). Infant communicative development: Evidence from adoptive and biological families for genetic and environmental influences on rate differences. *Developmental Psychology, 21*, 378–385.

Harkness, S., and Super, C. M. (1983). The cultural construction of child development: A framework for the socialization of affect. *Ethos, 11*, 221–231.

Harkness, S., and Super, C. M. (1985). Child-environment interactions in the socialization of affect. In M. Lewis and C. Saarni (Eds.), *The socialization of emotions* (pp. 21–36). New York: Plenum.

Harris, P. L. (1983). Infant cognition. In P. H. Mussen (Series Ed.), M. M. Haith and J. J. Campos (Vol. Eds.), *Handbook of child psychology: Vol. 2. Infancy and developmental psychobiology* (3rd ed., pp. 689–782). New York: Wiley.

Hart, B., and Risley, T. R. (1995). *Meaningful differences in the everyday experience of young American children*. New York: Paul H. Brookes.

Hart, B., and Risley, T. R. (1999). *The social world of children learning to talk*. New York: Paul H. Brookes.

Harwood, R. L. (1992). The influence of culturally derived values on Anglo and Puerto Rican mothers' perceptions of attachment behavior. *Child Development, 63*, 822–839.

Harwood, R. L., Miller, J. G., and Irizarry, N. L. (1995). *Culture and attachment: Perceptions of the child in context*. New York: Guilford.

Héroard, J. (1868). *Journal de Jean Héroard sur l'enfance et la jeunesse de Louis XIII (1601–1628). [Jean Héroard's journal of the childhood and youth of Louis XIII (1601–1628)]*. Paris: Eud. Soulie et Ed. de Barthelemy.

Hill, C. R., and Stafford, F. P. (1980). Parental care of children: Time diary estimate of quantity, predictability and variety. *Journal of Human Resources, 15*, 219–239.

Hirshberg, L. M., and Svejda, M. (1990). When infants look to their parents: I. Infants' social referencing of mothers compared to fathers. *Child Development, 61*, 1175–1186.

Ho, H. Z. (1987). Interaction of early caregiving environment and infant developmental status in predicting subsequent cognitive performance. *British Journal of Developmental Psychology, 5*, 183–191.

Hodapp, R. M., Goldfield, E. C., and Boyatzis, C. J. (1984). The use and effectiveness of maternal scaffolding in mother–infant games. *Child Development, 55*, 772–781.

Hofferth, S. L., and Hayes, C. D. (Eds.). (1987). *Risking the future: Adolescent sexuality, pregnancy, and childbearing* (Vol. 2). Washington, DC: National Academy of Sciences Press.

Hoff-Ginsberg, E. (1991). Mother–child conversation in different social classes and communicative settings. *Child Development*, *62*, 782–796.

Holden, G. W., and Miller, P. C. (1999). Enduring and different: A meta-analysis of the similarity in parents' child rearing. *Psychological Bulletin*, *125*, 223–254.

Hopkins, B., and Westra, T. (1990). Motor development, maternal expectation, and the role of handling. *Infant Behavior and Development*, *13*, 117–122.

Hornik, R., Risenhoover, N., and Gunnar, M. (1987). The effects of maternal positive, neutral, and negative affective communications on infant responses to new toys. *Child Development*, *58*, 937–944.

Hrdy, S. B. (1999). *Mother nature: A history of mothers, infants, and natural selection*. New York: Pantheon Books.

Ingersoll, E. W., and Thoman, E. B. (1999). Sleep/wake states of preterm infants: Stability, developmental change, diurnal variation, and relation with caregiving activity. *Child Development*, *70*, 1–10.

Jackson, S. (1987). Great Britain. In M. E. Lamb (Ed.), *The father's role: Cross-cultural perspectives* (pp. 29–57). Hillsdale, NJ: Lawrence Erlbaum Associates.

Jacobson, J. L., Boersma, D. C., Fields, R. B., and Olson, K. L. (1983). Paralinguistic features of adult speech to infants and small children. *Child Development*, *54*, 436–442.

Jaeger, S. (1985). The origin of the diary method in developmental psychology. In G. Eckhardt, W. G. Bringmann, L. Sprung (Eds.), *Contributions to a history of developmental psychology* (pp. 63–74). Berlin: Mouton.

Jakobson, R. (1969). *Child language, aphasia, and phonological universals*. New York: Humanities Press. (Original work published 1941.)

Jakobson, R. (1971). Why "Mama" and "Papa"? In A. Bar-Adon and W. F. Leopold (Eds.), *Child language* (pp. 212–217). Englewood Cliffs, NJ: Prentice-Hall.

Jennings, K. D., Stagg, V., Connors, R. E. (1991). Social networks and mothers' interactions with their preschool children. *Child Development*, *62*, 966–978.

Johnson, W., Emde, R. N., Pennbrook, B., Stenberg, C., and Davis, M. (1982). Maternal perception of infant emotion from birth through 18 months. *Infant Behavior and Development*, *5*, 313–322.

Kagan, J. (1971). *Change and continuity in infancy*. New York: Wiley.

Kagan, J. (1984). *The nature of the child*. New York: Basic Books.

Kagan, J. (2000). *Three seductive ideas*. Cambridge, MA: Harvard University Press.

Kagan J., Snidman, N., Arcus, D., and Reznick, J. S. (1997). *Galen's prophecy: Temperament in human nature*. New York: Basic Books.

Kawasaki, C., Nugent, J. K., Miyashita, H., Miyahara, H., and Brazelton, T. B. (1994). The cultural organization of infants' sleep. *Children's Environments Quarterly*, *11*, 135–141.

Kent, R. D. (1984). The psychobiology of speech development: Co-emergence of language and a movement system. *American Journal of Physiology*, *246*, R888–R894.

Kerig, P. K., Cowan, P. A., and Cowan, C. P. (1993). Marital quality and gender differences in parent–child interaction. *Developmental Psychology*, *29*, 931–939.

Klein, P. S. (1988). Stability and change in interaction of Israeli mothers and infants. *Infant Behavior and Development*, *11*, 55–70.

Klinnert, M., Campos, J. J., Sorce, J., Emde, R. N., and Svejda, M. (1983). Emotions as behavior regulators: Social referencing in infancy. In R. Plutchik and H. Kellerman (Eds.), *Emotions in early development* (Vol. 2, pp. 57–86). New York: Academic.

Kojima, H. (1986). Japanese concepts of child development from the mid-17th to mid-19th century. *International Journal of Behavioral Development*, *9*, 315–329.

Kotelchuck, M. (1976). The infants' relationship to the father: Experimental evidence. In M. E. Lamb (Ed.), *The role of the father in child development* (pp. 329–344). New York: Wiley.

Kuchuk, A., Vibbert, M., and Bornstein, M. H. (1986). The perception of smiling and its experiential correlates in 3-month-old infants. *Child Development*, *57*, 1054–1061.

Lamb, M. E. (1998). Nonparental childcare: Context, quality, correlates, and consequences. In W. Damon (Series Ed.), I. E. Sigel and K. A. Renninger (Vol. Eds.), *Handbook of child psychology: Vol. 4. Child psychology in practice* (5th ed., pp. 73–133). New York: Wiley.

Lamb, M. E., and Easterbrooks, M. A. (1981). Individual differences in parental sensitivity: Origins, components, and consequences. In M. E. Lamb and L. R. Sherrod (Eds.), *Infant social cognition: Empirical and theoretical considerations* (pp. 127–153). Hillsdale, NJ: Lawrence Erlbaum Associates.

Lamb, M. E., Frodi, A. M., Frodi, M., and Hwang, C.-P. (1982). Characteristics of maternal and paternal behavior in traditional and nontraditional Swedish families. *International Journal of Behavioral Development*, *5*, 131–141.

Landry, S. H. (1995). The development of joint attention in premature low birthweight infants. Effects of early medial complications and maternal attention-directing behaviors. In C. Moore and P. J. Dunham (Eds.) *Joint Attention: Its origins and role in development* (pp. 223–250). Hillsdale, NJ: Lawrence Erlbaum Associates.

Leach, P. (1997). *Your baby and child: From birth to age five*. New York: Knopf.

Leiderman, P. H., Tulkin, S. R., and Rosenfeld, A. (Eds.). (1977). *Culture and infancy: Variations in the human experience.* New York: Academic.

Lerner, R. M. (1989). Developmental contextualism and the lifespan view of person-context interaction. In M. H. Bornstein and J. S. Bruner (Eds.), *Interaction in human development* (pp. 217–239). Hillsdale, NJ: Lawrence Erlbaum Associates.

Lerner, R. M. (1997). *Concepts and theories of human development.* Mahwah, NJ: Lawrence Erlbaum Associates.

LeVine, R. A. (1977). Childrearing as cultural adaptation. In P. H. Leiderman, S. R. Tulkin, and A. Rosenfeld (Eds.), *Culture and Infancy: Variations in the human experience* (pp. 15–27). New York: Academic.

LeVine, R. A. (1988). Human parental care: Universal goals, cultural strategies, individual behavior. In R. A. LeVine, P. M. Miller, and M. M. West (Eds.), *Parental behavior in diverse societies* (pp. 3–12). San Francisco: Jossey-Bass.

LeVine, R. A., and Miller, P. M. (Eds.). (1990). Cross-cultural validity of attachment theory [Special issue]. *Human Development, 33,* 2–80.

Lewis, M. (1997). *Altering fate: Why the past does not predict the future.* New York: Guilford.

Lightfoot, C., and Valsiner, J. (1992). Parental belief systems under the influence: Social guidance of the construction of personal cultures. In I. E. Sigel, A. V. McGillicuddy-De Lisi, and J. J. Goodnow (Eds.), *Parental belief systems: The psychological consequences for children* (2nd ed., pp. 393–414). Hillsdale, NJ: Lawrence Erlbaum Associates.

Lorenz, K. (1935/1970). *Studies in animal and human behavior* (R. Martin, Trans.). London: Methuen.

Lounsbury, M. L., and Bates, J. E. (1982). The cries of infants and different levels of perceived temperamental difficultness: Acoustic properties and effects on listeners. *Child Development, 53,* 677–686.

Lyons-Ruth, K., Zoll, D., Conell, D., and Grunebaum, H. U. (1986). The depressed mother and her one-year-old infant: Environment, interaction, attachment and infant development. In E. Tronick and T. Field (Eds.), *Maternal depression and infant disturbance* (pp. 61–83). San Francisco: Jossey-Bass.

Lytton, H., and Romney, D. M. (1991). Parents' differential socialization of boys and girls: A meta-analysis. *Psychological Bulletin, 109,* 267–296.

Maccoby, E. E., and Martin, J. A. (1983). Socialization in the context of the family: Parent–child interaction. In P. H. Mussen (Series Ed.), E. M. Hetherington (Vol. Ed.), *Handbook of child psychology: Vol. 4. Socialization, personality, and social development* (3rd ed., pp. 1–101). New York: Wiley.

Mahler, M., Pine, A., and Bergman, F. (1975). *The psychological birth of the human infant.* New York: Basic Books.

Main, M. (1991). Metacognitive knowledge, metacognitive, monitoring, and singular (coherent) vs. multiple (incoherent) models of attachment: Findings and directions for future research. In C. M. Parkes, J. Stevenson-Hinde, and P. Marris (Eds.), *Attachment across the life cycle* (pp. 127–159). London: Routledge.

Martin, J. A. (1989). Personal and interpersonal components of responsiveness. In M. H. Bornstein (Ed.), *Maternal responsiveness: Characteristics and consequences* (pp. 5–14). San Francisco: Jossey-Bass.

Mayes, L. C., and Bornstein, M. H. (1995). Developmental dilemmas for cocaine-abusing parents and their children. In M. Lewis and M. Bendersky (Eds.), *Mothers, babies, and cocaine: The role of toxins in development* (pp. 251–272). Hillsdale, NJ: Lawrence Erlbaum Associates.

McCall, R. B. (1981). Nature-nurture and the two realms of development: A proposed integration with respect to mental development. *Child Development, 52,* 1–12.

McGillicuddy-De Lisi, A. V. (1992). Parents' beliefs and children's personal–social development. In I. E. Sigel, A. V. McGillicuddy-De Lisi, and J. J. Goodnow (Eds.), *Parental belief systems: The psychological consequences for children* (2nd ed., pp. 115–142). Hillsdale, NJ: Lawrence Erlbaum Associates.

McLaughlin, B., White, D., McDevitt, T., and Raskin, R. (1983). Mothers' and fathers' speech to their young children: Similar or different? *Journal of Child Language, 10,* 245–252.

McLoyd, V. C., and Wilson, L. (1990). Maternal behavior, social support, and economic conditions as predictors of distress in children. *New Directions in Child Development, 46,* 49–70.

Mead, M., and MacGregor, F. C. (1951). *Growth and culture.* New York: Putnam's.

Mead, M., and Newton, N. (1967). Cultural patterning of perinatal behavior. In S. Richardson and A. Guttmacher (Eds.), *Childbearing: Its social and psychological aspects.* Baltimore: Williams and Wilkins.

Mendelson, M. J. (1990). *Becoming a brother: A child learns about life, family, and self.* Cambridge, MA: MIT Press.

Michelsson, K., Rinne, A., and Paajanen, S. (1990). Crying, feeding, and sleeping patterns in 1 to 12 month old infants. *Child: Care, Health, and Development, 16,* 99–111.

Miller, S. (1988). Parents' beliefs about children's cognitive development. *Child Development, 59,* 259–285.

Minnett, A. M., Vandell, D. L., and Santrock, J. W. (1983). The effects of sibling status on sibling interaction: Influence of birth order, age spacing, sex of child, and sex of sibling. *Child Development, 54,* 1064–1072.

Montemayor, R. (1982). The relationship between parent-adolescent conflict and the amount of time adolescents spend alone with parents and peers. *Child Development, 53,* 1512–1519.

Moore, C., and Dunham, P. J. (Eds.), (1995). *Joint attention: Its origins and role in development* (pp. 223–250). Hillsdale, NJ: Lawrence Erlbaum Associates.

Morelli, G. A., and Tronick, E. Z. (1991). Parenting and child development in the Efe foragers and Lese farmers of Zaire. In M. H. Bornstein (Ed.), *Cultural approaches to parenting* (pp. 91–113). Hillsdale, NJ: Lawrence Erlbaum Associates.

Murdock, G. P. (1959). Cross-language parallels in parental kin terms. *Anthropological Linguistics, 1*, 1–5.

Murphey, D. A. (1992). Constructing the child: Relations between parents' beliefs and child outcomes. *Developmental Review, 12*, 199–232.

Murray, L., and Trevarthen, C. (1985). Emotional regulation of interactions between two-month-olds and their mothers. In T. M. Field and N. A. Fox (Eds.), *Social perception in infants* (pp. 177–197). Norwood, NJ: Ablex.

Nadel, J., and Butterworth, G. (Eds.) (1999). *Imitation in infancy.* New York: Cambridge University Press.

National Center for Health Statistics (2000). *Births: Final data for 1998* (National Vital Statistics Rep. Vol. 48, No. 3). Atlanta, GA: Centers for Disease Control and Prevention.

National Center for Health Statistics (2001). Available E-mail: http://www.cdc.gov/nchs/fastats/birthwt.htm or http://www.cdc.gov/growthcharts/. Atlanta, GA: Centers for Disease Control and Prevention.

Nelson, C. A. (1987). The recognition of facial expressions in the first two years of life: Mechanisms of development. *Child Development, 58*, 889–909.

Nicely, P. Tamis-LeMonda, C. S. and Bornstein, M. H. (1999). Mothers' attuned responses to infant affect expressivity promote earlier achievement of language milestones. *Infant Behavior and Development, 22*, 557–568.

Ninio, A. (1980). Picture-book reading in mother–infant dyads belonging to two subgroups in Israel. *Child Development, 51*, 587–590.

Ochs, E. (1988). *Culture and language development: Language acquisition and language socialization in a Samoan village.* New York: Cambridge University Press.

Olson, S. L., Bates, J. E., and Bayles, K. (1984). Mother–infant interaction and the development of individual differences in children's cognitive competence. *Developmental Psychology, 20*, 166–179.

Osofsky, J. D., Hann, D. M., and Peebles, C. (1993). Adolescent parenthood: Risks and opportunities for parents and infants. In C. Zeanah (Ed.), *Handbook of infant mental health* (pp. 106–119). New York: Guilford.

Osterholm, P., Lindeke, L. L., and Amidon, D. (1983). Sleep disturbance in infants aged 6 to 12 months. *Pediatric Nursing, 9*, 269–271.

Palacios, J. (1990). Parents' ideas about the development and education of their children. Answers to some questions. *International Journal of Behavioral Development, 13*, 137–155.

Papoušek, M., Papoušek, H., and Bornstein, M. H. (1985). The naturalistic vocal environment of young infants: On the significance of homogeneity and variability in parental speech. In T. M. Field and N. Fox (Eds.), *Social perception in infants* (pp. 269–297). Norwood, NJ: Ablex.

Parke, R. D., and Sawin, D. B. (1975, April). *Infant characteristics and behavior as elicitors of maternal and paternal responsibility in the newborn period.* Paper presented at the biennial meeting of the Society for Research in Child Development, Denver.

Parke, R. D., and Sawin, D. B. (1980). The family in early infancy: Social interactional and attitudinal analyses. In F. A. Pedersen (Ed.), *The father–infant relationship: Observational studies in the family setting* (pp. 44–70). New York: Praeger Special Studies.

Parks, P. L., and Smeriglio, V. L. (1986). Relationships among parenting knowledge, quality of stimulation in the home and infant development. *Family Relations, 35*, 411–416.

Pedersen, F. A. (1975, September). *Mother, father and infant as an interactive system.* Paper presented at the annual convention of the American Psychological Association, Chicago.

Pepler, D., Corter, C., and Abramovitch, R. (1982). Social relations among children: Comparison of sibling and peer interaction. In K. H. Rubin and H. S. Ross (Eds.), *Peer relationships and social skills in childhood* (pp. 209–227). New York: Springer-Verlag.

Pettit, G. S., and Bates, J. (1984). Continuity of individual differences in the mother–infant relationship from 6 to 13 months. *Child Development, 55*, 729–739.

Piaget, J. (1952). *The origins of intelligence in children.* New York: Norton.

Plato (1970). *The laws* (T. J. Saunders, Trans.). Harmondsworth, Middlesex, England: Penguin. (Original work written *ca.* 355 B.C.)

Plomin, R. (1989). Environment and genes: Determinants of behavior. *American Psychologist, 44*, 105–111.

Plomin, R. (1999). Behavioral genetics. In M. Bennett (Ed.), *Developmental psychology: Achievements and prospects* (pp. 231–252). Philadelphia: Psychological Press/Taylor & Francis.

Plomin, R., and DeFries, J. C. (1985). *The origins of individual differences in infancy: The Colorado Adoption Project.* New York: Academic.

Population Reference Bureau. (2000). Available E-mail: http://www.prb.org. Washington, DC: Population Reference Bureau.

Porter, R. H. (1991). Mutual mother–infant recognition in human. In P. G. Hepper (Ed.), *Kin recognition* (pp. 413–432). Cambridge, England: Cambridge University Press.

Porter, R. H., and Levy, F. (1995). Olfactory mediation of mother–infant interactions in a selected mammalian species. In R. Wong (Ed.), *Biological perspectives on motivated activities* (pp. 77–110). Norwood, NJ: Ablex.

Porter, R. H., and Winberg, J. (1999). Unique salience of maternal breast odors for newborn infants. *Neuroscience and Biobehavioral Reviews, 23*, 439–449.

Powell, D. R. (1980). Personal social networks as a focus for primary prevention of child maltreatment. *Infant Mental Health Journal, 1*, 232–239.

Power, T. G. (1985). Mother– and father–infant play: A developmental analysis. *Child Development, 56*, 1514–1524.

Preyer, W. (1882/1888–1889). *Die seele des kindes.* Leipzig: Grieben. Published in English in 1888–1889 as *The mind of the Child, Parts 1 and 2.* (H. W. Brown, Trans.). New York: Appleton. Reprint edition 1973 by Arno, New York.

Prochner, L., and Doyon, P. (1997). Researchers and their subjects in the history of child study: William Blatz and the Dionne quintuplets. *Canadian Psychology, 38*, 103–110.

Ratner, N. B., and Pye, C. (1984). Higher pitch in BT is not universal: Acoustic evidence from Quiche Mayan. *Journal of Child Language, 11*, 512–522.

Raver, C. C. (1996). Success at catching and keeping toddlers' attention: An examination of joint attention among low-income mothers and their 2-year olds. *Early Development and Parenting, 5*, 225–236.

Rochat, P., and Striano, T. (1999). Social–cognitive development in the first year. In P. Rochat (Ed.), *Early social cognition* (pp. 3–34). Mahwah, NJ: Lawrence Erlbaum Associates.

Rohner, R. (1985). *The warmth dimension.* Beverly Hills, CA: Sage.

Rondal, J. A. (1980). Fathers' and mothers' speech in early language development. *Journal of Child Language, 7*, 353–369.

Rousseau, J. J. (1762). *Emile.* New York: Barron's Educational Series.

Rubenstein, J., and Howes, C. (1976). The effects of peers on toddler interaction with mother and toys. *Child Development, 47*, 597–605.

Rubin, J., Provenzano, F., and Luria, Z. (1974). The eye of the beholder: Parents' view of sex of newborns. *American Journal of Orthopsychiatry, 43*, 720–731.

Russell, G. (1983). *The changing role of fathers?* St. Lucia, Queensland, Australia: University of Queensland Press.

Russell, G., and Russell, A. (1987). Mother–child and father–child relationships in middle childhood. *Child Development, 58*, 1573–1585.

Rutter, M., and the English and Romanian Adoptees Study Team (1998). Developmental catch-up and delay, following adoption after severe global early privation. *Journal of Child Psychology and Psychiatry, 39*, 465–476.

Sameroff, A. J. (1983). Developmental systems: Contexts and evolution. In P. H. Mussen (Series Ed.), W. Kessen (Vol. Ed.), *Handbook of child psychology: Vol. 1. History, theory, and methods* (3rd ed., pp. 237–294). New York: Wiley.

Sameroff, A. J., and Feil, L. A. (1985). Parental concepts of development. In I. E. Sigel (Ed.), *Parental belief systems: The psychological consequences for children* (pp. 83–100). Hillsdale, NJ: Lawrence Erlbaum Associates.

Scarr, S., and McCartney, K. (1983). How people make their own environments: A theory of genotype-environment effects. *Child Development, 54*, 424–435.

Schellenbach, C. J., Whitman, T. L., and Borkowski, J. G. (1992). Toward an integrative model of adolescent parenting. *Human Development, 35*, 81–99.

Scheper-Hughes, N. (1989). Death without weeping. *Natural History, 98*, 8–16.

Seifer, R., Schiller, M., Sameroff, A. J., Resnick, S., Riordan, K. (1996). Attachment, maternal sensitivity, and infant temperament during the first year of life. *Developmental Psychology, 32*, 12–25.

Shakin, M., Shakin, D., and Sternglanz, S. H. (1985). Infant clothing: Sex labeling for strangers. *Sex Roles, 12*, 955–963.

Simons, R. L., Whitbeck, L. B., Conger, R. D., and Wu, C.-I. (1991). Intergenerational transmission of harsh parenting. *Developmental Psychology, 27*, 159–171.

Singer, J. L. (1995). Imaginative play in childhood: Precursor of subjunctive thought, daydreaming, and adult pretending games. In A. D. Pellegrini (Ed.), *The future of play theory* (pp. 187–219). Albany, NY: State University of New York Press.

Slater, P. G. (1977–78). From the cradle to the coffin: Parental bereavement and the shadow of infant damnation in Puritan society. *The Psychohistory Review, 6*, 4–24.

Snow, C. E. (1977). Mothers' speech research: From input to interactions. In C. E. Snow and C. A. Ferguson (Eds.), *Talking to children: Language input and acquisition* (pp. 31–49). Cambridge, England: Cambridge University Press.

Sorce, J. F., and Emde, R. N. (1981). Mother's presence is not enough: Effect of emotional availability on infant exploration. *Developmental Psychology, 17*, 737–745.

Spemann, H. (1938). *Embryonic development and induction.* New Haven, CT: Yale University Press.

Spitze, G., and Logan, J. (1992). Helping as a component of parent–adult-child relations. *Research on Aging, 14*, 291–312.

Spock, B., Parker, S. J., Parker, S., and Scotland, S. (1998). *Dr. Spock's baby and childcare.* New York: Pocket Books.

Sroufe, L. A., and Fleeson, J. (1986). Attachment and the construction of relationships. In W. W. Hartup and Z. Rubin (Eds.), *Relationships and development* (pp. 51–72). Hillsdale, NJ: Lawrence Erlbaum Associates.

Steiner, J. E. (1979). Human facial expressions in response to taste and smell stimulation. In H. Reese and L. Lipsitt (Eds.), *Advances in child development and behavior* (Vol. 13). New York: Academic.

Stern, D. (1985). *The interpersonal world of the infant.* New York: Basic Books.

Stern, D. (1990). *Diary of a child.* New York: Basic Books.

Stewart, R. B. (1983). Sibling interaction: The role of the older child as teacher for the younger. *Merrill-Palmer Quarterly, 29*, 47–68.

Stewart, R. B. (1990). *The second child: Family transition and adjustment*. Newbury Park, CA: Sage.

Stoolmiller, M. (1999). Implications of the restricted range of family environments for estimates of heritability and nonshared environment in behavior genetic adoptions studies. *Psychological Bulletin, 125*, 392–409.

Strauss, S., and Stavey, R. (1981). U-shaped behavioral growth: Implications for theories of development. In W. W. Hartup (Ed.), *Review of child development research* (Vol. 6, pp. 547–599). Chicago: University of Chicago Press.

Sulloway, F. J. (1997). *Born to rebel: Birth order, family dynamics, and creative lives*. New York: Vintage Books.

Super, C. M., and Harkness, S. (1986). Temperament, development, and culture. In R. Plomin and J. Dunn (Eds.), *The study of temperament: Changes, continuities, and challenges* (pp. 131–149). Hillsdale, NJ: Lawrence Erlbaum Associates.

Szalai, A. (Ed.). (1972). *The use of time: Daily activities of urban and suburban populations in twelve countries*. The Hague: Mouton.

Taine, H. A. (1877). Taine on the acquisition of language by children. *Mind, 2*, 252–259.

Tamis-LeMonda, C. S., and Bornstein, M. H. (1994). Specificity in mother–toddler language–play relations across the second year. *Developmental Psychology, 30*, 283–292.

Tamis-LeMonda, C. S., Bornstein, M. H., Cyphers, L., Toda, S., and Ogino, M. (1992). Language and play at one year: A comparison of toddlers and mothers in the United States and Japan. *International Journal of Behavioral Development, 15*, 19–42.

Tamis-LeMonda, C. S., and Cabrera, N. (1999). Perspectives on father involvement: Research and policy. *Social Policy Report, Society for Research in Child Development, 13*, 1–25.

Teti, D. M. (1992). Sibling interaction. In V. B. Van Hasselt and M. Hersen (Eds.), *Handbook of social development: A lifespan perspective. Perspectives in developmental psychology* (pp. 201–226). New York: Plenum.

Teti, D. M., Bond, L. A., and Gibbs, E. D. (1986). Sibling-created experiences: Relationships to birth-spacing and infant cognitive development. *Infant Behavior and Development, 9*, 27–42.

Teti, D. M., and Gelfand, D. M. (1991). Behavioral competence among mothers of infants in the first year: The mediational role of maternal self-efficacy. *Child Development, 62*, 918–929.

Teti, D. M., O'Connell, M. A., and Reiner, C. D. (1996). Parenting sensitivity, parental depression and child health: The mediational role of parental self-efficacy. *Early Development and Parenting, 5*, 237–250.

Thelen, E., and Smith, L. B. (1998). Dynamic systems theories. In W. Damon (Series Ed.), R. M. Lerner (Vol. Ed.), *Handbook of child psychology: Vol. 1. Theoretical models of human development* (5th ed., pp. 563–634). New York: Wiley.

Thoman, E. B. (1990). Sleeping and waking states in infants: A functional perspective. *Neuroscience and Biobehavioral Reviews, 14*, 93–107.

Thomas, A., Chess, S., Birch, H., Hertzig, M., and Korn, S. (1963). *Behavioral individuality in childhood*. New York: New York University Press.

Tiedemann, D. (1787). Beobachtungen über die Entwicklung der Seelenfähigkeiten bei Kindern. *Hessische Beiträge zur Gelehrsamkeit und Kunst, 2*, 313–315 and *3*, 486–488. (Observations on the development of the mental faculties of children. *Pedagogical Seminary*, 1927, *34*, 205–230.)

Tinbergen, N. (1951). *The study of instinct*. Oxford, England: Oxford University Press.

Tinbergen, N. (1963). On aims and methods of ethology. *Zeitschrift für Tierpsychologie, 20*, 410–433.

Trehub, S. E., and Hsing-Wu, C. (1977). Speech as reinforcing stimulation for infants. *Developmental Psychology, 13*, 121–124.

Trevarthen, C. (1979). Communication and cooperation in early infancy: A description of primary intersubjectivity. In M. Bullowa (Ed.), *Before speech: The beginning of interpersonal communication* (pp. 321–347). Cambridge, England: Cambridge University Press.

Trevarthen, C. (1993). The self born in intersubjectivity: The psychology of an infant communicating. In U. Neisser (Ed.), *The perceived self* (pp. 121–173). New York: Cambridge University Press.

Trevarthen, C., and Hubley, P. (1978). Secondary intersubjectivity: Confidence, confiding and acts of meaning in the first year. In A. Lock (Ed.), *Action, gesture and symbol* (pp. 182–229). New York: Academic.

Tronick, E. Z., and Gianino, A. F. (1986). The transmission of maternal disturbance to the infant. In E. Z. Tronick and T. Field (Eds.), *Maternal depression and infant disturbance* (pp. 5–11). New York: Wiley.

Turkheimer, E., and Waldron, M. (2000). Nonshared environment: A theoretical, methodological, and quantitative review. *Psychological Bulletin, 126*, 78–108.

UNICEF (1993). *Facts for life*. New York: UNICEF.

Valsiner, J. (Ed.). (1987). *Cultural context and child development*. Norwood, NJ: Ablex.

Vandell, D. L., and Wilson, K. S. (1987). Infants' interactions with mother, sibling, and peer: Contrasts and relations between interaction systems. *Child Development, 58*, 176–186.

Van den Boom, D., and Hoeksma, J. (1994). The effect of infant irritability on mother–infant interaction: A growth curve analysis. *Developmental Psychology, 30*, 581–590.

Van IJzendoorn, M. H. (1992). Intergenerational transmission of parenting: A review of studies in nonclinical populations. *Developmental Review, 12*, 76–99.

Vygotsky, L. (1978). *Mind in society*. Cambridge, MA: Harvard University Press.

Wachs, T. D. (2000). *Necessary but not sufficient: The respective roles of single and multiple influences on individual development*. Washington DC: American Psychological Association.

Wachs, T. D., and Camli, O. (1991). Do ecological or individual characteristics mediate the influence of the physical environment upon maternal behavior. *Journal of Environmental Psychology, 11*, 249–264.

Wachs, T. D., and Chan, A. (1986). Specificity of environmental action, as seen in environmental correlates of infants' communication performance. *Child Development, 57*, 1464–1474.

Waddington, C. H. (1962). *New patterns in genetics and development*. New York: Columbia University Press.

Wallace, D. B., Franklin, M. B., and Keegan, R. T. (1994). The observing eye: A century of baby diaries. *Human Development, 37*, 1–29.

Watson, J. B. (1924/1970). *Behaviorism*. New York: Norton.

Werner, E. E. (1979). *Cross-cultural child development: A view from planet Earth*. Monterey, CA: Brooks-Cole.

White, B. L., Kaban, B., Shapiro, B., and Attanucci, J. (1977). Competence and experience. In I. Č. Užgiris and F. Weizmann (Eds.), *The structuring of experience* (pp. 115–152). New York: Plenum.

Whiting, J. W. (1981). Environmental constraints on infant care practices. In R. H. Munroe, R. L. Munroe, and B. B. Whiting (Eds.), *Handbook of cross-cultural human development* (pp. 155–179). New York: Garland STPM Press.

Winnicott, D. W. (1957). *Mother and child: A primer of first relations*. New York: Basic Books.

Winnicott, D. W. (1965). *The maturational processes and the facilitating environment: Studies in the theory of emotional development*. New York: International Universities Press.

Yogman, M. W. (1982). Development of the father–infant relationship. In H. E. Fitzgerald, B. M. Lester, and M. W. Yogman (Eds.), *Theory and research in behavioral pediatrics* (pp. 221–280). New York: Plenum.

Young, K. T. (1991). What parents and experts think about infants. In F. S. Kessel, M. H. Bornstein, and A. J. Sameroff (Eds.), *Contemporary constructions of the child* (pp. 79–90). Hillsdale, NJ: Lawrence Erlbaum Associates.

Zajonc, R. B. (1983). Validating the confluence model. *Psychological Bulletin, 93*, 457–480.

# 2

# Parenting Toddlers

Carolyn Pope Edwards
Wen–Li Liu
*University of Nebraska-Lincoln*

## INTRODUCTION

The age period bridging between infancy and early childhood (the 18-month or 2-year period between approximately 12 and 36 months of age) is often referred to as *toddlerhood*. Although toddlerhood is unquestionably a time of rapid growth and change, there exists no professional consensus as to exactly when it begins and ends or even whether it is a full-fledged developmental period, or stage, of childhood. A *stage* is a distinct time of development bounded by fundamental reorganizations in cognitive and socioemotional capacities and characterized by its own unique pattern of developmental issues, tasks, and achievements. If toddlerhood cannot be considered a genuine stage, then at least it must be a prominent transitional phase or substage on the cusp of infancy and childhood. In that case, it can be asked whether toddlers are more properly classified with infants or with young children with regard to the capabilities and limitations—the particular delights and puzzlements—they present to caregiving adults.

This uncertainty about whether or not toddlerhood is a distinct stage of childhood can be illuminated by a quick look at the professional literature. For example, many older developmental and early childhood education texts (especially those less influenced by the psychoanalytic perspective) do not include a major section on the toddler period (e.g., Gardner, 1978). Some recent texts continue to follow that older pattern and divide their material on childhood into three major periods, *infancy*, *early childhood*, and *middle childhood* (e.g., Craig and Kermis, 1995; Feldman, 2001; Santrock, 2000). In contrast, however, other newer texts follow the lead of Stone and Church (1973) and treat the infant and the toddler periods separately (Dehart, Sroufe, and Cooper, 2000; Newcombe, 1996). Still others combine them but recognize two major substages by using a chapter heading such as, "Infancy and Toddlerhood" (e.g., Berk, 1999; Papalia, Olds, and Feldman, 1999; J. Schickedanz, Schickedanz, Forsyth, and Forsyth, 2001). When infancy and toddlerhood are treated in a combined way, the boundary age marking the transition to early childhood is most often placed at the beginning of the third year (24 months), but when toddlerhood is treated as a separate period, then the boundary age moves forward to the middle or the end of the third year (30 or 36 months).

Experts writing for parents of young children have tended increasingly to recognize the uniqueness of toddler characteristics and issues by giving them explicit attention in parenting guides, such as those prepared by the American Academy of Child and Adolescent Psychiatry (1998), Brazelton (1989), and Leach (1997). This increasing attention is mirrored in the applied fields of early childhood education, care, and intervention, in which there is a burgeoning literature on infants and toddlers that recognizes a toddler period yet generally sees toddler needs as closer to those of infants than those of older children. Many newer texts in early childhood education have separate chapters on curriculum and guidance for infants versus toddlers (e.g., Hildebrand, 1997; Seefeldt and Barbour, 1998), but others combine the two age periods (e.g., Morrison, 1998). The *Guidelines for Developmentally Appropriate Practice in Early Childhood Programs* from the National Association for the Education of Young Children (Bredekamp and Copple, 1997) are divided into three separate sections for the age periods, birth through 3, 3 through 5, and 6 through 8 years. State regulations for licensing childcare programs require higher staff–child ratios for the 15- to 33-month age group than for 3- to 4-year-old children, yet not so high as those required for children under 15 months of age. In the United States, public recognition of the importance of the earliest years of life finally led in 1995 to the establishment of a national, federally funded program, Early Head Start, to serve economically disadvantaged infants and toddlers and their families. In European countries such as Italy, however, there have flourished since the 1970s strong systems of public, inclusionary, family-centered care and education for children under the age of 3—services separate from but complementary to those for children aged 3 to 6 years (Edwards, Gandini, and Forman, 1998; Gandini and Edwards, 2001).

Thus recent years have witnessed a sharpening interest in and awareness of the special capacities and requirements of toddlers, as research on the second and the third years of life has exploded and more very young children have come under the supervision of professional educators, caregivers, and clinicians. Clearly there is a consensus of practical opinion and applied professional belief in contemporary America that the tasks of nurturing and guiding children just past the threshold of mobility and language present significantly different challenges than these tasks do of either infants or older children.

Indeed, these practical opinions track and correspond rather closely to the portrait of toddlers painted by the American research literature. In this chapter we review several of the classic and emerging theoretical perspectives on development during the toddler period. Then we discuss important issues addressed by current research on the parenting of children during their second and third years of life. We close with a brief analysis of how new theories and findings about toddler development have been translated into practical advice for parents. Theorists from many perspectives—psychoanalytic, cognitive, attachment, and systems theories—have made attempts to define the central psychosocial and/or cognitive tasks of the toddler period, and their efforts have been subjected to the theoretical scrutiny of critics versed in childrearing customs in non-Western societies. Empirical researchers, meanwhile, have attempted to operationalize the themes of the toddler period in behavioral terms and establish the underlying processes of developmental change, including the processes of socialization that most affect toddler growth and development. Finally, writers seeking to offer the benefits of new thinking and new knowledge to parents have offered their opinions—often based as much on personal experience and observation as on empirical evidence—to successive generations of anxious mothers and fathers. After briefly reviewing the theoretical perspectives, we survey the empirical findings concerning toddler development and socialization and then briefly appraise several advice books to parents that have been most popular as well as esteemed by both professionals and the general public. Thus three portraits of parenting toddlers are here put forward for consideration.

# THEORETICAL PERSPECTIVES ON TODDLER DEVELOPMENT

It is clear at the outset that much current child development literature features a common vocabulary and presents overlapping images of the defining developmental tasks confronting toddlers and their parents. From the parental point of view, of course, the hallmarks of the toddler period are weaning, walking, and talking—in academic language, separation–individuation, motility, and communicative competence. The scientific perspective incorporates this commonsense parental perspective and then goes beyond it by hypothesizing underlying structural changes that are most fundamental to healthy growth and development for the child. Parental support, guidance, and structure help the child navigate the toddler period. The child faces several developmental tasks those major issues on the child's developmental agenda and occupying much of the child's emotional and interactional energy. Cultural communities may differ in the order and timing of developmental tasks and the significance they place on each task for describing the maturity of the child, but the tasks can be predicted to be universal. Although different theorists cast these tasks in slightly different ways, the following tasks, or developmental themes, are most frequently named in the current literature:

(1) *autonomy and independence*, or the emergence of capacities to function at one remove (physical and psychological) from the parent and to begin to master simple skills of daily living, such as feeding and dressing, toileting and personal hygiene, sleeping apart from the mother, and playing without adult facilitation

(2) *categorical self-concept and beginning self-reflection*, or the capacity for self-recognition in the mirror, awareness of the self as a source of actions, ideas, words, and feelings, and beginning reflective self-evaluation

(3) *impulse control, or emotion regulation*, or the emergence of capacities related to affective and behavioral regulation and compliance with parent expectations, including abilities to wait, self-comfort, resist temptation, defer gratification, and follow rules and directions even when not immediately monitored

(4) *empathy, morality, and standards*, or the emergence of abilities related to becoming prosocial and taking into account others' perspective and needs, learning rules and standards, and feeling anxiety or distress when standards are violated

(5) *gender identity and gender-role identification*, or the emergence of capacities to label and identify the gender of self and others, know some of the appropriate behaviors and attributes of males and females of various ages, understand the stability of gender over the life course, and prefer to imitate and affiliate with others of one's gender

(6) *becoming connected to others and a member of society*, or establishing close relationships and one's place as a member of a larger family or kinship grouping, including functioning in a sibling or peer group and learning how to engage appropriately in social interaction across a variety of domains, such as teaching and learning, dominance and responsibility, nurturance and dependency, play and sociability

## Psychoanalytic and Neopsychoanalytic Theories

The aforementioned six themes have grown out of the classic and the emerging theoretical literature on parenting and toddler development. Psychoanalytic theorists were perhaps the first to define developmental tasks for the second and the third years of life and strongly shaped our thinking in regard to the developmental tasks of autonomy and impulse control. The classic psychoanalytic account of the period of childhood just past infancy focuses on issues surrounding control of aggression and bodily functions. Sigmund Freud portrayed young children as assertive and willful beings whose strivings for independence and sexual gratification bring them into inevitable conflict with socializing, restraining parents. It is in the context of the parent–child relationship that the child masters and controls primitive impulses and functions. In the first edition of *Three Essays on the Theory of Sexuality*, Freud (1901–1905; collected 1953) defined latency as all of childhood up to puberty and claimed that there were but two interruptions of latency before puberty: infantile orality and preschool genitality (see Mueller and Cohen, 1986). In later writings, however, Freud (1920, 1949) argued that the sexual impulse increases progressively all through the early years, expressed in three overlapping waves: the *oral* phase of the first year; the *sadistic–anal* phase peaking in the second or third year, in which satisfaction is sought in aggression and in excretion; and the *phallic* phase of the fourth and fifth years. Freud (1920) discussed how, during the sadistic–anal phase, the outer world is first seen by children as a hostile force opposed to their pursuit of pleasure. Battles with parents over when and how to express aggression and to pass their excretions are children's first hint of external and internal conflict (Freud, 1920, p. 324). Thus an important legacy of Freud's theory is the centrality of issues of conflict to our understanding of toddler experience.

Several other psychoanalysts after Freud considered infant development and elaborated his ideas regarding developments during the second and the third years of life, always making conflict a central point of interest. Erikson (1950), for example, accepted Freud's proposal that transformations in aggressive and sexual drives form the core of the emerging personality, but he reconceived the psychosexual stages as *psychosocial* and saw the body zones as modalities for parent–child encounters in cultural context. Influenced by anthropological research, Erikson described how in many traditional rural cultures parents are casual about elimination and leave it to older children to gradually lead children out to the bush, whereas in Western middle-socioeconomic households, pressures for cleanliness, order, and punctuality sometimes lead to excessively early and/or harsh toilet training. Erikson highlighted the conflict issue by claiming that the necessary alternation of first retaining, then expelling, the products of the bowels gives the anal modality its special potential for creating both internal and external tension. In laying out *eight psychosocial stages of humankind*, he elaborated on this duality through the metaphor of *autonomy versus shame and doubt* as representing the pivotal issue of the second and the third years of life. Parents, Erikson argued, support their children through this crisis by letting their toddlers make choices in ways that do not harm themselves or others, by helping them to play and assert themselves safely and independently, and by rewarding and sharing in their accomplishments. Ever since the work of Erikson, the focus on the battle for autonomy has dominated American understanding of toddler development, with at least preliminary awareness of the role of the family and culture in intensifying or attenuating toddlers' struggles for maturity.

The themes of autonomy and conflict were taken up by neopsychoanalytic theorists such as Spitz (1965) and Mahler (Mahler, Pine, and Bergman, 1975), whose theories encompass the first three years of life but differentiate more substages than Freud and Erikson. Thus the toddler period becomes subdivided into two or three phases. For example, Mahler, Pine, and Bergman (1975) conceptualized the process of ego development during infancy as involving two parallel but intertwined strands they called separation and individuation. The toddler period involves the three stages of *practicing* (a drive toward separateness based on the exhilarating discovery of walking), *rapprochement* (an ambivalent, contested reengagement with the mother), and *individuation* (a lasting sense of separateness from mother coupled with a balanced sense of personal powers and dependencies). As with autonomy, the child is helped toward individuation by a mother who tolerates ambivalence and negativism and responds flexibly to conflicting demands.

Recent writers in the psychoanalytic tradition have put less emphasis on themes of sexuality, aggression, and autonomy and more on themes of individuality and personal meaning (Emde and Robinson, 2000). Emde has framed a "developmental–psychoanalytic" scheme that lays out how primary, universal motives (including activity, self-regulation, cognitive assimilation, affective monitoring, and connecting to others) are transformed during infancy and toddlerhood into more advanced human moral motives. This transformation takes place and requires a context of close, extended relationships between infants and their emotionally available caregivers.

## Cognitive Theories

Piaget's (1952) cognitive–structural theory of the growth of intelligence during childhood has been the second major influence shaping the contemporary understanding of the developmental tasks of toddlerhood. According to this theory, the sensorimotor stage of infancy concludes at approximately 18 to 24 months of age, with the attainment of representational thought, or *symbolization*, an event ushering in the long preoperational stage that does not culminate until the achievement of concrete operational intelligence. The attainment of sensorimotor intelligence is evident in pervasive changes in toddlers' behavior, related to new abilities to carry out actions mentally. For example, children older than approximately 18 months of age believe that other people and things are permanent and mentally compute a missing object's displacements. They can imitate actions observed at an earlier time, engage in pretend play, show "insight" in problem solving (i.e., solve means-ends problems and invent new means through mental combinations), and use symbols detached from their original contexts. These emerging behaviors provide many possibilities for parent–infant play and quickly become the focus of delightful games of imitation, peekaboo, hiding, and pretend, part of an ancient repertory of beloved "nursery games."

The toddler period in Piaget's theory is not differentiated as a separate phase. Instead, younger toddlers (under approximately 18 months of age) are expected to be sensorimotor infants, and older toddlers (18 to 36 months of age) are expected to resemble symbolic preschool children. The cognitivist revolution has led, in the United States, to an urgent sense that parents *should* facilitate and support the development of their older toddlers' representational competencies—language and symbolic play. Parents should provide a cognitively rich and stimulating environment (which invites children to ask and answer their own questions; Duckworth, 1972); partnership and intersubjectivity in object play and exploration (Hubley and Trevarthen, 1979); dialogue that promotes concept formation and abstraction ("cognitive distance" between subjective and objective, self and others, objects and their properties, ideas and actions; Sigel, 1986); and a social environment supportive of curiosity, self-directed play and investigation, and competence motivation.

Contemporary cognitivists (e.g., Case, 1992, 1998; Fischer, 1980; Fischer and Bidell, 1998; Flavell, 1994; Haith and Benson, 1998) have continued to find much to agree with Piaget's (1952) substantive descriptions of early development and, more generally, with the hypothesis that parents assist children in gradually building conceptual and representational competence. Conceptual skills are acquired gradually, with each level of understanding building on previous ones. Parents and children are seen as active partners in the process of the children's learning and acquiring knowledge, through sensory and motoric exploration. In attempting to correct or refine Piaget's stage theory and descriptions, some cognitive researchers have formulated alternative frameworks based on their own empirical findings (e.g., Case, 1992; Fischer, 1980). These theories contain points of overlap with one another but do not exactly match in number of discrete stages or in times of transition between stages; they agree in presenting a more domain-specific and highly age-graded account of toddlerhood than did Freud, Erikson, and Piaget. Furthermore, they highlight and extend Piaget's hypotheses about the construction of a categorical self-concept (understanding of the self as a distinct entity and agent; theme 2 in the list at the beginning of this section) and elaborate how children construct identities for themselves and others (Fischer, Hand, Watson, Van Parys, and Tucker, 1984).

Theorists coming from an information-processing perspective, in contrast, have sought to specify the ways in which the toddler acquires new mental strategies, maps them onto old contexts, refines them, and executes them in an increasingly skillful way (Chen and Siegler, 2000). The toddler is able to handle and manipulate the information presented by the environment about physical objects and events, space, time, number, and categories (Haith and Benson, 1998). Through their criticism of Piaget's grand theory, information-processing theorists have been largely successful in undermining the prevailing notion that researchers should try to formulate broad, general stages in children's thinking. Instead, researchers turned to describing developmental changes that are microdevelopmental and local.

Nevertheless, the success of these critics has not discouraged others from continuing to draw insight from Piaget's descriptions of infant and toddler cognition. For example, Sroufe (1979) reinterpreted the development of affect and attachment through a perspective informed by both psychoanalytic and cognitive–structural theories. Kopp (1982) outlined discontinuous phases of *coping and self-regulation* from a social skills perspective, synthesizing the findings on early childhood cognitive advances documented by many investigators. From the ages of approximately 12 to 18 months, the young toddler achieves *control*, or abilities to initiate, maintain, and terminate physical acts based on elementary awareness of the social demands of a situation. Initial self-monitoring, self-inhibition of previously prohibited behavior, and compliance appear. For example, in the presence of something dangerous that toddlers have been taught not to touch, they will look toward their mothers and back away from the object. From the ages of approximately 24 to 36 months, older toddlers achieve *self-control*, that is, the ability to comply with requests, to delay specific activities because of either self-instruction or another's demand, and to monitor their behavior according to caregiver expectations in the absence of the caregiver. Such children will shake their heads, "no," and refrain from touching the dangerous object even when their mothers are out of sight. The achievement of self-control involves major growth in self-awareness, knowledge of social standards, recall memory, and ability to delay or inhibit responding.

## Attachment Theories

A third loosely connected group of theories clarified another central issue for the toddler period: children's *entry into larger social systems beyond the mother–infant dyad* (theme 6 in the list at the beginning of this section), involving relationships with immediate and extended family members, as well as with peers, secondary caregivers, neighbors, and others outside the family. Attachment theory, first proposed by Bowlby (1969), proved a useful corrective to the prevailing behavioristic view that the child's orientation toward caregivers was based on "dependency motives" conditioned through satisfaction of the child's primary and secondary needs (Gewirtz, 1972). Attachment theory lays out developmental phases of the child's progressive entry into widening social networks. Infancy, it can be summarized, is the preeminent time for the mother–child dyad (Barnard and Solchany, in Vol. 3 of this *Handbook*; Bornstein, in Vol. 1 of this *Handbook*). Infants show passing interest and pleasure in people other than parents, but they do not function well or for long out of visual and auditory range of an attachment figure. They may enjoy interacting with persons other than an attachment figure, but they do not require such playmates for optimal development. During the toddler period, in contrast, when children have accomplished the developmental work involved in establishing mature mother–infant reciprocity and partnership (Sander, 1962) on the basis of shared rhythms, intentions, and memory (Kaye, 1982), they now begin to display appetite for establishing strong and lasting relationships—attachments and friendships—with other persons, too. Mueller and Cohen (1986) referred to "peer hunger" as being seen first during the toddler period, but perhaps it is "people hunger," a desire for exciting long-term partners with whom to establish reciprocal relationships and gain social experience, skill, knowledge, and confidence. Mothers and other family members play a key role in mediating toddlers' entry into these wider social relationships and influencing the affective responses, communicative styles, and social repertoires that their children bring to forming meaningful and sustainable relationships and associations (Barnard and Solchany, in Vol. 3 of this *Handbook*; Ladd, Profilet, and Hart, 1992). They may also help by providing their child with opportunities for making friends, supervising their child's play, or coaching them in sharing, entering a group, and solving disputes (Parke, Cassidy, Burks, Carson, and Boyum, 1992).

Attachment theory, however, provided more than another discourse to discuss the outlines of toddler development. It also provided hypotheses about the importance of developmental transitions themselves as opportunities for early intervention to correct disturbances in parent–child interaction. Brazelton's (1992) framework interpreted, or reframed, the stressful periods of the parent–child relationship that predictably occur at transition points as the most positive and productive moments (*touchpoints*) for professionals to help parents gain insight into their children and support their development of competence and individuality. Touchpoints are culturally universal and predictable times that occur just before major spurts of motor, cognitive, or emotional growth, and they are characterized by behavioral disintegration and regression in the child and by stress on the parent–child system. With regard to the toddler period, these points normatively occur at the ages of 12 months, 15 months, 18 months, 2 years, and 3 years. Thus, for Brazelton, both infancy and toddlerhood represented particularly rich times for outside intervention precisely because both age periods contain many transitions and moments of disorganization and reorganization.

## Systems Theories

In recent years, several theories were put forward to describe development from a systems perspective, as the product of dynamic interaction between the child as a complex whole and the multiple facets of the environment. Certainly development has long been recognized as a multidetermined, multidirectional process. Systems theories go beyond that holistic intuition to provide more rigorous frameworks for conceptualizing and studying that complexity. For example, *ecological systems theory* (Bronfenbrenner, 1979; Bronfenbrenner and Morris, 1998) offered an analysis of the changing settings that surround the developing person and relate dynamically to that person and each other over time. Five different categories of systems (*microsystem, mesosystem, exosystem, macrosystem, chronosystem*) exist at different levels of immediacy to the person, each engaging the developing person in different direct and indirect ways. The theory specified ways in which toddlers may be influenced by relations within and among such contexts as home, childcare, and parent's place of employment (e.g., Edwards, Logue, Loehr, and Roth, 1986, 1987), but it did not offer principles for explaining the processes of developmental change. *Interactive systems theory* focused on the reciprocal nature of the parent–child relationship and the bidirectional influence of infantcare practices on parent and child development. For instance, Sander (1962) proposed that the early mother–infant relationship develops through five stages on the basis of the child's unfolding competencies and initiatives; this formulation proved useful in guiding systematic observation of parent–child interactions and relationships and also intervention with dyads at risk. Finally, *dynamic systems theory* (Fischer and Bidell, 1998; Thelen and Fogel, 1989; Thelen and Smith, 1998) represented a new approach growing out of physics and biology that conceptualized behavior and development as emergent processes—partially predicable, but also partially indeterminate. Addressing the infant–toddler period, Fogel (1993) described how child–parent communication is controlled mutually by both partners and leads to both gradual changes and sudden developmental leaps.

## Critiques from a Cross-Cultural Perspective

Each of these theoretical perspectives on toddlerhood has received criticism from different quarters, and each has continually evolved on the basis of new research and dialogue within the scientific community. As Maccoby (1992) noted, socialization theories have shown striking continuities but also sweeping changes over this century. They have generally evolved from grand and inclusive to modest and domain specific. They have changed from unidirectional (parent behaviors as causes, child behaviors as effects) to bidirectional and transactional. Explanations of the underlying causes and processes of development have evolved from simple to complex.

Socialization theories have also evolved in response to concerns about cultural limitation and bias. These theories were criticized as being too heavily based on narrow empirical research and on philosophical and psychological assumptions of advanced Western societies. Three such lines of criticism focused specifically on the toddler period.

One line of criticism addressed the classic account of the toddler's drive for autonomy and separateness (theme 1 in the list at the beginning of this section). This account now appears incorrect or oversimplified when considered as a universal description (Edwards, 1989). For example, in many non-Western communities, such as the Mayan community of Zinacantan in Chiapas, Mexico, the transition from infancy to early childhood is not typified by resistant toddlers demanding and asserting control over toileting and other self-help skills (the familiar "No! *I* can do it!"), but instead by watchful, imitative children who acquire elements of self-care with a minimum of fuss. Clothing is simple; dirt floors and yards can be easily swept; the emotions of pride, shame, and guilt do not seem to be at issue. Zinacanteco toddlers appear not to assert separateness and to push away from encircling mothers, but rather the opposite. They struggle to cope with an unsought physical distancing initiated by mothers who until then had kept them calm, quiet, and peaceful by carrying them under a shawl on the back and by nursing them frequently. Now their previously all-giving mothers devote themselves to the new babies. The displaced toddlers, often appearing listless and dejected, frequently hover in their mothers' vicinity. They face the twin shocks of being weaned from the breast and weaned from the back and, as a result, losing the pleasures of nursing, close contact by day, and sleeping next to their mothers at night. After an extended period of adjustment, however, these children seem to accept their change in status and to rebound as active members of the children's multiage courtyard play group. Mothers in Zinacantan, as in other similar cultures, do not see themselves as playmates or conversational partners for their infants and young children; rather they delegate these roles to siblings and other family members (Edwards, 1993; Edwards and Whiting, 1993). Greenfield, Brazelton, and Childs (1989), describing Zinacanteco infancy, hypothesized that the infantcare practices lay the groundwork for the development of toddlers who watch closely, imitate elders, and respond, taking the initiative to make others respond to them:

The descriptions of Zinacanteco toddlerhood correspond in rough outline to many other descriptions of toddler behavior in rural, non-Western communities (DeLoache and Gottlieb, 2000; Edwards, 1993; Farver, 1993; Whiting and Edwards, 1988). Albino and Thompson (1956) made intensive clinical observations of how Zulu toddlers reacted to the customary practice of sudden weaning and noted the following disturbances: clinging, refusals to respond, aggression toward mother, sucking of objects, repetitive behavior (such as rocking), messing and naughtiness (such as playing with fire, spilling food, throwing dirt), fretfulness or crying, disturbed sleep and bed wetting, subdued apathy. Following the period of disturbance, however, Zulu children quite suddenly developed behaviors normally expected of older children, such as helping with household tasks, increased facility in speech, and a greater independence from adult support.

It seems that, in many non-Western communities, after weaning toddlers begin to function without constant maternal attention and to play well and get most of their needs met within the multiage playgroup of siblings and courtyard cousins. This is illustrated in the following description by Sigman et al. (1988, p. 1259) of Embu children living in Kenya:

> The influence of siblings and peers appears to be quite important for the Embu toddlers' development. Older sisters were frequently the caregivers who listened to and talked to their younger sibling. Furthermore, those toddlers most involved in sustained social interaction developed the most rapidly, and social interactions almost always involved other children rather than adults.

These descriptions do not fit well the portrait of a self-initiated drive for autonomy and separateness—what Brazelton (1989) called the "Declaration of Independence" of the 1-year-old child—widely accepted in American child development and parenting literature as the normative pattern.

In place of the psychoanalytic account, Weisner (1989a, 1989b, 1993) suggested that the language of increasing "interdependence" (or "shared social support") rather than "independence" best describes the developmental goal of parents in many cultures around the world. Whiting and Edwards (1988; Edwards, 1992, 1993; Whiting, 1980, 1983) proposed examining without theoretical presumption the cross-cultural universals and variations in behavior that young children demonstrate to and elicit from social partners, using as a point of reference the four major age grades defined by Margaret Mead: the *lap child* (infant), *knee child* (toddler), *yard child* (preschooler), and *community child* (schoolchild). They then theorized about age-specific *developmental agendas*, such as seeking responsiveness from others (lap child), discovering the limits of the physical and social environments (knee child), establishing a position in the childhood pecking order (yard child), and seeking symbolic knowledge and to compete with same-gender peers (community child).

Findings from comparative studies of parental developmental expectations make clear that parents from different cultures do not agree on the expected age at which children should acquire various competencies nor on how crucial these various competencies are for maturity (Goodnow, in Vol. 3 of this *Handbook*). For example, Americans regard social skills with peers and verbal articulateness and assertiveness to be very important for young children, and they push for early achievement of these skills. In contrast, Italians regard sensitivity to the needs of others and graciousness in entering and exiting from social situations to be signs of maturity (Edwards, 1992; Edwards, Gandini, and Giovannini, 1993). Super and Harkness (1986; Harkness and Super, 1983, 1993, in Vol. 2 of this *Handbook*) likewise argued that developmental stages are influenced by cultural experiences and demarcated differently around the world. Cultures vary in how they make socialization demands, what different aspects of development they see as critical for growth, and how developmental timetables are subjected to socialization pressure or left to unfold at their own pace (Deloache and Gottlieb, 2000).

The bottom line of these arguments is that, before concluding what is *the* central or defining developmental task of the toddler period, we need more complete information on toddler development and behavior in a wide variety of cultural settings. Thus, even the list of six themes proposed at the beginning of this section—autonomy, self-awareness, impulse control, emergence of standards, gender identity, and becoming a member of society—should be considered tentative and subject to cross-cultural validation.

Rogoff (1998; Rogoff, Mistry, Gönçu, and Mosier, 1991, 1993) developed a second line of criticism of the standard theoretical accounts, focusing on issues of cognitive development. Drawing on Vygotsky's (1962, 1978) theory of cognitive development, Rogoff argued that cognitive as well as social development occurs in cultural contexts, through interaction of children with more competent partners in situations of *guided participation*. The Piagetian account, Rogoff claimed, leads researchers to attend chiefly to situations in which a parent and a young child interact around a toy or engage face to face in talk or play. In reality, at least for many children around the world, most learning and development take place not in situations in which adults and children are focused on each other but rather jointly participate in a task or social activity that engages their shared interest, such as cooking, weaving, visiting, or celebrating. In studies of toddlers in four cultures (Rogoff et al., 1993), adults are seen to *scaffold* their children's ("apprentices") learning, first through choosing and structuring their activities, then through various forms of tacit communication and explicit verbal guidance. The kinds of behaviors that adults can exhibit to extend toddlers' cognitive competence include recruiting the child's interest in a task, simplifying the task, motivating the child to maintain effort, calling attention to important discrepancies between what the child has accomplished and the ideal solution, controlling frustration and risk, and demonstrating the ideal solution (Wood, Bruner, and Ross, 1976). However, the preferred way in which the adult scaffolds the toddler's learning is strongly affected by culture (Rogoff et al., 1993). In some contexts, for example, among Mayan families in the Highlands of Guatemala, caregivers and toddlers *jointly* and *mutually* contribute to the direction of activity in everyday moments of problem solving. The caregivers orient their toddlers to an activity, monitor what unfolds, and offer help and suggestions when needed, but meanwhile they also *simultaneously* attend to other persons present or activities taking place (such as with older children). Mayan toddlers, for their part, watch closely the progress of events taking place around them and sensitively share the leadership for problem solving. In contrast, in other contexts, such as among middle-socioeconomic Turkish and European American families, caregivers and toddlers prefer to take turns and *alternate*, rather than share, the task of directing activity, and both mother and child focus *exclusively* on one activity and one social partner at a time. Such findings are proving fruitful in opening up new lines of research on the ways in which children appropriate their culture through processes of participation and negotiation with more competent experts (Farver, 1993).

A third line of criticism was drawn from the work of developmental sociolinguists. Ochs and Schieffelin (1984) called for a new conceptualization of childhood socialization based on merging this domain with the study of language acquisition. The forms, functions, and message content of children's early language in natural settings, they argued, should be documented and examined for "the ways in which they *organize* and *are organized by* culture" (p. 276). Using Ochs's transcripts of Samoan adult–child speech, Schieffelin's transcripts of the Kaluli of Papua, New Guinea, and a synthesis of American child language studies, they created three very different portraits of early parent–child communication patterns. They saw not one choreography of normal parent–toddler speech but rather many (within and across societies), shaped by the interaction of biological pre-dispositions with cultural role and rule systems. Sociolinguistic research yielded a growing cor-pus of ethnographic studies detailing the socialization of early communication in cultural context (Schieffelin and Ochs, 1986).

## Summary

The classic and more recent theoretical descriptions of the toddler period together yield a fairly integrated picture of developmental tasks faced during the second and the third years. Such tasks, which occupy much of the emotional and interactional energy of the developing child, include (1) learning to function autonomously, that is, at one remove from the caregiver, and beginning to help in an appropriate way as defined by family and culture with the ordinary routines of self-care and daily living; (2) categorical self-concept and beginning self-reflection; (3) impulse and self-control, the precursors of self-regulation in the absence of the caregiver; (4) the beginnings of moral conscience, including sensitivity to the violation of standards and organized emotional themes of hurt feelings, empathy toward the plight of others, fear of punishment, guilt, shame, and desire to repair; (5) gender identity, beginning knowledge of gender roles, and beginning preference for acting like and affiliating with others of one's gender; and (6) becoming a member of society in the sense of taking a place in the larger family and kinship network and in a childhood play group.

Critiques of this literature by anthropologists, cross-cultural psychologists, and sociolinguists made the point that toddler development cannot be adequately described without introducing further theoretical perspectives based on Vygotsky's (1962, 1978) writings and using naturalistic obser-vations that clarify the meaning systems and communication processes involved in socialization. Furthermore, whereas certain developmental tasks may be universal, cultural groups may nevertheless differ in what age and order they impose these tasks on the child, and in how significant or insignificant they claim each task to be in evaluating a child's maturity. Moreover, cultures differ in whether their ultimate goal is interdependence or independence and to whom (mother versus child) they assign the leading role in the push for separateness (Greenfield and Suzuki, 1998). Whereas people in North America and Western Europe tend to see the drive for autonomy as coming from the toddler who needs to push away from the mother, people in rural village communities from sub-Saharan Africa, South America, and Central America place the mother in charge of creating psychological separation and distance—against the toddler's expected resistance (Edwards, 1989).

## CLASSICAL AND MODERN RESEARCH ON TODDLER DEVELOPMENT AND PARENTING TODDLERS

Recent years have also witnessed, in addition to the strides made in theorizing about the develop-mental tasks of the toddler period, an outpouring of empirical research focusing on toddler be-havioral development and parent–child interaction during the second and the third years of life. The research findings provide further insight on how children move through the developmental tasks already discussed. However, in current developmental texts, the discussions of findings are not usually organized by developmental tasks or themes, but rather by behavioral domains that can readily be operationalized and observed. In the remainder of this chapter, research findings relevant to parenting toddlers are reviewed, and the subheadings commonly found in the child development literature are used: (1) self-concept and self-reflection, (2) compliance and noncompliance, (3) empathy and the emergence of standards, (4) gender identity and gender-role identification, and (5) cognitive and communicative competence. Of course, the topics of self-concept, emergence of standards, and gender identity (themes 1, 3, and 4 in the list at the beginning of the previous section) obviously correspond to earlier themes. The topics of compliance and noncompliance correspond to the developmental task or theme of impulse control and emotion regulation. The topic of cognitive and communicative competence relates not to any one single theme; the issues here are broader than psychosocial tasks and underlie all of them simultaneously. Yet, two other well-studied topics that could be reviewed, attachment and temperament, are addressed elsewhere (Cummings and Cummings, in Vol. 5 of this *Handbook*; Putnam, Sanson, and Rothbart, in Vol. 1 of this *Handbook*).

## Self-Concept and Self-Reflection

Extensive studies of children's self-recognition by Lewis and his colleagues (Lewis and Brooks-Gunn, 1979; Lewis, Sullivan, Stranger, and Weiss, 1989) established that toddlers between approximately 15 and 18 months of age begin to respond to their mirror image as if they know it is their own face they are seeing. At first, however, they may not understand that the mirror image is a *representation* of the self (Povinelli, Landau, and Periloux, 1996), but their symbolic capacities grow quickly. Looking at the mirror, they label themselves by name or use personal pronouns, such as I and me (Baldwin, 1897; Kagan, 1981). These behaviors are taken as evidence that the child has formed a "categorical self-concept," or the awareness that the self is a separate, physical entity and a source of actions, words, ideas, and feelings. Whereas the infant's capacity to distinguish self from other is primitive (based on the different "affordances" discovered in his or her own body versus in other physical entities encountered), the toddler's sense of self is truly interpersonal because it involves self-conscious emotions and capacities for perspective taking and pretend play (Asendorpf, Warkentin, and Baudonniere, 1996; Pipp-Siegel and Foltz, 1997). However, not until the preschool years does the child acquire a sense of the self's continuity and endurance through time, based on autobiographical memory and a "narrative" sense of self (Povinelli and Simon, 1998).

The toddler's categorical concept of the self as entity and agent, in turn, serves as the basis for a second major achievement, the beginning of reflective self-evaluation, that is, the ability to reflect on whether or not one can meet an achievement standard or accomplish a task, such as fulfilling a parent's request. Stipek, Recchia, and McClintic (1992) found that, as children approached the age of 2, they showed prideful responses when succeeding with a toy (such as pushing shapes into a sorting box or hammering pegs into a pounding bench), and they sought recognition by calling their mothers' attention to their accomplishments. Mothers who tended to praise their toddlers more frequently had children who spontaneously showed more pride (even when not being praised) in the laboratory setting. In another study, intrusive mothers had boys who were relatively less responsive and "internalizing" when confronting failure (Belsky, Domitrovich, and Crnic, 1997). Nevertheless, competitive standards of success ("winning" and "losing" against someone else) seem to have little meaning to toddlers before the age of 3. In speculating about the implications of their findings for parenting, Stipek et al. (1992) commented that the capacity for reflective self-evaluation opens the child up to learning about parental and cultural values. Parents' approval and disapproval teaches children, first, that some things they do can please other people as well as themselves, and, second, about desirable outcomes and standards. The children "should become at least somewhat dependent on adults to identify socially valued outcomes" (Stipek et al., 1992, p. 19), and they should begin to internalize the forms in which praise and blame are expressed to them, for example, the words, postures, and emotions commonly used with them should become their working models for proper emotional expression in evaluating self and others (Kitayama and Markus, 1994).

## Compliance and Noncompliance

During the second year of life, children become capable of learning their family's and community's standards for proper and desirable behavior. Indeed, socialization pressures begin in earnest during the second or the third year of life in most cultural communities around the world (Kopp, 1982; Maccoby and Martin, 1983; Whiting, 1983; Whiting and Edwards, 1988). Some demands for mature behavior are elicited by 2-year-old toddlers' budding interest in the world around them, desire to participate in adult work (Reingold, 1982), and new abilities to imitate complex adult and peer routines that evidence competence (Kuczynski, Zahn-Waxler, and Radke-Yarrow, 1987). Other socialization pressures arise in response to the management problems presented by toddlers' emerging mobility and exploratory behaviors. Toddlers elicit many commands from both adults and older children that serve to protect them from physical dangers ("Stay away from the fire"), infection ("Stop eating dirt"), and wandering too far ("Don't cross the road"). Toddlers also receive frequent admonishments concerning cleanliness and hygiene ("go wash yourself"), basic etiquette ("Greet your grandmother"), care of clothing and household property ("That will break"), and other simple rules and standards. If what they are doing is perceived as annoying or intrusive, they receive commands to go away, to desist, or not to interrupt. In some cultural communities, 3-year-old toddlers may even begin to receive commands related to meaningful household and subsistence tasks; in such places, assigning the toddler a chore or errand is seen as nurturant and complimentary—a way to flatter children as grownups and include them in the family group (Edwards and Whiting, 1993: Weisner, 1989a). Thus he study of the growth of compliance, the ability and willingness to modulate behavior in accordance with caregiver commands and expectations, has been one of the most active areas of toddler research. One limitation, however, is that most of the research relates to North American families, the types most likely to believe in continuing high levels of parent–child interaction during the toddler period. The findings therefore would not seem to apply to the kinds of rural subsistence communities, as mentioned in the subsection on cross-cultural perspectives, that use the toddler period as a time to wean the child from mother's bed, back, and breast, and redirect much of the child's dependency out toward the family as a whole. Compliance issues are certainly present in the latter, too, but the close analyses of mother–child communication and interaction surrounding growth of self-regulation have yet to be conducted in such non-Western settings.

Developmental studies of resistance and negativism are not new in the United States; they were prevalent in the 1920s and 1930s (Kopp, 1992). This work, along with Gesell's (1940) findings, firmly established the stereotype of "the terrible twos." Taken together, earlier studies do reveal a peak of resistant and negativistic behaviors when a child is approximately 2 years old, with a steady decline by the age of 4 years (Dubin and Dubin, 1963; Spitz, 1957; Wenar, 1982).

In response to maternal requests for cooperation, child compliance increases from toddler to preschool to school years (Whiting and Edwards, 1988). Across cultures, girls are more cooperative and responsive to maternal commands and requests and earlier involved in responsible tasks. Toddler boys are more likely than girls to approach injury-risk hazards and less obedient to their mothers' redirections, perhaps explaining why they suffer more accidents and injuries (Morrongiello and Dawber, 1998). However, compliance is a usual part of the toddler repertory. In play situations, even children under the age of 2 years comply when they understand a command and do not comply when they do not understand (Kaler and Kopp, 1990). Commands and requests usually activate not simply cooperation but actual joyful enthusiasm from children aged 18 to 24 months, especially when accompanied by clarity, sensitivity about interrupting the children's ongoing behavior, and appreciative and attentive feedback to the children's performance (Reingold, Cook, and Kolowitz, 1987). The pleasure taken in mastery and in fitting their actions to the words of the adults seems to account for toddlers' readiness to do what parents ask.

However, when the situation is nonplayful or when the adult forcefully insists on breaking contact or interaction with the child, toddler behavior is not always so cooperative (Power and Chapieski, 1986). Schneider-Rosen and Wenz-Gross (1990) studied age changes in toddler compliance to both mothers and fathers in a variety of tasks typical of situations with which children are often confronted: told to play independently and not interrupt a busy parent; told to stop playing in order to read a book with the parent; told to clean up toys and put them away; told to sit quietly and not touch a toy; and told to work on a difficult problem alone. The different tasks elicited different patterns of responses and age trends, suggesting different underlying task demands. Neither fathers nor mothers elicited more cooperation overall. Age relations were complex, and the authors interpreted the findings as pointing to a transition and behavioral reorganization when a child is approximately 24 months old. Before this age, behavior is under the control of external monitors (adults), and children are very motivated to comply. When the child is beyond the age of 2, behavior may be influenced more by the child's sense of autonomy and internal control systems involving language, memory, and the ability to inhibit responding.

Many studies have documented developmental changes in the ways that young children express their noncompliance. Passive noncompliance and direct defiance are the strategies typical of younger toddlers, whereas bargaining, negotiation, and direct refusal are the more mature strategies typical of older toddlers and preschool children (Kopp, 1992; Kuczynski and Kochanska, 1990; Kuczynski, Kochanska, Radke-Yarrow, and Girnius-Brown, 1987). These changes in noncompliant behavior are accompanied by changes in the control strategies used by mothers. Simple distraction and physical guidance (e.g., showing, leading by the hand) are used more by mothers of young toddlers, whereas verbal suggestion, reasoning, and counternegotiation are used more by the mothers of older, more verbal children (Kuczynski et al., 1987). Thus both mothers and children show evolving "techniques of persuasion" that they use with each other.

Crying and tantrums are other forms of resistant noncompliance often seen in toddlers. Brazelton (1992) argued that temper tantrums in the second year reflect the child's inner turmoil and struggle between dependence and independence and are best handled by parents who stand back and allow their child to regain control. By moving beyond crying and tantrums, the child demonstrates emotional regulation, which is an important component of self-regulation. Matheny (reported in Kopp, 1992) observed children in laboratory settings for the Louisville Twin Study and found negative emotional tone to increase sharply when children were between 12 and 18 months of age, to decline somewhat by 24 months of age, and to shift strongly back toward more positive tone by 30 months of age. Similarly, Kopp (1992), in home and laboratory observations, found a peak for crying (both short bouts and longer tantrums) when children were 18 to 21 months of age, with a clear drop by 36 months.

Besides providing a window into the development of self-regulation, the study of compliance and noncompliance offers a way to examine the development of reciprocity in parent–child relations (Parpal and Maccoby, 1985). Affective reciprocity has been amply documented; for example, highly negative London 2- to 4-year-old children were found to have more negative mothers (Dowdney and Pickles, 1991), but the cause-and-effect relations within the cycle of reciprocity are complex. Maccoby and Martin (1983) made a useful distinction between "situational" compliance (immediate obedience, often based on factors such as threat of punishment or promise of reward) and "receptive" compliance (a long-term reciprocity-based readiness to cooperate with expectations). Power-assertive techniques, such as yelling and punishment, they argued, may well be effective in the short run because they generate some degree of fear and submission to authority, yet less effective in the long run because they must be resorted to more and more frequently as time goes on and they do not create a general cooperative attitude on the part of the child—what Maccoby and Martin (1983) called a "readiness to be socialized." In support of this hypothesis, both Power and Chapieski (1986) and Crockenberg and Litman (1990) found better compliance in 2-year-old toddlers to be associated with mothers' use of guidance and nonassertive methods of control, whereas defiance was associated with power-assertive techniques and physical punishment. Donovan, Leavitt, and Walsh (2000) found that mothers who greatly overestimated their control and used high negative control had toddlers who quickly became defiant when exercising their autonomy. Lytton's (1979) study of $2\frac{1}{2}$-year-old boys based on parents' "compliance diaries" found consistent enforcement of rules and frequency of joint play and cooperative activities to be related to high levels of compliance, and love withdrawal and other forms of psychological punishment related to low compliance.

"Responsiveness," however, is a quality that children together with parents create in relationship. Ritchie (1999) found that mothers greatly dislike extended "power bouts" with their toddlers, and that children prone to engage in such struggles elicit more negative perceptions from their mothers. Similarly, mothers of toddlers rated high in "negative reactivity" tend to be more controlling and less guiding in style, and their children are less compliant (Braungart-Rieker, Garwood, and Stifter, 1997). Some extremely difficult toddlers, who are aggressive, unyielding, and unruly in the face of their parents' attempts at guidance, help create the devastating "cycles of coercion," as analyzed by Patterson (1982; Patterson and Fisher, in Vol. 5 of this *Handbook*).

The key to enlisting the toddler's willing compliance, suggested Westerman (1990), may be more than simple reciprocity but instead interaction behaviors that are *well coordinated* with the child's, in the sense that parent behaviors scaffold the child's effort, fit with what the child is doing, add to it, and set the stage for what the child might do next. Mothers of 3- to 4-year-old toddlers, who were identified as having compliance problems, were compared with other mothers at the same preschools, and the former were judged less successful in coordinating with their children on a block task (Westerman, 1990). Parpal and Maccoby (1985) trained mothers in responsive play that scaffolded their children's play with toys and found that these children subsequently increased in compliance. The point, then, may not be simply that parents should apply firm, responsive control (following Baumrind's, 1972, well-known paradigm for authoritative parenting). Rather, parents need to work toward a certain type of control, within a context of generally positive emotion and sense of well-being, that leads the toddler toward learning and success.

## Empathy and the Emergence of Standards

During children's second year, an early moral sense, including sensitivity to flawed objects and distress when a standard is violated or cannot be met, clearly emerges (Kagan, 1981). This moral sense parallels their new capacities for self-reflective evaluation, described in the subsection on self-concept. Children show anxiety ("Something is wrong!") when they see someone hurt, an object broken, or an important rule violated. At first children exhibit a strong, unspecific arousal and may not be sure whether to react with positive or negative emotion (Zahn-Waxler, Radke-Yarrow, Wagner, and Chapman, 1992), but at the age of 2 their reactions become more differentiated. By the age of 3, they find that a number of organized socioemotional themes have emerged to serve as the basis of childhood morality and conscience: shame, guilt, reparation, empathy, pride, hurt feelings (Eisenberg and Valiente, in Vol. 5 of this *Handbook*; Emde, Biringen, Clyman, and Oppenheim, 1991).

Research has determined the effects of different parental behaviors in influencing children's responses and in helping them modulate and organize their emotional responses into constructive actions, such as apologizing, offering sympathy or comfort, seeking to assist or repair, going for help, and inhibiting future transgression. Maternal modeling is important. Maternal sensitivity and reasoning have been found to relate positively to empathetic, prosocial responses during the child's second year of life. For example, when mothers show concern and talk about who was hurt, and why, their toddlers show more empathy and attempts to help someone in pain (Zahn-Waxler, Radke-Yarrow, and King, 1979). Conversely, parents who subject their toddlers to abuse at home have children who do not show concern in response to the distress of a daycare classmate, but instead react with disturbing and unusual sorts of behavior (not seen in comparable nonabused children), such as with physical attacks, fear, and anger at the victim (Azar, in Vol. 4 of this *Handbook*; Main and George, 1985).

Girls and boys do not respond identically to the distress of others, however, even during the toddler period. Although boys are as prosocially active as girls (often offering instrumental help or seeking to repair), girls show more empathetic concern and tend to mirror or copy the affective experience of the other more (Zahn-Waxler et al., 1992, p. 134): "Typically, these are seen as indicators of joining in the emotional experience of others, and there is a long history of discussion regarding why females are sometimes more prone than males to participate in others' affective states."

Temperament may be another factor besides gender that affects how a child feels when a standard is violated and that may predict how parents can most effectively get the child to comply (Putnam et al., in Vol. 1 of this *Handbook*). Kochanska (1993) proposed that individuals vary in intensity of *affective discomfort* (arousal, fear, shame, anxiety, guilt, remorse) occasioned by transgression (committed or anticipated). Evidence from several laboratories suggests that there are stable individual differences in inhibitory or effortful control that correspond to consistent physiological patterns, endure over time, and display consistent gender differences favoring girls (Deinstbier, 1984; Feinman, 1982; Goldsmith and Campos, 1986; Kochanska, 1991; Kochanska, Murray, and Coy, 1997). From maternal reports, temperament can change considerably during infancy, but is very stable when the child is between the ages of 2 and 4 (Lemery, Goldsmith, Klinnert, and Mrazek, 1999). The different temperaments may call for different parenting styles to ensure optimal development of a moral self and conscience. Subtle, gentle methods of socialization may work well with an anxious child who responds quickly to parental disapproval. Such a child becomes early motivated by the affects of shame and guilt. However, a more effortful approach to moral socialization may be required for underaroused, imperturbable children. For them, parental disapproval is less motivating, and they learn better through positive emotions such as pride, challenge and excitement, and pleasure in pleasing adults. Otherwise, parents of less perturbable children may find themselves resorting to higher and higher levels of anger and punishment to control their child. The stage will be set for a negative cycle of coercion and formation of an aggressive, uncontrollable child (Patterson, 1982).

## Gender Identity and Gender-Role Identification

During the second and the third years of life, children take several important steps along the road to constructing a *gender identity* (the knowledge that one is and always will be a male or female) and *gender-role identification* (consisting of gender-role knowledge and preferences). Parents of children this age may be becoming more mindful of their child's masculinity or femininity; as toddlers' language development accelerates, parents may correct children's use of gender labels and pronouns, and parents may find that the clothes and toys available or that their children prefer are more obviously gender linked (Leaper, in Vol. 1 of this *Handbook*). Issues of gender, nevertheless, are not yet as central and exciting to the toddler as they will be during preschool and adolescent eras. Instead, age groups (baby, child, adult) stand out as the most salient and interesting social categories to toddlers because they point to what toddlers feel are the most noteworthy distinctions in people's size, competence, and activities (for instance, who gets fed a bottle, sleeps in a crib, wears a diaper, rides a bike, drives a car, and so on; see Edwards, 1986).

By the age of $2\frac{1}{2}$ or 3 years, most children have become fairly accurate in labeling photographs of themselves and others by gender (Etaugh, Grinnell, and Etaugh, 1989). Toddlers typically master gender nouns (boy, girl, man, woman) before they master pronouns (he, she, and so forth) and correctly apply labels to others before consistently labeling themselves. Their gender labeling does not yet involve the concept of stability over time, and 3-year-old toddlers will make comments like that of Lisa, age 3, "I'm a girl, but when I'm four, I'll be a boy" (Edwards, 1986, p. 58). By the age of 3 or 4 years, children are certain about their own gender; they have formed one of the most stable self-categorizations they will make in their lifetimes (Kohlberg, 1966).

During the same period, from watching television, reading books, and observing the world around them, children are beginning to construct gender-role knowledge and stereotypes. They are also aware of what qualities their society stigmatizes, already knowing, for example, that "thin is good, fat is bad" (Cramer and Steinwert, 1998). By the age of 3, children have been found to be aware of gender-role differences for adult possessions, adult tasks, and children's toys (Weinraub et al., 1984). Toddler "gender schemas" are not tight logical structures, however, but loosely organized clusters of information picked up from multiple sources and connected to emerging concepts of "male" and "female" (Fagot, 1995; Martin, 1993).

Gender-typed preferences and behaviors also emerge early. Around the age of 2 for girls and 3 for boys, children begin to direct more of their social approaches to same-gender play partners. Without yet seeking to exclude or avoid opposite-gender children, toddlers yet show a beginning attraction or preference for others of their own gender, especially when in group situations (Maccoby, 1988; Whiting and Edwards, 1988).

What causes these differences? The role of parental socialization in gender-role development has been closely studied and debated for many years (Fagot, 1995; Leaper, in Vol. 1 of this *Handbook*). Current evidence strongly indicates that both gender identification and preference for same-gender partners are driven by cognitive processes rather than social reinforcement (Maccoby, 1988, 1999). The drawing apart of boys and girls in social play is seen universally across cultures whenever children are present in sufficient numbers for choice to be a factor; gender segregation is always strongest in same-age rather than in mixed-aged groups and hence is a more dominant feature of play at school than within the home or nearby yards (Whiting and Edwards, 1988). Rather than being created by adult reinforcement, gender segregation seems lessened when an adult is present (e.g., when several children of both genders gather around a teacher to hear a story at nursery school; Maccoby, 1988).

The role of reinforcement in helping produce gender-typed behavior is not discounted, but it does need to be understood in new and more complex ways. First, when children are at the age of 2, already reinforcements for gender-typed behavior are most effective when processed in terms of gender (Fagot, 1985). Boys' peer groups early start defining and sanctioning nonmasculine behaviors, causing boys to seek to avoid doing things defined as not male. Second, although parental socialization is no longer believed to account for gender differences in dominance and aggressive behaviors (now understood to be hormonally mediated), nevertheless parents surely play a role in children's development of some gender labeling and gender-typed behavior. Current research examines parents as coparticipants with children in a system of preferences and meanings; parent emotional reactions sometimes "steer" toddlers toward gender-typed behavior (e.g., Weitzman, Birns, and Friend, 1985). Parents also "join" with the children in influential ways and modify their attention and interest patterns. For example, Caldera, Huston, and O'Brien (1989) found parents of toddlers (observed in the laboratory) to follow their children in play with either same-gender or cross-gender toys, but they became more involved and excited with same-gender toys. The gender-stereotyped toys, moreover, themselves elicited gender-typed play: Trucks evoked different, noisier, more active play than did play with feminine toys, no matter the gender of parent or the gender of child. These findings are reminiscent of the claim of Whiting and Edwards (1988) that, from a cross-cultural perspective, parents exert their strongest gender-role socialization through the settings and activities to which they assign boys versus girls, rather than through praise or reprimands that are intended to modulate behavior. Moreover, parents are not the only adults influential in young children's gender-role development, and many studies (e.g., Fagot, Hagan, Leinbach, and Kronsberg, 1985) have found that adults act in more gender-stereotyped ways when they do not know a child well and hence are in a more ambiguous situation. Relatives, neighbors, new acquaintances, and media models may play heightened roles in creating worlds of gendered meaning for very young children.

## Cognitive and Communicative Competence

Throughout the 1960s and early 1970s, the vulnerability of infants and young children to environmental deprivation was a rallying cry for researchers, educators, and policymakers. Hunt (1961), Fowler (1962), and others, resonating to the social idealism of the times, galvanized a wave of early intervention programs and evaluation research aimed at understanding and eradicating educational disadvantages ascribed to socioeconomic background. In the 1980s, however, the earlier optimism was not so much vanquished as tempered and transformed into more cautious and narrowly defined efforts aimed at specific target populations, for example, early intervention efforts for infants and toddlers with disabilities or identified risks, child abuse prevention and treatment, and early treatment of speech and communication disorders. Knowledge about form and process in developmental change during a child's first three years of life exploded, but experts were more aware of, first, the complexities of the questions and the limits of what we know, second, the contribution the child makes to situations and interactions, and, third, the huge range in normal childrearing environments found throughout history and around the world.

During the 1990s, a solid body of findings accumulated, fulfilling the promise of what can be found through more complex designs with a longitudinal component, multiple measures and methods, representative samples including diverse and/or at-risk populations, and hypotheses based on better understanding of gene–environment interactions. In general, the findings suggested that toddlers and caregivers jointly contribute to developing cognitive and communicative competence. For example, Bradley et al. (1989) reported on an extensive 3-year longitudinal study involving six sites and three ethnic groups in North America. Correlations between mental test scores and the Home Observation for Measurement of the Environment inventory (Caldwell and Bradley, 1978; a measure of the quality of the physical and social environment) increased during the child's second year of life and then stabilized during the third. Parental responsivity and availability of stimulating play materials were more strongly related to subsequent mental test scores than were the socioeconomic status variables. Cross-lag correlations supported the interpretation of bidirectional influences, but with more evidence of the environment's shaping the child than of the child's shaping the environment. In another study, the cross-national team behind the Twins Early Development Study found high group heritability for both verbal and performance delays in toddler and preschool children. Environmental factors were also influential, but with the magnitude of their effect differing for each kind of delay (Eley et al., 1999).

Many experts on infancy, such as Kagan (1971) and Fogel (1984), however, stopped believing that early experiences are inherently more important than experiences at any other time in life; instead, self-righting forces in the individual and in the environment are operative throughout the lifespan. Others (e.g., Fowler, 1986) claimed that early experiences are important and formative, but that the hard problem is to identify phenomena of a magnitude sufficient to make a long-term impact— sufficient to override the continuing accumulation of multiple, competing experiences. Fowler (1986) argued that research must be more focused and ask more complex, multivariate questions, looking at specific experiences, and also their exact timing and duration, in relation to particular outcomes.

McCall (1981) proposed a model that attributes causal power to dimensions of the environment but in different ways before versus after the second year of life. The model portrays early development as looking like a shovel or scoop (narrow at the top, then rapidly widening out). McCall argued that, during the first 18 months of life, development proceeds along a fairly narrow, fixed, species-typical path, at least as long as species-typical, appropriate environments prevail. After this earliest period, however, environmental influences and organismic factors (such as temperament or learning style) are more likely to have a formative impact, and children's development fans out into a greater variety of normal types of outcomes. Thus, the toddler period, from 18 months to 3 years of age, represents the time when cultural, socioeconomic, familial, and organismic differences become more implicated in the case of children's development. For example, a longitudinal study of African American children from low-income homes followed the cognitive performances of the children from 6 months to 8 years of age. The factors associated with more optimal development were intensive early educational childcare, responsive stimulation at home, and higher maternal IQ (Burchinal, Campbell, Bryant, Wasik, and Ramey, 1997). For these children, higher quality of center-based care was related to higher Bayley IQ scores, language development, and communication skills across time, even after the researchers adjusted for family and child characteristics (Burchinal et al., 2000). Moreover, environmental risk factors (such as family income and disorganization and neighborhood poverty) do not operate in a linear, additive way, but rather in complex, compounding ways.

Whichever model of the influence of early experiences turns out to be correct, evidence is accumulating for the relation of specific experiences to specific outcomes in cognitive and language development.*Environmental specificity* occurs when certain aspects of the environment promote specific types of competencies or are more influential with some categories of children. For example, Wachs (1982) found that exploratory play skills in children's second and third years are best enhanced by caregivers' providing contingently responsive objects (such as rattles and balls), as well as an overall variety of objects, during children's first year. The development of spatial relations and perspective taking are best predicted by the avoidance of noise, confusion, and environmental overcrowding during the children's first two years. Males may be more vulnerable to the effects of environmental stress. Early exposure to a variety of exploratory materials and toys (especially ones that provide contingent feedback to the child's actions) leads to improved problem-solving and exploratory play when the child is 2 years old (Yarrow, Rubenstein, and Pedersen, 1975). Wachs and Gruen (1982) argued that some forms of stimulation should be introduced at specific ages and others eliminated. Early experiences require later reinforcement to remain influential: "The vast majority of early experiences, *taken in isolation*, will not have lasting effects unless later experiences occur which stabilize the effects of the initial experiences" (Wachs and Gruen, 1982, p. 220).

There is also evidence for specificity in the social environment–organism interaction, although these relations are not always confirmed as predicted (e.g., Bornstein, Vibbert, Tal, and O'Donnell, 1992). For instance, in a longitudinal, experimental design, Slade (1987) found that mothers' availability for interactive play and conversation contributed to toddlers' symbolic (pretend) play, across the age period from 20 to 28 months. *Semantic contingency*, an immediate matching of adult speech to the topic or content of the child's utterance (e.g., "You like that truck across the street? It's a big dump truck!"), has repeatedly been found to be effective in promoting more rapid language development in toddlerhood (Bohannon and Stanowicz, 1988; Cross, 1978; Rice, 1989; Smolak and Weinraub, 1983). The adult may repeat the child's utterance, expand on it, use the child's word in a question, repeat a child's phrase with grammatical correction, or request clarificaton. Vocabulary development during toddlerhood has been related to the overall amount of parent speech (Huttenlocher, Haight, Bryk, Seltzer, and Lyons, 1991) and to adults' tendencies to describe aspects of the environment that are at that moment occupying the child's attention (e.g., "Yes, that bird [you're looking at] is big and blue") (Dunham and Dunham, 1992; Valdez-Menchaca and Whitehurst, 1988). Social interactive routines, such as book reading, are strongly supportive of vocabulary development and emergent print literacy (Bus and van IJzendoorn, 1988). As Fogel (1984, p. 287) concluded, "Maternal vocalization, contingent responsiveness, and involvement become important between six and twenty-four months, after which a lack of restrictiveness and providing opportunities to interact with other people are the best predictors of cognitive and language development." Early intervention programs for children at risk for language delays have been successful when they involve training parents to talk (more often and more responsively) and read and discuss pictures with their children; and the effects are compounded over time. Recognition of the overriding importance of parents in children's lives has led to an approach to early intervention that is family focused rather than child focused—involving partnership and sharing of responsibility and expertise between the family and the professionals.

## Summary

Several content areas of toddler development and parenting have received intensive psychological study. Researchers have built a strong knowledge base for understanding the underlying processes related to toddler self-concept, compliance/noncompliance, moral development, gender identity, and cognitive and language development, and their implications for parenting. Moreover, theoretical analyses of these content areas have shown strong and encouraging signs of a maturing field of knowledge. There has been a synthesis of findings and joining of vocabularies across formerly separate research traditions. For example, in work on the growth of self-regulation (e.g., Kopp, 1982,

1992), analyses of the cognitive underpinnings were drawn together from the Genevan tradition, Vygotskian and Russian psychology, and the American functionalist point of view.

Antecedent-consequent relations, however, still remained difficult to nail down. The standards for what is considered convincing evidence of parental causation were increased, and bidirectional, multicausational models became the goal. Both research investigators and textbook writers became increasingly cautious in generalizing about socialization effects and lasting influences of early experience.

## TRANSLATION OF THEORY AND RESEARCH INTO PRACTICAL INFORMATION FOR PARENTING TODDLERS

During recent years, many of the major findings on toddler development became available to parents in summary and simplified form through the medium of advisory literature. Parents who wanted expert advice on care and guidance of their toddlers had many books from which to choose, including trade books devoted entirely to the toddler period. Women's and parenting magazines often featured articles addressing toddler issues and developments, with much attention devoted to selecting high-quality childcare and providing appropriate intellectual stimulation.

Many works focused on emotional development. Fraiberg's (1959) *The Magic Years* was a psychoanalytic account of childhood between 18 months and 3 years of age, when parents guide children in acquiring selfhood, conscience, and self-control. Brazelton's (1989) *Toddlers and Parents* integrated an Eriksonian perspective on autonomy into a framework that explored temperamental differences among children and addressed contemporary childrearing issues such as maternal employment and single parenthood. *First Feelings* by Greenspan and Greenspan (1985) described six emotional milestones during the preschool years. This book was intended to help parents understand such problems as supporting a rich emotional life, setting limits, and coping with fears. Brazelton's (1992) *Touchpoints* reframed childhood problems into strengths and stressful transitions into open moments of opportunity for change on the part of both parents and children. Brazelton joined forces with Greenspan to publish *The Irreducible Needs of Children: What Every Child Must Have to Grow, Learn, and Flourish* (Brazelton and Greenspan, 2000). Meanwhile, Deloache and Gottlieb (2000) offered parents a new way to look at the field of expert advice. In *A World of Babies: Imagined Childcare Guides for Seven Societies*, they presented a set of fictionalized accounts of how various societies believe socialization should take place—each account prepared in the how-to style of a parental guidebook. The book gave parents a way to step back and gain perspective on the "rights and wrongs" of weaning, managing sleep, and the other practical aspects of parenting, by seeing some alternative ways that cultural communities in other times and places have found to help infants and toddlers survive and enter society.

Lickona's (1994) *Raising Good Children*, one of the few parenting books to start from a cognitive–structuralist theoretical base, built on the author's work on character education in schools. He used Kohlberg's (1969) model of moral judgment development to assist parents to understand typical childhood reasoning, achieve fairness in conflict resolution, reason and communicate with children, and use books and television to aid moral education. Lickona summarized the toddler years as laying the foundation for moral development, including acquiring respect for authority and an attitude of cooperation with reasonable rules and requests.

Books that described toddler development for parents in a comprehensive way included Leach's (1997) *Your Baby and Child, What to Expect, The Toddler Years* by Eisenberg, Murkoff, and Hathaway (1994), *The Baby Book* by Sears and Sears (1993), and Fisher's (1988) *From Baby to Toddler*. These books presented child development norms, medical information, and guidance on common behavior problems, management issues, daily routines, and learning activities. The enduring legacy of psychoanalytic theory was still seen in the strong concern with emotions, but tempered by themes more properly attributed to other lines of research focused on symbolic thinking, language, exploration, and play. In the wake of exploding public interest in medical research on brain development during the child's first 3 years, several experts spoke to what this research really did—and did not—say to parents. For example, Ramey and Ramey (1999) helped parents to interpret realistically the research on brain development and early learning, and suggested to them how to foster intellectual and emotional development, without falling prey to expensive fads and distortions involving commercial products.

All of this expert advice to parents, then, provided another kind of synthesis of what has been learned in the past few decades of theorizing and research on toddler development. Moreover, although presented without scholarly annotation, the advisory literature also integrated what the professionals believed about how parents can best deal with age-old childrearing problems as well as the current sticking points of contemporary life and society.

## CONCLUSIONS

The past 30 years have witnessed an explosion of new knowledge about the second and the third years of life, accompanied by growing awareness of the special issues of this age period and the effects of differing parenting strategies. Toddlerhood is more and more recognized as a separate phase or stage of child development, bounded by infancy on the one side and early childhood on the other; some authorities even subdivide toddlerhood into discrete subphases, although there is no consensus on whether there are two or three subphases and what is the normative age of transition between subphases.

There is substantial agreement, however, on the developmental tasks faced during the second and the third years, which include the following:

(1) learning to function independently or interdependently (at one remove from the caregiver) and beginning to help in an appropriate way as defined by family and culture with the ordinary routines of self-care and daily living
(2) self-concept and beginning self-reflection
(3) impulse control and emotion regulation, the precursors to self-control in the absence of the caregiver
(4) the beginnings of moral conscience, including sensitivity to the violation of standards and organized emotional themes of hurt feelings, empathy toward the plight of others, fear of punishment, guilt, shame, and desire to repair
(5) gender identity, beginning knowledge of gender roles, and beginning preference for acting like and affiliating with others of one's gender
(6) becoming connected to others in society and taking a place in the larger family and childhood play group

Cultures appear to differ in the age at which they expect mastery of these competencies by the child, their order, and how significant each is considered in defining the child's maturity. Moreover, cultures differ in whether the ultimate goal of socialization is autonomy or interdependence and whether they put on the parent or on the child the responsibility for leading the way toward the child's more self-reliant functioning.

The content areas of toddler development that have been most studied by developmental scientists include compliance/noncompliance, moral development, gender identity, language development, and cognitive development. A great deal is now known about the descriptive details of development, for both typically and nontypically developing toddlers. Moreover, theoretical writings about the underlying processes and antecedent-consequences relations show increasing syntheses of findings across formerly separate traditions and a joining of vocabularies, as in the work on the growth of self-control and emotion regulation.

Although socialization processes in the field of toddler development are by no means fully understood, nevertheless standards are higher for what is considered convincing evidence, and bidirectional, multicausational, and transactional models have become the goal. Parents are no longer made the "whipping boys" for all childhood disabilities and disturbed outcomes. Researchers and textbook writers have become more conservative in speculating about how socialization takes place and the lasting impacts of early experience. As a result, in advisory books and articles for parents, socialization is increasingly talked of as a two-way street, and parents' expectations for what they can (or should) accomplish through their childrearing efforts are more moderate than they were for the previous generation. Moreover, greater knowledge about many details of toddler development has translated into a greater quantity and quality of popular literature about this age period. More information has become available to parents to assist them in negotiating everyday problems, understanding their individual child's temperament, growth, and development, and making good decisions on behalf of their children to introduce them to the wider world.

It still remains the case, however, that despite the linguistic and cultural diversity within American society and despite our increasing understanding about varied ways of childrearing, the definition of good parenting put forward in the expert literature remains fairly unitary and standardized. The definition complements widely shared American ideals and goals for healthy child development. The literature helps parents to facilitate their child's early and continued school success, friendships with peers, self-confidence, increasing independence from one's family of origin, individuality and emotional autonomy, capacity for intimacy, pleasure in work and play, and achievement motivation. As yet there is only beginning recognition of the legitimate role that ethnic heritage might play in parental values and decision making. Similarly, there is only limited consideration given to what kind of toddler parenting might lead toward alternative values that may be required in future generations, such as moderated appetite for individual choices and consumer goods, lifelong interdependency with extended family, and a more calm and unhurried lifestyle with more continuity of meaningful relationships and fewer transitions and stresses on children. Perhaps these alternative questions represent areas of future inquiry. In the study of socialization, history indicates that greater knowledge inevitably creates new concerns and a questioning of assumptions that limit the validity of that knowledge.

## REFERENCES

Albino, R. C., and Thompson, V. J. (1956). The effects of sudden weaning on Zulu children. *British Journal of Medical Psychology, 29,* 177–210.

American Academy of Child and Adolescent Psychiatry. (1998). *Your child: Emotional, behavioral, and cognitive development from birth to preadolescence.* New York: HarperCollins.

Asendorpf, J. B., Warkentin, V., and Baudonniere, P. M. (1996). Self-awareness and other awareness II: Mirror self-recognition, social contingency awareness, and synchronic imitation. *Developmental Psychology, 32,* 313–321.

Baldwin, J. M. (1897). *Social and ethical interpretations in mental development.* New York: Macmillan.

Baumrind, D. (1972). Socialization and instrumental competence in young children. In W. W. Hartup (Ed.), *The young child: Reviews of research* (Vol. 2, pp. 202–274). Washington, DC: National Association for the Education of Young Children.

Belsky, J., Domitrovich, C., and Crnic, K. (1997). Temperament and parenting antecedents of individual differences in three-year-old boys' pride and shame reactions. *Child Development, 68,* 456–466.

Berk, L. E. (1999). *Infants, children, and adolescents* (3rd ed.). Needham Heights, MA: Allyn and Bacon.

Bohannon, J. N. III, and Stanowicz, L. (1988). The issue of negative evidence: Adult responses to children's language errors. *Developmental Psychology, 24,* 684–689.

Bornstein, M. H., Vibbert, M., Tal, J., and O'Donnell, K. (1992). Toddler language and play in the second year: Stability, covariation, and influences of parenting. *First Language, 12,* 323–338.

Bowlby, J. (1969). *Attachment.* New York: Basic Books.

Bradley, R. H., Caldwell, B. M., Rock, S. L., Barnard, K. E., Gray, C., Hammond, M. A., Mitchell, S., Siegel, L., Ramey, C. R., Gottfried, A. W., and Johnson, D. L. (1989). Home environment and cognitive development in the first 3 years of life: A collaborative study involving six sites and three ethnic groups in North America. *Developmental Psychology, 25*, 217–235.

Braungart-Rieker, J., Garwood, M. M., and Stifter, C. A. (1997). Compliance and noncompliance: The roles of maternal control and child temperament. *Journal of Applied Developmental Psychology, 18*, 411–428.

Brazelton, T. B. (1989). *Toddlers and parents: A declaration of independence.* New York: Dell.

Brazelton, T. B. (1992). *Touchpoints.* Reading, MA: Addison-Wesley.

Brazelton, T. B., and Greenspan, S. (2000). *The irreducible needs of children: What every child must have to grow, learn, and flourish.* Boulder, CO: Perseus.

Bredekamp, S., and Copple, C. (1997). *Developmentally appropriate practice in early childhood programs* (Rev. ed.). Washington, DC: National Association for the Education of Young Children.

Bronfenbrenner, U. (1979). *The ecology of human development.* Cambridge, MA: Harvard University Press.

Bronfenbrenner, U., and Morris, P. A. (1998). The ecology of developmental processes. In W. Damon (Series Ed.) and R. M. Lerner (Ed.), *Handbook of child psychology: Vol. 1. Theoretical models of human development* (5th ed., pp. 993–1028). New York: Wiley.

Burchinal, M. R., Campbell, F. A., Bryant, D. M., Wasik, B. H., and Ramey, C. T. (1997). Early intervention and mediating processes in cognitive performance of children of low-income African American families. *Child Development, 68*, 935–954.

Burchinal, M. R., Roberts, J. E., Riggins, R., Zeisel, S. A., Neebe, E., and Bryant, D. (2000). Relating quality of center-based child care to early cognitive and language development longitudinally. *Child Development, 71*, 339–357.

Bus, A. G., and van IJzendoorn, M. H. (1988). Mother-child interactions, attachment, and emergent literacy: A cross-sectional study. *Child Development, 59*, 1262–1272.

Caldera, Y. M., Huston, A. C., and O'Brien, M. (1989). Social interactions and play preferences of parents and toddlers with feminine, masculine, and neutral toys. *Child Development, 60*, 70–76.

Caldwell, B., and Bradley, R. (1978). *Home observation for measurement of the environment: Administration manual.* Little Rock, AR: University of Arkansas Press.

Case, R. (1992). *The mind's staircase: Exploring the conceptual underpinnings of children's thought and knowledge.* Hillsdale, NJ: Lawrence Erlbaum Associates.

Case, R. (1998). The development of conceptual structures. In W. Damon (Series Ed.) and D. Kuhn and R. S. Siegler (Eds.), *Handbook of child psychology: Vol. 2. Cognition, perception, and language* (5th ed., pp. 745–800). New York: Wiley.

Chen, Z., and Siegler, R. S. (2000). Across the great divide: Bridging the gap between understanding of toddlers' and older children's thinking. *Monographs of the Society for Research in Child Development, 65* (2, Serial No. 261).

Craig, G. J., and Kermis, M. D. (1995). *Children today.* Upper Saddle River, NJ: Prentice-Hall.

Cramer, P., and Steinwert, T. (1998). Thin is good, fat is bad: How early does it begin? *Journal of Applied Developmental Psychology, 19*, 429–451.

Crockenberg, S. C., and Litman, C. (1990). Autonomy as competence in 2-year-olds: Maternal correlates of child defiance, compliance, and self-assertion. *Developmental Psychology, 26*, 961–971.

Cross, T. G. (1978). Mothers' speech and its association with rate of language acquisition in young children. In N. Waterson and C. Snow (Eds.), *The development of communication* (pp. 199–216). London: Wiley.

Dehart, G., Sroufe, L. A., and Cooper, R. (2000). *Child development: Its nature and course* (4th ed.). New York: McGraw-Hill.

Deinstbier, R. A. (1984). The role of emotion in moral socialization. In C. Izard, J. Kagan, and R. B. Zajonc (Eds.), *Emotions, cognitions, and behaviors* (pp. 484–513). New York: Cambridge University Press.

Deloache, J. S., and Gottlieb, A. (Eds.). 2000. *A world of babies: Imagined childcare guides for seven societies.* New York: Cambridge University Press.

Donovan, W. L., Leavitt, L. A., and Walsh, R. O. (2000). Maternal illusory control predicts socialization strategies and toddler compliance. *Developmental Psychology, 36*, 402–411.

Dowdney, L., and Pickles, A. R. (1991). Expression of negative affect within disciplinary encounters: Is there dyadic reciprocity? *Developmental Psychology, 27*, 606–617.

Dubin, E. R., and Dubin, R. (1963). The authority inception period in socialization. *Child Development, 34*, 885–898.

Duckworth, E. (1972). The having of wonderful ideas. *Harvard Education Review, 42*, 217–231.

Dunham, P., and Dunham, F. (1992). Lexical development during middle infancy: A mutually driven infant–caregiver process. *Developmental Psychology, 28*, 414–420.

Edwards, C. P. (1986). *Promoting social and moral development in young children: Creative approaches for the classroom.* New York: Teachers College.

Edwards, C. P. (1989). The transition from infancy to early childhood: A difficult transition, and a difficult theory. In V. R. Bricker and G. H. Gossen (Eds.), *Ethnographic encounters in Southern Mesoamerica: Essays in honor of Evon Z. Vogt, Jr.* (pp. 167–175). Austin, TX: University of Texas Press.

Edwards, C. P. (1992). Cross-cultural perspectives on family-peer relations. In R. D. Parke and G. W. Ladd (Eds.), *Family-peer relationships: Modes of linkage* (pp. 285–316). Hillsdale, NJ: Lawrence Erlbaum Associates.

Edwards, C. P. (1993). Behavioral sex differences in children of diverse cultures: The case of nurturance to infants. In M. Pereira and L. Fairbanks (Eds.), *Juveniles—Comparative socioecology* (pp. 327–338). New York: Oxford University Press.

Edwards, C. P., Gandini, L., and Forman, G. (Eds.). (1998). *The hundred languages of children (2nd ed.): The Reggio Emilia approach, advanced reflections*. Stamford, CT: Ablex.

Edwards, C. P., Gandini, L., and Giovannini, D. (1993). The contrasting developmental timetables of parents and preschool teachers in two cultural communities. In S. Harkness and C. Super (Eds.), *Parental cultural belief systems* (pp. 270–288). New York: Guilford.

Edwards, C. P., Logue, M. E., Loehr, S., and Roth, S. (1986). The influence of model infant group care on parent/child interaction at home. *Early Childhood Research Quarterly, 1,* 317–332.

Edwards, C. P., Logue, M. E., Loehr, S., and Roth, S. (1987). The effects of day care participation on parent/infant interaction at home. *American Journal of Orthopsychiatry, 57,* 33–36.

Edwards, C. P., and Whiting, B. B. (1993). "Mother, older sibling, and me": The overlapping roles of caregivers and companions in the social world of two- to three-year-olds in Ngeca, Kenya. In K. MacDonald (Ed.), *Parent–child play: Descriptions and implications* (pp. 305–329). Albany, NY: State University of New York Press.

Eisenberg, A., Murkoff, H. E., and Hathaway, S. E. (1994). *What to expect, the toddler years*. New York: Workman.

Eley, T. C., Bishop, D. V. M., Dale, P. S., Oliver, B., Petrill, S. A., Price, T. S., Purcell, S., Saudino, K. J., Simonoff, E., Stevenson, J., and Plomin, R. (1999). Genetic and environmental origins of verbal and performance components of cognitive delay in 2-year-olds. *Developmental Psychology, 35,* 1122–1131.

Emde, R. N., Biringen, Z., Clyman, R. B., and Oppenheim, D. (1991). The moral self of infancy: Affective core and procedural knowledge. *Developmental Review, 11,* 251–270.

Emde, R. N., and Robinson, J. L. (2000). Guiding principles for a theory of early intervention: A developmental-psychoanalytic perspective. In S. J. Meisels, and J. P. Shonkoff (Eds.), *Handbook of early childhood intervention* (pp. 160–178). New York: Cambridge University Press.

Erikson, E. (1950). *Childhood and society*. New York: Norton.

Etaugh, C., Grinnell, K., and Etaugh, A. (1989). Development of gender labeling: Effect of age of pictured children. *Sex Roles, 21,* 769–773.

Fagot, B. I. (1985). Beyond the reinforcement principle: Another step toward understanding sex role development. *Developmental Psychology, 21,* 1097–1104.

Fagot, B. I. (1995). Psychosocial and cognitive determinants of early gender-role behavior. *Annual Review of Sex Research, 6,* 1–31.

Fagot, B. I., Hagan, R., Leinbach, M. D., and Kronsberg, S. (1985). Differential reactions to assertive and communicative acts of toddler boys and girls. *Child Development, 56,* 1499–1505.

Farver, J. M. (1993). Cultural differences in scaffolding pretend play: A comparison of American and Mexican mother–child and sibling–child pairs. In K. MacDonald (Ed.), *Parent–child play: Descriptions and implications* (pp. 349–366). Albany, NY: State University of New York Press.

Feinman, S. (1982). Social referencing in infancy. *Merrill-Palmer Quarterly, 28,* 445–470.

Feldman, R. S. (2001). *Child development* (2nd ed.). Upper Saddle River, NJ: Prentice-Hall.

Fischer, K. W. (1980). A theory of cognitive development: The control and construction of hierarchies of skills. *Psychological Review, 87,* 477–531.

Fischer, K. W., and Bidell, T. R. (1998). Dynamic development of psychological structures in action. In W. Damon (Series Ed.) and R. M. Lerner (Ed.), *Handbook of child psychology: Vol. 1. Theoretical models of human development* (5th ed., pp. 467–562). New York: Wiley.

Fischer, K. W., Hand, H. H., Watson, M. W., Van Parys, M. M., and Tucker, J. L. (1984). Putting the child into socialization. In L. Katz (Ed.), *Current topics in early childhood education* (Vol. 5, pp. 27–72). Norwood, NJ: Ablex.

Fisher, J. J. (Ed.). (1988). *Johnson and Johnson: From baby to toddler, the essential month by month guide to your child's first two years*. New York: Berkeley.

Flavell, J. H. (1994). Cognitive development: Past, present, and future. In R. D. Parke, P. A. Ornstein, J. J. Rieser, and C. Zahn-Waxler (Eds.), *A century of developmental psychology* (pp. 569–588). Washington, DC: American Psychological Association.

Fogel, A. (1984). *Infancy: Infant, family, and society*. St. Paul, MN: West Publishing.

Fogel, A. (1993). *Developing through relationships*. Chicago: University of Chicago Press.

Fowler, W. (1962). Cognitive learning in infancy and early childhood. *Psychological Bulletin, 59,* 116–152.

Fowler, W. (Ed.). (1986). *Early experience and the development of competence*. San Francisco: Jossey-Bass.

Fraiberg, S. H. (1959). *The magic years: Understanding and handling the problems of early childhood*. New York: Scribner's.

Freud, S. (1920). *A general introduction to psychoanalysis* (J. Riviere, Trans.). New York: Washington Square.

Freud, S. (1949). *An outline of psycho-analysis* (J. Strachey, Trans.). New York: Norton.

Freud, S. (1953). *Three essays on the theory of sexuality*. In J. Strachey (Ed. and Trans.), *The standard edition of the complete psychological works of Sigmund Freud* (Vol. 7, pp. 125–230). London: Hogarth. (Original work published 1901–1905).

Gandini, L., and Edwards, C. P. (2001). *Bambini: The Italian approach to infant–toddler care*. New York: Teachers College Press.

Gardner, H. (1978). *Developmental psychology*. Boston: Little, Brown.

Gesell, A. (1940). *The first five years of life: A guide to the study of the preschool child*. New York: Harper and Brothers.

Gewirtz, J. L. (Ed.). (1972). *Attachment and dependency*. Washington, DC: Winston.

Goldsmith, H. H., and Campos, J. J. (1986). Fundamental issues in the study of early temperament: The Denver Twin Temperament Study. In M. E. Lamb, A. L. Brown, and B. Rogoff (Eds.), *Advances in developmental psychology* (Vol. 4, pp. 231–283). Hillsdale, NJ: Lawrence Erlbaum Associates.

Greenfield, P. M., Brazelton, T. B., and Childs, C. P. (1989). From birth to maturity in Zinacantan: Ontogenesis in cultural context. In V. R. Bricker and G. H. Gossen (Eds.), *Ethnographic encounters in Southern Mesoamerica: Essays in honor of Evon Z. Vogt, Jr.* (pp. 177–216). Austin, TX: University of Texas Press.

Greenfield, P. M., and Suzuki, L. K. (1998). Culture and human development: Implications for parenting, education, pediatrics, and mental health. In W. Damon (Series Ed.) and I. E. Sigel and K. A. Renninger (Eds.), *Handbook of child psychology: Vol. 4. Child psychology in practice* (5th ed., pp. 1059–1112). New York: Wiley.

Greenspan, S., and Greenspan, N. T. (1985). *First feelings*. New York: Viking.

Haith, M. M., and Benson, J. B. (1998). Infant cognition. In W. Damon (Series Ed.) and D. Kuhn and R. S. Siegler (Eds.), *Handbook of child psychology: Vol. 2. Cognition, perception, and language* (5th ed., pp. 199–254). New York: Wiley.

Harkness, S., and Super, C. M. (1983). The cultural construction of child development: A framework for the socialization of affect. *Ethos, 11*, 221–231.

Harkness, S., and Super, C. M. (Eds.). (1993). *Parental cultural belief systems*. New York: Guilford.

Hildebrand, V. (1997). *Introduction to early childhood education* (6th ed.). Upper Saddle River, NJ: Prentice-Hall.

Hubley, P., and Trevarthen, C. (1979). Sharing a task in infancy. In I. E. Užgiris (Ed.), *Social interaction and communication during infancy* (pp. 57–80). San Francisco: Jossey-Bass.

Hunt, J. M. (1961). *Intelligence and experience*. New York: Ronald.

Huttenlocher, J., Haight, W., Bryk, A., Seltzer, M., and Lyons, T. (1991). Early vocabulary growth: Relation to language input and gender. *Developmental Psychology, 27*, 236–248.

Kagan, J. (1971). *Change and continuity in infancy*. New York: Wiley.

Kagan, J. (1981). *The second year: The emergence of self-awareness*. Cambridge, MA: Harvard University Press.

Kaler, S. R., and Kopp, C. (1990). Compliance and comprehension in very young toddlers. *Child Development, 61*, 1997–2003.

Kaye, K. (1982). *The mental and social life of babies*. Chicago: University of Chicago Press.

Kitayama, S., and Markus, H. R. (1994). *Emotion and culture: Empirical studies of mutual influence*. Washington DC: American Psychological Association.

Kochanska, G. (1991). Socialization and temperament in the development of guilt and conscience. *Child Development, 62*, 250–263.

Kochanska, G. (1993). Toward a synthesis of parental socialization and child temperament in early development of conscience. *Child Development, 64*, 325–347.

Kochanska, G., Murray, K., and Coy, K. C. (1997). Inhibitory control as a contributor to conscience in childhood: From toddler to early school age. *Child Development, 68*, 263–277.

Kohlberg, L. (1966). A cognitive-developmental analysis of children's sex-role concepts and attitudes. In E. E. Maccoby (Ed.), *The development of sex differences* (pp. 82–173). Stanford, CA: Stanford University Press.

Kohlberg, L. (1969). Stage and sequence: The cognitive developmental approach to socialization. In D. A. Goslin (Ed.), *Handbook of socialization theory and research* (pp. 347–480). Chicago: Rand McNally.

Kopp, C. B. (1982). The antecedents of self-regulation: A developmental perspective. *Developmental Psychology, 18*, 199–214.

Kopp, C. B. (1992). Emotional distress and control in young children. In N. Eisenberg and R. A. Fabes (Eds.), *Emotion and its regulation in early development* (pp. 41–56). San Francisco: Jossey-Bass.

Kuczynski, L., and Kochanska, G. (1990). Development of children's noncompliance strategies from toddlerhood to age 5. *Developmental Psychology, 26*, 398–408.

Kuczynski, L., Kochanska, G., Radke-Yarrow, M., and Girnius-Brown, O. (1987). A developmental interpretation of young children's noncompliance. *Developmental Psychology, 23*, 799–806.

Kuczynski, L., Zahn-Waxler, C., and Radke-Yarrow, M. (1987). Development and content of imitation in the second and third years of life: A socialization perspective. *Developmental Psychology, 23*, 276–282.

Ladd, G. W., Profilet, S. M., and Hart, C. H. (1992). Parents' management of children's peer relations. In R. D. Parke and G. W. Ladd (Eds.), *Family–peer relationships: Modes of linkage* (pp. 215–281). Hillsdale, NJ: Lawrence Erlbaum Associates.

Leach, P. (1997). *Your baby and child: From birth to age five*. New York: Knopf.

Lemery, K. S., Goldsmith, H. H., Klinnert, M. D., and Mrazek, D. A. (1999). Developmental models of infant and childhood temperament. *Developmental Psychology, 35*, 189–204.

Lewis, M., and Brooks-Gunn, J. (1979). *Social cognition and the acquisition of self*. New York: Plenum.

Lewis, M., Sullivan, M., Stranger, C., and Weiss, M. (1989). Self-development and self-conscious emotions. *Child Development*, *60*, 146–156.

Lickona, T. (1994). *Raising good children*. New York: Bantam.

Lytton, H. (1979). Disciplinary encounters between young boys and their mothers: Is there a contingency system? *Developmental Psychology*, *15*, 256–268.

Maccoby, E. E. (1988). Gender as a social category. *Developmental Psychology*, *24*, 755–765.

Maccoby, E. E. (1992). The role of parents in the socialization of children: An historical overview. *Developmental Psychology*, *28*, 1006–1017.

Maccoby, E. E. (1999). *The two sexes: Growing up apart, coming together*. Cambridge, MA: Harvard University Press.

Maccoby, E. E., and Martin, J. A. (1983). Socialization in the context of the family: Parent-child interaction. In P. H. Mussen (Series Ed.) and E. M. Hetherington (Ed.), *Handbook of child psychology: Vol. 4. Socialization, personality, and social development* (4th ed., pp. 1–101). New York: Wiley.

Mahler, M., Pine, F., and Bergman, A. (1975). *The psychological birth of the human infant*. New York: Basic Books.

Main, M., and George, C. (1985). Responses of abused and disadvantaged toddlers to distress in agemates: A study in the day care setting. *Developmental Psychology*, *21*, 407–412.

Martin, C. A. (1993). New directions for investigating children's gender knowledge. *Developmental Review*, *13*, 184–204.

McCall, R. B. (1981). Nature–nurture and two realms of development: A proposed integration with respect to mental development. *Child Development*, *52*, 1–12.

Morrison, G. S. (1998). *Early childhood education today* (7th ed.). Upper Saddle River, NJ: Merrill.

Morrongiello, B. A., and Dawber, T. (1998). Toddlers' and mothers' behaviors in an injury-risk situation: Implications for sex differences in childhood injuries. *Journal of Applied Developmental Psychology*, *19*, 625–639.

Mueller, E. C., and Cohen, D. (1986). Peer therapies and the little latency: A clinical perspective. In E. C. Mueller and C. R. Cooper (Eds.), *Process and outcome in peer relations* (pp. 161–183). New York: Academic.

Newcombe, N. (1996). *Child development: Change over time* (8th ed.). Needham Heights, MA: Allyn and Bacon.

Ochs, E., and Schieffelin, B. B. (1984). Language acquisition and socialization. In R. A. Shweder and R. A. LeVine (Eds.), *Culture theory: Essays on mind, self, and emotion* (pp. 276–320). New York: Cambridge University Press.

Papalia, D. E., Olds, S. W., and Feldman, R. (1999). *A child's world* (8th ed.). New York: McGraw-Hill.

Parke, R. D., Cassidy, J., Burks, V. M., Carson, J. L., and Boyum, L. (1992). Familial contributions to peer competence among young children: The role of interactive and affective processes. In R. D. Parke and G. W. Ladd (Eds.), *Family–peer relationships: Modes of linkage* (pp. 107–134). Hillsdale, NJ: Lawrence Erlbaum Associates.

Parpal, M., and Maccoby, E. E. (1985). Maternal responsiveness and subsequent child compliance. *Child Development*, *56*, 1326–1334.

Patterson, G. R. (1982). *Coercive family process*. Eugene, OR: Castalia.

Piaget, J. (1952). *The origins of intelligence in children*. New York: International Universities Press.

Pipp-Siegel, S., and Foltz, C. (1997). Toddlers' acquisition of self/other knowledge: Ecological and interpersonal aspects of self and other. *Child Development*, *68*, 69–79.

Povinelli, D. J., Landau, K. R., Periloux, H. K. (1996). Self-recognition in young children using delayed versus live feedback: Evidence of a developmental asynchrony. *Child Development*, *67*, 1540–1554.

Povinelli, D. J., and Simon, B. B. (1998). Young children's understanding of briefly versus extremely delayed images of the self: Emergence of the autobiographical stance. *Developmental Psychology*, *34*, 188–194.

Power, T. G., and Chapieski, M. L. (1986). Childrearing and impulse control in toddlers: A naturalistic investigation. *Developmental Psychology*, *22*, 271–275.

Ramey, C. T., and Ramey, S. L. (1999). *Right from birth: Building your child's foundation for life birth to 18 months*. New York: Goddard.

Reingold, H. (1982). Little children's participation in the work of adults: A nascent prosocial behavior. *Child Development*, *53*, 114–125.

Reingold, H., Cook, K., and Kolowitz, V. (1987). Commands activate the behavior and pleasure of 2-year-old children. *Developmental Psychology*, *23*, 146–151.

Rice, M. L. (1989). Children's language acquisition. *American Psychologist*, *44*, 149–156.

Ritchie, K. L. (1999). Maternal behaviors and cognitions during discipline episodes: A comparison of power bouts and single acts of noncompliance. *Developmental Psychology*, *35*, 580–589.

Rogoff, B. (1998). Cognition as a collaborative process. In W. Damon (Series Ed.) and D. Kuhn and R. S. Siegler (Eds.), *Handbook of child psychology: Vol. 2. Cognition, perception, and language* (5th ed., pp. 679–744). New York: Wiley.

Rogoff, B., Mistry, J., Gönçu, A., and Mosier, C. (1991). Cultural variation in the role relations of toddlers and their families. In M. H. Bornstein (Ed.), *Cultural approaches to parenting* (pp. 173–183). Hillsdale, NJ: Lawrence Erlbaum Associates.

Rogoff, B., Mistry, J., Gönçu, A., and Mosier, C. (1993). Guided participation in cultural activity by toddlers and caregivers. *Monographs of the Society for Research in Child Development*, *58* (8, Serial No. 236).

Sander, L. W. (1962). Issues in early mother–child interaction. *Journal of the American Academy of Child Psychiatry*, *1*, 141–166.

Santrock, J. W. (2000). *Children* (6th ed.). New York: McGraw-Hill.

Schickedanz, J. A., Schickedanz, D. I., Forsyth, P. D., and Forsyth, G. A. (2001). *Understanding children and adolescents* (4th ed.). Needham Heights, MA: Allyn and Bacon.

Schieffelin, B. B., and Ochs, E. (1986). *Language socialization across cultures.* Cambridge, England: Cambridge University Press.

Schneider-Rosen, K., and Wenz-Gross, M. (1990). Patterns of compliance from eighteen to thirty months of age. *Child Development, 61,* 104–112.

Sears, W., and Sears, M. (1993). *The baby book: Everything you need to know about your baby from birth to age two.* Boston, MA: Little, Brown.

Seefeldt, C., and Barbour, N. (1998). *Early childhood education: An introduction* (4th ed.). Upper Saddle River, NJ: Merrill.

Sigel, I. E. (1986). Early social experience and the development of representational competence. In W. Fowler (Ed.), *Early experience and the development of competence* (pp. 49–65). San Francisco: Jossey-Bass.

Sigman, M., Neumann, C., Carter, E., Cattle, D. J., D'Souza, S. D., and Bwibo, N. (1988). Home interactions and the development of Embu toddlers in Kenya. *Child Development, 59,* 1251–1261.

Slade, A. (1987). A longitudinal study of maternal involvement and symbolic play during the toddler period. *Child Development, 58,* 367–375.

Smolak, L., and Weinraub, M. (1983). Maternal speech: Strategy or response? *Journal of Child Language, 10,* 369–380.

Spitz, R. (1957). *No and yes: On the genesis of human communication.* New York: International Universities Press.

Spitz, R. (1965). *The first year of life.* New York: International Universities Press.

Sroufe, L. A. (1979). Socioemotional development. In J. Osofsky (Ed.), *Handbook of infant development* (pp. 462–516). New York: Wiley.

Stipek, D., Recchia, S., and McClintic, S. (1992). Self-evaluation in young children. *Monographs of the Society for Research in Child Development, 57* (1, Serial No. 226).

Stone, L. J., and Church, J. (1973). *Childhood and adolescence: A psychology of the growing person* (3rd ed.). New York: Random House.

Super, C. M., and Harkness, S. (1986). The developmental niche: A conceptualization at the interface of child and culture. *International Journal of Behavioral Development, 9,* 545–569.

Thelen, E., and Fogel, A. (1989). Toward an action-based theory of infant development. In J. Lockman and N. Hazen (Eds.), *Action in social context: Perspectives on early development* (pp. 23–64). New York: Plenum.

Thelen, E., and Smith, L.B. (1998). Dynamic systems theories. In W. Damon (Series Ed.) and R. M. Lerner (Eds.), *Handbook of child psychology: Vol. 1. Theoretical models of human development* (5th ed., pp. 563–634). New York: Wiley.

Valdez-Menchaca, M. C., and Whitehurst, G. J. (1988). The effects of incidental teaching on vocabulary acquisition by young children. *Child Development, 59,* 1451–1459.

Vygotsky, L. S. (1962). *Thought and language.* Cambridge, MA: MIT Press.

Vygotsky, L. S. (1978). *Mind in society: The development of higher psychological processes.* Cambridge, MA: Harvard University Press.

Wachs, T. D. (1982). Early experience and early cognitive development: The search for specificity. In I. U. Užgiris and J. Hunt (Eds.), *Research with scales of psychological development in infancy.* Champaign, IL: University of Illinois Press.

Wachs, T. D., and Gruen, G. E. (1982). *Early experience and human development.* New York: Plenum.

Weinraub, M., Clemens, L. P., Sockloff, A., Ethridge, T., Gracely, E., and Myers, B. (1984). The development of sex role stereotypes in the third year: Relationships to gender labeling, gender identity, sex-typed toy preference, and family characteristics. *Child Development, 55,* 1493–1503.

Weisner, T. (1989a). Cultural and universal aspects of social support for children: Evidence from the Abaluyia of Kenya. In D. Belle (Ed.), *Children's social networks and social supports* (pp. 70–90). New York: Wiley.

Weisner, T. (1989b). Comparing sibling relationships across cultures. In P. G. Zukow (Ed.), *Sibling interaction across cultures* (pp. 11–22). New York: Springer-Verlag.

Weisner, T. (1993). Overview: Sibling similarity and difference in different cultures. In C. W. Nuckolls (Ed.), *Siblings in South Asia* (pp. 1–18). New York: Guilford.

Weitzman, N., Birns, B., and Friend, R. (1985). Traditional and nontraditional mothers' communication with their daughters and sons. *Child Development, 56,* 894–898.

Wenar, C. (1982). On negativism. *Human Development, 25,* 1–23.

Westerman, M. A. (1990). Coordination of maternal directives with preschoolers' behavior in compliance-problem and healthy dyads. *Developmental Psychology, 26,* 621–630.

Whiting, B. B. (1980). Culture and social behavior: A model for the development of social behavior. *Ethos, 8,* 95–116.

Whiting, B. B. (1983). The genesis of prosocial behavior. In D. L. Bridgeman (Ed.), *The nature of prosocial development: Interdisciplinary theories and strategies* (pp. 221–242). New York: Academic.

Whiting, B. B., and Edwards, C. P. (1988). *Children of different worlds: The formation of social behavior.* Cambridge, MA: Harvard University.

Wood, D., Bruner, J., and Ross, G. (1976). The role of tutoring in problem-solving. *Journal of Child Psychology and Psychiatry*, *17*, 89–100.

Yarrow, L. J., Rubenstein, J. L., and Pedersen, F. A. (1975). *Infant and environment: Early cognitive and motivational development*. Washington, DC: Hemisphere.

Zahn-Waxler, C., Radke-Yarrow, M., and King, R. A. (1979). Child-rearing and children's prosocial initiations toward victims in distress. *Child Development*, *50*, 319–330.

Zahn-Waxler, C., Radke-Yarrow, M., Wagner, E., and Chapman, M. (1992). Development of concern for others. *Developmental Psychology*, *28*, 126–136.

# 3

# Parenting During Middle Childhood

W. Andrew Collins
Stephanie D. Madsen
Amy Susman-Stillman
*University of Minnesota*

## INTRODUCTION

Parents of children between the ages of 5 and 12 years—the period commonly referred to as middle childhood—face challenges arising from both maturational changes in children and from socially imposed constraints, opportunities, and demands impinging on them. Children in diverse societies enter a wider social world at approximately the age of 5 years and begin to determine their own experiences, including their contacts with particular others, to a greater degree than previously. Between the age of 5 years and adolescence, transitions occur in physical maturity, cognitive abilities and learning, the diversity and impact of relationships with others, and exposure to new settings, opportunities, and demands. These changes inevitably alter the amount, kind, content, and significance of interactions between parents and children. In this chapter we address the impact of the distinctive challenges and achievements of middle childhood on parent–child relationships and on the processes of socialization within families.

The chapter includes five main sections. The first section provides a brief overview of historical considerations in the study of parenting of 5- to 12-year-old children. The second section outlines key normative changes in children that affect parenting during middle childhood. The third section reviews changes in parent–child relationships in which parenting issues are embedded. The fourth section distills findings from research on the issues of parenting and of parent–child relationships that are especially linked to the distinctive changes of the period. These include adapting processes of control, fostering self-management and responsibility, facilitating positive relationships outside the family, and maintaining contacts with schools and other out-of-home settings. The concluding section underscores the key themes from research and notes persistent questions about the distinctiveness of parenting during middle childhood.

## HISTORICAL CONSIDERATIONS IN MIDDLE CHILDHOOD PARENTING

In diverse cultures, early–middle childhood historically has marked a major shift in children's relationships with adults. The age of 6 or 7 years was the time at which children were absorbed into the world of adults, helping to shoulder family responsibilities and working alongside their elders. Well into the 18th century in Western nations, many children left home by the age of 6 or 7 years to work as servants in other households (Aries, 1962). If children remained at home, their parents became more like supervisors or overseers. The assumption that children were capable of tasks now largely reserved for adults was consistent with a general attitude toward forcing infants and young children toward behavioral rectitude and submissiveness to authority (see French, in Vol. 2 of this *Handbook*).

Only in recent times have changing concepts of the family and the advent of formal schooling removed children of this age from wide participation in adult society. In industrialized nations today, the ages of 5 to 12 years have continued to be set apart from younger ages because they correspond to the beginning of compulsory schooling. Schooling provides a distinctive social definition of children and social structures that constrain and channel development during this period. This secular change has meant that, rather than taking on adult responsibilities, as was the case in earlier periods, children in middle childhood are primarily concerned with preparation for eventual responsibility. Children's preparation for adulthood is conducted not only by parents, but also by institutions and persons outside of the family. Thus the central contemporary issue of parenting during middle childhood is how parents most effectively adjust their interactions, cognitions, and affectional behavior to the changing characteristics of children in order to maintain appropriate influence and guidance during age-graded transitions toward greater autonomy (Maccoby, 1992). The next section outlines these changes and some implications for parent–child relationships.

## NORMATIVE CHANGES IN CHILDREN DURING MIDDLE CHILDHOOD

To most parents in industrialized societies, middle childhood is less distinctive as a period of development than infancy, toddlerhood, or adolescence. The ages of 5 to 12 years nevertheless universally are set apart by major transition points in human development (Rogoff, Pirrotta, Fox, and White, 1975). In this section we briefly review changes in children that set the stage for transitions in parenting during middle childhood. These changes include cognitive competence and the growth of knowledge, transitions in social contexts and relationships, increased vulnerability to stress, altered functions of the self, and self-regulation and social responsibility.

### Cognitive Competence and the Growth of Knowledge

Cognitive changes greatly expand children's capacities for solving problems and gaining necessary information to become increasingly competent and resourceful. For parents, changes in children's cognitive competence necessitate alterations ranging from the content of conversations, strategies for control and influence over children's behavior, and expectations regarding competence and self-regulation.

Three characteristic changes of middle childhood are noteworthy. One is a growing ability to reason in terms of abstract representations of objects and events. For children younger than 5 to 7 years old, cognition characteristically involves limitations on the number of objects that can be thought about at one time, and systematic or abstract reasoning is relatively rare (Edwards and Liu, in Vol. 1 of this *Handbook*). Between the ages of 5 and 9 years, most children gain capacities that enable them to reason effectively about increasingly complex problems and circumstances; and by 10 to 12 years of age, children begin to show increased abilities for generalizing across concrete instances and for systematic problem solving and reasoning. Second, children begin to organize tasks more maturely and independently than in early childhood. This more planful behavior entails adopting goals for activities, subordinating knowledge and actions in the service of a superordinate plan, and monitoring one's own activities and mental processes. Third, increases occur in both the opportunity and the capacity for acquiring information and for using new knowledge in reasoning, thinking, problem solving, and action. Compared with younger children, 5- to 12-year-old children thus can solve more difficult, abstract intellectual problems in school and can master increased, more complex responsibilities at home and in other common settings (Case, 1998; DeLoache, Miller, and Pierroutsakos, 1998; Fischer and Bullock, 1984).

These cognitive expansions are accompanied by increased challenges to integrate knowledge and abilities for understanding self and others, relationships, communities, and societies. Children in middle childhood contrast sharply with younger children in their abilities for greater social under-standing. Compared with younger children, 6- to 12-year-old children evaluate others with greater accuracy and more often view classmates as teachers and other children do (Malloy, Sugarman, Montvilo, and Ben-Zeev, 1995; Malloy, Yarlas, Montvilo, and Sugarman, 1996). Children in middle childhood also increasingly distinguish among psychological traits (e.g., shy–outgoing, nice–mean, active–inactive) (Heyman and Gelman, 2000). In interactions with others, 5- to-12-year-old chil-dren, relatively more than younger children, adopt the perspectives of others, which helps them to infer possible reasons for others' behaviors (Crick and Dodge, 1994; Dunn and Slomkowski, 1992). These growing social cognitive skills underlie the further growth of social competence during middle childhood, including skills for describing and explaining conditions and events (e.g., Whitehurst and Sonnenschein, 1981), for deceiving others and for detecting their deceptions (e.g., DePaulo, Jordan, Irvine, and Laser, 1982; Watson and Valtin, 1997), and for predicting the behavior of other children (e.g., Droege and Stipek, 1993; Heyman and Dweck, 1998). Whereas preschool children are "ruthless stereotypers" (E. Maccoby, personal communication, October 12, 1996), children in middle child-hood increasingly recognize similarities as well as differences in female and male gender roles (Serbin, Powlishta, and Gulko, 1993; Welch-Ross and Schmidt, 1996). Concepts of parent–child relationships move toward the idea that parents and children mutually have responsibilities to each other, rather than focus on parents as those who satisfy children's needs (Selman, 1980).

Children in middle childhood, in addition to growth in interpersonal understanding, increasingly understand many broader conditions of life. Compared with younger children, 5- to 12-year-old children generally grasp basic notions related to fundamental life experiences such as conception, illness, and death (Bibace and Walsh, 1981; Lazar and Torney-Purta, 1991), although many of their beliefs about human biology remain inaccurate and simplistic (Morris, Taplin, and Gelman, 2000). At the group and the societal levels, 5- to 12-year-old children generally manifest a strong sense of fairness, both in the distribution of resources and in equal treatment under the law (Helwig, 1998; McGillicuddy-De Lisi, Watkins, and Vinchur, 1994). Moreover, they increasingly believe in the right of children of their age to some degree of self-determination and self-expression (Helwig, 1997; Ruck, Abramovitch, and Keating, 1998).

For parents generally, the characteristic reasoning patterns of 5- to 12-year-old children necessitate more elaborate and compelling explanations and justifications in order to have the same degree of impact that, in earlier years, parents could achieve by distracting or admonishing a child.

The experiences of adoptive parents of 5- to 12-year-old children illustrate some of the challenges stemming from cognitive changes. Preschool children can and often do label themselves as adopted, but greater cognitive capacities in middle childhood make it possible to form a more complex understanding of what adoption means. For example, only after the age of 6 years do children typically identify adoption and birth as alternative paths to parenthood (Brodzinsky, Smith, and Brodzinsky, 1998). Later, children recognize that their adoptive parents' joy in having them as children necessarily involves the loss of parenting rights for their birth parents, which sometimes precipitates a sense of loss for their biological family. Children in middle- to late-middle childhood (ages 8 to 12.5 years) question their parents about a significantly greater number of adoption-related issues than younger children do (Wrobel, Kohler, Grotevant, and McRoy, 1998), and parents face pressing decisions about how to address the child's curiosity while preserving a positive view of the child's adoptive status and heritage (Brodzinsky and Pinderhughes, in Vol. 1 of this *Handbook*). Thus cognitive change underlies distinctive patterns of behavior and responsiveness during middle childhood and, consequently, alters the demands on parents.

## Social Contexts and Relationships

Parents of 5- to 12-year-old children also encounter additional burdens and responsibilities because social *networks* expand significantly during middle childhood. Whereas most of children's exchanges with others during infancy and early childhood occur in their families, 5- to 12-year-old children spend less time in the company of adults and family members, relative to peers and other adults outside of the family. The shifts are most pronounced between the ages of 5 and 9 years. Not until early adolescence, however, do contacts with peers, rather than those with adults, dominate social networks (Feiring and Lewis, 1991a, 1991b; Steinberg and Silk, in Vol. 1 of this *Handbook*).

Middle childhood experiences exert considerable pressure to create and maintain connections with peers (Hartup, 1996; Ladd and Pettit, in Vol. 5 of this *Handbook*). Entering school especially increases the number and kinds of developmental tasks and influences that children encounter. For parents, these experiences outside the family often necessitate their monitoring children's activities and choices of companions at a distance and create new challenges in fostering positive behavior and development (also see Crouter and Head, in Vol. 3 of this *Handbook*).

The need for *social support* from a variety of others, moreover, is more apparent in middle childhood than in earlier years. Contrary to stereotypes, perceptions of parents as sources of both emotional support and instrumental help typically remain stable across age groups during middle childhood (Hunter and Youniss, 1982). Children from 5 to 12 years old, however, recognize that others, some of them outside the family, serve significant social needs in their lives (Bryant, 1985; Furman and Buhrmester, 1992; Reid, Landesman, Treder, and Jaccard, 1989; Zarbatany, Hartmann, and Rankin, 1990).

To maintain these extended networks, children must learn to cooperate on more complex tasks and to work without extensive oversight by adults (Ladd and Pettit, in Vol. 5 of this *Handbook*). By the ages 10 to 12 years, children become notably more skilled in using goal-directed planful strategies to initiate, maintain, and cooperate within peer relationships. One implication of these skills is greater ability to manage conflicts with peers (Parker and Gottman, 1989; Selman and Schultz, 1989). Consequently, parents may spend less time in direct management of peer relations. Children who do not gain these skills are at a disadvantage for optimal social development and at risk for a variety of later problems (Parker and Asher, 1987).

Peer relationships play a role that is increasingly complementary to that of parents during middle childhood (Hartup, 1996). Over the years from age 5 to age 12, children increasingly view their peers as important sources of intimacy, as well as companionship. Although parents and peers influence children toward similar values and behaviors in most cases, peers also often provide experience and expectations in areas in which families typically have limited impact, especially in areas based on an understanding of give-and-take with others of equal power and status (e.g., collaborative tasks). For the most part, however, parental and peer influences are reciprocal: Families provide children with basic skills for smooth, successful peer relationships; and children often "import" knowledge, expectations, and behavioral tactics from their interactions with peers that stimulate parents' adjustments to their children's maturing abilities (Collins, 1995; Youniss, 1980; also see Ladd and Pettit, in Vol. 5 of this *Handbook*).

Parents' roles increasingly involve facilitating children's lives at school. Classrooms, playgrounds, and school buses provide ready access to peers and also opportunities for more diverse contacts than many children would otherwise encounter (Hartup, 1996). Varying settings between elementary and middle schools, however, may complicate children's efforts to form and maintain stable relationships with peers (Eccles, Lord, and Buchanan, 1996; Epstein, 1989). The social field for children initially is the classroom, and most interactions are with only one teacher and the same group of students throughout the day, whereas in the later grades the entire school is the social field, with multiple teachers, classrooms, and common spaces (Minuchin and Shapiro, 1983). For parents, monitoring of school experiences may entail more effort as the number of teachers and settings increases (see Crouter and Head, in Vol. 3 of this *Handbook*). Additionally, many parents must arrange for and interact with out-of-home childcare personnel and with adults who provide instruction and supervision in out-of-school learning and recreational settings (Dryfoos, 1999; Honig, in Vol. 5 of this *Handbook*; Vandell and Shumow, 1999). Clearly the transitions of middle childhood generate new tasks for parents as well as developmental challenges for children.

## Risks and Coping

The problems of parenting during middle childhood are exacerbated by an increase in risks and stressors for children, relative to early childhood. Although children between the ages of 5 and 12 years are generally the healthiest segment of the population in industrialized countries (Shonkoff, 1984), for many the physical transitions of middle childhood and the secular trend toward earlier puberty hasten exposure to some of the health risks of adulthood. Accidents, the major cause of death during childhood, increase between the ages of 5 and 12 years. During the past two decades, tobacco, alcohol, and other drug use have become more common for children in the middle childhood age group; moreover, middle childhood experiences increase the risk of beginning to use alcohol and tobacco by middle adolescence (Dishion, Capaldi, and Yoerger, 1999; Shonkoff, 1984).

*Neighborhoods.*    The broadening of opportunities for children to interact in environments outside the home frequently also broadens potential sources of risk. Children's perceptions of the neighborhood are linked to their socioemotional adjustment. Reported feelings of loneliness vary with children's perceptions of their neighborhood as problematic or child friendly and by the degree of perceived support from neighbors. Negative neighborhood characteristics are linked to poorer socioemotional functioning (Chase-Lansdale, Gordon, Brooks-Gunn, and Klebanov, 1997). Inner-city 9- to 12-year-old children who rated their neighborhoods high on economic disadvantage and personal exposure to stressful life events and low on personal support tend to be more involved in antisocial behavior and drug use (Dubow, Edwards, and Ippolito, 1997).

The impact of neighborhood characteristics on middle childhood development is often difficult to pin down, perhaps because familial influences are consistent and more direct sources of influence that frequently either extend or actively counteract neighborhood influences (Chase-Lansdale et al., 1997; Chase-Lansdale and Gordon, 1996; Dubow et al., 1997; Duncan, Brooks-Gunn, and Klebanov, 1994). For example, parents with negative perceptions of their neighborhoods supervise children more closely (Dubow et al., 1997). On the other hand, neighborhood characteristics can exacerbate familial difficulties. Low-income African American children living in a single-parent family show especially high levels of aggression if they also live in a financially disadvantaged neighborhood, whereas children from similar economic and family conditions in a middle-income neighborhood are no more aggressive than other children (Kupersmidt, Griesler, DeRosier, Patterson, and Davis, 1995). Middle-income neighborhoods do not unequivocally serve as a protective factor or potentiator of developmental opportunities, however; the particular opportunities and limitations impinging on children are more important than economic advantage per se.

*Exposure to violence.*    The broader environments of middle childhood carry, for many children, increased risk of exposure to violence (Finkelhor and Dziuba-Leatherman, 1994; Lorion and Saltzman, 1993; Osofsky, Wewers, Hann, and Fick, 1993; Richters and Martinez, 1993). Studies show the risk of exposure to violence to be as great for 5- to 8-year-old children as for 10- to 12-year-old children. The ready availability of weapons to individuals of all ages increases the likelihood of being a victim or a perpetrator of violence during the middle childhood years. Although the impact of violence surely concerns parents, even parents in high-risk neighborhoods seriously underestimate the extent to which their children report exposure to violence (Hill and Jones, 1997).

Experiencing violence, as a victim or a witness, influences children's sense of security and hope in the world (Lewis and Osofsky, 1997). Ethnographic research with African American children in an urban school revealed that children persistently discuss daily violent events in their community, and their discussions reflect the insidious presence of these experiences in the children's minds (Towns, 1996). Children's perceptions of violence in their communities are correlated positively with their reports of fearfulness, distress, and depression at home and at school (Bell and Jenkins, 1993; Hill, Levermore, Twaite, and Jones, 1996; Martinez and Richters, 1993; Osofsky et al., 1993). Exposure to violence and victimization at home are associated with a variety of emotional and behavior problems and diminished school performance (Emery, 1989).

Parents may play a role by monitoring the degree of risk associated with extrafamilial settings and by imposing appropriate safety measures, including training children to respond to high-risk situations. Furthermore, parents are critical sources of social support to children in coping with risky, threatening conditions. Children who perceive that persons are available with whom they can talk, discuss problems, and so forth, cope more effectively with the stress of multiple personal and social changes during middle childhood and the transition to adolescence (Dubow and Tisak, 1989; Dubow, Tisak, Causey, Hryksho, and Reid, 1991; Hirsch and Rapkin, 1987).

## Development of Self-Concept, Self-Regulation, and Social Responsibility

Parents and other significant adults (e.g., teachers, coaches) also play a significant role in the growing capacities of 5- to 12-year-old children for functioning as responsible individuals (Eccles, 1999). Attaining mature self-regulatory capacities requires knowledge of the self, emotions, and cognitive capacities to focus on long-term goals and to take account of others' views and needs.

*Self and self-regulation.*   During middle childhood, children's descriptions of themselves become more stable and more comprehensive (Byrne and Shavelson, 1996; Damon and Hart, 1988). This shift partly reflects the growth of cognitive concepts and awareness of cultural norms and expectations for performance. In addition, self-evaluation intensifies as exposure to more varied persons and social contexts stimulates comparisons among self and others and provides evaluative feedback about characteristics, skills, and abilities (Eccles, 1999; Pomerantz, Ruble, Frey, and Greulich, 1995). Linked to changing concepts of self are greater capacities for self-control and self-regulation. For most children, impulsive behavior declines steadily from early childhood into middle childhood (Maccoby, 1984).

Parents and adult mentors can further capacities for self-regulation by exposing children to standards of conduct and models of socially valued behaviors and by providing rewards and punishments in accord with those standards (Smith and Smoll, 1990). Parents' and teachers' impact on motivation is greatest when their encouragement emphasizes opportunities for learning and mastery rather than stresses the need to succeed at social or task goals (Erdley, Cain, Loomis, Dumas-Hines, and Dweck, 1997; Kamins and Dweck, 1999). Furthermore, parents can stimulate cognitive components of self-regulation through discussion and reasoning that invoke principles for discerning right from wrong and that emphasize the consequences of transgressions (Chapman and McBride, 1992; Dunn and Slomkowski, 1992; Eisenberg and Valiente, in Vol. 5 of this *Handbook*; Walker and Taylor, 1991).

As self-regulation increases during middle childhood, parents develop new expectancies (see Goodnow, in Vol. 3 of this *Handbook*). Parents ordinarily expect more autonomy and independence in tasks at school and at home, including peer-group activities (Hartup, 1984). Parents gradually allow children to assume more responsibility for interacting with health care personnel and for mastering and acting on information and instructions about medication, specific health practices, and evolving life-style issues with implications for physical and mental well-being (Shonkoff, 1984; also see

Hickson and Clayton, in Vol. 5 of this *Handbook*; Meadow-Orlans, in Vol. 4 of this *Handbook*; Melamed, in Vol. 5 of this *Handbook*). These transitions lay the groundwork for greater autonomy in adolescence and young adulthood.

*Vulnerability and coping.* Children from 5 to 12 years old generally may be vulnerable to different stressors than children of other ages (Compas, 1987; Maccoby, 1984). For example, children of these ages generally are less distressed by short-term separations from parents than are younger children, but they grieve more intensely and over a longer period of time over the death of a parent (Rutter, 1983). Certain resources for coping with stress, moreover, may be more readily available to 5- to 12-year-old children than to younger children (Rudolph, Dennig, and Weisz, 1995). Among these are greater knowledge of strategies for coping with uncontrollable stress, which may modulate the degree of children's vulnerability (Altshuler and Ruble, 1989; Band and Weisz, 1988; Finnegan, Hodges, and Perry, 1996) and availability of social support (Dubow et al., 1991).

## NORMATIVE CHANGES IN PARENT–CHILD RELATIONSHIPS

Concurrent with these individual changes of middle childhood are characteristic patterns of parent–child interactions and relationships that distinguish this period from earlier and later years of life.

### Interactions and Affective Expression

Interactions between parents and children become less frequent in middle childhood. Parents are with children less than half as much as before their children started in school (Hill and Stafford, 1980). This decline in time together is relatively greater for parents with lower levels of education.

When parents and children are together, moreover, parents and children both show less overt affection during middle childhood than previously (McNally, Eisenberg, and Harris, 1991; Newson and Newson, 1968, 1976; Roberts, Block, and Block, 1984). Children also report that parents are less accepting toward them, especially during the later years of middle childhood (Armentrout and Burger, 1972). Despite a decrease in displays of physical affection, when their children are between the ages of 3 and 12 years, however, parents report little change in their enjoyment of parenting, having positive regard for their child, or having respect for the child's opinions and preferences (McNally et al., 1991; Roberts et al., 1984).

Parents and children alike are less likely to display and experience negative emotions in these interactions. Emotional outbursts, such as temper tantrums and coercive behaviors of children toward other family members, ordinarily begin to decline in early childhood (Goodenough, 1931; Newson and Newson, 1968, 1976; Patterson, 1982). This trend continues during middle childhood, and the frequency of disciplinary encounters also decreases steadily between the ages of 3 and 9 years (Clifford, 1959). Nevertheless, several emotional characteristics of interactions with 5- to 12-year-old children may complicate parents' management of their relationships with children. Compared with preschool children, 5- to 12-year-old children are more likely to sulk, become depressed, avoid parents, or engage in passive noncooperation with their parents (Clifford, 1959). Furthermore, children become increasingly likely to say that their conflicts with parents come about because parents provide inadequate help or do not spend enough time with the child, or (among older children) because parents fail to meet parent role expectations or there is a lack of consensus on familial and societal values (Fisher and Johnson, 1990).

### Mother–Child and Father–Child Relationships

Some aspects of relationships are differentiated by gender. In general, mothers and children spend more time together than do fathers and children (Collins and Russell, 1991; Parke, in Vol. 3 of this

*Handbook*). When both parents are with the child, however, mothers and fathers initiate interaction with children with equal frequency, and children initiate similar numbers of interactions with each parent (Noller, 1980; Russell and Russell, 1987). As in early life, fathers typically are involved relatively more in physical/outdoor play interactions, whereas mothers interact more frequently in connection with caregiving and household tasks. In observational studies with both parents present, though, fathers and mothers engaged in caregiving to a similar degree.

Both positive and negative emotional expressions and conflictual interactions are more likely in mother–child than in father–child interactions (Bronstein, 1984; Russell and Russell, 1987). This may reflect the greater amount of time and greater diversity of shared activities involving mothers. There is some indication that interactions of mothers with sons are marked by greater emotional expression than those of mothers with daughters, although whether these emotions are relatively more positive or negative is inconsistent across studies (for reviews, see Collins and Russell, 1991; Lytton and Romney, 1991).

Researchers frequently fail to find evidence of several differences commonly expected for interactions of children with mothers and with fathers. Both mothers and fathers increase their attention to school achievement and homework during middle childhood (McNally et al., 1991; Roberts et al., 1984). Furthermore, studies of parental reinforcements for instances of behaviors such as competitiveness, autonomous achievement, or competence in cognitive or play activities generally show negligible differences between mothers and fathers (Bronstein, 1984; Russell and Russell, 1987). Collins and Russell (1991) argued that few parental differences first emerge in middle childhood. Furthermore, the degree to which mother–child and father–child relationships are complementary, rather than overlapping, is more likely to change during adolescence than during middle childhood.

## Mutual Cognitions

Parents' and children's cognitions about each other and about issues of mutual relevance also change during middle childhood, especially the latter part of the period. Parents' knowledge of their children's daily activities and preferences increase during the middle childhood years (Crouter, Helms-Erikson, Updegraff, and McHale, 1999; Miller, Davis, Wilde, and Brown, 1993; also see Crouter and Head, in Vol. 3 of this *Handbook*). Children from 10 to 11 years of age and their parents tend to agree on the topics for which parents' authority is legitimate, but disagreement becomes more likely during adolescence (Smetana, 1989). Late-middle childhood is an important time for achieving more mutual cognitions. Alessandri and Wozniak (1987) found that 10- to 11-year-old children perceived their parents' beliefs about them less accurately than 15- to 16-year-old children did. Following those same 10- to 11-year-old children for 2 years, however, the researchers found that the children, who were now aged 12 to 13 years, were more accurate in their perceptions of what their parents believed about them (Alessandri and Wozniak, 1989).

Maccoby (1984; Maccoby and Martin, 1983) and Collins (1995) have speculated that mutual cognitions are more significant determinants of relationship qualities in middle childhood than in earlier periods. By the time a child reaches middle childhood, shared experiences have created extensive expectancies about the probable reactions of both parents and children. These expectancies then guide each person's behavior in interactions with the other. The rapid changes of late-middle childhood, in particular, stimulate both parents and children to adapt their beliefs and perceptions about the other to maintain their relationship over time.

To summarize, changes in parent–child relationships create new paradigms for interaction that affect when and how parents will respond to the behavior of children during middle childhood. Although partly resulting from adaptations to developmental changes that have already occurred, these relational patterns also affect responses to further changes during and beyond middle childhood. In the next section we examine findings from research on parenting of 5- to 12-year-old children.

## ISSUES IN PARENTING DURING MIDDLE CHILDHOOD

Changes in children and parent–child relationships raise the question of whether middle childhood is a distinctive period of parenting. This section addresses two related questions: What distinctive tasks devolve on parents during the middle childhood years, and what characteristics of effective parenting have emerged in studies of 5- to 12-year-old children? These questions are examined in research findings on four central issues of parenting entailed by the developmental changes of middle childhood: adapting control processes, fostering self-management and a sense of responsibility, facilitating positive relationships with others, and managing experiences in extrafamilial settings.

### Adapting Control Processes

Changes in interactions between parents and children, together with changing demands from age-graded activities and experiences, necessitate different strategies for exerting influence over children's behavior. These strategies may involve different disciplinary practices than those of childhood, more extensive shared regulation of children's behavior, and altered patterns for effective control.

*Disciplinary practices.*   Parenting young children typically involves distraction and physically assertive strategies for preventing harm and gaining compliance. When their children are in middle childhood, however, parents report less frequent physical punishment and an increasing use of techniques such as deprivation of privileges, appeals to children's self-esteem or sense of humor, arousal of children's sense of guilt, and reminders that children are responsible for what happens to them (Clifford, 1959; Newson and Newson, 1976; Roberts et al., 1984). These techniques may reflect changes in parents' attributions about the degree to which children should be expected to control their own behavior and also a greater tendency to regard misbehavior as deliberate and thus warranting both parental anger and punishment (Dix, Ruble, Grusec, and Nixon, 1986).

Maccoby (1984) speculated that children's responses to parents' control attempts during middle childhood are affected by changes in children's concepts of the basis for parental authority. Whereas preschoolers view parental authority as resting on the power to punish or reward, children in early-middle childhood increasingly believe parental authority derives from all the things that parents do for them. After the age of approximately 8 years, children invoke parents' expert knowledge and skill also as reasons to submit to their authority (Braine, Pomerantz, Lorber, and Krantz, 1991). Maccoby (1984) speculated that parental appeals based on fairness, the return of favors, or reminders of the parents' greater knowledge and experience may become more effective during middle childhood, with parents less often feeling compelled to resort to promises of reward or threats of punishment. This line of reasoning implies that, during their children's middle childhood, parents may find it easier to follow the disciplinary practices that have been found most effective in fostering patterns of self-regulated, socially responsible behavior, namely, an emphasis on the implications of children's actions for others (induction), rather than on use of parents' superior power to coerce compliance (Hoffman, 1994).

Parents' effectiveness as disciplinarians depends in part on the clarity with which they communicate expectations and reprimands (Grusec and Goodnow, 1994). Children tend to "tune out" when instructions and reprimands are conveyed in an ambiguous manner, as when a parent is inexplicit or reprimands the child while smiling. Such ineffective messages often result from a parent's sense of powerlessness or lack of control over the child's behavior, but also exacerbate behaviors parents wish to correct (Bugental, Blue, and Cruzcosa, 1989; Bugental, Lyon, Lin, McGrath, and Bimbela, 1999).

*Coregulation.*   Decreasing face-to-face interactions during middle childhood put additional pressures on parents' strategies for exerting control over children's behavior. Different methods are appropriate because of the age and the capabilities of children and also because children must be trained to regulate their own behavior for longer periods of time. At the same time, children's increased capabilities to be planful and goal directed and to communicate plans and wishes to parents more effectively permit greater collaboration on mutually acceptable plans and more effective monitoring through conversations about children's activities (Maccoby, 1984, 1992).

Maccoby (1984) specified the responsibilities of both parents and children in this cooperative process. First, parents must stay informed about events occurring outside their presence and must coordinate agendas, that link the daily activities of parents and child. Second, they must effectively use the times when direct contact does occur for teaching and feedback. Third, they must foster the development of abilities that will allow children to monitor their own behavior, to adopt acceptable standards of good and bad behavior, to avoid undue risks, and to know when they need parental support or guidance. This process is reciprocal: Children must be willing to inform parents of their where abouts, activities, and problems so that parents can mediate and guide when necessary.

*Effective control in middle childhood.*   Maccoby's formulation implies that effective parental control processes are tantamount to training of skills for self-regulation. A key component of effective control is parental *monitoring*, which requires careful attention to children's behavior and associated contingencies. Monitoring is integral to *child-centered* control techniques, in which parents exert influence by sensitively fitting their behavior to behavioral cues from children, rather than allowing the parents' own needs to drive parent–child interactions (Maccoby and Martin, 1983). Ineffective parental monitoring repeatedly has been linked to antisocial behavior in middle childhood and adolescence (Patterson, 1982, 1986; Tolan and Loeber, 1993; see Crouter and Head, in Vol. 3 of this *Handbook*).

The effectiveness of monitoring, however, depends on the parents' general style of control. Children are most likely to manifest positive developmental outcomes when parents practice child-centered patterns of discipline, accompanied by clearly communicated demands, parental monitoring, and an atmosphere of acceptance toward the child (authoritative parenting) (Baumrind, 1989; Maccoby and Martin, 1983; Maccoby, 1992). For example, attentive, responsive care appears to be positively linked to the development of self-esteem, competence, and social responsibility. The meager evidence now available from other cultures indicates that optimal childrearing practices frequently include somewhat more restrictiveness than is usually implied by North American findings with middle-socioeconomic families (e.g., Chao, 1994; Chao and Tseng, in Vol. 4 of this *Handbook*; Rohner and Pettingill, 1985; Rohner and Rohner, 1981). In every society, however, responsiveness to children's needs and support for their development appears to foster competent, responsible behaviors (see Steinberg and Silk, in Vol. 1 of this *Handbook*; Harkness and Super, in Vol. 2 of this *Handbook*). Darling and Steinberg (1993) have argued that a context of responsive, supportive, child-centered parental style affects the impact of specific parental practices, such as monitoring of children's behavior.

The research findings on which these generalizations are based generally do not provide definitive evidence that parenting characteristics *cause* particular constellations of child characteristics, but studies from which causal effects can be inferred imply that the characteristics above constitute the currently best description of effective parenting (Collins, Maccoby, Steinberg, Hetherington, and Bornstein, 2000). A striking example comes from a prevention program intended to foster more effective parenting following divorce (Forgatch and DeGarmo, 1999). School-age sons of recently divorced single mothers often manifest increased academic, behavioral, social, and emotional problems relative to sons of nondivorced mothers, and the divorced mothers themselves commonly behave toward their sons in a more coercive and less positive manner than nondivorced mothers do (Hetherington, Bridges, and Insabella, 1998). The prevention program provided yearlong training and discussion groups that encouraged mothers to use the effective parenting principles previously described during this postdivorce period. No intervention was provided to the children. At the end of 12 months, treatment group mothers generally showed less coercive behavior toward children and fewer declines in positive behavior than control-group mothers. Moreover, the degree of *change* in the mothers' behavior over the course of 12 months significantly predicted the degree of *change* in the children's behaviors, both at home and at school. By changing the mothers' behavior, these researchers changed the children's behavior, thus demonstrating that effective parenting causes improved child behavior.

Parents of 5- to 10-year-old children describe their childrearing along two dimensions: nurturance–restrictiveness (ranging from positive, facilitating reactions to negative, interfering reactions) and power (amount of active control exerted by the parent, including both rewards and punishments) (Dekovic and Janssens, 1992; Emmerich, 1962). Researchers have found no evidence of change in parents' behavior on these dimensions during middle childhood (e.g., Emmerich, 1962). Moreover, children's perceptions of firmness of control show little variation across groups from ages 9 to 13 years (Armentrout and Burger, 1972). Most experts now believe that firmness alone is an inadequate indicator of effective control. Lewis (1981) argued that, in many families, firmness of control coexists with responsive, child-centered parenting, which in turn enhances children's motivation to respond positively to their parents.

To summarize, middle childhood does not induce dramatic changes in parents' typical styles of childrearing. As in other periods, effective childrearing entails both attentiveness and responsiveness to children's needs and expectations of age-appropriate behavior. Nevertheless, during middle childhood patterns from earlier life are altered in ways that fundamentally affect the exchanges between parents and children and the implications of those exchanges for further development. These changes involve a gradual transition toward greater responsibility for children in regulating their own behavior and interactions with others.

## Fostering Self-Management and Social Responsibility

Alterations in parents' management and control activities partly result from children's own developing self-management skills. Although parents do not abruptly relinquish control any more than children abruptly become autonomous, children's enhanced self-management skills probably contribute to a gradual transition from parental regulation of children's behavior to self-regulation by the child (Maccoby, 1984, 1992).

This implicit transfer of regulatory responsibility is a hallmark of adolescent development (Steinberg and Silk, in Vol. 1 of this *Handbook*), but Maccoby (1984) has argued that the transfer process begins earlier and lasts longer than has commonly been assumed. She contends that the transfer of power from parents to children involves a three-phase developmental process: parental regulation, coregulation, and, finally, self-regulation. In the intermediate period of *coregulation*, parents retain general supervisory control but expect children to exercise gradually more extensive responsibilities for moment-to-moment self-regulation. This coregulatory experience in turn lays the groundwork for greater autonomy in adolescence and young adulthood.

In several formulations (Collins, Gleason, and Sesma, 1997; Grusec and Goodnow, 1994; Kuczynski, Marshall, and Schell, 1997), coregulation, rather than autonomous self-regulation, is treated as the norm for both parent–child and other relationships. Interdependence is essential to social relationships at every age, and socialization entails more mature and complex forms of interdependence with age. Maccoby (1992, p. 1013) has characterized the effective goal of authoritative parenting as "inducting the child into a system of reciprocity." Training for autonomy is seen, not as preparing children for freedom from the regulatory influences of others, but as enhancing capabilities for responsible exercise of autonomy, while recognizing one's interdependence with others (Collins et al., 1997). Thus parenting in middle childhood is less a matter of gradually yielding control than of transforming patterns of responsibility in response to new characteristics and challenges.

Variations in parents' behavior toward children are correlated with several distinctive aspects of self-management and responsibility: incidence of prosocial and undercontrolled, often antisocial, behavior; internalization of moral values; and increasing responsibility for self-care and for collective well-being. These links are discussed in the following three subsections.

*Incidence of prosocial and antisocial behavior.* For most children, behaviors that benefit others increase and those that harm others decline beginning in early childhood (for a review, see Coie and Dodge, 1998). During middle childhood several common changes imply that prosocial behavior probably becomes more likely and undercontrolled antisocial behavior less likely. Among these are declining tendencies to behave impulsively, increases in planfulness and other executive processes, greater capacity for understanding the impact of one's actions on others, and knowledge of what is required for helpfulness (Barnett, Darcie, Holland, and Kobasigawa, 1982). Children in middle childhood also increasingly know the appropriate conditions for displaying anger and aggression (Underwood, Coie, and Herbsman, 1992).

Parents contribute to the development of prosocial norms in several ways. Parents' own positive coping with frustration and distress serve to influence children's regulation of their emotions (Kliewer, Fearnow, and Miller, 1996). Parents' use of explanations that emphasize the implications of children's behavior for others also is associated with helpful, emotionally supportive behavior toward others (Hoffman, 1994). Furthermore, parents generally are perceived as sources of social support (Furman and Buhrmester, 1992). When children perceive that they can talk with others, discuss problems with them, and so forth, they generally are more likely to show prosocial behaviors and attitudes, such as empathy, tolerance of differences, and understanding of others (Bryant, 1985).

Middle childhood is especially significant in the development of the control of hostile aggressive actions. Although the overall likelihood of aggressive behavior is reduced relative to early childhood, 5- to 12-year-old children's aggression is more often hostile and person oriented than in early childhood (Hartup, 1974). Parental behaviors and family environments marked by harsh parental discipline repeatedly have been associated with the likelihood of antisocially aggressive behavior (Pinderhughes, Dodge, Bates, Pettit, and Zelli, 2000; Tolan and Loeber, 1993). A key linking the two appears to be the development of a bias toward interpreting the actions of others as intentionally harmful (Dodge, Bates, and Pettit, 1990). Children generally regard acts that are unintended, unforeseeable, and unavoidable as less blameworthy and less deserving of retaliation than other actions. Habitually aggressive children frequently show biases toward attributing hostile intent to others in ambiguous situations (Dodge, 1980). These biases are most likely in children who have experienced a history of harsh parental discipline in early childhood (Weiss, Dodge, Bates, and Pettit, 1992). In general, antisocial behavior is highly likely when children have repeatedly experienced indifferent, unresponsive behavior from their parents (Patterson, 1982). Antisocial tendencies place children at risk for peer rejection and school failure during middle childhood and for involvement in antisocial behavior in adolescence and young adulthood (Patterson, DeBaryshe, and Ramsey, 1989). Thus antisocial behavior is the nexus of a longitudinal process linking ineffective parenting and personal and social dysfunction (Finkelhor and Dziuba-Leatherman, 1994).

Mass media portrayals of antisocial and prosocial behavior consistently have been shown to influence spontaneous behavior after viewing. Children who spend relatively small amounts of time with television and other electronic media generally show fewer antisocial behaviors and fare better on many school and other tasks (Wright et al., in press). On the average, children in middle childhood devote 3 to 4 hr per day to television viewing, more time than any other age group in the first two decades of life. This amount varies greatly, however, depending on the child's gender, socioeconomic status, and many other factors. Parents' own viewing habits and the degree to which they attempt to regulate their children's viewing influence both the amount and the kind of exposure to media models of positive and negative social behaviors (Dorr, Rabin, and Irlen, in Vol. 5 of this *Handbook*; Huston and Wright, 1998). Parents can help to reduce the negative impact of television viewing by watching programs with children, providing explanations for complex situations and events, helping children differentiate between reality and fiction, and encouraging children to make responsible choices about the content of media.

*Internalization of moral values.*   Parents enhance social understanding by appealing to concerns for others and stimulating more cognitively complex reasoning about moral issues (Hoffman, 1994; Walker and Taylor, 1991). During middle childhood these parental techniques may become more ef-fective, because of children's increasing abilities for understanding others' experiences and feelings (Flavell and Miller, 1998). The implications for behavior come from the well-established correlation between parental disciplinary approaches based on warmth, other-oriented induction, and infrequent use of coercive discipline without explanations and signs of "conscience"—confessing misdeeds, offering reparations, feeling guilty (Eisenberg and Valiente, in Vol. 5 of this *Handbook*; Turiel, 1998).

The term responsibility encompasses broad behavioral expectations, including" ... (a) follow-ing through on specific interpersonal agreements and commitments, (b) fulfilling one's social role obligations, and (c) conforming to widely held social and moral rules of conduct" (Ford, Wentzel, Wood, Stevens, and Siesfeld, 1989, p. 405). Parental practices associated with the development of prosocial behavior and acquisition of moral values during middle childhood can be regarded as factors in the development of responsibility generally (Eisenberg and Valiente, in Vol. 5 of in this *Handbook*).

More specific strategies, however, involve parental expectations regarding household tasks and other activities considered relevant to the welfare of the family as a whole. Parents generally believe that expecting children to carry out household tasks not only provides valuable work experience, but also teaches about expected relationships with others (Goodnow, in Vol. 3 of this *Handbook*; Goodnow and Collins, 1990). Goodnow (1988) views division of responsibility for household tasks as an instance of distributive justice, referring not only to the distribution of labor for efficiency's sake, but also distribution in the sense of relational goals such as obligation, justice, and reciprocity. Warton and Goodnow (1991) found developmental progressions from middle childhood into adolescence in the understanding of distribution principles, such as direct-cause responsibility ("people should take care of the areas that they mess up"). This progression involves moving from a direct assertion of responsibility (e.g., "It's Mom's job") or an emphasis on some concrete details of the situation, to the understanding of the principle ("John should clean up the playroom because he and his friends were playing down there, and I wasn't involved"), followed by a move toward a modified, rather than rigid, use of the principle (e.g., "John made this mess, but he has to do his paper route on time; he'll help me out some other time"). Although parents of 5- to 12-year-old children are most likely to be dealing with the first two phases of this progression, discussions emphasizing the third view of equality may have impact on the growth of concepts of responsibility during middle childhood. Amato (1989) reported that, for 8- to 9-year-old children, rearing environments characterized by high levels of parental control and parental support, along with high allocation of household responsibility, are associated with broad competence at tasks.

To summarize, fostering self-management and responsibility probably involves a more gradual process than is implied by the common image of parents' transferring control to their children. Coreg-ulatory processes, in which parents allocate responsibilities for gradually broader self-management to children while retaining oversight, probably influence children through two key processes: (1) training for effective self-management and (2) enhancing capacities for interdependence, both with persons more powerful than they and with persons of equal power (Baumrind, 1989).

## Facilitating Positive Relationships

Parents' relationships with their children during middle childhood and also in earlier periods influence the development of supportive relationships during middle childhood and also enhance competence in and beyond the ages 5 to 12 years. This is apparent from the impact of parents on their children's relationships with each other and on their relationships with peers.

*Sibling relationships.*   Sibling relationships become increasingly positive, egalitarian, and companionable during middle childhood (Dunn, 1992; Dunn and McGuire, 1992). The degree to which this occurs, however, is related to parental interactions with both siblings. In a study of 10- to 11-year-old girls and their 7- to 9-year-old sisters, the daughters whose mothers were above average in responsiveness to their daughters' needs showed more prosocial behavior and less hostility toward their siblings than the daughters of mothers who were below average in responsiveness (Bryant and Crockenberg, 1980). In other studies, rates of positive, negative, and controlling behaviors directed by mothers toward each child are correlated positively with the rates of such behaviors directed by siblings toward each other (Stocker, Dunn, and Plomin, 1989).

Parents' treating siblings differently has also been linked to negative relationships between the siblings. This is apparent from several related research findings. One such finding is that the children of parents who responded more extensively to one child over the other were more likely to behave with hostility toward one another (e.g., Bryant and Crockenberg, 1980). Another is that rates of fathers' and mothers' positive behavior directed to each child were associated with siblings' positive behavior toward each other; and both negative parental behavior generally and differences in behavior toward the children were associated with negative sibling interactions (Brody, Stoneman, and McCoy, 1992). This was especially likely when one child's temperament was more difficult than the other child's (Brody, Stoneman, and Gauger, 1996).

It is not possible to say whether parents' treating children differently during middle childhood affects sibling relationships more than differential behavior in other life periods. Children who perceive that they are treated less positively than their sibling, however, are somewhat more likely than their sibling to show negative personality adjustment in adolescence (Daniels, Dunn, Furstenberg, and Plomin, 1985).

*Peer relationships.*   Parents facilitate their children's positive peer relationships indirectly and directly throughout childhood (Parke, MacDonald, Beitel, and Bhavnagri, 1988). Indirect or stage-setting effects subsume the advantages of positive, accepting, secure parent–child relationships on children's capacities for forming and maintaining smooth, prosocial relationships with others (e.g., Contreras, Kerns, Weimer, Gentzler, and Tomich, 2000; Dishion, 1990). Direct or intervention effects refer to parents' management of their children's relations with other children and the transmission of specific social skills for effective interactions with peers (Parke and Bhavnagri, 1989).

In general, the parental correlates of positive relations with peers in middle childhood parallel the more extensive findings from studies of preschool children (Hartup, 1984). In middle childhood, mothers and fathers of well-liked children are emotionally supportive, infrequently frustrating and punitive, and discouraging of antisocial behavior in their children (e.g., Dekovic and Janssens, 1992). The families of these children are generally low in tension and are marked by affection toward, and parental satisfaction with, their children. Furthermore, social skills that are significant to successful peer relationships (e.g., self-confidence, assertiveness, and effectiveness with other children) are correlated with a history of affection from both parents and dominance from the same-gender parent (Parke et al., 1988). In research with 8- and 9-year-old children and their parents, popularity with peers was positively correlated with children's perceptions of positive relationships with parents and observational measures of fathers' receptivity to children's proposed solutions on a teaching task (Henggeler, Edwards, Cohen, and Summerville, 1991).

These findings imply both direct and indirect links between parent and peer relationships, but leave open the question of how such links come about. Relevant evidence on one possible process comes from a study of 5- and 6-year-old middle-socioeconomic European American children and their parents (Cassidy, Parke, Butkovsky, and Braungart, 1992). The children in this study were more cooperative and interacted more smoothly with peers if their parents were emotionally expressive. The relation was most pronounced for children who showed understanding of emotions, including emotional expressions, experiences, conditions, and effective action and feeling responses. Thus the impact of the emotional tenor of parent–child relationships may be especially great for those children who are capable of inferring positive principles of interpersonal behavior from experiences with parents and siblings. Later research revealed that positive relationships with parents contribute to children's developing abilities for regulating their emotions, and this ability in turn makes the child more effective in interactions with peers (Contreras et al., 2000).

Parent–child interaction patterns also have been linked to less positive behavior in middle childhood (Dishion, 1990; McFadyen-Ketchum, Bates, Dodge, and Pettit, 1996; Patterson, 1982, 1986; Patterson and Bank, 1989; Schwartz, Dodge, Pettit, and Bates, 1997; Vuchinich, Bank, and Patterson, 1992). In two cohorts of boys, aged 9 to 10 years, Dishion (1990) found that erratic monitoring and ineffective disciplinary practices marked the families of rejected boys, as did higher levels of family stress, lower socioeconomic status, and evidence of more behavioral and academic problems for the boys themselves. Parents' ineffective disciplinary practices increased the likelihood of peer rejection by enhancing the likelihood of antisocial behavior and academic failure. Later analyses of these data, along with data from a 2-year follow-up (Vuchinich et al., 1992), showed a reciprocal relation between parental ineffectiveness and child behavior: Parental discipline in these families was ineffective partly because the children behaved antisocially, but the ineffective discipline also helped to maintain these antisocial tendencies.

In addition to the association between parenting and antisocial behavior, the family environment, including parents' marital conflict and parental disagreement on childrearing standards and practices, has been linked to children's antisocial tendencies and poor relationships with peers (Gonzales, Pitts, Hill, and Roosa, 2000; Grych, in Vol. 4 of this *Handbook*; McCloskey, Figueredo, and Koss, 1995). These diverse pieces of evidence indicate that parent–child and peer relationships are linked through complex, multiple processes (Ladd and Pettit, in Vol. 5 of this *Handbook*).

*Timing of effects.*   Considerable uncertainty exists about whether links between parent–child relationships and interpersonal competence during middle childhood reflect concurrent relationships or the longer history of interactions between parent and child. Current longitudinal research indicates impressive stabilities between parent–child relationships in infancy and early childhood and extrafamilial relationships in middle childhood (e.g., Elicker, Englund, and Sroufe, 1992; Sroufe, Carlson, and Shulman, 1993). These findings come from research on *attachment* or individuals' feeling of confidence in the responsiveness of one person in particular (see Bornstein, in Vol. 1 of this *Handbook*; Cummings and Cummings, in Vol. 5 of this *Handbook*).

In these studies, security of attachment to caregivers when children were 12 and 18 months old was associated with a variety of indicators of children's competence with peers at 10 to 12 years of age (Elicker et al., 1992; Sroufe et al., 1993; Sroufe, Egeland, and Carlson, 1999). The securely attached children were more likely to be rated highly by adults on broad-based social and personal competence and were less dependent on adults. These children also spent more time with peers, were more likely to form friendships, and were more likely to have friendships characterized by openness, trust, coordination, and complexity of activity. They also spent more time in, and functioned more effectively in, groups and were more likely to follow implicit rules of peer interactions than children with histories of insecure attachment. An example comes from research on same-gender versus cross-gender peer interactions. During middle childhood, frequency of cross-gender interactions is negatively correlated with social skills and popularity. Insecurely attached children more frequently engaged in cross-gender interactions than securely attached children did (Sroufe, Bennett, Englund, Urban, and Shulman, 1993). In general, the links between security of attachment and social competence with peers in middle childhood are similar to links found in preschool (Sroufe et al., 1993; Sroufe et al., 1999). That is, at the ages of 5 to 12, children show similar patterns of orientation to peers and teachers as they did in early childhood; and both the early and the middle childhood patterns are correlated with attachment measures taken during the first 2 years of life.

These correlations may mean that relationships with parents have similar characteristics across time. Parents who provide responsive, child-centered care in infancy might be more likely to adapt those patterns of care to the support and the guidance needed by children in later years, thus providing continuity of care. The researchers suggest two other possibilities. One is that the patterns of behavior formed in early relationships may persist, eliciting characteristically different patterns of reactions from others in later life. That is, positive relationships with peers may result from skillful interpersonal behavior by the securely attached child. A second possibility is that children carry forward from early relationships an internal working model of interpersonal relationships (Bowlby, 1973). Internal working models are inferred cognitive representations or prototypes of one's key relationships that incorporate behaviors, feelings, and expectancies of reactions from others.

These possibilities are not mutually exclusive, and all three may contribute to the complex linkages between familial and peer relationships. Longitudinal analyses imply that early relationships are probably linked to middle childhood peer competence by means of internal working models (Fury, Carlson, and Sroufe, 1997). Children's internal working models of relationships were assessed at the ages of 4, 8, and 12 years. There were clear contrasts among groups varying in early attachment scores in early and middle childhood measures of internal working models. Together, infant attachment scores and later measures of internal working models accounted for 44% of the variance in ratings of social competence when children were at the age of 12 years; early attachment alone, however, was not reliably related to later social competence. Important questions remain, such as whether and how representations themselves are affected by variations in relationships after infancy, but findings to date imply that parenting in middle childhood partly is rooted in relational patterns established in earlier periods of life.

*Beyond middle childhood.* It should be noted that temporal linkages between familial and extrafamilial relationships run forward, as well as backward, in time. Rejection by peers, which consistently has been linked to relationships with parents and siblings in childhood, is a compelling marker of long-term developmental disadvantage (Parker and Asher, 1987). Individuals with unsatisfactory peer relationships in childhood face greater risks for behavioral problems, school failure, and emotional maladjustment in childhood and adolescence and for mental health problems and criminality in adulthood. Parent–child relationships appear to affect these developmental outcomes by their impact on antisocial behavior and academic failure in middle childhood (Patterson et al., 1989) and even on long-term unemployment in adulthood (Kokko and Pulkinnen, 2000).

More positive linkages to parent–child relationships have also been documented. Franz, McClelland, and Weinberger (1991) reported longitudinal follow-ups of individuals who were first studied at the age of 5 years, together with their mothers. The participants were measured at the age of 41 years on an indicator of "conventional social accomplishment," defined as having a long, happy marriage, children, and relationships with close friends at midlife (Vaillant, 1977). Having a warm and affectionate father and mother at the age of 5 years was correlated with affiliative behaviors and reports of good relationships with significant others 36 years later. These characteristics of parents also were associated with higher levels of generativity, work accomplishment, psychological well-being, lower level of strain and less use of emotion-focused coping styles in adulthood. In a separate analysis with this same sample, parents' characteristics when individuals were 5 years old were associated with these same individuals' empathic concern at the age of 31 years (Koestner, Franz, and Weinberger, 1990). As in the shorter-term longitudinal findings previously described, a variety of possible processes may account for this link between middle childhood familial relationships and these varied adult characteristics.

*Parent–peer cross pressures.* One widely invoked possible linkage between parent–child and peer relationships in middle childhood is an inverse one: namely, that increasing involvement with peers may be associated with decreasing engagement with and influence of parents. This linkage, though, has only limited and narrow support in the literature. A more common finding is that attitudes toward both parents and peers are more favorable than unfavorable throughout middle childhood and adolescence (Collins, 1995; Steinberg and Silk, in Vol. 1 of this *Handbook*). Within this general stability, however, some change does occur. For example, the number of children reporting positive attitudes toward parents declines moderately during middle childhood, although attitudes toward peers generally do not become more favorable during this period.

With respect to endorsement of attitudes held by parents versus peers, the inverse relation occurs only for antisocial behavior and, furthermore, is not especially intense before to puberty (Hartup, 1984). In a cross-sectional study of children aged 9, 12, 15, and 17 years, Berndt (1979) charted age-related patterns of conformity to parents and peers regarding prosocial, neutral, and antisocial behaviors. Antisocial behavior, in this instance, referred to such activities as cheating, stealing, trespassing, and minor destruction of property. Children and adolescents alike conformed to both parents and friends regarding prosocial behavior; there was some decline across ages in conformity to parents, but not peers, on neutral behaviors; and conformity to peers regarding antisocial behaviors increased between the ages of 8 and 15, but not beyond. Thus there is relatively little evidence that pronounced parent–peer cross pressures are the norm in middle childhood.

More disruptive shifts may occur in families in which parents fail to maintain age-appropriate, child-centered control patterns. Several studies indicate that conformity to peers may be more likely in families in which relationships with parents are perceived as unsatisfactory. Fuligni and Eccles (1993) collected self-report questionnaires on this topic from 1,771, children from 12 to 13 years old. They found that children who believed their parents continued the same patterns of power assertion and restrictiveness they had used in earlier years were higher in an extreme form of peer orientation. Furthermore, those who perceived few opportunities to be involved in decision making, as well as no increase in these opportunities, were higher in both extreme peer orientation and peer advice seeking. Studies of school-age children and early adolescents who are on their own in the afterschool hours also show greater susceptibility to peer influence cross pressures when parent–child relationships are less warm and involve less regular parental monitoring (Galambos and Maggs, 1991; Steinberg, 1986).

*Social support for parents.*   Parents' perceptions of a supportive network beyond the family also influence their behavior and children's development (Cochran and Niego, in Vol. 4 of this *Handbook*). For example, interventions with troubled families are more effective when parents perceive that social support is available to them (Wahler, 1980), whereas isolation from community support systems often typifies abusive families (e.g., Azar, in Vol. 4 of this *Handbook*; Emery and Laumann-Billings, 1998).

To summarize, qualities of relationships with parents have significant implications for development in and beyond middle childhood. Furthermore, linkages to other periods indicate that middle childhood experiences are inextricable from developmental influences and processes across the lifespan. A variety of possible processes may link middle childhood family relationships to both earlier and later functioning.

## Managing Extrafamilial Experiences

As children move into settings beyond the family, parents increasingly must monitor extrafamilial settings and negotiate with nonfamilial adults on behalf of children. Of these settings, the most prominent is school. In addition, many parents must arrange for afterschool care by others or must establish and monitor arrangements for self-care by children.

*School.*   Children in the United States typically spend almost as much time in school as at home. Schools advance both academic knowledge and knowledge of cultural norms and values and provide essential supports for learning literacy skills, which greatly extend cognitive capacities in many different areas (Fischer and Bullock, 1984). Experiences in school also affect children's views of their own abilities to learn and their actual achievement and adjustment (Eccles, Wigfield, and Schiefele, 1998).

Family experiences are linked to children's successful adaptation to the demands of schooling (Epstein and Sanders, in Vol. 5 of this *Handbook*). A history of shared work and play activities with parents is positively linked to a smooth entry into school, whereas early interactions characterized by a controlling parent and a resisting child, or by a directing child, are correlated with poor adjustment

(Barth and Parke, 1993; Pianta and Nimetz, 1991). Several parental characteristics are linked to both short-term and long-term academic motivation: providing a cognitively stimulating home environment, regardless of socioeconomic level (Gottfried, Fleming, and Gottfried, 1998), values favoring the development of autonomy rather than conformity (Okagaki and Sternberg, 1993), and emphasizing goals associated with learning, rather than goals associated with performance and evaluation (Ablard and Parker, 1997).

Children express more satisfaction with school when the authority structure of classrooms is similar to the authority practices they encounter at home (Epstein, 1983; Hess and Holloway, 1984). Furthermore, parenting styles consistently have been linked to school success. Authoritative styles that emphasize encouragement, support for child-initiated efforts, clear communication, and a child-centered teaching orientation in parent–child interactions are associated with higher achievement than are strategies characterized by punishment for failure, use of a directive teaching style, and discouragement of child-initiated interactions (Baumrind, 1989; Pianta and Nimetz, 1991). These correlations occur in studies with both European American and African American families and with adolescents as well as with younger children (Steinberg, Elmen, and Mounts, 1989). These latter findings implicate authoritative parenting in higher school grades and lower incidence of behavior problems in school, compared with authoritarian or permissive parenting styles. In addition to parental control strategies, lower school achievement during middle childhood has been linked with family environments characterized by interparent and parent–child hostility (Feldman and Wentzel, 1990).

Parents' expectations regarding children's achievement also are implicated in school success (Stevenson and Newman, 1986). Expectations have an impact from the beginning of schooling. Entwisle and Hayduk (1982) examined United States parents' expectations for their children's school performance each year between the ages of 5 and 9. For middle-socioeconomic children and children of blue-collar parents, parents' expectations were strong influences on children's first marks. The influence of blue-collar parents on children after the age of 6 years appeared to be considerably less than that of their middle-class counterparts (Alexander and Entwisle, 1988; Hoff, Laursen, and Tardif, in Vol. 2 of this *Handbook*).

In European American middle class families, parental expectations are correlated with achievement into the preadolescent years (Frome and Eccles, 1998; Stevenson and Newman, 1986). Changes in expectations often occur during the early school years, however, and these changes are difficult to explain. Children's performances in school may affect these expectations, of course. Alexander and Entwisle (1988) found a significant impact of first-grade (age 6 years ) achievement on parents' subsequent expectations for children's school performance. In other instances, contrasting expectations emerge for children who are equivalent in classroom grades and in test scores. For example, although parents' expectations for math performance do not differ by gender at the beginning of school, males are expected to do better than females by the beginning of the second grade (age 7) (Entwisle and Baker, 1983).

High parental expectations also appear to be key factors in cross-national differences in school achievement during middle childhood. Stevenson and Lee (1990) examined parental correlates of substantially lower levels of academic achievement by children in the United States, compared to China and Japan. They found that parents in the United States have lower expectations for and assign less importance to school achievement than Asian parents do; furthermore, mothers in the United States are more likely to regard achievement primarily as a reflection of innate ability, whereas Asian mothers emphasize the importance of hard work in attaining academic excellence. Compared with parents in China and Japan, as well as immigrant parents in the United States, parents born in the United States are more likely to believe that general cognitive development, motivation, and social skills are more important than academic skills (Huntsinger, Jose, Liaw, and Ching, 1997; Okagaki and Sternberg, 1993; Stevenson and Lee, 1990). Thus, not only expectations about children's achievement, but the importance assigned to mastery of school tasks per se, affect the impact of parents on their children's school experiences (Huntsinger, Jose, and Larson, 1998).

Family difficulties, such as divorce, are also linked to children's school learning and to their emerging self-concepts (Hetherington and Stanley-Hagan, in Vol. 3 of this *Handbook*). In the first year or two after a divorce, children from one-parent families frequently miss school, study less effectively, and disrupt their classrooms more often. Furthermore, teachers observe difficulties in their general social behavior, including their relations with friends. Girls are seen to be more dependent, and boys are perceived as more aggressive and less able to maintain attention and effort at assigned tasks and, in general, to be less competent academically. On the other hand, one important context may compensate for difficulties in the other, as when family members provide support for school difficulties, or teachers and classmates help to buffer children's distress over family problems (Hetherington et al., 1998; Hetherington and Stanley-Hagan, in Vol. 3 of this *Handbook*).

Parents' involvement with schools and with children's school-related tasks also is correlated positively with children's school achievement in middle childhood. Parental involvement is variously defined as expectations of school performance, verbal encouragement, direct reinforcement of school-relevant behaviors, general academic guidance or support, and children's perceptions of parents' influence on school progress (Fehrmann, Keith, and Reimers, 1987). Correlations are less impressive in the secondary grades (usually after the age of 12), perhaps because common forms of parental involvement are perceived as intrusions on autonomy.

The most studied area of parental involvement in schooling is homework. Leone and Richards (1989) found that 11- and 12-year-old students in the top one third of their classes spent significantly more time on homework, including time spent working with a parent on school assignments. Other studies have shown negative correlations, perhaps because parents are more likely to become involved in homework when children have not been doing well on their own. Even under these conditions, though, test scores generally improved when parents became involved, especially when parents have been trained in how best to help their children complete homework assignments (Miller and Kelley, 1991). Parental attitudes toward the importance of homework, like attitudes toward the importance of school achievement generally, vary cross nationally. For example, parents in China, Japan, and Taiwan value school achievement more highly than U.S. parents do (Chao and Tseng, in Vol. 4 of this *Handbook*; Chen and Stevenson, 1989).

Several factors influence the impact of parental involvement. One factor is parents' general style of childrearing. Among authoritative parents (those who characteristically showed responsive, child-centered behavior and clear expectations for child behavior), involvement was highly correlated with academic achievement, in comparison with involvement of authoritarian (restrictive, parent-centered, controlling) parents. Authoritative parents' involvement is likely perceived as reflecting interest in and support for children's school-related activities, whereas authoritarian parents' involvement may be interpreted as intrusive, controlling, and implying disrespect and lack of trust for the child (Darling and Steinberg, 1993).

*Afterschool care.* At the start of the 21st century, 78% of parents with children aged 6 to 13 years participate in the workforce. Because children spend only 6 hr each day in school and these 6 hr frequently do not correspond to parents' work schedules, large numbers of children are alone without immediate adult supervision for significant amounts of time (Capizzano, Tout, and Adams, 2000; Vandell and Shumow, 1999). Estimates put the number of children who spend unsupervised time at 3.6 to 4 million. Afterschool childcare arrangements vary by age of children, ethnicity, parents' availability and whether parents have traditional or nontraditional work hours.

Parents' and children's reports offer discrepant views of typical afterschool arrangements, with children reporting more time alone and less happiness with the arrangements and whether or not the child actually adhered to the arrangement (Belle, 1999). Frequent changes occur in afterschool arrangements, because of unsatisfactory arrangements, changing age, ability and desires of the child, expense, perceived danger, degree of structure in the arrangements, and balancing children's needs with familial or parental work needs. In the latter years of middle childhood (ages 10 to 12 years), many families from all ethnic and income groups begin a transition to letting children be on their own, rather than being supervised directly by an adult, during the afterschool hours (Capizzano et al., 2000; Kerrebrock and Lewis, 1999; Vandell and Shumow, 1999).

Few general differences in academic performance or psychosocial status are apparent when children in adult-care arrangements are compared with those in self-care arrangements. Vandell and Corasaniti (1988) reported that 8- and 9-year-old children in center care showed lower academic achievement and lower acceptance by peers than children in other care arrangements, including mother care. Surprisingly, "latchkey" children—children who are at home alone after school—were not generally disadvantaged relative to mother-care children. The reasons for the deficits observed in children cared for in centers are not clear.

Negative effects are most likely when children on their own are not monitored regularly and when they are free to spend time away from home with peers (Galambos and Maggs, 1991; Steinberg, 1986; Vandell and Shumow, 1999). These arrangements are more common in the preadolescent years than the early elementary years. Older children are more susceptible to peer influences and more likely to engage in problem behaviors than children who stay at home and those who are in regular telephone contact with parents. The negative effects from being allowed to roam may result partly from generally less positive parent–child relationships. For girls particularly, permissive self-care arrangements are associated with lowered perceptions of parental acceptance and higher levels of parent–child conflicts (Galambos and Maggs, 1991). Among these preadolescents and younger children alike, regular arrangements for parental monitoring and clear expectations for letting parents know where the child is seem to overcome the potential negative effects of self care (Galambos and Maggs, 1991; Steinberg, 1986; Vandell and Corasaniti, 1988).

By contrast, school-age childcare programs clearly benefit children's development compared with self-care. Although this conclusion may reflect the generally more positive developmental course of the middle-socioeconomic children who participate, the greatest benefits clearly come from programs that are well suited to the developmental level of the child, that offer flexible programs, and that feature a well-educated staff and low child-to-staff ratios (Vandell and Shumow, 1999). One study showed that 11- to 13-year-old children who participated for 2 years in an afterschool enrichment program with a comparable group of children who did not had improved attitudes toward school, improved behavior at school, better grades, and less tension at home (Dryfoos, 1999; also see Huston et al., 2001).

In summary, parents' involvement in children's lives away from home entails many of the same principles and processes that determine their effectiveness in direct interactions. Appropriate monitoring, in the context of warm, accepting relationships, is associated with positive school adjustment and academic achievement and with benign impact of self-care arrangements. Children with better relationships with their parents appear to be better able to understand the necessity for afterschool care, even if it is not their preference (Belle, 1999). Although these areas of children's lives require different forms of parental involvement, the general style of parents' relationships with children is a key factor in the impact of out-of-home experiences on development during middle childhood.

## CONCLUSIONS

Parenting during middle childhood encompasses adaptation to distinctive transformations in human development that affect not only the current well-being of children, but carry significant implications for later life. The age of 5 to 7 years is universally regarded as "the age of reason" (Rogoff et al., 1975). In non-Western cultures children are assumed to develop new capabilities at this age and are often assigned expanded roles and responsibilities in their families and communities. Although the transition to adultlike responsibilities is less pronounced in Western industrialized societies, 5- to 12-year-old children are expected to show greater autonomy and responsibility in some arenas.

The unique experiences of individual children in middle childhood partly reflect changes experienced by virtually all children of this age and also the interpersonal relationships and the characteristics of particular communities and social institutions. Such factors as urban versus rural residence, family and domestic group status, parental and nonparental childcare arrangements, tasks typically assigned to children, and the role of women in the society have all been demonstrated to affect important dimensions of childhood socialization in both industrialized and developing countries.

Common changes in children and in relationships have raised two key questions that underlie the framework outlined in the chapter. One is the question of whether parenting during middle childhood is distinctively different from parenting in other age periods. Although the particular forms of parental behavior and parent–child interaction vary considerably, certain issues arise in virtually all families of 5- to 12-year-old children in industrialized societies: exercising regulatory influence while facilitating increasing self-regulation, maintaining positive bonds while fostering a distinctive sense of self, providing groundwork for effective relationships and experiences outside of the family (Collins, 1984, 1995). These issues are integral to parent–child relationships from a child's birth, although often in less obtrusive or more rudimentary forms than in middle childhood, and they remain central in the adolescent years and, to a lesser degree, in early adulthood (White, Speisman, and Costos, 1983).

The distinctiveness of parenting 5- to 12-year-old children largely arises from the relative novelty and salience of issues specific to this age period. Middle childhood is a period of intensifying transitions, many of which require parents to extend their activities on behalf of the child to interactions with others, including teachers, peers, and other families. In addition, behaviors of children toward parents change as the result of cognitive, emotional, and social transitions. Consequently, both the scope of the issues and the methods available for addressing them are altered in middle childhood.

Current models of socialization imply that the most effective parental responses to changes in children's behavior combine child-centered flexibility and adherence to core values and expectancies for approved behavior (Baumrind, 1989; Darling and Steinberg, 1993; Dix, 1991; Grusec and Goodnow, 1994; Hoffman, 1994; Maccoby, 1992). This combination may be more complex in middle childhood than in other periods. Furthermore, the balance between ensuring continuity and adapting to child-driven change may be more difficult to maintain in and after middle childhood than in early childhood. The capacity for age-appropriate adaptation, however, probably is not exclusive to effective parenting in this period, but is inherent in the characteristics of effective parenting at every age.

One question that is not directly addressed in this chapter concerns the linkages between parenting and individual development during middle childhood and in later periods. These associations are more often implicit than explicit. Nevertheless, research findings have documented some key connections. The most extensively duplicated finding is that parenting styles marked by authoritativeness toward children, but clearly child-centered attitudes and concerns, are correlated with a variety of positive outcomes that attain salience in middle childhood and that are predictive of successful adaptation in later life. These include peer acceptance, school success, competence in self-care, and competence and responsibility in a broad array of tasks. Equally well established is the finding that parenting behavior and attitudes dominated by parental concerns, rather than child characteristics and needs, are associated with less positive outcomes on all of these variables. The latter must be regarded as middle childhood risk factors for long-term dysfunction.

A caveat is that studies do not tell us whether experiencing negative conditions for the first time in middle childhood affects later development differently in either kind or degree than experiencing parenting problems over a longer period. Nevertheless, the documented consequences of these negative conditions for 5- to 12-year-old children leave little doubt that effective parenting powerfully affects development both during and after middle childhood.

# REFERENCES

Ablard, K. E., and Parker, W. D. (1997). Parents' achievement goals and perfectionism in their academically talented children. *Journal of Youth and Adolescence, 26,* 651–668.

Alessandri, S. M., and Wozniak, R. H. (1987). The child's awareness of parental beliefs concerning the child: A developmental study. *Child Development, 58,* 316–323.

Alessandri, S. M., and Wozniak, R. H. (1989). Continuity and change in intrafamilial agreement in beliefs concerning the adolescent: A follow-study. *Child Development, 60,* 335–339.

Alexander, K. L., and Entwisle, D. R. (1988). Achievement in the first 2 years of school: Patterns and processes. *Monographs of the Society for Research in Child Development, 53* (2, Serial No. 218).

Altshuler, J. L., and Ruble, J. L. (1989). Developmental changes in children's awareness of strategies for coping with uncontrollable stress. *Child Development, 60,* 1337–1349.

Amato, P. R. (1989). Family processes and the competence of adolescents and primary school children. *Journal of Youth and Adolescence, 18,* 39–53.

Aries, P. (1962). *Centuries of childhood.* New York: Knopf.

Armentrout, V. A., and Burger, G. K. (1972). Children's reports of parental child-rearing behaviors at five grade levels. *Developmental Psychology, 7,* 44–48.

Band, E. B., and Weisz, J. R. (1988). How to feel better when it feels bad: Children's perspectives on coping with everyday stress. *Developmental Psychology, 24,* 247–253.

Barnett, K., Darcie, G., Holland, C., and Kobasigawa, A. (1982). Children's cognitions about effective helping. *Developmental Psychology, 18,* 267–277.

Barth, J. M., and Parke, R. D. (1993). Parent–child relationship influences on children's transition to school. *Merrill-Palmer Quarterly, 39,* 173–195.

Baumrind, D. (1973). The development of instrumental competence through socialization. In A. D. Pick (Ed.), *Minnesota symposia on child psychology* (Vol. 7, pp. 3–46). Minneapolis: University of Minnesota Press.

Baumrind, D. (1989). Rearing competent children. In W. Damon (Ed.), *Child development today and tomorrow* (pp. 349–378). San Francisco: Jossey-Bass.

Bell, C. C., and Jenkins, E. J. (1993). Community violence and children on Chicago's Southside. *Psychiatry, 56,* 46–54.

Belle, D. (1999). *The after-school lives of children: Alone and with others while parents work.* Mahwah, NJ: Lawrence Erlbaum Associates.

Berndt, T. J. (1979). Developmental changes in conformity to peers and parents. *Developmental Psychology, 15,* 608–616.

Bibace, R., and Walsh, M. (1981). Children's conceptions of illness. In R. Bibace and M. Walsh (Eds.), *Children's conceptions of health, illness, bodily functions: New directions for child development* (No. 14). San Francisco: Jossey-Bass.

Bowlby, J. (1973). *Attachment and loss: Vol. 2. Separation.* New York: Basic Books.

Braine, L. G., Pomerantz, E., Lorber, D., and Krantz, D. H. (1991). Conflicts with authority: Children's feelings, actions, and justifications. *Developmental Psychology, 27,* 829–840.

Brody, G. H., Stoneman, Z., and McCoy, J. K. (1992). Associations of maternal and paternal direct and differential behavior with sibling relationships: Contemporaneous and longitudinal analyses. *Child Development, 63,* 82–92.

Brody, G. H., Stoneman, Z., and Gauger, K. (1996). Parent–child relationships, family problem-solving behavior, and sibling relationship quality: The moderating role of sibling temperaments. *Child Development, 67,* 1289–1300.

Brodzinsky, D. M., Smith, D. W., and Brodzinsky, A. B. (1998). *Children's Adjustment to Adoption: Developmental and Clinical Issues.* Thousand Oaks, CA: Sage.

Bronstein, P. (1984). Differences in mothers' and fathers' behaviors toward children: A cross-cultural comparison. *Developmental Psychology, 20,* 995–1003.

Bryant, B. (1985). The neighborhood walk: Source of support in middle childhood. *Monographs of the Society for Research in Child Development, 50* (3, Serial No. 210).

Bryant, B., and Crockenberg, S. (1980). Correlates and dimensions of prosocial behavior: A study of female siblings with their mothers. *Child Development, 51,* 529–544.

Bugental, D. B., Blue, J., and Cruzcosa, M. (1989). Perceived control over caregiving outcomes: Implications for child abuse. *Developmental Psychology, 25,* 532–539.

Bugental, D. B., Lyon, J. E., Lin, E. K., McGrath, E. P., and Bimbela, A. (1999). Children "tune out" in response to the ambiguous communication, style of powerless adults. *Child Development, 70,* 214–230.

Byrne, B. M., and Shavelson, R. J. (1996). On the structure of social self-concept for pre-, early, and late adolescents: A test of the Shavelson, Hubner, and Stanton (1976) model. *Journal of Personality and Social Psychology, 70,* 599–613.

Capizzano, J., Tout, K., and Adams, G. (2000). Child care patterns of school-age children with employed mothers. *Assessing the New Federalism* (Occasional Paper No. 41). Washington, DC: Urban Institute.

Case, R. (1998). The development of conceptual structures. In D. Kuhn and R. S. Siegler (Vol. Eds.) and W. Damon (Ed.), *Handbook of child psychology: Vol. 2. Cognition, perception, and language* (5th ed., pp. 745–800). New York: Wiley.

Cassidy, J., Parke, R. D., Butkovsky, L., and Braungart, J. M. (1992). Family-peer connections: The roles of emotional expressiveness within the family and children's understanding of emotions. *Child Development, 63*, 603–618.

Chao, R. K. (1994). Beyond parental control and authoritarian parenting style: Understanding Chinese parenting through the cultural notion of training. *Child Development, 65*, 1111–1119.

Chapman, M., and McBride, M. L. (1992). The education of reason: Cognitive conflict and its role in intellectual development. In C. U. Shantz and W. W. Hartup (Eds.), *Conflict in child and adolescent development* (pp. 36–69). New York: Cambridge University Press.

Chase-Lansdale, P. L., and Gordon, R. A. (1996). Economic hardship and the development of five and six year-olds: Neighborhood and regional perspectives. *Child Development, 67*, 3338–3367.

Chase-Lansdale, P. L., Gordon, R. A., Brooks-Gunn, J., and Klebanov, P. K. (1997). Neighborhood and family influences on the intellectual and behavioral competence of preschool and early school-age children. In J. Brooks-Gunn, G. J. Duncan, and J. L. Aber (Eds.), *Neighborhood poverty: Context and consequences for children.* (Vol. 1, pp. 79–118). New York: Russell Sage Foundation.

Chen, C., and Stevenson, H. W. (1989). Homework: A cross-cultural examination. *Child Development, 60*, 551–561.

Clifford, E. (1959). Discipline in the home: A controlled observational study of parental practices. *Journal of Genetic Psychology, 95*, 45–82.

Coie, J., and Dodge, K. A. (1998). Aggression and antisocial behavior. In N. Eisenberg (Vol. Ed.) and W. Damon (Ed.), *Handbook of child psychology. Vol: 3. Social, emotional, and personality development* (5th ed., pp. 779–862). New York: Wiley.

Collins, W. A. (Ed.) (1984). *Development during middle childhood: The years from six to twelve.* Washington, DC: National Academy of Sciences U.S.A.

Collins, W. A. (1995). Relationships and development: Family adaptation to individual change. In S. Shulman (Ed.), *Close relationships and sociemotional development* (pp. 128–154). Norwood, NJ: Ablex.

Collins, W. A., Gleason, T., and Sesma, A., Jr. (1997). Internalization, autonomy, and relationships: Development during adolescence. In J. E. Grusec and L. Kuczynski (Eds.), *Parenting and children's internalization of values* (pp. 78–102). New York: Wiley.

Collins, W. A., Maccoby, E. E., Steinberg, L., Hetherington, E. M., and Bornstein, M. H. (2000). Contemporary research on parenting: The case for nature *and* nurture. *American Psychologist, 53*, 218–232.

Collins, W. A., and Russell, G. (1991). Mother–child and father–child relationships in middle childhood and adolescence. *Developmental Review, 11*, 99–136.

Compas, B. D. (1987). Coping with stress during childhood and adolescence. *Psychological Bulletin, 101*, 393–403.

Contreras, J. M., Kerns, K. A., Weimer, B. L., Gentzler, A. L., and Tomich, P. L. (2000). Emotion regulation as a mediator of associations between mother–child attachment and peer relationships in middle childhood. *Journal of Family Psychology, 14*, 111–124.

Crick, N. R., and Dodge, K. A. (1994). A review and reformulation of social information-processing mechanisms in children's social adjustment. *Psychological Bulletin, 115*, 74–101.

Crouter, A. C., Helms-Erikson, H., Updegraff, K., and McHale, S. M. (1999). Conditions underlying parents' knowledge about children's daily lives in middle childhood: Between- and within-family comparisons. *Child Development, 70*, 246–259.

Damon, W., and Hart, D. (1988). *Self-understanding in childhood and adolescence.* New York: Cambridge University Press.

Daniels, D., Dunn, J., Furstenberg, F. F., Jr., and Plomin, R. (1985). Environmental differences within the family and adjustment differences within pairs of adolescent siblings. *Child Development, 56*, 764–774.

Darling, N., and Steinberg, L. (1993). Parenting style as context: An integrative model. *Psychological Bulletin, 113*, 487–496.

Dekovic, M., and Janssens, J.M.A.M. (1992). Parents' child-rearing style and child's sociometric status. *Developmental Psychology, 28* (5), 925–932.

DeLoache, J. S., Miller, K. F., and Pierroutsakos, S. L. (1998). Reasoning and problem solving. In D. Kuhn and R. S. Siegler (Vol. Eds.) and W. Damon (Ed.), *Handbook of child psychology. Vol. 2. Cognition, perception, and language* (5th ed., pp. 801–850). New York: Wiley.

DePaulo, B., Jordan, A., Irvine, A., and Laser, P. (1982). Age changes in the detection of deception. *Child Development, 53*, 701–709.

Dishion, T. J. (1990). The family ecology of boys' peer relations in middle childhood. *Child Development, 61*, 874–892.

Dishion, T. J., Capaldi, D. M., and Yoerger, K. (1999). Middle childhood antecedents to progressions in male adolescent substance use: An ecological analysis of risk and protection. *Journal of Adolescent Research, 14*, 175–205.

Dix, T. (1991). The affective organization of parenting: Adaptive and maladaptive process. *Psychological Bulletin, 110*, 3–25.

Dix, T., Ruble, D., Grusec, J., and Nixon, S. (1986). Social cognition in parents: Inferential and affective reactions to children of three age levels. *Child Development, 57*, 879–894.

Dodge, K. A. (1980). Social cognition and children's aggressive behavior. *Child Development, 51*, 162–170.

Dodge, K. A., Bates, J. E., and Pettit, G. S. (1990). Mechanisms in the the cycle of violence. *Science, 250*, 1678–1683.

Droege, K. L., and Stipek, D. J. (1993). Children's use of dispositions to predict classmates' behavior. *Developmental Psychology, 29*, 646–654.

Dryfoos, J. (1999). The role of the school in children's out-of-school time. *The Future of Children, 9,* 117–134.

Dubow, E. F., Edwards, S., and Ippolito, M. F. (1997). Life stressors, neighborhood disadvantage, and resources: A focus on inner-city children's adjustment. *Journal of Clinical Child Psychology, 26,* 130–144.

Dubow, E. F., and Tisak, J. (1989). The relation between stressful life events and adjustment in elementary school children: The role of social support and social problem-solving skills. *Child Development, 60,* 1412–1423.

Dubow, E. F., Tisak, J., Causey, D., Hryksho, A., and Reid, G. (1991). A two-year longitudinal study of stressful life events, social support, and social problem-solving skills: Contributions to children's behavioral and academic adjustment. *Child Development, 62,* 583–599.

Duncan, G. J., Brooks-Gunn, J., and Klebanov, P. (1994). Economic deprivation and early childhood development. *Child Development, 65,* 296–318.

Dunn, J. (1992). Sisters and brothers: Current issues in developmental research. In F. Boer and J. Dunn (Eds.), *Children's sibling relationships: Developmental and clinical issues* (pp. 1–17). Hillsdale, NJ: Lawrence Erlbaum Associates.

Dunn, J., and McGuire, S. (1992). Sibling and peer relationships in childhood. *Journal of Child Psychology and Psychiatry, 33,* 67–105.

Dunn, J., and Slomkowski, C. (1992). Conflict and the development of social understanding. In C. U. Shantz and W. W. Hartup (Eds.), *Conflict in child and adolescent development* (pp. 70–92). New York: Cambridge University Press.

Eccles, J. S. (1999). The development of children ages 6 to 14. *The Future of Children, 9,* 30–44.

Eccles, J. S., Lord, S., and Buchanan, C. M. (1996). School transitions in early adolescence: What are we doing to our young people? In J. Graber, J. Brooks-Gunn, and A. C. Petersen (Eds.), *Transitions through adolescence: Interpersonal domains and context* (pp. 251–284). Mahwah, NJ: Lawrence Erlbaum Associates.

Eccles, J. S., Wigfield, A., and Schiefele, U. (1998). Motivation to succeed. In W. Damon (Eds.) and N. Eisenberg (Vol. Eds.), *Handbook of child psychology: Vol. 3. Social, emotional, and personality development* (5th ed., pp. 1017–1096). New York: Wiley.

Elicker, J., Englund, M., and Sroufe, L. A. (1992). Predicting peer competence and peer relationships in childhood from early Parent–child relationships. In R. D. Parke and G. W. Ladd (Eds.), *Family-peer relationships: Modes of linkage* (pp. 77–106). Hillsdale, NJ: Lawrence Erlbaum Associates.

Emery, R. (1989). Family violence. *American Psychologist, 44,* 321–328.

Emery, R. E., and Laumann-Billings, L. (1998). An overview of the nature, causes, and consequences of abusive family relationships: Toward differentiating maltreatment and violence. *American Psychologist, 53,* 121–135.

Emmerich, W. (1962). Variations in the parent roles as a function of parents' sex and the child's sex and age. *Merrill-Palmer Quarterly, 8,* 1–11.

Entwisle, D., and Baker, D. P. (1983). Gender and young children's expectations for performance in arithmetic. *Developmental Psychology, 29,* 200–209.

Entwisle, D., and Hayduk, L. (1982). *Early schooling.* Baltimore: Johns Hopkins University Press.

Epstein, J. L. (1983). Longitudinal effects of family-school-person interactions on student outcomes. In A. Kerckhoff (Ed.), *Research in Sociology of education and socialization* (Vol. 4, pp. 90–130). Greenwich, CT: JAI.

Epstein, J. L. (1989). The selection of friends: Changes across the grades and in different school environments. In T. J. Berndt and G. W. Ladd (Eds.), *Peer relationships in child development* (pp. 158–187). New York: Wiley.

Erdley, C. A., Cain, K. M., Loomis, C. C., Dumas-Hines, F., and Dweck, C. (1997). Relations among children's social goals, implicit personality theories, and responses to social failure. *Developmental Psychology, 33,* 263–272.

Fehrmann, P. G., Keith, T. Z., and Reimers, T. M. (1987). Home influence on school learning: Direct and indirect effects of parental involvement on high-school grades. *Journal of Educational Research, 80,* 330–337.

Feiring, C., and Lewis, M. (1991a). The development of social networks from early to middle childhood: Gender differences and the relation to school competence. *Sex Roles, 25,* 237–253.

Feiring, C., and Lewis, M. (1991b). The transition from middle childhood to early adolescence: Sex differences in the social network and perceived self-competence. *Sex Roles, 24,* 489–509.

Feldman, S. S., and Wentzel, K. R. (1990). Relations among family interaction patterns, classroom self-restraint, and academic achievement in preadolescent boys. *Journal of Educational Psychology, 82,* 813–819.

Finkelhor, D., and Dziuba-Leatherman, J. (1994). Victimization of children. *American Psychologist, 49,* 173–183.

Finnegan, R. A., Hodges, E. V. E., and Perry, D. G. (1996). Preoccupied and avoidant coping during middle childhood. *Child Development, 67,* 1318–1328.

Fischer, K. W., and Bullock, D. (1984). Cognitive development in school-age children: Conclusions and new directions. In W. A. Collins (Ed.), *Development during middle childhood: The years from six to twelve* (pp. 70–146). Washington, DC: National Academy of Sciences U.S.A.

Fisher, C. B., and Johnson, B. L. (1990). Getting mad at mom and dad: Children's changing views of family conflict. *International Journal of Behavioral Development, 13,* 31–48.

Flavell, J. H., and Miller, P. H. (1998). Social cognition. In D. Kuhn and R. S. Siegler (Vol. Eds.) and W. Damon (Ed.), *Handbook of child psychology: Vol. 2. Cognition, perception, and language* (5th ed., pp. 851–898). New York: Wiley.

Ford, M. E., Wentzel, K. R., Wood, D., Stevens, E., and Siesfeld, G. A. (1989). Processes associated with integrative social competence: Emotional and contextual influences on adolescent social responsibility. *Journal of Adolescent Research, 4,* 405–425.

Forgatch, M. S., and DeGarmo, D. S. (1999). Parenting through change: An effective prevention program for single mothers. *Journal of Consulting and Clinical Psychology, 67,* 711–724.

Franz, C. E., McClelland, D. C., and Weinberger, J. (1991). Childhood antecedents of conventional social accomplishment in midlife adults: A 36-year prospective study. *Journal of Personality and Social Psychology, 60,* 586–595.

Frome, P. M., and Eccles, J. S. (1998). Parents' influence on children's achievement-related perceptions. *Journal of Personality and Social Psychology, 74,* 435–452.

Fuligni, A. J., and Eccles, J. S. (1993). Perceived Parent–child relationships and early adolescents' orientation toward peers. *Developmental Psychology, 29,* 622–632.

Furman, W., and Buhrmester, D. (1992). Age and sex differences in perceptions of networks of personal relationships. *Child Development, 63,* 103–115.

Fury, G., Carlson, E. A., and Sroufe, L. A. (1997). Children's representations of attachment relationships in family drawings. *Child Development, 68,* 1154–1164.

Galambos, N. L., and Maggs, J. L. (1991). Out-of-school care of young adolescents and self-reported behavior. *Developmental Psychology, 27,* 644–655.

Gonzales, N. A., Pitts, S. C., Hill, N. E., and Roosa, M. W. (2000). A mediational model of the impact of interparental conflict on child adjustment in a multiethnic, low-income sample. *Journal of Family Psychology, 14,* 365–379.

Goodenough, F. L. (1931). *Anger in young children.* Minneapolis: University of Minnesota Press.

Goodnow, J. J. (1988). Children's household work: Its nature and functions. *Psychological Bulletin, 103,* 5–26.

Goodnow, J. J., and Collins, W. A. (1990). *Development according to parents: The nature, sources, and consequences of parents' ideas.* London: Lawrence, Erlbaum Associates.

Gottfried, A. E., Fleming, J. S., and Gottfried, A. W. (1998). Role of cognitively stimulating home environment in children's academic intrinsic motivation: A longitudinal study. *Child Development, 69,* 1448–1460.

Grusec, J., and Goodnow, J. J. (1994). The impact of parental discipline methods on the child's internalization of values: A reconceptualization of current points of view. *Developmental Psychology, 30,* 4–19.

Hartup, W. W. (1974). Aggression in childhood: Developmental perspectives. *American Psychologist, 29,* 226–341.

Hartup, W. W. (1984). The peer context in middle childhood. In W. A. Collins (Ed.), *Development during middle childhood: The years from six to twelve* (pp. 240–282). Washington, DC: National Academy of Sciences U.S.A.

Hartup, W. W. (1996). The company they keep: Friendships and their developmental significance. *Child Development, 67,* 1–13.

Helwig, C. C. (1997). The role of agent and social context in judgments of freedom of speech and religion. *Child Development, 68,* 484–495.

Helwig, C. C. (1998). Children's conceptions of fair government and freedom of speech. *Child Development, 69,* 518–531.

Henggeler, S. W., Edwards, J. J., Cohen, R., and Summerville, M. B. (1991). Predicting changes in children's popularity: The role of family relations. *Journal of Applied Developmental Psychology, 12,* 205–218.

Hess, R. D. and Holloway, S. D. (1984). Family and school as educational institutions. In R. D. Parke (Ed.), *Review of child development research: The family* (Vol. 7, pp. 179–222). Chicago: University of Chicago Press.

Hetherington, E. M., Bridges, M., and Insabella, G. M. (1998). What matters? What does not? Five perspectives on the association between marital transitions and children's adjustment. *American Psychologist, 53,* 167–184.

Heyman, G. D., and Dweck, C. S. (1998). Children's thinking about traits: Implications for judgments of the self and others. *Child Development, 64,* 391–403.

Heyman, G. D., and Gelman, S. A. (2000). Beliefs about the origins of human psychological traits. *Developmental Psychology, 36,* 663–678.

Hill, C. R., and Stafford, F. P. (1980). Parental care of children: Time diary estimate of quantity, predictability and variety. *Journal of Human Resources, 15,* 219–239.

Hill, H. M., and Jones, L. P. (1997). Children's and parents' perceptions of children's exposure to violence in urban neighborhoods. *Journal of the National Medical Associaton, 89,* 270–276.

Hill, H. M., Levermore, M., Twaite, J., and Jones, L. P. (1996). Exposure to community violence and social support as predictors of anxiety and social and emotional behavior among African American children. *Journal of Child and Family Studies, 5,* 399–414.

Hirsch, B. J., and Rapkin, B. D. (1987). The transition to junior high school: A longitudinal study of self-esteem, psychological symptomatology, school life, and social support. *Child Development, 58,* 1235–1243.

Hoffman, M. L. (1994). Discipline and internalization. *Developmental Psychology, 30,* 26–28.

Hunter, F. T., and Youniss, J. (1982). Changes in functions of three relations during adolescence. *Developmental Psychology, 18,* 806–811.

Huntsinger, C. S., Jose, P. E., and Larson, S. L. (1998). Do parent practices to encourage academic competence influence the social adjustment of young European American and Chinese American children? *Developmental Psychology, 34*, 747–756.

Huntsinger, C. S., Jose, P. E., Liaw, F.-R., and Ching, W.-D. (1997). Cultural differences in early mathematics learning: A comparison of Euro-American, Chinese-American, and Taiwan-Chinese families. *International Journal of Behavioral Development, 21*, 371–388.

Huston, A. C., Duncan, G. J., Granger, R., Bos, J., McLoyd, V. C., Mistry, R., Crosby, D., Gibson, C., Magnuson, K., Romich, J., and Ventura, A. (2001). Work-based anti-poverty programs for parents can enhance the school performance and social behavior of children. *Child Development, 72*, 318–336.

Huston, A. C., and Wright, J. C. (1998). Mass media and children's development. In I. E. Sigel and K. A. Renninger (Vol. Eds.) and W. Damon (Ed.), *Handbook of child psychology: Vol. 4. Child psychology in practice* (5th ed., pp. 999–1058). New York: Wiley.

Kamins, M. L., and Dweck, C. S. (1999). Person versus process praise and criticism: Implications for contingent self-worth and coping. *Developmental Psychology, 35*, 835–847.

Kerrebrock, N. and Lewit, E. M. (1999). Child Indicators: Children in self-care. *The Future of Children, 9*, 151–160.

Kliewer, W., Fearnow, M. D., and Miller, P. A. (1996). Coping socialization in middle childhood: Tests of maternal and paternal influences. *Child Development, 67*, 2339–2357.

Kokko, K., and Pulkinnen, L. (2000). Aggression in childhood and long-term unemployment in adulthood: A cycle of maladaptation and some protective factors. *Developmental Psychology, 36*, 463–472.

Koestner, R., Franz, C., and Weinberger, J. (1990). The family origins of empathic concern: A 26-year longitudinal study. *Journal of Personality and Social Psychology, 58*, 709–717.

Kuczynski, L., Marshall, S., and Schell, K. (1997). Value socialization in a bidirectional context. In J. E. Grusec and L. Kuczynski (Eds.), *Parenting and children's internalization of values* (pp. 23–50). New York: Wiley.

Kupersmidt, J. B., Griesler, P. C., DeRosier, M. E., Patterson, C. J., and Davis, P. W. (1995). Childhood aggression and peer relations in the context of family and neighborhood factors. *Child Development, 66*, 360–375.

Lazar, A., and Torney-Purta, J. (1991). The development of the subconcepts of death in young children: A short-term longitudinal study. *Child Development, 62*, 1321–1333.

Leone, C. M., and Richards, M. H. (1989). Classwork and homework in early adolescence: The ecology of achievement. *Journal of Youth and Adolescence, 18*, 531–548.

Lewis, C. C. (1981). The effects of parental firm control: A reinterpretation of findings. *Psychological Bulletin, 90*, 547–564.

Lewis, M., and Osofsky, J. (1997). Violent cities, violent streets: Children draw their neighborhoods. In J. D. Osofsky (Ed.), *Children in a violent society* (pp. 277–299). New York: Guilford.

Lorion, R. P., and Saltzman, W. (1993). Children's exposure to community violence: Following a path from concern to research to action. *Psychiatry, 56*, 55–65.

Lytton, H., and Romney, D. M. (1991). Parents' differential socialization of boys and girls: A meta-analysis. *Psychological Bulletin, 109*, 267–296.

Maccoby, E. E. (1984). Middle childhood in the context of the family. In W. A. Collins (Ed.), *Development during middle childhood: The years from six to twelve* (pp. 184–239). Washington, DC: National Academy of Sciences U.S.A.

Maccoby, E. E. (1992). The role of parents in the socialization of children: An historical overview. *Developmental Psychology, 28*, 1006–1017.

Maccoby, E. E., and Martin, J. A. (1983). Socialization in the context of the family: Parent–child interaction. In P. H. Mussen (Series Ed.) and E. M. Hetherington (Vol. Ed.), *Handbook of child psychology: Vol. 4. Socialization, personality, and social development* (3rd ed., pp. 1–101). New York: Wiley.

Malloy, T. E., Sugarman, D. B., Montvilo, R. K., and Ben-Zeev, T. (1995). Children's interpersonal perceptions: A Social Relations Analysis of perceiver and target effects. *Journal of Personality and Social Psychology, 68*, 418–426.

Malloy, T. E., Yarlas, A., Montvilo, R. K., and Sugarman, D. B. (1996). Agreement and accuracy in children's interpersonal perceptions: A Social Relations Analysis. *Journal of Personality and Social Psychology, 71*, 692–702.

Martinez, P. and Richters, J. E. (1993). The NIMH Community Violence Project II: Children's distress symptoms associated with violence exposure. *Psychiatry, 56*, 22–35.

McCloskey, L. A., Figueredo, A. J., and Koss, M. P. (1995). The effects of systemic family violence on children's mental health. *Child Development, 66*, 1239–1261.

McFadyen-Ketchum, S. A., Bates, J. E., Dodge, K. A., and Pettit, G. S. (1996). Patterns of change in early childhood aggressive-disruptive behavior: Gender differences in predictions from early coercive and affectionate Mother–child interactions. *Child Development, 67*, 2417–2433.

McGillicuddy-De Lisi, A. V., Watkins, C., and Vinchur, A. J. (1994). The effect of relationship on children's distributive justice reasoning. *Child Development, 65*, 1694–1700.

McNally, S., Eisenberg, N., and Harris, J. D. (1991). Consistency and change in maternal childrearing practices and values: A longitudinal study. *Child Development, 62*, 190–198.

Miller, D. L., and Kelley, M. L. (1991). Interventions for improving homework performance: A critical review. *School Psychology Quarterly, 6*, 174–185.

Miller, S. A., Davis, T. L., Wilde, C. A., and Brown, J. (1993). Parents' knowledge of their children's preferences. *International Journal of Behavioral Development, 16*, 35–60.

Minuchin, P., and Shapiro, E. (1983). The school as a context for social development. In P. H. Mussen (Series Ed.) and E. M. Hetherington (Vol Ed.), *Handbook of child psychology: Vol. 4. Socialization, personality, and social development* (3rd ed., pp. 197–274). New York: Wiley.

Morris, S. C., Taplin, J. E., and Gelman, S. A. (2000). Vitalism in naïve biological thinking. *Developmental Psychology, 36*, 582–595.

Newson, J., and Newson, E. (1968). *Four years old in an urban community*. Chicago: Aldine de Gruyter.

Newson, J., and Newson, E. (1976). *Seven years old in the home environment*. New York: Wiley.

Noller, P. (1980). Cross-gender effects in two-child families. *Developmental Psychology, 16*, 159–160.

Okagaki, L., and Sternberg, R. J. (1993). Parental beliefs and children's school performance. *Child Development, 64*, 36–56.

Osofsky, J. D., Wewers, S., Hann, D. M., and Fick, A. C. (1993). Chronic community violence: What is happening to our children? *Psychiatry, 56*, 36–45.

Parke, R. D., and Bhavnagri, N. P. (1989). Parents as managers of children's peer relationships. In D. Belle (Ed.), *Children's social networks and social supports* (pp. 241–259). New York: Wiley.

Parke, R. D., MacDonald, K. B., Beitel, A., and Bhavnagri, N. (1988). The role of the family in the development of peer relationships. In R. Peters and R. J. McMahon (Eds.), *Social learning systems approaches to marriage and the family* (pp. 17–44). New York: Brunner Mazel.

Parker, J. G., and Asher, S. R. (1987). Peer relations and later personal adjustment: Are low-accepted children "at risk?" *Psychological Bulletin, 102*, 357–389.

Parker, J. G., and Gottman, J. M. (1989). Social and emotional development in a relational context: Friendship interactions from early childhood to adolescence. In T. J. Berndt and G. W. Ladd (Eds.), *Peer relationships in child development* (pp. 95–131). New York: Wiley.

Patterson, G. R. (1982). *Coercive family processes*. Eugene, OR: Castalia.

Patterson, G. R. (1986). Performance models for antisocial boys. *American Psychologist, 41*, 432–444.

Patterson, G. R., and Bank, L. (1989). Some amplifier and dampening mechanisms for pathologic processes in families. In M. R. Gunnar and E. Thelen (Ed.), *Systems and development: Vol. 22. The Minnesota symposia on child psychology* (pp. 167–210). Hillsdale, NJ: Lawrence Erlbaum Associates.

Patterson, G. R., DeBaryshe, B. D., and Ramsey, E. (1989). A developmental perspective on antisocial behavior. *American Psychologist, 44*, 329–335.

Pianta, R. C., and Nimetz, S. L. (1991). Relationships between children and teachers: Associations with classroom and home behavior. *Journal of Applied Developmental Psychology, 12*, 379–393.

Pinderhughes, E. E., Dodge, K. A., Bates, J. E., Pettit, G. S., and Zelli, A. (2000). Discipline responses: Influences of parents' socioeconomic status, ethnicity, beliefs about parenting, stress, and cognitive-emotional processes. *Journal of Family Psychology, 14*, 380–400.

Pomerantz, E. M., Ruble, D. N., Frey, K. S., and Greulich, F. (1995). Meeting goals and confronting conflict: Children's changing perceptions of social comparison. *Child Development, 66*, 723–738.

Reid, M., Landesman, S., Treder, R., and Jaccard, J. (1989). "My family and friends": Six- to twelve-year old children's perceptions of social support. *Child Development, 60*, 896–910.

Richters, J. E., and Martinez, P. (1993). The NIMH Community Violence Project: I. Children as victims and witnesses to violence. *Psychiatry, 56*, 7–21.

Roberts, G. C., Block, J. H., and Block, J. (1984). Continuity and change in parents' child-rearing. *Child Development, 55*, 586–597.

Rogoff, B. S., M., Pirrotta, S., Fox, N., and White, S. (1975). Age of assignment of roles and responsibilities in children: A cross-cultural survey. *Human Development, 18*, 353–369.

Rohner, R. P., and Pettengill, S. M. (1985). Perceived parental acceptance–rejection and parental control among Korean adolescents. *Child Development, 56*, 524–528.

Rohner, R. P., and Rohner, E. C. (1981). Parental acceptance–rejection and parental control: Cross-cultural codes. *Ethnology, 20*, 245–260.

Ruck, M. D., Abramovitch, R., and Keating, D. P. (1998). Children's and adolescents' understanding of rights: Balancing nurturance and self-determination. *Child Development, 64*, 404–417.

Rudolph, K. D., Dennig, M. D., and Weisz, J. R. (1995). Determinants and consequences of children's coping in the medical setting: Conceptualization, review, and critique. *Psychological Bulletin, 118*, 328–357.

Russell, G., and Russell, A. (1987). Mother–child and father–child relationships in middle childhood. *Child Development, 58*, 1573–1585.

Rutter, M. L. (1983). Stress, coping, and development: Some issues and some questions. In N. Garmezy and M. Rutter (Eds.), *Stress, coping, and development in children* (pp. 1–41). New York: McGraw-Hill.

Schwartz, D., Dodge, K. A., Pettit, G. S., and Bates, J. E. (1997). The early socialization of aggressive victims of bullying. *Child Development, 68,* 665–675.

Selman, R. (1980). *The growth of interpersonal understanding: Developmental and clinical applications.* New York: Academic.

Selman, R., and Schultz, L. H. (1989). Children's strategies for interpersonal negotiation with peers: An interpretive/empirical approach to the study of social development. In T. J. Berndt and G. W. Ladd (Eds.), *Peer relationships in child development* (pp. 371–406). New York: Wiley.

Serbin, L. A., Powlishta, K. K., and Gulko, J. (1993). The development of sex-typing in middle childhood. *Monographs of the Society for Research in Child Development, 58* (2, Serial No. 232).

Shonkoff, J. P. (1984). The biological substrate and physical health in middle childhood. In W. A. Collins (Ed.), *Development during middle childhood: The years from six to twelve* (pp. 24–69). Washington, DC: National Academy of Sciences U.S.A.

Smetana, J. G. (1989). Adolescents' and parents' reasoning about actual family conflict. *Child Development, 60,* 1052–1067.

Smith, R. E., and Smoll, F. L. (1990). Self-esteem and children's reactions to youth sport coaching behaviors: A field study of self-enhancement processes. *Developmental Psychology, 26,* 987–993.

Sroufe, L. A., Bennett, C., Englund, M., Urban, J., and Shulman, S. (1993). The significance of gender boundaries in preadolescence: Contemporary correlates and antecedents of boundary violation and maintenance. *Child Development, 64,* 455–466.

Sroufe, L. A., Carlson, E., and Shulman, S. (1993). The development of individuals in relationships: From infancy through adolescence. In D. C. Funder, R. D. Parke, C. Tomlinson-Keasey, and K. Widaman (Eds.), *Studying lives through time: Approaches to personality and development* (pp. 315–342). Washington, DC: American Psychological Association.

Sroufe, L. A., Egeland, B., and Carlson, E. A. (1999). One social world: The integrated development of Parent–child and peer relationships. In W. A. Collins and B. Laursen (Eds.), *Relationships as developmental contexts: The Minnesota symposia on child psychology* (Vol. 30, pp. 241–261). Mahwah, NJ: Lawrence Erlbaum Associates.

Steinberg, L. (1986). Latchkey children and susceptibility to peer pressure: An ecological analysis. *Developmental Psychology, 22,* 433–439.

Steinberg, L., Elmen, J. D., and Mounts, N. S. (1989). Authoritative parenting, psychosocial maturity, and academic success among adolescents. *Child Development, 60,* 1424–1436.

Stevenson, H. W., and Lee, S. Y. (1990). Contexts of achievement. *Monographs of the Society for Research in Child Development, 55* (1–2, Serial No. 221).

Stevenson, H. W., and Newman, R. S. (1986). Long-term prediction of achievement and attitudes in mathematics and reading. *Child Development, 57,* 646–659.

Stocker, C., Dunn, J., and Plomin, R. (1989). Sibling relationships: Links with child temperament, maternal behavior, and family structure. *Child Development, 60,* 715–727.

Tolan, P. H., and Loeber, R. (1993). Antisocial behavior. In P. H. Tolan and B. Cohler (Eds.), *Handbook of clinical research and practice with adolescents* (pp. 307–331). New York: Wiley.

Towns, D. P. (1996). "Rewind the World!": An ethnographic study of inner-city African American children's perceptions of violence. *Journal of Negro Education, 65,* 375–389.

Turiel, E. (1998). The development of morality. In W. Damon (Ed.) and N. Eisenberg (Vol. Ed.), *Handbook of child psychology: Social, emotional, and personality development* (5th ed., pp. 863–932). New York: Wiley.

Underwood, M. K., Coie, J. D., and Herbsman, C. R. (1992). Display rules for anger and aggression in school-age children. *Child Development, 63,* 366–380.

Vaillant, G. E. (1977). *Adaptation to life.* Boston: Little, Brown.

Vandell, D. L., and Corasaniti, M. A. (1988). The relation between third graders' after-school care and social, academic, and emotional functioning. *Child Development, 59,* 868–875.

Vandell, D. L. and Shumow, L. (1999). After-school child care programs. *The Future of Children, 9,* 64–80.

Vuchinich, S., Bank, L., and Patterson, G. R. (1992). Parenting, peers, and the stability of antisocial behavior in preadolescent boys. *Developmental Psychology, 28,* 510–521.

Wahler, R. G. (1980). Parent insularity as a determinant of generalization success in family treatment. In S. Salzinger, J. Antrobus, and J. Glick (Eds.), *The ecosystem of the sick child* (pp. 187–200). New York: Academic.

Walker, L. J., and Taylor, J. H. (1991). Family interactions and the development of moral reasoning. *Child Development, 62,* 264–283.

Warton, P. M., and Goodnow, J. J. (1991). The nature of responsibility: Children's understanding of "your job." *Child Development, 62,* 156–165.

Watson, A. J., and Valtin, R. (1997). Secrecy in middle childhood. *International Journal of Behavioral Development, 21,* 431–452.

Welch-Ross, M. K., and Schmidt, C. R. (1996). Gender-schema development and children's constructive story memory: Evidence for a developmental model. *Child Development, 67,* 820–835.

Weiss, B., Dodge, K. A., Bates, J. E., and Pettit, G. S. (1992). Some consequences of early harsh discipline: Child aggression and a maladaptive social information processing style. *Child Development, 63*, 1321–1335.

White, K. M., Speisman, J. C., and Costos, D. (1983). Young adults and their parents. In H. D. Grotevant and C. R. Cooper (Eds.), *Adolescent development in the family: New directions in child development* (No. 22, pp. 61–76). San Francisco: Jossey-Bass.

Whitehurst, G. J., and Sonnenschein, S. (1981). The development of informative messages in referential communication: Knowing when versus knowing how. In W. P. Dickson (Ed.), *Children's oral communication skills* (pp. 127–142). New York: Academic.

Wright, J. C., Huston, A. C., Murphy, K. C., St. Peters, M., Piñon, M., Scantlin, R., and Kotler, J. (in press). The relations of early television viewing to school readiness and vocabulary of children from low income families: The Early Window Project. *Child Development.*

Wrobel, G. M., Kohler, J. K, Grotevant, H. D., and McRoy, R. G. (1998). Factors related to patterns of information exchange between adoptive parents and children in mediated adoptions. *Journal of Applied Developmental Psychology, 19*, 641–657.

Youniss, J. (1980). *Parents and peers in social development: A Sullivan–Piaget perspective.* Chicago: University of Chicago Press.

Zarbatany, L., Hartmann, D. P., and Rankin, D. B. (1990). The psychological functions of preadolescent peer activities. *Child Development, 61*, 1067–1080.

# 4

# Parenting Adolescents

Laurence Steinberg
Jennifer S. Silk
*Temple University*

## INTRODUCTION

The family's transition out of middle childhood brings with it a new set of issues and concerns for parents and children that arise when the interpersonal equilibrium established during middle childhood is perturbed by the intraindividual and contextual changes associated with early adolescence. Although the vast majority of families are able to negotiate this transition successfully, establishing a new equilibrium as well as surviving the temporary period of disequilbrium that precedes it, this period challenges the emotional resources of even the most well-functioning families. Indeed, when parents are asked which period in their child's development that they are most nervous and apprehensive about, adolescence tops the list (Pasley and Gecas, 1984).

Part of parents' anxiety about adolescence no doubt stems from widespread and erroneous stereotypes of adolescents as difficult, oppositional, and moody—stereotypes that pervade popular culture, fill the pages of parenting magazines, and define the content of advice books aimed at parents with teenagers. Even a cursory glance at the titles of the books and articles aimed at this market suggests that surviving, rather than thriving, is the goal toward which parents should strive. The contrast between the tenor of books written about parenting infants and those written about parenting adolescents is striking. As we have noted elsewhere (Steinberg, 2001), the parenting sections of bookstores are stocked with books advising parents on how to enjoy and promote the development of their cuddly infants alongside volumes on how to discipline their spiteful and problem-ridden teenagers.

Although some portion of parents' apprehensiveness about adolescence is rooted in misinformation, not all of it is. Some measure of parental anxiety is no doubt warranted by the very real fact that adolescence is a period of dramatic change in the child's physical, cognitive, emotional, and social competencies and concerns. With the possible exception of toddlerhood (Edwards and Liu, in Vol. 1 of this *Handbook*)—the other period in the child's development about which parents are often unsure—no developmental period brings with it such remarkable or rapid transformation in the child as does adolescence. The fact that this transformation typically occurs during a time when parents themselves may be grappling with a new set of difficult psychological issues, brought on by their own passage into midlife, makes the family's transition into adolescence all the more challenging for both the parent and the adolescent (Steinberg and Steinberg, 1994).

In the pages that follow, we update and extend the chapter on adolescence that appeared in the previous (1995) edition of this *Handbook*. Our perspective is influenced by several theoretical orientations, including those used by scholars of the family life cycle (e.g., Rodgers, 1973), by family systems theorists (e.g., Minuchin, 1974), and by human ecologists (e.g., Bronfenbrenner, 1979). From family life cycle theorists we take the position that families, like individuals, move through distinct, qualitatively different stages over the course of time that are defined by unique sets of individual and interpersonal phenomena. Accordingly, in the next section of this chapter we ask what it is about the child's adolescent years that makes this a unique period for the family.

From family systems theorists, we take the view that the family is best understood as a system of relationships that change in response to the changing needs and concerns of family members. Like other living systems, families attempt to maintain a sense of equilibrium in their relationships. As the family moves from one stage of the family life cycle to the next—for example, from middle childhood into adolescence—the equilibrium established during the former stage is often disrupted, or perturbed, by changes in one or more family members or in the context in which the family lives. Thus we view the challenge of adolescence for families as revolving around the need to establish a new, qualitatively different, equilibrium. In view of this, and consistent with the extant literature on parent–adolescent relationships, our emphasis in this chapter is on early and middle adolescence, the likely periods, respectively, of disequilibrium and reestablished equilibrium in family relationships.

Finally, from the study of the ecology of human development we take the view that the internal workings of the family take place within a broader context that shapes family functioning. This context includes the other settings in which family members function (e.g., the adolescent's school, the parents' workplace), the immediate community in which the family lives, and the more distal influences of culture, economics, and historical time. A discussion of these contextual influences on parenting during adolescence is beyond the scope of this chapter (see Harkness and Super, in Vol. 2 of this *Handbook*; Hoff, Laursen, and Tardif, in Vol. 2 of this *Handbook*; Lerner, Rothbaum, Boulos, and Castellino, in Vol. 2 of this *Handbook*), but the reader should bear in mind that much of what we say about parenting adolescents here is derived from research and theory about parent–adolescent relationships in contemporary industrialized society.

We begin this chapter with a discussion of the primary sources of perturbation in the family system as a child enters adolescence. These perturbations include developmental changes in the adolescent, such as the physical, cognitive, self-definitional, and social changes that typically accompany a child's transition into adolescence. Changes in the child's social context during adolescence, as well as changes in the parent's life as the child reaches adolescence, are also discussed as important sources of pertubation in family life. In the second section of the chapter we review historical perspectives on the task of reestablishing an equilibrium between parent and child in response to the perturbations previously discussed. Building on the current view of adolescence as a time of normative developmental changes and renegotiation of relationships, in the third section we review normative changes with respect to three primary dimensions of the parent–adolescent relationship: autonomy, harmony, and conflict. We discuss individual differences in these dimensions as functions of demographic and socioeconomic characteristics of families in the fourth section. In the fifth section, we take up the question of whether and in what ways individual differences in parent–adolescent relationships and parenting practices are associated with differences in psychosocial adjustment among adolescents. We end this chapter with some remarks regarding directions for future research and a few concluding comments.

## SOURCES OF PERTURBATION IN THE FAMILY AT ADOLESCENCE

Three sets of interrelated developments combine to perturb the equilibrium established in most families by the end of middle childhood: (1) developmental changes associated with the child's passage from childhood into adolescence, (2) changes in the child's social context at adolescence, and (3) developmental changes associated with the parent's experience of midlife.

### Developmental Changes of Adolescence

*Pubertal changes and implications for parents.*   Perhaps the most obvious developmental change of adolescence is the onset of puberty. Physical and sexual maturation profoundly affect the way that adolescents view themselves and the way that they are viewed and treated by others, including their parents. The chief physical manifestations of puberty include a rapid acceleration in growth, the development of primary and secondary sex characteristics, changes in body composition, and changes in the circulatory and respiratory systems (Marshall, 1978). These changes result in dramatic increases in height and weight and in the quantity and distribution of fat and muscle. Reproductive maturation involves the maturation of the gonads as well as changes in the genitals and breasts; the growth of pubic, facial, and body hair; and the further development of the sex organs. The timing of pubertal events varies between girls and boys and also varies within gender. The onset of puberty can occur as early as 7 years of age in girls and $9\frac{1}{2}$ in boys or as late as 13 in girls and $13\frac{1}{2}$ in boys.

Pubertal changes are stimulated by an increase in sex hormones during puberty. Popular portrayals warn parents to expect dramatic mood swings from their teenage children, who are depicted as powerless against the "raging hormones" coursing through their veins. Evidence for hormonally driven moodiness in adolescence, however, is far weaker than popular stereotypes would suggest (Brooks-Gunn, Graber, and Paikoff, 1994; Buchanan, Eccles, and Becker, 1992; Richards and Larson, 1993). When studies do find a connection between hormones and mood it is typically in early adolescence, during which fluctuations in hormones are associated with greater irritability and aggression among males and depression among females (Buchanan et al., 1992). Rapid mood swings during adolescence, to the extent that they do occur, are not driven by hormonal changes, however, but are closely linked to adolescents' behaviors, companions, and other situational factors, suggesting that adolescents may be moodier than adults because they change activities and contexts more often than adults do.

Although adolescence may not be associated with greater moodiness than childhood (Buchanan et al., 1992; Larson, Csikszentmihalyi, and Graef, 1980; Larson and Lampman-Petraitis, 1989), it is clearly associated with increases in negative affect. Adolescents report experiencing negative moods more often than preadolescents or adults do (Larson and Asmussen, 1991; Larson et al., 1980; Larson and Lampman-Petraitis, 1989). The increase in negative affect during adolescence indeed poses a challenge for parents of teenagers, but this challenge has been vastly exaggerated in popular accounts and cultural stereotypes. In effect, parents can expect their adolescents to spend more time "down in the dumps" at this developmental juncture. As a result, parents may need to recalibrate their reactions to their children's negative emotions.

Although hormonal changes appear to have few direct effects on adolescent emotionality or behavior, pubertal changes may perturb the parent–adolescent relationship in a more indirect fashion, by changing family members' views of themselves and each other (Brooks-Gunn et al., 1994; Paikoff and Brooks-Gunn, 1990; Peterson and Taylor, 1980; Steinberg and Steinberg, 1994). First, the biological changes of puberty cause changes in the adolescent's self-image, which in turn may affect how she or he behaves toward parents. Second, physical maturation leads to changes in appearance that, in turn, lead to changes in treatment by parents (Leffert and Petersen, 1996; Steinberg, 1988). The changes associated with puberty are a constant and visible reminder to parents that their child is growing up. Often physical changes may be asynchronous with cognitive or emotional changes, leading parents to overestimate or underestimate their adolescent's needs and capabilities.

In many families, puberty seems to create emotional distance between parents and their adolescents. As youngsters mature from childhood toward the middle of puberty, distance between adolescents and parents increases and conflict intensifies (Laursen, Coy, and Collins, 1998; Paikoff and Brooks-Gunn, 1991). The change that takes place is reflected in an increase in "negatives" (e.g., conflict, complaining, anger) and, to a lesser extent, a decrease in "positives" (e.g., support, smiling, laughter) (e.g., Flannery, Torquati, and Lindemeier, 1994; Holmbeck and Hill, 1991a). Because this connection between pubertal maturation and parent–child distance is not affected by the age at which the adolescent goes through puberty, it suggests that something about puberty in particular may transform the parent–child bond. Interestingly, puberty increases distance between children and their parents in most species of monkeys and apes, and some have argued that the pattern seen in human adolescents may have an evolutionary basis (Steinberg, 1989). Although puberty seems to distance adolescents from their parents, it is not associated with familial "storm and stress," and rates of outright conflict between parents and children are not dramatically higher during adolescence than before or after (Laursen et al., 1998).

*Cognitive changes and implications for parents.*    In addition to noticing that their children look more like adults, parents of adolescents begin to notice that their children are also thinking more like adults. Developmentalists assert competing theories about the exact nature of cognitive change during adolescence; however, most agree that adolescents think in ways that are more advanced, more efficient, and generally more effective than those of younger children. During adolescence individuals become better able than children to think about the abstract and the hypothetical. Advances in "metacognition" also occur, such that adolescents begin thinking about the process of thinking itself. Finally, adolescent thinking becomes more multidimensional and relativistic (Keating, 1990).

Like the physical changes of puberty, the cognitive changes of adolescence perturb the equilibrium established by the parent and the child during middle childhood. Adolescents bring a new cognitive frame to family discussions, decisions, and arguments, thus challenging the way the family functions in discussing affairs and making decisions. As children mature cognitively, they may want to be treated more like adults and to have greater say in family decisions. A reorganized equilibrium will entail that parents recognize the adolescent's increased cognitive capacities—as well as some remaining intellectual limitations—and allow for gradual increases in decision-making opportunities.

In addition to changes in the way adolescents approach decision making, parents will find that adolescents begin to view social conventions and moral standards in a more relativistic fashion. A temporary period of conflict may accompany the adolescent's realization of the subjectivity of social conventions and moral standards. During adolescence, absolutes and rules come to be questioned, as the young person begins to see that moral standards and social conventions are subjective and sometimes arbitrary. According to Smetana, this "discovery" may underlie the bickering and squabbling over mundane issues often seen in families with adolescents (Smetana, 1988a, 1988b, 1989; Smetana and Asquith, 1994; Yau and Smetana, 1996). When teens and parents argue about attire, curfews, or tattoos, each may define the point of contention differently. Parents are likely to see these as issues of "right" and "wrong" by social custom or convention; adolescents, in contrast, are likely to define these same issues as matters of personal choice. Smetana believes that teenagers and their parents often clash more over the *definition* of the issue (that is, as a matter of custom versus a matter of personal choice) than over the specific details. The struggle, then, is over who has the authority—and into whose "jurisdiction" the issue falls (Smetana, 1995). As a consequence of normal cognitive development, a child who is willing to accept parents' views of right and wrong—who does not question his or her mother when she says, "We do not leave clothes on the floor"—grows into an adolescent who understands that some issues are matters of personal choice, rather than social convention ("It's *my* room, so why should it bother *you*?").

Parents are understandably distraught as they watch their adolescents challenge and reject valued rules and regulations. Some parents may feel as though their adolescent is rejecting their own value and judgment as a parent. For the adolescent, arguments over values and rules serve to "flex" newly developed cognitive muscles; but from the standpoint of the parent, such arguments may be experienced as matters of personal rejection or failure as a parent (Steinberg, 2001). In most families, this period of conflict is gradually resolved as older adolescents come to see the value in many social conventions and parents come to respect the authority and jurisdiction of their maturing child.

*Self-definitional changes.* As adolescents mature cognitively and physically, they begin to search for a firm sense of who they are and how they fit into the social world in which they live. The establishment of autonomy and identity are normative developmental tasks of adolescence, the effects of which may also reverberate throughout the family. The normal drive of adolescents to establish themselves as separate individuals with unique identities may clash with the parents' desire to maintain their children's dependence and impart their own set of values. Furthermore, the increased responsibility, independence, and freedom that accompany the transition from childhood to adulthood, combined with the attainment of an adultlike physical appearance, lead adolescents to feel as though they should be treated more like adults. Parents may not be ready to grant adolescents the autonomy or independence that they seek, leading to conflicts over rules, regulations, and rights.

*Social changes.* Adolescents' physical, cognitive, and self-definitional changes are accompanied by developmental transitions within the social realm. As children enter the teenage years, they begin to spend less time with their families (Larson, Richards, Moneta, Holmbeck, and Duckett, 1996). This decrease remains throughout the middle school and high school years and is attributed to increasing opportunities for recreational, academic, and social activities outside the family setting. As adolescents interact less with their parents, peer relationships take on greater importance in adolescents' lives (Berndt, 1989; Buhrmester, 1996; Savin-Williams and Berndt, 1990). Although parents typically remain very important influences in adolescents' lives, peers begin to take on roles that previously fell almost entirely within the parent's domain. Peers act as emotional confidantes (Gottman and Mettetal, 1986), provide each other with advice and guidance (Buhrmester, 1996), and serve as influential models of behavior and attitude (Sussman et al., 1994). Parents may find it difficult to share such important roles and may begin to feel shut out of their adolescents' lives. Families may have a tough time adjusting to the adolescent's increasing interest in forgoing family activities for peer activities. Furthermore, whereas parents likely exerted a strong influence in determining which individuals their children developed friendships with during childhood, in adolescence, peer associations are often beyond the realm of parents' control. Thus parents may find their teenage children seeking advice from or modeling themselves after peers whom the parents find objectionable.

Even when parents approve of their teenagers' friends (and teenagers more often than not choose friends with values similar to those of their parents), they may find that peer influences on their adolescents' behaviors are not always consonant with their own judgments or preferences. Although peers can and do influence each other in positive ways (e.g., Mounts and Steinberg 1995; Wentzel and Caldwell 1997), the influence of peers may also lead the adolescent toward experimentation with tobacco, alcohol, and other drugs, as well as delinquency (Urberg, Degirmencioglu, and Pilgrim, 1997). The adolescent peer context also begins to encompass interaction with opposite-gender peers and the initiation of dating. As the adolescent makes a developmentally appropriate transition into a peer-oriented youth culture, the parent is thus confronted with an entirely new set of worries and concerns about their child (e.g. drugs, alcohol, delinquency, driving, sexual activity). Although this picture sounds bleak for the parent of an adolescent, evidence suggests that parents continue to influence the behaviors and the decisions of their children well into the teen years in extremely important ways (Blum and Rinehart, 2000; Collins, Maccoby, Steinberg, Hetherington, and Bornstein, 2000).

In sum, normative developmental changes often perturb the family system in ways that challenge parents and teens to renegotiate their relationships. The onset of puberty leads to transformations in appearance and stature that change the way parents perceive their offspring. Additionally, hormonal changes result in sexual maturation as well as increased negative affect, both of which present new challenges to the parent. Pubertal changes are also followed by an increase in emotional distance between parents and their adolescent children. Cognitive developments during adolescence necessitate changes in decision-making practices within families. In particular, the adolescent's increasing understanding of the subjectivity of conventions and moral standards may lead the teenager to challenge previously accepted parental rules and regulations. As adolescents begin to look and think more like adults, they also begin to perceive themselves as autonomous individuals and may attempt to assert this autonomy in ways that parents are not yet prepared for. This period requires a balance between the adolescent's desire for independence and parents' desire to maintain a sense of control over their teen's decisions and activities. Socially, adolescents become less interested in spending time with their parents, instead devoting the bulk of their social interest and energies to their same-gender and opposite-gender peers. Parents must adjust to their new role as important but less salient figures in their teen's life. As we have suggested, these perturbations in multiple domains of adolescent development often destabilize the parent–adolescent relationship for a period of time, as both teens and parents find ways to renegotiate a relationship that is appropriate to the teen's increasingly adultlike appearance, intellect, and social interests.

## Changes in the Child's Social Context

Just as adolescence brings with it a set of developmental transitions for the individual, it also signals transitions within the surrounding social context. In fact, a near-universal aspect of adolescence is some sort of recognition that the individual's status has changed—a social redefinition of the individual. Indeed, some theorists have argued that the nature of adolescence is far more influenced by the way in which society defines the economic and the social roles of young people than by the biological or cognitive changes of the period. As a result of this change in social definition, adolescents in Western industrialized society experience a loosening of restrictions and increased autonomy and opportunity in a number of realms. Adolescents may welcome this newfound freedom, but parents may find such social transitions a challenge to their ability to monitor and control behaviors, influences, and activities in their teenagers' lives.

*Increases in unsupervised time.*   Researchers studying how individuals utilize their time have noted that unconstrained or "free" time is greater during adolescence than during any other period of life (Kleiber and Rickards, 1985). Leisure occupies more of the typical adolescent's waking hours than do school and work combined (Larson, 2000). For the adolescent, much of this free time is spent in activities that go unsupervised by adults. This increase in unsupervised activity results both from greater autonomy seeking on the part of the adolescent and a loosening of societal and structural restrictions imposed on younger children (see Collins, Madsen, and Susman-Stillman, in Vol. 1 of this *Handbook*). For example, younger children typically spend the afterschool hours in structured afterschool programs, at home, or in the neighborhood under the supervision of parents (the neighbor's parents if not their own). In contrast, there are far fewer opportunities for teenagers to engage in structured afterschool activities. Part-time jobs appear to offer adult supervision, but in-depth research shows that most jobs occupied by teenagers afford little opportunity for adult interaction (Greenberger and Steinberg, 1981). For many adolescents, changing societal norms and restrictions give rise to greater geographic mobility—they can take public transportation by themselves and, by middle adolescence, they can obtain a driver's license.

How do parents deal with the new "licenses," vehicular and otherwise, that society grants teenagers? The adolescent's geographic mobility and decreased supervision make it more difficult for parents to monitor their children's whereabouts and control their activities. Even if the teen holds an afterschool job, parents have little control over the adolescent's interactions, influences, and activities while they are at work. This period tests the boundaries of trust within the parent–adolescent relationship, as parents must allow their teens some leeway to make their own decisions (and mistakes) regarding how, where, and with whom to spend their free time. Parental concern about adolescents' time in unsupervised and unstructured activity is warranted, in that antisocial behavior is more frequent among adolescents whose free time is so characterized (Osgood, Wilson, O'Malley, Bachman, and Johnston, 1996). Evidence suggests, however, that well-adjusted adolescents (those who do well in school and report fewer problem behaviors) tend to have parents who know who their friends are, where they spend free time, and what kinds of things they do (e.g., Pettit, Bates, Dodge, and Meece, 1999). Parents are challenged to find ways of *monitoring* adolescent activities without being able to directly supervise or control these activities. This entails a new equilibrium in which parents and adolescents strike a balance between autonomy and control in the adolescent's daily activities.

*Increased expectations for autonomy in school.*   This balance between autonomy and control must also be established with regard to the adolescent's academic activities. The transition from elementary to secondary school is generally accompanied by greater expectations for autonomy and self-management by the adolescent on the part of the school system and the parent. In elementary school, teachers often provide parents with direct information about important assignments and school activities as well as frequent feedback about children's school performances. Parents of adolescents, however, must rely more on the child to keep them informed about what is going on in school and to request their assistance when necessary. Again, the parent and the adolescent must find an effective balance between autonomy and control. Ideally, in this balance, the parent fosters self-direction and autonomy in academic endeavors, but also monitors the adolescent's educational activities enough to ensure that academic needs and potentials are met (Steinberg, Lamborn, Dornbusch, and Darling, 1992).

*Increased exposure to self-selected mass media.*   The lower level of parental control found at home and in school applies to adolescents' recreational activities as well. Adolescents spend an enormous amount of recreational time utilizing mass media, including television, movies, music, magazines, and the Internet (Roberts, Foehr, Rideout, and Brodie, 1999). Adolescents are typically allowed to exert greater control over the content of their media consumption than younger children, whose choice of TV, movies, and music is monitored more by parents and cultural restrictions (e.g., ratings on movies and compact disks). This increased control over media consumption on the part of adolescents results in a process of self-socialization, whereby teens are socialized by influences of their own choosing. It becomes increasingly difficult for parents to supervise, control, or even keep abreast of such influences. The majority of teens, in fact, have access to mass media from within the privacy of their own bedrooms—making parental monitoring especially difficult (Roberts et al., 1999). Furthermore, the content of mass media may contribute to parents' anxieties about adolescent well-being. The lyrics of many popular songs, for example, send messages to teens that may be in direct contradiction to the messages that parents have attempted to instill.

In sum, changes within the adolescent's social context also may perturb the parent–adolescent relationship. Increases in unsupervised free time and mobility both serve to decrease parental knowledge and authority over adolescent activities and companions. Adolescents spend much of this free time utilizing self-selected mass media, such as music and TV, that may not be consonant with parents' socialization goals or values. Monitoring, rather than direct supervision, becomes the primary way for parents to stay abreast of their teen's recreational activities, although parents must rely on their adolescents to keep them informed of academic developments and activities as well. Teenagers have many choices about how to spend their time, and parents have much less of a role in facilitating or determining how this time is spent compared with when their children were younger. Parents may have difficulty relinquishing much of their control of their adolescents' recreational and academic contexts and may find themselves in disagreement over their teens' decisions about how to spend their time.

## The Adolescent's Parents at Midlife

Much scholarship throughout the past two decades has been devoted to the developmental challenges encountered by the adolescent and changes in the adolescent's social context; however, few researchers have seriously considered the developmental needs of the parent at this stage of life. The literature on adolescent development suggests that children may actually navigate the transition into adolescence with relative ease, whereas it is *parents* that find adolescence to be a weathering journey (Steinberg, 2001). In families with middle-aged adults, adjusting to adolescence appears to take more of a toll on the mental health of parents than on the mental health of adolescents (Steinberg and Steinberg, 1994). Several studies have found this period in the family life cycle to be a low point in parents' marital and life satisfaction, as well as a period of heightened risk for divorce (Gecas and Seff, 1990; Gottman and Levenson, 2000). Repetitive bickering over mundane issues appears to have a cost for parental mental health, especially among mothers, who bear the brunt of the frontline action in most households (Silverberg and Steinberg, 1987). The deidealization of the parent by the adolescent is especially difficult for many parents to cope with (Steinberg and Steinberg, 1994). These findings highlight the need for a closer look at the developmental challenges that confront many parents around the time their children become adolescents.

Today, the typical parent is close to 40 years old when her or his first child enters early adolescence. A growing body of evidence suggests that the period surrounding the age of 40 (sometimes referred to as a midlife crisis) can be a potentially difficult time for many adults (Farrell and Rosenberg, 1981; Levinson, 1978). Many families experience a clash between the psychological issues of adolescence and the psychological issues of midlife (Steinberg and Steinberg, 1994). For example, at the same time that adolescents are entering into a period of rapid physical growth, sexual maturation, and, ultimately, the period of the lifespan that society has labeled one of the most physically attractive, their parents are beginning to feel increased concern about their own bodies, about their physical attractiveness, and about their reproductive ability or sexual appeal (Gould, 1972).

A second overlap of crises concerns perceptions of time and the future. At the same time that adolescents are beginning to develop the capability to think systematically about the future, their parents are beginning to feel that the possibilities for change are limited. Whereas adolescents' ideas about the future are becoming more expansive, their parents' ideas are probably becoming more limited. One reason for this shift may be that midlife adults are reminded of their mortality because they see their own parents aging. In fact, adolescence is often a time in which three generations (the adolescent, the middle-aged parent, and the older grandparent) are simultaneously undergoing developmental transitions that involve the appraisal and reappraisal of life goals, leaving the adolescent's parent feeling "sandwiched." Adolescents are on the threshold of gaining a great deal of status. Their careers and marriages lie ahead of them, and their choices seem limitless. For their parents, in contrast, many choices have already been made—some successfully, others perhaps less so. Most adults reach their occupational plateau during midlife, and many must deal with whatever gap exists between their early aspirations and their actual achievements (Gould, 1972). In sum, for adolescents, this phase in the family life cycle is a time of boundless horizons; for their parents, it is a time of coming to terms with choices made when they were younger. This overlap of crises is likely to have an impact on family life, again potentially upsetting the interpersonal equilibrium established in middle childhood (Hamill, 1994; Steinberg and Steinberg, 1994).

A parent may be especially adversely affected by the transition of the child into adolescence if the child is the same-gender. Mothers of daughters and fathers of sons, for example, show more psychological distress, report less satisfaction with their marriage, and experience more intense midlife identity concerns as their children begin to mature physically, get involved in dating relationships, and distance themselves from their parents emotionally. Parents who are deeply involved in work outside the home or who have an especially happy marriage may be buffered against some of these negative consequences, whereas single mothers may be especially vulnerable to these effects (Kalil and Eccles, 1993; Koski and Steinberg, 1990; MacDermid and Crouter, 1995; Silverberg, Marczak, and Gondoli, 1996; Silverberg and Steinberg, 1987, 1990; Steinberg and Silverberg, 1987; Steinberg and Steinberg, 1994). These studies of factors that influence parental mental health during the adolescent years are important, because research shows that parents who are emotionally distressed (e.g., depressed, anxious, self-doubting) feel and are less effective as parents (Gondoli and Silverberg, 1997).

In sum, the parent of an adolescent is often faced with a set of personal developmental changes that can make the task of parenting a teenager especially challenging. Adults at midlife may feel increased concern about their physical appearance or life choices. These issues are especially salient in the face of their adolescent's budding opportunities and physical and sexual maturation. Additionally, parent–adolescent bickering over mundane issues, as well as parental deidealization, may take a toll on parents' mental health. The period in which one's child enters adolescence has been characterized as a low point in life satisfaction for parents, and it appears especially difficult for parents of the same gender as that of their adolescent.

## FEATURES OF THE NEW PARENT–CHILD EQUILIBRIUM AT ADOLESCENCE: HISTORICAL PERSPECTIVES

Although scholars of adolescence have long agreed that the parent–child relationship is transformed as the child moves into adolescence, there have been important shifts over time in how the process and the outcome of this transformation have been described. In actuality, there has been a remarkable shift over the past half-century in our view of what constitutes healthy family functioning in adolescence. Whereas early, psychoanalytically guided conceptualizations of family functioning emphasized parent–adolescent conflict as necessary and adolescent detachment as the desirable outcome of the process, contemporary models view conflict as far from inevitable, associate intense parent–adolescent conflict with problematic development, and see the healthy endpoint of the family's transition into adolescence as one in which the adolescent has established a sense of individuality within the context of close, not distant, family relationships.

### Detachment and Psychoanalytic Theory

Orthodox psychoanalytic perspectives on adolescent development (e.g., Freud, 1958) held that the healthy adolescent's task was to "detach" from her or his parents. Detachment, triggered by the biological changes of puberty and their sexual sequelae, was characterized by intrafamilial storm and stress, and adolescent rebellion was viewed as both an inevitable and normative response to puberty—the "second Oedipal" event (Adelson and Doehrman, 1980; see Lerner et al., in Vol. 2 of this *Handbook*). From the analytic vantage point, intense parent–adolescent conflict was seen as normative, and parent–adolescent harmony, at least in the extreme, was viewed as developmentally stunting and symptomatic of intrapsychic immaturity. According to this view, parenting that tolerated and permitted detachment would facilitate adaptive psychosocial development among adolescents.

The psychoanalytic view held that adolescent detachment abruptly terminates the latency, or preadolescent, period. In response to the resurgence of latent drives, the formerly obedient and respectful young adolescent "regresses" to a more psychologically primitive state and turns spiteful, vengeful, oppositional, and unpredictable (Freud, 1958). This disjunctive view of adolescence implies that a history of parent–child harmony immediately before adolescence was more or less irrelevant to the development of inevitably stormy parent–child relations in adolescence.

## Individuation and Neoanalytic Theory

Orthodox analytic views of the detachment process gave way to more tempered, neoanalytic theories that emphasized the process of adolescent "individuation" rather than detachment. The normative goal of adolescence shifted from overt detachment and conflict to more of an intrapsychic separation from the parent. Blos (1979) described individuation as the adolescent's development of a more distinct sense of herself or himself as psychologically separate from her or his parents. The process of individuation, which begins during infancy and continues well into late adolescence, involves a gradual, progressive sharpening of one's sense of self as autonomous, as competent, and as separate from one's parents. Neoanalytic perspectives generally downplay the behavioral storminess of the adolescent's movement toward emotional and behavioral emancipation stressed in orthodox psychoanalytic models (Adelson and Doehrman, 1980).

In Blos's view, the individuation process is marked by the repudiation of parents, but much of the process is cognitive, not behavioral, and successful individuation is not necessarily accompanied by overt rebellion or oppositionalism (Josselson, 1980). According to the neoanalytic perspective, day-to-day squabbling and bickering between the adolescent and parents are reflective of the adolescent's inner turmoil as she or he negotiates the intrapsychic process of individuation. Although the healthy endpoint in this model is individuation rather than detachment, the basic premise still holds that parent–adolescent conflict is the chief mechanism through which relationships are transformed. Furthermore, the new equilibrium that ensues involves a more "separate" adolescent who has rejected her or his parent, if only in a cognitive or intrapsychic sense.

## Integrating Individuality and Connectedness

Psychoanalytic and neoanalytic models of parent–adolescent relationships came under attack in the late 1970s and early 1980s on the basis of a growing body of empirical evidence that challenged the view that detachment was desirable, or even typical. The weight of the empirical evidence to date indicates that the portrait of family storm and stress painted by early analytic writers is excessively pessimistic. Most research indicates that, among the 25% of teenagers and parents who report having problems during adolescence, approximately 80% had problematic relationships during childhood (Rutter, Graham, Chadwick, and Yule, 1976). In fact, only approximately 5% of families who enjoy positive relationships during childhood can expect to develop serious problems during adolescence (Steinberg, 1990). The view that adolescent detachment and family strain are inherent features of family life during adolescence may accurately describe families of adolescents with problems, but does not apply to the normal population of young people and their parents.

In light of these findings, new models of adolescent–parent relationships acknowledge the adolescent's need to individuate and establish a sense of emotional autonomy, but view this process as one that is healthiest when it occurs in the context of an emotionally close parent–child relationship. The term transformation replaces the term severing as a more accurate descriptor of relationship change at this stage of the life cycle (Grotevant, 1998). The new equilibrium is one in which a healthily individuated adolescent (responsible, independent, competent) enjoys warm and close relationships with parents who have gradually permitted increases in the adolescent's autonomy. Conflict is one possible route to this endpoint, but it is not the only one, nor necessarily the most desirable. In psychoanalytic and neoanalytic frameworks, parents were more or less passive participants in the individuation/detachment process. They were "objects" from which the adolescent separated. In new models, parents are seen as active participants in the process who can facilitate healthy emotional development by granting age-appropriate autonomy while maintaining a warm and involved relationship.

This is not to deny that adolescence is often a time of heightened conflict and perturbation of the family system. As mentioned previously, the early adolescent period is characterized by heightened bickering and squabbling and diminished levels of positive interaction. However, these perturbations in family relationships typically do not threaten the emotional cohesion of the parent–child bond. Generally speaking, families with psychologically competent teenagers interact in ways that permit family members to express their autonomy while remaining attached, or "connected," to other family members (Grotevant, 1998; Rathunde, 1996; Silverberg, Tennenbaum, and Jacob, 1992). In these families, verbal give-and-take is the norm, and adolescents (as well as parents) are encouraged to express their own opinions, even if this sometimes leads to disagreement. At the same time, however, the importance of maintaining close relationships in the family is emphasized, and individuals are encouraged to consider how their actions may affect other family members (Rueter and Conger, 1995a, 1995b).

The balance between individuality and connectedness may be facilitated by a recognition of the reciprocity of the parent–adolescent relationship (Youniss and Smollar, 1985). Both parties (parent and adolescent) actively participate in the mutual and reciprocal process of redefining the relationship. As Youniss and colleagues have noted, transformation of the relationship from one of unilateral authority to one of cooperative negotiation is necessary for the adolescent's social and psychological development to proceed on course; a severing of the parent–adolescent bond jeopardizes this process. In healthy families, adolescents remain responsive to parental authority and continue to seek parental advice, but they do so against a backdrop of greater freedom.

In support of these models, evidence shows that adolescents who are permitted to assert their own opinions within a family context that is secure and loving develop higher self-esteem and more mature coping abilities. In contrast, adolescents whose autonomy is squelched are at risk for developing feelings of depression, and those who do not feel connected are more likely than their peers to develop behavior problems (Allen, Hauser, Bell, and O'Conner, 1994; Allen, Hauser, Eickholt, Bell, and O'Conner, 1994; Hauser, Powers, and Noam, 1991).

## DEVELOPMENTAL CHANGES IN THE PARENT–ADOLESCENT RELATIONSHIP: AUTONOMY, HARMONY, AND CONFLICT

These models of transformations in the parent–adolescent relationship all highlight scholars' consensus that family relationships during this period differ in significant ways from family relations before to the perturbations of adolescence. Researchers interested in tracking changes in parent–child relationships during adolescence have focused primarily on three overarching dimensions: (1) autonomy (the extent to which the adolescent is under the control of the parents), (2) harmony (the extent to which the parent–adolescent relationship is warm, involved, and emotionally close), and (3) conflict (the extent to which the parent–adolescent relationship is contentious and hostile). Within the study of autonomy, distinctions are usually drawn between psychological control (control of the adolescent's opinions, feelings, and thoughts) and behavioral control (control of the adolescent's activities) because they appear to have different effects on adolescent development, with adolescents profiting from relatively less psychological control and relatively more behavioral control. Although one could make comparable distinctions among different aspects of harmony (e.g., affection, involvement, emotional closeness) or among different aspects of conflict (e.g., hostility, contentiousness, coercion), empirical study indicates that drawing such distinctions does not typically result in an improved understanding of the parent–adolescent relationship or its impact on adolescent development.

### Developmental Changes in Parenting and Adolescent Autonomy

The shift toward increased autonomy in adolescence is probably the most salient of all the relational changes to occur. In most families, there is a movement during adolescence from patterns of influence and interaction that are asymmetrical and unequal to ones in which parents and their adolescent children are on a more equal footing. As we noted earlier, the development of autonomy within the parent–adolescent relationship can be seen more as a realignment than a detachment or severing of ties (Guisinger and Blatt, 1994). In general, autonomous adolescents report that they are quite close to their parents, enjoy doing things with their families, have few conflicts with their mothers and fathers, feel free to turn to their parents for advice, and say they would like to be like their parents (Kandel and Lesser, 1972). Strained family relationships appear to be associated with a lack of autonomy during adolescence, rather than with its presence (Bomar and Sabatelli, 1996).

Adolescents gain autonomy vis-à-vis their parents gradually throughout the adolescent years. Yet, the term autonomy is used in different ways by different writers. Emotional autonomy, for example, refers to aspects of independence that are related to changes in the individual's close relationships with parents. An important aspect of emotional autonomy is the process of deidealizing one's parents (Steinberg and Silverberg, 1986). Unlike younger children, adolescents realize that their parents are fallible and, furthermore, that they are real people rather than omniscient and omnipotent figures. This realization is more likely to lead to a more balanced and accurate view of parents than a repudiation or rejection of parental authority (Youniss and Smollar, 1985). Nevertheless, as they grow older, adolescents are more likely to see and point out their parents' shortcomings (Feldman and Gehring, 1988), a phenomenon that is a source of irritation and upset to many parents (Steinberg and Steinberg, 1994). Emotionally autonomous adolescents also become more self-reliant and less dependent on their parents and lead more individuated lives in which they feel there are things that their parents do not know about them.

Behavioral autonomy, in contrast to emotional autonomy, refers to the capacity to make independent decisions and follow through with them. Adolescents' early attempts at establishing behavioral autonomy within the family are often a frequent source of conflict between parents and teenagers. Studies of family interaction suggest that early adolescence, in particular, may be a time during which young people begin to try to play a more forceful role in the family but when parents may not yet acknowledge the adolescents' input. As a result, young adolescents may interrupt their parents more often but have little impact—a state of affairs that may lead to escalating conflict in family discussions (Steinberg, 1981). By middle adolescence, however, teenagers act and are treated much more like adults. They have more influence over family decisions, but they do not need to assert their opinions through interruptions or immature behavior (Grotevant, 1998). They are also permitted to spend more time outside direct parental supervision.

Parents of adolescents differ in their willingness to grant autonomy, of both a psychological and a behavioral nature. Parents who attempt to squelch the adolescent's desire for autonomy are referred to as psychologically controlling. Psychological control involves attempts on the parent's part to control the adolescent's attitudes, feelings, and thoughts (Barber, 1996). Behavioral control, in contrast, involves the management of adolescent behaviors and activities. As we discuss in a later section on individual differences, parents of adolescents differ from each other along these dimensions, and such variation influences adolescent adjustment and mental health (Barber, 1992, 1996; Gray and Steinberg, 1999).

## Developmental Changes in Parent–Adolescent Harmony

Changes in family harmony also occur during the transition into adolescence, although there is less research and consensus on the extent of changes in positive affect than in autonomy or, as we shall see, conflict. The small body of existing evidence suggests that relationships become somewhat less close during the transition into adolescence. The lessening of positive interaction typically takes the form of fewer shared activities and less frequently expressed affection. Diminished closeness is more likely to be manifested in increased privacy on the part of the adolescent and diminished physical affection between teenagers and parents, rather than any serious loss of love or respect between parents and children (Montemayor, 1983, 1986). Some have found that a temporary withdrawal of positive affect seems to precede pubertal events, such as the attainment of menarche in girls

(Holmbeck and Hill, 1991a), although this pattern has not always been found (Montemayor, Eberly, and Flannery, 1993). Research suggests that the distancing effect of puberty is temporary and that relationships may become less conflicted and more intimate during late adolescence (Thornton, Orbuch, and Axinn, 1995). After a decrease in early adolescence, older teens report more positive affect during family interactions (Larson et al., 1996).

Despite temporary decreases in positive affect and positive interchanges among parents and young adolescents, the relative level of emotional cohesion across families generally remains unchanged during adolescence. That is, children who had warm relationships with their parents during preadolescence are likely to remain close and connected with their parents during adolescence, even though the frequency and the quantity of positive interactions may be somewhat diminished. It is also important to emphasize that the magnitude of the decline in positive affect is very small. Although some adolescents and their parents have serious interpersonal problems, the overwhelming majority of adolescents feel close to their parents, respect their parents' judgment, feel that their parents love and care about them, and have a great deal of respect for their parents as individuals (Public Agenda, 1999; Steinberg, 2001). In fact, one fifth of American teenagers say that their top concern is that they do not have enough time with their parents (YMCA, 2000).

## Developmental Changes in Parent–Adolescent Conflict

Of all of the interpersonal transitions that take place in the family during adolescence, conflict between parents and teens has received the lion's share of attention from scholars and parents alike. Despite firmly held popular notions and pervasive media portrayals of conflict as the hallmark of family relations during this period, research has clearly established that frequent, high-intensity, angry fighting is not normative during adolescence (Steinberg, 1990). Also, parents and adolescents, in contrast to popular views, do not hold widely conflicting views about important political, social, or religious matters. Even in periods of political and social upheaval, most arguments between teens and their parents have revolved around the mundane issues of daily life such as chores, attire, and curfew (Montemayor, 1983). Thus, although fighting is not a central feature of normative family relationships in adolescence, nattering or bickering is.

Many of the frustrations associated with parent–adolescent conflict may be related less to the content of the conflict and more to the manner in which conflict is typically resolved. Conflicts between teenagers and parents tend to be resolved not through compromise but through submission (i.e., giving in) or disengagement (i.e., walking away), neither of which enhances the quality of their relationship or the adolescent's problem-solving abilities (Laursen and Collins, 1994; Montemayor and Hanson, 1985). Adolescents whose parents model constructive conflict resolution are able to resolve conflict with their peers more productively (Cooper, 1988), suggesting that family conflict has the potential to teach adolescents important conflict-resolution skills. Data indicating that parent–adolescent conflict is not typically resolved through constructive means suggest that most parents and teenagers are missing important opportunities to facilitate the adolescent's ability to resolve conflicts in other arenas.

Researchers have explored how changes in the adolescent's social–cognitive abilities may affect parent–adolescent conflict. As noted earlier, changes in the ways adolescents view family rules and regulations may contribute to increased conflict over the jurisdiction of particular issues (Smetana, 1989). Research also indicates that early adolescence is a time of changes in youngsters' views of family relationships and in family members' expectations of each other. Collins (1988, 1990) studied the changes in children's and parents' expectations for each other that take place during adolescence and how "violations" of these expectations can cause family conflict. Indeed, different members of the family have different views of parent–adolescent conflict and are differentially affected by it (Larson and Richards, 1994). A child may enter adolescence expecting that it will be a time of great freedom, for example, whereas the parents may view the same period as one in which tighter reins are necessary. Differences in expectations about what adolescence is going to be like can escalate into arguments and misunderstandings; in fact, differences in developmental expectations are associated with relatively more conflict in the parent–adolescent relationship (Dekovic, Noom, and Meeus, 1997). Mismatches in developmental expectations are highest during early adolescence, with views beginning to converge over time (Collins, Laursen, Mortensen, Luebker, and Ferreira, 1997).

Researchers have attempted to chart the trajectory of parent–child conflict as youngsters develop from middle childhood through late adolescence, although making sense out of this literature has been difficult owing to variations in the ways researchers operationalize both conflict and development (Laursen and Collins, 1994). Until recently, it was widely assumed that parent–child conflict followed the course of an inverted U-shaped curve across the adolescent period (e.g. Hall, 1904; Montemayor, 1983). However, although current research provides solid evidence that mild conflict does in fact increase in early adolescence, there is debate about the trajectory of conflict in middle and late adolescence. A meta-analysis of studies of parent–adolescent conflict failed to support the commonly held view that parent–child conflict rises and then falls across adolescence (Laursen et al., 1998). The results of the meta-analysis suggest that we may need to consider both frequency and affective intensity of conflict in attempting to chart its trajectory accurately. The analysis indicated a linear decline in conflict *rate* and total conflict with age, but an increase in conflict *affect* with both age and pubertal maturation. Thus the curvilinear pattern in conflict reported by some investigators may be the result of a blurring of distinctions between conflict frequency (which may decline) and conflict intensity (which may rise). Also unclear is the extent to which changes in rate or intensity of conflict are associated with pubertal change as opposed to age (Laursen et al., 1998; Paikoff and Brooks-Gunn, 1991).

It is also likely that families differ from one another in their patterns of conflict during adolescence. Smetana (1996) used cluster analyses to identify three patterns of parent–adolescent conflict among families from the United States and Hong Kong. The largest group of families were "frequent squabblers"; they reported high rates of conflict, but of relatively mild intensity. A smaller group of families, labeled placid, reported that conflicts were rare. A final group of families, labeled tumultuous, reported frequent conflict like the squabblers, but was distinguished by extreme affective intensity during conflict. Smetana suggests that the squabblers may represent the typical family during this period of perturbation, with the smaller group of placid families representing the subset of families that have already successfully renegotiated relationships. The tumultuous families may represent a subgroup of families that are at risk for adolescent psychopathology or problems in adjustment. Although further research is needed to replicate these findings in other types of samples, this classification fits well with current theoretical perspectives on parent–adolescent conflict.

In sum, intense and frequent conflict is not normative during adolescence; however, bickering or nattering over mundane issues such as chores, curfews, clothing, or rules and regulations appears to be fairly typical in the households of teenagers and their parents. Much of this conflict can be understood as an outgrowth of adolescents' cognitive maturation, particularly their realization of the subjectivity of social convention. Additionally, conflicts often center around violations of both adolescents' and parents' expectations for each other. Such conflicts are typically resolved through submission or disengagement rather than negotiation or compromise, often leaving the involved parties dissatisfied and irritated as a result. Conflict appears to decrease in frequency from early to middle adolescence, although it increases in intensity during this same period. Future research is needed to clarify the trajectory of parent–adolescent conflict throughout the adolescent years.

## INDIVIDUAL DIFFERENCES IN PARENTING ADOLESCENTS

Although research has indicated that there are changes in autonomy, harmony, and conflict between parents and children as the family moves into and through the adolescent years, there is also considerable variability among families with respect to the nature and quality of the parent–adolescent relationship. Among the most commonly cited sources of variation are gender (of the parent, of the child, and the interaction of the two), family structure (i.e., the parents' marital status and the household's composition), ethnicity, and social class. Because these topics receive extended coverage in other chapters within the *Handbook* (Hetherington and Stanley-Hagan, Vol. 3; Hoff et al., Vol. 2; Garcia Coll and Pachter, Vol. 4; Leaper, Vol. 1; Weinraub, Horvath and Gringlas, Vol. 3), we provide only a brief overview of the major findings as they pertain to autonomy, harmony, and conflict in adolescence.

## Gender of Parent and Gender of Child

Gender differences in parent–adolescent relationships have been examined across the four family dyads: mother–daughter, mother–son, father–daughter, and father–son. Surprisingly, few effects have been found as a function of the gender of the teenager (Russell and Saebel, 1997; Silverberg et al., 1992; Steinberg, 1987a). Although there are occasional exceptions to the rule, sons and daughters report similar degrees of closeness to their parents, similar amounts of conflict, similar types of rules and conflicts, and similar patterns of activity (Hill and Holmbeck, 1987; Montemayor and Brownlee, 1987; Youniss and Ketterlinus, 1987). Observational studies of interactions between parents and adolescents also indicate that sons and daughters interact with their parents in remarkably similar ways (Cooper and Grotevant, 1987; Hauser et al., 1987).

In contrast, reviews of studies of adolescent–parent relations indicate that teenagers—females and males alike—have very different relationships with mothers than with fathers (Collins and Russell, 1991; Holmbeck et al., 1995). Mothers spend more time with their teenagers than fathers do, and when fathers are involved, it is more often in leisure activities than in caregiving roles (Collins and Russell, 1991). Adolescents tend to be closer to their mothers, spend more time alone with them, and feel more comfortable talking to them about problems and other emotional matters. Fathers are more likely to be perceived as relatively distant authority figures who may be consulted for "objective" information (such as help with homework) but who are rarely sought for support or guidance (such as help for problems with a boyfriend or girlfriend). In general, adolescents' relationships with their mothers can be characterized as more intense than those with fathers; this intensity includes not only greater closeness but also more charged and more frequent conflict (Larson and Richards, 1994; Laursen, 1995; Montemayor et al., 1993). The father–daughter relationship, in particular, stands out as especially distant (Larson and Richards, 1994). Daughters often perceive fathers as distant authority figures, and their relationship is characterized by affective blandness and minimal interaction (Youniss and Smollar, 1985). Adolescent boys, on the other hand, turn to their fathers for support more often than do daughters, but there is less intimacy in the father–son than in the mother–son dyad.

## Family Structure

The past four decades have witnessed dramatic changes in the structure of the American family. Today many adolescents grow up with single parents—either divorced or never married—or in blended families in which one or both parents have remarried (Hetherington and Stanley-Hagan, in Vol. 3 of this *Handbook*; Weinraub et al., in Vol. 3 of this *Handbook*). Scholars have attempted to explore how such variations in family structure may have an impact on the task of parenting an adolescent. This question has proven complicated, with many factors such as the adolescent's relationship with the noncustodial parent or stepparent, the degree of conflict involved in the marital transition, and the amount of time passed since the transition all emerging as important factors in predicting both parenting and adolescent adjustment (Amato and Rezac, 1994; Hetherington et al., 1992; Maccoby, Buchanan, Mnookin, and Dornbusch, 1993).

Evidence suggests that divorced mothers of adolescents often undergo a temporary period of disorganized or disrupted parenting in the years immediately following the divorce (Hetherington et al., 1992). Divorced mothers, as well as never-married single mothers, appear to monitor their children's activities less closely than married mothers do (Astone and McLanahan, 1991; Hetherington, 1987). Researchers also have explored the ways in which the process of developing autonomy may differ for adolescents whose parents have divorced (Sessa and Steinberg, 1991; Wallerstein and Kelly, 1974; Weiss, 1979). These writers argue that having divorced parents prompts the adolescent to grow up "faster"—to deidealize parents at an earlier age and to take on increased responsibility. As a consequence, adolescents from divorced homes may begin the process of individuation somewhat earlier than their peers. Evidence suggests that divorced mothers, compared with married mothers, delegate higher levels of responsibility to both sons and daughters (Hetherington 1987, 1989). Other research suggests that adolescents living in single-mother families are given greater decision-making authority than adolescents from two-parent families (Dornbusch et al., 1985; Steinberg, 1987b). The effects of comparatively greater levels of autonomy granting in single-mother families are not known, although this may account in part for higher rates of problem behavior among adolescents from single-parent households.

The evidence is somewhat mixed with regard to parent–adolescent conflict in single-parent and remarried families. During the first 2 years following a divorce, for example, parent–adolescent conflict appears especially high, although it may return to levels comparable with those in intact families over time (Hetherington, Cox, and Cox, 1978, 1982; Hetherington et al., 1992). Whereas some studies find that parent–adolescent conflict continues at a relatively higher rate beyond the initial adjustment years (Baer, 1999; Zastowny and Lewis, 1990), others report that parents and adolescents argue less in single-parent than in married households (Smetana, Yau, Restrepo, and Braeges, 1991). Furthermore, Gringlas and Weinraub (1995) find no differences in mother–adolescent conflict between households with never-married versus married mothers. More conclusive evidence suggests that conflict is particularly high in households in which adolescents must adjust to parental remarriage. Many adolescents find it difficult to adjust to a new authority figure's moving into the household, especially if that person has different ideas about rules and discipline (Buchanan, Maccoby, and Dornbusch, 1996; Hetherington, Henderson, and Reiss, 1999).

Although levels of conflict may be heightened in divorced families with adolescents, it also appears that warmth and closeness are more intense in single-parent families than in divorced families. Mother–adolescent relationships in divorced-mother families may be regarded as emotionally intense, including high levels of both conflict and harmony (Hetherington et al., 1992). Adolescents in divorced, single-parent families describe their parents as friendlier than do adolescents whose parents are married and are in a relatively more positive mood when with their family than when with friends (Asmussen and Larson, 1991). At the same time, divorced mothers may have relatively greater difficulty in adapting to their adolescent's emotional maturation toward adulthood, especially in families with girls, as this may foreshadow an end to a close friendship as well as a change in the parent–adolescent relationship (Steinberg and Steinberg, 1994).

Again, establishing harmonious relationships between adolescents and stepparents can be a challenging task. Many stepparents find it difficult to join a family and not be accepted immediately as the new parent (Vuchinich, Hetherington, Vuchinich, and Clingempeel, 1991). Although many stepfathers and their adolescent stepchildren do eventually establish positive relations, the lack of a biological connection between stepparent and stepchild—coupled with the stresses associated with divorce and remarriage—may make this relationship especially vulnerable to problems (Hetherington et al., 1999).

## Ethnicity

Far less is known about systematic variations in adolescent autonomy, conflict, and harmony across ethnic groups (see Chao and Tseng, in Vol. 4 of this *Handbook*; Harwood, Leyendecker, Carlson, Asencio, and Miller, in Vol. 4 of this *Handbook*; McAdoo, in Vol. 4 of this *Handbook*). In general, researchers find that authoritative parenting—a style of parenting characterized by a combination of warmth and control—is less prevalent among African American, Asian American, or Latin American families than among European American families, no doubt reflecting the fact that parenting practices are often linked to cultural values and beliefs (Dornbusch, Ritter, Leiderman, Roberts, and Fraleigh, 1987; Steinberg, Dornbusch, and Brown, 1992; Steinberg, Mounts, Lamborn, and Dornbusch, 1991; Yau and Smetana, 1996). Research has also indicated that authoritarian parenting (high in control but low in warmth) is more prevalent among ethnic minority than among European American families, even after ethnic differences in socioeconomic status are taken into account (Chao, 1994; Dornbusch et al., 1987; Steinberg et al., 1992). Some researchers have found that conflict between adolescents and parents is less frequent in ethnic minority than in nonminority families, although the topics of disagreement are similar across ethnic groups (Barber, 1994; Kupersmidt, Burchinal, Leff, and Patterson, 1992). African American single mothers have been found to expect more independent and autonomous behavior from their children than European American single mothers do (McKenry and Fine, 1993).

## Social Status

Researchers have also studied the impact on adolescents of growing up amidst chronic economic disadvantage (Brody et al., 1994; Magnuson and Duncan, in Vol. 4 of this *Handbook*; Felner et al., 1995). In general, both persistent poverty and temporary economic strain undermine parental effectiveness, making mothers and fathers harsher, more depressed, less vigilant, and, if married, more embroiled in marital conflict.

Under conditions of economic disadvantage, parents of adolescents in well-functioning families often use a combination of "promotive" strategies, which attempt to strengthen the adolescent's competence through effective childrearing within the home environment, and "restrictive" strategies, which attempt to minimize the child's exposure to dangers in the neighborhood (Furstenberg, Cook, Eccles, Elder, and Sameroff; 1999; Jarrett, 1995). Studies indicate that promotive strategies as well as moderately (but not overly) restrictive strategies may be beneficial to adolescent development. Although adolescents in poor neighborhoods benefit from consistent parental monitoring— perhaps even from monitoring that is more vigilant than that used by families from more advantaged communities—they do not thrive when their parents exercise control that is excessive (McCarthy, Lord, Eccles, Kalil, and Furstenberg, 1992).

Studies of economic loss find that financial hardship often takes a toll on the affective climate of the parent–adolescent relationship, as manifested in higher levels of conflict and rejection and lower levels of warmth and responsiveness (Elder, Van Nguyyen, and Caspi, 1985; Lempers, Clark-Lempers, and Simons, 1989). These studies provide evidence that economic loss diminishes parenting in samples of European American, two-parent families. McLoyd (1990) has suggested that the same process can be extended to low-income African American families living in chronic poverty. Financial strain increases mothers' and fathers' feelings of depression, worsens parents' marriages, and causes conflicts between parents and adolescents over money. These consequences, in turn, make parents more irritable, which adversely affects the quality of their parenting. Studies show that parents under economic strain are less involved, less nurturing, harsher, and less consistent in their discipline (McLoyd, 1990).

## PARENTING AND ADOLESCENT ADJUSTMENT

It has long been posited that variations in parent–adolescent relationships have implications for adolescent adjustment, including adolescent mental health, academic achievement, and social adjustment. In the following subsection we address several challenges to this widely accepted assertion and provide evidence for associations among parent–adolescent autonomy, harmony and conflict, and adolescent adjustment. The implications of variations in each of these dimensions of the parent–adolescent relationship for adolescent adjustment are considered, as well as the correlates and consequences of exposure to different styles of childrearing, such as authoritative, authoritarian, or indulgent parenting.

## Do Parents Matter?

The assertion that variations in how parents interact with their adolescent have implications for the adolescent's development and well-being, a view that has been widely accepted among researchers and practitioners alike (not to mention parents), came under strong attack in the late 1990s within the scientific journals and the popular press. The argument advanced in the scientific journals was based on the work of numerous behavioral geneticists, who claimed that much (if not most) of the observed correlation between parenting practices and adolescent outcomes was due to genetic transmission rather than to socialization. Thus, for example, the observed correlation between parental hostility and adolescent antisociality could be attributed to the fact that hostile parents and antisocial adolescents share a similar set of genes that predispose them toward aggressive behavior and that the parents' actual behavior played only a small, if any, role in producing the adolescent outcome.

The notion that parents have a modest or even negligible impact on adolescent behavior and adjustment was extended and popularized by Harris (1995, 1998), who argued the case against "nurture" on two additional fronts. In addition to the claim that much of the putative relation between parenting and adolescent adjustment was due to genetic transmission, Harris suggested that much of what researchers had interpreted as parental effects on the adolescent was actually the reverse. Thus, for example, instead of interpreting the link between warm parenting and adolescent adjustment as indicative of the impact of parental warmth on adolescent well-being, one might very reasonably conclude from the same observation that well-adjusted teenagers elicit warm parenting from their mothers and fathers. Because most research on parenting and adolescent adjustment is cross—sectional, the direction of effects is not always obvious. Second, Harris argued that socialization researchers had greatly underestimated the influence of peers and other nonfamilial socialization agents, such as the mass media. In support of this assertion she noted that siblings in the same family (who ostensibly are exposed to the same parental influence) often differ from each other considerably and pointed out that friends (who are not exposed to the same parents) are often rather similar.

Although Harris's contention that experts have overemphasized the impact of parenting on adolescent behavior and adjustment is reasonable, her argument that parents have little, if any, impact on their teenagers' development has been questioned on several grounds (see Collins et al., 2000). First, the behavioral genetics evidence she and others cite is not nearly as conclusive or consistent as the writings suggest. Most of this work does not examine gene-by-environment interactions, account for gene–environment correlations, or explain why heritability estimates vary considerably as a function of measures, samples, or approaches to data analyses. For instance, heritability estimates tend to be higher when studies use self-report measures, homogeneous middle-socioeconomic samples, and statistical models that exclude the possibility of gene-by-environment interactions (Collins et al., 2000). Second, although it is true that the majority of studies on the links between parenting and adolescent adjustment are correlational in design, not all of them are, and both longitudinal studies (which assess parenting at one point in time and adjustment at some later date) and experimental research (in which parenting practices are altered through some sort of educational or clinical intervention) provide evidence that parenting practices affect, and not simply reflect, adolescent adjustment (see Collins et al., 2000, for a brief review of this work). Indeed, the available evidence indicates that the single most consistent predictor of adolescent mental health and well-being is the quality of the relationship the young people have with their parents (Resnick et al., 1997).

## Parenting Style and Parenting Practices

To better understand the relation between parenting and adolescent adjustment, it is useful to draw a distinction between *parenting style* and *parenting practices*. As discussed by Darling and Steinberg (1993), parenting style refers to the overall emotional climate of the parent–child relationship—an affective context of sorts that sets the tone for the parent's interactions with the adolescent. The parenting climate is defined by variations in autonomy, harmony, and conflict, preferably assessed simultaneously. Just as one requires information about several dimensions of the weather (e.g. temperature, humidity, winds) to decide whether the climate can be described as good or bad (e.g., a high temperature under conditions of high humidity or a cold temperature accompanied by gusty breezes is much more uncomfortable than heat without humidity or cold without wind), knowledge about parents' standing on multiple dimensions is needed to understand the overall emotional climate of the parenting relationship.

Parenting practices, in contrast, are specific goal-directed attempts by the parent to socialize the adolescent in a particular fashion—toward high academic achievement or away from experimentation with alcohol, for instance. Reviewing an adolescent's homework, checking in with a teenager by telephone after school, or setting a relaxed curfew are all examples of parenting practices. They are more or less independent from parenting style, in that the practices can be carried out against very different stylistic backdrops (e.g., one parent may check over a child's homework in a way that is intrusive and affectively hostile, whereas another may do so in a way that is relaxed and cheerful; one parent may set a relaxed curfew within the context of a harmonious and close emotional relationship whereas another may do so within a relationship that is distant and aloof). The distinction between parenting style and parenting practices is important, because there is some evidence that the same parenting practice may have very different outcomes when implemented with one style than when implemented with another (Darling and Steinberg, 1993; Steinberg, Lamborn, et al., 1992). In other words, it is not just what parents do that matters, but the emotional context in which they do it.

Within the study of parenting style, researchers have taken two different approaches. In the dimensional approach, links between parenting and adolescent adjustment are examined for specific dimensions of parenting. Thus studies have examined the impact of autonomy granting on achievement, or the effects of parent–adolescent harmony on self-esteem, or the impact of conflict on depression. In this tradition, researchers have studied the independent or, less often, the interactive effects of autonomy, harmony, and conflict on adolescent adjustment.

## Links Between Dimensions of Parenting and Adolescent Adjustment

*Autonomy.*    Within the realm of autonomy, healthy identity development is more likely to occur within families in which adolescents are encouraged both to be "connected" to their parents and to express their own individuality (Cooper, Grotevant, and Condon, 1983; Grotevant and Cooper, 1986). Adolescents fare best when their relationships at home strike the right balance between autonomy and connectedness (Hodges, Finnegan, and Perry, 1999). Healthy individuation and positive mental health are fostered by close, not distant, family relationships (Allen, Hauser, Eickholt, et al., 1994; Bomar and Sabatelli, 1996).

The need for parents to strike the right balance between autonomy and connectedness can be seen in the work of Hauser and Allen, who have studied videotapes of parent–adolescent discussions (Allen and McElhaney, 2000; Allen, Hauser, O'Connor, Bell, and Eickholt, 1996; Hauser et al., 1991; Hauser and Safyer, 1994). The tapes were coded for two specific types of behavior related to adolescent autonomy: *enabling behavior* and *constraining behavior*. Parents who are highly enabling accept their adolescents but at the same time help them to develop and state their own ideas through questions, explanations, and the tolerance of differences of opinion. In contrast, parents who use a great deal of constraining behavior have difficulty accepting their child's individuality and react to expressions of independent thinking with remarks that are distracting, judgmental, or devaluing. Adolescents whose parents use a great deal of enabling and relatively little constraining are more individuated and score higher on measures of ego development and psychosocial competence.

The same balance can be seen in the research on decision making; adolescents fare better when their families engage in joint decision making (in which the adolescent plays an important role but parents remain involved in the final say) rather than unilateral decision making by the parent or adolescent (Lamborn, Dornbusch, and Steinberg, 1996). Monitoring is also an important vehicle through which parents remain involved in their adolescent's live without constraining them (Crouter and Head, in Vol. 3 of this *Handbook*). Research indicates that parental monitoring and supervision are highly related to positive adjustment and academic achievement among adolescents (Lamborn, Mounts, Steinberg, and Dornbusch, 1991; Linver and Silverberg, 1997; Patterson and Stouthamer-Loeber, 1984), although some researchers have questioned whether the positive effects of monitoring are due to monitoring per se or to the impact of having a harmonious relationship, which tends to facilitate both parental knowledge about their adolescent as well as healthy adolescent development (Kerr and Stattin, 2000).

On the other hand, adolescents whose parents are intrusive or overprotective may have difficulty individuating from them, which may lead to depression, anxiety, and diminished social competence (Allen and McElhaney, 2000; Holmbeck et al., 2000). Whereas excessive behavioral control is associated primarily with rebellion and externalizing problems among adolescents, excessive psychological control is associated with both internalizing problems (Garber, Robinson, and Valentiner, 1997) and externalizing problems (Barber, 1996; Conger, Conger, and Scaramella, 1997).

Studies of autonomy highlight the importance of including multiple dimensions of parenting in studies of adolescent adjustment. The granting of emotional autonomy, for example, appears to have vastly different effects on the adolescent, depending on the level of harmony in the parent–adolescent relationship. Adolescents who become emotionally autonomous, but who also feel distant or detached from their parents, score poorly on measures of psychological adjustment, whereas adolescents who demonstrate the same degree of emotional autonomy, but who still feel close and attached to their parents, are psychologically healthier than their peers (Allen et al., 1996; Chen and Dornbusch, 1998; Fuhrman and Holmbeck, 1995; Lamborn and Steinberg, 1993; Ryan and Lynch, 1989).

*Harmony.* The literature on the relation between harmony in the parent–child relationship and adolescent adjustment is straightforward and unsurprising. Adolescents who report feeling relatively closer to their parents score higher than their peers on measures of psychosocial development, including self-reliance (Steinberg and Silverberg, 1986); behavioral competence, including school performance (Hill, 1980; Maccoby and Martin, 1983); and psychological well-being, including self-esteem (Harter, 1983). Not surprisingly, they score lower on measures of psychological or social problems (including drug use, depression, deviant behavior, and impulses control) (Allen, Hauser, Eickholt, et al., 1994; Garber et al., 1997; Ge, Best, Conger, and Simons, 1996; Jessor and Jessor, 1977).

*Conflict.* We noted earlier that conflict, although less intense and frequent than once thought, is a characteristic aspect of the relationship between early adolescents and their parents (Laursen and Collins, 1994). Some have argued that such mild conflict may actually serve a functional role in the adolescent's development. From a sociobiological perspective, bickering and squabbling at puberty may have evolved as a mechanism to ensure that adolescents will spend time away from the family of origin and mate outside the natal group (Steinberg, 1989). At an interpersonal level, disagreement may be a mechanism through which adolescents inform their parents about changing self-conceptions and expectations (Holmbeck and Hill, 1991a; Steinberg, 1990). It appears that adolescents' identity development and interpersonal skills are more advanced in families in which members are willing to express their own points of view and tolerate disagreements with each other (Cooper et al., 1983). Conflict with parents may also facilitate the development of conflict-resolution skills, assertiveness, and role-taking skills (Cooper et al., 1983; Smetana, Yau, and Hanson, 1991).

In research on conflict, we again see the importance of examining multiple dimensions of parenting simultaneously, however, as the positive effects of conflict appear only in parent–adolescent relationships that are also characterized by a high degree of cohesion or harmony (Cooper, 1988). Parent–child conflict has negative effects on adolescent development when it occurs within the context of hostile and contentious interchanges. It may be the affective intensity of the conflict, rather than its frequency or content, that distinguishes adaptive from maladaptive parent–adolescent conflict (Smetana, 1996).

## Typological Approaches

Studies of the links among adolescent adjustment and various dimensions of the parent–adolescent relationship clarify the benefit of simultaneously examining multiple parenting dimensions in order to obtain a more accurate reading of the emotional climate of the parent–adolescent relationship. Baumrind's (1978) approach groups parents into four categories based on levels of parental responsiveness (similar to the harmony dimension) and demandingness (similar to control). Parents who are both responsive and demanding are labeled authoritative. Most researchers agree that authoritative parenting is composed of three main components: *warmth* (the degree to which the adolescent is loved and accepted), *structure* (the degree to which the adolescent is supervised and has expectations and rules for her or his behavior), and *autonomy support* (the degree to which parents accept and encourage the adolescent's individuality) (Barber, 1994; Gray and Steinberg, 1999). Parents who are very demanding but not responsive are *authoritarian*. Authoritarian parents place a high value on obedience and conformity and tend to favor more punitive, absolute, and forceful disciplinary measures. They tend not to encourage independent behavior and, instead, place a good deal of importance on restricting the child's autonomy. A parent who is very responsive but not at all demanding is labeled *indulgent* (or permissive). Indulgent parents place relatively few demands on the child's behavior, giving the child a high degree of freedom to act as she or he wishes. Parents who are neither demanding nor responsive are labeled *indifferent*. Indifferent parents minimize the time and the energy that they must devote to interacting with their child. In extreme cases, indifferent parents may be neglectful.

Generally speaking, young people who have been reared in authoritative households are more psychosocially competent than peers who have been reared in authoritarian, indulgent, or indifferent homes (Steinberg, 2001; Steinberg and Morris, 2001). Adolescents in authoritative homes are more responsible, more self-assured, more adaptive, more creative, more curious, more socially skilled, and more successful in school. Adolescents from authoritative homes achieve more in school, report less depression and anxiety, score higher on measures of self-reliance and self-esteem, and are less likely to engage in antisocial behavior, including delinquency and drug use. Furthermore, the disadvantages of nonauthoritative parenting accumulate over time.

Why is authoritative parenting associated with healthy adolescent development? First, authoritative parents provide an appropriate balance between restrictiveness and autonomy, giving the adolescent opportunities to develop self-reliance while providing the standards, limits, and guidelines that developing individuals need (Rueter and Conger, 1995a, 1995b, 1998). Authoritative parenting promotes the development of adolescents' competence (Glasgow, Dornbusch, Troyer, Steinberg, and Ritter, 1997; Steinberg, Elmen, and Mounts, 1989) and enhances their ability to withstand a variety of potentially negative influences, including life stress (Barrera, Li, and Chassin, 1995; McIntyre and Dusek, 1995) and exposure to antisocial peers (Curtner-Smith and MacKinnon-Lewis, 1994; Mason, Cauce, Gonzales, and Hiraga, 1994; Mounts and Steinberg, 1995). Second, because authoritative parents are more likely to engage their children in verbal give-and-take, they are likely to promote the sort of intellectual development that provides an important foundation for the development of psychosocial competence (Rueter and Conger, 1998). Authoritative parents, for example, are less likely than other parents to assert their authority by turning adolescents' personal decisions into "moral" issues (Smetana, 1995; Smetana and Asquith, 1994). Family discussions in which decisions, rules, and expectations are explained help the adolescent to understand social systems and social relationships. This understanding plays an important part in the development of reasoning abilities, role taking, moral judgment, and empathy (Baumrind, 1978; Krevans and Gibbs, 1996). The verbal give-and-take characteristic of parent–child exchanges in authoritative families fosters cognitive and social competence, thereby enhancing the child's functioning outside the family. Third, the nurturance and parental involvement provided by authoritative parents render the adolescent more receptive to parental influence, enabling more effective and efficient social-ization (Darling and Steinberg, 1993; Reimer, Overton, Steidl, Rosenstein, and Horowitz, 1996; Sim, 2000).

It is not difficult to see why the sort of give-and-take that is found in authoritative families is well suited to the child's transition into adolescence. Gradual changes in family relationships that permit the young person more independence and encourage more responsibility but that do not threaten the emotional bond between parent and child—in other words, changes that promote increasing emotional autonomy—are relatively easy to make for a family that has been flexible and has been making these sorts of modifications in family relationships all along (Baumrind, 1978; Vuchinich, Angelelli, and Gatherum, 1996).

Adolescents reared in authoritarian homes, in contrast, are more dependent, more passive, less socially adept, less self-assured, and less intellectually curious. In authoritarian households, in which rules are rigidly enforced and seldom explained to the child, adjusting to adolescence is more difficult for the family. Authoritarian parents may see the child's increasing emotional independence as rebellious or disrespectful, and they may resist their adolescent's growing need for independence. In families in which excessive parental control is accompanied by extreme coldness and punitiveness, the adolescent may rebel against parents' standards explicitly, in an attempt to assert her or his independence in a visible and demonstrable fashion (Hill and Holmbeck, 1986). Such rebellion is not indicative of genuine emotional autonomy, though; it is more likely to be a demonstration of the adolescent's frustration with her or his parents' rigidity and lack of understanding (Lamborn and Steinberg, 1993).

At the other extreme, parenting that is indifferent, neglectful, or abusive has been shown con-sistently to have harmful effects on the adolescent's mental health and development, leading to depression and a variety of behavior problems (Crittenden, Claussen, and Sugarman, 1994; Sheeber, Hops, Alpert, Davis, and Andrews; 1997; Strauss and Yodanis, 1996). Adolescents reared in in-different homes are often impulsive and more likely to be involved in delinquent behavior and in precocious experiments with sex, drugs, and alcohol (Fuligni and Eccles, 1993; Kurdek and Fine, 1994; Lamborn et al., 1991; Steinberg, Lamborn, Darling, Mounts, and Dornbusch, 1994; Steinberg, 2001). In both indulgent families and indifferent families, parents do not provide suf-ficient guidance for their children, and, as a result, youngsters do not acquire adequate standards for behavior. Adolescents reared in indulgent households are often less mature, more irresponsible, more conforming to their peers, and less able to assume positions of leadership. The problems of parental permissiveness, however, are exacerbated by a lack of closeness, as is the case in indifferent families.

An important question examined over the past decade is whether the benefits of authoritative parenting transcend the boundaries of ethnicity, socioeconomic status, and household composition (Steinberg et al., 1991). Although occasional exceptions to these general patterns have been noted, the evidence linking authoritative parenting and healthy adolescent development is remarkably strong, and it has been found in studies of a wide range of ethnicities, cultures, regions, social strata, and family structures (e.g., Carson, Chowdhury, Perry, and Pati, 1999; Forehand, Miller, Dutra, and Chance, 1997; Ge et al., 1996; Hetherington et al., 1999; Juang and Silbereisen, 1999; Pilgrim, Luo,

Urberg, and Fang, 1999; Slicker, 1998; Steinberg et al., 1991; Weiss and Schwartz, 1996). As a general rule, adolescents fare better when their parents are authoritative regardless of their racial or social background or their parents' marital status. This finding has now been confirmed in samples from countries around the world and as diverse in their value systems as the United States, China, Hong Kong, Scotland, Australia, and Argentina (Feldman, Rosenthal, Mont-Reynaud, Lau, and Leung, 1991; Shek, 1996; Shucksmith, Hendry, and Glendinning, 1995).

## FUTURE DIRECTIONS

Two primary implications follow from the review we have just presented. First, it is likely that psychologists can do much to reduce parental anxieties and public concerns about adolescence by providing accurate information about what to expect during this developmental phase. Overdrawn and inaccurate portrayals of family conflict and "normative disturbance" in adolescence have driven parents to seek information about the period, but much of the information that parents receive about rearing teenagers is conflicting and confusing. Misinformation and erroneous stereotypes about adolescence fill bookstores, flood the Internet, and dominate portrayals of teenagers and their parents in the news, on television, and in film (Steinberg, 2001). Contrary to popular belief, it appears that only a very small proportion of families—somewhere between 5% and 10%—experience a dramatic deterioration in the quality of the parent–child relationship during adolescence. Parents need to know what healthy adolescence is, how to assess whether their child is on a healthy trajectory, how to facilitate their adolescent's healthy development, and how to get help when problems arise (Steinberg, 2001). Providing parents with accurate information is also important in light of the role that expectancies appear to play in parent–adolescent conflict (e.g. Collins et al., 1997). Parents expecting a storm during adolescence may pull in the reins and behave in ways counterproductive to the development of autonomy and healthy individuation. Parental fears and anxieties may become self-fulfilling prophecies, leading to undue stress, negativity, and conflict.

Second, future researchers must pay more attention to the developmental needs of parents with teenage children. Rather than focusing exclusively on the psychological adjustment of teenagers to adolescence, future research on transformations in family relationships at adolescence needs to examine how this transition has an impact on the mental health and parenting effectiveness of the parent. Furthermore, researchers and clinicians need to ask what can be done to assist parents at this stage of life.

## CONCLUSIONS

We have argued that the child's transition from middle childhood into adolescence introduces new issues and concerns into family functioning that perturb the parent–child relationship and necessitate the renegotiation of a new interpersonal equilibrium. Salient sources of perturbation include the physical, cognitive, social, and self-definitional changes associated with adolescent development, as well as changes in the adolescent's social context. Additionally, family relationships may be perturbed by the developmental changes of adulthood, as many parents of adolescents are struggling with issues related to their passage into midlife. Parental mental health may also be adversely affected by the bickering and nattering that occurs during adolescence, by perceived rejection by teenage children of parents' values and goals, and by the process of parental deidealization.

Early psychoanalytic theory held that the changes of adolescence called for a severing of bonds between parent and adolescent, with the adolescent essentially detaching from her or his parents at this stage of the life cycle. Contemporary researchers have largely rejected this view, arguing instead that the goal of the parent–adolescent dyad is to forge a sense of autonomy and individuality for the adolescent while maintaining a core emotional connection and bond between parent and teenager. This renegotiated equilibrium has been measured and tracked by researchers along three important dimensions of the parent–adolescent relationship: autonomy, harmony, and conflict. In general, adolescent autonomy increases during the teen years as parent–adolescent harmony decreases, although the reader should bear in mind that these changes vary between families and are not abrupt or absolute. Changes in parent–adolescent conflict have proven more difficult to track, with inconsistent results reported. It appears that that the rate of conflict decreases from early to middle adolescence but the intensity of conflict increases from early to middle adolescence. Although the trajectory of conflict during adolescence remains to be clearly charted, researchers agree that conflict is higher among parents and adolescents than among parents and younger children. Contrary to earlier notions about the storm and stress of adolescence, however, this conflict is generally mild and typically concerns mundane issues. Changes along the dimensions of autonomy, harmony, and conflict appear to follow from the developmental changes associated with adolescence, and several theorists have argued that changes such as increases in autonomy and conflict or decreases in harmony may be adaptive for adolescent cognitive and/or social development.

Individual differences in parent–adolescent autonomy, harmony, and conflict are associated with other family characteristics, including family structure, gender of child and gender of parent, ethnicity, and social status, although much remains to be learned about the processes that account for such associations. Variations in parenting tracked along the dimensions of autonomy, harmony, and conflict, as well as measured with typological approaches to parenting have been demonstrated to affect adolescent adjustment. Researchers have accrued enough evidence to conclude that adolescents benefit from having parents who are authoritative: warm, firm, and accepting of their needs for psychological autonomy. This assertion holds regardless of the family's structure, ethnicity, or social status. The challenge ahead lies not in continuing to search for the most effective ways to parent adolescents—social scientists have already discovered these—but in educating adults in how to be authoritative, in helping those who are not authoritative to develop more effective parenting skills, and in understanding the best approaches for disseminating this information on a broad scale (Steinberg, 2001).

Psychologists may reassure parents that they will likely remain important sources of influence, guidance, and support throughout their child's teen years. Glib assertions that "parents don't matter" or that "it's all genetic" need to be countered with the wealth of evidence showing that parents do matter and that environmental factors moderate the expression of even the strongest inherited predispositions. Blum and Rinehart (2000, p. 31) made the following conclusion on the basis of a comprehensive study of the lives, behavior, and health of 90,000 American teenagers:

> Across all of the health outcomes examined, the results point to the importance of family and the home environment for protecting adolescents from harm. What emerges most consistently as protective is the teenager's feeling of connectedness with parents and family. Feeling loved and cared for by parents matters in a big way.

To be sure, the developmental challenges of adolescence necessitate transformations and realignments in parents' relationships with their teenagers. Yet these perturbations are temporary, and flexible parents and adolescents can adapt to these challenges in ways that maintain rewarding relationships and facilitate the adolescent's development of competence in multiple domains. Based on what we have learned from a quarter-century of solid and systematic research on parent–adolescent relationships, parents should not approach adolescence with a sense of dread, but should look forward to the development of a new and more adultlike relationship with their child characterized by continued connectedness and mutual respect, and they should savor the joys of watching their child develop into a mature and autonomous young adult.

# REFERENCES

Adelson, J., and Doehrman, M. (1980). The psychodynamic approach to adolescence. In J. Adelson (Ed.), *Handbook of adolescent psychology* (pp. 99–116). New York: Wiley.

Allen, J., Hauser, S., Bell, K., and O'Connor, T. (1994). Longitudinal assessment of autonomy and relatedness in adolescent-family interactions as predictors of adolescent ego development and self-esteem. *Child Development, 65,* 179–194.

Allen, J., Hauser, S., Eickholt, C., Bell, K., and O'Connor, T. (1994). Autonomy and relatedness in family interactions as predictors of expressions of negative adolescent affect. *Journal of Research on Adolescence, 4,* 535–552.

Allen, J., Hauser, S., O'Connor, T., Bell, K., and Eickholt, C. (1996). The connection of observed hostile family conflict to adolescents' developing autonomy and relatedness with parents. *Development and Psychopathology, 8,* 425–442.

Allen, J, and McElhaney, K. (2000, March). *Autonomy in discussions vs. autonomy in decision-making as predictors of developing close friendship competence.* Paper presented at the Biennial Meeting of the Society for Research on Adolescence, Chicago, IL.

Amato, P. R., and Rezac, S. J. (1994). Contact with nonresidential parents, interparental conflict, and children's behavior. *Journal of Family Issues, 15,* 191–207.

Asmussen, L., and Larson, R. (1991). The quality of family time among young adolescents in single-parent and married-parent families. *Journal of Marriage and the Family, 53,* 1021–1030.

Astone, N. M., and McLanahan, S. S. (1991). Family structure, parental practices, and high school completion. *American Sociological Review, 56,* 309–220.

Baer, J. (1999). The effects of family structure and SES on family processes in early adolescence. *Journal of Adolescence, 22,* 341–354.

Barber, B. K. (1992). Family, personality, and adolescent problem behaviors. *Journal of Marriage and the Family, 54,* 69–79.

Barber, B. (1994). Cultural, family, and personal contexts of parent–adolescent conflict. *Journal of Marriage and the Family, 56,* 375–386.

Barber, B. K. (1996). Parental psychological control: Revisiting a neglected construct. *Child Development, 67,* 3296–3319.

Barrera, M., Jr., Li, S., and Chassin, L. (1995). Effects of parental alcoholism and life stress on Hispanic and non-Hispanic Caucasian adolescents: A prospective study. *American Journal of Community Psychology, 23,* 479–507.

Baumrind, D. (1978). Parental disciplinary patterns and social competence in children. *Youth and Society, 9,* 239–276.

Berndt, T. J. (1989). Obtaining support from friends during childhood and adolescence. In D. Belle (Ed.), *Children's social networks and social supports* (pp. 308–331). New York: Wiley.

Blos, P. (1979). *The adolescent passage.* New York: International Universities Press.

Blum, R., and Rinehart, P. (2000). *Reducing the risk: Connections that make a difference in the lives of youth.* Minneapolis: Division of General Pediatrics and Adolescent Health, University of Minnesota.

Bomar, J., and Sabatelli, R. (1996). Family system dynamics, gender, and psychosocial maturity in late adolescence. *Journal of Adolescent Research, 11,* 421–439.

Brody, G., Stoneman, Z., Flor, D., McCrary, C., Hastings, L., and Conyers, O. (1994). Financial resources, parent psychological functioning, parent co-caregiving, and early adolescent competence in rural two-parent African-American families. *Child Development, 65,* 590–605.

Bronfenbrenner, U. (1979). *The ecology of human development.* Cambridge, MA: Harvard University Press.

Brooks-Gunn, J., Graber, J. A., and Paikoff, R. L. (1994). Studying links between hormones and negative affect: Models and measures. *Journal of Research on Adolescence, 4,* 469–486.

Buchanan, C. M., Eccles, J. S., and Becker, J. B. (1992). Are adolescents the victims of raging hormones: Evidence for activational effects of hormones on moods and behavior at adolescence. *Psychological Bulletin, 111,* 62–107.

Buchanan, C., Maccoby, E., and Dornbusch, S. (1996). *Adolescents after divorce.* Cambridge, MA: Harvard University Press.

Buhrmester, D. (1996). Need fulfillment, interpersonal competence, and the developmental contexts of early adolescent friendship. In W. Bukowski, A. Newcomb, and W. Hartup (Eds.), *The company they keep* (pp. 158–185). New York: Cambridge University Press.

Carson, D., Chowdhury, A., Perry, C., and Pati, C. (1999). Family characteristics and adolescent competence in India: Investigation of youth in southern Orissa. *Journal of Youth and Adolescence, 28,* 211–233.

Chao, R. K. (1994). Beyond parental control and authoritarian parenting style: Understanding Chinese parenting through the cultural notion of training. *Child Development, 65,* 1111–1119.

Chen, Z.-Y., and Dornbusch, S. M. (1998). Relating aspects of adolescent emotional autonomy to academic achievement and deviant behavior. *Journal of Adolescent Research, 13,* 293–319.

Collins, W. A. (1988). Research on the transition to adolescence: Continuity in the study of developmental processes. In M. Gunnar (Ed.), *21st Minnesota symposium on child psychology* (pp. 1–15). Hillsdale, NJ: Lawrence Erlbaum Associates.

Collins, W. A. (1990). Parent–child relationships in the transition to adolescence: Continuity and change in interaction, affect, and cognition. In R. Montemayor, G. Adams, and T. Gullotta (Eds.), *Advances in adolescent development: Vol. 2. The transition from childhood to adolescence.* Beverly Hills, CA: Sage.

Collins, W. A., Laursen, B., Mortensen, N., Luebker, C., and Ferreira, M. (1997). Conflict processes and transitions in parent and peer relationships: Implications for autonomy and regulation. *Journal of Adolescent Research, 12,* 178–198.

Collins, W. A., Maccoby, E., Steinberg, L., Hetherington, E. M., and Bornstein, M. (2000). Contemporary research on parenting: The case for nature *and* nurture. *American Psychologist, 55,* 218–232.

Collins, W. A., and Russell, G. (1991). Mother–child and father–child relationships in middle adolescence: A developmental analysis. *Developmental Review, 11,* 99–136.

Conger, K. J., Conger, R. D., and Scaramella, L. V. (1997). Parents, siblings, psychological control, and adolescent adjustment. *Journal of Adolescent Research, 12,* 113–138.

Cooper, C. (1988). Commentary: The role of conflict in adolescent parent relationships. In M. Gunnar (Ed.), *21st Minnesota symposium on child psychology* (pp. 181–187). Hillsdale, NJ: Lawrence Erlbaum Associates.

Cooper, C., and Grotevant, H. (1987). Gender issues in the interface of family experience and adolescents' friendship and dating identity. *Journal of Youth and Adolescence, 16,* 247–264.

Cooper, C., Grotevant, H., and Condon, S. (1983). Individuality and connectedness in the family as a context for adolescent identity formation and role-taking skill. In H. Grotevant and C. Cooper (Eds.), *Adolescent development in the family: New directions for child development* (No. 22, pp. 43–59). San Francisco: Jossey-Bass.

Crittenden, P., Claussen, A., and Sugarman, D. (1994). Physical and psychological maltreatment in middle childhood and adolescence. *Development and Psychopathology, 6,* 145–164.

Curtner-Smith, M., and MacKinnon-Lewis, C. (1994). Family process effects on adolescent males' susceptibility to antisocial peer pressure. *Family Relations, 43,* 462–468.

Darling, N., and Steinberg, L. (1993). Parenting style as context: An integrative model. *Psychological Bulletin, 113,* 487–496.

Dekovic, M., Noom, M. J., and Meeus, W. (1997). Expectations regarding development during adolescence: Parental and adolescent perceptions. *Journal of Youth and Adolescence, 26,* 253–272.

Dornbusch, S. M., Carlsmith, J. M., Bushwall, S. J., Ritter, P. L., Leiderman, H., Hasdorf, A. H., and Gross, R. T. (1985). Single parents, extended households, and the control of adolescents. *Child Development, 56,* 326–341.

Dornbusch, S., Ritter, P., Leiderman, P., Roberts, D., and Fraleigh, M. (1987). The relation of parenting style to adolescent school performance. *Child Development, 58,* 1244–1257.

Elder, G. H. J., Van Nguyyen, T., and Caspi, A. (1985). Linking family hardship to children's lives. *Child Development, 56,* 361–375.

Farrell, M., and Rosenberg, S. (1981). *Men at midlife.* Boston: Auburn House.

Feldman, S., and Gehring, T. (1988). Changing perceptions of family cohesion and power across adolescence. *Child Development, 59,* 1034–1045.

Feldman, S. S., Rosenthal, D. A. Mont-Reynaud, R., Lau S, and Leung, K (1991). Ain't misbehavin': Adolescent values and family environments as correlates of misconduct in cross-national study of Chinese, Australian, and American youth. *Journal of Research on Adolescence, 1,* 109–134.

Felner, R., Brand, S., DuBois, D., Adan, A., Mulhall, P., and Evans, E. (1995). Socioeconomic disadvantage, proximal environmental experiences, and socio-emotional and academic adjustment in early adolescence: Investigation of a mediated effects model. *Child Development, 66,* 774–792.

Flannery, D., Torquati, J., and Lindemeier, L. (1994). The method and meaning of emotional expression and experience during adolescence. *Journal of Adolescent Research, 9,* 8–27.

Forehand, R., Miller, K., Dutra, R., and Chance, M. (1997). Role of parenting in adolescent deviant behavior: Replication across and within two ethnic groups. *Journal of Consulting and Clinical Psychology, 65,* 1036–1041.

Fuhrman, T., and Holmbeck, G. (1995). A contextual-moderator analysis of emotional autonomy and adjustment in adolescence. *Child Development, 66,* 793–811.

Fuligni, A., and Eccles, J. (1993). Perceived parent–child relationships and early adolescents' orientation toward peers. *Developmental Psychology, 29,* 622–632.

Furstenberg, F., Jr., Cook, T., Eccles, J., Elder, G., Jr., and Sameroff, A. (1999). Managing to make it: *Urban families and adolescent success.* Chicago: University of Chicago Press.

Freud, A. (1958). Adolescence. *Psychoanalytic Study of the Child, 13,* 255–278.

Garber, J., Robinson, N. S., and Valentiner, D. (1997). The relation between parenting and adolescent depression: Self-worth as a mediator. *Journal of Adolescent Research, 12,* 12–33.

Ge, X., Best, K. M., Conger, R. D., and Simons, R. L. (1996). Parenting behaviors and the occurrence and co-occurrence of adolescent depressive symptoms and conduct problems. *Developmental Psychology, 32,* 717–731.

Gecas, V., and Seff, M. (1990). Families and adolescents: A review of the 1980s. *Journal of Marriage and the Family, 52,* 941–958.

Glasgow, K., Dornbusch, S., Troyer, L., Steinberg, L., and Ritter, P. (1997). Parenting styles, adolescents' attributions, and educational outcomes in nine heterogeneous high schools. *Child Development, 68,* 507–529.

Gondoli, D. M., and Silverberg, S. B. (1997). Maternal emotional distress and diminished responsiveness: The mediating role of parenting efficacy and parental perspective taking. *Developmental Psychology, 33,* 861–868.

Gottman, J. M., and Levenson, R. W. (2000). The timing of divorce: Predicting when a couple will divorce over a 14-year period. *Journal of Marriage and the Family, 62*, 737–745.

Gottman, J., and Mettetal, G. (1986). Speculations about social and affective development: Friendship and acquaintanceship through adolescence. In J. Gottman and J. Parker (Eds.), *Conversations with friends: Speculations on affective development* (pp. 192–237). New York: Cambridge University Press.

Gould, R. (1972). The phases of adult life. *American Journal of Psychiatry, 129*, 521–531.

Gray, M., and Steinberg, L. (1999). Unpacking authoritative parenting: Reassessing a multidimensional construct. *Journal of Marriage and the Family, 61*, 574–587.

Greenberger, E., and Steinberg, L. (1981). The workplace as a context for the socialization of youth. *Journal of Youth and Adolescence, 10*, 185–210.

Gringlas, M., and Weinraub, M. (1995). The more things change... single parenting revisited. *Journal of Family Issues, 16*, 29–52.

Grotevant, H. (1998). Adolescent development in family contexts. In W. Damon (Series Ed.) and N. Eisenberg (Vol. Ed.), *Handbook of child psychology: Vol. 3. Social, emotional, and personality development.* (5th ed., pp. 1097–1150). New York: Wiley.

Grotevant, H. and Cooper (1986). Individuation in family relationships: A perspective on individual differences in the development of identity and role-taking skill in adolescent. *Human Development, 29*, 82–100.

Guisinger, S., and Blatt, S. (1994). Individuality and relatedness: Evolution of a fundamental dialectic. *American Psychologist, 49*, 104–111.

Hall, G. S. (1904). *Adolescence.* New York: Appleton.

Hamill, S. (1994). Parent–adolescent communication in sandwich generation families. *Journal of Adolescent Research, 9*, 458–482.

Harris, J. R. (1995). Where is the child's environment? A group socialization theory of development. *Psychological Review, 102*, 458–489.

Harris, J. R. (1998). *The nurture assumption: Why children turn out the way they do.* New York: Free Press.

Harter, S. (1983). Developmental perspectives on the self-system. In E. M. Hetherington (Ed.), *Handbook of child psychology: Vol. 4. Socialization, personality, and social development* (3rd ed., pp. 275–385). New York: Wiley.

Hauser, S., Book, B., Houlihan, J., Powers, S., Weiss-Perry, B., Follansbee, D., Jacobson, A., and Noam, G. (1987). Sex differences within the family: Studies of adolescent and parent family interactions. *Journal of Youth and Adolescence, 16*, 199–220.

Hauser, S., Powers, S., and Noam, G. (1991). Adolescents and their families. New York: Free Press.

Hauser, S., and Safyer, A. (1994). Ego development and adolescent emotions. *Journal of Research on Adolescence, 4*, 487–502.

Hetherington, E. M. (1987). Family relations six years after divorce. In K. Pasley and M. Ihinger-Tallman (Eds.), *Remarriage and stepparenting: Current research and theory* (pp. 185–205). New York: Guilford.

Hetherington, E. M. (1989). Coping with family transitions: Winners, losers, and survivors, *Child Development, 60*, 1–14.

Hetherington, E. M., Cox., M., and Cox, R. (1978). The aftermath of divorce. In J. Stevens, J. H. and M. Matthews (Eds.), *Mother–child, father–child relations* (pp. 110–155). Washington, DC: National Association for the Education of Young Children.

Hetherington, E. M., Cox., M., and Cox, R. (1982). Effects of divorce on parents and children. In M. E. Lamb (Ed.), Nontraditional families: *Parenting and child development* (pp. 233–288). Hillsdale, NJ: Lawrence Erlbaum Associates.

Hetherington, E. M., Clingempeel, W., Anderson, E., Deal, J., Hagan, M., Hollier, E., and Lindner, M. (1992). Coping with marital transitions: A Family systems perspective. *Monographs of the Society for Research in Child Development, 57* (Serial No. 227).

Hetherington, E. M., Henderson, S., and Reiss, D. (1999). Adolescent siblings in stepfamilies: Family functioning and adolescent adjustment. *Monographs of the Society for Research in Child Development, 64* (Serial No. 259).

Hill, J. P. (1980). The family. In M. Johnson (Ed.), *Toward adolescence: The middle school years. The 79th Yearbook of the National Society for the Study of Education* (pp. 32–55). Chicago: University of Chicago Press.

Hill, J. P., and Holmbeck, G. N. (1986). Attachment and autonomy during adolescence. In G. T. Whitehurst (Ed.), *Annals of child development* (Vol 3., pp. 145–189). Greenwich CT: JAI.

Hill, J., and Holmbeck, G. (1987). Disagreements about rules in families with seventh-grade girls and boys. *Journal of Youth and Adolescence, 16*, 221–246.

Hodges, E., Finnegan, R., and Perry, D. (1999). Skewed autonomy-relatedness in preadolescents' conceptions of their relationships with mother, father, and best friend. *Developmental Psychology, 35*, 737–748.

Holmbeck, G. N., and Hill, J. P. (1991a). Conflictive engagement, positive affect, and menarche in families with seventh-grade girls. *Child Development, 62*, 1030–1048.

Holmbeck, G. N., and Hill, J. P. (1991b). Rules, rule behaviors, and biological maturation in families with seventh-grade boys and girls. *Journal of Early Adolescence, 11*, 236–257.

Holmbeck, G., Paikoff, R., and Brooks-Gunn, J. (1995). Parenting adolescents. In M. Bornstein (Ed.), *Handbook of parenting: Vol. 1: Children and Parenting* (pp. 91–118). Mahwah, NJ: Erlbaum.

Holmbeck, G., Shapera, W., Westhoven, V., Johnson, S., Millstein, R., and Hommeyer, J. (2000, March). *A longitudinal study of observed and perceived parenting behaviors and autonomy development in families of young adolescents with spina bifida*. Paper presented at the biennial meeting of the Society for Research on Adolescence, Chicago, IL.

Jarrett, R. (1995). Growing up poor: The family experiences of socially mobile youth in low-income African American neighborhoods. *Journal of Adolescent Research, 10*, 111–135.

Jessor, R. and Jessor, S. (1977). *Problem behavior and psychosocial development: A longitudinal study of youth*. New York: Academic.

Josselson, R. (1980). Ego development in adolescence. In J. Adelson (Ed.), *Handbook of adolescent psychology* (pp. 188–210). New York: Wiley.

Juang, L., and Silbereisen, R. (1999). Supportive parenting and adolescent adjustment across time in former East and West Germany. *Journal of Adolescence, 22*, 719–736.

Kalil, A., and Eccles, J. (1993, March). *The relationship of parenting style and conflict to maternal well-being in single and married mothers of school-aged children*. Paper presented at the biennial meetings of the Society for Research in Child Development, New Orleans, LA.

Kandel, D., and Lesser, G. (1972). Youth in two worlds. San Francisco: Jossey-Bass.

Keating, D. (1990). Adolescent thinking. In S. Feldman and G. Elliott (Eds.), At the threshold: *The developing adolescent* (pp. 54–89). Cambridge, MA: Harvard University Press.

Kerr, M., and Stattin, H. (2000). What parents know, how they know it, and several forms of adolescent adjustment: Further support for a reinterpretation of monitoring. *Developmental Psychology, 36*, 366–380.

Kleiber, D. A., and Rickards, W. H. (1985). Leisure and recreation in adolescence: Limitations and potential. In M. G. Wade (Ed.), *Constraints on leisure* (pp. 289–317). Springfield, IL: Thomas.

Koski, K. J., and Steinberg, L. (1990). Parenting satisfaction of mothers during midlife. *Journal of Youth and Adolescence, 19*, 465–474.

Krevans, J., and Gibbs, J. (1996). Parents' use of inductive discipline: Relations to children's empathy and prosocial behavior. *Child Development, 67*, 3263–3277.

Kupersmidt, J., Burchinal, M., Leff, S., and Patterson, C. (1992, March). *A longitudinal study of perceived support and conflict with parents from middle childhood through adolescence*. Paper presented at the biennial meetings of the Society for Research on Adolescence, Washington, DC.

Kurdek, L., and Fine, M. (1994). Family acceptance and family control as predictors of adjustment in young adolescents: Linear, curvilinear, or interactive effects. *Child Development, 65*, 1137–1146.

Lamborn, S. D., Dornbusch, S. M., and Steinberg, L. (1996). Ethnicity and community context as moderators of the relations between family decision making and adolescent adjustment. *Child Development, 67*, 283–301.

Lamborn, S. D., Mounts, N. S., Steinberg, L., and Dornbusch, S. M. (1991). Patterns of competence and adjustment among adolescents from authoritative, authoritarian, indulgent, and neglectful families. *Child Development, 62*, 1049–1065.

Lamborn, S., and Steinberg, L. (1993). Emotional autonomy redux: Revisiting Ryan and Lynch. *Child Development, 64*, 483–499.

Larson, R. (2000). Toward a psychology of positive youth development. *American Psychologist, 55*, 170–183.

Larson, R., and Asmussen, L. (1991). Anger, worry, and hurt in early adolescence: An enlarging world of negative emotions. In M. E. Colten and S. Gore (Eds.), *Social institutions and social change* (pp. 21–41). New York: Aldine de Gruyter.

Larson, R., Csikszentmihalyi, M., and Graef, R. (1980). Mood variability and the psychosocial adjustment of adolescents. *Journal of Youth and Adolescence, 9*, 469–490.

Larson, R., and Lampman-Petraitis, C. (1989). Daily emotional states as reported by children and adolescents. *Child Development, 60*, 1250–1260.

Larson, R., and Richards, M. H. (1994). *Divergent realities: The emotional lives of mothers, fathers, and adolescents*. New York: Basic Books.

Larson, R. W., Richards, M. H., Moneta, G., Holmbeck, G., and Duckett, E. (1996). Changes in adolescent's daily interactions with their families from ages 10 to 18: Disengagement and transformation. *Developmental Psychology, 32*, 744–754.

Laursen, B. (1995). Conflict and social interaction in adolescent relationships. *Journal of Research on Adolescence, 5*, 55–70.

Laursen, B., and Collins, W. (1994). Interpersonal conflict during adolescence. *Psychological Bulletin, 115*, 197–209.

Laursen, B., Coy, K., and Collins, W. A. (1998). Reconsidering changes in parent–child conflict across adolescence: A meta-analysis. *Child Development, 69*, 817–832.

Leffert, N., and Petersen, A. C. (1996). Biology, challenge, and coping in adolescence: Effects on physical and mental health. In M. H. Bornstein and J. L. Genevro (Eds.), *Child development and behavioral pediatrics: Crosscurrents in contemporary psychology* (pp. 129–154). Mahwah, NJ: Lawrence Erlbaum Associates.

Lempers, J. D., Clark-Lempers, D., and Simons, R. L. (1989). Economic hardship, parenting, and distress in adolescence, *Child Development, 60,* 25–39.

Levinson, D. (1978). *Seasons of a man's life.* New York: Knopf.

Linver, M. R., and Silverberg, S. B. (1997). Maternal predictors of early adolescent achievement-related outcomes: Adolescent gender as moderator. *Journal of Early Adolescence, 17,* 294–318.

Maccoby, E. E., Buchanan, C. M., Mnookin, R. H., and Dornbusch, S. M. (1993). Postdivorce roles of mothers and fathers in the lives of their children. *Journal of Family Psychology, 7,* 24–38.

Maccoby, E. E., and Martin, J. (1983). Socialization in the context of the family: Parent–child interaction. In P. H. Mussen (Series Ed.) and E. M. Hetherington (Vol. Ed.), *Handbook of child psychology: Vol. 4. Socialization, personality, and social development* (4th ed., pp. 1–101). New York: Wiley.

MacDermid, S., and Crouter, A. C. (1995). Midlife, adolescence, and parental employment in family systems. *Journal of Youth and Adolescence, 24,* 29–54.

Marshall, W. (1978). Puberty. In F. Falkner and J. Tanner (Eds.), *Human growth* (Vol. 2). New York: Plenum.

Mason, C., Cauce, A., Gonzales, N., and Hiraga, Y. (1994). Adolescent problem behavior: The effect of peers and the moderating role of father absence and the mother–child relationship. *American Journal of Community Psychology, 22,* 723–743.

McCarthy, K., Lord, S., Eccles, J., Kalil, A., and Furstenberg, F., Jr. (1992, March). *The impact of family management strategies on adolescents in high risk environments.* Paper presented at the biennial meeting of the Society for Research on Adolescence, Washington.

McIntyre, J., and Dusek, J. (1995). Perceived parental rearing practices and styles of coping. *Journal of Youth and Adolescence, 24,* 499–510.

McKenry, P., and Fine, M. (1993). Parenting following divorce: A comparison of Black and White single mothers. *Journal of Comparative Family Studies, 24,* 99–111.

McLoyd, V. C. (1990). The impact of economic hardship on black families and children: Psychological distress, parenting, and socioemotional development. *Child Development, 61,* 311–346.

Melby, J. N., and Conger, R. D. (1996). Parental behaviors and adolescent academic performance: A longitudinal analysis. *Journal of Research on Adolescence, 6,* 113–137.

Minuchin, S. (1974). *Families and family therapy.* Cambridge, MA: Harvard University Press.

Montemayor, R. (1983). Parents and adolescents in conflict: All families some of the time and some families most of the time. *Journal of Early Adolescence, 3,* 83–103.

Montemayor, R. (1986). Family variation in parent–adolescent storm and stress. *Journal of Adolescent Research, 1,* 15–31.

Montemayor, R., and Brownlee, J. (1987). Fathers, mothers, and adolescents: Gender-based differences in parental roles during adolescence. *Journal of Youth and Adolescence, 16,* 281–292.

Montemayor, R., Eberly, M., and Flannery, D. J. (1993). Effects of pubertal status and conversation topic on parent and adolescent affective expression. *Journal of Early Adolescence, 13,* 431–447.

Montemayor, R., and Hanson, E. (1985). A naturalistic view of conflict between adolescents and their parents and siblings. *Journal of Early Adolescence, 5,* 23–30.

Mounts, N. S., and Steinberg, L. (1995). An ecological analysis of peer influence on adolescent grade point average and drug use. *Developmental Psychology, 31,* 915–922.

Osgood, D., Wilson, J., O'Malley, P., Bachman, J., and Johnston, L. (1996). Routine activities and individual deviant behavior. *American Sociological Review, 61,* 635–655.

Paikoff, R. L., and Brooks-Gunn, J. (1990). Physiological processes: What role do they play during the transition to adolescence? In R. Montemayor and G. R. Adams (Eds.), *From childhood to adolescence: A transitional period?* (pp. 63–81). Newbury Park, CA: Sage.

Paikoff, R., and Brooks-Gunn, J. (1991). Do parent–child relationships change during puberty? *Psychological Bulletin, 110,* 47–66.

Pasley, K., and Gecas, V. (1984). Stresses and satisfactions of the parental role. *Personnel and Guidance Journal, 2,* 400–404.

Patterson, G., and Stouthamer-Loeber, M. (1984). The correlation of family management practices and delinquency. *Child Development, 55,* 1299–1307.

Petersen, A., and Taylor, B. (1980). The biological approach to adolescence: Biological change and psychological adaptation. In J. Adelson (Ed.), *Handbook of adolescent psychology* (pp. 117–155). New York: Wiley.

Pettit, G. S., Bates, J. E., Dodge, K. A., and Meece, D. W. (1999). The impact of after-school peer contact on early adolescent externalizing problems is moderated by parental monitoring, perceived neighborhood safety, and prior adjustment. *Child Development, 70,* 768–778.

Pilgrim, C., Luo, Q., Urberg, K. A., and Fang, X. (1999). Influence of peers, parents, and individual characteristics on adolescent drug use in two cultures:. *Merrill-Palmer Quarterly, 45,* 85–107.

Public Agenda. (1999). *Kids these days '99: What Americans really think about the next generation.* New York: Public Agenda.

Rathunde, K. (1996). Family context and talented adolescents' optimal experience in school-related activities. *Journal of Research on Adolescence, 6,* 605–628.

Reimer, M., Overton, W., Steidl, J., Rosenstein, D., and Horowitz, H. (1996). Familial responsiveness and behavioral control: Influences on adolescent psychopathology, attachment, and cognition. *Journal of Research on Adolescence, 6,* 87–112.

Resnick, M., Bearman, P., Blum, R., Bauman, K., Harris, K., Jones, J., Tabor, J., Beuhring, T., Sieving, R., Shew, M., Ireland, M., Bearinger, L., and Udry, J. (1997). Protecting adolescents from harm: Findings from the National Longitudinal Study of Adolescent Health. *Journal of the American Medical Association, 278,* 823–832.

Richards, M. H., and Larson, R. (1993). Pubertal development and the daily subjective states of young adolescents. *Journal of Research on Adolescence, 3,* 145–169.

Roberts, D., Foehr, U., Rideout, V., and Brodie, M. (1999). *Kids and media @ the new millennium.* Menlo Park, CA: Kaiser Family Foundation.

Rodgers, R. (1973). *Family interaction and transaction: A developmental approach.* Englewood Cliffs, NJ: Prentice-Hall.

Rueter, M., and Conger, R. (1995a). Interaction style, problem-solving behavior, and family problem-solving effectiveness. *Child Development, 66,* 98–115.

Rueter, M., and Conger, R. (1995b). Antecedents of parent-adolescent disagreements. *Journal of Marriage and the Family, 57,* 435–448.

Rueter, M., and Conger, R. (1998). Reciprocal influences between parenting and adolescent problem-solving behavior. *Developmental Psychology, 34,* 1470–1482.

Russell, A., and Saebel, J. (1997). Mother–son, mother–daughter, father–son, and father–daughter: Are they distinct relationships? *Developmental Review, 17,* 111–147.

Rutter, M., Graham, P., Chadwick, F., and Yule, W. (1976). Adolescent turmoil: Fact or fiction? *Journal of Child Psychology and Psychiatry, 17,* 35–56.

Ryan, R., and Lynch, J. (1989). Emotional autonomy versus detachment: Revisiting the vicissitudes of adolescence and young adulthood. *Child Development, 60,* 340–356.

Savin-Williams, R., and Berndt, T. (1990). Friendship and peer relations. In S. Feldman and G. Elliott (Eds.), *At the threshold: The developing adolescent* (pp. 277–307). Cambridge, MA: Harvard University Press.

Sessa, F., and Steinberg, L. (1991). Family structure and the development of autonomy in adolescence. *Journal of Early Adolescence, 11,* 38–55.

Sheeber, L., Hops, H., Alpert, A., Davis, B., and Andrews, J. (1997). Family support and conflict: Prospective relations to adolescent depression. *Journal of Abnormal Child Psychology, 25,* 333–344.

Shek, D. T. (1996) Mental Health of Chinese Adolescents. In S. Lau (Ed)., *Growing up the Chinese way.* Beijing: Chinese University Press.

Shucksmith, J., Hendry, L., and Glendinning, A. (1995). Models of parenting: implications for adolescent well-being within different types of family contexts. *Journal of Adolescence, 18,* 253–270.

Silverberg, S., Marczak, M., and Gondoli, D. (1996). Maternal depressive symptoms and achievement-related outcomes among adolescent daughters: Variations by family structure. *Journal of Early Adolescence, 16,* 90–109.

Silverberg, S., and Steinberg, L. (1987). Adolescent autonomy, parent–adolescent conflict, and parental well-being. *Journal of Youth and Adolescence, 16,* 293–312.

Silverberg, S., Tennenbaum, D., and Jacob, T. (1992). Adolescence and family interaction. In V. Van Hasselt and M. Hersen (Eds.), *Handbook of social development: A lifespan perspective* (pp. 347–370). New York: Plenum.

Sim, T. (2000). Adolescent psychosocial competence: The importance and role of regard for parents. *Journal of Research on Adolescence, 10,* 49–64.

Slicker, E. (1998). Relationship of parenting style to behavioral adjustment in graduating high school seniors. *Journal of Youth and Adolescence, 27,* 345–372.

Smetana, J. (1988a). Concepts of self and social convention: Adolescents' and parents' reasoning about hypothetical and actual family conflicts. In M. Gunnar (Ed.), *21st Minnesota symposium on child psychology* (pp. 79–122). Hillsdale, NJ: Lawrence Erlbaum Associates.

Smetana, J. (1988b). Adolescents' and parents' conceptions of parental authority. *Child Development, 59,* 321–335.

Smetana, J. (1989). Adolescents' and parents' reasoning about actual family conflict. *Child Development, 60,* 1052–1067.

Smetana, J. G. (1995). Parenting styles and conceptions of parental authority during adolescence. *Child Development, 66,* 299–316.

Smetana, J. G. (1996). *Adolescent–parent conflict: Implications for adaptive and maladaptive development.* Rochester, NY: University of Rochester Press.

Smetana, J., and Asquith, P. (1994). Adolescents' and parents' conceptions of parental authority and personal autonomy. *Child Development, 65,* 1147–1162.

Smetana, J., Yau, J., and Hanson, S. (1991). Conflict resolution in families with adolescents. *Journal of Research on Adolescence, 1,* 189–206.

Smetana, J., Yau, J., Restrepo, A., and Braeges, J. (1991). Adolescent–parent conflict in married and divorced families. *Developmental Psychology, 27,* 1000–1010.

Steinberg, L. (1981). Transformations in family relations at puberty. *Developmental Psychology, 17,* 833–840.

Steinberg, L. (1987a). Recent research on the family at adolescence: The extent and nature of sex differences. *Journal of Youth and Adolescence*, *16*, 191–198.

Steinberg, L. (1987b). Single parents, stepparents, and the susceptibility of adolescents to antisocial peer pressure. *Child Development*, *58*, 269–275.

Steinberg, L. (1988). Reciprocal relation between parent–child distance and pubertal maturation. *Developmental Psychology*, *24*, 122–128.

Steinberg, L. (1989). Pubertal maturation and parent–adolescent distance: An evolutionary perspective. In G. Adams, R. Montemayor, and T. Gullotta (Eds.), *Advances in adolescent development* (Vol. 1, pp. 71–97). Beverly Hills, CA: Sage.

Steinberg, L. (1990). Autonomy, conflict, and harmony in the family relationship. In S. Feldman and G. Elliot (Eds.), *At the threshold: The developing adolescent* (pp. 255–276). Cambridge: Harvard University Press.

Steinberg, L. (2001). We know some things: Adolescent–parent relationships in retrospect and prospect. *Journal of Research on Adolescence*, *11*, 1–20.

Steinberg, L., Dornbusch, S., and Brown, B. (1992). Ethnic differences in adolescent achievement: An ecological perspective *American Psychologist*, *47*, 723–729.

Steinberg, L., Elmen, J. D., and Mounts, N. S. (1989). Authoritative parenting, psychosocial maturity, and academic success among adolescents. *Child Development*, *60*, 1424–1436.

Steinberg, L., Lamborn, S., Darling, N., Mounts, N., and Dornbusch, S. (1994). Over-time changes in adjustment and competence among adolescents from authoritative, authoritarian, indulgent, and neglectful families. *Child Development*, *65*, 754–770.

Steinberg, L., Lamborn, S., Dornbusch, S, and Darling, N. (1992). Impact of parenting practices on adolescent achievement: Authoritative parenting, school involvement, and encouragement to succeed. *Child Development*, *63*, 1266–1281.

Steinberg, L. and Morris, A. S. (2001). Adolescent development. *Annual Review of Psychology*, *52*, 83–110.

Steinberg, L., Mounts, N. S., Lamborn, S., and Dornbusch S., M. (1991). Authoritative parenting and adolescent adjustment across varied ecological niches. *Journal of Research on Adolescence*, *1*, 19–36.

Steinberg, L., and Silverberg, S. (1986). The vicissitudes of autonomy in early adolescence. *Child Development*, *57*, 841–851.

Steinberg, L., and Silverberg, S. (1987). Influences on marital satisfaction during the middle stages of the family life cycle. *Journal of Marriage and the Family*, *49*, 751–760.

Steinberg, L., and Steinberg, W. (1994). *Crossing paths: How your child's adolescence triggers your own crisis*. New York: Simon and Schuster.

Strauss, M., and Yodanis, C. (1996). Corporal punishment in adolescence and physical assaults on spouses in later life: What accounts for the link? *Journal of Marriage and the Family*, *58*, 825–841.

Sussman, S., Dent, C., McAdams, L., Stacy, A., Burton, D., and Flay, B. (1994). Group self-identification and adolescent cigarette smoking: A 1-year prospective study. *Journal of Abnormal Psychology*, *103*, 576–580.

Thornton, A., Orbuch, T. L., and Axinn, W.G. (1995). Parent–child relationships during the transition to adulthood. *Journal of Family Issues*, *16*, 538–564.

Urberg, K. A., Degirmencioglu, S. M., and Pilgrim, C. (1997). Close friend and group influence on adolescent cigarette smoking and alcohol use. *Development Psychology*, *33*, 834–844.

Vuchinich, S., Angelelli, J., and Gatherum, A. (1996). Context and development in family problem solving with preadolescent children. *Children Development*, *67*, 1276–1288.

Vuchinich, S., Hetherington, E., Vuchinich, R., and Clingempeel, W. (1991). Parent–child interaction and gender differences in early adolescents, adaptation to stepfamilies. *Development Psychology*, *27*, 618–626.

Wallerstein, J. S., and Kelly, J. (1974). The effects of parental divorce: The adolescent experience. In E. J. Anthony and C. Koupernick (Eds.), *The child in his family* (Vol. 3). New York: Wiley.

Weiss, R. (1979). Growing up a little faster: The experience of growing up in a single parent household. *Journal of Social Issues*, *35*, 97–111.

Weiss, L., and Schwartz, J. (1996). The relationship between parenting types and older adolescents, personality, academic achievement, adjustment, and substance use. *Child Development*, *67*, 2101–2114.

Wentzel, K., and Caldwell, K. (1997). Friendships, peer acceptance, and group membership: Relations to academic achievement in middle school. *Child Development*, *68*, 1198–1209.

Yau, J., and Smetana, J. (1996). Adolescent–parent conflict among Chinese adolescents in Hong Kong. *Child Development*, *67*, 1262–1275.

YMCA. (2000). *Telephone survey conducted for the White House Conference on Teenagers*. Chicago: YMCA.

Youniss, J., and Ketterlinus, R. (1987). Communication and connectedness in mother– and father–adolescent relationships. *Journal of Youth and Adolescence*, *16*, 265–292.

Youniss, J., and Smollar, J. (1985). *Adolescent relations with mothers, fathers, and friends*. Chicago: University of Chicago Press.

Zastowny, T. R., and Lewis, J. L. (1990). Family interactional patterns and social support systems in single-parent families. *Journal of Divorce*, *13*, 1–37.

# 5

# Parent–Child Relationships in Adulthood and Later Years

Steven H. Zarit
David J. Eggebeen
*Pennsylvania State University*

## INTRODUCTION TO PARENT–CHILD RELATIONSHIPS OVER THE LIFESPAN

Parent–child relationships are a lifespan issue. Rather than ceasing when children are launched from the family, these relationships endure with often complex patterns of interaction, support, and exchange that wax and wane around key transitions in the adult years. Indeed, family issues such as intergenerational conflict, mutual assistance, and inheritance have a timeless feel to them. Several trends in contemporary society, however, have made these issues different and more complex. Changes in mortality and morbidity have resulted in more people who live longer, often with disabilities. Altered patterns of marriage and divorce have also meant that more individuals enter old age without the support of a spouse. Finally, lower rates of savings and accumulation of wealth are likely to affect the economic prospects of younger generations and cause a decline in confidence that extrafamilial institutions will help.

In this chapter, we review the most recent research on the nature of relationships between older parents and their adult children. Reflecting the basic premises of a life course perspective, we assume that ties between older parents and their adult children are a two-way street, that is, not only do children provide support and care to parents, but parents continue to support their children long after those children have been launched into adulthood. We examine the circumstances under which adult children provide assistance to older parents with disabilities and, conversely, those under which older parents continue giving extensive help to their adult children.

During recent years, a primary focus of research in gerontology has been on family caregiving and, specifically, the assistance provided to an older person with disabilities. The need for, and provision of, care to older individuals by other family members is a momentous event in later life. With ever-increasing costs of medical and long-term care of older people, assistance by family members is often essential to the security and the well-being of an older parent. Unfortunately, for

135

many families this involvement is stressful, with ramifications that can adversely affect a caregiver's life in many different ways. Assisting a parent with a severe disability may interfere with children's own employment, family life and/or well-being or reawaken long-standing conflicts with parents or siblings (Aneshensel, Pearlin, Mullan, Zarit, and Whitlatch, 1995).

Although caregiving is a critically important event for families, many researchers are becoming convinced that focusing only on caregiving does not capture the reciprocal, contingent nature of parent–child ties across the lifespan. A life course perspective implies that caregiving evolves from a long history of interactions and exchanges between parents and children. Parents provide a variety of kinds of assistance to their adult children, including financial and emotional support. Even when children are assisting a parent with disabilities, the parent may still be returning some support as well. We believe that examination of these complementary patterns of exchange contributes a fuller understanding of intergenerational relationships in later life than would a focus on the caregiving of older people alone, because most relationships of parent and adult child do not involve caregiving, and when care is needed, it develops in the context of long-standing relationships with their unique histories of exchange, affection, and values.

We begin this chapter with an examination of the demographic changes that have dramatically altered the structure of the family and family relationships over the adult years. Based on these trends, critical issues in intergenerational relationships are identified. We then briefly examine theoretical perspectives that illuminate the exploration of family relationships in adulthood. Turning to research, we consider what is known about patterns of assistance from parents to children during the adult years under routine circumstances and then the types of assistance rendered from children to parents. We next review the extensive literature on caregiving, including who provides care, stresses associated with caregiving, and determinants and mediators of caregiving stress. We end this section with a discussion of the clinical implications of stresses and strains that inevitably are a part of caregiving situations. Finally, we speculate about the future of ties between the generations. As we look ahead, should we be optimistic or pessimistic about the ability of families to support and care for each other across generational lines?

## HOW DEMOGRAPHIC CHANGES HAVE AFFECTED FAMILY TIES

The demographic revolution of the past century changed family structure in substantial ways. Increased life expectancy and decreased family size resulted in an aging of the population and the family. Having an older person in the family had once been relatively rare; now, it is usual and expected. In the United States in 1900, life expectancy at birth was 49 years for women and 46.4 years for men. Currently, women have an expected lifespan of 79.4 years and men 73.6 years (Hoyert, Kochanek, and Murphy, 1999). Life expectancy at the age of 65 shows a similar increase, from 12.2 years for women in 1900 to 19.2 years now, and from 11.5 years for men in 1900 to 15.9 years currently (Anderson, 1999; U.S. Bureau of the Census, 1992c). Thus not only are people living longer, but the later years now represent a greater proportion of the lifespan.

The effect of these trends has been an increase in the number and the proportion of older people in the population. In 1900, only 4.1% of the population was aged 65 years or older. As of May 2000, 12.7% of the population are estimated to be aged 65 years or older (Population Estimates Program, 2000). This figure is expected to increase as the post-World War II baby boom reaches its later years. By the year 2030, it is expected that one out of every five Americans will be over the age of 65 years (Population Projections Program, 2000).

Among non-European Americans there is a smaller proportion of older people than in the European American population. This difference is due primarily to two factors: The non-European American population has higher rates of mortality before the age of 65 years and non-European Americans, on average, have more children. In the coming decades, however, the numbers of non-European American older people are likely to increase somewhat faster than for European American older people. Based on recent Census Bureau projections, the number of European American older people is expected to increase by 90% from 2000 to 2030. In contrast, the number of African American older people is expected to increase 160% and Latin American older people nearly 296% (Population Estimates Program, 2000).

Other noteworthy characteristics of the older population can be identified from demographic trends. Of particular importance for family life is the growth of the number of "oldest old," those people in their 80s and older. This age group has been growing at a faster rate than any other in the population. Currently, 3.3% of the United States population is aged 80 years or older, with the figure expected to rise to 9.3% by the year 2030 (Population Estimates Program, 2000). Based on current mortality estimates, 34% of the people in a birth cohort will live to 85 years or more (Anderson, 1999). The significance of this age group is that they are more likely to have disabilities that necessitate daily assistance with a variety of activities.

Another important trend is that the older population is predominately female. Because women have greater life expectancies than men, they outnumber men by a 3:2 ratio among all people aged 65 years and older (U.S. Bureau of the Census, 1996). This gender gap increases with advancing age such that the preponderance of females is perhaps the defining characteristic of the oldest-old population. Currently, there are only 43 men aged 85 years and older for every 100 women aged 85 years and older (Population Estimates Program, 2000). However, this gender gap is expected to abate somewhat in the coming decades as the mortality differences between men and women narrow. By 2050, the ratio of men to women among the oldest-old population is expected to increase to approximately 60:100 (U.S. Bureau of the Census, 1996).

These gender differences in survivorship, combined with the fact that women tend to marry men 2 or more years older than themselves, means that older women are much more likely to be widowed. At the end of the 20th century, nearly 73% of men aged 65 years and older are married, whereas 45% of older women are widowed (U.S. Bureau of the Census, 2000). These differences in marital status are why elderly women are much more likely to live alone, become institutionalized at earlier ages, have incomes below the poverty line, and to be more likely in need of support from family (U.S. Bureau of the Census, 1996).

Most older people are healthy and live independently, but a substantial minority have limitations in functioning that require regular assistance. The proportion of those needing assistance increases with age. For example, in 1995 among noninstitutionalized persons 70 years of age and older, 32% had difficulty performing and 25% were unable to perform at least one of nine physical activities. However, persons 85 years of age and older were 2.6 times as likely as persons aged 70 to 74 years to be unable to perform physical activities (Kramarow, Lentzner, Rooks, Weeks, and Saydah, 1999). As would be expected, the proportion of individuals living in nursing homes rises in a similar way with advanced age and varies by race and gender. In 1997, the proportion of European American women residing in nursing homes was 1.1% for those aged 65 to 74 years, 5.2% for those aged 75–84 years, and 22.3% among women aged 85 years and older (Kramarow et al., 1999). The corresponding figures for men are less than 1% for ages 65 to 74 years, 3.3% among those aged 75 to 84 years, and 11.7% for men aged 85 years and older. The greater likelihood that older men are married contributes to their lower rates of nursing home residence.

The economic status of older people overall is probably better now than at any time in history. The poverty rate for persons aged 65 years and older was 10.5% in 1998. This rate is considerably below the rate for children (18.9%) and compares favorably with that of working age adults (10.5%) (U.S. Bureau of the Census, 1999). The economic circumstances of older people vary widely, however. Persons who are 75 years old and older have poverty rates that are more than one third higher than young-old persons (aged 65 to 74 years). Poverty rates are also higher for single, divorced, and widowed women and minority older people, groups that have increasingly characterized older people (U.S. Bureau of the Census, 1996).

Finally, momentous changes in marriage and fertility are having a profound impact on later-life families. Birth rates declined steadily from 1900 until the end of World War II, reversing during the 1950s and early 1960s, before falling to the current average of approximately two children born per woman (Ventura, Martin, Curtin, Mathews, and Park, 2000). Although the baby boom was characterized by a decline in childlessness, the proportion of large families (six or more children) continued to fall. These fertility fluctuations have meant that current cohorts of older people are comparatively advantaged in terms of availability of having at least one child. This will change, however, as the baby boomers—whose rates of childbearing are substantially below those of their parents—begin to enter their later years at the end of the first decade of the millennium.

High rates of marital dissolution are also changing the intergenerational family experiences of older Americans. Divorced children often need help from their parents and are less able to provide caregiving assistance. In addition, a small, but growing, proportion of older individuals are themselves divorced. In 1998, 7.3% of older women were currently divorced (U.S. Bureau of the Census, 2000). However, this represents more than a threefold increase since 1970, when only 2.3% of older women were currently divorced. Furthermore, demographers project that older divorcees will continue to become more common such that by 2030 over 15% of older women will likely be divorced (U.S. Bureau of the Census, 1996). These shifts are significant, given available evidence that shows that older people who are divorced are significantly worse off on a number of indicators, both economic and social, than older people who are married or widowed (Pezzin and Schone, 1999; Uhlenberg, Cooney, and Boyd, 1990).

These demographic trends have resulted in a situation in which multigenerational families are common. Adult children are likely to have elderly parents, who may provide occasional or regular assistance to them and their children. In turn, increased life expectancy means that more people survive to ages when they will have chronic illnesses and need assistance. With smaller families and potentially greater needs than resources among adult children, caregiving may place a greater strain on the family. As the population ages, caregivers themselves will be older. Thus current trends suggest an increasing need for assistance on the part of adults who are growing older. Unfortunately, this trend is occurring at the same time that there appear to be declining family resources to provide help, particularly smaller family size and economic trends that leave children dependent on their parents for longer periods of time during adulthood.

## CRITICAL ISSUES IN PARENT–CHILD RELATIONSHIPS IN LATER LIFE

Several critical issues emerge from examination of parent–child relationships across the adult years:

(1) Demographic trends suggest that the needs of older family members may be increasing. Older generations live longer and are more likely to become disabled at some point in their lives. The legacy of the divorce revolution of the mid-1960s through the 1970s is a growing number of individuals entering their later years who are vulnerable both socially and economically.

(2) Although the need for routine or usual kinds of support, as well as caregiving demands on the family, are increasing, there are a number of social changes that suggest a diminished capacity on the part of younger generations to provide assistance. Younger generations may be less in a position to provide help because they may need help themselves. Young adults are more likely to experience spells of economic vulnerability that are due to poorer prospects for high-paying jobs. This is especially true for the "forgotten half"—those young adults who do not receive a college degree. A high risk of divorce as well as the fact that nonmarital childbearing is increasingly common also raises the spector of more and more young adults who need help from their aging parents. Given the time limits imposed by the 1996 welfare reforms, support from parents may be even essential.

(3) Although a small segment of the population, children with chronic mental or physical disabilities have increased life expectancy and ongoing needs for assistance during their adulthood.

As a result, parents may provide essential assistance to a child with special needs long into their own later years.

(4) Support from middle-aged children may be less forthcoming. There is a growing "time bind" among middle-aged adults, driven by fundamental changes in work life (e.g., the growth of women's labor force participation, the increase in work hours). These time constraints mean less opportunity to meet the needs of older parents.

(5) When care is needed, it emerges from long-standing patterns of interactions and exchanges. The configuration of assistance in families with grown children is complex, typically involving reciprocity rather than a transfer of resources and assistance in only one direction. Helping patterns that emerge in later life need to be understood in the context of ongoing patterns of reciprocity, rather than reduced to simple notions of "reverse parenting" or other such concepts.

(6) The contributions of adult children to caring for older parents vary considerably, depending on family structure and their position in the family. Rather than one pattern, we find some children helping as secondary caregivers to their other parent or to a sibling, some trying to manage care while living at a distance from the parent, and some functioning as primary caregivers while receiving varying amounts of assistance from their own spouses, children, siblings, and other relatives.

(7) Caregiving for an older person with a disability is often very stressful for everyone involved. The antecedents of caregiving stress have been described extensively, but there is less agreement on what can be done to help families or what the appropriate interface of family and formal services ought to be.

## THEORETICAL APPROACHES TO PARENT–CHILD RELATIONSHIPS

Our examination of family relationships in later years is guided by two main perspectives: a life course perspective on changes in the family and the application of stress theory to family caregiving.

A life course perspective emphasizes that individuals and families develop over time and the course of development and change is influenced by the social and historical context (Elder, 1974, 1978, 1997). This approach draws attention to variations both within cohorts or generations and between them. A major source of within-cohort heterogeneity is variations in the timing of transitional life events (e.g., marriage, childbirth, job or career events). Parent–child relationships as well as the exchange of assistance are significantly moderated by life course transitions—both the event and its timing. For example, the birth of a (grand)child is an important life event that triggers parental assistance to adult children. However, the timing and the context of the birth are important determinants of the kinds and the amount of assistance rendered. Equally important is the premise that change over time is ubiquitous, because people go through major transitional events. Needs of adult children change as they move through childbearing and as their children mature. Financial constraints of early adulthood may diminish for some as work careers stabilize. For others, however, unexpected changes or crises (such as divorce, job loss, or illness) may abruptly change ongoing patterns of parent–child relationships. Parents' experiences change as well. Retirement, death of a spouse, changes in health, or residential changes are all transitions that affect relationships, the ability of parents to provide resources, and their own need for help.

A life course perspective also assumes important variations between cohorts or generations. Historical events (economic depressions, wars), demographic changes (declining mortality, fluctuations in fertility), and cultural revolutions uniquely stamp successive cohorts. Thus the lifespan profile of parent–child relationships experienced by individuals who today are in their 70s was neither the same as that of cohorts before them nor will it necessarily be typical of succeeding cohorts. Important cohort differences in contemporary society include increased participation of women in the workplace and decreased economic opportunities for young adults compared with those for their parents.

Finally, a life course perspective implies that life events in one generation have implications for life events in contiguous generations. It is not just the life course transitions of children or their parents that matter, but how they interlock (Elder, 1985). For example, the ability or the desire of parents to help their adult child cope with a newborn may be powerfully moderated by the timing of events in their own lives (e.g., work, health, and/or marital transitions). Complicating the picture further may be events in the lives of other siblings of the adult child or even the caregiving needs of an older parent of the parent (Bengtson, Rosenthal, and Burton, 1996; Logan and Spitze, 1996; Ward and Spitze, 1998). Parent–child relationships are lifelong processes of interchanges among individuals, influenced by their respective biographies and embedded in family, social, economic, and historical contexts.

The life course perspective provides a broad framework for viewing family interactions. In turn, stress theory can illuminate the process of adaptation of families giving care to an older person (Aneshensel et al., 1995; Cohler, Groves, Borden and Lazarus, 1989; Kinney and Stephens, 1989; Vitaliano, Maiuro, Ochs, and Russo, 1989; Zarit, 1989; 1992). Caregiving involves chronic long-term stressors that have cumulative and generally adverse effects over time. There are, however, considerable individual differences in how family members adapt to the caregiving role and in the degree of emotional distress and disruption they experience in their lives. Children assisting parents with very similar kinds of disabilities may show widely varying patterns of adaptation (e.g., Aneshensel et al., 1995; Aneshensel, Pearlin, and Schuler, 1993; Zarit, 1992). The notion that a particular type of parent care consistently results in similar strains or adaptational patterns is not supported by the evidence.

Three key concepts are useful for understanding these individual differences. First is the notion of stress proliferation (Pearlin, Mullan, Semple, and Skaff, 1990). Caregiving involves specific activities of assisting a disabled parent that are stressful to varying degrees. These primary stressors have both physical (e.g., lifting) and emotional (e.g., conflict with the parent over care, feelings of loss) dimensions. Over time, these demands can take a toll on the psychological, social, and economic resources of the caregiver. In other words, these primary-care stressors proliferate or spill over into other areas of the person's life. Caregivers may experience role conflict, for instance, having difficulty meeting the demands of caregiving and work or their own marriage. They may also experience psychological strains, such as feeling engulfed by the caregiving role (Skaff and Pearlin, 1992). As stresses proliferate, they may take a toll on psychological well-being or even physical health (Schulz and Beach, 1999).

The degree of proliferation varies considerably, however, depending on the personal circumstances of the caregiver, as well as factors that may mitigate or lessen the impact of stressors. This stress-containment process is the second factor leading to individual differences in adaptation. Protective factors that contain or limit the impact of stressors include using optimal coping strategies to manage everyday problems and pressures and receiving timely social support and assistance from others (Aneshensel et al., 1995).

The third concept is that caregiving is a career with entry and exit points and key transitions around which expectations for behavior change (Pearlin, 1993). Caregivers are socialized to the role over time, acquiring adaptive strategies as new or changed circumstances arise. Critical transitions, such as nursing home placement, restructure key features of the caregiving role, but usually do not lead to the end of the family's involvement (Rosenthal, Sulman and Marshall, 1993; Zarit and Whitlatch, 1992). Even after the care recipient dies, caregiving stressors can continue to take a toll (Aneshensel et al., 1995).

A central premise of stress theory is that the emotional distress experienced by caregivers is not due to caregiving per se, but to the beliefs, meaning, resources and coping strategies of families and the larger family context in which care is given (Aneshensel et al., 1995; Cohler et al., 1989). Some of the factors that increase the risk of stress proliferation or that contain it are potentially modifiable, for example, the help and the emotional support provided by other family members. Even when a parent is suffering from a challenging and irreversible disorder such as Alzheimer's disease, there will be modifiable aspects of the situation that can lessen the impact on the caregiver.

In summary, stress theory provides a framework for understanding the caregiving experiences of family members. The explanatory power of this framework is considerably enhanced, however, when caregiving is viewed in context—something that a life course perspective is particularly suited to do. This perspective sensitizes us to grapple with more than just the characteristics of a single caregiver. We need instead to consider the stresses and the challenges of caregiving in the context of other family members, the cumulative history of the caregiver and recipient, including prior assistance between parent and child, and larger social and historical trends.

## ASSISTANCE PARENTS GIVE TO THEIR ADULT CHILDREN

The substance of parent–child relationships consists of what one does for another. How typical are exchanges between generations in contemporary American families? Is support from parents or children in times of need forthcoming? Is assistance effective? What patterns are evident over the lifespan of children and their parents? What factors structure the amount and the kinds of help rendered? We address these questions in the next subsections by first reviewing research focused on parental help to adult children, including routine kinds of assistance, help to dependent adult children, and assistance in times of need. In subsequent subsections, we discuss research that concentrates on adult children's assistance to parents, including both routine help and care in times of dependence or need.

What assistance do parents give to their adult children? This question is not as straightforward as it seems. There are three dimensions to exchanges between generations that need to considered. First, there is the accounting period. Research done on kin ties in the 1960s often asked if the respondent had "ever" participated in exchanges of support with other family members. In part this research was designed to test the degree of social isolation of the nuclear family. Work done in the 1980s focused on "potential" exchanges, attempting to measure whether the respondent would be able to get help in times of need. Often this work examined kin availability (e.g., number, distance, quality of the relationship, or perceived availability on the part of the respondent). Finally, in the past decade or so a number of researchers have attempted to assess the nature of "routine" exchanges of assistance across generations. Often this construct was operationalized as whether some type of assistance was given or received in the past month or two.

A second consideration is what is being exchanged. Somewhat reflecting disciplinary pulls, economists have been most interested in exchanges of money and inheritances, sociologists have mostly looked at the exchange of help and services, psychologists have leaned toward the exchange of psychosocial support, and most social gerontologists have focused on caregiving. The availability in the past decade of large, nationally representative data sets containing a rich set of exchange indicators that cut across economic, social, and psychological domains have led to more interdisciplinary work in this area and attempts to assess the linkages among these domains (Eggebeen and Davey, 1998; Parrott and Bengtson, 1999; Silverstein and Bengtson, 1997).

Finally, the question of how much help parents give their adult children cannot be fully addressed without consideration of the context of intergenerational assistance. In general, what individuals say about the availability of support, what support they routinely give and receive from other family members, and the nature of help rendered in an emergency are not strongly related to each other. For example, families that show evidence of few exchanges of routine support (e.g., little or no giving or receiving of help in the past month) may still be very responsive and supportive in a crisis (e.g., a health emergency or the death of a family member) (Eggebeen and Davey, 1998). What these findings mean is that generalizing about the overall nature of intergenerational support in American families based on only one of these situations is hazardous.

## Routine Help Parents Give Their Adult Children

What do we know about patterns of routine help given by older parents to their adult children? Most surveys that ask about routine assistance find that a majority of parents have given at least some form of help to at least one of their adult children in the recent past (e.g., within the past month). Estimates from the 1988/1992 National Survey of Families and Households (NSFH)—perhaps the most widely utilized data set for studying intergenerational exchanges—are that the majority (62%) of parents of adult children had given them some form of help (e.g., money, household assistance, advice or emotional support, or childcare) within the past month. This finding—that a majority of parents routinely give some help to their independent living adult children—is echoed in other data. Research on specific communities such as Boston and Albany, New York, essentially corroborate the notion that routine help to children characterizes the majority of parent–child ties (Logan and Spitze, 1996; Rossi and Rossi, 1990).

The fact that more than half of parents are engaged in supporting their children should not necessarily be interpreted to mean that this support is either typical or responsive to needs. For example, data from the NSFH show that the proportion of parents who give a particular kind of assistance to any adult child never typifies the majority of parents. Parents are most likely to give advice (46%), whereas assisting with childcare or household tasks characterizes approximately one third of parents (Eggebeen, 1992). Monetary transfers are the rarest. Evidence from the Asset and Health Dynamics (AHEAD) study showed that only approximately one fourth of adult children have received at least $500 in the past year from their parents (McGarry and Schoeni, 1997). The Albany area survey, which focused on help between parents and a particular child (rather than any child), found routine giving of specific kinds of assistance never to typify more than one fourth of the parents (Logan and Spitze, 1996). This study also assessed the frequency of giving each type of help and respondents' estimates of the amount of time spent in an average week helping a child. The median frequency of help given is approximately once a month, and the average number of hours per week is 1.22.

Evidence drawn from cross-sectional data of the responsiveness of parental support in times of need is mixed. Data from the 1988 wave of the NSFH suggest that a child's poverty status, single parenthood, poor physical health, or unemployment are not associated with a greater likelihood of parental support (Eggebeen and Wilhelm, 1995). However, McGarry and Schoeni (1997), drawing on detailed data from the AHEAD study on exchanges between a parent and each of their adult children show that poor adult children are significantly more likely to receive financial help from a parent than their better-off siblings are.

If needs do not automatically spur parental giving, what does? There are several strong predictors of parental giving, including the life cycle stage of the child, the quality of the parent–child relationship, and how far apart parents and children live. Of particular importance, though, are parental resources. Parents with the most resources (married, highly educated, high income or wealth) are significantly more likely to help at least one of their children (Eggebeen, 1992; Eggebeen and Wilhelm, 1995; Hogan, Eggebeen and Clogg, 1993). In short, the propensity to give to children appears to be driven more by the capacity of parents to give than the children's needs.

## Life Course Variations in Help Given by Parents to Their Children

Giving to children is moderated by the life course characteristics of children as well as those of parents. One of the surest ways to receive parental support is for the adult child to have a child, as those with preschool-aged children are the most likely to get help from their parents (Eggebeen, 1992; Eggebeen and Hogan, 1990; Hogan, Eggebeen, and Clogg, 1993; Spitze and Logan, 1992). As grandchildren age, however, parental giving declines, even when the parent's age is taken into account (Eggebeen and Hogan, 1990). This change occurs partly because grandparents are an important source of childcare, which recedes in importance as grandchildren mature. Other forms of help, such as financial assistance, help with household chores, and even emotional support and advice, also decline as grandchildren age (and their parents enter midlife). By the time the last grandchild is 19 years of age or older, older (grand)parents tend to receive more assistance from their adult children than they give (Eggebeen and Hogan, 1990; Smith and Drew, in Vol. 3 of this *Handbook*).

Evidence suggests that giving to children is also affected by changes in the life course of parents. Most significantly, as parents age, they tend to give less to their children (Eggebeen, 1992; Cooney and Uhlenberg, 1992). Much of the decline in giving as individuals age can be explained by factors associated with aging (e.g., declines in health, death of spouse, changing needs of children as they age). Yet the monotonic decline in the likelihood of giving help to children by age persists even when these other factors are taken into account (Cooney and Uhlenberg, 1992; Eggebeen, 1992; Rossi and Rossi, 1990; Spitze and Logan, 1992).

The flow of assistance to adult children is also disturbed by changes in the older parents' marital status. There is some evidence that widowhood is associated with less support to children (Eggebeen, 1992; Rossi and Rossi, 1990). However, other research has found that widowhood per se is not related to reduced assistance once changes in the parent's socioeconomic status and health are taken into account (Morgan, 1983; Spitze and Logan, 1992). Divorce and remarriage, however, appear to hurt ties between the generations. There is relatively consistent evidence that marital disruption decreases contact between parents and children, the quality of relationships, and the support rendered to adult children (Amato, Rezac, and Booth, 1995; Aquilino, 1994; Cooney and Uhlenberg, 1990; Furstenberg, Hoffman, and Shrestha, 1995; Hetherington and Stanley-Hagen, in Vol. 3 of this *Handbook*, Lye, Klepinger, Hyle, and Nelson, 1995; White, 1992, 1994). Some of these studies find that the divorce effects are stronger for fathers than for mothers (Aquilino, 1994; White, 1992). However, the timing of the marital transition appears to moderate this gender differential. Furstenberg et al. (1995) found, for instance, that when children are young adults at the time of the parental divorce, there are no differences in intergenerational ties by gender of the parent. Finally, there is some evidence that remarriage does not restore intergenerational support deficits evident among divorced families (White, 1992, 1994).

An important, but often overlooked, transition in the lives of middle-aged adults is the death of their parents (Winsbourgh, Bumpass, and Aquilino, 1991). The midlife transition to the top of the generational ladder has implications for assistance to children. As parents cope with the health declines and the eventual death of their parents, they tend to give less assistance to children than when both their parents were alive or after both have died (Hogan, Eggebeen, and Snaith, 1996).

Finally, and inevitably, the death of the parent spurs a "final" intergenerational transfer—inheritance of the parent's estate. In general, social scientists have ignored this feature of the life course, despite some evidence that the potential for a bequest probably affects parent–child relationships (Bernheim, Shleifer, and Summers, 1985; Kotlikoff and Spivak, 1991). Economists, with their interest in intergenerational wealth transfers, however, have developed theories and models of bequests (see Eggebeen and Wilhelm, 1995). Available evidence suggests that parents typically treat their children equally in bequests (Menchik, 1980). Wilhelm (1996) also found substantial evidence of equal division, but those who did not give equally did not systematically give more to the child with lower earnings. Unfortunately, detailed information on the effects of future inheritance on current behavior and the determinants of patterns of bequests is difficult to come by.

## Variations in Patterns of Assistance Due to Race and Gender

We have thus far ignored subgroup variations in order to highlight overall patterns of assistance. We turn now to a brief discussion of differentials in support of children by the important features of race and gender.

Ethnographic studies and specialized surveys document extensive social support networks among African American families (Dilworth-Anderson, 1992; Stack, 1974; Taylor, 1986). These findings have led some researchers to conclude that African Americans have stronger kin networks than European Americans do (Stack, 1974; Wilson, 1986). Recent work based on nationally representative data that systematically compare kin assistance of African Americans and European Americans have generally not found superior support networks among minority families even when socioeconomic differences are taken into account (Eggebeen, 1992; Hofferth, 1984; Hogan, Eggebeen, and Clogg, 1993; Hogan, Hao, and Parish, 1990; Jayakody 1998; McGarry and Schoeni, 1997).

There are two possible explanations for these discrepant findings. It may be that research based on small, nonrepresentative samples overestimated the significance of kin ties among minority families and that research based on more representative samples can be interpreted as correcting the erroneous characterization that African American families have exceptionally strong and effective kin networks. A more plausible explanation is that the economic and the social circumstances of the African American community worsened during the 1980s and early 1990s. The erosion of neighborhoods and communities within cities, declining employment prospects of young African American males, and accelerating changes in family structure have meant that increasing numbers of African American families find themselves in situations in which needs are many but resources are few (Greenwell and Bengtson, 1997; Jayakody, 1998; Wilson, 1987). The results of studies that indicate that by the early 1990s support networks among African American families were comparatively weak probably says more about how much changed in African American America during the 1980s than about faulty conclusions drawn from ethnographic research.

Whether the increased prosperity of the 1990s has significantly reversed these trends, particularly for family support, remains to be determined. Two emerging social changes in the 1990s have brought new challenges to African American families. The 1996 federal welfare reforms mandated time limits to state cash assistance programs. Research on prereform welfare suggested that assistance from family members was somewhat responsive when welfare benefits ended, but family transfers were typically inadequate by themselves in addressing needs (Chin, 2000; Hao, 1994). As of this writing, however, the actual responsiveness of aging parents to an adult child moving off of Temporary Assistance to Needy Families (TANF) because of having reached the time limits is unknown. In other words, are older parents up to the challenge of supporting children who have exhausted their TANF benefits? A second social change of importance to understanding social support is the rise of the African American middle class. A fast-growing proportion of African Americans, those with critical job skills and higher education, have been able to take advantage of the booming economy of the mid- to late-1990s. Will this growing prosperity lead to greater intergenerational transfers?

A second source of variation in giving to children is that of gender. A number of studies show that women are more involved in kin-keeping activities that structure family events and maintain contact among family members (Eggebeen, 1992; Rossi and Rossi, 1990). There is also evidence of cross-generational gender differences in relationships, with mother–daughter ties being stronger than other dyads (Rossi and Rossi, 1990; Whitbeck, Hoyt, and Huck, 1994). When specific components of exchange are scrutinized, evidence suggests that giving tends to mirror traditional gender-role expectations. Men are found to be more likely to give financial help and women to dominate in providing childcare and emotional support (Eggebeen, 1992; Silverstein, Parrott, and Bengtson, 1995).

Finally, small numbers of older parents provide extensive assistance to children with special needs. Examples of these special groups include individuals with developmental disabilities, severe mental illness, and traumatic brain or spinal injuries. This type of care is often physically and emotionally demanding (e.g., Friss, 1990). When parents are the primary support for these individuals with special needs, the parents' own aging can underscore the fragility of the care arrangements.

In summary, recent research on routine parental support of children shows the following patterns: Most parents are routinely involved in support of at least one of their adult children. The likelihood of providing support appears to be influenced more by parental resources than by children's need. However, support to children is strongly related to changes in their life course. Support of children lessens as parents age, independent of disturbances caused by divorce or death, or health problems, although these transitions also have a major impact on giving to children. Recent work based on sample surveys indicates lower levels of support among African American families relative to

European Americans. However, social changes in the 1990s raised new questions about the nature of intergenerational family support in African American families. Finally, there is consistent evidence that support rendered to children differs by gender of the parent.

## ADULT CHILDREN'S ASSISTANCE TO PARENTS

Next to spouses, adult children are the most important source of support for older adults. Older adults are two to three times more likely to pick children over anyone else as someone they would turn to in an emergency (Hogan and Eggebeen, 1995). Children are also the first line of defense in times of illness recovery or when older persons need a place to live. We begin with a discussion of relationships between children and their healthy normal parents, that is, patterns of routine assistance. Clearly this is the dominant form of ties, yet the research on these exchanges is comparatively sparse. Following the discussion on routine ties, we review special literatures on assistance to dependent populations.

### Routine Assistance of Children to Parents

Evidence from a number of studies over the past decade indicates that a substantial minority of older American parents typically have received some routine assistance from their adult children in the past month or so (Davey and Eggebeen, 1998; Eggebeen, 1992; Eggebeen and Davey, 1998; Logan and Spitze, 1996; Rossi and Rossi, 1990). Getting emotional support or advice is the most common form of assistance received by parents, followed by help around the house and help with shopping and errands. Receiving financial help tends to be rare. In the NSFH, for example, fewer than 3% of parents reported receiving a gift or loan of $200 or more from any of their children in the past 5 years (Eggebeen, 1992).

Several points need to be kept in mind when one is interpreting these numbers. First, as noted in the previous section, parents are much more likely to give assistance to their children than to receive it, at least until late in life, when growing needs for help with daily living and eventually caregiving change this balance. For example, evidence from the NSFH shows that parents are 1.7 times more likely to give than to receive routine kinds of help from children (Eggebeen, 1992). Spitze and Logan (1992) report an even greater imbalance in their data, with parents 2.6 times more likely to give than receive help. Thus routine help from children is less frequent than assistance *to* children when parents are in good health.

There seems to be little reason to view these comparatively low rates of help from children with alarm, however. There is little evidence that parents are isolated. Data from the NSFH show that the average level of parent–child contact on a scale of 1 to 6 is 5.4 (Eggebeen, 1992). Furthermore, parents' subjective assessments of their relationships with adult children tend to be overwhelmingly positive (Eggebeen and Davey, 1998). Finally, when parents are asked whom they see as a potential source of support, they pick their children by a wide margin over friends, siblings, or other kin (Hogan and Eggebeen, 1995). In short, many middle-aged parents, it would seem, are in frequent contact with at least some of their adult children, interpret their relationships with children as positive, and because they have few needs that their children can help with, are not regularly soliciting aid.

When needs arise, however, there is good evidence that support from children is forthcoming. Drawing on the panel design of the NSFH, Eggebeen and Davey (1998) found that, aside from previous levels of support, the quality of the relationships, or the number or availability of adult children, the likelihood of older parents getting help from their children is significantly higher in the context of a crisis.

Of course, these generalizations about patterns of assistance obscure considerable variation by age, family size, gender, and marital status. It is these patterns we turn to discussing now. Even if the likelihood of giving help to children declines monotonically with age, receipt of assistance appears to slowly become more commonplace, accelerating in frequency after the age of 70 years (Logan and Spitze, 1996; Spitze and Logan, 1992). Much of this increase among the very old is related to growing dependence from increases in limitations on physical activities, poor health, or death of a spouse. It is these events that transform the kinds of support activities children have typically given their parents from routine help into caregiving. It should be noted, however, that increases in help occur even after one controls for decline in health or the death of a spouse (Eggebeen, 1992).

The strongest predictor of older parents' receiving routine help is number of children (Eggebeen, 1992). Even in modern industrialized societies, it appears that having many children is a reasonable strategy to ensure support in old age.

It has been argued that the greater investment on the part of women in kin relations throughout their life course results in their receiving more social support and assistance than men when they are old (Longino and Lipman, 1981; Spitze and Logan, 1989). Data from the NSFH show that men are much less likely than women to receive help from children (Eggebeen, 1992). Some of this difference is accounted for by the very different relationships relative to women that divorced men maintain with their children. Cooney and Uhlenberg (1990) found that the diminished contact men have with children postdivorce has implications into old age: They are significantly less likely than nondivorced men and women to have contact with their adult children. However, even when marital status is taken into account, women maintain a considerable advantage over men in receiving support from children (Eggebeen, 1992).

Divorce will become increasingly salient for future cohorts of older persons. Little research has investigated the plight of divorced older people, in part because they were not a large proportion of the older population until recently (Uhlenberg, 1990). Over the past decade, however, there has emerged a number of studies that have focused on the intergenerational consequences of divorce (Cooney and Uhlenberg, 1990; Eggebeen, 1992; Furstenberg, Hoffman, and Shrestha, 1995; Lye et al., 1995; Pezzin and Schone, 1999). The consensus among these studies is that divorce decreases the amount of intergenerational exchanges and damages the quality of the parents' relationship with children.

By comparison, there is considerable evidence that widowed older parents receive more assistance from their children than do married parents (Eggebeen, 1992; Lopata, 1979; Rossi and Rossi, 1990; Stoller and Earl, 1983). Of course, the elevated levels of support are largely due to their greater tangible needs (Crimmins and Ingegneri, 1990; Morgan, 1983).

In summary, parents on balance give more assistance to their children than they receive, but this pattern probably reflects the comparatively fewer needs middle-aged parents have relative to their children. As parents age, their needs grow and assistance from children appears responsive, especially in the event of a health crisis, death of spouse, or a severe economic dislocation. Among oldest-old people, in which the need for support from children becomes more acute, patterns of routine care are transformed and many adult children face a period of intense caregiving.

## Children's Assistance to Dependent Parents

An extensive literature describes family caregiving, including who provides care and the stresses associated with it. Helping patterns between children and their older parents are characterized by considerable heterogeneity. The amount of help needed and assistance provided range from very minimal to extensive around-the-clock responsibilities. At any single point in time, most older people need little or no regular assistance, so the amount of help being provided by children will be minimal. On occasions, however, even these minimal involvements can be very stressful, with children perceiving that their parents are making excessive demands on them. These situations are probably best viewed as an extension of parent–child relationships that have been characterized by long-standing personal and family conflict, rather than as the result of aging or dependency.

Families sometimes have to mobilize resources around a crisis, for example, if the parent is hospitalized or dies unexpectedly. As hospital stays have become increasingly brief, families are confronted with complex decisions about where and how to provide acute and rehabilitation care. During these transitions, families must make difficult decisions about a parent's medical care and post-hospital living arrangements for which they may have little information or preparation. Adding to the stress, families may not have good skills for making decisions or may disagree over what decisions to make and who should make them. The decisions made during these crisis events can, of course, have long-range consequences for everyone involved. Unfortunately, not much is known about how families mobilize and respond to these types of events, in part because they are difficult to anticipate and because the family's intensive involvement usually has a short duration.

The most typical caregiving situation, and the one that current research extensively addresses, involves providing long-term assistance. A parent's chronic disability can develop as the result of an acute problem, such as a sudden illness or accident. More typically, however, functional limitations associated with chronic disease accumulate gradually over a long period of time. Eventually the older person and family recognize the need for regular assistance with everyday tasks.

*Who becomes a caregiver?*   When the need for assistance develops, help is most often provided by a family member. Social norms are strong not only about providing care, but also concerning which family member will become the caregiver. The belief that families are responsible for the care of their older relatives has long been a central tenet in many cultures (e.g., Habib, Sundström, and Windmiller, 1993). With the emergence of modern nuclear families, there has been a concern that families will pull back from their traditional obligation to care for parents and instead turn over their care to formal institutions. Although historical trends are difficult to determine, it appears that families remain highly involved, even when extensive formal services are available (Habib et al., 1993). Indeed, given the increased probability of becoming a caregiver and assisting someone for a long period of time, families may be providing more help than ever before. One index of care is the proportion of older people in nursing homes and other institutional settings, which has remained constant at 5% in the United States over the past 40 years.

Most people endorse attitudes of filial obligation, indicating their belief that children should be involved in their parents' lives and provide assistance when needed (e.g., Brody, Johnsen, and Fulcomer, 1984; Brody, Johnsen, Fulcomer, and Lang, 1983; Stein et al., 1998; Youn, Knight, Jeong, and Benton, 1999). Many children, however, prefer not having to share a household with a parent. Correspondingly, many older people say they do not want to be a burden to their children and also prefer not sharing a household with them (Brody et al., 1984). In one study of three generations of women, Brody et al. (1983) found that the oldest generation was more accepting of receiving help from formal sources, whereas the youngest generation was the least accepting of having help provided that way.

Not everyone feels the same sense of obligation. Daughters report a stronger obligation to care for a parent than do sons (Stein et al., 1998). In some cultures, the expectation that children will care for parents remains very strong. Korean Americans, for example, feel a stronger sense of obligation to their parents than do European Americans (Youn et al., 1999).

When an older person needs assistance, one person typically assumes primary responsibility for care, with other family members playing a secondary or supplementary role and providing less or intermittent assistance. On rare occasions, two children may share the care tasks relatively equally, or the older person may move from one household to another on a regular schedule.

The role of primary caregiver is more likely to be assumed by some family members than by others. If an older person has a surviving spouse, the spouse would typically take on the primary caring responsibility. In those instances, children may play a secondary caregiving role, assisting their parents with some tasks. When the older person has no spouse, then a daughter is more likely to assume the primary caregiving role. Sons become primary caregivers when there are no daughters,

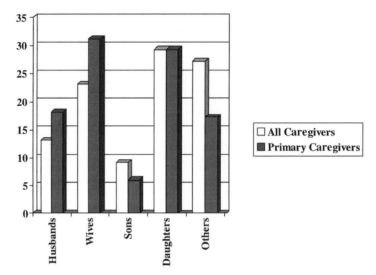

FIGURE 5.1. Kin relationship of family caregivers to the care recipient.

performing tasks similar to those of daughters in those circumstances (Williamson and Schulz, 1990). When they are in a secondary role, sons often assume some traditional masculine tasks, such as managing finances and household repairs (Cantor, 1983). In the absence of any adult children or when adult children are unable to take on primary caregiving responsibilities, then other relatives or, in some instances, friends or acquaintances, may do so.

This pattern is borne out by data from a national survey of family caregivers (Stone, Cafferata, and Sangl, 1987). In this sample, caregivers were assisting with at least one activity of daily living. Figure 5.1 shows the relationship between caregiver and older person for both all caregivers (both primary and secondary) and for primary caregivers. Looking at all caregivers, we see that the largest group was husbands or wives of the older person (36% of the sample of all caregivers). Daughters were the next most common group (29%). A small percentage (8%) were sons. Additionally, some daughters-in-law and sons-in-law, who were included in the "other" category, were providing care. If we consider only primary caregivers, the proportion of spouses rises to 49%, compared with 29% who were daughters and 6% who were sons. That increase for spouses is due to the fact that nearly all of them were the primary caregiver. By comparison, only 70% of caregiving daughters and slightly less than half of the sons had the main responsibility for their parent. Thus adult children, and particularly daughters, may find themselves in either a primary-care role, or, frequently, as secondary caregivers assisting a parent or a sibling.

The profile of characteristics of adult children caregivers that emerges in this survey is somewhat different from the media's image of a "sandwich generation" caught between the demands of parents and young children. Instead, consistent with the increased life expectancy of their parents' generation, most adult child caregivers are older and their children are grown and out of the house. Caregiving daughters were, on average, 52 years old, and sons were 49 years old (Stone et al., 1987). It is noteworthy that 13% of daughters and 9% of sons were themselves over the age of 65 years. Three fourths of adult children in the caregiving role did not have children under the age of 18 years living in the household. Conflict between caregiving and parenting roles does occur, as subsequently described, but it is not as frequent as often presented.

Although we previously noted that both parents and children prefer to live separately, the most common care arrangement when help is needed is for the older parent and the adult child to share the same residence. This was the case for 61% of daughters and sons (Stone et al., 1987). Workforce participation was lower than one might expect: 44% of daughters and 55% of sons were currently employed (Stone et al., 1987).

These summaries do not, of course, reflect the full variation in patterns of family care. Caregiving varies among social and ethnic groups, but also can differ within groups. As an example, in the African American community, the amount and the type of help that the primary caregiver receives from family and friends can vary considerably (Dilworth-Anderson, Williams, and Cooper, 1999). Of particular importance in coming years will be how single parenthood and high rates of divorce and remarriage affect the ties felt by adult children to help a parent, particular a father. Another trend found in inner-city African American families is compression between generations, such that grandparents, who may be in their 30s and 40s, rear their grandchildren and also assist their own older parents and grandparents (Burton and Sörensen, 1993). These types of variations in family care are important to consider when one is assessing a family or planning interventions.

*Stresses of caregiving.*    The point at which a parent begins to experience difficulty living independently is a critical transition for both the parent and his or her children. Most older parents and adult children are unaware of the range of options available for specialized housing and community services to assist someone who is disabled, and they may not know where to find this type of information. Physicians are the professionals most people ask first in this situation, but many doctors, unfortunately, are ill informed about aging services (MaloneBeach, Zarit, and Spore, 1992). Community-based services, such as a homemaker or nurse's aide who assists an older person in the home with specific tasks or an adult daycare program, can be a valuable way of helping an older person remain at home. The availability, quality, and cost of these services can vary widely from one locale to another. Typically, however, family members perform the main tasks needed in caring for an elder.

A special set of circumstances, which arises frequently in modern society, is that in which children live at some distance from a parent or parents whose daily living skills are deteriorating. The child living at a distance faces the problem of obtaining reliable information about the parent's situation, identifying and assessing local resources that might help the parent, and deciding when to intervene. Because social services can vary so much from one region to another, finding out quickly what services are available and which agencies provide better-quality home care can present a formidable and time-consuming task. Care managers for older people are increasingly available and can provide care coordination for an older person whose children live at some distance. This service, however, is not reimbursed by Medicare or most other insurance.

When it is difficult to arrange for or monitor services at a long distance, children may consider moving a parent closer to them or into their house. In this situation, children are painfully cognizant of the problems the parent is having at home, but they often are unaware of the pitfalls associated with a move. On the positive side, a move can address children's concerns about their parent's safety. They can more directly monitor their parent and any paid help hired to assist the parent. A move will also cut down travel time and make children more accessible to a parent in the event of an emergency. On the downside, however, moving a parent from a community in which that parent has lived for many years can disrupt the parent's familiar routines and severe ties with old friends and neighbors. A common problem is that adult children may unrealistically expect the parent to function independently in the new setting. The unfamiliarity of a new place and new routine can overwhelm an older person whose functioning is already compromised. The result may be greater dependency on children than the children have anticipated. Parents may also unrealistically insist they could have maintained in their own home and resent their children's efforts to relocate them.

Much of research literature has focused on how chronic stressors affect the caregiver's emotional well-being and health. The risks for caregivers as a group have been well established. Being a caregiver is associated with decreased well-being, increased rates of depression, other types of emotional distress, greater vulnerability to health problems and increased mortality (e.g., Anthony, Zarit, and Gatz, 1988; Gallagher, Rose, Rivera, Lovett, and Thompson, 1989; George and Gwyther, 1986; Kiecolt-Glaser, Dura, Speicher, Trask, and Glaser, 1991; Lévesque, Cossette, and Laurin, 1995; Pot, Deeg, and van Dyck, 1997; Schulz and Beach, 1999; Schulz, Williamson, Morycz, and Biegel, 1993).

Many studies combine caregivers into a single group and do not examine how kin relationship (i.e., being a child or a spouse) may affect emotional well-being and health. As a result, it is difficult to differentiate the specific problems of and risks to adult children compared with those of other caregivers. The available research suggests overall that adult child caregivers experience a degree of emotional distress similar to that of spouse caregivers and report higher levels of distress than do age-matched samples of noncaregivers. Two factors, however, temper these findings. First, gender is strongly related to reports of emotional distress. Wives and daughters who are caregivers report higher levels of distress than husbands or sons, even after one controls for the severity of the parent's disease (e.g., Anthony-Bergstone et al., 1988; Schulz et al., 1993; Williamson and Schulz, 1990; Zarit and Whitlatch, 1992). Second, adult children appear quite similar to spouse caregivers in their vulnerability when sharing a household with their parent (Deimling, Bass, Townsend, and Noelker, 1989).

Some aspects of caregiving are more stressful than others. Caregivers are typically more distressed when a parent has behavioral or emotional problems, than when only routine assistance with everyday tasks is required (e.g., Haley, Brown, and Levine, 1987; Ory, Hoffman, Yee, Tennstedt, and Schulz, 1999; Pruchno and Resch, 1989a). Notably, people caring for an older person with a dementing illness such as Alzheimer's disease or with a mental disorder are more likely to experience emotional distress than caregivers of people with physical disabilities and no mental health comorbidity (Birkel, 1987; Pearson, Verma, and Nellett, 1988).

When considering how the stresses of caregiving can proliferate into other areas of the adult child's life, we find that the most common problems are restriction of social and leisure activity, increased conflict with spouses and other family members, and increased difficulties at work (Brody, Hoffman, Kleban, and Schoonover, 1989; Deimling et al., 1989; Miller and Montgomery, 1990; Scharlach and Boyd, 1989; Semple, 1992; Stephens, Townsend, Matire, and Druly, 2000; Stone et al., 1987; Suitor and Pillemer, 1993).

Conflict with other family members is fairly common (Brody et al., 1989; MaloneBeach and Zarit, 1995). Semple (1992) examined three dimensions of family conflict: (1) around definitions of the older person's illness and strategies for care, (2) over family members' attitudes and behavior toward the patient, and (3) over family members' behavior and attitudes toward the caregiver. All three types of conflict were more commonly reported by adult children than by spouse caregivers. In turn, higher levels of conflict were associated with feelings of depression and anger for the primary caregiver.

Other studies have found that the relationship between caregiving daughters and their siblings is a major source of interpersonal stress (Brody et al., 1989; Pillemer and Suitor, 1993). When the sisters of caregiving daughters were also interviewed, they reported high levels of guilt over not doing more (Brody et al., 1989). Many caregivers find that the advice and information they get from relatives is stressful, even though this type of help is often considered a form of social support (MaloneBeach and Zarit, 1995). This counterintuitive finding may indicate that families do not listen to or find out what caregivers need, but instead push their own suggestions and agenda for handling the situation.

For many adult children, the increasing demands of caregiving can interfere with work. Some leave the workforce when taking on responsibility for care of a parent (Stone et al., 1987). In one survey of caregivers of people with neurological disorders, approximately half the daughters in the sample reported giving up their jobs (Petty and Friss, 1987). Among those people continuing to work, it is not uncommon to have absences, to reduce work hours, or to report other disruptions of work that result from caregiving activities (Brody, Kleban, Johnsen, Hoffman, and Schoonover, 1987; Scharlach and Boyd, 1989; Stone et al., 1987). Having a child at home under the age of 18 years adds to this pressure (Scharlach and Boyd, 1989).

Comparisons of working daughters who are employed and those who are not have shown, not surprisingly, that the former provide less overall care and are more likely to use formal services to assist the parent (Brody and Schoonover, 1986; Matthews, Werkner, and Delaney, 1989). Brody et al. (1987) distinguished four groups of daughters who were caregivers: (1) traditional homemakers,

(2) women who left employment to become caregivers, (3) women who were employed and reported conflict over their continued employment, and (4) women who were employed but had no conflict. Conflicted workers were those women who had reduced their work hours or were considering quitting their jobs as a result of caregiving. The women who left work or were conflicted over work were caring for mothers who were more severely disabled. They also reported higher levels of strain and disruption in their lives than the other two groups.

Comprehensive studies of role conflict in caregiving were conducted by Stephens and Townsend (1997; Stephens, Townsend, Martire, and Druly, 2000). The sample included women who were caring for a parent or parent-in-law and who simultaneously held roles as parent, wife, and employee. Of the sample, 62% reported some conflict between their other roles and caregiving. Of the daughters reporting conflict between caregiving and other roles, 34% indicated that the most conflict was with caring for their own children, 28% said it was with their husband, and 38% had the most conflict with their work role. Not surprisingly, greater conflict was associated with poorer psychological well-being. Employment, however, appeared to buffer the stresses associated with caregiving.

In addition to leading to role strain and conflict, the stresses of caregiving may proliferate in another way by threatening one's psychological sense of self (Pearlin et al., 1990). Examples of these types of changes include feeling trapped or feeling a loss of identity in the role of caregiver (Aneshensel et al., 1995; Johnson and Catalano, 1983; Miller and Montgomery, 1990; Robinson and Thurnher, 1979; Skaff and Pearlin, 1992). These factors have been found to be the strongest predictors of placing a disabled older person into a nursing home (Aneshensel et al., 1993).

Counter to stress proliferation are resources that contain or limit the effect of stressors. One of the most important resources is social support, either from one's inflormal network or from formal service providers. Siblings typically assist each other in caregiving (Brody et al., 1989; Suitor and Pillemer, 1993), although as previously noted, there may also be conflict over this help. When siblings help, it is associated with decreased strain and depression for the primary caregiver (Li, Seltzer, and Greenberg, 1999). Friends may also be an important source of emotional support (Suitor and Pillemer, 1993). Spouses provide critical support to caregivers. Brody et al. (Brody, Litvin, Hoffman, and Kleban, 1992) studied married daughters who were caring for a parent with daughters who were not married (including separated or divorced, widowed, and never married). Married caregivers reported more support, less financial strain, and less depression than did the unmarried daughters.

Formal help is a very important source of assistance for caregivers and may be used more frequently by adult children caregivers than by spouse caregivers (Johnson and Catalano, 1983; Zarit, Stephens, Townsend, Greene, and Leitsch, 1999). In general, however, rates of using services are fairly low for all caregivers (Aneshensel et al., 1995). Factors affecting utilization include the cost of care, difficulties in finding appropriate and good-quality services and reluctance by family caregivers to turn responsibilities over to someone else (MaloneBeach et al., 1992; Mullan, 1993). A major reason for low service use is that Medicare and other third-party payers do not reimburse for most long-term care services, including nursing homes. Caregivers' emotional states may also affect service use. Caregivers who are depressed and may thus have the most need for assistance use formal services the least (Mullan, 1993). Their depression and concomitant feelings of helplessness and hopelessness may act as barriers to obtaining assistance.

Another important resource for containing stress is how caregivers cope with daily stresses and challenges. It has generally been suggested that people with better problem-solving skills, who can distance themselves somewhat from problems and think about alternative courses of action, will function better than caregivers who respond emotionally to their situation (e.g., Johnson and Catalano, 1983; Niederehe and Funk, 1987; Pruchno and Resch, 1989b; Vitaliano, Becker, Russo, Magana-Amato, and Maiuro, 1988–1989; Zarit, Orr, and Zarit, 1985). As an example, Li et al. (1999) found that daughters who were higher in mastery used more problem-focused coping strategies in caring for a parent, and that led to less depression over an 18-month period. When one is coping with

Alzheimer's disease or other long-term degenerative conditions, cognitive coping strategies, such as finding meaning in the situation or seeking comfort in one's religious beliefs, can be very helpful (Pruchno and Resch, 1989b).

Caregiving activities may span several years, shifting in intensity in response to changes in the parent's condition and other circumstances in the caregiver's. Only a few longitudinal studies have been conducted to date on the course of adult caregiving. These investigations suggest that caregivers can follow different trajectories, with some showing increased problems and stress-related symptoms, but others improving, even as the older person's condition worsens (e.g., Aneshensel et al., 1995; Schulz et al., 1993; Townsend, Noelker, Deimling, and Bass, 1989; Zarit, Todd, and Zarit, 1986). Improvement may be related to adopting more effective strategies for managing stress (Zarit, Todd, and Zarit, 1986).

Probably the most difficult transition in caregiving is the decision to place a parent in a nursing home or similar facility. Despite the changes that have occurred in family structure and the greater involvement of women in the workplace, placing a parent remains a last choice for most people. Children may feel guilty and depressed about the prospects of placement. They also encounter realistic barriers, including the fact that some long-term care facilities do not provide adequate care and that most care is not covered by Medicare or other insurance.

In recent years, new types of care facilities, often called assisted living, have been developed to offer older people more autonomy and a better quality of life (Zarit, Dolan, and Leitsch, 1998). Rather than operating on the medical model as nursing homes do, assisted living emphasizes the social aspects of daily life and tries to help people maintain their involvement in ordinary activities. Although the best of these facilities offer an excellent housing option for older people, many are plagued with the same problems as nursing homes, such as staff shortages and turnover, inadequately trained staff, and unimaginative activities. They are also expensive. The emotional difficulty of placement is thus compounded by the limited number of good housing options.

Placement also does not mean the end of a caregiver's involvement. Children typically remain involved, visiting their parent frequently, in some cases assisting their parent with daily activities such as feeding or dressing, and interacting with staff to ensure good care (Zarit and Whitlatch, 1992). Although placement relieves some features of emotional distress associated with caregiving, many caregivers continue to experience high levels of depression and other problems after institutionalization of a spouse or parent (Zarit and Whitlatch, 1992). These feelings may persist for two years or longer after placement (Zarit and Whitlatch, 1993).

Contemporary research on family caregiving has established a foundation for understanding the experience of adult children and the problems they encounter when caring for an older parent or parents. This research, however, is not without its limitations. An important limiting factor is that research has almost exclusively focused on people who are the primary or main providers of care. Much less is known about the problems and stresses of being in a secondary role or how primary and secondary caregivers can interact effectively. The relationships between primary and secondary caregivers lend themselves to certain kinds of difficulties, for example, misunderstandings among the various helpers about the older person's disabilities and needs and about the type and schedule of assistance to the primary caregiver. As we have seen, conflict among siblings on these issues can be a major source of stress. Because many adult children find themselves in a secondary helping role, either to a parent or to a sibling, there needs to be a better understanding of the factors that lead to effective collaboration or to problems in these relationships.

## Clinical Implications of Research on Family Caregiving

Adult caregiving is a major event in family life, with many potential hazards as well as the possibility for fulfillment that comes from believing that one is meeting obligations to a parent. Many types of formal social services that provide part of the care to an older person with disabilities along with clinical interventions directed at the older person, caregiver, or the wider family may be helpful to alleviate or prevent the development of excessive strain on caregivers.

Working with older people and their families requires special skills that go beyond basic clinical competencies (Zarit and Zarit, 1998). These skills are important for gaining an adequate understanding of the older person and the problems faced by the family and form a foundation for interventions with caregivers. These skills include the following:

(1) Assessment of disorders of aging. Clinicians working with older people should be familiar with assessment procedures for disorders of aging. In particular, they need to be able to differentiate memory and cognitive problems that are due to dementia from problems of normal aging or reversible conditions such as depression (e.g., Kaszniak, 1990; Zarit and Zarit, 1998). When families raise questions about the competency of an older individual, it is essential to be able to differentiate when there are real problems from situations in which families may be using the parent's age to redress old grievances or to change the distribution of resources in the family.

(2) Understanding of diseases and medications. Working with older people requires an understanding of the course and the consequences of major illnesses associated with aging and the effects of common medications (Zarit and Zarit, 1998). Clinicians need to be able to distinguish between what is possible to achieve with treatment and what is not. As an example, rehabilitation for severe losses of vision is often possible, and older people can benefit from a variety of vision aids (Genensky and Zarit, 1993). In contrast, a person with Alzheimer's disease or another dementing disorder will be able to make only very limited functional gains. In those instances, more of the focus of treatment will be on how the family can change to cope effectively with the strains caused by the disease, rather than trying to improve the functioning of the "patient."

(3) Awareness of one's own feelings about aging. Because aging is associated with many negative expectations and beliefs, clinicians should be aware of their own concerns and reactions. As in dealing with any other family situation, it is important not to ally oneself with one generation over another. Some clinicians hold strong negative beliefs about older people, which color their assessments and cause them to side inappropriately with children against their parents. Clinicians can also err in the direction of taking the side of the older people against children. Knight (1986) discussed these and other "countertransference" issues that can arise when one is working with older people.

(4) Knowledge of the aging service system. Social services and other resources are available to assist older people and their families. When a parent needs assistance or supervision on a regular basis, a program like adult daycare can be of enormous value (Zarit, Stephens, Townsend, and Greene, 1998). Programs, eligibilities, and costs, however, vary considerably from one part of the country to another. Clinicians working with older people should familiarize themselves with these resources or collaborate with other clinicians or case managers who are aware of current programs and benefits. A central issue is that Medicare does not cover many important services. As previously noted, for example, Medicare does not pay for most nursing home stays. As a result, nursing home placement has significant financial consequences for families. Placement should never be suggested in a casual way, and planning should be undertaken with an understanding of the alternatives for paying for it.

Many different clinical strategies are useful when one is working with adult children and their older parents (Smyer, Zarit, and Qualls, 1990; Zarit and Zarit, 1998). The following approaches are useful for addressing the stresses of caregiving:

(1) Education. Clinicians often play an educative role, helping families to understand the older person's problems and the consequences of those problems. Counseling sessions can be useful

for clarifying families' goals and values regarding caregiving and helping them understand the alternatives that are available.

(2) Improving management of the care situation. Many stressful aspects of care situations can be brought under better control by families. As an example, common behavioral disturbances associated with Alzheimer's disease, such as agitation, will often respond to behavioral management strategies (Zarit et al., 1985; Zarit and Zarit, 1998). Agitation may follow long periods of inactivity. By identifying inactivity as an antecedent of agitation, a family can plan activities to involve and stimulate the patient in order to head off the problem. Typically, a wide range of social and behavioral strategies can help improve the older person's mood and behavior while lowering the strain on caregivers.

(3) Change the amount and type of help provided by family members. Although care usually falls primarily on one person in the family, assistance from other family members can often make the situation more manageable. They may not, however, understand the need for help or the type of help the primary caregiver would like. Family meetings led by a psychologist or social worker can clarify the older person's problems for the family while addressing the caregiver's needs. This type of approach has been found to be an effective way of mobilizing family resources and helping families keep a relative at home longer (Mittelman et al., 1993, 1995, 1996; Whitlatch, Zarit, and von Eye, 1991; Zarit et al., 1985).

(4) Bringing in new resources. In addition to mobilizing help within the family, obtaining formal social services to provide care to the older person can reduce strain on caregivers. Programs such as adult daycare, overnight respite care, or home helpers who assist the older person with activities in the home can be quite valuable. Families, however, may be reluctant to use formal services, believing either that someone else cannot do a good enough job or that the older person will not accept help. Usually a clinician can work through these sorts of objections by examining them and suggesting alternative ways of thinking about using formal services (Zarit et al., 1985). Sometimes, however, the barriers are realistic, such as when a family cannot afford the cost of a program or when services are not available or reliable.

Although an empirical literature on the effectiveness of treatment of family problems in later life is limited, some initial findings are available. In particular, a family systems approach that addresses patterns of interaction around caregiving and seeks to increase the amount of assistance being provided has shown promise (Mittelman et al., 1993, 1995, 1996; Whitlatch et al., 1991; Zarit et al., 1985). Helping caregivers learn how to manage their relative's depressive symptoms and behavior problems can also be very helpful (Teri, Logsdon, Uomoto, and McCurry, 1997). A frequent source of help for caregivers is support groups. Although these groups may be very useful for helping family members understand their situation and the alternatives available to them, they may not alleviate depression or emotional distress (Zarit and Teri, 1991).

Scharlach (1987) conducted an intervention with daughters who reported problematic relationships with their mothers. In this study, daughters were enrolled into either a support group or a group emphasizing cognitive behavioral skills. The evaluation of outcome focused on both the daughters and their mothers. The results indicated that the cognitive behavioral approach reduced stress among daughters and decreased loneliness among their mothers. This type of study, which examines the effects of treatment on both child and parent, is promising for identifying useful strategies for working with families.

We should not omit the role of formal services. Adult daycare has been found to relieve strain and depression among caregivers of people with dementia (Zarit et al., 1998). Other respite services are also effective in relieving caregivers' stress (Montgomery and Kosloski, 1995; Zarit and Leitsch, 2001).

All too often, however, families do not find out about these types of services when they might be of most help to them. Treatment as usual often consists of telling caregivers there is nothing they can do. As we have stressed throughout, however, there are often modifiable features of the stress process. Well-planned interventions that reduce risks and increase protective factors can contain the effects of caregiving stressors and allow children to provide good quality care to their parents without excessive cost or burden to themselves.

## FUTURE TRENDS IN PARENT–CHILD RELATIONSHIPS IN LATER LIFE

What will intergenerational support and family caregiving look like in the future? Should we be optimistic or pessimistic that current patterns will suffice to meet the needs of adult children and dependent, older parents? Speculating about the future is always a risky prospect; unexpected historical events happen, the economy can move in unpredicted ways, political winds can abruptly shift. Yet, because of the demographic "momentum" of some of the social changes previously discussed— changes that will have a direct bearing on the form and the nature of current intergenerational support and caregiving—we can make some reasonable assertions.

The ongoing sociodemographic changes may make it difficult to be optimistic about the continued ability of families to bear a disproportionate burden of caregiving. Indeed, it is likely that a growing proportion of the elderly will be in need of care at the same time that the capacity of their children to provide support will be diminished.

At the same time, ever-spiralling costs of medical care for society as a whole, and specifically for older people, mean that it is unlikely that there will be a large diversion of funds into support of social programs that provide assistance to family caregivers or to other approaches that encourage caring for older people in the community. Consensus reigns about the need for alternatives to institutionalization and the benefits of caring for older people in the community. Programs that share some portion of the care, such as adult daycare, have been growing at a steady pace in the United States. Coverage of supportive community-based services under Medicare or through special programs in some states has grown gradually. Additional increments can be expected, but it is unlikely that there will be any substantial increase of funds for these programs in the upcoming years.

As previously described, some promising and relatively cost-effective approaches for addressing the problems of family caregivers and older people with disabilities have been identified. It is particularly important to examine benefits simultaneously for both the older people and their families at large. Service systems that are not unduly bureaucratic or confusing are also needed, ones that offer flexible solutions to the problems older people face. All too often, we try to fit people's problems into preexisting categories of services rather than make programs responsive to specific needs.

At a more basic level, we need to consider what the role of the family ought to be: That is, how much can adult children be expected to provide for parents with disabilities and what portion of assistance should come from the public sector, such as an enhanced Medicare program? In the Scandinavian countries, for example, it is assumed that the state will take care of the needs of the older population, and although families continue to provide substantial amounts of assistance, governments support high levels of formal care (e.g., Hokenstad and Johannson, 1990). As we examine our own circumstances, we need to ask what the relative contributions should be from families and from formal services and how should the latter be funded. Unfortunately, there is little consensus either about the amount of formal help that should be available or how to pay for it.

Looking to the future, we can expect that families will continue to provide older adults with extensive assistance. However, the unprecedented demands placed on adult caregivers by older people with severe disabilities, the adult caregiver's other responsibilities, and their reduced economic and personal resources mean that new forms of family care and new patterns of assistance between formal and informal helpers need to be developed. The success of these approaches will have critical implications for the quality of family life in this century.

## CONCLUSIONS

Demographic changes in mortality, morbidity, marriage, and fertility have profoundly altered the context of intergenerational family ties. Declines in mortality means that adult child–older parent ties are commonplace. On the other hand, greater survivorship has come partly at the expense of higher risks of chronic illness and dependency. Higher divorce rates among both adult children and their parents imply potentially more needs and fewer resources to share. Finally, the baby boom cohorts will face old age with comparatively fewer adult children than their parents had to rely on for support.

The majority of parents give assistance to their children on a routine basis. The strongest predictors of parental support are the birth of a (grand)child, the quality of the aging parent–adult child relationship, how far apart parents and children live, and parental resources. Also important are the age and the marital status of the parents—parents give less as they age and married parents tend to give more than widowed or divorced parents do. There is also evidence of substantial variations in patterns of routine assistance by race and gender. Survey research finds little evidence of more extensive older parent–adult child ties among African Americans relative to European Americans. Women evidence stronger ties and engage in more extensive kin-keeping activities. Men are found to give financial help; women are more likely to provide emotional support and childcare.

On balance, parents tend to give more than to get routine help from adult children. Children are most likely to offer emotional support and advice and are least likely to provide financial help. Given the overall positive ratings of relationships and the high levels of contact, it appears that the low rates of support probably reflect the comparatively lower need of older parents for routine assistance. Although giving to adult children declines with age, the reception of help from children becomes more common with the passing years.

Number of children, gender, and marital status considerably influence the extent of the support given to parents. Parents with large numbers of children receive much more assistance than parents of few adult children. Women receive more help from their children than men do. Divorced men are particularly at a disadvantage when it comes to assistance from adult children. Considerable evidence exists showing that widowhood mobilizes support from children.

Disability of an older parent represents a major life transition for families. Adult children are involved in caring for parents in a variety of ways. Some children assist their other parent who has assumed the primary responsibility for care. In other instances, adult children take on the primary-care role or help a sibling who has done so. Taking on long-term responsibilities of caring for an older person is often stressful and may be disruptive to other relationships and activities in one's life. Caregiving can become an all-consuming involvement, which quickly exceeds a caregiver's physical, emotional, and financial resources. Long-term caregiving has been found to be associated with several different kinds of negative consequences, including increased rates of depression and other emotional distress, increased risk of health problems, and increased strain or conflict with other family members and at work, as well as feelings of losing one's identity or being trapped in the role of caregiver.

Support from family and friends as well as good coping resources can lessen the negative impact on caregivers. Clinical interventions that help families work more effectively together to support the primary caregiver while being sensitive to the needs of the older parent represent a promising approach to reducing strain on everyone involved. Supportive services, such as adult daycare, can also relieve some of the daily pressures for care from the family.

Despite the growing attention that family caregiving has received, it is difficult to be optimistic about future prospects. Demographic trends suggest that the number of older people with disabilities will grow while the resources of families to assist them will diminish. Increased rates of divorce, remarriage and stepparent families complicate the picture of how much family care will be available in subsequent generations. New approaches are needed that support the efforts of family caregivers to assist parents or other older relatives. These approaches need to strike a balance among the interests of the older person, the family, and society, so that the last years of life can represent a fulfillment of family relationships, rather than a threat to the family's survival.

## ACKNOWLEDGMENTS

Partial support for this chapter was provided by National Institute on Aging grant 1 RO1 AG11345, "Mental Health of Caregivers of the Elderly: Day Care Use" (Steven H. Zarit, principal investigator), and by National Institute of Mental Health grant 1 RO1 MH59027, "Reducing Behavior Problems in Dementia: Day Care Use."

## REFERENCES

Amato, P. R., Rezac, S. J., and Booth, A. (1995). Helping between parents and young adult offspring: The role of parental marital quality, divorce, and remarriage. *Journal of Marriage and the Family, 57,* 363–374.

Anderson, R. N. (1999). *United States Life Tables, 1997: National Vital Statistics Reports* (Vol. 47, No. 28). Hyattsville, MD: National Center for Health Statistics.

Aneshensel, C. S., Pearlin, L. I., and Schuler, R. M. (1993). Stress, role captivity and the cessation of caregiving. *Journal of Health and Social Behavior, 34,* 54–70.

Aneshensel, C. S., Pearlin, L. I., Mullan, J. T., Zarit, S. H., and Whitlatch, C. J. (1995). *Profiles in caregiving.* San Diego: Academic.

Anthony, C. R., Zarit, S. H., and Gatz, M. (1988). Symptoms of distress among caregivers of dementia patients. *Psychology and Aging, 3,* 245–248.

Aquilino, W. S. (1994). Later life parental divorce and widowhood: Impact on young adults' assessment of parent–child relations. *Journal of Marriage and the Family, 56,* 908–922.

Bengtson, V., Rosenthal, C., and Burton, L. (1996). Paradoxes of families and aging. In R. Binstock and L. George (Eds.), *Handbook of aging and the social sciences* (3rd ed., pp. 263–287). New York: Academic.

Bernheim, B. D., Shleifer, A., and Summers, L. H. (1985). The strategic bequest motive. *Journal of Political Economy, 96,* 1045–1076.

Birkel, R. C. (1987). Toward a social ecology of the home-care household. *Psychology and Aging, 2,* 294–301.

Brody, E. M., Hoffman, C., Kleban, M. H., and Schoonover, C. (1989). Caregiving daughters and their local siblings: Perceptions, strains, and interactions. *Gerontologist, 29,* 529–538.

Brody, E. M., Johnsen, P. T., and Fulcomer, M. C. (1984). What should adult children do for elderly parents? Opinions and preferences in three generations of women. *Journal of Gerontology, 39,* 736–746.

Brody, E. M., Johnsen, P. T., Fulcomer, M. C., and Lang, A. M. (1983). Women's changing roles and help to the elderly: Attitudes of three generations of women. *Journal of Gerontology, 38,* 597–607.

Brody, E. M., Kleban, M. H., Johnsen, P. T., Hoffman, C., and Schoonover, C. B. (1987). Work status and parent care: A comparison of four groups of women. *Gerontologist, 27,* 201–208.

Brody, E. M., Litvin, S. J., Hoffman, C., and Kleban, M. H. (1992). Differential effects of daughters marital status on their parent–care experiences. *Gerontologist, 32,* 58–67.

Brody, E. M., and Schoovoner, C. B. (1986). Patterns of parent–care when adult daughters work and they they do not. *Gerontologist, 26,* 372–381.

Burton, L. M., and Sörensen, S. (1993). Temporal context and the caregiver role: Perspectives from ethnographic studies of multigeneration African American families. In S. H. Zarit, L. I. Pearlin, and K. W. Schaie (Eds.), *Caregiving systems: Informal and formal helpers* (pp. 47–65). Hillsdale, NJ: Lawrence Erlbaum Associates.

Cantor, M. H. (1983). Strain among caregivers: A study of experience in the United States. *Gerontologist, 23,* 597–604.

Chin, M. (2000). *Kin support and public assistance to single mother families: Longitudinal analyses.* Unpublished doctoral dissertation. Pennsylvania State University.

Cohler, B. J., Groves, L., Borden, W., and Lazarus, L. (1989). Caring for family members with Alzheimer's disease. In E. Light and B. Lebowitz (Eds.), *Alzheimer's disease treatment and family stress: Directions for research* (pp. 50–105). Washington, DC: U.S. Government Printing Office.

Cooney, T. M., and Uhlenberg, P. R. (1990). The role of divorce in men's relations with their adult children after mid-life. *Journal of Marriage and the Family, 52,* 677–688.

Cooney, T. M., and Uhlenberg, P. R. (1992). Support from parents over the life course. *Social Forces, 71,* 63–84.

Crimmins, E. M., and Ingegneri, D. G. (1990). Interaction and living arrangements of older parents and their children. *Research on Aging, 12,* 3–35.

Davey, A., and Eggebeen, D. J. (1998). Patterns of intergenerational exchange and mental health. *Journal of Gerontology: Psychological Sciences, 53*, P86–P95.

Deimling, G. T., Bass, D. M., Townsend, A. L., and Noelker, L. S. (1989). Care-related stress: A comparison of spouse and adult-child caregivers in shared and separate households. *Journal of Aging and Health, 1*, 67–82.

Dilworth-Anderson, P. (1992). Extended kin networks in Black families. *Generations, 17*, 29–32.

Dilworth-Anderson, P., Williams, S. W., and Cooper, T. (1999). Family caregiving to elderly African Americans: Caregiver types and structures. *Journal of Gerontology: Social Sciences, 54B*, S237–S241.

Eggebeen, D. J. (1992). Family structure and intergenerational exchanges. *Research on Aging, 14*, 427–447.

Eggebeen, D. J., and Davey, A. (1998). Do safety nets work? The role of anticipated support in times of need. *Journal of Marriage and the Family, 60*, 939–950.

Eggebeen, D. J., and Hogan, D. P. (1990). Giving between generations in American families. *Human Nature, 1*, 211–232.

Eggebeen, D. J., and Wilhelm, M. O. (1995). Patterns of support given by older Americans to their children. In S. A. Bass (Ed.), *Aging and active: Dimensions of productive engagement among older Americans* (pp. 122–168). New Haven, CT: Yale University Press.

Elder, G. H., Jr. (1974). *Children of the great depression*. Chicago: University of Chicago Press.

Elder, G. H., Jr. (1978). Family history and the life course. In T. Haraven (Ed.), *Transitions: The family and life course in historical perspective* (pp. 17–64). New York: Academic.

Elder, G. H., Jr. (1985). Perspectives on the life course. In G. H. Elder, Jr. (Ed.), *Life course dynamics, trajectories, and transitions, 1968–1980* (pp. 23–49). Ithaca, NY: Cornell University Press.

Elder, G. H., Jr. (1998). The life course and human development. In R. Lerner (Ed.), *Handbook of child psychology: Vol. 1: Theoretical models of human development* (pp. 939–991). New York: Wiley.

Friss, L. (1990). A model state-level approach to family survival for caregivers of brain-impaired adults. *Gerontologist, 30*, 121–125.

Furstenberg, F. F. Jr., Hoffman, S. D., and Shrestha, L. (1995). The effect of divorce on intergenerational transfers: New evidence. *Demography, 32*, 319–334.

Gallagher, D., Rose, J., Rivera, P., Lovett, S., and Thompson, L. W. (1989). Prevalence of depression in family caregivers. *Gerontologist, 29*, 449–456.

Genensky, S. M., and Zarit, S. H. (1993). Low-vision care in a clinical setting. In A. A. Rosenbloom, Jr. and M. W. Morgan (Eds.), *Vision and aging* (2nd ed., pp. 424–444). Boston: Butterworth-Heinemann.

George, L. K., and Gwyther, L. P. (1986). Caregiver well-being: A multidimensional examination of family caregivers of demented adults. *Gerontologist, 26*, 253–259.

George, L. K., and Gold, D. T. (1991). Life course perspectives on intergenerational connections. *Marriage and Family Review, 16*, 67–83.

Greenwell, L., and Bengston, V. L. (1997). Geographic distance and contact between middle-aged children and their parents: The effects of social class over 20 years. *Journal of Gerontology: Social Sciences, 52B*, S13–S26.

Habib, J., Sundström, G., and Windmiller, K. (1993). Understanding the pattern of support for the elderly: A comparison between Israel and Sweden. *Journal of Aging and Social Policy, 5*, 187–206.

Haley, W. E., Brown, S. L., and Levine, E. G. (1987). Family caregiver appraisals of patient behavioral disturbance in senile dementia. *Clinical Gerontologist, 6*, 25–34.

Hao, L. (1994). *Kin support, welfare, and out-of-wedlock mothers*. New York: Garland.

Hofferth, S. (1984). Kin networks, race, and family structure. *Journal of Marriage and the Family, 46*, 791–806.

Hogan, D. P., and Eggebeen, D. J. (1995). Sources of emergency help and routine assistance in old age. *Social Forces, 73*, 917–936.

Hogan, D. P., Eggebeen, D. J., and Clogg, C. C. (1993). The structure of intergenerational exchanges in American families. *American Journal of Sociology, 98*, 1428–1458.

Hogan, D. P., Eggebeen, D. J., and Snaith, S. (1996). The well-being of aging Americans with very old parents. In T. Haraven (Ed.). *Aging and Intergenerational Relations Over the Life Course* (pp. 327–346). New York: Walter de Gruyter.

Hogan, D. P., Hao, L.-X., and Parish, W. L. (1990). Race, kin networks, and assistance to mother-headed families. *Social Forces, 68*, 797–812.

Hokenstad, M. C., and Johansson, L. (1990). Caregivers for the elderly in Sweden: Program challenges and policy initiatives. In D. E. Biegel and A. Blum (Eds.), *Aging and caregiving: Theory, research, and policy* (pp. 254–269). Newbury Park, CA: Sage.

Hoyert, D. L., Kochanek, D. L., and Murphy, S. L. (1999). *Final Data for 1997: National Vital Statistics Reports* (Vol. 47, No. 19). Hyattsville, MD: National Center for Health Statistics.

Jayakody, R. (1998). Race differences in intergenerational financial assistance. *Journal of Family Issues, 19*, 508–533.

Johnson, C. L., and Catalano, D. J. (1983). A longitudinal study of family supports to impaired elderly. *Gerontologist, 23*, 612–618.

Kaszniak, A. W. (1990). Psychological assessment of the aging individual. In J. E. Birren and K. W. Schaie (Eds.), *Handbook of the psychology of aging* (3rd ed., pp. 427–445). New York: Academic Press.

Kiecolt-Glaser, J. R., Dura, J. R., Speicher, C. E., Trask, O. J., and Glaser, R. (1991). Spousal caregivers of dementia victims: Longitudinal changes in immunity and health. *Psychosomatic Medicine, 53,* 345–362.

Kinney, J. M., and Stephens, M. A. P. (1989). Caregiving hassles scale: Assessing the daily hassles of caring for a family members with dementia. *Gerontologist, 29,* 328–332.

Knight, B. (1986). *Psychotherapy with older adults.* Newbury Park, CA: Sage.

Kotlikoff, L. J., and Spivak, A. (1991). The family as an incomplete aunnuities market. *Journal of Political Economy, 89,* 706–732.

Kramarow, E., Lentzner, H., Rooks, R., Weeks, J., and Saydah, S. (1999). *Health and Aging Chartbook, Health, United States, 1999.* Hyattsville, MD: National Center for Health Statistics.

Lévesque, L., Cosette, S., and Laurin, L. (1995). A multidimensional examination of the psychological and social well-being of caregivers of a demented relative. *Research on Aging, 17,* 332–360.

Li, L. W., Seltzer, M. M., and Greenberg, J. S. (1999). Change in depressive symptoms among daughter caregivers: An 18-month longitudinal study. *Psychology and Aging, 14,* 206–219.

Logan, J., and Spitze, G. (1996). *Family ties: Enduring relations between parents and their grown children.* Philadelphia: Temple University Press.

Longino, C. F., and Lipman, A. (1981). Married and spouseless men and women in planned retirement communities: Support network differentials. *Journal of Marriage and the Family, 43,* 169–177.

Lopata, H. Z. (1979). *Women as widows: Support systems.* Chicago: Elsevier.

Lye, D. N., Klepinger, D. H., Hyle, P. D., and Nelson, A. (1995). Childhood living arrangements and adult children's relations with their parents. *Demography, 32,* 262–280.

MaloneBeach, E. E., and Zarit, S. H. (1995). Dimensions of social support and social conflict as predictors of caregiver depression. *International Psychogeriatrics, 7,* 39–50.

MaloneBeach, E. E., Zarit, S. H., and Spore, D. L. (1992). Caregivers' perceptions of case management and community-based services: Barriers to service use. *Journal of Applied Gerontology, 11,* 146–159.

Matthews, S. H., Werkner, J. E., and Delaney, P. J. (1989). Relative contributions of help by employed and nonemployed sisters to their elderly parents. *Journal of Gerontology: Social Sciences, 44,* S36–S44.

McGarry, K., and Shoeni, R. F. (1997). Transfer behavior within the family: Results from the Asset and Health Dynamics Study. *The Journals of Gerontology Series B, 52B* [Special Issue], 83–92.

Menchik, P. L. (1980). Primogeniture, equal sharing, and the U.S. distribution of wealth. *Quarterly Journal of Economics, 94,* 299–316.

Miller, B., and Montgomery, A. (1990). Family caregivers and limitations in social activities. *Research on Aging, 12,* 72–93.

Mittelman, M. S., Ferris, S. H., Steinberg, G., Shulman, E., Mackell, J. A., Ambinder, A., and Cohen, J. (1993). An intervention that delays institutionalization of Alzheimer's disease patients: Treatment of spouse-caregivers. *Gerontologist, 33,* 730–740.

Mittelman, M. S., Ferris, S. H., Shulman, E., Steinberg, G., Ambinder, A., Mackell, J., and Cohen, J. (1995). A comprehensive support program: Effect on depression in spouse-caregivers of AD patients. *Gerontologist, 35,* 792–802.

Mittelman, M. S., Ferris, S. H., Shulman, E., Steinberg, G., Ambinder, A., Mackell, J., and Cohen, J. (1996). A family intervention to delay nursing home placement of patients with Alzheimer disease: A randomized controlled trial. *Journal of the American Medical Association, 276,* 1725–1731.

Montgomery, R. J. V., and Kosloski, K. (1995). Respite revisited: Re-assessing the impact. In P. R. Katz, R. L. Kang, and M. D. Mezey (Eds.), *Quality care in geriatric settings* (pp. 47–67). New York: Springer.

Morgan, L. A. (1983). Intergenerational economic assistance to children: The case of widows and widowers. *Journal of Gerontology, 38,* 725–731.

Mullan, J. T. (1993). Barriers to the use of formal services among Alzheimer's caregivers. In S. H. Zarit, L. I. Pearlin and K. W. Schaie (Eds.), *Caregiving systems: Informal and formal helpers* (pp. 241–260). Hillsdale, N.J.: Lawrence Erlbaum Associates.

Niederehe, G., and Funk, J. (1987, August). *Family interaction with dementia patients: Caregiver styles and their correlates.* Paper presented at the annual meeting of the American Psychological Association, New York.

Ory, M. G., Hoffman, R. R., Yee, J. L., Tennstedt, S., and Schulz, R. (1999). Prevalence and impact of caregiving: A detailed comparison between dementia and nondementia caregivers. *Gerontologist, 39,* 177–185.

Parrott, T. M., and Bengtson, V. L. (1999). The effects of earlier intergenerational affection, normative expectations and family conflict on contemporary exchanges of help and support. *Research on Aging, 21,* 73–105.

Pearlin, L. I. (1993). The careers of caregivers. *Gerontologist, 32,* 647.

Pearlin, L. I., Mullan, J. T., Semple, S. J., and Skaff, M. M. (1990). Caregiving and the stress process: An overview of concepts and measures. *Gerontologist, 30,* 583–594.

Pearson, J., Verma, S., and Nellett, C. (1988). Elderly psychiatric patient status and caregiver perceptions as predictors of caregiver burden. *Gerontologist, 28,* 79–83.

Petty, D., and Friss, L. (1987, October). A balancing act of working and caregiving. *Business and Health,* 22–25.

Pezzin, L. E., and Schone, B. S. (1999). Parental marital disruption and intergenerational transfers: An analysis of lone elderly parents and their children. *Demography, 36,* 287–297.

Population Estimates Program. (2000). Resident population estimates of the United States by age and sex: April 1, 1990 to July 1, 1999, with short term projection to May 1, 2000. Washington DC: Population Division, U.S. Census Bureau.

Population Projections Program. (2000). Projections of the total resident population by 5-year age groups and sex with special age categories: Middle series, 2025–2045. Washington DC: Population Division, U.S. Census Bureau.

Pot, A. M., Deeg, D. J. H., and van Dyck, R. (1997). Psychological well-being of informal caregivers of elderly people with dementia: Changes over time. *Aging and Mental Health, 1*, 261–268.

Pruchno, R. A., and Resch, N. L. (1989a). Aberrant behaviors and Alzheimer's disease: Mental health effects on spouse caregivers. *Journal of Gerontology: Social Sciences, 44*, S177–S182.

Pruchno, R. A., and Resch, N. L. (1989b). Mental health of caregiving spouses: Coping as mediator, moderator, or main effect? *Psychology and Aging, 4*, 454–463.

Robinson, B., and Thurnher, M. (1979). Taking care of aged parents: A family cycle transition. *Gerontologist, 19*, 586–593.

Rosenthal, C. J., Sulman, J., and Marshall, V. W. (1993). Depressive symptoms in family caregivers of long-stay patients. *Gerontologist, 33*, 249–257.

Rossi, A. S., and Rossi, P. H. (1990). *Of human bonding: Parent–child relations across the life course*. New York: Aldine de Gruyter.

Scharlach, A. E. (1987). Relieving feelings of strain among women with elderly mothers. *Psychology and Aging, 2*, 9–13.

Scharlach, A. E., and Boyd, S. L. (1989). Caregiving and employment: Results of an employee survey. *Gerontologist, 29*, 382–387.

Schulz, R., and Beach, S. R. (1999). Caregiving as a risk factor for mortality: The caregiver health effects study. *Journal of the American Medical Association, 282*, 2215–2219.

Schulz, R., Williamson, G. M., Morycz, R., and Biegel, D. E. (1993). Changes in depression among men and women caring for an Alzheimer's patient. In S. H. Zarit, L. I. Pearlin and K. W. Schaie (Eds.), *Caregiving systems: Informal and formal helpers* (pp. 119–140). Hillsdale, NJ: Lawrence Erlbaum Associates.

Semple, S. J. (1992). Conflict in Alzheimer's caregiving families: Its dimensions and consequences. *Gerontologist, 32*, 648–655.

Silverstein, M., and Bengston, V. L. (1997). Intergenerational solidarity and the structure of adult child–parent relationships in American families. *American Journal of Sociology, 103*, 429–460.

Silverstein, M., Parrott, T. A., and Bengtson, V. L. (1995). Factors that predispose middle-aged sons and daughters to provide social support to older parents. *Journal of Marriage and the Family, 57*, 465–475.

Skaff, M. M., and Pearlin, L. I. (1992). Caregiving: role engulfment and the loss of self. *Gerontologist, 32*, 656–664.

Smyer, M. A., Zarit, S. H., and Qualls, S. H. (1990). Psychological intervention with aging individuals. In J. E. Birren and K. W. Schaie (Eds.), *Handbook of the psychology of aging* (3rd ed., pp. 375–403). New York: Academic.

Spitze, G., and Logan, J. (1989). Gender differences in family support: Is there a payoff? *Gerontologist, 29*, 108–113.

Spitze, G., and Logan, J. (1992). Helping as a component of parent-adult child relations. *Research on Aging, 14*, 291–312.

Stack, C. (1974). *All our kin: Strategies for survival in the black community*. New York: Harper & Row.

Stein, C. H., Wemmerus, V. A., Ward, M., Gaines, M. E., Freeberg, A. L., and Jewell, T. C. (1998). "Because they're my parents": An intergenerational study of felt obligation and parental caregiving. *Journal of Marriage and the Family, 60*, 611–622.

Stephens, M. A. P., and Townsend, A. L. (1997). Stress of parent care: Positive and negative effects of women's other roles. *Psychology and Aging, 12*, 376–386.

Stephens, M. A. P., Townsend, A. L., Martire, L. M., and Druley, J. A. (2000). Balancing parent care with other roles: Interrole conflict of adult daughter caregivers. *Journal of Gerontology: Psychological Sciences, 56B*, P24–P34.

Stoller, E. P., and Earl, L. L. (1983). Help with activities of everyday life: Sources of support for the non-institutionalized elderly. *Gerontologist, 23*, 64–70.

Stone, R., Cafferata, G. L., and Sangl, J. (1987). Caregivers of the frail elderly: A national profile. *Gerontologist, 27*, 616–626.

Suitor, J. J., and Pillemer, K. (1993). Support and interpersonal stress in the social networks of married daughters caring for patients with dementia. *Journal of Gerontology: Social Sciences, 48*, S1–S8.

Taylor, R. J. (1986). Receipt of support from family among Black Americans. *Journal of Marriage and the Family, 48*, 67–77.

Teri, L., Logsdon, R. G., Uomoto, J., and McCurry, S. M. (1997). Behavioral treatment of depression in dementia patients: A controlled clinical trial. *Journal of Gerontology: Psychological Sciences, 52B*, P159–P166.

Townsend, A., Noelker, L., Deimling, G., and Bass, D. (1989). Longitudinal impact of interhousehold caregiving on adult children's mental health. *Psychology and Aging, 4*, 393–401.

Uhlenberg, P. R. (1990, October). *Implications of increased divorce for the elderly*. Paper presented at the United Nations International Conference on Aging Population in the Context of the Family, Kitakyushu, Japan.

Uhlenberg, P. R., Cooney, T. M., and Boyd, R. L. (1990). Divorce for women after midlife. *Journal of Gerontology: Social Sciences, 45*, S3–S11.

U.S. Bureau of the Census. (1992). Sixty-five plus in America, *Current Population Reports, Special Studies* (Series No. P23–178). Washington, DC: U.S. Government Printing Office.

U.S. Bureau of the Census. (1996). 65+ in the United States. *Current Population Reports, Special Studies* (Series No. P23–190). Washington DC: U.S. Government Printing Office.

U.S. Bureau of the Census. (1999). Poverty in the United States: 1998. *Current Population Reports* (Series No. P60–207). Washington, DC: U.S. Government Printing Office.

U.S. Bureau of the Census. (2000). Marital status and living arrangements: March 1998. *Current Population Reports* (Series No. P20–514). Washington DC: U.S. Government Printing Office.

Ventura, S. J., Martin, J. A., Curtin, S. C., Mathews, T. J., and Park, M. M. (2000). Births: Final Data for 1998. *National Vital Statistics Reports* (Vol. 48, No. 3). Hyattsville, MD: National Center for Health Statistics.

Vitaliano, P. P., Becker, J., Russo, J., Magana-Amato, A., and Maiuro, R. D. (1988–1989). Expressed emotion in spouse caregivers of patients with Alzheimer's disease. *Journal of Applied Social Sciences, 13*, 216–250.

Vitaliano, P. P., Maiuro, R. D., Ochs, H., and Russo, J. (1989). A model of burden in caregivers of DAT patients. In E. Light and B. Lebowitz (Eds.), *Alzheimer's disease treatment and family stress: Directions for research* (pp. 267–291). Washington, DC: U.S. Government Printing Office.

Ward, R.A., and Spitze, G. (1998). Sandwiched marriages: The implications of child and parent relations for marital quality at midlife. *Social Forces, 77*, 647–666.

Whitbeck, L. B., Hoyt, D. R., and Huck, S. M. (1994). Early family relationships, intergenerational solidarity, and support provided to parents by their adult children. *Journal of Gerontology: Social Sciences, 49*, S85–S94.

White, L. K. (1992). The effect of parental divorce and remarriage on parental support for adult children. *Journal of Family Issues, 13*, 234–250.

White, L. K. (1994). Stepfamilies over the life course: Social support. In A. Booth and J. Dunn (Eds.), *Stepfamilies: Who benefits? Who does not?* Hillsdale, NJ: Lawence Erlbaum Associates.

Whitlatch, C. J., Zarit, S. H., and von Eye, A. (1991). Efficacy of interventions with caregivers: A reanalysis. *Gerontologist, 31*, 9–14.

Wilhelm, M. O. (1996). Bequest behavior and the effect of heirs' earnings: Testing the altruistic model of bequests. *American Economic Review, 86*, 874–892.

Williamson, G. M., and Schulz, R. (1990). Relationship orientation, quality of prior relationship, and distress among caregivers of Alzheimer's patients. *Psychology and Aging, 5*, 502–509.

Wilson, M. (1986). The Black extended family: An analytical consideration. *Developmental Psychology, 22*, 246–258.

Wilson, W. J. (1987). *The truly disadvantaged.* Chicago: University of Chicago Press.

Winsborough, H. H., Bumpass, L. L., and Aquilino, W. S. (1991). *The death of parents and the transition to old age* (National Survey of Families and Households Working Paper 39). Madison, WI: Center for Demography and Ecology, University of Wisconsin-Madison.

Youn, G., Knight, B. G., Jeong, H.-S., and Benton, D. (1999). Differences in familism values and caregiving outcomes among Korean, Korean American, and White American dementia caregivers, *Psychology and Aging, 14*, 355–364.

Zarit, S. H. (1989). Issues and directions in family intervention research. In E. Light and B. Lebowitz (Eds.), *Alzheimer's disease treatment and family stress: Directions for research* (pp. 458–486). Washington, DC: U.S. Government Printing Office.

Zarit, S. H. (1992). Concepts and measures in family caregiving research. In B. Bauer (Ed.), *Conceptual and methodological issues in family caregiving research* (pp. 1–19). Toronto: University of Toronto.

Zarit, S. H., Dolan, M. M., and Leitsch, S. A. (1998). Interventions in nursing homes and other alternative living settings. In I. H. Nordhus, G. VandenBos, S. Berg , and P. Fromholt (Eds.), *Clinical geropsychology* (pp. 329–344). Washington, DC: American Psychological Association.

Zarit, S. H., and Leitsch, S. A. (2001). Developing and evaluating community based intervention programs for Alzheimer's patients and their caregivers. *Aging and Mental Health, 5 (Suppl)*, S84–S98.

Zarit, S. H., Orr, N. K., and Zarit, J. M. (1985). *The hidden victims of Alzheimer's disease: Families under stress.* New York: New York University Press.

Zarit, S. H., Stephens, M. A. P., Townsend, A., and Greene, R. (1998). Stress reduction for family caregivers: Effects of day-care use. *Journal of Gerontology: Social Sciences, 53B*, S267–S277.

Zarit, S. H., Stephens, M. A. P., Townsend, A., Greene, R., and Leitsch, S. A. (1999). Patterns of adult day service use by family caregivers: A comparison of brief versus sustained use. *Family Relations, 48*, 355–361.

Zarit, S. H., Todd, P. A., and Zarit, J. M. (1986). Subjective burden of husbands and wives as caregivers: A longitudinal study. *Gerontologist, 26*, 260–270.

Zarit, S. H., and Teri, L. (1991). Interventions and services for family caregivers. *Annual Review of Gerontology and Geriatrics, 11*, 287–310.

Zarit, S. H., and Whitlatch, C. J. (1992). Institutional placement: Phases of the transition. *Gerontologist, 32*, 665–672.

Zarit, S. H., and Whitlatch, C. J. (1993). Short and long-term consequences of placement for caregivers. *Irish Journal of Psychology, 14*, 25–37.

Zarit, S. H., and Zarit, J. M. (1998). *Mental disorders in older adults: Fundamentals of assessment and treatment.* New York: Guilford.

# PART II

## PARENTING CHILDREN OF VARYING STATUS

# 6

# Parenting Siblings

Wyndol Furman
*University of Denver*
Richard Lanthier
*The George Washington University*

## INTRODUCTION

When a second child is born, family dynamics change, and the joys and responsibilities of parenting undergo dramatic transformations. One no longer has *a* child, but instead one has *children*. These children can be quite different from one another. The parenting practices used with one child may need to be modified for the second and subsequent children. The children may differ, and the parents themselves may change as they continue to develop. Therefore it is not surprising to discover that parents treat their latterborn children differently from their firstborn or from an only child. The nature of the relationship that develops between siblings can also influence how parents rear siblings.

Furman (1995) examined the literature on the potential influences that siblings have on parenting and parent–child relationships. Since the time of that review, researchers have continued to conduct research relevant to the issue. In this chapter, we review these studies, as well as the prior ones, and discuss how parenting may be influenced by having siblings. We focus on nontwin siblings, as Lytton with Gallagher (in Vol. 1 of this *Handbook*) discuss twin relationships extensively. In the first section of this chapter we present a brief history of the field, outlining the central theories, research trends, and major conceptual issues in research on parenting siblings. After this historical analysis, we summarize the empirical literature on four broad topics: how parent–child relationships may vary as a function of family constellation variables, such as birth order and family size; how relationships change with the birth of another child; how the nature of the sibling relationship may be related to parenting; and how consistent parental treatment of two children is. We close by discussing future directions for research in the field.

## A BRIEF HISTORY OF SIBLING RESEARCH

Limited attention was paid to the role of siblings until Adler (1931) wrote about the importance of family structure. In his theory of individual psychology, Adler suggested that children's birth order in the family has profound influences on their experience growing up. Like other psychodynamic theorists, Adler (1931) believed childhood experiences shaped mature personality (see also Ansbacher and Ansbacher, 1956). Adler observed that oldest children have two quite distinct experiences as they develop. The oldest begin life as only children and receive full attention from their parents. When second children are born, the firstborns are "dethroned" and must suddenly share their parents' attention and affection with siblings. A rivalry naturally develops as the oldest children fight back for their mothers' love.

This battle can be enacted in several ways. In one case a coercive pattern of interaction with the mother and the firstborn develops. In another case the firstborn may develop a preference for and identification with the father. Adler believed that, because of the experience of dethronement, firstborn children are the most likely to develop problem behaviors. Specifically, he noted that the oldest children are more likely to show insecurity or asocial tendencies, particularly in regard to their younger siblings. On the other hand, Adler acknowledged that such fates were not inevitable. When oldest children feel certain of their parents' love and are well prepared for the transition that will occur with the birth of the sibling, they may identify with the parental role and take a protective, nurturing stance with younger siblings.

Secondborns have an older sibling by definition. Secondborns therefore must share their parents' attention with other siblings and do not benefit from a period of unilateral attention and support. Accordingly, Adler expected secondborns to be more cooperative. At the same time, their older siblings establish a set of expectations for what the children in the family will be like and what they should accomplish. These expectations often lead to ambitiousness and competitiveness on the part of the secondborns. Like their oldest siblings, secondborns undergo dethronement if more children come into the family. In these cases, however, Adler believed the dethronement was less traumatic for them than firstborns because secondborns had never been only children.

The youngest children never experience displacement or dethronement by other siblings. As such, the youngest are the babies in the families and are often pampered and spoiled. Outcomes for the youngest child vary; in some instances, the stimulation and chances for competition among siblings can influence them to excel, but in other cases, the spoiling leads to maladjustment, neuroses, or feelings of inferiority.

Adler also discussed the fate of only children. He thought that because only children never have sibling rivals, the feelings of competition are frequently directed toward their fathers. Adler thought that only children develop mother complexes in which they are tied to their mothers' apron strings and alienate the fathers from the family system. Only children frequently desire to be the center of attention and feel that such attention is their right.

In spite of the fact that Adler was primarily concerned with potential birth-order effects, he discussed some potential moderators of these effects within families. For example, he pointed out that wide age spacing among siblings can lead each child to have some of the features of an only child. Adler also briefly discussed the impact of the gender of siblings on development. A boy who only has sisters may feel quite different and isolated in a family of mostly women. An only girl among boys may become either very feminine or very masculine; frequently she feels insecure or helpless.

Adler's theory stimulated a significant amount of research on the effects of birth order on personality, IQ, and adjustment. In addition, the impact of Adler's work is still very strong in the popular press and among laypeople. In their definitive review of the empirical literature on birth order, Ernst and Angst (1983) examined nearly 1,500 studies published from 1946 to 1980. They observed that the research, although very prolific, was not very systematic. Birth order often appeared to be included in a larger study because it was easy to do, and consequently many studies were not guided by theory. Significant birth-order effects were also commonly interpreted after the fact. Overall, the scientific yield of this research proved disappointing. In fact, many reviewers have concluded that birth order or other family constellation variables are not major contributors to development and adjustment (Ernst and Angst, 1983; Schooler, 1972).

One result of the growing disenchantment with family constellation research was that researchers in the 1980s began to examine the features or characteristics of sibling relationships such as warmth, conflict, and rivalry. Some of this work examined how birth order or other constellation variables related to these features of sibling relationships; but this work differed from most past research by directly measuring the relationship features rather than inferring what the relationships are like based on the family constellation variables. Studies began to examine how the birth of a second child influences patterns of interactions within the family system. This focus on relationship characteristics led to the important recognition that a relationship between two children cannot be characterized as just one relationship. The two siblings have different perspectives and experiences in the relationship. Moreover, other family members or other outside observers have different perspectives on a particular relationship. Paralleling research that examines convergence among different raters for psychological adjustment (e.g., Achenbach, McConaughy, and Howell, 1987), research found that relationship measures from different perspectives that do not always converge empirically. Moreover, theoretically they should not be expected to be identical (Furman, Jones, Buhrmester, and Adler, 1988).

At this time, researchers also became interested in identifying variables beyond the family constellation that might affect the nature of the sibling relationship. Parent–child relationships and parenting practices emerged as key factors that shape the nature of sibling relationships. Although the general field of parenting had grown to recognize that children influence their parents and parenting (Bell, 1968, 1971; Lewis and Rosenblum, 1974), it seems fair to say that most of the work on siblings has been guided by an implicit model of parenting that affects sibling relationships. As we discuss in this chapter, however, many of the findings concerning seeming parental influences could reflect the influences that sibling relationships have on parents.

As researchers became more interested in the qualitative features of family relationships, investigators approached the topic of sibling relationships from a number of varied theoretical perspectives. Attachment theory, social learning theory, role theory, and family systems theory have all guided work in the field. Interestingly, the empirical research on siblings has not generated many new theoretical views. One noteworthy exception is Kreppner's theory, which integrates child developmental and family developmental perspectives in an account of changes in the family with the birth of a second child (Kreppner, 1989; Kreppner, Paulsen, and Schuetze, 1982).

More recently, Plomin and his colleagues (Plomin and Daniels, 1987; Rowe and Plomin, 1981) observed that two siblings are similar in personality, intelligence, and other characteristics because of the similarity in the genetic makeup. However, once the genetic influences are taken into account, the siblings are no more similar to each other than two unrelated children are. That is, the initial evidence suggested that there was little effect of any "shared" environmental influences that stem from being reared in the same house by the same parents. Although more recent evidence has tempered this conclusion (Reiss, Neiderhiser, Hetherington, and Plomin, 2000), the research has underscored the importance of "nonshared" environmental influences on development and adjustment. Such nonshared factors may include family structural variables, differential parental treatment, differential sibling interactions, extrafamilial network influences, and accidental factors (Rowe and Plomin, 1981). Nonshared and shared environmental influences on development, relationships, and adjustment are some of the most vital areas of research today.

A focus on diversity represents a final development in the study of siblings. Until recently, most of the research had been conducted with middle-socioeconomic-status (SES), European American families. Investigators have, however, begun to examine understudied populations, such as ethnic minorities or lower-SES families. For example, Watson (1998) argued that the sibling subsystem is extremely important in African American culture, yet it has been largely ignored by social scientists. This omission is especially worrisome as it is commonly thought that older siblings often provide care for their younger siblings in African American families (e.g., Brody, Stoneman, Smith, and Gibson, 1999). In light of this potential difference in African American family processes, Brody et al. (1999) tested a family process model for linking parenting processes and self-regulation to sibling relationships in rural African American families.

Similarly, other investigators have begun to examine the roles that SES and family income may play in parenting and sibling relationships. For example, Baydar, Hyle, and Brooks-Gunn (1997) report that the effects of a birth of a sibling are particularly detrimental to economically disadvantaged youth. On the other hand, Dunn, Deater-Deckard, Pickering, Golding, and the ALSPAC Study Team (1999) found that income bore little relation to the quality of parent–child relationships, sibling relationships, or the links between them. They argue that other contextual variables may moderate the association between income and these variables. For example, they suggest that income may be more important in single-parent families and stepfamilies.

The studies of different ethnic and SES populations in the United States have been complemented by research in cultures outside of the United States, Canada, and Western Europe. Several volumes have now been published on such cross-cultural research (Nuckolls, 1993; Zukow, 1989). In one such study, Whittemore and Beverly (1989) describe how siblings in the Mandinka of Senegal engage in much caregiving as the mothers tend the rice fields and engage in other economic pursuits. Thus an older sibling clearly has a major impact on the kind of caregiving that a child receives (see Zukow-Goldring, in Vol. 3 of this *Handbook*, for further discussion of sibling caregiving).

The research on cultural factors is likely to have important implications for our understanding of how siblings may influence parenting. Specifically, it will provide us information about the generalizability of our findings. It will reveal what effects are specific to particular cultures or subcultures and what ones may be more universal in nature. Such research can indicate how cultural factors interact with other variables to shape the course of parenting. Finally, an examination of diverse cultures will also provide a number of "natural experiments." For example, at the present time, most Chinese families are permitted to have only one child; it will be interesting to know what effect this societal policy has had on parenting.

Our brief review of the history of sibling research indicates that the questions of interest and the dominant methodological approaches have changed substantially over the course of time. Indeed, they continue to change as our understanding of genetic and environmental influences increases. In the sections that follow we review research that examines the links between siblings and parenting.

## FAMILY CONSTELLATION VARIABLE EFFECTS ON PARENTING

Many studies have examined the effects of birth-order, spacing of siblings, family size, and other family constellation variables (Ernst and Angst, 1983). Most of this literature, however, is not directly relevant to the question of how siblings may influence parenting. The typical family constellation research study compares children or adults of different birth-orders on some individual characteristic, such as a personality trait. Observed differences among birth orders are commonly interpreted in terms of differences in parent–child relationships. The characteristics of the parent–child relationships are rarely measured directly—rather, inferences are made on the basis of the birth-order difference. On the basis of these studies, we cannot determine if particular characteristics of parent–child relationships are responsible for the effects of family constellation variables on individual characteristics. In fact, we cannot attribute any birth-order effects to the parent–child relationship per se. For example, differences in firstborns' or latterborns' sibling relationships could also be responsible for any birth-order effect. In fact, Adler often conceptualized the effects of birth order in terms of differences in sibling relationships as well as differences in parent–child relationships. For example, secondborns were thought to be envious of firstborns and struggled to surpass them. Because of the limitations of inferring relationship characteristics from family constellation variables, the review that follows focuses on studies that directly examine differences in family relationships.

## Ordinal Position, Gender of Sibling, and Age-Spacing Effects

Many investigators have found that firstborns receive more attention and higher-quality care as infants and toddlers than latterborns do (see Ernst and Angst, 1983; Grossman, Eichler, and Winickoff, 1980; Parke and O'Leary, 1975). These differences may be especially pronounced when the secondborn is female or of the same gender as the firstborn (Dunn and Kendrick, 1981a; 1981b; Jacobs and Moss, 1976). The difference in attention and quality of care is particularly likely when the age spacing is between 19 and 30 months (Lewis and Kreitzberg, 1979).

Belsky and his colleagues conducted some of the most extensive studies of parental treatment and birth order. They collected naturalistic observations of families who had just had their first child and families who had just had their second child (Belsky, Gilstrap, and Rovine, 1984; Belsky, Taylor, and Rovine, 1984). Compared with parents of firstborn children, those of latterborn children responded to, stimulated, and expressed positive affection less often. Interestingly, no differences were observed in firstborn and latterborn infants' behavior or temperament, indicating that the parenting effects did not reflect responding to differences in infants' behavior per se. These differences in parents' behavior increased with time since the birth of the secondborn, perhaps reflecting the fact that newborns, regardless of ordinal status within the family, demand more time and attention. The differences in the treatment of firstborn and latterborn children were much greater for fathers than for mothers. Belsky and colleagues suggested that this parental gender difference may be due to mothers' needing to be with the newborns to breastfeed them and serve as primary caregivers, whereas fathers may take responsibility for their older children. Other research suggests that by the time the infants reach toddlerhood, mothers are more involved with firstborn toddlers than with latterborn toddlers (Bradley and Caldwell, 1984). In a longitudinal study, however, Lasko (1954) reported that the first child enjoys a more child-centered environment in the first 2 years of life, but by 3 or 4 years of age the firstborn child is treated less warmly than secondborns at that age. These developmental trends probably reflect the fact that many families at that stage have a new child who needs their attention as well. Further support for this explanation comes from the literature, which indicates that only children receive more parental attention throughout their development (see next subsection).

In the preschool years, differences remain in the relationships of firstborns and latterborns with their parents, even though the relative amount of attention to firstborns may decline with age and the emergence of new siblings. For example, parents often have higher achievement expectations for their firstborns compared with those for their latterborn children (Ernst and Angst, 1983; Kammeyer, 1967). Firstborns are given more cognitively complex explanations and pressured more on achievement tasks than are latterborn children (Rothbart, 1971). These expectations can be unrealistic and may be rooted in the parents' initial inexperience with children and with being a parent. For example, parents with one child underestimate the age at which children begin to speak a complete sentence or sleep through the night (Waddell and Ball, 1980).

Mothers appear to be less tolerant and supportive and more controlling, demanding, intrusive, and inconsistent with their firstborns (see Ernst and Angst, 1983; Ward, Vaughn, and Robb, 1988), especially when the firstborn is a daughter (Baskett, 1984; Rothbart, 1971). Perhaps they treat children differently because of differences in expectations or because they encourage firstborns to be more independent at earlier ages (see Ernst and Angst, 1983). Most of these studies were conducted with preschool children, and it is less clear if such differences occur later in development. For example, many of Lasko's (1954) ordinal position effects were found only when the children were of preschool age and not later when they were in school.

Fathers are more likely to play the role of disciplinarian with adolescent firstborns than with latterborns (Henry, 1957). Firstborn preadolescents and adolescents also report greater parental control than latterborns do, but these variations may reflect differences in family size (see Ernst and Angst, 1983, and subsequent subsection).

One study found that mothers with children close in age to each other treat them more rationally, democratically, and with more understanding than do mothers with children who are widely spaced (Lasko, 1954). On the other hand, another study of adolescents found almost the opposite pattern (Kidwell, 1981). Unfortunately, such inconsistent results are not uncommon in the field.

Similarly, the literature has yielded relatively inconsistent results concerning parental favoritism and affection (Ernst and Angst, 1983). Some investigators have reported that the youngest child is more likely to be favored (Furman and Buhrmester, 1985; Harris and Howard, 1985), but others have found firstborns to be favored or no differences among firstborns, middleborns, or lastborns (see Kiracofe and Kiracofe, 1990). Further complicating the picture, Koch (1960) reported that perceptions of favoritism vary as a function of genders of the children and the magnitude of differences in their ages.

Firstborns appear to be more influenced by their parents and to be more parent or adult oriented (Baskett, 1984). In their review of the literature, Sutton-Smith and Rosenberg (1970) concluded that firstborns are more similar to their parents and identify more with their parents; however, such differences, like the findings for parental control reported earlier, may reflect differences in family size or SES (Ernst and Angst, 1983).

Finally, whereas most of the studies reviewed here have compared firstborns and latterborns of the same age, other work has examined parents' behavior when the two children were of different ages. Not surprisingly, parents display age-appropriate adjustments in their play or interaction with their two children (e.g., Stevenson, Leavitt, Thompson, and Roach, 1988). Mothers also direct more behavior toward younger siblings than toward older siblings in triadic interactions (Brody, Stoneman, and Burke, 1987; Brody, Stoneman, and McCoy, 1992). It is less clear if that difference reflects an age-appropriate adjustment or if the children actually construe it that way, even if it were. The issue of differential parental treatment is discussed subsequently.

## Only Children

Another way to examine the influences of siblings on parenting is to look at parent–child relationships with only children. Many of the studies on birth order have not distinguished between only children and firstborns who have siblings. In some instances, however, only children have been compared with firstborns or various categories of latterborns.

In a pair of metanalyses of approximately 20 studies, Falbo and Polit (1986) and Polit and Falbo (1987) reported that only children tend to have more positive relationships with their parents. For instance, mothers of an only child spend more time with them than do mothers with two children (Falbo and Cooper, 1980). Parents with singletons tend to engage in more conversation during meals than do parents with two or three children (Lewis and Feiring, 1982). The magnitude of such differences, however, is relatively small (mean effect size $d = .20$ and mean effect size weighted by sample size $= .13$). Moreover, only children's relationships primarily differ from those of children from large families (five children or more) and not from those in two-child families (mean $ds = .20$ versus .08). Comparisons with firstborns have also yielded relatively small effects (mean $d = .08$). Together, these findings suggest that family size may be a stronger determinant of parent–child relationships than whether parents have only one child.

## Family Size

In their study of large families, Bossard and Boll (1956) reported that parenting in large families is "extensive" rather than "intensive." They argued that children in large families are loved, but their sheer number prohibits concentrated care on any one child other than when it is specifically needed (e.g., when a child is younger or ill). The emphasis in these large families is on the family as a whole rather than on any particular individual in the family. Obedience and discipline are stressed as children are expected to conform and cooperate with parents and elder siblings who have dominant roles. Competition and rivalry are discouraged because of their divisive and damaging effects on the family. We should note that the conclusions of Bossard and Boll were drawn from an in-depth study of 100 large families and not from direct comparisons of large and small families. However, many of their observations have been replicated in subsequent studies. For example, family size is negatively associated with the amount of attention parents pay to any particular child and to the amount of attention parents pay to each other (Lewis and Feiring, 1982). These effects on attention appear to be quite robust as they are found even after researchers control for potential confounds such as parental education, SES, and mother's participation in the labor force (Lindert, 1978).

As family size increases, parents become more autocratic (Elder, 1962; Sears, Maccoby, and Levin, 1957). Perhaps by necessity, fathers are more involved in childrearing (Lewis and Feiring, 1982). They are more likely to be the disciplinarian and the dominant decision maker (Elder and Bowerman, 1963; Sears et al., 1957). Parents with small families are less restrictive of their children's autonomy and more encouraging of their independence and self-direction than are parents with large families (Elder and Bowerman, 1963; Nye, Carlson, and Garrett, 1970). Similarly, family size is positively related to perceptions of parental punitiveness and rejection and negatively related to perceptions of parental love and support (Kidwell, 1981; Nye et al., 1970; Peterson and Kunz, 1975; Scheck and Emerick, 1976). In comparison with these studies, other research suggests that such family size effects are not present when parental education, occupation, race, intactness of the family, or SES are controlled for (Bell and Avery, 1985; Blake, 1989).

## Methodological Problems in Family Constellation Research

Before our review of research in family constellation effects concludes, it is important to point out some methodological limitations in this research. Some of these problems may underlie the often contradictory findings observed within this line of work. In addition, some of these issues may explain why comparatively little research is currently being conducted with family constellation variables.

Dissatisfaction with interpretation of family constellation effects is not new, and several authors have summarized the difficulties inherent in interpreting such effects (see Adams, 1972; Ernst and Angst, 1983; Kammeyer, 1967; Schooler, 1972). The key problem is that one cannot attribute any observed differences to the family constellation variable per se, even when the associations between parenting and family constellation variables are directly observed. Family structure studies are inherently correlational, thus making causal inferences impossible. For example, family size may affect parenting by diluting the amount of attention children can receive from their parents; however, it is just as plausible that parents' experiences in rearing children may influence the likelihood of having more children. For example, parents who find that rearing a child takes little attention or energy may be more likely to have many children than those who find it takes an enormous amount of time and energy.

By the same reasoning, it is hard to discern the causal links between parenting and birth order. Of course, parenting does not directly influence birth order, as children have already been born first, second, or latter before the beginning of the parenting they experience. Yet, as with family size, prior parenting experiences can affect the likelihood that a parent decides to have more children and thus affects the likelihood that a child is of a certain ordinal position. Consider the finding that parents have more supportive and tolerant relationships with latterborns (see Ernst and Angst, 1983). One explanation of this finding is that birth order affects parenting. For example, parents may have more reasonable expectations for a secondborn and thus are more able to develop a supportive and tolerant relationship with the secondborn. Alternatively, parenting experiences may affect the likelihood of having a secondborn. Those who had a supportive relationship with a firstborn may be more likely to have a second child than those who had a negative experience. If this is true and if supportive parenting of one child is predictive of supportive parenting of another child, then we would expect more supportive relationships with secondborns than with firstborns. That is, those who had a supportive relationship with their firstborn are likely to have a supportive relationship with their secondborn. Those who did not have a supportive relationship with their first child would be less likely to have a secondborn. Consequently, the proportion of secondborn children who have supportive relationships with parents is greater than the proportion of firstborn children. In this case, we could have a "birth-order effect," even if individual parents treated their firstborns and their secondborns identically. The "effect" would stem from the difference between those who chose to have secondborns and those who chose not to have one.

Family constellation variables are also intercorrelated, which of course wreaks havoc with correlational research. In fact, Eysenck and Cookson (1970) estimated the correlation between birth order and family size to be as high as .70. It is easy to understand such a high correlation when one considers that, even though all families with children must have a firstborn, only larger ones have fourthborns, fifthborns, or sixthborns. Studies have repeatedly shown that family size is associated with a wide range of variables, such as parental education, maternal IQ, likelihood of divorce, SES, religious affiliation, and population density (Barger and Hall, 1966; Blake, 1981; Ernst and Angst, 1983; Falbo, 1978b; Schooler, 1972; Udry, 1978). As such, firstborns are also more likely to be from middle-SES, non-Catholic, urban families than are latterborns. So is the effect a birth-order effect or a family size effect? Some investigators have tried to control for this problem by equating the number of children in studies of ordinal position, but such matching generates as many problems as it solves (see subsequent discussion).

Whatever the approach taken, controlling for the number of siblings does not eliminate the fact that other variables are correlated with ordinal position, such as age of parent, family income, and childrearing expenses (see Adams, 1972; Ernst and Angst, 1983). Even comparisons of children within the same family may be confounded by these factors.

The correlations among family constellation variables may have subtle effects as well. For example, the average age spacing between secondborn and thirdborn children is greater than that between firstborn and secondborn children; as a consequence, secondborns may not receive as much parental attention as their older *or* younger siblings, which may lead to greater dependency on their part (McGurk and Lewis, 1972). Although such a finding may appear as a birth-order effect, it could actually reflect differences in spacing.

Difficulties in interpreting structural differences between only children and other children also exist (see Falbo, 1978a). Only children are more likely to have a mother who works outside the home and are more likely to come from single-parent families. The economic conditions of families of only children are not clear. On the one hand, the childrearing expenses are less, but on the other hand, economic difficulties could lead some parents to have only one child. Moreover, some parents with only one child may have wished to have larger families. The proportion of voluntary and involuntary one-child families is not well known and may be changing with the increase in women's participation in the labor force and changing attitudes about contraception and abortion.

As already mentioned, some investigators have tried to eliminate the effects of confounding variables by matching on the confounding variable or controlling for it statistically by partial correlation techniques or analysis of covariance. Even if we knew all the confounding variables (an obviously implausible assumption), such procedures would not permit us to make accurate causal inferences with correlational designs (Meehl, 1970). Matching on one variable can lead to mismatching on another variable. For example, matching small and large families on social class may increase the likelihood that they differ in religious background, which creates a new and perhaps unmeasured confound. One solution to this issue is to see if patterns of results are the same when confounding variables are covaried or matched and when they are not. The inferences are strengthened if they are the same, but unfortunately they often are not (e.g., Bell and Avery, 1985).

A more contemporary approach has been to use structural equation modeling (SEM) techniques to evaluate the plausibility of various models that depict the causal relations among a set of variables.

Although such procedures have promise, it is not clear that they solve the problem of confounding variables because they too rely on partial correlation techniques. Moreover, accurate inferences are based on two vital assumptions: accurate specification of the time lags (Gollob and Reichardt, 1987) and causal closure, i.e., all relevant variables are included in the model (James, Mulaik, and Brett, 1982). Unfortunately, one can confidently say that neither assumption is ever met. In addition, structural modeling techniques evaluate the fit of a specified model to data. Other models that fit the data equally well may exist. Thus, although SEM techniques have merit, it is important to realize their limitations.

Researchers interested in parenting and family structure face one other vexing methodological problem—the confounding of age and birth order. When comparing firstborn and latterborn children's interactions with their parents, the appropriate comparison is unclear. When interactions between parents and children are observed at any one time, the children will differ in age as well as in ordinal position. Parents are likely to treat children of different ages differently regardless of their ordinal position. The alternative is to examine the parent–child interactions of firstborns and latterborns when the children are of the same age (e.g., comparing interactions between parents and a 6-year-old firstborn and between parents and a 6-year-old latterborn). Such comparisons, however, are confounded by potential cohort or time of observation effects—a classic instance of the problem of matching on one variable (age) and mismatching on another. Moreover, it is not clear what the phenomenologically relevant comparisons are. For example, if I am a 6-year-old secondborn child, do I compare how my parents treat me with how my parents treated my firstborn sibling when that sibling was 6 years old or how they treat the firstborn now that the sibling is 8 years old? Children may make some adjustments for age, but anecdotal evidence clearly indicates that they also make comparisons of parents' contemporaneous behavior toward a sibling. What parent has not heard the complaint from their younger child that she or he is not being allowed to do something a sibling was permitted to do? Latterborn children may feel they always have fewer privileges than their older siblings do, even if their parents treat them identically when they are the same age.

Ultimately, studies of birth order or other family constellation variables are inherently correlational. Birth order is not experimentally manipulated nor are people randomly assigned to different ordinal positions. Although inferences about causality are limited, the work remains important. It is of value to know how parent–child interactions or other variables may be associated with birth order. At the very least, such work may provide clues about potential causal mechanisms.

## Concluding Comments

Although the literature on family constellation variables has yielded some consistent patterns of results, the interpretation of these findings is not clear because of methodological problems inherent in this kind of work. Interestingly, these variables often are presumed to have great explanatory power among the lay public, even though the research indicates they often only account for less than 10%, or even less than 5%, of the variance in outcomes of interest. Although small effects can be theoretically interesting (Abelson, 1985), the documented explanatory power of these variables seems to stand in striking contrast to the layperson's views of the importance of family constellation variables. How often, for example, have we heard someone say, "of course, she's a firstborn," and then nod with understanding? Intuitively, it seems likely that individuals' experiences in childhood would differ depending on whether they had a sister or brother, if they were older or younger than a sibling, or if they came from a large family or one with no siblings.

Of course, it is quite possible that some important distinctions have been missed, that our models have been incorrectly specified, or that our measurement is not accurate enough. Many studies, for example, have lumped all latterborns into a single category, a decision that may mask important differences. In support of this possibility, Kidwell (1981) found that middleborn adolescents reported more parental punitiveness and less parental support and reasonableness than either firstborns or lastborns did. Similarly, middleborn children receive less caregiving than either firstborns or lastborns do (Lindert, 1978). Greater progress in this area would be made if large sample sizes were used to examine all the constellation variables simultaneously. Some work suggests that constellation effects may interact with other variables in meaningful ways. For example, the effects of ordinal position may differ for males and females (Miller and Maruyama, 1976; Paulhus and Shaffer, 1981). Although such efforts are important, the studies that have considered all the combinations of constellation variables have not yielded stronger or clearer effects. Often, in fact, the results of such studies are so complex that they baffle the most clever post hoc theorist.

Perhaps parents and laypeople are wrong and have simply confirmed their beliefs by remembering only the instances that meet their expectations. Such reasoning has been convincingly demonstrated across a broad array of domains in social psychology (see, e.g., Tversky and Kahneman, 1990). Before accepting that such beliefs are simply the result of biases in the human reasoning system, however, we should entertain the possibility that a family constellation variable may lead to any number of different experiences, rather than to any particular one. For example, some parents may think that older siblings should serve as caregivers and encourage such a role, but other parents may not think that older siblings should have that responsibility. The literature has shown that parents have expectations for what children of different ordinal positions are like (Baskett, 1985), but the size of those effects in practice also indicates that there is considerable variability in such expectations. In addition, cultures vary in their expectations regarding sibling roles (see Zukow, 1988; Zukow-Goldring, in Vol. 3 of this *Handbook*), and it seems equally plausible to expect variation within cultures. Accordingly, we should examine family members' beliefs about role expectations directly, rather than inferring them from the family constellation variables. Greater progress was made in the field when the characteristics of sibling relationships were assessed directly rather than inferred from the family constellation variables. Perhaps if expectations and their impact on individuals are directly examined, the scientist's and the layperson's views can be reconciled.

## BIRTH OF A SIBLING

The effects of siblings on parenting can also be determined by an examination of the changes in the family after the birth of a sibling. In this approach, patterns of interactions with the firstborn are observed before and after the new child's birth. This strategy of examining changes as the result of the birth of a sibling does not have some of the interpretive problems that are inherent in comparisons of one- and two-child families, which differ on variables other than the presence of a second child. Nevertheless, it too has problems in interpretation. Interactions with the firstborn may change over time for reasons other than the birth of a second child. Perhaps the most obvious reason is that the firstborn child is older, although sometimes the prebirth and the postbirth observations are close enough in time to make this interpretation unlikely (Dunn and Kendrick, 1982). The birth of another child also brings on other changes, such as increased economic demands.

Interpretative problems notwithstanding, a consistent pattern of changes in interactions with firstborns has been observed. Mothers and their firstborns interact less frequently after the birth of the second child than before (Dunn and Kendrick, 1980; Stewart, 1991; Stewart, Mobley, Van Tuyl, and Salvador, 1987). One might expect such changes in light of the mother's additional responsibilities and the increased economic demands on the parents (Baydar, Greek, and Brooks-Gunn, 1997). Consistent with this idea, mothers initiate fewer conversations and play less than before, whereas firstborns make a greater number of initiations (Dunn and Kendrick, 1980). Finally, the tenor of the interactions changes. Both mothers and their firstborns display less warmth and more neutral affect after the birth of the second child (Baydar, Greek, and Brooks-Gunn, 1997; Taylor and Kogan, 1973). Firstborns deliberately misbehave more often, and mothers make more prohibitions, as confrontations occur more often (Baydar, Greek, and Brooks-Gunn, 1997; Dunn and Kendrick, 1980; Kendrick and Dunn, 1980). These confrontations typically occur when the mother is occupied with the newborn and not when she is away from the baby. Yet the number of positive interchanges between firstborn and mother is also greater when the mother is holding or feeding the newborn than when she is not with the baby. Thus the birth of a sibling changes the frequency, nature, and context of the interactions between mother and firstborn, which may account for the instability in attachment classifications of firstborns following the birth of a sibling (Touris, Kromelow, and Harding, 1995).

These changes vary from family to family. When higher levels of confrontation existed before the birth, the families show greater increases in confrontation and maternal prohibition (Dunn and Kendrick, 1982). The escalation in conflict with mother and decrease in joint attention are more marked when the father and the firstborn have a close relationship (Dunn and Kendrick, 1982). The decrease in positive attention to the older sibling is greater when the spacing of births is small (Baydar, Greek, and Brooks-Gunn, 1997).

Not only may the demands of a newborn lead to significant changes in the mother's behavior toward the firstborn, but the firstborns themselves may also play a role. Many are more distressed or develop behavioral problems (Baydar, Hyle, and Brooks-Gunn, 1997; Dunn, Kendrick, and MacNamee, 1981; Nadelman and Begun, 1982; Thomas, Birch, Chess, and Robbins, 1961). Young preschoolers, particularly boys, are especially likely to have such difficulties (Dunn et al., 1981; Nadelman and Begun, 1982), whereas toddlers are not as troubled (Thomas et al., 1961). Children who have difficult temperaments before the birth are also more likely to have an increased number of problems after the birth (Dunn et al., 1981; Thomas et al., 1961). These "regressive" behaviors may be an effort to regain the parents' attention and investment (Stewart, 1991). Whereas an increase in behavior problems is common, some children do not develop such problems and may even improve in behavior (Nadelman and Begun, 1982). Over half begin to act more maturely and may become independent in terms of feeding or toilet training (Dunn et al., 1981). In either case, the birth of a sibling seems to lead to firstborns' acting differently.

Most of the research on the birth of a sibling has focused on mother–child interactions, and only one study has examined father–child interactions. Stewart and his colleagues found that talk between father and firstborn gradually decreased over the course of the secondborn's first year of life (Stewart, 1991; Stewart et al., 1987).

Another limitation of the literature is that investigators have primarily examined changes from a month or two before the second birth to the first year afterward. Changes may have already begun earlier in the pregnancy. For instance, mothers interact differently with firstborns when they are expecting a second child than when they are not (Nadelman and Begun, 1982).

Few investigators have examined whether the changes that occur with the birth of a sibling last or whether they change in nature over time, although some research suggests that the decrease in positive interactions and the increase in behavior problems may be temporary (Baydar, Greek, and Brooks-Gunn, 1997; Baydar, Hyle, and Brooks-Gunn, 1997). Kreppner et al. (1982) proposed that the changes in the family from a triadic to a tetradic system entail three phases. During the first phase (0 to 8 months following birth), the infant is initially integrated into the family. The family focuses on home management as the parents redistribute their efforts because of the increased responsibilities. The second phase occurs with the onset of crawling and walking by the second child (9 to 16 months). The management of the interactions between siblings becomes important as the young one becomes more autonomous and involved with others. In the final phase (17 to 24 months), the family substems become more differentiated. The parents are no longer parents of a child and an infant, but instead are parents of two children.

According to Kreppner et al. (1982), families use any of three strategies to adjust for the birth of a new child. Sometimes the father takes an increased amount of responsibility for the firstborn, allowing the mother to focus on the secondborn. Sometimes the father takes more responsibility for household tasks and the mother remains primarily responsible for both children. Finally, some sets of parents are more interchangeable in their roles, with both father and mother taking responsibilities for the two children and household work. Kreppner's conceptualization appears promising, but as yet only a limited amount of research has examined the differences in how families respond to the birth of another child (Kreppner, 1990).

In summary, it is clear that the birth of a second child is associated with changes in the interactions between mother and firstborn. Such evidence is consistent with the idea that siblings influence parenting. As yet, however, little is known about individual differences in the changes that occur with the birth of a sibling, the changes in father–child interactions, or the long-term impact of a sibling on parenting.

## SIBLING RELATIONSHIP CHARACTERISTICS

Thus far, we have examined the potential influence that birth order or other family constellation variables may have on parenting siblings. That research suggested that the sheer existence of siblings may have an influence on parenting and that parenting may differ by sibling. Not all siblings or sibling relationships are alike, however. In the following subsections, we examine how the characteristics of sibling relationships may be related to parenting or other facets of the family system.

### Features of Sibling Relationships

Before the associations among family relationships are examined, it is important to consider how sibling relationships vary. Furman and Buhrmester (1985) interviewed children about the salient qualities in these relationships. Children commonly mentioned the following qualities: companionship, prosocial behavior, similarity, admiration of (or by) sibling, affection, nurturance by (or of) sibling, antagonism, quarreling, competition, dominance by (or over) sibling, parental partiality, and a general evaluation of the relationship. From these interviews, we developed the Sibling Relationship Questionnaire to assess sibling relationships. Factor analyses of children's questionnaire ratings yielded four dimensions: warmth/closeness, conflict, relative status/power, and rivalry. These dimensions (or subsets of them) have commonly appeared in other questionnaires and observational studies of children's sibling relationships (e.g., Minnett, Vandell, and Santrock, 1983; Stocker and McHale, 1992) and adults' sibling relationships (Stocker, Lanthier, and Furman, 1997). In fact, it appears that these are manifestations of dimensions that underlie most forms of personal relationships as the dimensions appear to characterize parent–child relationships, friendships, and mentoring relationships (Adler and Furman, 1988; Lanthier and Williams, 2000).

The study of relationship qualities provides us with a different picture from that we obtained by examining family constellation variables in that relationship qualities are not exclusively or even primarily determined by family constellation variables. In fact, although each of the qualitative factors is related to constellation variables, only status/power is strongly related to them (Furman and Buhrmester, 1985); as one might expect, the older sibling of the dyad is perceived to have more power and status than the younger one. Variables such as the personality traits of the siblings predict the other relationship qualities better than family constellation variables do (Furman and Lanthier, 1996). In effect, sibling relationships vary considerably within any particular type of family constellation as well as between different family constellations. Accordingly, just as we might expect family constellation variables to be related to parenting, we might also expect the variation in sibling relationship quality to be related to parenting as well.

### Parent–Child Relationships and Sibling Relationships

There are many reasons why we should expect sibling relationships and parent–child relationships to be related. First, according to family systems theory, the functioning of any one subsystem in the family is influenced by interactions within other subsystems (Minuchin, 1974). Second, the two may be linked through behavioral contagion effects. For example, conflicts between siblings could lead siblings to react angrily toward their parents. Third, parents are likely to react to the emotional tone of the sibling relationship. If the siblings frequently fight, parents may feel less positively toward them and treat them with less affection. Alternatively, parents may feel particularly close and affectionate toward their children when the children are getting along well with each other. Finally, parents' disciplinary strategies and efforts may be influenced by patterns of sibling interaction. For example, sibling conflicts may lead to more punitive discipline.

Given the strong expectations for relations between relationships, it is not surprising that a large number of investigators have examined the links between them. Like the literature on family constellation effects, however, almost all the literature is correlational in nature, making it impossible to infer causality. Most of the literature seems to stem from an implicit model that parenting affects sibling relationships, but the reverse is possible as well. Accordingly, this literature may provide some ideas about the potential contributions of sibling relationships to parenting.

Studies have shown that the relations between sibling relationships and parent–child relationships can be seen quite early, even when one child is an infant. When a preschool child and infant are both securely attached to their mother, they are most likely to have a nonantagonistic relationship with each other. When both children are insecurely attached, they are least likely to have such a relationship (Teti and Ablard, 1989).

The evidence for links between relationships with parents and siblings is particularly striking in the preschool and the school years. In one of the first studies on the topic, Bryant and Crockenberg (1980) reported that prosocial behavior between siblings is positively associated with maternal responsiveness, whereas antisocial behavior is negatively related. Similarly, verbal aggression and physical conflict are associated with parental physical punishment (Felson, 1983; Patterson, 1986). Stocker and McHale (1992) assessed sibling and parent–child relationships by interviewing family members and periodically calling them about the day's interactions. Sibling hostility and rivalry were negatively related to warmth in relationships with both mothers and fathers. Sibling affection was positively related to paternal warmth.

In studying 10- to 12-year-old children, Furman and Giberson (1995) found that maternal perceptions of sibling relationship warmth were positively associated with three indices of warmth in mother–child relationships. Maternal perceptions of sibling conflict were associated with perceptions of maternal power assertion. In a follow-up study, similar links were found with both mother–child and father–child relationships when assessed by either parent or child report. Additionally, observational ratings of sibling warmth were positively related with three observational indices of warmth in mother–child relationships and negatively related with power assertion. The reverse pattern of relations was found for sibling conflict. Similar patterns of relations were found in a third study of sibling relationships of preschoolers (5 to 6 years old) (Katz, 1992). These studies have revealed a consistent pattern of links between the features of sibling relationships and parent–child relationships. The links between parental discipline and sibling relationships may vary developmentally, however, as different strategies may be more or less effective at different ages (Kramer, Perozynski, and Chung, 1999).

Several longitudinal studies have examined the links between sibling and parent–child relationships in young children. Vandell and Wilson (1987) reported that 6-month-old infants' turn takings with mothers were associated with the infants' interactions with their preschool siblings when the infants were 6 months and 9 months old, but the interactions with their siblings when they were 6 months of age were not predictive of their subsequent interactions with mothers when they were 9 months old. Similarly, Kendrick and Dunn (1983) found that maternal interventions in young siblings' conflicts were predictive of hostile interactions between siblings 6 months later, but hostile interactions between siblings were not predictive of their mothers' behavior subsequently. These results suggest that, at least in early development when infants are just learning the rudimentary facets of interactions, the direction of effects may go from interactions with mother to interactions with siblings.

Longitudinal studies have also examined the relations between parent–child and sibling relationships in older children. In a follow-up study of their research on early family interactions, Volling and Belsky (1992) collected home observations of families when the older child was approximately 6 years old. Conflict between siblings was concurrently associated with higher conflict between the mother and the children, but not between the father and the children. Sibling conflict was also associated with the firstborn's having an insecure attachment to the mother at the age of 1 year and maternal intrusiveness toward the firstborn at the age of 3 years. Paternal attachment was not related, but father support and facilitation of the firstborn at the age of 3 years was associated with prosocial behavior in the sibling dyad. In another longitudinal study that began when the two siblings averaged 7 and 9 years of age (Brody, Stoneman, McCoy, and Forehand, 1992), ratings of low family harmony were associated with perceptions of sibling conflict and observations of negative interactions, both contemporaneously and 1 year later. In a second follow-up of the same sample, Brody, Stoneman, and McCoy (1994) found that parent–child relationships with younger sibling were predictive of sibling relationship quality 4 years later. Finally, a longitudinal study in the United Kingdom found consistent contemporaneous links between parent–child relationships and sibling relationships (Dunn et al., 1999). Although the links between parent–child relationships and sibling relationships are clear, the directionality of such effects remains unclear. Unfortunately, the longitudinal links between sibling relationships and subsequent parent–child interactions have been examined in studies of only very young children (Kendrick and Dunn, 1983; Vandell and Wilson, 1987).

## Differential Treatment

The characteristics of sibling relationships are also associated with differences in parents' relationships with the two children. For example, when children are disparaging and discomforting to one another, mothers are more likely to attend to one child's needs and not to the other's than if the children are not disparaging (Bryant and Crockenberg, 1980). The child in the dyad who is more negative toward her or his sibling is also likely to be disciplined more than the other child (McHale, Crouter, McGuire, and Updegraff, 1995). Similarly, low rates of positive sibling interactions and high rates of negative interactions are associated with differences in the degree to which mothers interact positively or communicate with their two children (Brody et al., 1987; Hetherington, 1988; Stocker, Dunn, and Plomin, 1989). Sibling relationships are also described less positively by mothers who are rated as being differentially responsive to their children (Stocker et al., 1989). Frequent sibling conflict and low sibling warmth are associated with differences in maternal warmth, when assessed by either questionnaires or observational measures (Furman and Giberson, 1995). Similarly, when the older sibling in the dyad is less positively involved and more conflictual than older siblings in other dyads, he or she is disciplined more (Volling and Elins, 1998).

The ties with differences in the fathers' relationships with the two children have not been examined as extensively. Most of the existing studies, however, have found links similar to those found for mothers (Brody, Stoneman, and McCoy, 1992; McHale et al., 1995; Volling and Elins, 1998), although not in all cases (Furman and Giberson, 1995). Finally, maternal and paternal differential treatment are not only associated contemporaneously with perceptions of sibling conflict and ratings of negative behavior between siblings, but they also predict such scores a year later (Brody, Stoneman, McCoy, and Forehand, 1992).

Differential treatment has not been examined directly in studies of very young sibling dyads, but the findings of several studies suggest similar patterns of relations may exist. For example, frequent maternal play and attention toward the firstborn shortly after the secondborn's birth is predictive of low rates of interaction or negative interaction between the two siblings old (Dunn and Kendrick, 1981a, 1981b). Similarly, maternal interaction with an infant is negatively related to positive interactions between the infant and the preschool child (Howe and Ross, 1990).

Although a significant amount of research has been conducted on differential treatment, most of it has not examined the links between sibling relationships and differential treatment. Instead the emphasis has been on how differential treatment may be related to other factors, such as marital conflict (Deal, 1996) or stress (Crouter, McHale, and Tucker, 1999). Some issues regarding the links between differential treatment and sibling relationship qualities need further investigation. For example, the links may vary as a function of how the differential treatment is construed. Those children who viewed their parents' differential treatment as unfair have been found to report more conflict and less warmth in their relationship with each other (Kowal and Kramer, 1997). When the differential treatment was perceived as fair, however, the sibling relationship was not more conflictual or less warm. Further work is needed to determine when siblings' interchanges with each other may trigger differential treatment perceived as fair and when they may trigger seemingly unfair treatment.

## Indirect Links Between Sibling Relationships and Parenting

As noted previously, family system theorists expect all of the family subsystems to be interrelated (Minuchin, 1974). Accordingly, the quality of children's sibling relationships should be associated with the quality of the marital relationship, and research indicates that it is. In both married and divorced families, more positive sibling interactions are linked to more positive spousal and exspousal relationships (MacKinnon, 1989). Similarly, perceived sibling conflict is positively related to perceived marital conflict, whereas perceived warmth is negatively related (Deal, 1996, Furman and Giberson, 1995; Stocker, Ahmed, and Stall, 1997; Stocker and Youngblade, 1999). Furthermore, Dunn et al. (1999) found that measures of the marital relationship obtained *before* the younger child's birth predicted the quality of the sibling relationship 4 years later. Such links between marital relationships and sibling relationships are not always found, however. In a study of adolescent twins conducted in Australia (Noller, Feeney, Sheehan, and Peterson, 2000), marital conflict patterns were not associated with conflict patterns in sibling relationships.

## Concluding Comments

It is clear that characteristics of sibling relationships are associated with similar characteristics of parent–child relationships. The links between differential parental treatment and disharmony in sibling relationships are particularly well documented. It also appears that the characteristics of the parents' marriage and the children's sibling relationship may be related to one another, although that issue has received less empirical attention until quite recently.

Although the links are evident, what is less clear is the direction of effects among the various family relationships. One might intuitively expect bidirectional effects, but the few existing studies that looked for such effects did not find any evidence of bidirectionality. Moreover, little is known about the mechanisms or the processes that might link the different relationships. For example, do characteristics of sibling relationships have direct effects on marriages, or do they have indirect effects by influencing parent–child relationships, which in turn influence marriages? In either case, should the links be explained in terms of imitation, behavioral contagion, working models, or some other process? The question of process is discussed subsequently.

## CONSISTENCY IN PARENTS' RELATIONSHIPS WITH THEIR CHILDREN

A final consideration we address is the consistency in parents' behavior toward their children. Evidence that various children are treated differently would be consistent with the idea that children's characteristics influence parenting or that parents change with siblings. Consistency across children would suggest, although by no means prove, that such characteristics do not matter, at least in terms of studying parenting. To some degree, investigators who study family constellation variables and the qualitative features of relationships have examined these questions in their studies of differences within or across families. A significant difference in how parents treat children implies that parents are not completely consistent in how they treat their children, but it does not tell us about how consistent or inconsistent they are.

An early investigation on the topic found relatively low levels of consistency in mothers' affective relationships toward their children, but relatively high levels of consistency in general childrearing (Lasko, 1954). In a study of firstborn and secondborn infants, mothers were somewhat consistent in their social, affectionate, and caregiving behavior toward each, although the magnitude of consistency varied markedly across specific variables (Jacobs and Moss, 1976). Similarly, consistency occurs in mothers' rates of playful and attentive behavior toward their firstborn and secondborn children when each is 1 year old (Dunn and Kendrick, 1982). Mothers' behaviors toward their 2-year-old and their 4- to 6-year-old children are relatively consistent, especially when the children are of the same sex (Abramovitch, Pepler, and Corter, 1982).

Another test for parental consistency is to examine concordance rates for attachment classifications, although this is only a rough estimate of consistency as children contribute to the quality of attachment relationships as well as parents. In any case, maternal attachment classifications are relatively concordant for firstborns and secondborns; specifically, 57% of the siblings are classified the same, whereas one would expect only 34% to be the same by chance (Ward et al., 1988). The similarity or concordance is particularly striking in light of the fact that stability of attachment classification over time for the same child is only 60%. Significant relations also exist between mothers' supportive and helpful behaviors toward their firstborn and toward their secondborn when each child is 2 years old (Ward et al., 1988). Interestingly, these relations remain significant when similarity in the children's behaviors is controlled for, but the two children's behaviors are no longer correlated when the similarities in mothers' behavior is controlled for.

In a pair of studies, the Colorado Adoption Project team examined the correspondence of maternal behavior toward firstborns and secondborns when each child was 1 year of age (Dunn, Plomin, and Nettles, 1985) and when each was 2 years old (Dunn, Plomin, and Daniels, 1986). At both ages, relatively high levels of correlations exist in maternal affection and verbal responsiveness. Controlling behavior is somewhat consistent when the child is 1 year of age, but less so at the age of 2 years. Mothers' behavior toward the same child at 1 and 2 years of age is less correlated. Apparently, developmental changes in the children elicit different behaviors from mothers.

The Stanford Adolescent Custody Study examined parenting and parent–child relationships in divorced families (Monahan, Buchanan, Maccoby, and Dornbusch, 1993). The parenting of different children was less related than studies have found the parenting of different children in intact families to be, especially when the children in the divorced families lived apart.

The emphasis of Plomin and his colleagues on the importance of nonshared environmental influences has triggered work on the issue of consistencies and differences in parental treatment (Plomin and Daniels, 1987; Rowe and Plomin, 1981). Daniels and Plomin (1985) developed an inventory, the Sibling Inventory of Differential Experiences, to assess differential experiences. Although comparisons across scales must be made cautiously, it appears that adolescents and young adults perceive greater differences in their sibling and peer interactions than in their interactions with their parents. In fact, 56.5% reported they receive similar treatment, 34.5% reported "a bit" of difference, and only 9% indicated "much" difference. In a follow-up study, Daniels, Dunn, Furstenberg, and Plomin (1985) asked mothers and fathers to rate their closeness toward their two children and their two children's say in decisions. Relatively high levels of consistency across children exist in parents' reports, but when the two children are asked similar questions, their reports are only modestly correlated with one another. Similar patterns exist in children of divorced families (Monahan et al., 1993). Children who live apart after their parents' divorce differ more than children who live together, however, suggesting that there are shared as well as nonshared family influences (Monahan et al., 1993).

The degree of perceived consistency in parenting may also vary as a function of the domain of the relationship. For example, Volling and Elins (1998) found that the majority of parents report that they do not favor either child and that they find interactions with each of them equally enjoyable, yet they also are likely to discipline the older sibling substantially more.

Not surprisingly, the literature reviewed here provides evidence of both consistency and inconsistency in parenting behavior directed at siblings. The finding that different children are treated somewhat differently is certainly consistent with the idea that children's characteristics influence parenting. Such variability could, however, reflect changes in the parents as well. Additionally, comparisons of various studies do not lead to obvious conclusions about which facets of parenting are and are not consistent across children. Similarly, little is known about the factors that contribute to consistencies and inconsistencies in parenting. Accordingly, further work is needed before one can conclude if and how siblings may influence the consistency of parenting.

## FUTURE DIRECTIONS IN SIBLING RESEARCH

In this chapter, we have shown that parenting behavior is related to family constellation variables, the birth of additional children, and the quality of sibling relationships. The findings are consistent with the idea that siblings influence parenting, but alternative explanations could account for the results of these correlational studies. The task of identifying the direction of causality will always be challenging in this domain, but several types of studies may prove useful to understanding the nature of the correlations.

First, studies examining genetic influences on parents' interactions with their children can give clues about the direction of influence. A series of studies from the Colorado Adoption Project has shown that mothers interact more similarly toward their two biological children than toward two adopted children (Dunn et al., 1986; Dunn et al., 1985; Dunn and Plomin, 1986; Rende, Slomkowski, Stocker, Fulker, and Plomin, 1992). Twin studies of adolescents' perceptions of parental treatment have also found evidence of genetic influences (Pike, Manke, Reiss, and Plomin, 2000; Rowe, 1981, 1983). The similarity in biological children's behavior that stems from shared genes seems to lead to more similar treatment by their mothers. It is possible that mothers expect that genetically related children are more similar and treat them accordingly, although past twin studies have found that mothers respond to actual similarities rather than create them (Lytton, 1977; Lytton with Gallagher, in Vol. 1 of this *Handbook*). On the other hand, genetic analyses suggest that the links between parent–child relationships and sibling relationships may reflect shared environmental effects rather than genetic or nonshared effects (Bussell et al., 1999). Therefore family climate variables might underlie the associations among family relationship features, which suggests reciprocal influences between relationship spheres.

A second strategy to determine the causal direction of effect is to compare a mother's and a stranger's behavior toward the same child. If the mother and the stranger treat the child similarly, then one would infer that they are responding to some facet of the child's behavior or personality. Differences in maternal and stranger treatment would reflect the contributions the adults bring to the interactions, or alternatively, the contributions of the existing relationship between mother and child. For example, Thoman, Barnett, and Leiderman (1971) found that primiparous mothers took more intervals to feed their infant than multiparous mothers did, but nurses took equal amounts of time. These findings suggest that the primiparous mothers' inexperience is responsible for the difference between their feeding of firstborns and latterborns, rather than some infant characteristic.

A third strategy would be to manipulate the two children's behavior toward one another and observe the parent's response. This strategy has been commonly used to isolate the short-term effects of one child's behavior on a parent (or vice versa; see Bell and Harper, 1977), but it does not appear to have been used in studies of sibling relationships.

One might also obtain information regarding causality by observing a parent interacting with their two children. If no differences are observed in the parent's behavior toward the two children, then any differences in the children's behavior would be a reflection of the children's contribution to the interaction or the nature of their relationship. If the children's behavior is similar, then any differences in the parent's behavior would be attributed to the parent or the nature of their relationship. For example, Belsky and his colleagues found that parents of firstborns responded to their children more than parents of secondborns did, but the firstborn and the secondborn children did not differ in their behavior (Belsky, Gilstrap, and Rovine, 1984; Belsky, Taylor, and Rovine, 1984); thus the differences could be attributed to the parents. Such interpretations must be made cautiously, however, as it is possible that the children or parents differed on some other variable that was not measured. After all, one is left with the question of why the parents (children) responded differently if there were no differences in the other's behavior.

More generally, the social relations model of Kenny and La Voie (1984) can be used to separate out the contributions of different individuals. Using a round-robin procedure, one observes each person interacting with every other family member. One can then estimate actor effects (i.e., the consistency of a person's behavior in different dyads), partner effects (i.e., the extent to which behavior is elicited by a particular partner), and relationship effects (i.e., behavior specific to that dyad). One can also estimate the degree to which behaviors are reciprocated. In one such study of preschoolers, infant siblings, and their parents (Stevenson et al., 1988), the adjustments individuals made to one another (relationship effects) far outweighed either actor effects or partner effects. Some actor effects were found for children, but not for parents. Parents were more likely to adjust to their partners, suggesting that they were primarily responsible for the structuring that occurred in their interactions with their children. Although this methodological strategy has great promise, it leaves open the question of where relationship effects come from; that is, how did the past characteristics of the parent and the child contribute to the relationship that currently exists? Kramer and Baron (1995) found that retrospective accounts of parents' sibling relationships were related to how the parents interacted with their own children and also how the parents' children got along with each other. For example, mothers who reported negative relationships with their own siblings had children who got along better with their own siblings. Additionally, those mothers who reported that their own sibling relationships were negative were also less likely to use differential treatment with their own children. Because of the retrospective nature of this study, however, it will be important to verify these findings in a prospective study.

Although longitudinal studies are commonly called for in sibling studies, most of the existing work in this field has collected data at only one point in time. Moreover, the few longitudinal studies have focused primarily on comparisons of mean levels across time, rather than on examining correlations across time. When correlations have been examined, most investigators have looked at the links between only parent–child and subsequent sibling interactions, and not the reverse. Without knowing the ties from sibling interactions at one time to parent–child interactions at a subsequent time, it is hard to make causal inferences of any type. Although the longitudinal strategy has advantages over the collection of data at only one point, the limits of structural modeling techniques discussed previously should be kept in mind. Structural modeling is designed to rule out particular causal models, rather than to document causal links (Breckler, 1990).

Even when studies in which these different strategies are used suggest that the children may be affecting parenting, one should not necessarily conclude that it is something about a sibling or having a sibling that is responsible. For example, many investigators have reported differences in the treatment of male and female siblings (Leaper, in Vol. 1 of this *Handbook*). Although it is clear that the gender of the child has an impact on parenting, it is not as clear that the gender of the sibling matters. That is, differences between boys and girls in the same family may be the same as the differences between families of only girls and families of only boys. Thus one would need to compare differences in the treatment of a child when the sibling is the same or the opposite gender. Such comparisons exist for studies of personality characteristics (see Sutton-Smith and Rosenberg, 1970), but are relatively rare in the study of parent–child interactions. One exception is that mothers seem to interact less with secondborns when they are of the same gender as that of the firstborns (Kendrick and Dunn, 1982).

Similar problems exist in interpreting the literature on the differences in the personality characteristics of siblings (see Brody et al., 1987; Furman and Lanthier, 1996; Stocker et al., 1989). One problem is that the child's temperament seems to have an impact, but it is not as clear that the relative temperament of the child versus that of a sibling matters as well. Once again, one would need to determine whether variations in a sibling's temperament affect the parental treatment of a child.

Although the existing work sheds some light on the potential links between parenting and sibling relationships, further work is needed to specify the mechanisms responsible for such links (Furman and Giberson, 1995). One of the difficulties with family constellation constructs is that they are not direct indices of any family processes. At most, they are associated with or predictive of certain family processes. Thus identifying a significant effect of birth order does not tell us how or why there are birth-order differences. Do such effects reflect differences in parent–child relationships, sibling relationships, or other effects on family processes? Similarly, if parenting of the firstborn changes as a result of the birth of a sibling, is it because of the economic changes in the family, the extra parenting demands, or the older child's feelings of rivalry? Directly measuring the characteristics of parent–child and sibling relationships has led to progress, but even here much work remains. For example, imagine that warmth in sibling relationships has been demonstrated to affect warmth in parent–child relationships. How does one explain that? Numerous theoretical mechanisms, such as contagion effects or system effects, could account for it. Investigators need to develop means of ruling out alternative explanations. Finally, it is important to remember that our measures are snapshots of a system of variables that have a history of influence on one another. Moreover, they may have reached some state of relative homeostasis. It is not clear how well static pictures—even repeated ones—capture the process of change. Thus progress has been made, but the future presents some challenging problems to address.

## CONCLUSIONS

In this chapter, we addressed the interesting question of how sibling relationships affect parenting and parent–child relationships. We examined four approaches that have been used to examine this issue. First, Adler's (1931) theory of individual psychology triggered an extensive amount of research on how parent–child relationships may vary as a function of birth order, family size, and other family constellation variables. These studies found some differences, particularly when the children were young. The most consistent finding is that parents appear to be more involved, and are sometimes warmer, in their relationships with their firstborns. Somewhat paradoxically, however, parents also have higher expectations for and are more controlling of their firstborns. Only children also seem to have more positive relationships with their parents than other children—particularly children in large families. Family size may, in fact, be one of the more important variables as it seems that relationships are more autocratic and less intensive in larger families. Although parent–child relationships vary as functions of family constellation variables, it is important to remember that these differences are modest in size. Moreover, it is difficult to interpret these effects because they are inherently confounded with a number of other variables, such as SES. Perhaps as a result, relatively little work is now done on family constellation variables, other than using the variables as controls or sample strata.

We also examined the changes that occur in childrearing with the birth of subsequent children. Although relatively few such studies have been conducted, it has been found that interactions between firstborns and mothers are less frequent, less warm, and more conflictual after the birth of a sibling than before. Changes in father–child interactions seem similar, but they have been studied less frequently. It is also unclear how long the changes in parenting last after the birth of a sibling and whether the nature of the changes is consistent over time.

The third approach is to examine how the qualitative features or characteristics of sibling relationships are related to parenting. Warmth and positive interactions in sibling relationships are associated with warmth and positive interactions in parent–child relationships. Similarly, sibling conflict and hostility are linked with conflict and hostility between parents and children. Sibling warmth is also associated with similar treatment of children by parents, whereas sibling conflict is associated with differential treatment by parents. The quality of sibling relationships also seems related to the marital quality, although how the two relationships are linked is less clear. For that matter, it is not clear what processes are responsible for any of the observed relations between sibling relationships and other family relationships.

A fourth and final approach has been to examine the degree of consistency in parental treatment of two children. Research indicates that children are treated somewhat differently, which is consistent with the idea that children's characteristics may influence parenting. Such inconsistencies, however, could also stem from changes in parents' behaviors that are caused by other factors. Each of these four different approaches has led to a better appreciation of the links between siblings and parenting. At the same time, it is still difficult to draw firm causal inferences or to be able to specify the processes or theoretical mechanisms that are responsible for any observed links. Attention to those issues may lead to a greater understanding of parenting siblings.

## REFERENCES

Abelson, R. P. (1985). A variance explanation paradox: When a little is a lot. *Psychological Bulletin, 97*, 129–133.

Abramovitch, R., Pepler, D., and Corter, C. (1982). Patterns of sibling interaction among preschool-age children. In M. E. Lamb and B. Sutton-Smith (Eds.), *Sibling relationships: Their nature and significance across the life span* (pp. 61–86). Hillsdale, NJ: Lawrence Erlbaum Associates.

Achenbach, T. M., McConaughy, S. H., and Howell, C. T. (1987). Child/adolescent behavioral and emotional problems: Implications of cross-informant correlations for situation specificity. *Psychological Bulletin, 101*, 213–232.

Adams, B. N. (1972). Birth order: A critical review. *Sociometry, 35*, 411–439.

Adler, A. (1931). *What life should mean to you.* Boston: Little, Brown.

Adler, T. F., and Furman, W. (1988). A model for children's relationships and relationship dysfunctions. In S. W. Duck (Ed.), *Handbook of personal relationships* (pp. 211–229). New York: Wiley.

Ansbacher, H. L., and Ansbacher, R. R. (1956). *The individual psychology of Alfred Adler.* New York: Basic Books.

Barger, B., and Hall, E. (1966). The interrelationships of family size and socioeconomic status for parents of college students. *Journal of Marriage and the Family, 28*, 186–187.

Baskett, L. M. (1984). Ordinal position differences in children's family interactions. *Developmental Psychology, 20*, 1026–1031.

Baskett, L. M. (1985). Sibling status effects: Adult expectations. *Developmental Psychology, 21*, 441–445.

Baydar, N., Greek, A., and Brooks-Gunn, J. (1997). A longitudinal study of the effects of the birth of a sibling during the first six years of life. *Journal of Marriage and the Family, 59*, 939–956.

Baydar, N., Hyle, P., and Brooks-Gunn, J. (1997). A longitudinal study of the effects of the birth of a sibling during preschool and early grade school years. *Journal of Marriage and the Family, 59*, 957–965.

Bell, N. J., and Avery, A. W. (1985). Family structure and parent–adolescent relationships: Does family structure really make a difference? *Journal of Marriage and the Family, 47*, 503–508.

Bell, R. Q. (1968). A reinterpretation of the direction of effects in studies of socialization. *Psychological Review, 75*, 81–95.

Bell, R. Q. (1971). Stimulus control of parent or caretaker behavior by offspring. *Developmental Psychology, 4*, 63–72.

Bell, R. Q., and Harper, L. V. (1977). *Child effects on adults.* Hillsdale, NJ: Lawrence Erlbaum Associates.

Belsky, J., Gilstrap, B., and Rovine, M. (1984). The Pennsylvania infant and family development project. I: Stability and change in mother–infant and father–infant interaction in a family setting at one, three, and nine months. *Child Development, 55*, 692–705.

Belsky, J., Taylor, D., and Rovine, M. (1984). The Pennsylvania infant and family development project. II: The development of reciprocal interaction in the mother–infant dyad. *Child Development, 55*, 706–717.

Blake, J. (1981). The only child in America: Prejudice versus performance. *Population and Development, 1*, 43–54.

Blake, J. (1989). *Family size and achievement.* Berkeley, CA: University of California Press.

Bossard, J. H. S., and Boll, E. (1956). *The large family system.* Philadelphia: University of Pennsylvania Press.

Bradley, R. H., and Caldwell, B. M. (1984). The HOME inventory and family demographics. *Developmental Psychology, 20*, 315–320.

Breckler, S. J. (1990). Applications of covariance structure modeling in psychology: Cause for concern? *Psychological Bulletin, 107*, 260–273.

Brody, G., Stoneman, Z., and Burke, M. (1987). Child temperaments, maternal differential behavior, and sibling relationships. *Developmental Psychology, 23*, 354–362.

Brody, G., Stoneman, Z., and McCoy, J. K. (1992). Associations of maternal and paternal direct and differential behavior with sibling relationships: Contemporaneous and longitudinal analyses. *Child Development, 63*, 82–92.

Brody, G., Stoneman, Z., and McCoy, J. K. (1994). Contributions of family relationships and child temperaments to longitudinal variations in sibling relationship quality and sibling relationship styles. *Journal of Family Psychology, 8,* 274–286.

Brody, G., Stoneman, Z., McCoy, J. K., and Forehand, R. (1992). Contemporaneous and longitudinal associations of sibling conflict with family relationship assessments and family discussions about sibling problems. *Child Development, 63,* 391–400.

Brody, G., Stoneman, Z., Smith, T., and Gibson, N. M. (1999). Sibling relationships in rural African American families. *Journal of Marriage and the Family, 61,* 1046–1057.

Bryant, B. K., and Crockenberg, S. B. (1980). Correlates and dimensions of prosocial behavior: A study of female siblings with their mothers. *Child Development, 51,* 529–544.

Bussell., D. A., Neiderhiser, J. M., Pike, A., Plomin, R., Simmens, S., Howe, G. W., and Hetherington, E. M. (1999). Adolescents' relationship to siblings and mothers: A multivariate genetic analysis. *Developmental Psychology, 35,* 1248–1259.

Crouter, A. C., McHale, S. M., and Tucker, C. J. (1999). Does stress exacerbate parental differential treatment? A pattern analytic approach. *Journal of Family Psychology, 13,* 286–299.

Daniels, D., Dunn, J., Furstenberg, F. F., Jr., and Plomin, R. (1985). Environmental differences within the family and adjustment differences within pairs of adolescent siblings. *Child Development, 56,* 764–774.

Daniels, D., and Plomin, R. (1985). Differential experience of siblings in the same family. *Developmental Psychology, 21,* 747–760.

Deal, J. E. (1996). Marital conflict and differential treatment of siblings. *Family Process, 35,* 333–346.

Dunn, J., Deater-Deckard, K., Pickering, K., Golding, J., and the ALSPAC Study Team (1999). Siblings, parents, and partners: Family relationships within a community longitudinal study. *Journal of Child Psychology and Psychiatry, 40,* 1025–1037.

Dunn, J., and Kendrick, C. (1980). The arrival of a sibling: Changes in patterns of interaction between mother and firstborn child. *Journal of Child Psychology and Psychiatry, 21,* 119–132.

Dunn, J., and Kendrick, S. (1981a). Interaction between young siblings: Association with the interaction between mother and firstborn. *Developmental Psychology, 17,* 336–343.

Dunn, J., and Kendrick, C. (1981b). Social behavior of young siblings in the family context between same-sex and different-sex dyads. *Child Development, 52,* 1265–1273.

Dunn, J., and Kendrick, S. (1982). *Siblings: Love, envy, and understanding.* Cambridge, MA: Harvard University Press.

Dunn, J., Kendrick, C., and MacNamee, R. (1981). The reaction of firstborn children to the birth of a sibling: Mothers' reports. *Journal of Child Psychology and Psychiatry, 22,* 1–18.

Dunn, J., and Plomin, R. (1986). Determinants of maternal behavior towards 3-year-old siblings. *British Journal of Developmental Psychology, 4,* 127–137.

Dunn, J. F., Plomin, R., and Daniels, D. (1986). Consistency and change in mothers' behavior toward young siblings. *Child Development, 57,* 348–356.

Dunn, J. F., Plomin, R., and Nettles, M. (1985). Consistency of mothers' behavior toward infant siblings. *Developmental Psychology, 21,* 1188–1195.

Elder, G. H., Jr. (1962). Structural variations in the child-rearing relationship. *Sociometry, 25,* 241–262.

Elder, G. H., Jr., and Bowerman, C. E. (1963). Family structure and child-rearing patterns: The effects of family size and sex composition. *American Sociological Review, 28,* 891–905.

Ernst, C., and Angst, J. (1983). *Birth order: Its influence on personality.* New York: Springer-Verlag.

Eysenck, H. J., and Cookson, D. (1970). Personality in primary school children: Family background. *British Journal of Educational Psychology, 40,* 117–131.

Falbo, T. (1978a). Reasons for having an only child. *Journal of Population, 1,* 181–184.

Falbo, T. (1978b). Sibling tutoring and other explanations for intelligence discontinuities of only and last borns. *Journal of Population, 1,* 349–363.

Falbo, T., and Cooper, C. R. (1980). Young children's time and intellectual ability. *Journal of Genetic Psychology, 173,* 299–300.

Falbo, T., and Polit, D. (1986). Quantitative review of the only child literature: Research evidence and theory development. *Psychological Bulletin, 100,* 176–189.

Felson, R. B. (1983). Aggression and violence between siblings. *Social Psychology Quarterly, 46,* 271–285.

Furman, W. (1995). Parenting siblings. In M. Bornstein (Ed.), *Handbook of Parenting: Vol. 1. Children and Parenting* (pp. 143–162). Mahwah, NJ: Lawrence Erlbaum Associates.

Furman, W., and Buhrmester, D. (1985). Children's perceptions of the qualities of sibling relationships. *Child Development, 56,* 448–461.

Furman, W., and Giberson, R. S. (1995). Identifying the links between parents and their children's sibling relationships. In S. Shulman (Ed.), *Close relationships in social-emotional development* (pp. 95–108). Norwood, NJ: Ablex.

Furman, W., Jones, L., Buhrmester, D., and Adler, T. (1988). Children's, parents' and observers' perspectives on sibling relationships. In P. G. Zukow (Ed.), *Sibling interaction across culture* (pp. 165–183). New York: Springer-Verlag.

Furman, W., and Lanthier, R. (1996). Personality and sibling relationships. In G. Brody (Ed.), *Sibling relationships: Their causes and consequences* (pp. 127–146). Norwood, NJ: Ablex.

Gollob, H. F., and Reichardt, C. S. (1987). Taking account of time lags in causal models. *Child Development, 58,* 80–92.

Grossman, F., Eichler, L., and Winickoff, S. (1980). *Pregnancy, birth, and parenthood.* San Francisco: Jossey-Bass.

Harris, I., and Howard, K. (1985). Correlates of perceived parental favoritism. *Journal of Genetic Psychology, 146,* 45–56.

Henry, A. F. (1957). Sibling structure and perception of the disciplinary role of parents. *Sociometry, 20,* 67–85.

Hetherington, E. M. (1988). Parents, children, and siblings: Six years after the divorce. In R. A. Hinde and J. Stevenson-Hinde (Eds.), *Relationships within families* (pp. 311–331). Oxford, England: Oxford University Press.

Howe, N., and Ross, H. (1990). Socialization, perspective-taking, and the sibling relationship. *Developmental Psychology, 26,* 160–165.

Jacobs, S. M., and Moss, H. A. (1976). Birth order and sex of sibling as determinants of mother–infant interaction. *Child Development, 47,* 315–322.

James, L. R., Mulaik, S. A., and Brett, J. M. (1982). *Causal analysis: Assumptions, models, and data.* Beverly Hills, CA: Sage.

Kammeyer, K. (1967). Birth order as a research variable. *Social Forces, 46,* 71–80.

Katz, T. (1992). *Parents and siblings: Family relationships of young children.* Unpublished doctoral dissertation, University of Denver, Denver, CO.

Kendrick, C., and Dunn, J. (1980). Caring for a second baby: Effects on the interaction between mother and firstborn. *Developmental Psychology, 16,* 303–311.

Kendrick, C., and Dunn, J. (1982). Protest or pleasure: The response of firstborn children to interactions between their mothers and infant siblings. *Journal of Child Psychology and Psychiatry, 23,* 117–129.

Kendrick, C., and Dunn, J. (1983). Sibling quarrels and maternal responses. *Developmental Psychology, 19,* 62–70.

Kenny, D. A., and La Voie, L. (1984). The social relations model. In L. Berkowitz (Ed.), *Advances in experimental social psychology* (Vol. 18, pp. 141–182). New York: Academic.

Kidwell, S. (1981). Number of siblings, sibling spacing, sex, and birth order: Their effects on perceived parent–adolescent relationships. *Journal of Marriage and the Family, 43,* 315–332.

Kiracofe, N. M., and Kiracofe, H. N. (1990). Child-perceived favoritism and birth order. *Individual Psychology, 46,* 74–81.

Koch, H. L. (1960). The relation of certain formal attributes of siblings to attitudes held toward each other and toward their parents. *Monographs of the Society for Research in Child Development, 25* (4, Serial No. 78).

Kowal, A., and Kramer, L. (1997). Children's understanding of parental differential treatment. *Child Development, 68,* 113–126.

Kramer, L., Perozynski, L. A., and Chung, T. (1999). Parental responses to sibling conflict: The effects of development and parent gender. *Child Development, 70,* 1401–1414.

Kramer, L., and Baron, L. A. (1995). Intergenerational linkages: How experiences with siblings relate to the parenting of siblings. *Journal of Social and Personal Relationships, 12,* 67–87.

Kreppner, K. (1989). Linking infant development-in-context research to the investigation of life-span family development. In K. Kreppner and R. M. Lerner (Eds.), *Family systems and life-span development* (pp. 33–64). Hillsdale, NJ: Lawrence Erlbaum Associates.

Kreppner, K. (1990, October). *Differences in parents' cooperation patterns after the arrival of a second child.* Paper presented at the 21st Baby International Conference, Lisbon, Portugal.

Kreppner, K., Paulsen, S., and Schuetze, Y. (1982). Infant and family development: From triads to tetrads. *Human Development, 25,* 373–391.

Lanthier, R. P., and Williams, A. S. (2000, August). *Measuring and predicting the quality of mentor relationships.* Paper presented at the 2000 annual meeting of the American Psychological Association, Washington, DC.

Lasko, J. K. (1954). Parent behavior toward first and second children. *Genetic Psychology Monographs, 49,* 97–137.

Lewis, M., and Feiring, C. (1982). Some American families at dinner. In L. M. Laosa and I. E. Sigel (Eds.), *Families as learning environments for children* (pp. 115–145). New York: Plenum.

Lewis, M., and Kreitzberg, V. (1979). The effects of birth order and spacing on mother–infant interactions. *Developmental Psychology, 15,* 617–625.

Lewis, M., and Rosenblum, L. (Eds.). (1974). *The effect of the infant on its caregiver: The origins of behavior (Vol. 1).* New York: Wiley.

Lindert, P. H. (1978). *Fertility and scarcity in America.* Princeton, NJ: Princeton University Press.

Lytton, H. (1977). Do parents create, or respond to, differences in twins? *Developmental Psychology, 13,* 456–459.

MacKinnon, C. E. (1989). An observational investigation of sibling interactions in married and divorced families. *Developmental Psychology, 25,* 36–44.

McGurk, H., and Lewis, M. (1972). Birth order: A phenomenon in search of an explanation. *Developmental Psychology, 7,* 366.

McHale, S. M., Crouter, A. C., McGuire, S. A., and Updegraff, K. A. (1995). Congruence between mothers' and fathers' differential treatment of siblings: Links with family relations and children's well-being. *Child Development, 66,* 116–128.

Meehl, P. E. (1970). Nuisance variables and the *ex post facto* design. In M. Radner and S. Winokur (Eds.), *Minnesota studies in the philosophy of science* (Vol. 4, pp. 373–402). Minneapolis, MN: University of Minnesota Press.

Miller, N., and Maruyama, G. (1976). Ordinal position and peer popularity. *Journal of Personality and Social Psychology, 33*, 123–131.

Minnett, A. M., Vandell, D. L., and Santrock, J. W. (1983). The effects of sibling status on sibling interaction: Influence of birth order, age spacing, sex of child, and sex of sibling. *Child Development, 54*, 1064–1072.

Minuchin, S. (1974). *Families and family therapy.* Cambridge, MA: Harvard University Press.

Monahan, S. C., Buchanan, C. M., Maccoby, E. E., and Dornbusch, S. M. (1993). Sibling differences in divorced families. *Child Development, 64*, 152–168.

Nadelman, L., and Begun, A. (1982). The effect of the newborn on the older sibling: Mother questionnaires. In M. E. Lamb and B. Sutton-Smith (Eds.), *Sibling relationships: Their nature and significance across the life span* (pp. 13–38). Hillsdale, NJ: Lawrence Erlbaum Associates.

Noller, P., Feeney, J. A., Sheehan, G., and Peterson, C. (2000). Marital conflict patterns: Links with family conflict and family members' perceptions of one another. *Personal Relationships, 7*, 79–94.

Nuckolls, C. W. (Ed.). (1993). *Siblings in South Asia: Brothers and sisters in cultural context.* New York: Guilford.

Nye, I., Carlson, J., and Garrett, G. (1970). Family size, interaction, affection, and stress. *Journal of Marriage and the Family, 32*, 216–226.

Parke, R. D., and O'Leary, S. (1975). Father–mother–infant interaction in the newborn period: Some findings, some observations and some unresolved issues. In K. Riegel and I. Meacham (Eds.), *The developing individual in a changing world: Vol. 2. Social and environment issues.* The Hague, The Netherlands: Mouton.

Patterson, G. (1986). The contribution of siblings to training for fighting: A microsocial analysis. In D. Olweus, J. Block, and M. R. Radke-Yarrow (Eds.), *Development of antisocial and prosocial behavior: Research, theories, and issues* (pp. 235–261). New York: Academic.

Paulhus, D., and Shaffer, D. R. (1981). Sex differences in the impact of number of older and number of younger siblings on scholastic aptitude. *Social Psychology Quarterly, 44*, 363–368.

Peterson, E. T., and Kunz, P. R. (1975). Parental control over adolescents according to family size. *Adolescence, 10*, 419–427.

Pike, A., Manke, B., Reiss, D., and Plomin, R. (2000). A genetic analysis of differential experiences of adolescent siblings across three years. *Social Development, 9*, 96–114.

Plomin, R., and Daniels, D. (1987). Why are children in the same family so different from one another? *Behavioral and Brain Sciences, 10*, 1–22.

Polit, D. F., and Falbo, T. (1987). Only children and personality development: A quantitative review. *Journal of Marriage and the Family, 49*, 309–325.

Rende, R. D., Slomkowski, C. L., Stocker. C., Fulker, D. W., and Plomin, R. (1992). Genetic and environmental influences on maternal and sibling interaction in middle childhood: A sibling adoption study. *Developmental Psychology, 28*, 484–490.

Reiss, D., Neiderhiser, J. M., Hetherington, M., and Plomin, R. (2000). *The relationship code: Deciphering genetic and social influences on adolescent development.* Cambridge, MA: Harvard University Press.

Rothbart, M. K. (1971). Birth order and mother–child interaction in an achievement situation. *Journal of Personality and Social Psychology, 17*, 113–120.

Rowe, D. C. (1981). Environmental and genetic influences on dimensions of perceived parenting: A twin study. *Developmental Psychology, 17*, 203–208.

Rowe, D. C. (1983). A biometrical analysis of perceptions of family environment: A study of twin and singleton sibling kinships. *Child Development, 54*, 416–423.

Rowe, D. C., and Plomin, R. (1981). The importance of nonshared (E1) environmental influences in behavioral development. *Developmental Psychology, 17*, 517–531.

Scheck, D. C., and Emerick, R. (1976). The young male adolescent's perception of early child-rearing behavior: The differential effects of socioeconomic status and family size. *Sociometry, 39*, 39–52.

Schooler, C. (1972). Birth order effects: Not here, not now! *Psychological Bulletin, 78*, 161–175.

Sears, R. R., Maccoby, E. E., and Levin, H. (1957). *Patterns of child rearing.* Evanston, IL: Row, Peterson.

Stevenson, M. B., Leavitt, L. A., Thompson, R. H., and Roach, M. A. (1988). A social relations model analysis of parent and child play. *Developmental Psychology, 24*, 101–108.

Stewart, R. B., Jr. (1991). *The second child: Family transition and adjustment.* Newbury Park, CA: Sage.

Stewart, R., Mobley, L., Van Tuyl, S., and Salvador, M. (1987). The firstborn's adjustment to the birth of a sibling: A longitudinal assessment. *Child Development, 58*, 341–355.

Stocker, C., Ahmed, K., and Stall, M. (1997). Marital satisfaction and maternal emotional expressiveness: Links with children's sibling relationships. *Social Development, 6*, 373–385.

Stocker, C., Dunn, J., and Plomin, R. (1989). Sibling relationships: Links with child temperament, maternal behavior, and family structure. *Child Development, 60*, 715–727.

Stocker, C., Lanthier, R., and Furman, W. (1997). Sibling relationships in young adulthood. *Journal of Family Psychology*, *11*, 210–221.

Stocker, C. M., and McHale, S. M. (1992). The nature and family correlates of preadolescents' perceptions of their sibling relationships. *Journal of Social and Personal Relationships*, *9*, 179–195.

Stocker, C., and Youngblade, L. (1999). Marital conflict and parental hostility: Links with children's sibling and peer relationships. *Journal of Family Psychology*, *13*, 598–609.

Sutton-Smith, B., and Rosenberg, B. G. (1970). *The sibling*. New York: Holt, Rinehart & Winston.

Taylor, M., and Kogan, K. (1973). Effects of birth of a sibling on mother–child interaction. *Child Psychiatry and Human Development*, *4*, 53–58.

Teti, D. M., and Ablard, K. E. (1989). Security of attachment and infant–sibling relationships: A laboratory study. *Child Development*, *60*, 1519–1528.

Thoman, E. B., Barnett, C. R., and Leiderman, P. H. (1971). Feeding behaviors of newborn infants as a function of parity of mother. *Child Development*, *42*, 1471–1483.

Thomas, A., Birch, H. G., Chess, S., and Robbins, A. (1961). Individuality in responses of children to similar environment situations. *American Journal of Psychiatry*, *117*, 798–803.

Touris, M., Kromelow, S., and Harding, C. (1995). Mother–firstborn attachment and the birth of a sibling. *American Journal of Orthopsychiatry*, *65*, 293–297.

Tversky, A., and Kahneman, D. (1990). Judgment under uncertainty: Heuristics and biases. In P. K. Moser (Ed.), *Rationality in action: Contemporary approaches*. New York: Cambridge University Press.

Udry, J. R. (1978). Differential fertility by intelligence: The role of birth planning. *Social Biology*, *25*, 10–14.

Vandell, D. L., and Wilson, K. S. (1987). Infants' interactions with mother, sibling, and peer: Contrasts and relations between interaction system. *Child Development*, *58*, 176–186.

Volling, B. L., and Belsky, J. (1992). The contribution of mother–child and father–child relationships to the quality of sibling interaction: A longitudinal study. *Child Development*, *63*, 1209–1222.

Volling, B. L., and Elins, J. L. (1998). Family relationships and children's emotional adjustment as correlates of maternal and paternal differential treatment: A replication with toddler and preschool siblings. *Child Development*, *69*, 1640–1656.

Waddell, K. J., and Ball, F. L. (1980, August). *Parental knowledge questionnaire: The first two years*. Paper presented at the meetings of the American Psychological Association, Montreal, Quebec, Canada.

Ward, M. J., Vaughn, B. E., and Robb, M. D. (1988). Social–emotional adaptation and infant–mother attachment in siblings: Role of the mother in cross-sibling consistency. *Child Development*, *59*, 643–651.

Watson, M. F. (1998). African-American sibling relationships. In M. McGoldrick (Ed.), *Re-visioning family therapy: Race, culture, and gender in clinical practice* (pp. 282–294). New York: Guilford.

Whittemore, R. D., and Beverly, E. (1989). Trust in the Mandinka way: The cultural context of sibling care. In P. G. Zukow (Ed.), *Sibling interaction across cultures: Theoretical and methodological issues* (pp. 26–53). New York: Springer-Verlag.

Zukow, P. G. (Ed.). (1989). *Sibling interaction across cultures: Theoretical and methodological issues*. New York: Springer-Verlag.

# 7

# Parenting Girls and Boys

Campbell Leaper

*University of California at Santa Cruz*

## INTRODUCTION

We rarely, if ever, encounter a person for whom we are not permitted to determine "her" or "his" gender. If a child's gender is not apparent, we typically ask questions to find out. We may try an indirect method, such as asking for the child's name, or we may directly ask if the child is a girl or a boy. However, suppose that a person's gender was deliberately kept anonymous. That is the premise in Lois Gould's (1978) children's book, *X: A Fabulous Child's Story*:

> Once upon a time, a Baby named X was born. It was named X so that nobody could tell whether it was a boy or a girl. Its parents could tell, of course, but they couldn't tell anyone else.

The story poignantly highlights the challenges Ms. and Mr. Jones face when rearing a gender-neutral child. Difficulties arise the first day Baby X is visited by friends and relatives:

> The first thing they asked was what kind of baby X was. When the Joneses said, 'It's an X!' nobody knew what to say. They couldn't say, 'Look at her cute little dimples!' On the other hand, they couldn't say, 'Look at his husky little biceps!'

More problems arise later in the story when X becomes old enough for the first day of school:

> You couldn't tell what X was by its clothes. Overalls don't even button right to left, like girls' clothes, or left to right, like boys' clothes. And did X have a girl's short haircut or a boy's long haircut? As for the games X liked, either X played ball very well for a girl, or else played house very well for a boy. The children tried to find out by asking X tricky questions, like, 'Who's your favorite sports star?' X had two favorite sports stars: a girl jockey named Robyn Smith and a boy archery champion named Robin Hood.

After asking several questions, the children give up trying to figure out if X was a girl or a boy. However, by not fitting into the usual girl–boy rules, X is shunned by the other children:

> After school, X wanted to play with the other children. 'How about shooting baskets in the gym?' X asked the girls. But all they did was make faces and giggle behind X's back. 'Boy, is *he* weird,' whispered Jim to Joe. 'How about weaving some baskets in the arts and crafts room?' X asked the boys. But they made faces and giggled behind X's back, too. 'Boy, is *she* weird,' whispered Susie to Peggy.

X eventually begins to win over the other children as they begin to realize that by playing *both* boys' *and* girls' games, X is having twice the fun that they are. Consequently, the other children begin to wear overalls like X and to play with both girls' and boys' toys.

Lois Gould's story not only points out the barriers that parents must overcome to rear their children in a gender-neutral manner, but it also suggests some possible benefits of attempting this goal. Opportunities for fun and learning are systematically restricted when children are pressured to choose between "girls' stuff" and "boys' stuff." As illustrated in Gould's story, X enjoys a wider range of activities than the other children are allowed. However, as reviewed in this chapter, many parents adopt the dominant cultural prescriptions for girls and boys to be different. However, parents are not all alike. Therefore it is also possible to consider the extent to which variations in parents' behaviors are related to variations in their girls and boys.

The goal of this chapter is to review some of the ways that parents may contribute to the socialization of gender in their children. To do this, the larger cultural and historical contexts of parenting and gender development are considered first. Although conceptual models relevant to the study of parenting and gender development are noted, a comprehensive overview of theories is not offered. For theoretical and historical summaries, the reader is directed to several excellent reviews (e.g., Deaux and LaFrance, 1998; Fagot, 1995; Kimmel, 2000; Ruble and Martin, 1998). After the conceptual overview, the chapter assesses several aspects of child development associated with gender-related differences. Not only are overall gender effects on parenting practices examined, but important moderators and mediators of these influences are considered. As stated in the previous paragraph, there are considerable variations across mothers and fathers in their parenting practices in general (see Barnard and Solchany, in Vol. 3 of this *Handbook*; Parke, in Vol. 3 of this *Handbook*) and with regards to gender typing in particular.

The distinction between moderator and mediator variables is often blurred in the research literature (Baron and Kenny, 1986). A moderator is a third variable that affects the direction or the magnitude (or both) of the relation between the predictor and the outcome. To illustrate the impact of a moderator, consider the relation between the child's gender (predictor variable) and parent's encouragement of gender-typed play (outcome variable). Studies find that parents tend to encourage gender-stereotyped play activities in their children (Lytton and Romney, 1991). However, the effect tends to be more likely for fathers than mothers (Lytton and Romney, 1991; Siegal, 1987). Thus, the parent's gender is a moderator that influences the magnitude of the child gender effect on this aspect of parental behavior. In addition to parent gender, some of the relevant moderators of gender effects that are noted throughout this chapter include the parents' cultural background (Harkness and Super, in Vol. 2 of this *Handbook*), ethnicity (see Chao and Tseng, in Vol. 4 of this *Handbook*; Garcia, Coll and Pachter, in Vol. 4 of this *Handbook*; Harwood, Leyendecker, Carlson, Asencio, and Miller, in Vol. 4 of this *Handbook*; McAdoo, in Vol. 4 of this *Handbook*), socioeconomic status (Hoff, Laursen, and Tardif, in Vol. 2 of this *Handbook*; Magnuson and Duncan, in Vol. 4 of this *Handbook*), the parents' employment status (Gottfried, Gottfried, and Bathurst, in Vol. 2 of this *Handbook*), family structure (Brodzinsky and Pinderhughes, in Vol. 1 of this *Handbook*; Hetherington and Stanley-Hagan, in Vol. 3 of this *Handbook*; Patterson, in Vol. 3 of this *Handbook*; Weinraub, Horvath, and Gringlas, in Vol. 3 of this *Handbook*), and the marital relationship (Grych, in Vol. 4 of this Handbook).

In contrast, a mediator is an intervening process or variable that accounts for the relation between the predictor and the outcome variables. Moss's (1967) research on mother–infant interaction provides a useful example. Mothers were found to hold their sons more than their daughters when their infants were 3 weeks of age. However, sons also showed more irritability at this age than did daughters. When irritability was taken into account, there was no difference in the amount of holding of daughters versus sons. Thus, irritability may have been an intervening variable that mediated the relation between child gender and maternal holding. Specifically, sons were more likely to be irritable, and irritable babies were more likely to be held by their mothers. As noted throughout this chapter, child characteristics may account for many observed differences in parents' differential treatment of daughters and sons. During infancy and early childhood, gender-related differences in temperament or maturational level may evoke different behaviors in parents. Moreover, as girls and boys get older and develop their own preferences and skills, they influence their environments (including their parents) in more active ways.

## THE CULTURAL AND HISTORICAL CONTEXTS
## OF GENDER AND PARENTING

Ecological, sociocultural, and social–structural models emphasize the importance of the larger institutional and economic contexts for human behavior and its development (Lerner, Rothbaum, Boulos, and Castellino, in Vol. 2 of this *Handbook*). When we look at American and other Western societies, we can notice dramatic changes in gender relations over the past century. Although American women continue to lag behind men in high-status jobs and governmental positions, their numbers are increasing. In some other Western countries, women have more closely attained parity with men. The highest representation of women in positions of power can be found in Scandinavian countries such as Sweden, Finland, and Norway. In contrast, the lowest representation of women in industry or government tends to occur in most parts of Africa, the Middle East, and Latin America (Eisler, Loye, and Norgaard, 1995).

Despite dramatic changes in the status of women in Western societies during the past few decades, women remain largely responsible for the care of children. Although most mothers in the United States work outside the home, only modest increases have been seen in fathers' involvement in childcare (Coltrane, 2000). Dual-career couples may send their children to childcare centers during the day, but in the evenings and on the weekends, mothers typically end up working a "second shift" (Hochschild, 1989) by being the ones primarily responsible for childcare and housework.

To the extent that children use their parents as early gender role models, one of their first lessons will be that women nurture children (Chodorow, 1978). This observation is subsequently enacted when girls typically play house and care for their baby dolls. In these ways, girls practice being nurturant and affectionate caregivers. Boys are more likely to build towers and play sports and thereby practice the roles of instrumental and competitive workers. The idea that parental role modeling may influence children's developing conceptions of gender is supported by findings that daughters of single-parent mothers employed outside of the home tend to be less likely to adopt traditional gender stereotypes (Etaugh, 1993). By seeing a mother who is the primary breadwinner as well as a caregiver, they see an expanded role model for women. Sons of single-parent employed mothers are not as likely to show reduced gender stereotyping—perhaps because they are not being exposed to a nontraditional same-gender role model.

Some studies of households with primary caregiver fathers have not indicated a corresponding decrease in sons' gender stereotyping (e.g., Baruch and Barnett, 1986). It may be that boys are more resistant to nontraditional gender attitudes than are girls because of the higher status generally afforded men in the culture (Bussey and Bandura, 1999; Leaper, 2000a). Also, boys are apt to look outside of the family to infer the representativeness of their fathers as role models (see Bussey and Bandura, 1999). Thus, alternative role models may need to attain a high degree of representation in children's worlds before they have a strong impact on their developing understandings of gender.

What are the cultural variables associated with the social construction of gender in a society? When Best and Williams (1997) reviewed the cross-cultural research literature on gender development, they identified several cultural practices that appear to influence the behavior of women and men—and presumably of their children's development. The factors that appear to influence the degree of gender bifurcation in a society include the relative status of women and men, the division of labor by gender, fathers' involvement in caregiving, economic opportunities, and religious beliefs and values. For instance, the prevalence in a society of father involvement in childcare is negatively correlated with male dominance and men's violence (Best and Williams, 1997; Coltrane, 1988). In contrast, father involvement is associated with a higher endorsement of gender-egalitarian attitudes and practices. Transformations in cultural practices and parenting practices go hand in hand. With changes in both, we may expect corresponding effects on children's development.

## A CONCEPTUAL MODEL OF GENDER, PARENTING, AND CHILD DEVELOPMENT

To the extent that gendered parenting practices may reflect the gender divisions and the inequities in status that exist in the larger society (Best and Williams, 1997), a conceptual model is needed that addresses the link between society and the child's development. To this end, we can borrow from existing models and theories in developmental psychology. In particular, this chapter is guided by a combination of ecological (e.g., Bronfenbrenner, 1977; Bronfenbrenner and Morris, 1998), sociocultural (e.g., Rogoff, 1990), and social–cognitive (e.g., Bussey and Bandura, 1999) theoretical approaches.

Ecological and sociocultural models both emphasize the interrelation between everyday activity settings and larger cultural institutions. For instance, in Bronfenbrenner's (1977; Bronfenbrenner and Morris, 1998) ecological model of human development, levels of analysis ranged from the macrosystem to specific microsystems. The macrosystem refers to the cultural values and practices that define a society, such as its form of economy, political structure, traditions, and laws. Microsystems refer to particular environments in which the child may be found at a given moment. Examples of microsystems include the family home, the neighborhood, and the school. In a somewhat similar manner, sociocultural theory refers to the significance of everyday activity settings in particular microsystems during which cultural practices are learned. Examples of activity settings include playing with a parent or carrying out household chores in the home.

According to both ecological and sociocultural models, the macrosystem defines the particular opportunity structure for a particular community (Ogbu, 1981; Rogoff, 1990; Weisner, 1996). Childrearing strategies reflect adaptations by parents or other caregivers to help prepare children for success in the culture. The ecological–sociocultural model is useful for interpreting children's gender development. Specifically, the type of socialization practices directed toward girls and boys may reflect the existing opportunity structures for women and men in a particular community at a particular time in history. For example, if women are expected to be primarily responsible for rearing their children, childhood practices would be more apt to emphasize the practice of nurturant behaviors in girls than in boys. If men are expected to be primarily responsible for economic subsistence outside of the home, childhood practices would be more apt to emphasize the practice of independent behaviors in boys than girls. Indeed, cross-cultural studies do reveal that the division of labor according to gender is correlated with childrearing practices in societies (e.g., Best and Williams, 1997; Hewlett, 1991; Weisner, 1979; Whiting, 1986).

Given the link between cultural practices and child outcomes, Weisner (1996) has argued that the child's "cultural place" (cultural beliefs, practices, meanings, and ecological setting) should be in the foreground of any developmental inquiry. When applied to the study of gender development, it becomes necessary to consider how gender inequities in the larger society may shape the nature of children's and adults' microsystems. To the extent that children's development is largely an adaptation to their existing opportunities, it is also possible to consider how processes in children's macrosystems and microsystems can foster greater gender equality.

Comparisons of how societies vary from one another can be used to infer how features of the macrosystem are related to gender and children's development. Hewlett's (1991) study of Aka culture highlights the relation between the socioeconomic structure of a society and child development. The Aka people are a highly egalitarian, foraging society living in the central African rain forest. Both women and men spend much of their day mutually engaged in subsistence and childrearing tasks. Consider the following description of Aka mothers' and fathers' shared labor (Hewlett, 1991, p. 168):

> The Aka father's role can be characterized by its intimate, affectionate, helping-out nature. Aka fathers spend 47 percent of their day holding or within an arm's reach of their infants, and while holding the infant, father is more likely than mother to hug and kiss the infant. The father's caregiving often takes place while the mother is carrying a heavy load, collecting firewood, or preparing a meal.

Hewlett also observed that Aka fathers showed intrinsic satisfaction as caregivers. Furthermore, the active involvement of Aka fathers in caregiving has a corresponding impact on the development of the children. When asked with whom they played when they were children, adolescents referred equally to their mothers and fathers. Also, Aka boys did not reject what mainstream American culture generally considers feminine-stereotyped attributes and activities. Specifically, infant-care and food preparation were not viewed as "feminine" activities but rather as adult tasks for men as well as for women. The Aka culture shows that relatively egalitarian gender roles are possible in human societies, and highlights ways that gender arrangements in adulthood may influence children's construction of gender.

Another strategy for examining macrosystem–microsystem links is to look at variations within societies. Cultures are not monolithic entities. Although women in a given society may generally experience social and economic discrimination, typically there are variations in the degree to which these biases occur. For instance, within the United States, gender may be organized differently depending on socioeconomic factors such as income level, education level, race, and ethnicity (e.g., Chow, Wilkinson, and Baca Zinn, 1996; Leaper and Valin, 1996; Reid and Comas-Diaz, 1990) as well as structural variables such as marital status or maternal employment (e.g., Etaugh, 1993; Leaper, Leve, Strasser, and Schwartz, 1995; Risman, 2001; Stevenson and Black, 1988). Each of these factors influences the relative amounts of power, status, and resources that men and women can obtain in a society (Kimmel, 2000). Thus, gender, ethnicity (or race), and economic level are intertwined aspects of the macrosystem that partly define a person's status in society and can limit one's access to opportunities.

To illustrate, researchers have found that gender differences in attitudes and behaviors may be less common among African American children than among European American children (Albert and Porter, 1988; Bardwell, Cochran, and Walker, 1986). Among adults, African Americans are more likely than members of other ethnic groups to reject traditional gender-typed attitudes (Kane, 2000) and behaviors (Henley, 1995). However, African American men still may tend to adopt traditional gender attitudes (Kane, 2000). The greater likelihood of nontraditional gender attitudes and behavior among African American girls and women may be related to prevalent patterns of family structure. Most African American children are reared by a mother who is a single parent and employed outside the home (Brookins, 1985; Cauce, Hiraga, Graves, and Gonzales, 1996; Reid, 1985). Acting as both economic providers and caregivers, single-parent African American mothers may thereby present nontraditional, egalitarian gender role models to their daughters. In support of the hypothesis that family structure may be an important moderator in the gender-typing process, studies based on European Americans and other ethnic groups indicate that nontraditional gender-typing patterns are more likely for children reared in single-parent mother-headed households (Leaper et al., 1995; Stevenson and Black, 1988). Thus, social, cultural, and economic contexts collectively influence children's development.

Now that the interrelation between macrosystems and microsystems has been reviewed, the relevant psychological processes that operate within particular microsystems are considered next. Whereas ecological and social–structural models are helpful for conceptualizing how distal aspects of the macrosystem define cultural practices, social–cognitive (Bussey and Bandura, 1999) and sociocultural (Rogoff, 1990; Weisner, 1996) approaches are useful when one is articulating the socialization processes that occur within particular microsystems. One way that children learn about the social world is by observing who are the key characters. Additionally, children learn from the types of activities they practice and the incentives that follow. With regards to gender, parents may offer different role models and provide different experiences for girls and boys.

To the extent that mothers, fathers, or other caregivers are important figures in children's lives, they can inform children's impressions of what it means to be a woman or a man (Bussey and Bandura, 1999). Therefore, parents may influence children's development through *modeling*. Mothers and fathers have traditionally differed in roles and status. Fathers are seen as more powerful and separated from the family, whereas mothers are traditionally observed as caregivers and home managers (e.g., Goldman and Goldman, 1983; Weisner, Garnier, and Loucky, 1994). However, as women's roles and status have changed, it has been possible to observe corresponding changes in daughters' gender attitudes and aspirations (e.g., Etaugh, 1993; Fulcher, Sutfin, and Patterson, 2001; Weisner et al., 1994). Thus, the subsequent review considers the possible influences of parental modeling on children's gender development.

Compared with modeling, a more direct form of influence may occur through parents' *differential treatment* of daughters and sons. There are various forms that differential treatment may take. Four of them are highlighted here. First, one form of differential treatment occurs through the direct instruction or the guided participation of the child in cultural practices (Bussey and Bandura, 1999; Rogoff, 1990). Examples include a father teaching a son how to throw a ball or a mother teaching a daughter how to change a baby's diaper. A second form of differential treatment is through the type of expectations that a parent imposes on a child. For example, parents may convey gender-stereotyped expectations that science and mathematics are difficult for girls or that boys do not cry. As reviewed later, these messages are apt to influence children's own self-concept and motivation.

A third and potentially important way that parents may treat daughters and sons differently is through the types of opportunities they provide or encourage (Bussey and Bandura, 1999; Huston, 1985; Leaper, 2000a; Lytton and Romney, 1991). Access to particular activity settings gives children the opportunity to practice particular behaviors as well as to receive incentives for repeating the behaviors (Lott and Maluso, 1993). For example, feminine-stereotyped toys tend to emphasize practicing affiliative behaviors (e.g., feeding a baby doll), whereas masculine-stereotyped toys are more likely to induce instrumental behaviors (e.g., constructing a tower of blocks or competing in sports). To the extent that gender-differentiated experiences become regular in their lives, children's knowledge, expectations, preferences, and abilities are likely to be influenced.

Finally, parents may treat daughters and sons differently in how they monitor and manage the children's activities. As children get older and more autonomous, parents typically exert less direct control over their children. However, parental influence may continue through supervising their children's involvements outside of the home (Crouter and Head, in Vol. 3 of this *Handbook*). Differential treatment may occur in either the degree or the manner that parents supervise their children. For example, parents may place more overall restrictions on daughters than on sons, or they may monitor certain behaviors more closely in one gender than the other.

Thus, parents can variously act as gatekeepers of experience in children's lives. In any given activity setting, parents provide particular models, expectations, and situational constraints. In these ways, parents can influence their children's gender development. In the remainder of the chapter, parenting processes are interpreted in relation to various aspects of daughters' and sons' social–emotional and cognitive development. Additionally, aspects of the macrosystem will be considered as possible moderators of gender effects on parenting and child development. Relevant examples include the impact of family structure, ethnicity, parental roles, and socioeconomic status.

The review of parenting influences on girls' and boys' development is divided into two subsections. First, different aspects of child development during infancy and early childhood are considered. The topics include early emotional development, language and conceptual development, attachment and autonomy, emotion talk and expressiveness, gender-typed play, and household chores. The second subsection addresses gender-related differences in development that tend to emerge during later childhood or adolescence. With the onset of puberty and the increasing salience of adult gender roles, adolescence is viewed as a period of gender intensification (see Crouter, Manke, and McHale, 1995; Hill and Lynch, 1983; Steinberg and Silk, in Vol. 1 of this *Handbook*). Relevant topics include children's gender schemas, body image, athletic participation, mathematics and science achievement, peer-group affiliations, and emotional autonomy and closeness.

## PARENTING PROCESSES, GENDER, AND CHILD OUTCOMES

### Infancy and Early Childhood

*Early emotional communication and emotion regulation.*   Researchers have highlighted the importance of early parent–child interactions in emotional development (see Bornstein, in Vol. 1 of this *Handbook*; Cummings and Cummings, in Vol. 5 of this *Handbook*; Grolnick and Farkas, in Vol. 5 of this *Handbook*; Putnam, Sanson, and Rothbart, in Vol. 1 of this *Handbook*). The caregiver's attention and responsiveness to children's emotional expressions influences if and how children learn to regulate their emotions as well as their trust in social relationships (Eisenberg, Cumberland, and Spinrad, 1998). Studies of mothers' interactions with their infants suggest that mothers are more likely to respond contingently to emotional displays from sons than from daughters (Malatesta and Haviland, 1982; Tronick and Cohn, 1989; Weinberg, Tronick, Cohn, and Olson, 1999). Also, mothers may be more likely to maintain a consistent pattern of positive responding over time with infant sons than with infant daughters (Biringen et al., 1999). One interpretation of these findings is that boys are being socialized to control their emotions, whereas conversely girls are being encouraged to express a wider range of emotions: By responding more contingently and positively to sons than to daughters, mothers may be making an extra effort to ensure that their sons remain calm. In this way, mothers may thereby encourage greater emotional self-control in sons (Brody, 1999, 2000; Eisenberg et al., 1998; Haviland and Malatesta, 1981; Malatesta, Culver, Tesman, and Shepard, 1989).

To some extent, gender-related variations in mothers' responsiveness to their infants' emotions may derive from early temperamental differences. Boys tend to be higher than girls in negative emotionality during infancy (Kohnstamm, 1989; Moss, 1967; Osofsky and O'Connell, 1977). Relatedly, infant boys may have more difficulty than infant girls in regulating their emotions (Blackford and Walden, 1998; Carter, Mayes, and Pajer, 1990; Rosen, Adamson, and Bakeman, 1992; Weinberg et al., 1999). However, Haviland, and Malatesta (1981) argued that socialization pressures for boy infants to control emotion exceed whatever dispositional differences that may exist. Unfortunately, there have not been many efforts to covary infant temperament and differential treatment when child-gender effects on parenting were examined. At least one study made this type of analysis (Moss, 1967). In the initial analyses, mothers of 3-week-old infants were observed to hold, look at, arouse, and stimulate physically sons more than they did daughters. At this age, infant sons were also found to be more irritable than infant daughters. When infant irritability was covaried in the analyses, the differential effects for maternal holding and looking no longer obtained. However, mothers were still found to arouse and physically stimulate sons more than daughters.

The caregiver's own emotional state may moderate the likelihood of child-gender effects on parent–infant emotion communication. For example, Murray, Kempton, Woolgar, and Hopper (1993) compared depressed and nondepressed mothers who were interacting with their 2-month-old infants. Consistent with the findings from other studies, the nondepressed mothers directed more infant-focused speech to sons than to daughters. However, the reverse pattern was found with the depressed mothers. The authors suggested that if emotional regulation is more difficult for sons than for daughters, depressed mothers may withdraw from their sons' negative emotionality. Tronick and Weinberg (2000) similarly argued that infant sons with high negative emotionality may be especially vulnerable when their mothers or other primary caregivers are depressed.

In summary, to the extent that gender differences in infant temperament occur, girls and boys may tend to evoke different reactions from caregivers. Parental reactions may be influenced by both the child's temperament and gender. Negative emotionality may increase the likelihood of either parent's attempts to foster emotional regulation; moreover, negative emotionality in sons may elicit even greater parental pressures for self-control (Haviland and Malatesta, 1981).

*Language development.* Both parental modeling and differential treatment influences are indicated. The meta-analysis of Leaper, Anderson, and Sanders (1998) of parents' language behavior toward their children indicated gender-related variations in parents' verbal stimulation directed toward children (subsequently described). The effect sizes were significantly larger in magnitude during the children's infancy and toddler years, when language learning is greatest. Effect sizes were also moderated by the type activity setting observed (described later).

First, mothers may be more verbally stimulating than fathers when interacting with their young children. The meta-analysis of Leaper et al. (1998) indicated that across studies mothers tend to be more talkative with their children than are fathers. In this way, mothers and fathers may offer different role models to their children about the importance of verbal expression—which might both maintain and perpetuate the stereotype that women are more talk oriented than men.

Second, the meta-analysis indicated that mothers tended to be more talkative with daughters than with sons. There was not a corresponding comparison of fathers' talkativeness to daughters versus sons in the meta-analysis of Leaper et al. because of a paucity of relevant reports. However, among individual studies that are pertinent, there is some indication that fathers may be more talkative with daughters than with sons (Brachfeld-Child, Simpson, and Izenson, 1988; Brundin, Roedholm, and Larsson, 1988).

Besides the differential amounts of talkativeness that parents may demonstrate with daughters versus sons, there may be differences in parents' reactions to girls' and boys' communication initiatives. Fagot and Hagan (1991) found that, among parents of 18-month-old toddlers, sons received more negative comments in response to communication attempts than did daughters. Consequently, the authors suggested, boys may find it less enjoyable to initiate talk than do girls.

An important moderator and mediator of gender-related variations in parent–child language behavior is the interactive context. In the meta-analysis of Leaper et al. (1998), both the incidence and the magnitude of the parent-gender and the child-gender effects depended on the activity setting. In particular, gender differences occurred when unstructured settings were observed, but no average differences occurred in structured settings. In unstructured settings, the parent or the child selected the activity—which could have varied according to the child's gender. For example, a parent with a son may have selected a toy track to construct, and a parent with a daughter may have chosen to play house. In contrast, structured settings referred to assigned activities or tasks that everyone in the study was supposed to do (e.g., play with a puzzle). The mediating effect of activity setting on parent–child behavior has been directly tested in various studies, where it has been found that variations in language behavior are more strongly associated with the type of activity than with either the parent's or the child's gender (see Caldera, Huston, and O'Brien, 1989; Leaper, 2000a, 2000b; Leaper and Gleason, 1996; O'Brien and Nagle, 1987).

Although parents may initiate more verbal interaction with infant daughters than with sons, parents' behavior may be at least partly influenced by the child. There is some evidence that girls may acquire language earlier than boys (Bornstein and Haynes, 1998; also see Gleason and Ely, in press, for a review). Accordingly, it may be that parents are talking more to girls than to boys because girls are more likely to initiate and respond to verbal interaction. There is also some evidence that girls may score slightly higher in verbal ability later in childhood (see Gleason and Ely, in press; Hyde and Linn,

1988, for reviews). Based on their earlier acquisition of language and their subsequent advantage in language, some authors have speculated that females are biologically predisposed for greater verbal ability (see Gleason and Ely, in press, for a review). However, evidence for this hypothesis remains inconclusive, and it may also be possible that it is the greater amount of verbal stimulation directed toward girls that gives them whatever edge they might develop in verbal ability (Gleason and Ely, in press). Also, even if girls are born with a slightly greater propensity for language learning, the magnitude of the effect may be augmented through socialization. As with virtually every other type of development, language requires a supportive environment for development: Girls' as well as boys' vocabulary growth is related to the amount of parent speech to which they are exposed (Hart and Risley, 1995; Huttenlocher, Haight, Bryk, Seltzer, and Lyons, 1991; Weizman and Snow, 2001). Thus, child characteristics and parent influences may combine to exaggerate gender differences in children's language development somewhat analogous to the processes of emotion socialization described earlier (e.g., Brody, 1999, 2000).

*Early conceptual development.*   Once children acquire language, they are open to learning a new world of concepts. Researchers interested in children's cognitive and intellectual development have examined ways that parents' verbal interactions may help children's learning. One investigative approach is to consider how often parents initiate particular teaching strategies believed to facilitate learning and conceptual development. For instance, Sigel (1982) emphasized the importance of particular forms of didactic speech, known as distancing strategies, that encourage children to think beyond the immediate physical context. Because these forms of speech typically function to elicit information and thinking from children, they are also considered cognitively demanding. Distancing strategies or cognitively-demanding speech include open-ended questions, requests for explanations, directives, and explanations that foster the reconstruction of ideas as well as the ability to think about the past and future. Parents' use of these strategies is correlated with children's later success in abstract reasoning and mathematics (Sigel, Stinson, and Flaugher, 1991).

   Some studies indicate that fathers may be more likely than mothers to use certain types of cognitively demanding speech. Specifically, fathers have been observed to use more directives and to ask more open-ended questions than have mothers (see Gleason, 1987; Leaper et al., 1998; Mannle and Tomasello, 1987; McLaughlin, White, McDevitt, and Raskin, 1983). According to one view, fathers' greater use of cognitively demanding speech may prepare children for interacting with unfamiliar adults in outside environments such as school (Tomasello, Conti-Ramsden, and Ewert, 1990). However, this interpretation is contradicted by findings that parents' use of commands is inversely related to measures of cognitive and language development (Podmore, 1988).

   A second approach to studying teaching-related behavior is to consider parents' responsiveness to the child's learning needs. As proposed by Vygotsky and other sociocultural theorists (see Rogoff, 1990), simply maintaining high-level interactions does not help children learn. Instead, it is argued that optimal learning occurs when parents guide the child toward the successful solution of the task. In some cases, effective guidance may require providing a simpler explanation after the child shows difficulty. The process of building on the child's current cognitive level and encouraging the child's active learning is known as scaffolding.

   Some studies suggest that mothers tend to scaffold children's learning more than do fathers (Gleason, 1987; McLaughlin et al., 1983; Tenenbaum and Leaper, 1998). For example, Tenenbaum and Leaper (1998) found that mothers were more likely to adjust their responses following children's answers to earlier questions during play with a toy zoo. When children indicated a lack of understanding, mothers were more likely than fathers to follow up with a simpler question or explanation. Thus, mothers may place less overall cognitive demand on their children because they are more sensitive to their children's cognitive level (Gleason, 1987).

   In sum, fathers may tend to be more cognitively demanding overall compared with mothers, and mothers may be more likely than fathers to demonstrate scaffolding. Both patterns are compatible with traditional gender-role prescriptions that characterize men as independent problem solvers and women as interpersonally sensitive. To the extent that these observed differences are reliably found, girls and boys may infer corresponding lessons about their own gender by observing their parents.

In contrast to the findings regarding parent-gender effects, child-gender effects on parent teaching behaviors with young children are not highly robust across studies. Several studies indicate no differences in parents' treatment of daughters and sons during teaching tasks (Bee, Van Egeren, Streissguth, Nyman, and Leckie, 1969; Tenenbaum and Leaper, 1998). Moreover, at least two reports suggest that child-gender effects may vary for mothers and fathers (McGillicuddy-DeLisi, 1988; McLaughlin et al., 1983). In both studies, parents used more cognitively challenging verbal strategies with cross-gender children. If mothers tend to use less cognitively demanding speech with daughters than with sons, is there another form of speech they are using more with daughters? Flannagan and Baker-Ward (1996) found that mothers tended to talk about more interpersonal topics with daughters and discussed more teaching-related topics with sons.

Directives are one form of demanding speech that may be used with daughters more than with sons. Across studies, mothers tend to be less directive in their speech with sons than with daughters among school-age children (Leaper et al., 1998). Fathers also may be less directive with sons (Brachfeld-Child et al., 1988). Parents' use of direct commands with young children has been found to be negatively correlated with measures of children's cognitive and language development (Podmore, 1988). Thus, by using fewer directives with sons, parents may also be encouraging active problem solving in sons more than in daughters. Rather than emphasizing commands in teaching situations, some parents appear to use verbal strategies that promote active problem solving with sons more than with daughters (e.g., Frankel and Rollins, 1983; Weitzman, Birns, and Friend, 1985).

Sometimes it is important to consider more than the frequency that certain strategies are used. Specifically, it can be useful to know the manner and the context in which particular behaviors are used. For instance, whereas parental directives may generally impede children's active problem solving (Podmore, 1988), they may facilitate learning when combined with other teaching strategies (Frankel and Rollins, 1983). Some studies indicate a combination of directive behavior and cognitive involvement is more likely with sons than with daughters (Bronstein, 1999; Frankel and Rollins, 1983).

Child characteristics are yet another aspect of the context that may affect parents' teaching-related behavior. Two examples are described. First, Forman and Kochanska (2001) looked at 1-year-old toddlers' imitations of their mothers during a teaching task. Daughters were more likely than sons to imitate. The authors suggested that responsive imitation reflected the child's receptivity to socialization. If so, differences in how girls and boys respond to their mothers might affect their mothers' teaching behaviors over time.

Gender differences in children's emotional reactivity are offered as the second example of how child effects may affect parents' teaching behaviors. To the extent that young girls and boys tend to differ in emotional reactivity, there may be a corresponding impact on the parent's patience and willingness to help guide the child in learning situations. Maccoby, Snow, and Jacklin (1984) offered some support for this idea. They examined mothers' teaching efforts in assigned learning tasks with their child at 12 and 18 months of age. Difficult temperament mediated and moderated observed child-gender effects. The authors found that mothers of temperamentally difficult children—particularly sons—at 12 months of age subsequently reduced their teaching efforts compared with other mothers. Thus both child temperament and child gender contributed to mothers' behavior. The authors speculated that mothers' gender stereotypes may have led them to be less assertive with sons and that this effect was compounded with temperamentally difficult sons. However, there was some variation among mothers of difficult sons. When mothers did demonstrate high teaching efforts with difficult sons, these boys became less difficult over the course of the study. Thus, although child characteristics can affect the parents' teaching behaviors, it is possible for parents to work around these challenges.

If negative emotionality is more prevalent among infant and toddler boys than among girls, parents may be more apt to distance themselves from sons in ways that encourage more independent problem solving. Conversely, to the extent that girls may be slightly more advanced in language development during the toddler years, they may invite more active involvement from parents in general and during teaching situations in particular (Morisset, Barnard, and Booth, 1995). As explored in the next subsection, the child's emotionality may also mediate some gender effects that are related to attachment.

*Attachment.* There are few reported differences in girls' and boys' attachment classifications or in parental sensitivity toward girls and boys (Benenson, 1996; but see Barnett, Kidwell, and Leung, 1998; Fracasso, Busch-Rossnagel, and Fisher, 1994; Lippe and Crittenden, 2000, for exceptions). However, a few studies tentatively suggest that the correlates and consequences of attachment may vary somewhat for girls and boys. As described in the earlier subsection on emotion regulation, there is evidence indicating a tendency for gender differences in emotional development during infancy. Based on these early differences, attachment may sometimes have different precursors, correlates, and consequences for girls and boys (Biringen et al., 1999; van IJzendoorn et al., 2000).

Congruent with the greater likelihood of negative emotionality among boys than among girls during infancy, the research literature suggests that boys may be more vulnerable to emotional disruptions than are girls during the first few years. First, some studies indicate greater distress among sons than among daughters on separation from the caregiver (Brooks and Lewis, 1974; Fagot and Kavanagh, 1990a; Lollis, 1990). Second, attachment to the caregiver may be correlated with measures of emotional development in sons more strongly than in daughters. For instance, Lewis, Feiring, McGuffog, and Jaskir (1984) found that attachment to the mother when the child was 1 year old predicted the likelihood of later maladjustment in sons but not in daughters. However, it is unclear if it was the child's attachment that had a causal influence on later problems. Alternatively, those sons with high negative emotionality as infants may have been at risk for forming insecure attachments as well as for having later psychological difficulties (van den Boom, 1989). As highlighted in recent reviews, we need to disentangle child and parent effects (as well as their interaction) when explaining children's development (Collins, Maccoby, Steinberg, Hetherington, and Bornstein, 2000; Harris, 2000; Maccoby, 2000; Scarr and McCartney, 1983).

Other studies point to possible differences between girls and boys in how attachment is related to psychosocial functioning outside of the family. A recent meta-analysis indicated a moderate link between measures of child attachment and peer relations (Schneider, Atkinson, and Tardif, 2001). However, the analysis indicated minimal gender effects across studies. When gender-related variations are indicated in the literature, the association between attachment and measures of social competence is usually stronger for boys than for girls during the early childhood years (Cohn, 1990; DeMulder, Denham, Schmidt, and Mitchell, 2000; Kerns and Barth, 1995; LaFreniere, Provost, and Dubeau, 1992; Renken, Egeland, Marvinney, and Mangelsdorf, 1989; Turner, 1993). However, there are a few studies indicating a stronger association for girls than for boys (Barglow, Contreras, Kavesh, and Vaughn, 1998; Fagot and Kavanagh, 1990b; Kerns, Cole, and Andrews, 1998; Suess, Grossmann, and Sroufe, 1992). Future research is needed for us to understand the possible variables underlying these different findings.

Besides possibly being more strongly related to outcomes for one gender more than the other, attachment may predict different outcomes, depending on the child's gender. Turner (1991) found different patterns of correlation between attachment classifications and indices of social–emotional adjustment for preschool girls and boys. Compared with securely attached children, insecure boys were generally more aggressive and disruptive, whereas insecure girls were more dependent and demonstrated more positive expressive behavior. Thus, insecurely attached children were most likely to show negative gender-stereotyped behaviors—aggression in boys and dependency in girls. In contrast, the secure girls and boys exhibited moderate levels of assertion and compliance—a more balanced and integrated social–emotional style. However, before becoming confident with this inference, the findings must be replicated. The apparent inconsistencies also suggest the need to consider various factors that moderate the combined influences of attachment and gender.

Another relevant factor when gender-related variations in the attachment of children from two-parent families are considered is the employment status of each parent. Unfortunately, attachment studies generally consider the employment status of only the mother. Among these reports, it appears that maternal employment status is correlated with attachment-related variations in sons more than in daughters. For instance, studies tend to indicate that, in two-parent dual-career families, sons are more likely to have an insecure attachment to the father than are sons from traditional families (Belsky and Rovine, 1988; Braungart-Rieker, Courtney, and Garwood, 1999; Chase-Landsdale and Owen, 1987). There does not appear to be a corresponding effect on sons' attachment to mothers or on daughters' attachment to either parent. Authors have interpreted this as another sign of boys' greater emotional vulnerability during the early years (e.g., see Chase-Landsdale and Owen, 1987).

One study suggests some possible underlying factors that might explain when sons of dual-career parents show insecure attachments to their fathers. Braungart-Rieker et al. (1999) compared dual-career and traditional (i.e., husband as single earner) couples when their child was 4 and 12 months of age. Two findings are pertinent. First, fathers in dual-career marriages were less sensitive to their infant sons' signals than were fathers in single-earner marriages. Additionally, children of fathers in dual-career families were more likely than children of fathers in single-earner families to have insecure attachments to their fathers; there was no difference in the two family types in children's attachment to their mothers. One interpretation of the results is that fathers in dual-career marriages are not adequately sharing in the emotional care of their children in lieu of the mother's career involvement (Hochschild, 1989). It is unclear why fathers in dual-career marriages may tend to show less sensitivity to sons than to daughters. Perhaps the greater irritability sometimes associated with infant sons (reviewed earlier) poses relatively greater demands on fathers when mothers cannot or choose not to act as full-time caregivers. Therefore, rather than blaming mothers for working outside of the home, we may alternatively consider how well the father is coping with the demands of childcare in dual-career families (see Gottfried et al., in Vol. 2 of this *Handbook*).

*Early autonomy.* Theories of psychosocial development emphasize the importance of early attachment relationships as laying the foundation for children's autonomy (e.g., Bowlby, 1988; Cummings and Cummings in Vol. 5 of this *Handbook*; Erikson, 1963). Whereas emotional closeness with the parents is usually associated with the traditional development of girls, autonomy and self-assertion are associated more with the traditional development of boys (see Chodorow, 1978; Robinson and Biringen, 1995). However, the meta-analysis of Lytton and Romney (1991) indicated negligible average effect sizes associated with parents' treatment of daughters versus sons in the encouragement of either dependency or independence. However, the authors found a significantly higher number of studies indicating that parents encouraged dependency more in daughters than in sons. Thus averaging across studies did not reveal a robust effect of child gender on parents' socialization of autonomy, despite a pattern of significantly more studies that find more autonomy granting and less encouragement of dependency with sons than with daughters.

Quantitative reviews of the research literature can sometimes miss effects that depend on the age of the child, parent characteristics, or the activity setting (Fagot and Hagan, 1991). Indeed, the follow-up tests of Lytton and Romney as well as the meta-analysis of Leaper et al. (1998) revealed larger effects when particular moderators were taken into account. For instance, effect sizes were larger with observational than with self-report studies.

There are at least two specific ways that parents' differential encouragement of autonomy in daughters and sons can be noted. First, as reviewed earlier, parents may encourage greater self-control in sons than in daughters through early efforts to foster emotional regulation in those infant boys who show high negative emotionality. The child temperament effects may be further compounded by social prescriptions for males to control emotion (see Brody, 2000, and Haviland and Malatesta, 1981, for similar biosocial developmental models).

Second, mothers appear to be less verbally directive with sons than with daughters. Put simply, mothers are more likely to tell girls what to do. This was indicated in the meta-analysis of Leaper et al. (1998). Moreover, the magnitude of the effect was larger with school-age than with toddler or preschool-age children. Research suggests that mothers' use of power-assertive influence strategies may constrain the development of children's autonomy and self-efficacy (Crockenberg and Litman, 1990; Kuczynksi, Kochanska, Radke-Yarrow, and Girnius-Brown, 1987; Pomerantz and Ruble, 1998). If so, some mothers either deliberately or inadvertently may encourage differences in daughters' and sons' self-evaluations and autonomous functioning through their use of verbal directives.

Parents' differential socialization of autonomy in girls and boys may be mediated through the type of activity setting that is selected. Activities vary in their demand characteristics. Feminine-stereotyped activities tend to emphasize collaborative behaviors, whereas masculine-stereotyped activities tend to focus on instrumental behaviors (see Leaper, 1994). Accordingly, the meta-analysis of Leaper et al. (1998) found that gender effects were moderately large in relatively unstructured settings but tended to diminish in structured activities. Structured activities included the assignment of specific toys or problem-solving tasks, which would place similar demand characteristics on all participants. In contrast, in unstructured settings participants had more latitude to vary in activity choice. Indeed, studies systematically comparing parent–child interaction across contexts have indicated that the activity is typically a better predictor of behavior than either the child's or the parent's gender (Caldera et al., 1989; Leaper, 2000b; Leaper et al., 1995; Leaper and Gleason, 1996; Lewis and Gregory, 1987).

Finally, besides looking at the differential treatment of daughters and sons, another strategy is to consider how particular parenting styles affect girls and boys differently. When parents were permissive and did not place limits on their children's behavior, Baumrind (1989) found that children tended to develop poor self-control and scored low in independence and achievement. However, the effects were stronger for sons than for daughters. Perhaps the impact of permissive parenting was greater on sons, given the fewer restrictions traditionally placed on boys' behavior in society. However, it is also possible that it was the children who were influencing the parents more than the reverse. Boys who are highly impulsive and aggressive may exhaust their parents and lead them to adopt a permissive style (see Olweus, 1980).

*Affection.* Affectionate behavior is one way that relative degrees of attachment and autonomy may be expressed and fostered. The traditional gender stereotype is that affection is encouraged and tolerated in girls more than in boys. One might therefore expect to see more physical affection expressed through physical touch toward daughters than toward sons. However, studies comparing mothers' amounts of physical contact with daughters and sons during the first few months are mixed. Some studies indicate more contact with daughters (Goldberg and Lewis, 1969; Lindahl and Heimann, 1997; Robin, 1982). In contrast, there are other studies indicating more parental contact with sons than with daughters (Landerholm and Scriven, 1981; Lewis, 1972; Parke, O'Leary, and West, 1972); and still other studies indicate no child-gender effect (e.g., Baildum, Hillier, Menson, and Bamford, 2000). Given that infant boys as well as infant girls require persistent attention and handling from caregivers, perhaps it should not be surprising that child-gender effects on parent affection toward infants are not very consistent. Instead, we might expect differential treatment of daughters and sons in physical contact to be more likely during the toddler period when children depend less on the caregiver. That is what the research suggests.

More physical contact has been observed in mother–daughter than in mother–son pairs during the toddler years (Austin and Braeger, 1990; Clarke-Stewart and Hevey, 1981; Lamb, Frodi, Frodi, and Hwang, 1982) and early childhood (Benenson, Morash, and Petrakos, 1998). Fathers may also be more likely to make physical contacts and maintain closer proximity with daughters than with sons during the toddler years (Snow, Jacklin, and Maccoby, 1983) and possibly into adolescence and adulthood (Barber and Thomas, 1986; also see Barnard and Solchany, in Vol. 3 of this *Handbook*;

Parke, in Vol. 3 of this *Handbook*). Given the small number of studies as well as the varying ages and contexts sampled, we need to view these trends with caution. Additionally, the direction of effects—parent to child, child to parent, or a combination of both—remains unclear. We tend to assume that parents initiate gender-differentiated treatment, but it may also be that daughters elicit more affection and sons somehow discourage affection (e.g., Snow et al., 1983). Moreover, gender-related differences in parent–child physical proximity may be mediated by the selection of activity. Feminine-stereotyped play activities tend to foster closer proximity than masculine-stereotyped activities do (Caldera et al., 1989).

In addition to physical touch, simply talking to a child may foster a sense of closeness. If so, mothers appear to engage in more talk with daughters than with sons—as seen in the meta-analysis of Leaper et al. (1998). The effects were especially large from infancy through early childhood—which is notable because these are the years when children typically spend the most time with their mothers. To the extent that sons are engaging in fewer conversations with their mothers, they may develop a greater sense of separateness and independence. Once again, we must be cautious when interpreting the causal direction in the pattern of results.

A third way that parents may express affection is through the use of supportive statements. The meta-analysis of Leaper et al. (1998) uncovered some trends across studies. There was a small yet significant overall trend for mothers to use more supportive statements with daughters than with sons. The pattern of results is consistent with the relatively greater emphasis on affiliation associated with the socialization of girls compared with that of boys (e.g., Block, 1983; Leaper, 2000b; Leaper, Hauser, Kremen, Powers, Jacobson, Noam, Weiss-Perry, and Follansbee, 1989).

In sum, the research literature suggests that parents may express more physical and verbal affection with daughters than with sons. In these ways, parents may both initiate and encourage interpersonal closeness during girls' development. However, the research also indicates that a parent's affectionate behavior may depend at least partly on the parent's gender, the child's age, the child's behavior, or the activity setting.

In addition to the processes previously reviewed, another way that emotional closeness may develop between parents and children is through the discussion of emotional experiences. Gender-related variations in parent–child emotion talk and expressiveness are considered next.

*Emotion talk and emotional expressiveness.*   Women tend to be more verbally expressive of their feelings than are men (Goldschmidt and Weller, 2000). Do mothers and fathers provide gender-typed role models regarding emotion talk when interacting with their children? Some evidence suggests they may. Fivush, Brotman, Buckner, and Goodman (2000) observed that mothers discussed more emotional aspects of experiences and used more emotional words than did fathers when conversing with their children. However, other studies have not found differences between mothers' and fathers' emotional language when they were communicating with their children (Adams, Kuebli, Boyle, and Fivush, 1995; Fivush, 1998; Levin, Snow, and Lee, 1984).

Whereas the evidence for parent-gender differences in emotion talk may be mixed, studies more reliably show that parents' talk tends to be different with daughters and sons during early childhood. First, parents tend to discuss more emotional experiences and use more frequent and varied emotional words and references with their daughters than with their sons (Adams et al., 1995; Dunn, Bretherton, and Munn, 1987; Eisenberg, 1999; Fivush, 1998; Flannagan and Perese, 1998). Thus, parents may give their daughters more opportunities to practice emotion talk than they give their sons (see Melzi and Fernández, 2001, for a possible exception under different cultural conditions).

Second, in addition to differing in the amount of emotion talk, parents tend to vary in the type of emotional talk used with girls and boys. References to sadness or discussions of sad events are more likely with daughters than with sons (Adams et al., 1995; Fivush et al., 2000). In contrast, parent–child conversations about anger are more likely with sons than daughters (Brody, 1999; Fivush, 1991). Anger is a self-assertive emotion, and therefore its expression is congruent with the traditional masculine role. In contrast, sadness is a more passive and self-reflective state. The greater emphasis on talking about sadness with daughters is noteworthy in light of the higher incidence of depression among women than among men (Fivush and Buckner, 2000). Ruminating about sad and other negative events may be linked to women's greater risk for depression (Nolen-Hoeksema, Larson, and Grayson, 1999).

A third gender-related pattern seen in the literature is that parents may teach girls and boys to think differently about emotions. With daughters, parents may tend to emphasize the emotional situation and experience itself (Fivush, 1989); with sons, they tend to discuss the causes and consequences of the emotions (Cervantes and Callanan, 1998; Fivush, 1989). Parents may thereby strengthen the notion in their children that girls should be more emotionally sensitive and understanding, whereas boys should be in control of their emotions.

Is there any evidence that variations in parents' emotion talk with daughters and sons may affect their children's own emotional development? One study suggests that there may be a relation. Dunn, Brown, Slomkowski, Tesla, and Youngblade (1991) looked at mothers' conversations about feelings with their 2-year-old toddlers. They found that mothers tended to discuss and explain feelings more with their daughters than with their sons at this age. Approximately half a year later, there was a correlation between mothers' earlier emotion talk and the older child's level of emotion understanding. Of course, it is possible that daughters were already more advanced in emotional development at the younger age and that this influenced the mothers' behavior. Nonetheless, the findings of Dunn and her colleagues suggest that parents' behavior may have an impact on the child.

Three more studies provide some corroborating evidence for the potential influence of parents on the development of gender differences in emotion expression. First, Fuchs and Thelen (1988) examined school-age children's expected outcomes from their parents for expressing particular emotions and their stated likelihood of expressing emotions. Boys were more likely than girls to expect negative reactions for expressing sadness, and negative expectancies were related to being less likely of expressing sadness. Thus, boys may have internalized from their parents a display rule about the expression of sadness.

A second source for inferring possible parental influences comes from Bronstein, Briones, Brooks, and Cowan (1996). They carried out a longitudinal study of emotional development in children from fifth grade (11 years of age) into late adolescence. Overall, adolescent girls reported more support for emotional expression than did the adolescent boys. However, the adolescents also varied in expressiveness, depending on how emotionally expressive and accepting of emotion their families were. The adolescents from more emotionally expressive, and accepting families reported showing a greater range of emotions than that traditionally associated with their gender. Specifically, the girls reported a greater tendency to show anger, and the boys indicated a greater likelihood of crying. Crying was correlated with measures of adjustment for both girls and boys—but the direction of the correlation differed. For boys, crying was a positive indicator of adjustment; for girls, it was a negative indicator. In other words, cross-gender-typed patterns of emotional expression were associated with better adjustment. This finding underscores the proposition that traditional gender roles may hinder psychological development (see Block, 1973; Eccles, 1987; Leaper et al., 1989).

Finally, Brody (1997) offered evidence suggesting that nontraditional upbringings may influence girls' and boys' emotional development. She looked at the relation between fathers' amount of involvement with their children and the children's emotional expression. Fathers' involvement appeared to influence daughters and sons differently. Sons of highly involved fathers were more likely to express nontraditional emotions such as fear and warmth. Daughters of highly involved fathers were less likely to express fear and sadness. Thus, it would seem that involved fathers fostered tenderness in sons and self-confidence in daughters.

In sum, several studies indicate possible ways that parents may socialize emotional expression in girls and boys in the context of conversations about emotion. However, gender-related differences in parent–child emotion talk likely depend on various factors. Two examples are offered. First, gender differences in emotion talk may depend on the type of context examined. For example, gender effects may be more likely when participants are explicitly asked to discuss emotion-laden events (e.g., Fivush et al., 2000) than when more neutral materials are used (e.g., Denham, Cook, and Zoller, 1992). Second, daughters may evoke more emotion talk from their parents than do sons. As early as 24 months of age, girls tend to talk more frequently about varied emotional states than do boys (Adams et al., 1995; Cervantes and Callanan, 1998; Dunn et al., 1987; Fivush, 1998; Fivush et al., 2000). Gender differences in emotional development may also precede language acquisition (see previous subsection on emotional regulation). Brody's (1999, 2000) transactional model takes into account both temperamental and socialization processes in the development of gender differences in emotional expression.

*Gender-typed play.* Parents typically play in various ways with their children (see Tamis-LeMonda, Užgiris, and Bornstein, in Vol. 5 of this *Handbook*). Types of play can involve physical stimulation (e.g., lifting the child in the air, rough-and-tumble play), toy-mediated play (e.g., a toy food set or a construction set), sports, games, or teaching (e.g., reading a book). Studies generally find that fathers spend proportionally more of their time with children in play than do mothers (Lamb and Oppenheim, 1989). Furthermore, mothers and fathers tend to differ in the types of play they emphasize. Fathers are more likely to engage in physical play, whereas mothers are more apt to participate in toy-mediated or didactic forms of play (e.g., Labrell, 1996; McDonald and Parke, 1986; Power, 1985; Roopnarine and Mounts, 1985; Roopnarine, Talukder, Jain, Joshi, and Srivstav, 1990).

There is some indirect evidence that mothers' and fathers' role modeling during play may influence children's expectations. Fagot (1984) looked at $1\frac{1}{2}$- to 2-year-old and 3- to 5-year-old children as they interacted with an adult stranger. The older children—but not the younger children—acted differently depending on the adult's gender. With the man, the children were more apt to elicit ball play. In contrast, with the woman, they were more likely to ask for help. Fagot suggested that children learn different roles for adult women's and men's play in the home and subsequently use these expectations to guide their behavior outside of the home. This is only speculation and requires further test.

In addition to parent-gender differences, there are also child-gender effects on parents' play behavior. Rough physical play is especially more likely among fathers with their sons (Jacklin, DiPietro, and Maccoby, 1984; Lindsey, Mize, and Pettit, 1997; Tauber, 1979). Additionally, parents may actually discourage physical play in daughters compared with sons (Fagot, 1978). Given the apparent differences in the ways that parents may encourage gross motor physical activity in daughters and sons, one may wonder if parents are at least partly responsible for observed gender differences in children's activity levels. There is a small but significant gender difference in activity level that favors boys, beginning in infancy, and increases with age (Eaton and Enns, 1986). Thus, a small initial gender difference in infant temperament may exaggerate through socialization (Campbell and Eaton, 1999). If so, engaging sons in physical play may be one way that boys' activity levels are amplified. However, activity level itself does not appear to be correlated with children's later rough-and-tumble play (Campbell and Eaton, 1999). Therefore, highly active children are not necessarily the ones who engage in rough play or act aggressively—but they may be more prone to physical forms of play, including sports (addressed in the subsection on athletic participation).

Aside from physical forms of play, many child activities are centered around toys. Parents tend to give their children gender-stereotyped toys (Eisenberg, Wolchik, Hernandez, and Pasternack, 1985; Fisher-Thompson, 1993; Pomerleau, Bolduc, Malcuit, and Cossette, 1990; Rheingold and Cook, 1975; Robinson and Morris, 1986) and to encourage gender-typed play (see Lytton and Romney, 1991). However, there is variation among parents in how strongly they push traditional play in their daughters and sons. For example, Fagot, Leinbach, and O'Boyle (1992) noted that parents with gender-egalitarian views were less likely to encourage gender-typed toy play in their children. When parents do select gender-stereotyped toys, they are more apt to give boys sports equipment, tools, and vehicles. Conversely, they give girls more dolls, toy food sets, and toy furniture. Some parents have been found to purchase gender-stereotyped toys for their children within a few months of the child's birth (Pomerleau et al., 1990)—before the children express gender-typed toy preferences themselves.

Children begin to demonstrate preferences for gender-stereotyped toys between their first and second year. At the same time, parents have been found to communicate their approval of gender-stereotyped toy play nonverbally and verbally (e.g., Caldera et al., 1989; Eisenberg et al., 1985; Goldberg and Lewis, 1969; Langlois and Downs, 1980; Leaper et al., 1995; Roopnarine, 1986). Thus, as the child develops, a positive feedback loop between the parents' encouragement of gender-stereotyped play and the child's own preference for such play may occur. At least two studies have found a relation between mothers' and fathers' gender-stereotyped toy choices and toddler-age children's play (Eisenberg et al., 1985; Peretti and Sydney, 1984).

Parental gender typing of children's play tends to be stronger with sons than with daughters and with fathers than with mothers. In other words, sons tend to demonstrate gender-typed toy preferences earlier and maintain them more strongly than do girls (Robinson and Morris, 1986), and fathers are generally more concerned than are mothers with encouraging gender-typed behavior in children—especially in sons (see Siegal, 1987). The greater rigidity associated with boys' development is correlated with the higher status traditionally associated with males (see Leaper, 1994, 2000a).

When children are between the ages of 2 and 3 years, pretense becomes an important part of their play. As children enter the preschool years, sociodramatic play becomes a context for learning about and practicing social roles. Mothers may tend to favor this type of play more than fathers do (Roopnarine and Mounts, 1985). Also, both mothers and fathers may prefer this type of play with daughters more than with sons (Lindsey et al., 1997). To the extent that mother–daughter dyads are especially likely to engage in sociodramatic play, these interactions would involve practicing domestic roles (e.g., "playing house"), emphasize collaborative structures mediated through talk, and possibly reinforce the emotional bond between the pair. In these ways, mothers may contribute to their daughters' developing preferences for and skills in feminine-stereotyped affiliative domains (Leaper, 2000a, 2000b).

The impact of the activity setting is pertinent because of possible gender differences in activity preferences (e.g., Farver and Wimbarti, 1995). Mothers or daughters may be more likely than fathers or sons to choose activities that involve cooperative role playing (for example, pretending to have lunch together), whereas fathers or sons may be more likely than mothers or daughters to choose activities that are more task oriented (for example, putting together a toy car track). People typically communicate in ways that are functional for the activity. Thus, parent–child pairs playing with toy foods and plates are apt to create a dialogue that involves a cooperative back-and-forth structure. In contrast, parent–child pairs putting together a toy car track are more likely to focus on the task and to use more directive speech and relatively less speech overall (Leaper, 2000b).

Play is considered the work of children. Through play, children develop culturally meaningful forms of knowledge and social–cognitive skills (Carpenter, 1983; Huston, 1985). As they get older, life in the household may involve some real work in the form of household chores.

*Household chores.* Household chores, like play, are activity settings in which children engage in culturally meaningful practices. Studies of children's household work in the United States indicate a few patterns pertinent to gender socialization. First, parents tend to assign children gender-typed chores. Most notably, they typically assign childcare and cleaning to daughters and assign maintenance work to sons (Antill, Goodnow, Russell, and Cotton, 1996; Burns and Homel, 1989). Second, mothers and fathers typically model a traditional division of labor in their own household work (Hilton and Haldeman, 1991). Third, children are apt to prefer being assigned gender-stereotyped chores (Etauh and Liss, 1992). Fourth, girls are more likely than boys to be assigned household tasks during childhood and adolescence (Blair, 1992; Mauldin and Meeks, 1990; McHale, Bartko, Crouter, and Perry-Jenkins, 1990). The latter finding is congruent with the traditional assignment of females to the care of the household. Perhaps this helps explain a fifth point, which is that parental encouragement is more positively correlated with involvement in gender-typed chores for girls than boys (Antill et al., 1996). Finally, the degree and the manner to which daughters and sons are assigned household work often depend on the parents' socioeconomic level, marital status, employment, family size, and cultural background (Burns and Homel, 1989; Goodnow, 1988; Hilton and Haldeman, 1991; Lackey, 1989). For instance, in rural agrarian societies, older daughters are typically assigned childcare and older sons help outside the home (Whiting, 1986).

Some studies indicate that children's own preferences for gender-typed household chores may be guided by the role models they observe. Children who watch more television tend to have more traditional attitudes about the division of household labor than those who watch less television (Signorielli and Lears, 1992). Also, the type of role model that parents set themselves may influence children's attitudes (Gardner and LaBrecque, 1986; McHale et al., 1990). For example, adolescents of employed mothers held less traditional views about the division of household labor than did adolescents of homemaker mothers (Gardner and LaBrecque, 1986). Conversely, sons of traditional fathers who were assigned feminine-stereotyped chores experienced more stress about their responsibilities compared with sons of less traditional fathers (McHale et al., 1990).

Is there any evidence that the gender-typed assignment of household chores has an impact on children's development? There have been only a few studies attempting to examine the relation between children's assignments to household activities and their attitudes and behaviors. One study highlighted a possible connection: Ember (1973) considered variations among boys in Kenya between the ages of 7 and 16 years in being assigned feminine-stereotyped tasks such as childcare and household work. Those boys who were assigned more of the domestic tasks showed higher rates of feminine-stereotyped prosocial behaviors compared with those of other boys. Grusec, Goodnow, and Cohen (1996) similarly found a positive correlation between children's involvement in family-care work and their prosocial concern.

Emler and Hall (1994) argued that children's participation in gender-typed household chores in early childhood may contribute to their later notions of entitlement and obligation with regards to household work. To the extent that daughters are assigned more housework than sons, traditional expectations about the division of labor are fostered. Thus, gender differences in childhood opportunities may be viewed as early forms of discrimination that perpetuate the reproduction of gender inequities in adulthood. In other words, girls' and boys' participation in different play activities or household chores in childhood can be viewed as training for later role and status differences in adulthood (see Goodnow, 1988; Huston, 1985; Leaper, 2000a; Liss, 1983).

The assignment of household chores typically occurs when children are sufficiently mature to handle somewhat autonomous tasks. Accordingly, at this point, the review shifts to considering gender differences in children's development that tend to emerge during later childhood or adolescence.

## Middle Childhood and Adolescence

Adolescence marks a crossroads that is variously associated with gender intensification and increases in gender traditionalism (Hill and Lynch, 1983) or possibly with gender-role transcendence and increases in gender flexibility (Eccles, 1987). Some have argued that the pressures for traditional gender-role conformity become especially strong for adolescent girls (Archer, 1984; Hill and Lynch, 1983), whereas others have proposed that the male gender role continues to be more rigidly defined during adolescence (Massad, 1981). Regardless of who might be affected more negatively, adolescence poses challenges for both girls and boys as they begin to consider what it will mean to be adult women and men. Research suggests ways that parents may affect how their daughters' and sons' confront these trials. As described in the next subsection, parents may help shape children's general thinking about their own gender self-concept as well as shape their gender attitudes toward others.

*Gender schemas.*   Cognitive representations of gender, known as gender schemas, guide children's and adults' self-concepts, motivations, and expectations about others (Martin and Halverson, 1981; Ruble and Martin, 1998). A relevant question for this chapter is whether or not parents' gender schemas are related to their children's cognition or behavior. This issue was examined in the meta-analysis of Tenenbaum and Leaper (2001a). They reviewed studies that assessed the relation between parents' gender schemas and variations in child outcomes. Across studies, there was a small but sizable association between parents' gender cognitions and a variety of child outcome measures.

The relation between parents' gender schemas and child outcomes was even larger when particular moderators were taken into account. First, a distinction was made between gender schemas for self (i.e., gender self-concept) and gender schemas for others (i.e., gender stereotypes, traditional versus egalitarian attitudes) (Bigler, 1997; Signorella, 1999). Effect sizes were especially strong when either parents' gender attitudes (versus self-concept) were tested as a predictor or when children's gender attitudes were examined as an outcome measure. Thus, parents with more egalitarian gender attitudes may be more likely to foster less stereotyped beliefs in their children. Second, effect sizes were larger in parent–daughter than in parent–son pairs. This difference is consistent with other studies that indicate that gender attitudes are more rigid and resistant to change among boys and men than among girls and women (see Leaper, 1994, 2000a). Finally, the association between parent and child was stronger among parents of older children, adolescents, and young adults versus younger children. Eccles (1987) and others have argued that gender-role flexibility may be more likely during adolescence compared with childhood when the pressures of peer conformity are stronger. Therefore, parents' gender beliefs may be more salient during adolescence, when the maturing individual's gender identity undergoes some reexamination (Crouter et al., 1995).

One study highlights how social–structural factors in the family may underlie the connection between parents' and children's gender schemas. Fulcher et al. (2001) compared children of lesbian and heterosexual parents. They found that the division of labor among the parents—rather than the parents' gender composition—predicted children's gender stereotypes regarding future occupational choices. In both heterosexual and lesbian couples with a traditional division of labor (i.e., breadwinner and homemaker), children tended to have more traditional gender stereotypes. In contrast, there was less stereotyping of occupational choices among children in families whose parents shared roles and responsibilities.

Gender stereotypes and attitudes are potentially useful proxies of the degree to which cultural members have internalized the larger society's values, beliefs, and practices. Besides examining factors related to variations within culture in people's gender attitudes, it is sometimes useful to compare differences across societies to identify possible social–structural moderators. In this regard, the cross-national survey of Baxter and Kane (1995) indicated that traditional attitudes were correlated with women's degree of dependence on men in the society. For example, egalitarian attitudes were more likely in countries in which wives and husbands have relatively equal economic power. Also, having children is associated with more traditional attitudes in the United States—but not in Scandinavian countries. Fathers tend to be more involved in childcare, and affordable daycare is more accessible in Scandinavian nations. Thus we can see how social–structural factors possibly influence microsystem processes and children's development.

*Body image.*  Gender-role options are more rigidly defined for boys than for girls during childhood, as illustrated by the different connotations that the terms sissy and tomboy evoke (Martin, 1990). In this regard, Hill and Lynch (1983) emphasized adolescence as a period of "gender intensification" for girls, when there are increased demands for conformity in areas that were not previously subject to such pressure. They proposed that a major factor contributing to this intensification is girls' increasing concern with heterosexual attractiveness and physical appearance. These concerns are likely exaggerated by the pervasive cultural messages for girls and women to look pretty. In general, girls and women have more negative images of their bodies than do boys and men (e.g., Rozin and Fallon, 1988; Thompson, Corwin, Rogan, and Sargent, 1999). Relatedly, eating disorders are much more likely among girls and women than among boys and men (Rolls, Fedoroff and Guthrie, 1991).

Parents are agents for transmitting culture, and one of the cultural values that they may pass along is the emphasis on physical appearance for girls. The role of culture in this process is underscored when different ethnic groups are compared. Within the African American community, there is generally less value placed on thinness compared with that in the mainstream of European American society. It is notable therefore that gender-related differences in body image are less likely among African Americans (e.g., Thompson et al., 1999). Also, African American girls are less likely than European American girls to report expressions of weight concerns among their family or peers (Thompson et al., 1999). Although there may be ethnic group differences in their prevalence, many girls and women from all ethnic groups in the United States indicate dissatisfaction with their bodies (Robinson, Killen, Litt, and Hammer, 1996; Wilfley, Schreiber, Pike, and Striegel-Moore, 1996).

The possible reasons for girls' negative body images include pervasive media messages in television and magazine advertisements as well as peer norms that emphasize unrealistic notions of female beauty. There is also evidence that some parents may partly contribute to the problem. Smolak, Levine, and Schermer (1999) surveyed 10- to 11-year old children, and many reported that their parents—especially their mothers—made direct comments to the children about weight and shape concerns. Reports of these comments were negatively related to the children's own weight and appearance-related attitudes and behaviors. Moreover, the associations were stronger for girls. Similarly, Papini and Sebby (1988) found more parent–adolescent conflicts with daughters than with sons over appearance issues.

Besides responding to parents' stated concerns about appearance, distorted body image and eating disorders may also be indirect reactions to dysfunctional family dynamics. For example, Humphrey (1989) noted a characteristic pattern of parental communication with anorexic daughters. These mothers and fathers tended to give their daughters mixed messages. On the one hand, they provided nurturance and affection. On the other hand, they tended to ignore the daughter's individual needs and feelings. Thus, when compounded by the greater restrictions often placed on girls' autonomy in society, anorexia may become a means for girls in particularly dysfunctional families to seek some control in their lives.

Body image concerns may increase among girls after menarche. At that time, mothers may become an obvious source of information for postmenstrual girls. If a mother indicates satisfaction with her own appearance, she may be able to help her daughter feel more confident about her own changing body. In support of this hypothesis, Usmiani and Daniluk (1997) found a positive correlation between the body image scores of mothers and postmenstrual daughters; the association was not significant with mothers and premenstrual daughters.

Fathers may also play a role in accentuating daughters' concerns about weight. The survey by Schwartz, Phares, Tantleff-Dunn, and Thompson (1999) of college undergraduates indicated that women reported receiving more appearance-related comments from their fathers than did men. Also, both mothers' and fathers' comments about weight predicted women's—but not men's—body image.

As already noted, girls' body images are typically tied up with their notions of romantic attractiveness. As these girls enter adolescence, being popular with boys often becomes an important goal in itself as well as a sign of social status among peers for many girls (see Leaper, 1994). Researchers have found that adolescent girls often view popularity with boys as incompatible with doing well in athletic, academic, and other instrumental pursuits. Some of these areas are addressed next.

*Athletic participation.*    Since the establishment of Title IX of the U.S. Civil Rights Act in 1972 that bars gender discrimination in educational programs receiving federal aid, opportunities have increased for girls to participate in sports. However, these opportunities are not as widespread as the law allows. There remain institutional barriers in the schools. Additionally, there is evidence that parents tend to encourage athletic participation in boys more than in girls. Indeed, parental support is correlated with girls' levels of physical activity (Bungum and Vincent, 1997) and sports involvement (Lewko and Ewing, 1980). Sports participation, in turn, may positively benefit girls' body images and sense of self-efficacy (Richman and Shaffer, 2000).

Somewhat related to how people view their bodies is how they perceive their physical competence in athletics. In some ways, feeling good about one's body encompasses physical appearance and physical skill. Sports participation has been advocated as a way for children—perhaps especially girls—to gain a positive sense of self-efficacy in relation to their physical selves. Ironically, the forms of sports that have traditionally been more accessible to girls—ballet and gymnastics—emphasize maintaining a thin physique and often are associated with eating disorders (Garner, Rosen, and Barry, 1998).

Times are changing. Increasingly American girls are participating in various individual and team sports such as tennis and soccer. As girls catch up with boys in sports participation, we can consider how parents may have an impact on gender-related differences in children's participation and sense of self-efficacy in athletics. Not only may parents act differently with daughters and sons, parents' actions may influence girls and boys differently.

McElroy and Kirkendall (1981) considered early and middle adolescents' evaluations of their sports ability, their perceptions of their parents' judgments of their ability, and their self-esteem. Both girls and boys who viewed themselves as being high in sports ability tended to have lower self-esteem if they perceived their parents as having the opposite judgment of their ability. In other words, high-ability youth may feel let down if they do not feel their success has been acknowledged by their parents. In contrast, among those children who viewed themselves as being relatively low in sports ability, perceptions of parents' judgments were related to self-esteem for boys but not for girls. Boys who saw themselves as low in sports ability tended to have lower self-esteem if they viewed their parents as judging them as high in sports ability. Given the strong pressures on many American males to demonstrate their masculinity through sports (Messner, 1992), being nonathletic may be a risk factor for low esteem in boys when parents continue to push sports on their sons. In contrast, the pressures for athletic achievement may not be as great for most girls.

*Mathematics and science achievement.* During the elementary school years, girls and boys generally do equally well in mathematics and science. During adolescence, however, girls' achievement in these domains tends to decline. Although the reasons for these declines are complicated, there is some evidence that parents have a role. Studies show that parents tend to expect boys to do better than girls in mathematics (Eccles, Freedman-Doan, Frome, Jacobs, and Yoon, 2000) and science (Tenenbaum and Leaper, 2001b).

Early on, the types of toys that parents select and encourage in daughters and sons may indirectly influence academic interests and achievement. Serbin, Zelkowitz, Doyle, and Gold (1990) observed that access to masculine-stereotyped toys and activities in the home was a reliable predictor for academic achievement in girls and boys. The association was especially strong with regards to measures emphasizing visual–spatial ability.

As children get older, their parents' gender stereotypes regarding girls' and boys' abilities may lead to expectancy effects that influence the children's own academic beliefs and achievements. To illustrate, consider the longitudinal research of Eccles et al. (2000) on gender differences in children's mathematics achievementes. In the study of Eccles et al., parents generally endorsed the cultural stereotype that mathematics was more natural for boys than for girls. Also, despite the absence of gender differences in mathematics grades during elementary school, parents tended to underestimate girls' mathematics abilities and to overestimate boys' abilities. Eccles et al. found that, over time, girls' own self-perceptions reflected the parents' stereotypes. The girls increasingly lost confidence in their mathematics skills. At the same time, they lowered their evaluations of the usefulness of mathematics for their future. Thus, in high school, girls spent fewer years studying mathematics than boys did. These choices have likely consequences. Gender differences in mathematics self-efficacy in high school are related to later gender differences in occupational achievement. For example, Hackett (1985) found that high school mathematics self-efficacy was correlated with choosing a mathematics-related major in college.

Tenenbaum and Leaper (2001b) explored similar parent–child processes that may contribute to gender differences in science achievement in sixth and eighth graders (11- and 13-year-old children).

In addition to collecting attitudinal measures, they also observed actual parent–child conversations during science-related tasks. At the ages studied, they did not find a difference in the girls' and boys' science grades at school. However, they found that parents generally endorsed the view that boys were better at science than girls. Fathers, but not mothers, were also found to interact differently with daughters and sons: During the science tasks (but not during control tasks), fathers of sons used more explanations and scientific vocabulary than did fathers of daughters. Thus fathers demonstrated a gender bias in their encouragement of active problem solving in science activities. Gender biases in parents' encouragement of science may stretch back to early childhood. For example, Crowley, Callanan, Tenenbaum, and Allen (2001) observed child-gender effects on both mothers' and fathers' explanations to preschool-age children at a science museum. Parents were three times more likely to explain exhibits to sons than to daughters.

Once again, we need to remind ourselves that not all parents are the same. Updegraff, McHale, and Crouter (1996) compared the school achievement of young adolescents from families with either traditional and egalitarian parental roles. Marital equality was defined in relation to the two parents' relative involvement in child-oriented activities. The impact of parental roles appeared to be especially strong on girls during the transition to middle school. Girls with egalitarian parents maintained higher levels of academic achievement, especially in mathematics and science, compared to girls with traditional parents. Parental roles were not significantly related to boys' academic achievement.

In sum, parents may tend to foster self-confidence in mathematics and science for sons more than for daughters. Gender inequities in achievement in mathematics- and science-related achievements translate into corresponding gender inequities in later technological careers. When subordinate group members are denied access to certain opportunities and experiences, they are less apt to gain the confidence and the skill necessary to succeed in those areas from which they have been disenfranchised (Bandura, 1997)—as illustrated by the previously reviewed findings on gender inequities in mathematics achievement.

The preceding subsections have highlighted ways in which parents may influence girls' and boys' self-concepts and achievements. As Harter (1999) has shown, people's self-perceptions of their strengths in domains such as physical appearance, athletics, and academics contribute to their global sense of self-worth or self-esteem. The impact of parental gender typing on self-esteem is examined next.

*Self-esteem.*   Two recent meta-analyses reviewed the literature on gender differences in self-esteem (Kling, Hyde, Showers, and Buswell, 1999; Major, Barr, Zubek, and Babey, 1999). Both pointed out a small but significant overall trend for lower self-esteem among girls than among boys emerging during adolescence. No doubt the explanation for gender difference in self-esteem is multifaceted. However, there is some indication that parents can have some impact. Harter (1999) and others have argued for the importance of perceived positive regard from significant others as a contributor to children's sense of self-worth. Parents are one of the most important sources of perceived support. Perceived parental judgments and self-perceived competence may influence self-esteem differently for some girls and boys.

Generally, studies suggest that parenting styles may influence children's self-esteem. There are two gender-related patterns that tend to appear in the literature. First, researchers have observed in samples of children and adolescents that closeness with or perceived acceptance from the same-gender parent is correlated with higher self-esteem in daughters (Burnett and Demnar, 1996; Dickstein and Posner, 1978; Ohannessian, Lerner, Lerner, and von Eye, 1998; Zemore and Rinholm, 1989) and possibly to a lesser extent in sons (Dickstein and Posner, 1978; Zemore and Rinholm, 1989). Adolescence may be a period of gender intensification when time with and attention to same-gender parents increases (Crouter et al., 1995). If so, it would make sense that positive relationships with same-gender parents would be especially important to adolescents' self-esteem. However, at least one study indicated the opposite pattern with perceived acceptance from the cross-gender parent being more strongly associated with late adolescents' self-esteem (Richards, Gitelson, Petersen, and Hurtig, 1991). Factors underlying these correlations still need to be investigated.

A second gender-related pattern suggests that dimensions of parenting may predict self-esteem for girls and boys differently. Factors related to parent–child affiliation such as parental approval, acceptance, and support may be more strongly correlated with the self-esteem of daughters than that of sons during early and late adolescence (Buri, Louiselle, Misukanis, and Mueller, 1988; Eskilson and Wiley, 1987; Gecas and Schwalbe, 1986; Holmbeck and Hill, 1986; Openshaw, Thomas, and Rollins, 1984). In contrast, parental control and autonomy granting may be more strongly associated with self-esteem in sons than in daughters during early and late adolescence (Gecas and Schwalbe, 1986; Kawash, Keer, and Clewes, 1985). These apparent differences reflect traditional gender socialization patterns that emphasize greater closeness to parents for girls and greater independence from parents for boys. It therefore may be especially undermining for girls' self-esteem when they feel their parents are not emotionally supportive or for sons' self-esteem when they view their parents as not giving them adequate independence. However, daughters as well as sons suffer when they experience low parental support or overly restrictive parental control (e.g., Baumrind, 1989).

There are also some factors that may moderate or mediate the relation among parenting, gender, and children's self-esteem. First, the parents' marital relationship may influence the self-esteem of daughters and sons differently. For example, this was illustrated in a study by Amato (1986). During childhood, marital conflict may have a negative impact on the self-esteem of girls but not on that of boys. During adolescence, marital conflict had a weak negative effect on both girls' and boys' self-esteem. Perhaps daughters' traditionally closer ties to the family put young girls more at risk for negative self-appraisal when their parents got into conflict.

How equally partners share roles and responsibilities can affect how well spouses get along. Obeidallah, McHale, and Silbereisen (1996) considered this factor in relation to young adolescent girls' well-being. They found that girls who evaluated their parents' marriage as egalitarian were significantly lower in depression than were other girls. Thus, how gender is constructed in the family may have an indirect influence on children's self-development—perhaps especially on girls' development because girls remain closer to their families during adolescence than do boys.

Finally, financial strain is another potential stressor on many family relationships that may affect gender-related variations in children's self-esteem. Mayhew and Lempers (1998) found that economic difficulty tended to be negatively correlated with the parents' own self-esteem, and low parental self-esteem was associated with lower self-esteem among daughters—but not among sons. As previously suggested, if daughters tend to maintain a closer connection to the family than sons do, daughters may be more susceptible to parents' emotional states.

As Harter (1999) has shown, there are multiple pathways for attaining self-esteem. The key is feeling supported by significant figures and feeling competent in domains important to the self. Whereas boys have traditionally been encouraged to achieve through sports and career, girls have traditionally been directed to maintain close ties to the family. Consistent with these socialization emphases, the self-esteem of daughters tends to be influenced by family factors more than does the self-esteem of sons (Buri et al., 1988; Eskilson and Wiley, 1987; Gecas and Schwalbe, 1986; Mandara and Murray, 2000; Openshaw et al., 1984). Sports and career preparation tend to take sons outside of the home, where they can seek out the approval of other social supports such as coaches, teammates, and other peers (Eskilson and Wiley, 1987; Whitehead and Corbin, 1997). In contrast to boys, girls may therefore depend more on feeling supported by parents (Eskilson and Wiley, 1987) and possibly teachers (Burnett and Demnar, 1996) for their sense of self-esteem. However, as girls continue to increase their participation in sports and other extracurricular activities, we may see similar patterns between girls and boys in the relative impact of different sources of social support on self-esteem.

As the previously reviewed studies suggest, parents' support matters to adolescents' self-appraisals. Peers comprise another reference group that is important during adolescence. As discussed next, parents can moderate the influences that peers might have on their children.

*Monitoring and managing children's peer affiliations.*   As children become older and more autonomous, they increasingly turn to their peers for guidance and socioemotional support. Some authors have gone so far as to argue that parents are relatively insignificant sources of socialization compared with peers (Harris, 1995, 2000). Other researchers disagree (see Collins et al., 2000; Maccoby, 2000; Vandell, 2000). No one disputes the importance of peers, and most researchers would concede that parents' impact on their children has often been overstated. (Indeed, throughout this review, the potential influence of child effects on parents has been acknowledged.) However, there are many ways that parents appear to influence their children—many of them have been described in this chapter in relation to children's gender development. One more aspect of girls' and boys' development that parents may influence is their peer affiliations.

Although peers are highly influential socialization agents, parents may moderate the influence of peers through careful supervision and management (Brown, Mounts, Lamborn, and Steinberg, 1993; Crouter and Head, in Vol. 3 of this *Handbook*; Ladd, Le Sieur, and Profilet, 1993; Ladd and Pettit, in Vol. 5 of this *Handbook*; Parke, O'Neill, Isley, and Spitzer, 1998). Children and adolescents who receive low parental supervision are generally more susceptible to peer pressure (e.g., Steinberg, 1986). Additionally, several studies indicate a negative correlation between parental monitoring and rates of aggression and delinquency—especially (but not exclusively) for boys (Crouter, McHale, and Bartko, 1993; Goldstein, 1984; Griffin, Botvin, Scheier, and Diaz, 2000; Jacobson and Crockett, 2000; Li, Feigelman, and Stanton, 2000). A similar link has been observed between parental monitoring and child substance abuse (Fletcher, Darling, Steinberg, and Dornbusch, 1995; Thomas, Reifman, Barnes, and Farrell, 2000) and sexual risk taking (Li et al., 2000; Thomas et al., 2000).

Whereas parental monitoring appears to be important for reducing the likelihood of certain behavior problems in boys, parents' involvement may benefit girls in school. Fletcher and Shaw (2000) found that parents' relationships with both their 14-year-old children's peers and their peers' parents were related to daughters' greater involvements in school-based extracurricular activities. Given the traditionally closer ties of daughters to the family, girls may be less likely than boys to seek out extrafamilial activities. Parents may also impose more restrictions on girls' movements outside the family. Therefore parents' involvement in their children's lives outside of the family may have a stronger impact on daughters than on sons.

Monitoring children's behavior becomes especially challenging when parenting resources are stretched thin (see Crouter and Head, in Vol. 3 of this *Handbook*). For example, lower levels of parental monitoring often occur in single-parent households (Goldstein, 1984; Thomas et al., 2000), dual-career families (Jacobson and Crockett, 2000), and low-income urban households (Griffin et al., 2000; Li et al., 2000). Parental monitoring is associated with reduced likelihood of conduct problems in both single-parent mother-headed households (Goldstein, 1984) and in dual-career families (Jacobson and Crockett, 2000). Also, parental supervision in urban low-income homes is negatively correlated with aggression in girls and boys, alcohol abuse in boys, and tobacco smoking in girls (Griffin et al., 2000).

Parental monitoring may be especially important for sons in high-risk neighborhoods to the extent that various forms of risk taking are more likely among boys than among girls (Byrnes, Miller, and Schafer, 1999). Paradoxically, there may be less parental monitoring of boys than of girls in these settings (Li et al., 2000). Perhaps partly for these reasons, the importance of parental monitoring on reducing problem behaviors during the course of adolescence appears to increase for boys and to decrease for girls (Jacobson and Crockett, 2000).

There are some reports in the research literature of Child-Gender × Parent-Gender interaction effects on parental monitoring. Crouter, Helms-Erikson, Updegraff, and McHale (1999) found that parents who had two children between 8 and 11 years of age knew more about the activities of their same-gender than those of their cross-gender child. Thus, as children enter into adolescence, relationships with same-gender parents may increase in importance (Crouter et al., 1999). Given that fathers are typically less involved in childcare than are mothers, the implication is that same-gender parental monitoring may be less likely for sons than daughters. Paradoxically, monitoring may be more strongly related to positive child outcomes for sons than for daughters (Jacobson and Crockett, 2000).

In sum, parents can monitor and set restrictions on their children's and adolescents' peer affiliations. Parental supervision, in turn, may moderate many gender-related per influences on children. At some point, however, parents typically must let go and allow their children to stand on their own as adults. Accordingly, one of the topics of concern to many adolescence researchers is how parents negotiate and foster their daughters' and sons' emotional autonomy. This topic is taken up next.

*Emotional autonomy and closeness in adolescence and early adulthood.*   Adolescence is a period of emerging autonomy when offspring typically redefine their relationship with their parents (Steinberg and Silk, in Vol. 1 of this *Handbook*). The developmental challenge is to emerge into an independent adult while maintaining one's emotional closeness to the family. Theorists and researchers have noted that traditional patterns of gender development emphasize different patterns of attachment and autonomy for girls and boys (e.g., Block, 1973; Chodorow, 1978). As previously discussed, many parents may encourage closer ties to the family in daughters and relatively more autonomy in sons. These patterns can continue into adolescence and adulthood. For example, some studies indicate less autonomy from parents (especially from mothers) for daughters than for sons during adolescence (e.g., Ryan and Lynch, 1989) and adulthood (e.g., Brody, 1996; Frank, Avery, and Laman, 1988; Geuzaine, Debry, and Liesens, 2000). These effects may be especially strong in families of Latino and Asian descent (e.g., Chao and Tseng, in Vol. 4 of this *Handbook*; Fuligni, Tseng, and Lam, 1999; Harwood et al., in Vol. 4 of this *Handbook*).

Reported gender differences in emotional autonomy during adolescence and adulthood do not necessarily address if and how parents may have contributed to these outcomes. A few studies suggest some possibilities. Autonomy development during adolescence involves exploring and establishing one's sense of identity. To consider this process, Grotevant and Cooper (1985) examined the relation between family communication patterns and adolescents' identity explorations. They found a different set of correlations for daughters and sons. Daughters who scored highest on identity exploration tended to have fathers who demonstrated more separation (e.g., disagreement) and made more relevant comments to the adolescents' ideas during their interactions. One could interpret these fathers as emphasizing both individuality (through separation) and affiliation (by responding in relevant ways) with their daughters. In contrast, sons with the highest identity exploration were more likely to have fathers who responded with high mutuality to their sons' disagreements and suggestions. The fathers continued to engage their sons positively following their son's self-assertion moves. Fathers thereby allowed their sons to individuate in the context of providing them with positive feedback. Thus, fathers seemed to facilitate identity exploration by bridging the adolescents' needs for autonomy and affiliation in somewhat different ways with daughters and sons.

The findings of Grotevant and Cooper overlap somewhat with those reported by Leaper et al. (1989). They examined 14-year-old adolescents' conversations with their parents in relation to the adolescents' performance on Loevinger's measure of ego development over the next 4 years. A distinction was made between conformist-pathway and post-conformist-pathway adolescents. Block (1973) interpreted the conformist and the postconformist levels of ego development in relation to traditional and transcendent patterns of gender development, respectively. Psychosocial functioning at the conformist ego level reflects the adoption of mainstream standards with corresponding emphases on the expression of agency in boys and communion in girls. In contrast, the postconformist ego level reflects the development of autonomous values and standards with the integration of agency and communion. Leaper et al. (1989) found that parents' communication style with their 14-year-old children predicted gender-related variation in ego development over the next 4 years. Attaining the postconformist stage was associated with parental communications that emphasized separation with daughters and closeness with sons. Conversely, the reverse pattern of findings were obtained with the conformist-pathway adolescents. Conformist-pathway sons were more likely to have experienced communication that emphasized separation, and conformist-pathway daughters were more apt to have experienced parent communications that emphasized closeness. Thus, to reach the postconformist level, it may be helpful for parents to complement the pervasive socialization pressures on girls and boys to excel in gender-typed domains by helping their children practice in cross-gender-typed domains. For daughters this means a greater emphasis on independence, and for sons it means more emphasis on closeness.

Other studies have similarly highlighted the potential importance of emotional closeness to parents for sons' psychosocial adjustment during early adolescence (e.g., Kenny, Lomax, Brabeck, and Fife, 1998; Steinberg, 1987a). However, emotional support from parents—especially mothers—may be important for girls during late adolescence (Geuzaine et al., 2000). These possible Gender × Age interactions need to be considered more fully in relation to the importance and the impact of parental closeness for daughters and sons at different life phases.

Various parental and family factors are apt to moderate parental influences on the development of gender differences in autonomy. Among them are parents' gender attitudes. For example, Bumpus, Crouter, and McHale (2001) compared parents who held egalitarian and traditional gender attitudes, and they found that mothers with traditional gender attitudes tended to grant their daughters fewer autonomy opportunities than did mothers with less traditional attitudes. Some other potential moderators of parental influences on adolescent daughters' and sons' autonomy development include the parent's gender (e.g., Crouter et al., 1995; Grotevant and Cooper, 1985), family structure and marital status (e.g., Honess, Charman, Zani, Cicognani, Xeri, Jackson, and Bosma, 1997), the adolescent's pubertal timing and status (e.g., Bumpus et al., 2001; Steinberg, 1987b), and the adolescent's current dating status and history (Dowdy and Kliewer, 1998).

In sum, as their children grow into adults, mothers and fathers may affect the manner and the extent to which their daughters and sons balance their needs for autonomy and closeness. The greater encouragement traditionally given to daughters for closeness and to sons for independence has been congruent with the traditional gender divisions in society. However, some of the recent research suggests new possibilities. Sons as well as daughters may transcend traditional patterns. This theme is reiterated in the chapter's closing.

## CONCLUSIONS

The question of whether or not parents contribute significantly to children's socialization has stirred a healthy debate in developmental psychology (e.g., Collins et al., 2000; Harris, 1995, 2000; Maccoby, 2000; Vandell, 2000). Similarly, there are differing opinions regarding how important parents' influence on children's gender development may be (Block, 1983; Fagot and Leinbach, 1987; Leaper et al., 1998; Lytton and Romney, 1991; Maccoby and Jacklin, 1974). The impact of parents on children's development has often been overstated. At the same time, although caution is highly warranted, the evidence reviewed in this chapter strongly suggests that parents do matter in many important ways. The story is more complex than some might hope it to be. At least five points need to be taken into consideration when parenting influences on children's gender development are examined.

First, following the caveat raised in the preceding paragraph, we need to be more vigilant of possible child effects on parents when studying potential socialization influences (Scarr and McCartney, 1983). Sometimes girls and boys may act differently themselves and evoke corresponding different types of behaviors from their parents. Earlier in the chapter the example of early gender differences in infants' negative emotionality was discussed. To the extent that boys are more likely than girls to be born with difficult temperamental characteristics, they may evoke different behaviors from their parents. However, child effects on parents are not mutually exclusive with parent effects on children. Some models of gender socialization have considered the interplay between both sources of influence (e.g., Brody, 1999, 2000).

The second point to underscore is that detecting parenting influences on children's gender development requires taking a more fine-grained analysis than often occurs. When reviewers average effects across broad definitions of constructs, types of measures (e.g., observational versus self-report), child age levels, parent characteristics (e.g, parent gender, parent ethnicity, parent education), or activity settings (e.g., Lytton and Romney, 1991), the effect may be washed out (Fagot and Hagan, 1991). Alternatively, taking into account more of the developmental and the social contexts for parent–child interactions has revealed many interesting patterns of gender typing (e.g, Leaper et al., 1998).

Third, gender-related influences are frequently detected when predictors of development for girls and boys are compared. In many instances, similar parenting behaviors may affect daughters and sons differently because of gender-related differences in either children's dispositions or their prior socialization. Therefore, researchers need to examine the potential impact of family factors on girls and boys separately.

The importance of activity settings is the fourth point worth reiterating. When Lytton and Romney (1991) carried out their meta-analysis on parents' differential socialization of daughters and sons, the one area in which they detected a robust effect was in parents' encouragement of gender-typed activities. By itself, this is an important finding. Through experience in particular activities, children develop expectations, preferences, and skills. However, opportunities are defined by their access (Leaper, 2000a; Lott and Maluso, 1993). Therefore, to the extent that girls and boys have access to different opportunities—whether they be types of toys, play, social experiences, athletic or academic pursuits—they may develop corresponding gender differences in their intellectual and socioemotional developments. In these ways, childhood gender differences in activities may pave the way for later adult gender differences in roles and inequities in status.

The final point is that parenting practices vary according to the family ecology. Cultural and socioeconomic factors influence parents' conceptions of gender and their childrearing practices (Best and Williams, 1997; Whiting and Edwards, 1988). Within a given culture, there are social–structural variations in gender relations depending on people's education, social status, ethnic and religious traditions, as well as characteristics of the particular community. As we have seen, there are some parents whose practices may contribute to relatively greater bifurcation in girls' and boys' development, whereas there are other parents who may help their children transcend the restrictions of traditional gender roles and inequities. For instance, parents can help their daughters and sons balance and coordinate their needs for self-assertion and affiliation (Leaper, 2000b; Leaper et al., 1989). In these ways, parents and their children contribute to changes in the larger macrosystem.

In closing, recall the Story of X described at the beginning of the chapter. X was a child whose parents did not impose the traditional restrictions of having to choose between "girls' stuff" and "boys' stuff." X had the flexibility to choose both. However, X was only a fictional character in a children's book. Most children today are confronted with choosing between activities and practices that are stereotyped for one gender or the other. As women and men face fewer restrictions themselves as parents, their daughters and sons will explore and enjoy a wider world of possibilities.

## ACKNOWLEDGMENTS

The chapter is dedicated to the memory of Beverly Fagot for her pioneering research on parenting girls and boys. She was the author of the chapter on this topic in the first edition of the *Handbook of Parenting*. Margarita Azmitia, Kristen Etzler, and Harriet Tenenbaum are thanked for their comments or assistance during the preparation of this manuscript.

# REFERENCES

Adams, S., Kuebli, J., Boyle, P. A., and Fivush, R. (1995). Gender differences in parent–child conversations about past emotions: A longitudinal investigation. *Sex Roles, 33,* 309–323.

Albert, A. A., and Porter, J. R. (1988). Children's gender-role stereotypes: A sociological investigation of psychological models. *Sociological Forum, 3,* 184–210.

Amato, P. R. (1986). Marital conflict, the parent–child relationship and child self-esteem. Family relations. *Journal of Applied Family and Child Studies, 35,* 403–410.

Antill, J. K., Goodnow, J. J., Russell, G., and Cotton, S. (1996). The influence of parents and family context on children's involvement in household tasks. *Sex Roles, 34,* 215–236.

Archer, J. (1984). Gender roles as developmental pathways. *British Journal of Social Psychology, 23,* 245–256.

Austin, A. M. B., and Braeger, T. J. (1990). Gendered differences in parent's encouragement of sibling interaction: Implications for the construction of a personal premise system. *First Language, 10,* 181–197.

Baildum, E. M., Hillier, V. F., Menson, S., and Bamford, F. N. (2000). Attention to infants in the first year. *Child: Care, Health and Development, 26,* 199–216.

Bandura, A. (1997). *Self-efficacy: The exercise of control.* New York: Freeman.

Barber, B. K., and Thomas, D. L. (1986). Dimensions of fathers' and mothers' supportive behavior: The case for physical affection. *Journal of Marriage and the Family, 48,* 783–794.

Bardwell, J. R., Cochran, S. W., and Walker, S. (1986). Relationship of parental education, race, and gender to sex role stereotyping in five-year-old kindergartners. *Sex Roles, 15,* 275–281.

Barglow, P., Contreras, J., Kavesh, L., and Vaughn, B. E. (1998). Developmental follow-up of 6–7 year old children of mothers employed during their infancies. *Child Psychiatry and Human Development, 29,* 3–20.

Barnett, D., Kidwell, S. L., and Leung, K. H. (1998). Parenting and preschooler attachment among low-income urban African American families. *Child Development, 69,* 1657–1671.

Baron, R. M., and Kenny, D. A. (1986). The moderator–mediator variable distinction in social psychological research: Conceptual, strategic, and statistical considerations. *Journal of Personality and Social Psychology, 51,* 1173–1182.

Baruch, G. K., and Barnett, R. C. (1986). Fathers' participation in family work and children's sex-role attitudes. *Child Development, 57,* 1210–1223.

Baumrind, D. (1989). Rearing competent children. In W. Damon (Ed.), *Child development today and tomorrow* (pp. 349–378). San Francisco: Jossey-Bass.

Baxter, J., and Kane, E. W. (1995). Dependence and independence: A cross-national analysis of gender inequality and gender attitudes. *Gender and Society, 9,* 193–215.

Bee, H. L., Van Egeren, L. F., Streissguth, A. P., Nyman, B. A., and Leckie, M. S. (1969). Social class differences in maternal teaching strategies and speech patterns. *Developmental Psychology, 1,* 726–734.

Belsky, J., and Rovine, M. J. (1988). Nonmaternal care in the first year of life and the security of infant/parent attachment. *Child Development, 59,* 157–167.

Benenson, J. F. (1996). Gender differences in the development of relationships. In G. G. Noam and K. W. Fischer (Eds.), *Development and vulnerability in close relationships* (pp. 263–286). Mahwah, NJ: Lawrence Erlbaum Associates.

Benenson, J. F., Morash, D., and Petrakos, H. (1998). Gender differences in emotional closeness between preschool children and their mothers. *Sex Roles, 38,* 975–985.

Best, D. L., and Williams, J. E. (1997). Sex, gender, and culture. In J. W. Berry, M. H. Segall, and C. Kagitcibasi (Eds.), *Handbook of cross-cultural psychology: Vol. 3. Social behavior and applications* (pp. 163–212). Boston: Allyn and Bacon.

Bigler, R. S. (1997). Conceptual and methodological issues in the measurement of children's sex typing. *Psychology of Women Quarterly, 21,* 53–69.

Biringen, Z., Emde, R. N., Brown, D., Lowe, L., Myers, S., and Nelson, D. (1999). Emotional availability and emotion communication in naturalistic mother–infant interactions: Evidence for gender relations. *Journal of Social Behavior and Personality, 14,* 463–478.

Blackford, J. U., and Walden, T. A. (1998). Individual differences in social referencing. *Infant Behavior and Development, 21,* 89–102.

Blair, S. L. (1992). The sex-typing of children's household labor: Parental influence on daughters' and sons' housework. *Youth and Society, 24,* 178–203.

Block, J. H. (1973). Conceptions of sex role: Some cross-cultural and longitudinal perspectives. *American Psychologist, 28,* 512–526.

Block, J. H. (1983). Differential premises arising from differential socialization of the sexes: Some conjectures. *Child Development, 54,* 1335–1354.

Bornstein, M. H., and Haynes, O. M. (1998). Vocabulary competence in early childhood: Measurement, latent construct, and predictive validity. *Child Development, 69,* 654–671.

Bowlby, J. (1988). *A secure base: Parent–child attachment and healthy human development.* New York: Basic Books.

Brachfeld-Child, S., Simpson, T., and Izenson, N. (1988). Mothers' and fathers' speech to infants in a teaching situation. *Infant Mental Health Journal, 9*, 173–180.

Braungart-Rieker, J., Courtney, S., and Garwood, M. M. (1999). Mother– and father–infant attachment: Families in context. *Journal of Family Psychology, 13*, 535–553.

Brody, L. R. (1996). Gender, emotional expression, and parent–child boundaries. In R. D. Kavanaugh and B. Zimmerberg (Eds.), *Emotion interdisciplinary perspectives* (pp. 139–170). Mahwah, NJ: Lawrence Erlbaum Associates.

Brody, L. R. (1997). Gender and emotion: Beyond stereotypes. *Journal of Social Issues, 53*, 369–393.

Brody, L. R. (1999). *Gender, emotion, and the family.* Cambridge, MA: Harvard University Press.

Brody, L. R. (2000). The socialization of gender differences in emotional expression: Display rules, infant temperament, and differentiation. In A. H. Fischer (Ed.), *gender and emotion: Social psychological perspectives* (pp. 24–47). New York: Cambridge University Press.

Bronfenbrenner, U. (1977). Toward an experimental ecology of human development. *American Psychologist, 32*, 513–531.

Bronfenbrenner, U., and Morris, P. A. (1998). The ecology of developmental processes. In W. Damon (Series Ed.), and R. M. Lerner (Ed.), *Handbook of child psychology: Vol. 1. Theoretical models of human development* (5th ed., pp. 993–1028). New York: Wiley.

Bronstein, P. (1999). Differences in mothers' and fathers' behaviors toward children: A cross-cultural comparison. In L. A. Peplau and S. C. DeBro (Eds.), *Gender, culture, and ethnicity: Current research about women and men* (pp. 70–82). Mountain View, CA: Mayfield.

Bronstein, P., Briones, M., Brooks, T., and Cowan, B. (1996). Gender and family factors as predictors of late adolescent emotional expressiveness and adjustment: A longitudinal study. *Sex Roles, 34*, 739–765.

Brookins, G. K. (1985). Black children's sex-role ideologies and occupational choices in families of employed mothers. In M. B. Spencer, G. K. Brookins, and W. R. Allen (Eds.), *Beginnings: The social and affective development of black children* (pp. 257–271). Hillsdale, NJ: Lawrence Erlbaum Associates.

Brooks, J., and Lewis, M. (1974). Attachment behavior in thirteen-month-old, opposite-sex twins. *Child Development, 45*, 243–247.

Brown, B. B., Mounts, N., Lamborn, S. D., and Steinberg, L. (1993). Parenting practices and peer group affiliation in adolescence. *Child Development, 64*, 467–482.

Brundin, K., Roedholm, M., and Larsson, K. (1988). Vocal communication between parents and infants. *Early Human Development, 16*, 35–53.

Bumpus, M. F., Crouter, A. C., and McHale, S. M. (2001). Parental autonomy granting during adolescence: Exploring gender differences in context. *Developmental Psychology, 37*, 163–173.

Bungum, T. J., and Vincent, M. L. (1997). Determinants of physical activity among female adolescents. *American Journal of Preventive Medicine, 1*, 115–122.

Buri, J. R., Louiselle, P. A., Misukanis, T. M., and Mueller, R. A. (1988). Effects of parental authoritarianism and authoritativeness of self-esteem. *Personality and Social Psychology Bulletin, 14*, 271–282.

Burnett, P. C., and Demnar, W. J. (1996). The relationship between closeness to significant others and self-esteem. *Journal of Family Studies, 2*, 121–129.

Burns, A., and Homel, R. (1989). Gender division of tasks by parents and their children. *Psychology of Women Quarterly, 13*, 113–125.

Bussey, K., and Bandura, A. (1999). Social cognitive theory of gender development and differentiation. *Psychological Review, 106*, 676–713.

Byrnes, J. P., Miller, D. C., and Schafer, W. D. (1999). Gender differences in risk taking: A meta-analysis. *Psychological Bulletin, 125*, 367–383.

Caldera, Y. M., Huston, A. C., and O'Brien, M. (1989). Social interactions and play patterns of parents and toddlers with feminine, masculine, and neutral toys. *Child Development, 60*, 70–76.

Campbell, D. W., and Eaton, W. O. (1999). Sex differences in the activity level of infants. *Infant and Child Development, 8*, 1–17.

Carpenter, C. J. (1983). Activity structure and play: Implications for socialization. In M. B. Liss (Ed.), *Social and cognitive skills: Sex roles and children's play* (pp. 117–145). San Diego, CA: Academic.

Carter, A. S., Mayes, L. C., and Pajer, K. A. (1990). The role of dyadic affect in play and infant sex in predicting infant response to the still-face situation. *Child Development, 61*, 764–773.

Cauce, A. M., Hiraga, Y., Graves, D., and Gonzales, N. (1996). African American mothers and their adolescent daughters: Closeness, conflict, and control. In B. J. Ross Leadbeater and N. Way (Eds.), *Urban girls: Resisting stereotypes, creating identities* (pp. 100–116). New York: New York University Press.

Cervantes, C. A., and Callanan, M. A. (1998). Labels and explanations in mother–child emotion talk: Age and gender differentiation. *Developmental Psychology, 34*, 88–98.

Chase-Landsdale, P. L., and Owen, M. T. (1987). Maternal employment in a family context: Effects on infant–mother and infant–father attachments. *Child Development, 58*, 1505–1512.

Chodorow, N. (1978). *The reproduction of mothering: Psychoanalysis and the sociology of gender*. Berkeley, CA: University of California Press.

Chow, E., Wilkinson, D. Y., and Baca Zinn, M. (Eds.). (1996). *Race, class, and gender: Common bonds, different voices*. Thousand Oaks, CA: Sage.

Clarke-Stewart, K. A., and Hevey, C. M. (1981). Longitudinal relations in repeated observations of mother–child interaction from 1 to $2^1/_2$ years. *Developmental Psychology, 17*, 127–145.

Cohn, D. A. (1990). Child–mother attachment of six-year-olds and social competence at school. *Child Development, 61*, 152–162.

Collins, W. A., Maccoby, E. E., Steinberg, L., Hetherington, E. M., and Bornstein, M. H. (2000). Contemporary research on parenting: The case for nature and nurture. *American Psychologist, 55*, 218–232.

Coltrane, S. (1988). Father–child relationships and the status of women: A cross-cultural study. *American Journal of Sociology, 93*, 1060–1095.

Coltrane, S. (2000). Research on household labor: Modeling and measuring the social embeddedness of routine family work. *Journal of Marriage and the Family, 62*, 1208–1233.

Crockenberg, S., and Litman, C. (1990). Autonomy as competence in 2-year-olds: Maternal correlates of child defiance, compliance, and self-assertion. *Developmental Psychology, 26*, 961–971.

Crouter, A. C., Helms-Erickson, H., Updegraff, K., and McHale, S. M. (1999). Conditions underlying parents' knowledge about children's daily lives in middle childhood: Between- and within-family comparisons. *Child Development, 70*, 246–259.

Crouter, A. C., Manke, B. A., and McHale, S. M. (1995). The family context of gender intensification in early adolescence. *Child Development, 66*, 317–329.

Crouter, A. C., McHale, S. M., and Bartko, W. T. (1993). Gender as an organizing feature in parent–child relationships. *Journal of Social Issues, 49*, 161–174.

Crowley, K., and Callanan, M. A., Tenenbaum, H. R., and Allen, E. (2001). Parents explain more often to boys than to girls during shared scientific thinking. *Psychological Science, 12*, 258–261.

Deaux, K., and LaFrance, M. (1998). Gender. In D. T. Gilbert and S. T. Fiske (Eds.), *The handbook of social psychology, Vol. 1* (4th ed., pp. 788–827). New York: McGraw-Hill.

DeMulder, E. K., Denham, S., Schmidt, M., and Mitchell, J. (2000). Q-sort assessment of attachment security during the preschool years: Links from home to school. *Developmental Psychology, 36*, 274–282.

Denham, S. A., Cook, M., and Zoller, D. (1992). "Baby looks very sad": Implications of conversations about feelings between mother and preschooler. *British Journal of Developmental Psychology, 10*, 301–315.

Dickstein, E. B., and Posner, J. M. (1978). Self-esteem and relationship with parents. *Journal of Genetic Psychology, 133*, 273–276.

Dowdy, B. B., and Kliewer, W. (1998). Dating, parent-adolescent conflict, and behavioral autonomy. *Journal of Youth and Adolescence, 27*, 473–492.

Dunn, J., Bretherton, I., and Munn, P. (1987). Conversations about feeling states between mothers and their young children. *Developmental Psychology, 23*, 132–139.

Dunn, J., Brown, J., Slomkowski, C., Tesla, C., and Youngblade, L. M. (1991). Young children's understanding of other people's feelings and beliefs: Individual differences and their antecedents. *Child Development, 62*, 1352–1366.

Eaton, W. O., and Enns, L. R. (1986). Sex differences in human motor activity level. *Psychological Bulletin, 100*, 19–28.

Eccles, J. S. (1987). Adolescence: Gateway to gender-role transcendence. In D. B. Carter (Ed.), *Current conceptions of sex roles and sex typing: Theory and research* (pp. 225–241). New York: Praeger.

Eccles, J. S., Freedman-Doan, C., Frome, P., Jacobs, J., and Yoon, K. S. (2000). Gender-role socialization in the family: A longitudinal approach. In T. Eckes and H. M. Trautner (Eds.), *The developmental social psychology of gender* (pp. 333–360). Mahwah, NJ: Lawrence Erlbaum Associates.

Eisenberg, A. R. (1999). Emotion talk among Mexican American and Anglo American mothers and children from two social classes. *Merrill-Palmer Quarterly, 45*, 267–284.

Eisenberg, N., Cumberland, A., and Spinrad, T. L. (1998). Parental socialization of emotion. *Psychological Inquiry, 9*, 241–273.

Eisenberg, N., Wolchik, S. A., Hernandez, R., and Pasternack, J. F (1985). Parental socialization of young children's play: A short-term longitudinal study. *Child Development, 56*, 1506–1513.

Eisler, R., Loye, D., and Norgaard, K. (1995). *Women, men, and the global quality of life*. Pacific Grove, CA: Center for Partnership Studies.

Ember, C. R. (1973). Feminine task assignment and the social behavior of boys. Ethos, *1*, 424–439.

Emler, N. P., and Hall, S. (1994). Economic roles in the household system: Young people's experiences and expectations. In X. M. J. Lerner, and G. G. Mikula (Eds.), *Entitlement and the affectional bond: Justice in close relationships* (pp. 281–303). New York: Plenum.

Erikson, E. H. (1963). *Childhood and society* (2nd ed.). New York: Norton.

Eskilson, A., and Wiley, M. G. (1987). Parents, peers, perceived pressure, and adolescent self concept: Is a daughter a daughter all of her life? *Sociological Quarterly, 28*, 135–145.

Etaugh, C. (1993). Maternal employment: Effects on children. In J. Frankel (Ed.), *The employed mother and the family context* (pp. 68–88). New York: Springer.

Etaugh, C., and Liss, M. B. (1992). Home, school, and playroom: Training grounds for adult gender roles. *Sex Roles, 26,* 129–147.

Fagot, B. I. (1978). The influence of sex of child on parental reactions to toddler children. *Child Development, 49,* 459–465.

Fagot, B. I. (1984). The child's expectations of differences in adult male and female interactions. *Sex Roles, 11,* 593–600.

Fagot, B. I. (1995). Parenting boys and girls. In M. H. Bornstein (Ed.), *Handbook of parenting: Vol. 1. Children and parenting* (pp. 163–183). Mahwah, NJ: Lawrence Erlbaum Associates.

Fagot, B. I., and Hagan, R. (1991). Observations of parent reactions to sex-stereotyped behaviors: Age and sex effects. *Child Development, 62,* 617–628.

Fagot, B. I., and Kavanagh, K. (1990a). Sex differences in responses to the stranger in the Strange Situation. *Sex Roles, 23,* 123–132.

Fagot, B. I., and Kavanagh, K. (1990b). The prediction of antisocial behavior from avoidant attachment classification. *Child Development, 61,* 864–873.

Fagot, B. I., and Leinbach, M. D. (1987). Socialization of sex roles within the family. In D. B. Carter (Ed.), *Current conceptions of sex roles and sex typing: Theory and research* (pp. 89–100). New York: Praeger.

Fagot, B. I., Leinbach, M. D., and O'Boyle, C. (1992). Gender labeling, gender stereotyping, and parenting behaviors. *Developmental Psychology, 28,* 225–230.

Farver, J. M., and Wimbarti, S. (1995). Paternal participation in toddler's pretend play. *Social Development, 4,* 17–31.

Fisher-Thompson, D. (1993). Adult toy purchases for children: Factors affecting sex-typed toy selection. *Journal of Applied Developmental Psychology, 14,* 385–406.

Fivush, R. (1989). Exploring sex differences in the emotional content of mother–child conversations about the past. *Sex Roles, 20,* 675–691.

Fivush, R. (1991). Gender and emotion in mother–child conversations about the past. *Journal of Narrative and Life History, 1,* 325–341.

Fivush, R. (1998). Gendered narratives: Elaboration, structure, and emotion in parent–child reminiscing across the preschool years. In C. P. Thompson and D. J. Hermann (Eds.), *Autobiographical memory: Theoretical and applied perspectives* (pp. 79–103). Mahwah, NJ: Lawrence Erlbaum Associates.

Fivush, R., and Buckner, J. P. (2000). Gender, sadness, and depression: The development of emotional focus through gendered discourse. In A. H. Fischer (Ed.), *Gender and emotion: Social psychological perspectives* (pp. 232–253). New York: Cambridge University Press.

Fivush, R., Brotman, M. A., Buckner, J. P., and Goodman, S. H. (2000). Gender differences in parent–child emotion narratives. *Sex Roles, 42,* 233–253.

Flannagan, D., and Baker-Ward, L. (1996). Relations between mother–child discussions of children's preschool and kindergarten experiences. *Journal of Applied Developmental Psychology, 17,* 423–437.

Flannagan, D., and Perese, S. (1998). Emotional references in mother–daughter and mother–son dyads' conversations about school. *Sex Roles, 39,* 353–367.

Fletcher, A. C., Darling, N. E., Steinberg, L., and Dornbusch, S. (1995). The company they keep: Relation of adolescents' adjustment and behavior to their friends' perceptions of authoritative parenting in the social network. *Developmental Psychology, 31,* 300–310.

Fletcher, A. C., and Shaw, R. A. (2000). Sex differences in associations between parental behaviors and characteristics and adolescent social integration. *Social Development, 9,* 133–148.

Forman, D. R., and Kochanska, G. (2001). Viewing imitation as child responsiveness: A link between teaching and discipline domains of socialization. *Developmental Psychology, 37,* 198–206.

Fracasso, M. P., Busch-Rossnagel, N. A., and Fisher, C. B. (1994). The relationship of maternal behavior and acculturation to the quality of attachment in Hispanic infants living in New York City. *Hispanic Journal of Behavioral Sciences, 16,* 143–154.

Frank, S. J., Avery, C. B., and Laman, M. S. (1988). Young adults' perceptions of their relationships with their parents: Individual differences in connectedness, competence, and emotional autonomy. *Developmental Psychology, 24,* 729–737.

Frankel, M. T., and Rollins, H. A., Jr. (1983). Does mother know best?: Mothers and fathers interacting with preschool sons and daughters. *Developmental Psychology, 19,* 694–702.

Fuchs, D., and Thelen, M. H. (1988). Children's expected interpersonal consequences of communicating their affective state and reported likelihood of expression. *Child Development, 59,* 1314–1322.

Fulcher, M., Sutfin, E. L., and Patterson, C. J. (2001, April). *Parental sexual orientation, division of labor, and sex-role stereotyping in children's occupational choices.* Paper presented at the meeting of the Society for Research in Child Development, Minneapolis, MN.

Fuligni, A. J., Tseng, V., and Lam, M. (1999). Attitudes toward family obligations among American adolescents with Asian, Latin American, and European backgrounds. *Child Development, 70,* 1030–1044.

Gardner, K. E., and LaBrecque, S. V. (1986). Effects of maternal employment on sex role orientation of adolescents. *Adolescence, 21,* 875–885.

Garner, D. M., Rosen, L. W., and Barry, D. (1998). Eating disorders among athletes: Research and recommendations. *Child and Adolescent Psychiatric Clinics of North America, 7,* 839–857.

Gecas, V., and Schwalbe, M. L. (1986). Parental behavior and adolescent self-esteem. *Journal of Marriage and the Family, 48,* 37–46.

Geuzaine, C., Debry, M., and Liesens, V. (2000). Separation from parents in late adolescence: The same for boys and girls? *Journal of Youth and Adolescence, 29,* 79–91.

Gleason, J. B. (1987). Sex differences in parent–child interaction. In S. U. Philips, S. Steele, and C. Tanz (Eds.), *Language, gender, and sex in comparative perspective* (pp. 189–199). Cambridge, England: Cambridge University Press.

Gleason, J. B., and Ely, R. (in press). Gender differences in language development. To appear in A. V. McGillicuddy-DeLisi and R. DeLisi (Eds.), *Biology, society, and behavior: The development of sex differences in cognition.* Greenwich, CT: Ablex.

Goldberg, S., and Lewis, M. (1969). Play behavior in the infant: Early sex differences. *Child Development, 40,* 21–31.

Goldman, J. D., and Goldman, R. J. (1983). Children's perceptions of parents and their roles: A cross-national study in Australia, England, North America, and Sweden. *Sex Roles, 9,* 791–812.

Goldshmidt, O. T., and Weller, L. (2000). "Talking emotions": Gender differences in a variety of conversational contexts. *Symbolic Interaction, 23,* 117–134.

Goldstein, H. S. (1984). Parental composition, supervision, and conduct problems in youths 12 to 17 years old. *Journal of the American Academy of Child Psychiatry, 23,* 679–684.

Goodnow, J. J. (1988). Children's household work: Its nature and functions. *Psychological Bulletin, 103,* 5–26.

Gould, L. (1978). *X: A fabulous child's story.* New York: Daughters Publishing.

Griffin, K. W., Botvin, G. J., Scheier, L. M., and Diaz, T. (2000). Parenting practices as predictors of substance use, delinquency, and aggression among urban minority youth: Moderating effects of family structure and gender. *Psychology of Addictive Behaviors, 14,* 174–184.

Grotevant, H. D., and Cooper, C. R. (1985). Patterns of interaction in family relationships and the development of identity exploration in adolescence. *Child Development, 56,* 415–428.

Grusec, J. E., Goodnow, J. J., and Cohen, L. (1996). Household work and the development of concern for others. *Developmental Psychology, 32,* 999–1007.

Hackett, G. (1985). Role of mathematics self-efficacy in the choice of math-related majors of college women and men: A path analysis. *Journal of Counseling Psychology, 32,* 47–56.

Harris, J. R. (1995). Where is the child's environment? A group socialization theory of development. *Psychological Review, 102,* 458–489.

Harris, J. R. (2000). Socialization, personality development, and the child's environments: Comment on Vandell (2000). *Developmental Psychology, 36,* 711–723.

Hart, B., and Risley, T. R. (1995). *Meaningful differences in the everyday experience of young American children.* Baltimore, MD: Brookes.

Harter, S. (1999). *The construction of the self: A developmental perspective.* New York: Guilford.

Haviland, J. J., and Malatesta, C. Z. (1981). The development of sex differences in nonverbal signals: Fallacies, facts, and fantasies. In C. Mayo and N. M. Henley (Eds.), *Gender and Nonverbal Behavior* (pp. 183–208). New York: Springer-Verlag.

Henley, N. M. (1995). Ethnicity and gender issues in language. In H. Landrine (Ed.), *Bringing cultural diversity to feminist psychology: Theory, research, and practice* (pp. 361–395). Washington, DC: American Psychological Association.

Hewlett, B. S. (1991). *Intimate fathers: The nature and context of Aka Pygmy paternal infant care.* Ann Arbor, MI: University of Michigan Press.

Hill, J. P., and Lynch, M. E. (1983). The intensification of gender-related role expectations during early adolescence. In J. Brooks-Gunn and A. C. Petersen (Eds.), *Girls at puberty: Biological and psychological perspectives* (pp. 201–229). New York: Plenum.

Hilton, J. M., and Haldeman, V. A. (1991). Gender differences in the performance of household tasks by adults and children in single-parent and two-parent, two-earner families. *Journal of Family Issues, 12,* 114–130.

Hochschild, A. (1989). *The second shift: Working parents and the revolution at home.* New York: Viking.

Holmbeck, G. N., and Hill, J. P. (1986). A path-analytic approach to the relations between parental traits and acceptance and adolescent adjustment. *Sex Roles, 14,* 315–334.

Honess, T. M., Charman, E. A., Zani, B., Cicognani, E., Xeri, M. L., Jackson, A. E., and Bosma, H. A. (1997). Conflict between parents and adolescents: Variation by family constitution. *British Journal of Developmental Psychology, 15,* 367–385.

Humphrey, L. L. (1989). Observed family interactions among subtypes of eating disorders using structural analysis of social behavior. *Journal of Consulting and Clinical Psychology, 57,* 206–214.

Huston, A. C. (1985). The development of sex-typing: Themes from recent research. *Developmental Review, 5,* 1–17.

Huttenlocher, J., Haight, W., Bryk, A., Seltzer, M., and Lyons, T. (1991). Early vocabulary growth: Relation to language input and gender. *Developmental Psychology, 27,* 236–248.

Hyde, J. S., and Linn, M. C. (1988). Gender differences in verbal ability: A meta-analysis. *Psychological Bulletin, 104,* 53–69.

Jacklin, C. N., DiPietro, J. A., and Maccoby, E. E. (1984). Sex-typing behavior and sex-typing pressure in child/parent interaction. *Archives of Sexual Behavior, 13,* 413–425.

Jacobson, K. C., and Crockett, L. J. (2000). Parental monitoring and adolescent adjustment: An ecological perspective. *Journal of Research on Adolescence, 10*, 65–97.

Kane, E. W. (2000). Racial and ethnic variations in gender-related attitudes. *Annual Review of Sociology, 26*, 419–439.

Kawash, G. F., Kerr, E. N., and Clewes, J. L. (1985). Self-esteem in children as a function of perceived parental behavior. *Journal of Psychology, 119*, 235–242.

Kenny, M. E., Lomax, R., Brabeck, M., and Fife, J. (1998). Longitudinal pathways linking adolescent reports of maternal and paternal attachments to psychological well-being. *Journal of Early Adolescence, 18*, 221–243.

Kerns, K. A., and Barth, J. M. (1995). Attachment and play: Convergence across components of parent–child relationships and their relations to peer competence. *Journal of Social and Personal Relationships, 12*, 243–260.

Kerns, K. A., Cole, A., and Andrews, P. B. (1998). Attachment security, parent peer management practices, and peer relationships in preschoolers. *Merrill-Palmer Quarterly, 44*, 504–522.

Kimmel, M. S. (2000). *The gendered society.* New York: Oxford University Press.

Kling, K. C., Hyde, J. S., Showers, C. J., and Buswell, B. N. (1999). Gender differences in self-esteem: A meta-analysis. *Psychological Bulletin, 125*, 470–500.

Kohnstamm, G. A. (1989). Temperament in childhood: Cross-cultural and sex differences. In G. A. Kohnstamm and J. E. Bates (Eds.), *Temperament in childhood* (pp. 483–508). New York: Wiley.

Kuczynksi, L., Kochanska, G., Radke-Yarrow, M., and Girnius-Brown, O. (1987). A developmental interpretation of young children's noncompliance. *Developmental Psychology, 23*, 799–806.

Labrell, F. (1996). Paternal play with toddlers: Recreation and creation. *European Journal of Psychology of Education, 11*, 43–54.

Lackey, P. N. (1989). Adults' attitudes about assignments of household chores to male and female children. *Sex Roles, 20*, 271–281.

Ladd, G. W., Le Sieur, K. D., and Profilet, S. M. (1993). Direct parental influences on young children's peer relations. In S. Duck (Ed.), *Learning about relationships* (pp. 152–183). Thousand Oaks, CA: Sage.

LaFreniere, P. J., Provost, M. A., and Dubeau, D. (1992). From an insecure base: Parent–child relations and internalizing behaviour in the pre-school. *Early Development and Parenting, 1*, 137–148.

Lamb, M. E., Frodi, A. M., Frodi, M., and Hwang, C. (1982). Characteristics of maternal and paternal behavior in traditional and nontraditional Swedish families. *International Journal of Behavioral Development, 5*, 131–141.

Lamb, M. E., and Oppenheim, D. (1989). Fatherhood and father–child relationships: Five years of research. In S. H. Cath and A. Gurwitt (Eds.), *Fathers and their families* (pp. 11–26). Hillsdale, NJ: Lawrence Erlbaum Associates.

Landerholm, E. J., and Scriven, G. (1981). A comparison of mother and father interaction with their six-month-old male and female infants. *Early Child Development and Care, 7*, 317–328.

Langlois, J. H., and Downs, A. C. (1980). Mothers, fathers, and peers as socialization agents of sex-typed play behaviors in young children. *Child Development, 51*, 1217–1247.

Leaper, C. (1994). Exploring the consequences of gender segregation on social relationships. In C. Leaper (Ed.), *Childhood gender segregation: Causes and consequences.* (New Directions for Child Development, No. 65, pp. 67–86). San Francisco: Jossey-Bass.

Leaper, C. (2000a). The social construction and socialization of gender. In P. H. Miller and E. K. Scholnick (Eds.), *Toward a feminist developmental psychology* (pp. 127–152). New York: Routledge Press.

Leaper, C. (2000b). Gender, affiliation, assertion, and the interactive context of parent–child play. *Developmental Psychology, 36*, 381–393.

Leaper, C., Anderson, K. J., and Sanders, P. (1998). Moderators of gender effects on parents' talk to their children: A meta-analysis. *Developmental Psychology, 34*, 3–27.

Leaper, C., and Gleason, J. B. (1996). The relation of gender and play activity to parent and child communication. *International Journal of Behavioral Development, 19*, 689–703.

Leaper, C., Hauser, S. T., Kremen, A., Powers, S. I., Jacobson, A. M., Noam, G. G., Weiss-Perry, B., and Follansbee, D. (1989). Adolescent–parent interactions in relation to adolescents' gender and ego development pathway: A longitudinal study. *Journal of Early Adolescence, 9*, 335–361.

Leaper, C., Leve, L., Strasser, T., and Schwartz, R. (1995). Mother–child communication sequences: Play activity, child gender, and marital status effects. *Merrill-Palmer Quarterly, 41*, 307–327.

Leaper, C., and Valin, D. (1996). Predictors of Mexican-American mothers' and fathers' attitudes toward gender equality. *Hispanic Journal of Behavioral Sciences, 18*, 343–355.

Levin, H., Snow, C., and Lee, K. (1984). Nurturant talk to children. *Language and Speech, 27*, 147–162.

Lewis, C., and Gregory, S. (1987). Parents' talk to their infants: The importance of context. *First Language, 7*, 201–216.

Lewis, M. (1972). State as an infant–environment interaction: An analysis of mother–infant interaction as a function of sex. *Merrill-Palmer Quarterly, 18*, 95–121.

Lewis, M., Feiring, C., McGuffog, C., and Jaskir, J. (1984). Predicting psychopathology in six-year-olds from early social relations. *Child Development, 55*, 123–136.

Lewko, J. H., and Ewing, M. E. (1980). Sex differences and parental influence in sport involvement of children. *Journal of Sport Psychology, 2*, 62–68.

Li, X., Feigelman, S., Stanton, B. (2000). Perceived parental monitoring and health risk behaviors among urban low-income African-American children and adolescents. *Journal of Adolescent Health, 27*, 43–48.

Lindahl, L. B., and Heimann, M. (1997). Social proximity in early mother–infant interactions: Implications for gender differences? *Early Development and Parenting, 6*, 83–88.

Lindsey, E. W., Mize, J., and Pettit, G. S. (1997). Differential play patterns of mothers and fathers of sons and daughters: Implications for children's gender role development. *Sex Roles, 37*, 643–661.

Lippe, A., and Crittenden, P. M. (2000). Patterns of attachment in young Egyptian children. In P. M. Crittenden and A. H. Claussen (Eds.), *The organization of attachment relationships: Maturation, culture, and context* (pp. 97–114). New York: Cambridge University Press.

Liss, M. B. (1983). Learning gender-related skills through play. In M. B. Liss (Ed.), *Social and cognitive skills: Sex roles and children's play* (pp. 147–166). New York: Academic.

Lollis, S. P. (1990). Effects of maternal behavior on toddler behavior during separation. *Child Development, 61*, 99–103.

Lott, B., and Maluso, D. (1993). The social learning of gender. In A. E. Beall and R. J. Sternberg (Eds.), *The psychology of gender* (pp. 99–123). New York: Guilford.

Lytton, H., and Romney, D. M. (1991). Parents' differential socialization of boys and girls: A meta-analysis. *Psychological Bulletin, 109*, 267–296.

Maccoby, E. E. (2000). Parenting and its effects on children: On reading and misreading behavior genetics. *Annual Review of Psychology, 51*, 1–27.

Maccoby, E. E., and Jacklin, C. N. (1974). *The psychology of sex differences*. Stanford, CA: Stanford University Press.

Maccoby, E. E., Snow, M. E., and Jacklin, C. N. (1984). Children's dispositions and mother–child interaction at 12 and 18 months: A short-term longitudinal study. *Developmental Psychology, 20*, 459–472.

Major, B., Barr, L., Zubek, J., and Babey, S. H. (1999). Gender and self-esteem: A meta-analysis. In W. B. Swann Jr. and J. H. Langlois (Eds.), *Sexism and stereotypes in modern society: The gender science of Janet Taylor Spence* (pp. 223–253). Washington, DC: American Psychological Association.

Malatesta, C. Z., and Haviland, J. M. (1982). Learning display rules: The socialization of emotion expression in infancy. *Child Development, 53*, 991–1003.

Malatesta, C. Z., Culver, C., Tesman, J. R., and Shepard, B. (1989). The development of emotion expression during the first two years of life. *Monographs of the Society for Research in Child Development, 54*, 1–104.

Mandara, J., and Murray, C. B. (2000). Effects of parental marital status, income, and family functioning on African American adolescent self-esteem. *Journal of Family Psychology, 14*, 475–490.

Mannle, S., and Tomasello, M. (1987). Fathers, siblings and the bridge hypothesis. In K. E. Nelson and A. van Kleeck (Eds.), *Children's language* (Vol. 6, pp. 23–41). Hillsdale, NJ: Lawrence Erlbaum Associates.

Martin, C. L. (1990). Attitudes and expectations about children with nontraditional and traditional gender roles. *Sex Roles, 22*, 151–165.

Martin, C. L., and Halverson, C. F. (1981). A schematic processing model of sex typing and stereotyping in children. *Child Development, 52*, 1119–1134.

Massad, C. M. (1981). Sex role identity and adjustment during adolescence. *Child Development, 52*, 1290–1298.

Mauldin, T., and Meeks, C. B. (1990). Sex differences in children's time use. *Sex Roles, 22*, 537–554.

Mayhew, K. P., and Lempers, J. D. (1998). The relation among financial strain, parenting, parent self-esteem, and adolescent self-esteem. *Journal of Early Adolescence, 18*, 145–172.

McDonald, K., and Parke, R. D. (1986). Parent–child physical play: Effects of sex and age of children and parents. *Sex Roles, 15*, 367–378.

McElroy, M. A., and Kirkendall, D. R. (1981). Conflict in perceived parent/child sport ability judgments. *Journal of Sport Psychology, 4*, 244–247.

McGillicuddy-DeLisi, A. V. (1988). Sex differences in parental teaching behaviors. *Merrill-Palmer Quarterly, 34*, 147–162.

McHale, S. M., Bartko, W. T., Crouter, A. C., and Perry-Jenkins, M. (1990). Children's housework and psychosocial functioning: The mediating effects of parents' sex-role behaviors and attitudes. *Child Development, 61*, 1413–1426.

McLaughlin, B., White, D., McDevitt, T., and Raskin, R. (1983). Mothers' and fathers' speech to their young children: Similar or different? *Journal of Child Language, 10*, 245–252.

Melzi, G., and Fernández, C. (2001, April). *Emotion talk in Peruvian mother–child conversations*. Paper presented at the meeting of the Society for Research in Child Development, Minneapolis, MN.

Messner, M. A. (1992). *Power at play: Sports and the problem of masculinity*. Boston: Beacon.

Morisset, C. E., Barnard, K. E., and Booth, C. L. (1995). Toddlers' language development: Sex differences within social risk. *Developmental Psychology, 31*, 851–865.

Moss, H. A. (1967). Sex, age, and state as determinants of mother–infant interaction. *Merrill-Palmer Quarterly, 13*, 19–36.

Murray, L., Kempton, C., Woolgar, M., and Hopper, R. (1993). Depressed mother's speech to their infants and its relation to infant gender and cognitive development. *Journal of Child Psychology and Psychiatry, 34*, 1083–1101.

Nolen-Hoeksema, S., Larson, J., and Grayson, C. (1999). Explaining the gender difference in depressive symptoms. *Journal of Personality and Social Psychology, 77,* 1061–1072.

O'Brien, M., and Nagle, K. J. (1987). Parents' speech to toddlers: The effect of play context. *Journal of Child Language, 14,* 269–279.

Obeidallah, D. A., McHale, S. M., Silbereisen, R. K. (1996). Gender role socialization and adolescents' reports of depression: Why some girls and not others? *Journal of Youth and Adolescence, 25,* 775–785.

Ogbu, J. U. (1981). Origins of human competence: A cultural-ecological perspective. *Child Development, 52,* 413–429.

Ohannessian, C. M., Lerner, R. M., Lerner, J. V., and von Eye, A. (1998). Perceived parental acceptance and early adolescent self-competence. *American Journal of Orthopsychiatry, 68,* 621–629.

Olweus, D. (1980). Familial and temperamental determinants of aggressive behavior in adolescent boys: A causal analysis. *Developmental Psychology, 16,* 644–660.

Openshaw, D. K., Thomas, D. L., and Rollins, B. C. (1984). Parental influences of adolescent self-esteem. *Journal of Early Adolescence, 4,* 259–274.

Osofsky, J. D., and O'Connell, E. J. (1977). Patterning of newborn behavior in an urban population. *Child Development, 48,* 532–536.

Papini, D. R., and Sebby, R. A. (1988). Variations in conflictual family issues by adolescent pubertal status, gender, and family member. *Journal of Early Adolescence, 8,* 1–15.

Parke, R. D., O'Leary, S. E., and West, S. (1972). Mother–father–newborn interaction: Effects of maternal medication, labor and sex of infant. *Proceedings of the Annual Convention of the American Psychological Association, 7,* 85–86.

Parke, R. D., O'Neil, R., Isley, S., and Spitzer, S. (1998). Family-peer relationships: Cognitive, emotional, and ecological determinants. In M. Lewis and C. Feiring (Eds.), *Families, risk, and competence* (pp. 89–112). Mahwah, NJ: Lawrence Erlbaum Associates.

Peretti, P. O., and Sydney, T. M. (1984). Parental toy choice stereotyping and its effects on child toy preference and sex-role typing. *Social Behavior and Personality, 12,* 213–216.

Podmore, V. N. (1988). Mothers' interactive behaviours and their childrens' pre-school assessments: Relationships and issues. *New Zealand Journal of Educational Studies, 23,* 165–174.

Pomerantz, E. M., and Ruble, D. N. (1998). The multidimensional nature of control: Implications for the development of sex differences in self-evaluation. In J. Heckhausen and C. S. Dweck (Eds.), *Motivation and self-regulation across the life span* (pp. 159–184). New York: Cambridge University Press.

Pomerleau, A., Bolduc, D., Malcuit, G., and Cossette, L. (1990). Pink or blue: Environmental gender stereotypes in the first two years of life. *Sex Roles, 22,* 359–367.

Power, T. G. (1985). Mother– and father–infant play: A developmental analysis. *Child Development, 56,* 1514–1524.

Reid, P. T. (1985). Sex-role socialization of Black children: A review of theory, family, and media influences. *Academic Psychology Bulletin, 7,* 201–212.

Reid, P. T., and Comas-Diaz, L. (1990). Gender and ethnicity: Perspectives on dual status. *Sex Roles, 22,* 397–408.

Renken, B., Egeland, B., and Marvinney, D., and Mangelsdorf, S. (1989). Early childhood antecedents of aggression and passive-withdrawal in early elementary school. *Journal of Personality, 57,* 257–281.

Rheingold, H. L., and Cook, K. V. (1975). The contents of boys' and girls' rooms as an index of parents' behavior. *Child Development, 46,* 459–463.

Richards, M. H., Gitelson, I. B., Petersen, A. C., and Hurtig, A. L. (1991). Adolescent personality in girls and boys: The role of mothers and fathers. *Psychology of Women Quarterly, 15,* 65–81.

Richman, E. L., and Shaffer, D. R. (2000). "If you let me play sports": How might sport participation influence the self-esteem of adolescent females? *Psychology of Women Quarterly, 24,* 189–199.

Risman, B. J. (2001). Necessity and the invention of mothering. In R. Satow (Ed.), *Gender and social life* (pp. 26–31). Boston: Allyn and Bacon.

Robin, M. (1982). Neonate/mother interaction: Tactile contacts in the days following birth. *Early Child Development and Care, 9,* 221–236.

Robinson, C. C., and Morris, J. T. (1986). The gender-stereotyped nature of Christmas toys received by 36-, 48-, and 60-month-old children: A comparison between nonrequested vs. requested toys. *Sex Roles, 15,* 21–32.

Robinson, J. L., and Biringen, Z. (1995). Gender and emerging autonomy in development. *Psychoanalytic Inquiry, 15,* 60–74.

Robinson, T. N., Killen, J. D., Litt, I. F., and Hammer, L. D. (1996). Ethnicity and body dissatisfaction: Are Hispanic and Asian girls at increased risk for eating disorders? *Journal of Adolescent Health, 19,* 384–393.

Rogoff, B. (1990). *Apprenticeship in thinking: Cognitive development in social context.* New York: Oxford University Press.

Rolls, B. J., Fedoroff, I. C., and Guthrie, J. F. (1991). Gender differences in eating behavior and body weight regulation. *Health Psychology, 10,* 133–142.

Roopnarine, J. L. (1986). Mothers' and fathers' behaviors toward the toy play of their infant sons and daughters. *Sex Roles, 14,* 59–68.

Roopnarine, J. L., and Mounts, N. S. (1985). Mother–child and father–child play. *Early Child Development and Care, 20,* 157–169.

Roopnarine, J. L., Talukder, E., Jain, D., Joshi, P., and Srivstav, P. (1990). Characteristics of holding, patterns of play, and social behaviors between parents and infants in New Delhi, India. *Developmental Psychology*, *26*, 667–673.

Rosen, W. D., Adamson, L. B., and Bakeman, R. (1992). An experimental investigation of infant social referencing: Mothers' messages and gender differences. *Developmental Psychology*, *28*, 1172–1178.

Rozin, P., and Fallon, A. (1988). Body image, attitudes to weight, and misperceptions of ure preferences of the opposite sex: A comparison of men and women in two generations. *Journal of Abnormal Psychology*, *97*, 342–345.

Ruble, D. N., and Martin, C. L. (1998). Gender development. In W. Damon and N. Eisenberg (Eds.), *Handbook of child psychology: Vol. 3. Social, emotional, and personality development* (5th ed., pp. 933–1016). New York: Wiley.

Ryan, R. M., and Lynch, J. H. (1989). Emotional autonomy versus detachment: Revisiting the vicissitudes of adolescence and young adulthood. *Child Development*, *60*, 340–356.

Scarr, S., and McCartney, K. (1983). How people make their own environments: A theory of genotype-environment effects. *Child Development*, *54*, 424–435.

Schneider, B. H., Atkinson, L., and Tardif, C. (2001). Child–parent attachment and children's peer relations: A quantitative review. *Developmental Psychology*, *37*, 86–100.

Schwartz, D. J., Phares, V., Tantleff-Dunn, S., and Thompson, J. K. (1999). Kevin Body image, psychological functioning, and parental feedback regarding physical appearance. *International Journal of Eating Disorders*, *25*, 339–343.

Serbin, L. A., Zelkowitz, P., Doyle, A.-B., and Gold, D. (1990). The socialization of sex-differentiated skills and academic performance: A mediational model. *Sex Roles*, *23*, 613–628.

Siegal, M. (1987). Are sons and daughters treated more differently by fathers than by mothers? *Developmental Review*, *7*, 183–209.

Sigel, I. E. (1982). The relationship between parental distancing strategies and the child's cognitive behavior. In I. E. Sigel and L. M. Laosa (Eds.), *Families as learning environments for children* (pp. 47–86). New York: Plenum.

Sigel, I. E., Stinson, E. T., and Flaugher, J. (1991). Socialization of representational competence in the family. In L. Okagaki and R. J. Sternberg (Eds.), *Directors of development* (pp. 121–141). Hillsdale, NJ: Lawrence Erlbaum Associates.

Signorella, M. L. (1999). Multidimensionality of gender schemas: Implications for the development of gender-related characteristics. In W. B. Swann Jr. and J. H. Langlois, (Eds.), *Sexism and stereotypes in modern society: The gender science of J. T. Spence* (pp. 107–126). Washington, DC: American Psychological Association.

Signorielli, N., and Lears, M. (1992). Children, television, and conceptions about chores: Attitudes and behaviors. *Sex Roles*, *27*, 157–170.

Smolak, L., Levine, M. P., and Schermer, F. (1999). Parental input and weight concerns among elementary school children. *International Journal of Eating Disorders*, *25*, 263–271.

Snow, M. E., Jacklin, C. N., and Maccoby, E. E. (1983). Sex-of-child differences in father–child interaction at one year of age. *Child Development*, *54*, 227–232.

Steinberg, L. (1986). Latchkey children and susceptibility to peer pressure: An ecological analysis. *Developmental Psychology*, *22*, 433–439.

Steinberg, L. (1987a). Recent research on the family at adolescence: The extent and nature of sex differences. *Journal of Youth and Adolescence*, *16*, 191–197.

Steinberg, L. (1987b). Impact of puberty on family relations: Effects of pubertal status and pubertal timing. *Developmental Psychology*, *23*, 451–460.

Stevenson, M. R., and Black, K. N. (1988). Paternal absence and sex-role development: A meta-analysis. *Child Development*, *59*, 793–814.

Suess, G. J., Grossmann, K. E., and Sroufe, L. A. (1992). Effects of infant attachment to mother and father on quality of adaptation in preschool: From dyadic to individual organisation of self. *International Journal of Behavioral Development*, *15*, 43–65.

Tauber, M. A. (1979). Parental socialization techniques and sex differences in children's play. *Child Development*, *50*, 225–234.

Tenenbaum, H. R., and Leaper, C. (1998). Gender effects on Mexican-descent parents, questions and scaffolding during play: A sequential analysis. *First Language*, *18*, 129–147.

Tenenbaum, H. R., and Leaper, C. (2001a, April). *Effects of parents' gender-related schemas on children's cognition and behavior: A meta-analysis.* Paper presented at the meeting of the Society for Research in Child Development, Minneapolis, MN. (Also manuscript under review.)

Tenenbaum, H. R., and Leaper, C. (2001b, April). *Parent–child conversation about science: Socialization of gender inequities.* Paper presented at the meeting of the Society for Research in Child Development, Minneapolis, MN. (Also manuscript under review.)

Thomas, G., Reifman, A., Barnes, G. M., and Farrell, M. P. (2000). Delayed onset of drunkenness as a protective factor for adolescent alcohol misuse and sexual risk taking: A longitudinal study. *Deviant Behavior*, *21*, 181–210.

Thompson, S. H., Corwin, S. J., Rogan, T. J., and Sargent, R. G. (1999). Body size beliefs and weight concerns among mothers and their adolescent children. *Journal of Child and Family Studies*, *8*, 91–108.

Tomasello, M., Conti-Ramsden, G., and Ewert, B. (1990). Young children's conversations with their mothers and fathers: Differences in breakdown and repair. *Journal of Child Language*, *17*, 115–130.

Tronick, E. Z., and Cohn, J. F. (1989). Infant–mother face-to-face interaction: Age and gender differences in coordination and the occurrence of miscoordination. *Child Development, 60,* 85–92.

Tronick, E. Z., and Weinberg, M. K. (2000). Gender differences and their relation to maternal depression. In S. L. Johnson and A. M. Hayes (Eds.), *Stress, coping, and depression* (pp. 23–34). Mahwah, NJ: Lawrence Erlbaum Associates.

Turner, P. J. (1991). Relations between attachment, gender, and behavior with peers in preschool. *Child Development, 62,* 1475–1488.

Turner, P. J. (1993). Attachment to mother and behaviour with adults in preschool. *British Journal of Developmental Psychology, 11,* 75–89.

Updegraff, K. A., McHale, S. M., and Crouter, A. C. (1996). Gender roles in marriage: What do they mean for girls' and boys' school achievement? *Journal of Youth and Adolescence, 25,* 73–88.

Usmiani, S., and Daniluk, J. (1997). Mothers and their adolescent daughters: Relationship between self-esteem, gender role identity, and body image. *Journal of Youth and Adolescence, 26,* 45–62.

Vandell, D. L. (2000). Parents, peer groups, and other socializing influences. *Developmental Psychology, 36,* 699–710.

van den Boom, D. C. (1989). Neonatal irritability and the development of attachment. In G. A. Kohnstamm and J. E. Bates (Eds.), *Temperament in childhood* (pp. 299–318). New York: Wiley.

van IJzendoorn, M. H., Moran, G., Belsky, J., Pederson, D., Bakersmans-Kranenburg, M. J., and Kneppers, K. (2000). The similarity of siblings' attachments to their mother. *Child Development, 71,* 1086–1098.

Weinberg, M. K., Tronick, E. Z., Cohn, J. F., and Olson, K. L. (1999). Gender differences in emotional expressivity and self-regulation during early infancy. *Developmental Psychology, 35,* 175–188.

Weisner, T. S. (1979). Some cross-cultural perspectives on becoming female. In C. B. Kopp (Ed.), *Becoming female: Perspectives on development* (pp. 313–332). New York: Plenum.

Weisner, T. S. (1996). Why ethnography should be the most important method in the study of human development. In R. Jessor, A. Colby, and R. A. Shweder (Eds.), *Ethnography and human development: Context and meaning in social inquiry* (pp. 305–324). Chicago: University of Chicago Press.

Weisner, T. S., Garnier, H., and Loucky, J. (1994). Domestic tasks, gender egalitarian values and children's gender typing in conventional and nonconventional families. *Sex Roles, 30,* 23–54.

Weitzman, N., Birns, B., and Friend, R. (1985). Traditional and nontraditional mothers' communication with their daughters and sons. *Child Development, 56,* 894–898.

Weizman, Z. O., and Snow, C. E. (2001). Lexical output as related to children's vocabulary acquisition: Effects of sophisticated exposure and support for meaning. *Developmental Psychology, 37,* 265–279.

Whitehead, J. R., and Corbin, C. B. (1997). Self-esteem in children and youth: The role of sport and physical education. In K. R. Fox (Ed.), *The physical self: From motivation to well-being* (pp. 175–203). Champaign, IL: Human Kinetics.

Whiting, B. B. (1986). The effect of experience on peer relationships. In E. C. Mueller and C. R. Cooper (Eds.), *Process and outcome in peer relationships* (pp. 79–99). Orlando, FL: Academic.

Whiting, B. B., and Edwards, C. P. (1988). *Children of different worlds: The formation of social behavior.* Cambridge, MA: Harvard University Press.

Wilfley, D. E., Schreiber, G. B., Pike, K. M., and Striegel-Moore, R. H. (1996). Eating disturbance and body image: A comparison of a community sample of adult Black and White women. *International Journal of Eating Disorders, 20,* 377–387.

Zemore, R., and Rinholm, J. (1989). Vulnerability to depression as a function of parental rejection and control. *Canadian Journal of Behavioural Science, 21,* 364–376.

# 8

# Parenting Twins and the Genetics of Parenting

Hugh Lytton
*University of Calgary*
Lin Gallagher

## INTRODUCTION

Litters of offspring among animals must have been a familiar phenomenon to our nomadic and agricultural ancestors; hence multiple births (MBs) among humans cannot have been a surprising or mysterious occurrence. Nevertheless, twins figure as special human beings in myth and literature, and interest in them goes back as far as recorded history. The Bible tells of Jacob and Esau, who presumably were fraternal twins, since they displayed different physical characteristics (Esau being hairy and Jacob smooth). Greek mythology tells of Castor and Pollux, who form the Gemini constellation in the sky. Rome had its mythical twin founders: Romulus and Remus. Twins also figure in much of literature, from a Plautus comedy to Shakespeare to Thornton Wilder's (himself a twin) *The Bridge of San Luis Rey*.

Sometimes twin gods provide benefits (e.g., the Indian twin gods Acvin look after the weak and oppressed), but often twins are regarded as products of evil spirits, especially in Africa. On that continent (and among Native Americans too), one of a twin pair was sometimes killed (particularly the female partner), perhaps out of a fear of incest or the belief that incest had already occurred *in utero*. However, for some African tribes, a twin birth also is the occasion of a special joyous ceremony of welcome. Therefore it appears that there is no universal attitude to twins, either as omens of good or ill (see Scheinfeld, 1973).

Certainly by the late nineteenth century it was known how identical or "one-egg" (monozygotic or MZ) twins and fraternal or "two-egg" (dizygotic or DZ) twins were created, and hence their different genetic relatedness was appreciated. The idea of using twins in genetic analyses probably stems from Sir Francis Galton who, in 1875, wrote about twins as a criterion of the relative powers of nature and nurture. Since the days of Galton and Gesell, McGraw, and Newman near the turn of the twentieth century, innumerable investigations have compared MZ and DZ twins' intrapair correlations for height, weight, physiological and autonomic nervous system measures, and cognitive and socioemotional characteristics to determine the relative importance of environmental and genetic factors in development (see Mittler, 1971). Indeed, twins have been the foot soldiers of nature–nurture battles throughout the twentieth century to the present day.

More recently, the development of twins has been studied in its own right because their relationships to parents and to each other are marked by unique circumstances that make them different from those of singletons. Rearing twins—and *a fortiori* other MB sets—subjects their parents to stresses that singletons' parents are not subject to and tests, as it were, the limits of childrearing skills. Hence a comparison of twins' and singletons' experiences in their interactions with their parents throws light not only on the problems of rearing two children of the same age, but also on the processes involved in parent–child interaction and socialization in general. In the case of MZ twins, moreover, the impact of differential parental treatment in shaping twins' personalities is supposedly discernible and can theoretically be derived from any differences between the twin partners. Psychoanalysts have found twins especially attractive and have used child observation of twins as the canvas on which analytic reconstruction then paints a rich picture in order "... to advance psychoanalytic understanding of individuation, identification, self-image, identity, and psychopathology" (Dibble and Cohen, 1981, p. 45). Burlingham (1952), for instance, wrote a book that presented a detailed psychoanalytic study of the development of three pairs of identical twins.

The occurrence of MZ twinning (due to the splitting of a single ovum) is thought to be a random event, and, indeed, the MZ twinning rate is nearly constant at approximately 3.5 per thousand births all over the world. The occurrence of DZ twinning, on the other hand (due to double ovulation), is more frequent at later maternal ages (peak at approximately 37 years) and is due to greater secretion of pituitary gonadotrophin at those ages (Bulmer, 1970). The DZ twinning rate also varies widely across races; in the earlier part of the twentieth century, it was approximately 8 per thousand births in Eurasians—a level that it has now roughly recaptured—but it was approximately twice as large in Africans and approximately half as large in Mongoloid Asians. The rate is also approximately one and a half times as large for African Americans as for European Americans. The reasons for the differential DZ twinning rates are not known, but the ratios among races do not seem to have varied much in recent times (Bulmer, 1970; Inouye and Imaizumi, 1981).

Before 1970, DZ twinning rates were declining in a number of industrialized countries. It is thought that this was attributable to a changing age distribution of mothers, plus other factors (e.g., social status changes). However, between 1974 and 1990 the rates of MBs in Canada, for example, increased from 912 to 1,058 per 100,000 population. The rate of triplet and higher-order births grew by a remarkable 250%, but the twinning rate also rose. According to recent reports, these trends continued to increase over the late 1990s at an alarming rate. The increases are probably due to the use of ovulation-inducing drugs (fertility drugs), and similar trends have been found in the United States and Great Britain. There is, in fact, a narrow margin between a dose of fertility hormones that leads to a conception and one that produces multiple conceptions; so it is not surprising that 36% of mothers of triplets and 70% of mothers of quadruplets between 1982 and 1985 were reported to have received ovulation-inducing hormones.

In the 1980s, the proportion of twins born to women under the age of 25 years declined, but the proportion of twins born to women over the age of 30 years increased, and the rate of MBs out of all births to mothers over the age of 40 years was 22%. A shift of childbearing to higher ages among women in general and access to assisted conception are thought to have contributed to these increases in rate of MBs among women over 30 years old in the 1980s (Millar, Wadhera, and Nimrod, 1992).

A brief overview of the central issues and topics that will be discussed in detail in later sections is given next: The potential handicap that low-birthweight and preterm children—and twins are generally among them—may suffer from are discussed. Another section deals with the special problems that face parents in rearing two children of the same age. Then the way in which the development of social characteristics, language, and intelligence is affected by the "twoness" of the twin situation is examined. In particular, the evidence for the importance of biological versus environmental (parental childrearing) effects on twins' language and intelligence is assessed, and this question is discussed in the context of the more general question of what influence parents have on their children overall.

When we discuss differences between twins and singletons and between their respective parents, these are taken to apply to both MZ and DZ twins and also to same-sex and opposite-sex twins, unless one twin type (MZ or DZ) is specified.

## BIOLOGICAL HANDICAPS IN TWINS AND THEIR CONSEQUENCES

Twins' fetal development takes place in a more crowded womb, and they are born, on average, 3 weeks earlier than are singletons. Hence their average birthweight (which increased slightly between 1974 and 1990) is ~2,400 g (~5.3 lb versus the average singleton birthweight of ~3,500 g (~7.7 lb). Indeed, obstetric risk is naturally high for twins. They are at greater risk for congenital impairments and abnormalities than singletons are, owing to very premature birth and very low birthweight in a proportion of twins. Such impairments, which could include cerebral palsy and congenital heart defects, have also been linked to stress in the uterus, as multiple pregnancies are at greater risk of complications, such as toxemia, placenta previa, or fetal growth restriction.

Perinatal mortality in twins is approximately 4.5 times higher than in singletons, with prematurity being related to the cause of death in three fourths of the cases. Mortality is also often due to the twin–twin transfusion syndrome that occurs in some MZ twins. In those cases, the twins' fetal circulation systems are connected because they share a single chorion (membrane) in the womb, and one twin may donate blood to the other twin, with the blood donor becoming anemic and malnourished (Simonoff, 1992). In fact, MZ twins overall suffer from greater prenatal handicapping conditions and a higher mortality rate and lower birthweight than DZ twins do (Allen, 1955; Benirschke and Kim, 1973).

Low-birthweight children in later life tend to have more diseases, engage in less activity, and lose a greater number of school days to illness and poorer health status, although social factors may moderate this risk (see below) (Millar et al., 1992). (For attempts at remedying these adverse effects, see Goldberg and DiVitto, in Vol. 1 of this *Handbook*.) However, up to a point, "preterm," as normally defined, is not an adverse factor for twins, as the lowest risk for twins exists when gestation lasts 38 weeks rather than 40 weeks as in singletons (Rutter and Redshaw, 1991). Effects of biological adversities are always mediated by the social environment. This means that effects of low birthweight are particularly pronounced in lower socioeconomic environments, whereas in more privileged social environments low-birthweight children are hardly more at risk than normal-birthweight children are (Kopp, 1983).

An intriguing phenomenon is that the incidence of left-handedness is higher in twins than in singletons. One theory explains this by positing that left-handedness is associated with fetal exposure to elevated levels of testosterone (Geschwind and Behan, 1982), which is highest among same-sex male twins. Indeed, it has been found that the incidence of left-handedness decreases in order: male twins, female twins, male singletons, female singletons, an order somewhat consistent with the testosterone theory (Segal, 1999).

However, whatever their socioeconomic status, parents of MB babies must cope with many physical, mental, economic, and social stressors that can have adverse effects on family life. High demands are made on their time and efforts in looking after the twins—feed, wash, and diaper them—with breast-feeding them both presenting special difficulties; in addition, these parents have to put up with more than the usual interruptions of their nightly sleep. There is also considerable cost involved in caring for twins and transporting them. These difficulties are compounded when older siblings are in the house. All this means greater demands on parents' patience, efforts, time, and understanding (see the subsection on the quality of the environment for twins versus singletons, and the section on the development of language and intelligence).

# PROBLEMS IN REARING TWINS

The twoness of the twin situation creates for parents special problems and challenges in child-rearing.

## Demands on Twins' versus Singletons' Parents

Mothers of twins are generally much more involved with their offspring than mothers of singletons are. A detailed observational investigation of a few sets of families with MBs in Israel (Goshen-Gottstein, 1979) reports that mothers of twins spent 35% of their time on infant-centered activities during a 3-hr home visit versus ~25% for mothers of singletons. Care of the newborn babies was the most time-consuming task. Interestingly, Corter and Stiefel (1983) report that mothers of twins do *not* treat the pair as a unit more often than mothers of a sibship treat their children; in other words, they do not achieve economies of scale.

Lytton (1980) used naturalistic home observations to study the interactions of twins and singletons with their parents in a sample of 46 sets of male twins and 44 male singletons, 2 to 3 years of age. Behavior counts and impressionistic ratings for various kinds of behavior were derived from the observations. Not only are parents under greater time pressure when they have twins, they are also under greater stress. There often are inevitable conflicts between the twins—one twin biting the other as a method of attack or defense was reported by a number of parents of these 2-year-old toddlers, and parents naturally found this situation difficult to deal with—and then there are the twins' and other siblings' competing demands directed to the parents. However, transcending the conflicts, twins also acquire relative cohesion as a pair who often act and play together. Such intimacy may often mean that language becomes less important as a means of communication, and speech evolves into inarticulate grunts or monosyllables, unintelligible to others (the so-called secret language of twins). In general, their self-sufficiency will lead twins to seek less contact with others and hence to relative social isolation from adults. Nevertheless, their cohesion as a unit often fails to translate into a flow of chatter between them (e.g., in Lytton's [1980] study the mean number of utterances by one twin to the other over approximately 4 or 5 hr of observation was only 22).

Fathers are inevitably much more involved in childcare when twins arrive than with singletons. But even in MB families, Goshen-Gottstein (1979) reported that fathers helped only ~10% of the time—sometimes they were not at home during observations—and they spent more time on older children and general household duties than on infants. Siblings were also called on to help for longer hours in homes of twins than in those of singletons. Moreover, energy-saving devices, such as propping up bottles and confining children to cribs or playpens, were more in evidence in households of twins than in those of singletons.

Clearly, parents of twins and MBs experience both personal and financial difficulties (Segal, 1999). Three months after the twins' birth, many mothers in an Australian study reported that they were exhausted (76%), had no time to themselves (79%), and were depressed (30%)—these are much higher percentages than those found with singleton mothers (Hay and O'Brien, 1984). Such greater depression is still present when the children are 5 years old (Segal, 1999). Many American mothers of twins stressed the fatigue associated with caring for two babies simultaneously, especially the difficulties of feeding the two of them. Mothers also underlined the importance of help from fathers and even from grandmothers (Vandell, 1990). Only 16% of Australian parents had another child after they had the twins, although this was partly the result of the twins' tending to be the later children in the family. However, 32% of the sample had only twins, even though there would have been an opportunity to have other children (Hay and O'Brien, 1984). The stresses associated with twinrearing are also illustrated by the fact that there is a higher incidence of child abuse among twins than among singletons (Vandell, 1990).

Nevertheless, parents also recognize that benefits accrue from having twins, e.g., that they provide "instant families" and they enjoy the attention twins arouse (Segal, 1999).

## Quality of Environment for Twins Versus Singletons

Does the quality of the environment differ between households of twins and singletons, and if so, how does this affect the twins' development?

*Zajonc's confluence theory.*   The outstanding theory bearing on twins' cognitive development—almost the only one in this area—is Zajonc's "confluence model." This posits that children's cognitive development is very largely influenced by the intellectual climate in the family of rearing, and this will be a function of the number of children and their spacing. That is, the family's intellectual climate will be diluted the larger the number of children and the smaller the age gap between them, since the intellectual contribution of young children to newborns is bound to be small relative to that of parents or older sibling, something that will exert an adverse influence on the younger children in a sibship and on twins in particular. Zajonc and Mullally (1997) provided some confirmatory data for their theory from data aggregated at the birth-order level, and particularly cited the lower IQs of twins and triplets as examples and corroboration of this effect. However, the theory has not remained uncontested either in general (cf. Rodgers, 2001), or specifically, as it relates to twins, as we shall subsequently see. Many issues of parenting twins focus on the quality of the environment that parents are able to provide for two children of the same age, an issue that is central to this theory.

*Observations of families of twins.*   As several studies (e.g., Bornstein and Ruddy, 1984; Lytton, 1980) have demonstrated, the presence of two children of the same age in the home is likely to alter quite dramatically the climate of the relationships between children and parents; that is, this presence modifies the environmental contingencies to which children are exposed as well as the self-perceptions and family perceptions of the twins themselves.

The more important differences between twin and singleton groups that emerged in Lytton's study are shown in Table 8.1. (The twin and the singleton groups did not differ significantly in levels of mothers' education. Nevertheless, as the Table indicates, controlling for mothers' education has an effect on the twin-singleton difference for some behaviors. The influence of the "twin situation" is clearly quite pervasive, it is particularly noticeable in *parent* behavior, in which it is not swamped by socioeconomic effects. Twins experience fewer verbal interchanges with their parents overall, they receive fewer directions, either by way of commands or of suggestions, they receive fewer verbal justifications and generalizations of rules, and commands or prohibitions are less consistently followed through. Twins, too, meet with less praise and receive fewer overt expressions of affection, although this should not be interpreted as meaning that parents love their twins less than parents of singletons love their children—they simply have less time to show their affection. Mothers of twins, however, also display less appropriate sensitivity in responding to their children's distress or demands, verbally or nonverbally, than do mothers of singletons—very probably, they cannot afford to show the same sensitivity to their children's needs. Parents of twins also are far less verbally responsive to their children's initiations than are parents of singletons.

In general, the greater pressure on twins' parents' time—and, possibly also, the relative cohesion of the twin pair—seems to lead to parents' being less involved with their children, and, although this may indeed have some positive effects, it also means an impoverishment of the children's environment. We will see what effects this has on twins' speech and language skills in the section on language and intelligence.

The decreased quantity of mother–twin interaction compared with mother–singleton interaction is not due to twins' interacting more with each other—they tend to do little of this, as previously noted. Twins are more likely to initiate interactions with their mothers and to respond to mothers' initiations than to each other. Savic (1980) noted that not only the quantity but also the nature of interactions differs in households of twins from that in households of singletons. Thus twins have more choice whether or not to respond to mothers' initiations. Common occurrences, for instance,

TABLE 8.1
Some Important Twin–Singleton Differences at the Age of 2 Years

*Singletons Higher than Twins*

*Child Variables*

| | $p<$ | | $p<$ |
|---|---|---|---|
| Number of actions | .001 | Rate positive actions | .001 |
| Vocabulary IQ (Peabody Picture Vocabulary Test) | .05[a] | Rate negative actions | .001 |
| Compliance ratio | .05[a] | Speech maturity (rating) | .01 |
| Instrumental independence (rating) | .05[a] | Rate child speech | .001 |
| Internalized standards (rating) | .001 | Speech (% of actions) | .001 |

| *Mother Variables* | $p<$ | *Father Variables* | $p<$ |
|---|---|---|---|
| Command–prohibition— (% of actions[b]) | .001 | Command–prohibition (% of actions) | .001 |
| Use of reasoning (%) | .001 | Use of reasoning (%) | .001 |
| Affection (%) | .001 | Affection (%) | .001 |
| Consistency of enforcement (rating) | .01 | Consistency of enforcement (rating) | .01 |
| Suggestion (%) | .001 | Suggestion (%) | .001 |
| Positive action (%) | .001 | Positive action (%) | .01 |
| Love withdrawal (%) | .05 | Rate father–child speech | .001 |
| Rate mother–child speech | .001 | | |

*Twins Higher than Singletons*

| *Child Variables* | $p<$ | *Mother Variables* | $p<$ |
|---|---|---|---|
| Attachment behavior (% of actions) | .01 | Number of actions | .02 |
| Walking (%) | .01 | | |
| Expression of displeasure (%) | .001 | | |

*Note.* Adapted from Lytton (1980). Differences significant at the .05 level in two-tailed $t$ tests are shown.

[a]When the contribution of the mother's education was allowed for as a prior predictor, twinship no longer added significantly to the prediction for this variable in a multiple-regression analysis, indicating no significant twin–singleton difference ($p > .05$).

[b]"% of actions" and "%" denote percentage of the given agent's total actions.

are that mother addresses the pair, but only one twin responds, or that mother starts an interaction with twin A, but twin B takes over the interaction in the middle.

One of the disadvantages of being brought up as a twin is that twins have less prolonged uninterrupted interactions with their mothers than singletons do with theirs. This may arise because parents try to divide their attention equally between the two competing sets of demands or because of interruptions and demands from the other twin. In fact, sustained dyadic interaction and attention to one twin are rare, because the notion of "fair shares" is uppermost in mothers' minds. When mother is with both twins, many instances of shifts of attention between the two twins occur, and sometimes mother attempts to interact with both twins at the same time (e.g., handing a toy to twin A, while talking to twin B, telling him what to do) as mothers frequently do with siblings, too. In fact, mothers and twins rarely interact as triads, but are most likely to do so when they are brought together around a toy (Clark and Dickman, 1984; Lytton, 1980; Rutter and Redshaw, 1991; Savic, 1980; Vandell, 1990).

*Father–mother differences.*  Differences between mothers' and fathers' behavior toward their boys were noted in Lytton's (1980) study, but they were not analyzed separately for twins and singletons. Hence the following applies to both groups. When it comes to seeking nurturance—proximity or attention or help—the child clearly turns to mother on the whole rather than to father;

that is, both twins and singletons communicate their needs and demands, as well as their signals of distress, more to mother than to father, even allowing for father's shorter presence in the home. (Attachment behavior per se—in which twins and singletons differ—is subsequently discussed). When it comes to play, however, the situation is reversed: Father engages in far more play, and particularly rough-and-tumble play, with boys than mother does, even relative to his shorter time in the home (see Parke, in Vol. 3 of this *Handbook*). Part of the reason why play is such a salient activity for father in this study is no doubt the fact that the observations took place near supper time. When father comes home at this time, these mostly homemaker mothers, after a long tiring day with two lively twins, are glad to let him take over "play duty," and he is usually pleased to have this opportunity. Father generally also exhibits more affection and positively toned actions, partly, perhaps, as part of his extensive play with the children.

Mother enters into far more verbal communications of all kinds with the child than father does in families of both twins and singletons. Furthermore, mother plays a far more prominent role than father in attempting to change the child's behavior by commands, suggestions, or providing rationales for her directions. She considers this part of her duty as she goes through the day with the child. She evidently feels more reponsible for the child's behavior and welfare and hence intervenes more in the child's doings–on the child's behalf, as well as to restrain and change the child's behavior. The child reacts to this by sometimes turning a selectively deaf ear to her and complies less with her than with father's requests (Lytton, 1980).

In a questionnaire study of parents of 377 twin pairs, 1 to 6 years old, Cohen, Dibble, and Grawe (1977) found that mothers also tend to be less peremptory and overwhelmingly more child centered than fathers in the sense that they monitor their children's welfare and activities more.

*Effect of arrival of twins on older siblings.* The impact on a sibling, perhaps 1 to 3 years old, is one important aspect of the arrival of twins that parents often have to contend with. A toddler usually feels displaced in his parents' attention and affection by the arrival of a baby, but this effect is exacerbated when twins arrive on the scene, as was noted in several families in Lytton's (1980) study. (It is noteworthy that 64% of older siblings reacted negatively to twins' arrival in an Australian study (Hay and O'Brien, 1984.) Not only do twins, because of their more urgent needs, demand and get far more of the parents' attention than the older child does but by the time they are 2½ years old, they also tend to form a unit who play and act together, excluding the older child in the process, even though verbal interchanges between twins are sparse. In these cases, the older children, perceiving themselves isolated or downgraded by the twins, would develop intense feelings of rivalry. They would become the classical "difficult children," interfering with the interlopers and their play or throwing temper tantrums. It is a hard fact that, when three young children compete for parents' attention and time, it is the older singleton who gets the short end of the stick. Furthermore, it is notable that older brothers harbor more negative feelings toward new twin arrivals than do older sisters (Hay and O'Brien, 1984).

When mothers were more attentive and involved in joint play with elder daughters for approximately a year before the sibling's birth and when their firstborns had a secure rather than insecure attachment to their mothers, the older sibling's interaction with the newborn tended to be especially hostile and unfriendly, and sibling conflict, at slightly older ages, was particularly sharp. The reason may be that children with a history of supportive parent–child relationships experience a severe sense of loss when the parent now directs attention and affection that once was solely theirs to a younger sibling (Dunn and Kendrick, 1982; Volling and Belsky, 1992). These conclusions are based on studies of singletons, but they are likely to apply equally to the arrival of twins.

## Equal versus Differentiated Treatment

The essential question that parents of twins, in particular, ask themselves often quite consciously is this: How can we combine equal and fair distribution of resources with our desire to emphasize individuality and meet individual needs? It is clear from several reports that far more parents claim that they try to treat twins alike than say the opposite. Only rarely is one twin reported as receiving some kind of experience that differs from that accorded the other twin (Loehlin and Nichols, 1976). In self-ratings, too, parents report very high consistency of treatment between twin partners—$rs = .80$ or more. In fact, they do not differentiate their behaviors toward twin partners as much as they differentiate the twins' perceived personalities (Cohen et al., 1977). Such similarity of treatment is attempted in the service of equal and fair distribution of resources (for qualifications see below). Where differences do occur, the correlations between differences in parental treatment and differences in children's abilities, personality, and interests are very small. Overall, differential treatment, measured in a variety of ways, can account for only a tiny fraction of variance in personality; hence, parental treatment differences do not explain twins' behavioral differences (Loehlin and Nichols, 1976).

Behavior–genetic analyses attempt to estimate genetic and environmental components of variance in human characteristics by comparisons between MZ and DZ within-pair correlations or variances (see Plomin, DeFries, and McClearn, 1990). For these analyses to be valid, it has been claimed that the "equal environments assumption" has to be met. The argument goes like this: Suppose parents accorded more similar treatment to a pair of twins simply because of their knowledge that their twins are MZ, and not because the twins present very similar needs and demands, arising out of their genetic identity. Such an attitude, it has been thought, might give rise to spuriously greater similarity in these twins that, in a behavior–genetic analysis, would inflate the genetic component relative to the environmental component emerging from the analysis of a given characteristic (but see the previous paragraph about lack of effects of parental differential treatment).

MZ twins have repeatedly been found to receive more similar treatment in several respects than DZ twins (e.g., Cohen et al., 1977; Loehlin and Nichols, 1976; Rowe, 1981). Lytton (1980) found a similar result, but he also found that (1) parents do not introduce systematically greater similarity of treatment for MZ twins in actions that they initiate themselves and that are not contingent on the child's immediately preceding behavior and (2) when parents hold a mistaken belief about the twins' zygosity (i.e., think actual MZ twins to be DZ twins and vice versa), their treatment of the twins is more in line with the twins' actual than their perceived zygosity. It seems that regardless of parental expectations in regard to degree of behavioral similarity (MZ or DZ), young children with identical genetic endowment are likely to elicit somewhat similar parental behavior. In other words, parents respond to twins' genetic similarity or differences rather than create these (see also Cohen et al., 1977; Scarr and Carter-Saltzman, 1979).

Hence the somewhat greater similarity of treatment of MZ than of DZ twins does not invalidate behavior–genetic analyses. Nor does the existence of undoubted differences in socialization experiences between twins and singletons, in my opinion, invalidate the use of twins in behavior genetics because (1) there is no evidence that twins, as a group, differ systematically from singletons in genetic endowment or the structure of the genome, and (2) technically the differences in environment between twins and singletons are not relevant, as classical behavior–genetic analyses compare only variances of MZ and DZ twins, and no singleton variances enter into the calculations.

The conclusion that parents tend to accommodate their behavior to each twin's individuality—within the context of the goal of fair treatment—has also received support from mothers' interview responses, when they were asked whether they made differences between their 2-year-old twins and why (Lytton, 1980). Many mothers acknowledged that they treated the twins—both MZ and DZ—differently, but always attributed such differential treatment to the differing needs and personalities of the children. Typically, one child would be seen as needing more attention or warmth or as more mischievous, less easygoing, and less docile than the other. In two cases, differences in treatment were directly related to the fact that one twin suffered respiratory distress at birth and had to be kept in an incubator for some weeks, whereas the other one did not. The following extract is from some of the interviewer's notes for a MZ twin pair:

Mother doesn't think of them as twins—J has been behind. Their personalities warrant their being treated differently. The differences that mother makes are those they demand, or events produce. J is ten times worse than D in climbing on cupboards and tables and is usually spanked. Mother often has to spank J for things that D does not have to be spanked for. D is more sensitive—reponds to a look or being sent to his room. Mother spends about half an hour holding and cuddling D, and about 15 minutes with J or as much time as he'll allow.

At the age of 9 years (at follow-up), J still had allowances made for him because of his handicaps, namely a hearing defect and speech difficulties. In the follow-up phase of this investigation (Lytton, Watts, and Dunn, 1984), the problem of developing individuality and meeting individual needs within the context of overall equal and fair treatment elicited comments from a number of parents. In general, parents stressed that the rules were the same for both children and their overall aim was one of fairness, but within the limits of this general principle they made differences in response to the children's differing personalities and needs.

The principle of equality of basic rights, but differing responses to different personalities, was spelled out by this mother of DZ twins:

> Basically I try to treat them all equally in what I'm buying for them, getting for them. They may all get the same thing—different colors or sizes—so there's no fights. . . . I want them to be different, to have their own personalities, their own group of friends. When they started school I made it most definite that I wanted them in separate classrooms, from kindergarten on.

The reasons for making differences was clearly put by this mother of DZ twins:

> If there's differences, it's not because I make them. It's because they make them. . . . So the differences are because of their needs, not because of anything I figure I should change.

Another mother of DZ twins, stressed "They're so unalike that you would never treat them the same . . . ." The husband also said that he tends to baby one twin more, because this twin does not do as well as the other one academically and that he places more demands on the second twin because he responds more to that.

Parents of MZ twins are aware of the temptation to treat them as one and consciously force themselves to treat them as individuals. One mother of MZ twins made the following comments:

> I tend to treat them alike which is a pitfall with twins. It's easier to think of them as your third child. That was one of the problems when they went to Grade 1. Suddenly I had four children, and I always felt I had three. Because suddenly I had two teachers to see, two field trips to go on. . . . It's important to treat them differently, but it's very easy to fall into the habit of saying "the twins" and "they." And they speak that way, too. They say "we don't like him", or "Billy doesn't like us." You want them to enjoy being twins, but you also want them to be individuals. That's the biggest challenge of twins.

Another mother of MZ twins:

> I think we've tried to build up the difference because it's so slight. . . . Many times neighbors have discounted the fact that they are two different people—they call them the same name, etc. So we try to say "You don't have to dress alike, can have different toys, etc.". . . I try to make them stand on their own. They have a hard time doing that . . . If they are in trouble, they are in trouble together, and if they were doing something well, they're doing it together.

The questionnaires sent to parents of twins by Hay and O'Brien (1984) also shed light on the question of equal versus differentiated attitudes to, and treatment of, twin partners. To most questions (e.g., "To which twin do you feel closer?") the vast majority of parents answered "both." However, there were exceptions to which "both" was the answer offered by only a minority of parents, and these questions were "Which twin required more attention?" , "Which twin was easier to manage?", "Which twin was fussier?" , and "Which twin was more active and alert?". These questions clearly refer to aspects that might well be considered part of the twins' temperamental makeup that forced differentiation on parents (Putnam, Sanson, and Rothbart, in Vol. 1 of this *Handbook*).

It is of interest to note that mothers differentiate between children within a pair of DZ twins more than fathers do in areas such as consistency, monitoring, and parental temper and detachment. Mothers also differentiate more between partners in MZ pairs, perhaps because they are more intimately familiar with the individuality of each twin (Cohen et al., 1977).

*Favorites.*   Do parents have favorites among their twin children? Having children of the same age highlights contrasts as well as similarities between them. In an attempt to distinguish between what appear to be very similar personalities, parents may sometimes seek differences and accentuate preferences, rather than emphasize equality of treatment (Rutter and Redshaw, 1991). They may, for instance, emphasize different sets of skills for each twin, as one family did that rewarded and stressed mathematical skills for one twin and verbal skills for the other (Ainslie, 1985, cited in Vandell, 1990).

Indeed, if twins differ in nature, it is natural for mother (or father) to feel closer to one or to the other. In the study of 9-year-old twins, therefore, Lytton et al. (1984) made a subjective judgment as to the favorite status of one twin in cases in which this seemed warranted on the basis of parents' interview responses and impressions of especially close relationships observed during a structured family interaction task. There were no significant differences between the reported treatment of "favorites" versus "nonfavorites" by parents, but then parents would not be likely to admit such differential treatment in self-reports. However, there were some suggestive differences in children's characteristics. The favorite twins slightly exceeded the nonfavorite twins in verbal ability, and the latter had an edge over the former in nonverbal ability (neither difference was significant). It may be that the favorite twin's superiority in verbal communication made for closer ties with mother and that the nonfavorite twin compensated for this by more practical activities. Favorite twins were also rated as more attached to their mothers, and such differences in parent–child bonding and in verbal ability may be due to health factors, as it has been found that mothers attend and vocalize more to the healthier of the twins (Minde, Corter, and Goldberg, 1986—see subsequent discussion; Segal, 1999).

Mothers and fathers may also have separate favorites: Jouanjean-l'Antoene (1997), for instance, noticed preferential interactions between each twin and one parent that determined the nature of what a child learned. When Moilanen and Pennanen (1997) identified preferred twins at adolescence, they found that mothers' favorites had learned to speak earlier and were more often the psychological leader of the pair, whereas fathers' favorites tended to be the physical leaders of the pair.

Favorites in our study (Lytton et al., 1984) were also rated as slightly more compliant and, above all, as exhibiting fewer antisocial problems than their nonfavorite partners did. These differences were all plausible in that they provided explanations *why* one twin was more favored by his mother than the other was. It is naturally easier to love the child who is more compliant or less deviant in behavior. On the other hand, the possibility exists that greater attachment and compliance and fewer behavior problems flowed from the favorite status. We have no means of distinguishing between these hypotheses, but here, as so often, bidirectional influences are likely to be operating.

*Gender-typed rearing.*   This topic is a narrower part of the larger question of equal versus individually tailored treatment. Very little is known about the gender-typed treatment of opposite-sex twins. Where this aspect of parenting has been examined, few significant differences in behavior toward sons versus daughters have been found, strikingly fewer than differences between the behavior of mothers and fathers, for instance in the study by Cohen et al. (1977). Mothers were the more child-centered parent (shown in concern for the child's welfare and in the child's close supervision), but they were more child centered for boys than for girls. A unique observational study of a few families of twins, triplets, and quadruplets was carried out in Israel (Goshen-Gottstein, 1981). What emerged was a picture of a mix of unconscious, or at least nondeliberate, gender-equal treatment and of conscious gender-typed socialization (Leaper, in Vol. 1 of this *Handbook*). The results are somewhat counterintuitive. Mothers permitted more proximity seeking (dependence) in boys, encouraged more helping in girls, reinforced boys' and girls' aggression equally, and placed no emphasis on gender-typed toy play. Conscious gender-differentiating practices were differential hairstyle and clothing (e.g., skullcaps for boys), which came in only the third year of life. In strictly religious families, a very conscious and high degree of gender segregation in religious and school activities occurred (i.e., boys attended an all-male nursery school from the age of $2\frac{1}{2}$ years and had reading lessons in the fourth year of life, whereas girls attended a girls' nursery school from the age of 3 years and took reading lessons from the age of 6 years onward). Apart from this strict segregation in religious activities, the general trend of absence of systematic gender-typed treatment is consistent with the findings of Lytton and Romney (1991), except that these authors found one aspect of significant differential socialization, namely, the encouragement of same-gender-typed toy play.

Overall, we see how having twins poses some special problems that are, however, not insoluble for parents and how it makes parents walk a thin line between fair and equal distribution of resources and treatment tailored to each twin's individual needs.

## DEVELOPMENT OF SOCIAL CHARACTERISTICS

Attachment (usually to the mother), as a developmental function of the child is a concept and topic that, following Bowlby's conceptualization (e.g., Bowlby, 1958), has found wide acceptance among developmental psychologists. It attained especial popularity as an experimental paradigm with the development of a measurement tool, the Strange Situation, by Ainsworth, which provided a usable instrument for categorizing children as showing secure or insecure attachment (the latter being subdivided into avoidant or anxious) (Ainsworth, Blehar, Waters, and Wall, 1978).

### Security of Attachment in Twins

One might expect twins to display a higher incidence of insecure attachment than singletons do because the excessive demands placed on mother's care and attention by twins may lead some mothers to give them less than optimal maternal care. Following the reasoning of, for instance, Klaus and Kennell (1982), it has been suggested by some that a mother can form a successful intimate relationship with only one baby at a time and that mothers of twins may therefore encounter difficulty in meeting the needs of two infants simultaneously. Vandell, Owen, Wilson, and Henderson (1988) and Goldberg and Minde and their associates (Goldberg, Perrotta, Minde, and Corter, 1986; Minde et al., 1986) investigated the question of whether security of attachment in twins differed from that in singletons. The sample of Minde and Goldberg consisted of 26 twin pairs and 25 singleton controls, all of whom had birthweights of less than 1500 g, studied over the first year of life. The outcome was unusually clear: Neither low birthweight nor twinship imperiled security of attachment. The distribution of attachment categories in both the Vandell study of twins and the Minde and Goldberg study of low-birthweight babies did not differ significantly from those in other studies of normal-term babies in North America (approximately 70% secure, 10% avoidant, 20% resistant). Twins were no more likely than singletons were to be insecurely attached, and the processes contributing to attachment security in twins were found to be the same as those in singletons (Goldberg et al., 1986). However, a number of twins were in a "marginally secure" category, and the mothers of these marginally secure infants were rated lower on responsiveness and sensitivity (rated from observations) than all mothers of all other attachment categories. Such behavior would normally be expected to lead to insecure attachment in the infants. Goldberg et al. (1986) make the interesting suggestion

238

Lytton and Gallagher

that it is precisely the presence of a same-age peer that may be a protective factor, contributing to security of attachment, so that it pushes these twins into at least the marginally secure category.

Concordance in the category of attachment security allotted (secure, avoidant, or resistant) seems to be as high in DZ as in MZ twin pairs, a fact consistent with the theory that attachment quality is primarily a matter of maternal/paternal environment and relationships, not a matter of temperament (Vandell, 1990). Plomin and Rowe, in their (1979) behavior–genetic analyses, came to similar conclusions, namely that relationships with—and social behavior toward—mother were mainly shaped by experiences with mother.

In the study by Minde et al. (1986), mothers showed a slight preference for one of the twins, manifested by more positive statements about that twin, and more caregiving and visual and vocal attention to that twin, although the tendency was slight, not overpowering , and one that was hardly ever admitted to by the mother. The preference was demonstrably related to the medical status of the infant ( i.e., to the child's robustness and visual attention and responsiveness to the mother). However, preferences fluctuated over the first year, and a shift in preference occurred particularly when the initially nonpreferred infant was more attentive and sociable later on. The existence of a preference enhanced the probability of secure attachment, not only for the preferred, but, interestingly, also for the nonpreferred infant—it may even be a necessary condition for secure attachment, as all twin pairs in this study whose mothers showed no preference were later insecurely attached. Having a preference, according to Minde et al., may indicate that the mother is sensitive to the individualities of the twins and is committed to their individual needs, whereas apparent egalitarian treatment could be indicative of lesser interest and of lower intensity and rate of interactions (Minde et al., 1986).

Lytton (1980) quantified the *amount* of attachment behavior displayed by 2-year-old toddlers, expressed as a rate per unit of time, rather than classifying infants by categories of attachment security. He found that twins engaged in a greater amount of attachment behavior to their parents than singletons did. This result might be traced to parents' fewer displays of affection, as the twins may feel the need to reassure themselves of their parents' love. However, since it was mainly the nonverbal attachment behaviors of the younger twins (i.e., proximity seeking) that were manifested more often, the result may also be a consequence of twins' greater general immaturity.

At age 2 attachment behavior was indexed by the amount of such behavior toddlers showed to each parent and at the follow-up when the children were 9 years old by asking mothers and fathers to whom the child was more attached. At both 2 and 9 years of age, the majority of children (~60%) displayed more attachment to mother than to father. This was so despite the fact that fathers did a lot of romping and roughhousing with the children. Father, it seems, was the playmate, whereas mother was the comforter in distress overall.

There was one difference between the twins and the singletons at the age of 2 years: Relatively more twins than singletons were "father attached," in that they displayed more attachment behavior to fathers than to mothers. Why did these children buck the general trend? It may be that some of the twins were seeking an available attachment figure as a protective device against the lesser availability of the mother; indeed, in many twin pairs each of the partners appropriated their own attachment object. However, Lytton also found that the father-attached group had mothers who tended to exhibit less desirable qualities (e.g., a high propensity to physical punishment). Dibble and Cohen (1981) also found a frequent tendency for twins to attach themselves to separate parents.

Going by mothers' and fathers' reports on 9-year-old twins' attachment objects, it appears that there was a developmental shift from unilateral attachment to one parent when the twin was 2 years old to greater equality of attachment when the twin was 9 years old. Equal attachment was observed for 19% of the twins at the age of 2 years, but it was reported for an average of 59% when the twin was 9 years old, a change that can well be thought of as being due to the growth of greater independence and maturity. However, it might also be attributable to parents' wish to be "fair" to each other in their reports (Lytton, Watts, and Dunn, 1988).

Overall then, it would appear that the security of attachment relationships is not affected by the fact of twinship: that is, the fact that two children of the same age are being reared together.

## Twin–Twin Relationships

Although twins share the same home and the same parents, each twin has many unique experiences. It is sometimes said that this "nonshared" environment, which encompasses extrafamilial encounters such as in the classroom or with different friends, as well as differential treatment by parents is a more influential factor for the twins' personality development than is the environment that they share. However, as previously noted, Loehlin and Nichols (1976) found essentially no relation between individualized parental practices and twins' personalities.

Interactions between co-twins at the younger ages are not as frequent or intense as one might expect. If one compares the interactions of single-born siblings approximately $1\frac{1}{2}$ and $2\frac{1}{2}$ years old with those of $1\frac{1}{2}$-year-old twins, one finds more interaction in singleton dyads because of the greater social activity by the older sibling. Younger siblings also give to, share with, or imitate older siblings almost 3 times as much as twins do with one another (Corter and Stiefel, 1983).

As Savic (1980) found, an adult's presence can sometimes be the catalyst for bringing about twin–twin interaction. Both twins, for instance, might try to engage mother, and if she was nonresponsive, they would slide into interaction with each other instead; or, in an alternative scenario, one twin would interject himself or herself into an ongoing interaction between mother and the other twin. However, twins do not compensate for an insecure attachment to mother by more interaction with their co-twins: on the contrary, twins who are insecurely attached to mother are less likely to interact with their co-twins than are securely attached twins (Vandell, 1990).

Let us turn to competition between co-twins. In Lytton's observations of 2-year-old twins, competition for mother's attention occurred fairly regularly. Thus, if mother or father held twin A on their knee, twin B would cry "up, up," clamoring for the same privilege; or if one twin showed off his drawing to his mother, or was "cleaning" a chair, the other twin would want to do the same thing.

In one longitudinal study of twins' interactions at ages from 2 to 3 years, 25% of their time was taken up by joint play, such as sharing toys or run–chase games. When there was disharmony, the single most common theme was a struggle about objects. However, by the time they were 5 years old, almost no conflict was observed. The most common pattern was for shared play to occur, but some twins kept a wary distance from each other. In fact, it was those twins who had many conflicts at the age of 2 years who were more likely to ignore the other twin at the age of 5 years, in this way finding a conflict-free solution to their relationship (Wilson, 1987).

In the follow-up, by Lytton et al. (1984) of twins at the age 9 years, a structured family task provided the opportunity of noting competitiveness and cooperation between the twin partners: In only one third of the twin pairs did competitiveness predominate, and with them it tended to be pervasive and to extend into the twins' general interactions. The competitive twins were, for the most part, fraternal twins with obvious physical and behavioral differences and frequently with a marked discrepancy in skills in an area. But among the competitive twins there were also some MZ twins with poor social skills who interacted intensely because they had difficulty making other friends.

Being close to each other and joining in shared activities rather than having outgoing relationships with peers were more salient traits in these twins. Most twins found comfort and support in such a close relationship that held over and above temporary petty squabbles. Indeed, twins often prefer each other's company to being separate, and they worry about each other when they are separated. One of the pervasive fears and dislikes of the twins, as Lytton et al. (1984) found in recruiting twins for their follow-up, was being compared with each other in an evaluative (school) context, presumably because this might lead to feelings of inferiority, rivalry and hostility.

*Common identity versus individuation?* One perennial question is this: Should twins be placed in different classrooms at school to enhance individuality or should they be kept together for mutual support or other reasons? According to Koch (1966), separation of same-sex twins at school occurs approximately one third of the time, but opposite-sex twins are separated approximately half the time. At least in part, the separation or togetherness is the fulfilment of the twins' own wishes, according to some reports by mothers of twins. More male than female twins wish to be separated, but as many same-sex DZ as MZ twins (approximately two thirds of twins) wish to be together. The more vigorous, older, and aggressive twin pairs are more frequently separated, whereas the closer, more conforming, and scholastically able twins tend to be kept together—for obvious reasons. Typically, boys are much more likely to be separated than girls, partly as the outcome of their own wishes and partly because of their more vigorous and sometimes obstreperous natures, as Koch thinks. Schools may often believe this to be in the twins' own, as well as in the class's, interests. Research seems to show that better speech form and more freedom from stuttering are associated with placement of twins in different classes (Koch, 1966), which implies that twins who are closer to each other (e.g., interact more) have more speech and articulation problems than others (Hay and O'Brien, 1984). In any case, it is agreed—as it probably always has been—that the question of same or separate classroom placement for twins is best decided on a case-by-case basis, depending on the twins' individual characteristics and needs (Segal, 1999).

Constant companionship and similar needs and satisfactions for co-twins may result in great closeness and assimilation of behavior and traits, or they may have as their outcome deliberate attempts at "deidentification" (as in a striving for separate identities: Schacter, Gelutz, Shore, and Auler, 1978). MZ twins report, as one might expect, that they are closer; DZ twins say that they are more concerned with their own individual rights and show greater rivalry. Adult twins in general successfully develop separate identities (Vandell, 1990). However, extremes of common identity can sometimes be seen in older adult twins who not only have similar occupations and preferences, but who, at Twin Conferences, delight in showing themselves dressed in identical costume and jewellery.

In young twins closeness may manifest itself by secret language, or "cryptophasia," as it has been called. It may be that closeness relieves twins of the necessity of developing more intelligible means of communication, as understanding between them is facilitated by context, gestures, and common intention.

*Dominance.*   Of the mothers of 2-year-old male twins studied by Lytton (1980), 75% identified one twin as the more dominant, but many also qualified this by mentioning fluctuations in dominance according to situation and over time. Examining potential correlates of dominance in child characteristics, Lytton found no significant correlations with birthweight, vocabulary IQ, degree of compliance or attachment, or maternal practices. The only variable that showed a near-significant relation (at the .10 level) was the child's rate of speech. Confirmation of this finding comes from the fact that several mothers mentioned that the dominant twin talked more.

These findings suggest that the child's fluency is related to competence in dealing with the environment and hence to being perceived as a leader: This relation again highlights the importance of speech. In this sense, it is understandable that, in many twin pairs, one twin becomes the "Secretary for External Affairs," whereas the other one keeps the twin relationship going.

In the follow-up of twins at the age of 9 years, conducted by Lytton and his colleagues, the question of whether there is a leader and a follower among the twin partners was again raised. Only 57% of mothers identified one twin as the more dominant at this age: With greater age and more contact with others outside the family circle, a certain shift toward greater equality between the twins emerged. However, in two thirds of the pairs, the dominance or equality relationship remained unchanged over the 7-year time span, and in only three pairs was there a switch in the identity of the dominant partner. It seems therefore that such relationships between twin partners are fairly enduring (Lytton et al., 1988).

Koch (1966) who studied 90 pairs of twins of varying zygosity, aged 5 to 7 years, also reported dominance–submission relationships in 61% of twin pairs and found the relationship to be rather stable. Dominance in school-age twins, it appears, depends on many factors: intellectual ability , physical prowess, and interpersonal skills. In DZ opposite-sex pairs, it was the girl who predominated mostly, probably because of her advanced verbal and social skills.

## Peer and Adult Relationships

One might think that the pair situation among twins provides practice in interactional skills that might transfer to later peer relationships, but there is no evidence for such a helpful generalization. On the contrary, infant twins spent one third the time that singletons do in peer interaction in comparable playroom situations (Vandell et al., 1988). Also, Kim, Dales, Connor, Walters, and Witherspoon (1969), observing twins and singletons in nursery school, found twins to be less affectionate and less aggressive, as well as more solitary, than singletons at the age of 3 years, but none of these differences remained significant by the age of 5 years. Zazzo (1976) claimed that twins suffer from greater social isolation than singletons do because of the inward-turning nature of the "couple effect." Hay and O'Brien (1984) also found persistent problems in peer relationships for girl twins. Note that these negative findings come mainly from preschool children.

However, there are also some more optimistic reports—generally about older twins—in the literature: According to Koch (1966), twins' close relationships with each other do not interfere with their relationships with other children at school, in which twins are as involved with other children and with adults as singletons are. Often twins' relationships with peers have proved to be excellent, and teachers have reported that twins were less selfish and more friendly and helped teachers more than singletons did (Hay and O'Brien, 1984; Koch, 1966).

In the follow-up by Lytton, Watts, and Dunn (1987) of 9-year-old twins and singletons, none of the teacher ratings of social characteristics (e.g., compliance, independence, teacher dependence, peer relations) showed any difference between twins and singletons that even approached statistical significance nor did the ratings on a maladjustment questionnaire. Twins' peer relationships were rated as being even slightly better than those of singletons, so twins, it seems, are not necessarily less sociable than singletons are, as some authors (e.g., Zazzo, 1976) have claimed.

Which characteristics of twins predict the nature of peer relationships? First, involvement with other children is correlated with intelligence test scores. Second, security of attachment seems to predict good sibling/peer interactions: In the study by Vandell and colleagues, if at least one co-twin had a secure attachment relationship to mother, the pair played more with each other and more with unfamiliar peers than did those for whom only insecure attachments prevailed. Hence the relation between security of attachment and good peer relations seems confirmed. However, dyads composed of securely attached twins (assessed at the age of 12 months) spent more time in peer interaction at as early as 6 months of age. Perhaps both peer interaction and secure attachment are mediated by dispositional characteristics that predate both attachment and peer competence—and may be of biological origin (Vandell et al., 1988)?

## Psychopathology

Within a sample of children, all of whom had been referred to a mental health clinic, DZ, but not MZ, twins were diagnosed with relatively more conduct disorders than internalizing disorders, compared with other clinic-referred children (Simonoff, 1992). Some other studies have also found somewhat higher levels of externalizing problems, particularly attentional problems (e.g., attention deficit hyperactivity disorder [ADHD]), in twin than in singleton children (Gau, Silberg, Erickson, and Hewitt, 1992; Hay and O'Brien, 1987; Levy, Hay, McLaughlin, Wood, and Waldman, 1996). Some of these excess problems could be partly explained by social adversity and large family size. Also, lower reading level and language delay may be associated with ADHD (higher in twins), as these difficulties are associated in singletons (although it is not thought that the former causes the latter). However other studies, which used smaller samples selected from the population at large (Lytton et al., 1987) or larger samples (Levy et al., 1996; Van den Oord, Koot, Boomsma, Verhulst, and Orlebeke, 1995), found no differences in rated maladjustment or in most internalizing and externalizing psychopathology (except attentional problems) between twins and singletons. Hence, overall, twins present hardly any greater problems of psychopathology than do singletons.

To sum up: The relationships of twins to each other involve some special problems: How intensely do they want to achieve a common identity and to what degree do they want to develop a separate individuality? Twins will solve such problems according to their own inclinations. Twins vary in interpersonal skills, and hence in quality of peer relationships, just as singletons do, and, apart from their slight immaturity in the early school years, overall it seems that their twinship itself poses no special threat to their peer interactions.

As regards the incidence of behavior problems, we find that twin–singleton differences in community samples and in referral rates to clinics (twins higher) are much smaller than twin–singleton differences in language, reading, and IQ and hence are likely to be of little practical importance (Rutter and Redshaw, 1991).

## DEVELOPMENT OF LANGUAGE AND INTELLIGENCE IN TWINS

Twins' slight lag in language skills and verbal intelligence compared with that of singletons has always held a special fascination for psychologists because its explanation was in doubt: It could be attributable to twins' biological vulnerabilities or to the fact that they grow up as a pair (the latter explanation would exemplify Zajonc's confluence theory), or of course to a combination of these two factors.

### The Facts

There is consensus in the research literature that twins on average score 5 to 7 points lower on verbal intelligence tests than singletons do (Mittler, 1971; Myrianthopoulos, Nichols, and Broman, 1976; Record, McKeown, and Edwards, 1970). Moreover, among twins, MZ twins lag behind DZ twins on verbal tests (Koch, 1966). Language has also generally been found to be delayed in twins compared with that of singletons (Day, 1932; Hay, Prior, Collett, and Williams, 1987; Mittler, 1971), and, consequently, so has reading skill (Johnston, Prior, and Hay, 1984). Bornstein and Ruddy (1984), investigating a small sample in detail, reported that twins from infancy were lower than singletons on all measures of language development, and so did Tomasello, Mannle, and Kruger (1986). The effects are greater for male twins, in whom the negative consequences of being a twin are exacerbated by the greater vulnerability of males (Hay and O'Brien, 1984). The 2-year-old male twins in Lytton's (1980) study spoke less and their speech was marked by greater immaturity of construction and articulation than that of singletons, matched for age and maternal education (see Table 8.1). They also had lower scores on the Peabody Picture Vocabulary Test (PPVT). In addition, Conway, Lytton, and Pysh (1980) found that the complexity of twins' speech was less than that of matched singletons.

Much is sometimes made of twins' so-called secret language ("autonomous" language or cryptophasia), as if this were a systematically invented secret code. Bakker (1987), examining twins' actual speech, found that at least 90% of twins' vocabulary was traceable to parents' vocabulary. The secret language consisted of phonological distortions and of sounds that were simplified and made easier. Informal observations in Lytton's (1980) study also did not reveal any evidence for the existence of cryptophasia in twins at the age of 2 years, only of the use of immature, badly formed speech, such as Bakker (1987) described. This would sometimes be intelligible to co-twins, whose intentions and notions it expresses and who are in constant contact with each other, and not to the mother, in the same way that some children's unformed speech may be intelligible to mother when it is not to outsiders. As twins spend more time with others—in preschool and school, where they may often receive speech therapy—distortions and grammatical inaccuracies disappear. Hence the notion of a systematically invented secret language is probably a myth.

When the twins in Lytton's sample were compared with a fresh, matched group of singletons during a follow-up at the age of 9 years, the twins had significantly lower *verbal* intelligence test scores than the singletons did (see Table 8.2), even after the effects of maternal education were

TABLE 8.2
Twin–Singleton (9 Years Old) Differences on Cognitive Measures—Singletons Higher

| Measure | $p^a$ |
| --- | --- |
| Verbal intelligence[b] | .05 |
| Nonverbal intelligence[c] | .70 |
| Mathematics achievement[d] | .04 |
| Reading comprehension achievement[d] | .06 |
| Total achievement score[d] | .05[e] |
| Academic competence—teacher rating | .50 |
| Speech maturity—teacher rating | .95 |

*Note.* Adapted from Lytton, Watts, and Dunn (1987).
[a]Two-tailed $t$ tests, $df = 34$.
[b]Crichton Vocabulary Scale—percentiles.
[c]Raven's Colored Progressive Matrices—percentiles.
[d]Peabody Individual Achievement Test—Percentiles.
[e]When mothers' education was covaried, no significant twin–singleton difference remained for this variable.

removed; the same applied to mathematics achievement. However, the inferiority in verbal scores was entirely due to the MZ twins, as the DZ twins' scores were indistinguishable from those of the singletons. In *nonverbal* intelligence, the twins as a whole practically equalled the singletons, nor did they have significantly lower scores in tests of reading comprehension or in teachers' ratings of academic and speech competence (Lytton et al., 1987).

Although there has been repeated confirmation from a number of studies (e.g., Benirschke and Kim, 1973; Lytton et al., 1987; Mittler, 1971; Record et al., 1970) that twins are exposed to greater prenatal and perinatal hazards than singletons are, it should be noted that the 9-year-old twins in the follow-up by Lytton and his colleagues had fully overcome these initial handicaps in their physical development, as their height and weight when they were 9 years old were indistinguishable from those of singletons.

Research is also quite consistent in showing that parents have fewer verbal interchanges with each twin than singleton parents do with their children. Bornstein and Ruddy (1984) reported that mothers of 4-month-old twins encouraged attention to the environment less and that they were less likely to talk to their 12-month-old children than mothers of singletons were. Twins at 12 months of age then showed lower language skills than their singleton controls did, and the authors assume that this was the effect of earlier maternal behavior, as twins were the equals of singletons in maturity and habituation rate at 4 months of age (which generally predicted 12-month vocabulary).

Tomasello et al. (1986) similarly found, from another small sample, that although twin mothers spoke as much overall as did singleton mothers, on average individual twins had less speech specifically directed to them than did singleton children. Twins participated in fewer and shorter episodes of joint attentional focus and had fewer and shorter conversations with their mothers, who also exhibited a more directive style of interaction. These are important indicators because joint attentional episodes and the number of maternal utterances and questions were positively, but the number of directives was negatively, correlated with children's vocabulary in the sample as a whole. The slower language growth of twins, the authors concluded, is associated with the special pragmatic constraints on social and linguistic interactions in triadic situations (the twin situation) that form the postnatal family environment.

## The Effects of Biological and Postnatal Family Environment on Twins' Language

In general, when children are at the toddler stage, if one added parents' speech to both twins together, it would no doubt exceed in quantity the speech addressed to singletons. However, what affects the child is how much speech each twin receives, and a twin experiences fewer verbal interchanges of all kinds with his or her parents than a singleton does. Parents of twins in their socialization practices also, on average, are less psychologically minded and child centered than parents of singletons are. These kinds of socialization experiences might suffice to explain the twins' well-documented language deficit.

However, other possible explanations exist. One is the fact that twins tend to form a cohesive unit. The delay in using "I", for instance, it has been thought, may be due to merged, undifferentiated identities in twins (Zazzo, 1982). On the other hand, as Savic (1980) claims, it may simply be due to the complexity of the language task involved.

An alternative hypothesis would be to attribute twins' verbal deficit to their undoubtedly more adverse prenatal and perinatal experiences (e.g., lower birthweight, more pregnancy complications, and so forth). Conway et al. (1980) examined the contributions of both biological and postnatal environmental factors to the twin–singleton language differences, and found that, when children were 2 years old, biological prenatal factors explained ~8% of variance in the speech measures, but maternal speech measures explained 15% of variance. The simple amount of mother's speech was, in fact, the best predictor of children's speech ability. In other words, when children are 2 years old, the "twoness" of the twin situation seems a more powerful determinant of twins' lag in linguistic competence than are biological prenatal and perinatal difficulties. Such a conclusion is reinforced by the findings of an earlier study of twins who survived the death of their twin partners and were brought up as singletons, which reported that at the age of 11 years these surviving twins had a mean IQ at the singleton level, 5 points higher than that of twin pairs (Record et al., 1970).

These outcomes would also be in line with Breland's (1974) finding from large-scale studies of older children and adolescents that the close spacing of siblings results in more adverse effects on the intellectual development of the younger one than more generous spacing does. Twinship is, of course, the extreme instance of close spacing and shows the same results for both twins. It is findings such as these that inspired—and corroborated—Zajonc's confluence model of intellectual development (see previous discussion and Zajonc and Mullally, 1997).

However, evidence counter to the theory also exists. Lytton et al. (1987) in their follow-up study (see Table 8.2) tried to unravel the effects of biological birth hazards from the environmental effects of the twin situation and the effects of maternal education. Their analysis demonstrated that mothers' educational level and birth difficulties were significant influences on the verbal ability of twins at the age of 9 years, and when these factors *together* were held constant the twin–singleton difference in verbal ability was no longer significant. All these aspects together explained only 18.7% of the variance in verbal ability, but other factors that were not measured in the investigation (e.g., aspects of the home environment not captured by mothers' education or the twin–singleton dichotomy) must be operating too. It should be noted that the MZ performance in verbal ability and achievement remained significantly lower than either that of DZ twins or of singletons in this study. The essential point about these results is that by the age of 9 years the twins' lag in verbal competence can no longer be explained by the twin situation in view of the fact that this lag was confined entirely to MZ twins and was no longer present in DZ twins. Thus these findings disconfirm Zajonc's confluence hypothesis, discussed above, as did the findings of Brackbill and Nichols (1982), which failed to confirm the importance of birth interval in the intellectual status of 7-year-old children. Moreover, neither these authors nor a large-scale study on the twins of the Collaborative Perinatal Project (Myrianthopoulos et al., 1976) found any differences in IQ between single survivor twins, after their partner had died, and other twin pairs. It is not clear how the differences in outcomes between these and other studies that support Zajonc's model arose. (See Zajonc and Mullally, 1997, for a reconciliation; cf. also Rodgers, 2001.)

The change in explanatory factors for twins' lower verbal ability from 2 to 9 years of age in Lytton's investigations does not invalidate the earlier conclusion about the twin situation's being the crucial factor in speech. When children are 9 years old, parents no longer play such a predominant and near-exclusive role in their children's cognitive development because the children at that age will also derive a great deal of stimulation from the wider world of friends and school. The fact of being twins therefore recedes into the background as a determinant of verbal ability, but the effects of mothers' educational level and of possible perinatal handicapping conditions to some extent persist. We should also mention a study that contrasted 8-year-old language-impaired twins with non-language-impaired twins (Bishop, 1997). The researcher found that the groups did not differ in degree of perinatal hazard or birth condition, but the mothers of the language-impaired twins had suffered more from toxemia in pregnancy. If this was confirmed in other studies, the author thought, it pointed to a common genetic basis for immune disorders and developmental language delay.

In the final analysis, therefore, the data of Lytton et al. (1987) seem to indicate that socioeconomic status and education differences are more influential for verbal and cognitive development than the mere fact of being twins.

Although these findings confirm those of other investigations in showing that twins, and particularly MZ twins, still lag somewhat behind singletons in verbal ability and school achievement, the gap between twins and singletons narrows between the ages of 2 and 9 years. The twins also cannot be distinguished from singletons in nonverbal ability or in social development. The lag in verbal skills therefore has to be seen in perspective. From the history of many twins it is evident that most individual twins overcome any initial handicap, with the large majority growing into fully competent adults.

## ON REARING TWINS

What are the implications of multiple births for the quality of life of individuals? Medical professionals are developing a growing awareness of the medical, social, and economic problems caused by multiple births. Given recent developments in infertility treatment that lead to smaller numbers of ova or embryos that are transferred to the uterus, it is possible to achieve both high rates of pregnancy and a triplet rate of only 1%. Monitoring estrogen levels and choosing a carefully adapted fertility treatment method can therefore reduce the incidence of multiple births, and concern over the health implications of such births may, in fact, lead to changes in fertility treatments (Millar et al., 1992).

What are the main problems in rearing twins? It is by no means clear yet what the differences in psychological development, including language and cognitive development, between twins and singletons are due to. However, maybe the fact that parents have to divide their attention and resources between two children of the same age plays at least some part. If this is the case, parents may be able to mitigate some of the adverse effects by ensuring that each twin has a parent's undivided attention for a given time, thus making interaction more exclusive. They may do this by each parent allotting some time to each twin individually or by sharing care and attention with willing supporters, such as grandparents, in their social network.

A great deal having been written about the influence of parental environment on twins' development, the final question is this: What influence do parents have on their children anyhow? Twins who were found to be securely attached at the age of 12 months spent more time in peer interaction already at 6 months of age compared with that of insecurely attached pairs (Vandell et al., 1988; see previous discussions). Perhaps some dispositional characteristics, possibly of biological origin, are responsible for both peer competence and secure attachment. Parents' childrearing practices do not operate in a vacuum. They work in interaction with, and often as a reaction to, the child's predisposition. Lytton (1980), in a microanalysis of home observations, identified such mutual influences in concrete detail; examples are that mother's negative actions (criticism) increased the child's positive ones over time, and the child's positive actions eventually tended to reduce mother's negative ones; in this way, mother and child actions constituted a feedback loop. Ge et al. (1996) also showed how adoptees' antisocial behavior both influenced and was influenced by the parenting practices of the adoptive parents, thus demonstrating feedback loops. Reciprocal, recurrent interactions—called transactions—in which children's and parents' predispositions and mutual relationships are interwoven, occur continuously between parents and children, and they will have a large, cumulative effect on the development of ordinary children.

## A GENETIC PERSPECTIVE ON PARENTING

Sources of influence for different dimensions of socialization may differ. This can be illustrated, for instance, for the dimensions of (1) control and compliance and (2) acceptance, closely related to attachment. Lytton's (1980) observational study of child–parent interaction, for example, found that in the area of control–compliance the influence seemed to run mainly from parent to child, whereas in the area of attachment the influence seemed to run mainly in the opposite direction. Rowe (1981, 1983) confirmed similar relationships in genetic studies of older twins. In these studies, Rowe showed that when adolescent twins reported on their parents' acceptance–rejection the correlation between MZ twins was higher than that between DZ twins. This implied some genetic loading, arising from the *offspring's* genotypes, in parental behavior normally viewed as an environmental influence (i.e., parents' degree of acceptance was partly determined by their children's dispositions). However, such a genetic factor was not found in parents' control behavior.

Perhaps in the areas of attachment and acceptance–rejection the child is the dominant force, because most parents do not set out on a deliberate program to create or direct attachment to them, and acceptance is also largely a matter of the child's disposition and relationship with the parent. On the other hand, most parents do engage in a conscious, purpose-driven program of shaping and controlling the child's behavior—hence it is the parents' dispositions and goals that count more here. Nevertheless, in the case of extremes of externalizing behavior (conduct disorder), the child's predisposition often drives the parent–child interaction. This was suggested, for instance, by Anderson, Lytton, and Romney (1986) who found that mothers of both conduct-disordered (CD) and non-conduct-disordered (NCD) boys reacted more negatively to CD than to NCD boys.

Rowe's studies of twins pioneered a line of research within behavior genetics, which was designed to tease out genetic influences on ostensibly environmental factors impinging on the child, in particular parenting. Adoption studies, as we shall subsequently see, have also been used for this purpose. To anticipate, these studies all demonstrate that what we usually regard as measures of environmental impact, including such mundane activities as telling children the names of objects (Plomin, 1995), are often influenced by the genotypes of the children. In addition, it can also be reasonably assumed that parental practices will be partly determined by the parents own genes, as part of the parents' personalities. Moreover, if genetic factors play a role in some parental, ostensibly environmental, behaviors, then they may also affect the correlations between family influences and the child's development, and indeed several studies have now shown that they do. A review of the earlier studies in this area was written by Plomin (1995).

### Offspring Genetic Effects

Several studies of twins have shown that certain parental behavior, particularly warmth or support, is responsive to genetic variation among the children, whereas, typically, control is less so. This has been done by submitting the parental behavior to genetic analyses by use of the same methods that had been used for child behavior for many years. Not only have the differences between MZ and DZ twins' intrasibling correlations (MZ correlations higher) been employed for this purpose, but several investigations also used model-fitting structural equation methods to separate genetic from environmental components (e.g., Hur and Bouchard, 1995; Plomin, McClearn, Pedersen, Nesselroade, and Bergeman, 1988, who used older twins for their recollections of their own family environments). Furthermore, the Nonshared Environment and Adolescent Development (NEAD) project assembled a large sample (over 700 families), consisting not only of MZ and DZ twins, but also of full siblings in normal families and in stepfamilies, half-siblings, and genetically unrelated siblings. In this research the expected genetic relatedness of the pairs was entered into a model-fitting design to estimate the genetic and environmental contributions to parental behavior. Using questionnaires, Plomin, Reiss, Hetherington, and Howe (1994) demonstrated that positive and negative behavior by both mother and father were significantly genetically influenced, whereas monitoring, a form of control, was much less so. More than one fourth of the variance of parental "environmental" measures could be accounted for by genetic factors. Observation of parent–adolescent interaction in the same sample (O'Connor, Hetherington, Reiss, and Plomin, 1995) yielded very similar results. In addition, both adolescent and parental behavior also showed nongenetic influences, namely strong effects that arise from the nonshared environment (i.e., the unique experiences of each twin).

The Colorado Adoption Project has given rise to studies that compare adoptive with biological families, which, like the twin studies, have also revealed genetic contributions to ostensibly environmental measures. Thus Caldwell's HOME scales, which combine self-ratings by mothers and observations by an interviewer on such matters as mother's stimulation of the child, number of books in the home, and so forth, and Moos' Family Environment Scales (FES), which yield scales such as cohesion or family organization, have been used in both types of families; they have always generated higher correlations between siblings in biological than in adoptive families, suggesting a genetic component, with model-fitting analyses confirming these results (e.g. Braungart, Fulker, and Plomin, 1992; Coon, Fulker, DeFries, and Plomin, 1990). An observational study of play between siblings and of maternal interaction with them has additionally demonstrated genetic influences on observed sibling interactions, as well as on maternal interaction with the siblings. Here, as an exception to most other findings, the genetic contribution was manifest in attention and control, but not in warmth (Rende, Slomkowski, Stocker, Fulker, and Plomin, 1992). This appears to be the only study in which parental positive behavior or warmth lacks a genetic component.

## Associations between Environmental Measures and Children's Characteristics

Genetic influence can also be traced in the associations between environmental measures and children's developmental outcomes (e.g., between the HOME scale and Bayley's Mental Development Index, given to 2-year-old adoptive and biological siblings; Braungart et al., 1992), in which half the phenotypic correlation could be explained genetically and the rest seemed to be mediated by shared environmental factors. Similar relationships hold for the HOME scale and Wechsler's Intelligence Scale for Children, administered to 7-year-old children (Coon et al., 1990). Genetic contributions have also been found for the associations between the HOME scale and the FES, on the one hand, and, on the other, a temperament index, assessed for 1- and 2-year-old toddlers in an adoption study (Plomin, Loehlin, and DeFries, 1985). Such associations are called passive genotype–environment correlations because children are exposed to an environment created for them by parents who share 50% of their genes. Findings such as these appear to reduce the importance of external events, seen as environmental influences, but we should recall that the model-fitting analyses indicated that some of these measures (e.g., the HOME's organization measure) also acted as direct environmental input to children's IQs (Coon et al., 1990).

Children of a given genetic predisposition may evoke certain reactions from their environment (e.g., mentally sharp, curious children may evoke intellectual discussions, stimulation, and information, aggressive children may elicit harsh punishment). When such child characteristics and parents' behaviors are associated with each other, the effects are called evocative genotype–environment correlations. Such effects have emerged in the NEAD twin and sibling study, in which multivariate model-fitting analyses demonstrated a substantial (offspring-based) genetic loading in parents' negative behavior to their children, as well as in the covariance between parental negativity and adolescents' depressive symptoms and antisocial behavior. Nonshared environmental factors were also present, but were more modest in magnitude (Pike, McGuire, Hetherington, Reiss, and Plomin, 1996).

The most convincing case for evocative genotype–environment effects, however, has been made in adoption studies (e.g., Ge et al., 1996). This study observed adoptive parent–adolescent interactions and contrasted adolescents, one of whose biological parents exhibited substance abuse or antisocial personality with those whose parents did not. Their results showed the following characteristics: (1) Psychiatric disorders of biological parents were significantly related to their children's antisocial or hostile behaviors. (2) Biological parents' psychiatric disorders were associated with adoptive parents' parenting behavior. Children of biological parents with several psychiatric disorders received significantly higher levels of harsh or inconsistent discipline and lower levels of warmth and nurturance from adoptive fathers and mothers. (3) The association between biological parents' disorder and adoptive parents' behavior was substantially reduced when the adoptee's antisocial or hostile behavior was controlled—clear evidence of an evocative gene–environment correlation. (4) In addition, there was an independent, environmental influence running from mother's (although not father's) disciplinary practices to child's antisocial behavior.

The research of O'Connor, Deater-Deckard, Fulker, Rutter, and Plomin (1998) also evidenced evocative genotype–environment correlations by very similar methods as those used by Ge et al. (1996). These authors contrasted two groups of 7- to 12-year-old children from the Colorado Adoption Project, based on whether or not mothers had a self-reported history of antisocial behavior, and asked adoptive parents to complete reports on their own parenting practices and on adopted children's externalizing behavior. The genetic effect was not as strong as that in the study by Ge et al. (1996), but this may well have been attenuated by the fact that fathers' possible antisocial tendencies were not counted in the genetic risk (not enough data were available)—an important omission. As in the earlier study there also was an environmental effect in the relation between negative coercive control and children's externalizing behavior; hence the mutual influence model held for both these projects.

## Parent Genetic Effects

All the previously discussed studies showed genetic effects in the elicitation of parenting practices (i.e., certain parenting behaviors were at least partly elicited by specific genetic characteristics of the offspring). However, it would seem reasonable to assume that the provision of parenting would also be partly influenced by genetic characteristics of the parents. This hypothesis has indeed been confirmed by several recent investigations that used adult twin pairs who reported on the parenting practices that they themselves used in the rearing of their children. Perusse, Neale, Heath, and Eaves (1994) and Kendler (1996) asked several hundred adult twin pairs from the Virginia Twin Registry by a questionnaire about the parenting they provided for their children. In both studies genetic effects were apparent mainly for care or warmth, whereas protectiveness and authoritarianism were shaped more by the common environment that the twins experienced in their families of origin.

Another study (Losoya, Callor, Rowe, and Goldsmith, 1997) included adoptive and other biologically unrelated siblings, together with twin pairs, in their sample of parents who reported on parenting behavior toward their young children. They, too, found modest genetic effects on positive support (i.e., warmth), but also on control. Childrearing behavior was also related to most of the "Big Five" personality factors (e.g., positive support was positively related to all five personality dimensions). Here parental control showed genetic effects, based on *parental* genes, but when Rowe (1981, 1983) and others failed to find genetic effects in parental control they examined it from the perspective of *offspring* genetic similarity. These findings are expected from the general theory of disciplinary control, as discussed at the beginning of this section.

## CONCLUSIONS

The preceding discussion has concentrated on the relatively recent findings of the 1980s and 1990s that show that parenting practices contain some genetic components that can derive either from offspring or from parental genes. However, this does not negate the recognition that parenting is also partly an independent environmental force acting on children—who will react in their own particular ways. This has been demonstrated particularly clearly in the studies of Ge et al. (1996) and O'Connor et al. (1998). A convincing case for the importance of parenting, and, of course, reciprocal parent–child effects, has also been made by Collins, Maccoby, Steinberg, Hetherington, and Bornstein (2000).

For the creation of the ordinary characteristics of the ordinary child, parents' socializing efforts may well be the predominant influence overall. Thus less dictatorial techniques by parents may elicit more cooperation from the child, and parents can often by appropriate procedures and attitudes promote such things as more voluntary compliance with house rules, good "manners," or consideration for others. However, parents are influenced by the child's nature and accommodate their actions to the child's individuality and needs (e.g., by reacting to MZ twins more similarly than to DZ twins). They may also adapt their influence techniques to the degree of the child's person orientation or temperament (Bell, 1977; Kochanska, 1991) or encourage play with certain (gender-typed) toys when that is the child's preference (Lytton and Romney, 1991; Snow, Jacklin, and Maccoby, 1983).

Moreover, there are limits to parental influence. Severe psychopathology is not likely to arise from poor childrearing practices alone. Serious disorders, be they schizophrenia or conduct disorder, generally fit the "vulnerability–stress" model—a predisposition to a disorder is inherited, and this liability is then turned into reality by stressors in family life (e.g., poor parental discipline techniques) or rendered less likely by buffering factors (e.g., maternal affection) (Goldstein, 1988). In the case of pathological conditions, children's own predispositions may even be the stronger force that parental influence can sway only so much (see Lytton, 1990). However, twins' as well as other children's later personalities, in general, are best explained as outcomes of reciprocal and recurrent interactions over time between the organism and the environment.

## POSTSCRIPT: THE TWINS' FIRST YEAR

*By Lin Gallagher*

As the proud mother of four children, I have earned the privilege of being realistic regarding the finer points of parenting. Strangers often stop me and exclaim "Oh twins, you are so lucky!" Depending on the day, or rather the night, I may offer the stranger their pick for a week or respond lovingly in agreement.

The first few months since the birth of the twins have been a challenge. The beginning of any baby's life is sleepless and busy, but this is multiplied times two with twins. For the last six months the longest stretch of sleep I had at one time is three hours and this is rare. Even my husband is called into the act. I breast-fed for the first several months, which allowed him the opportunity to sleep through individual crying, but when a harmonious duet occurred we were both awakened. He at least could do pacifier duty until I was ready for number two.

Time has mellowed things around here. Both babies have begun smiling, playing with their older brothers, and even sleeping in longer stretches (occasionally). But I have resigned myself to the fact that my life right now revolves around my children's needs. In our house, there always seems to be too little time and energy and too much chaos and demands.

But like anything in life there is the good and the bad. Fortunately with twins there is a lot more of the good. I particularly enjoy watching them play together. They are a study in motion with eight little hands and feet whirling in the air. To them it really doesn't matter whose fingers or whose toes end up in whose mouth. Each will as contentedly suck on the other's fingers as their own. As they get older their interest in the other's antics increases and the beginnings of a very close relationship is unfolding before us.

Although I have raised two other children, parenting twins has brought a new set of issues. I used to worry about giving equal amounts of attention to each of the babies. But as they grow I realize I can relax and just try and meet the demands of each individual. Although Colin will sit and play by himself happily and is less demanding throughout the day, he makes sure he gets his time in other ways. He very often will awaken earlier in the morning for extra cuddles or will smile and gyrate so invitingly when you walk by you can't help but pick him up.

The twins also seem continuously to change who is the more contented and easier to care for. Right after birth, Kelsey was almost two pounds heavier than Colin, and seemed to be more relaxed and easier to settle. After a few months, Colin became the more contented baby. He enjoyed his own company, while Kelsey seemed to need constant reassurance that Mom was around. This is changing again, as Colin is demanding more and more stimulation and Kelsey is becoming very interested in developing her fine motor skills. Kelsey can now spend long stretches carefully examining a toy, her toes, or whatever is handy.

One thing reassuring about parenting twins is how different they are in personalities, needs, and responses. Colin is constantly in motion. His arms and legs are always going and his eyes open wide, sponging up any action around. He is quick to smile with a twinkle in his eye to attract the attention of any passers-by. He is a baby who is ready and willing to experience new situations.

Kelsey is the opposite, preferring quieter surroundings. She is cautious with new faces and surroundings, preferring the comfort of Mom's arms. Although she is less active she seems to spend more time taking in her surroundings. It is this difference that makes me realize that perhaps babies have a more important role to play in how they respond to the world around them than we give them credit for.

One thing for sure is the role they play in my response to them. My family may have doubled but so have the smiling, laughing faces to love. And on most days I think that my luck has doubled times two.

## Creating or Responding to Gender Differences at 8 Months of Age?

Our babies are starting to master many new feats, and we are amazed by the difference in their abilities and interests. Colin continues to be constantly on the go. He has started to crawl at $7\frac{1}{2}$ months, he is curious about everything around him, and when you play peekaboo he just cannot wait for you to pull off the blanket. Kelsey is the opposite. She has no interest in crawling yet and is content to sit and watch the action. When you play peek with her she waits patiently and greets you with a big smile as the blanket comes off.

Kelsey is the first girl in the family, and it is hard not to compare the twins with respect to gender. For the most part both the babies are encouraged in the same play and games. But we do treat Kelsey a little differently from Colin. She responds much more to gentle play or cradling in our laps. Although Colin enjoys being held and cuddled he is much happier crawling around. Colin really likes action; the louder the toy bangs the happier he is. When we play with Colin there is a lot more tickling and wrestling.

Kelsey also has a much higher level of separation anxiety than Colin. She will scream in outrage when Mom leaves the room. Around strangers Colin will become anxious if Mom strays too far, but isn't too bothered at home.

Being the only daughter in a family of four children does give Kelsey special status. For her first Christmas I felt compelled to give her a doll. We have decided that we will provide her with the opportunity to play with "girl" toys such as dolls and tea sets. But we plan to follow her lead whether she enjoys Barbies or Tonka trucks.

As a tomboy myself, I have no urge to push Kelsey into any particular play. Most childhood pursuits are very unisex like tricycle riding, modelling clay, etc. But there is no problem if Colin ends up playing dolls with Kelsey or Kelsey plays cars with Colin. Because of their interest in each other I suspect there will be a lot of compromise on both their parts. I think what is most important to me is that Kelsey and Colin direct their own interests. The twins reinforce for me how children differ right from birth, and I feel as their parent the need to be sensitive to what makes each child special.

## REFERENCES

Ainslie, R. C. (1985). The psychology of twinship. Lincoln: University of Nebraska Press.

Ainsworth, M. D. S., Blehar, M. C., Waters, E., and Wall, S. (1978). *Patterns of attachment: A psychological study of the strange situation*. Hillsdale, NJ: Lawrence Erlbaum Associates.

Anderson, K. E., Lytton, H., and Romney, D. M. (1986). Mothers' interactions with normal and conduct-disordered boys: Who affects whom? *Developmental Psychology, 22*, 604–609.

Allen, G. (1955). Comments on the analysis of twin samples. *Acta Geneticae Medicae et Gemellologiae, 4*, 143–159.

Bakker, P. (1987). Autonomous language in twins. *Acta Geneticae Medicae et Gemellologiae, 36*, 233–238.

Bell, R. Q. (1977). Socialization findings re-examined. In R. Q. Bell and R. V. Harper (Eds.), *Child effects on adults* (pp. 53–84). Hillsdale, NJ: Lawrence Erlbaum Associates.

Benirschke, K., and Kim, C. (1973). Multiple pregnancy (Part 1). *New England Journal of Medicine, 288*, 1278–1284.

Bishop, D. V. M. (1997). Pre- and perinatal hazards and family background in children with specific language impairments: A study of twins. *Brain and Language, 56*, 1–26.

Bornstein, M., and Ruddy, M. G. (1984). Infant attention and maternal stimulation: Prediction of cognitive and linguistic development in singletons and twins. In H. Bouma and D. G. Bouwhuis (Eds.), *Attention and performance X: Control of language processes* (pp. 433–445). Hillsdale, NJ: Lawrence Erlbaum Associates.

Bowlby, J. (1958). The nature of the child's tie to his mother. *International Journal of Psychoanalysis, 39*, 350–373.

Brackbill, Y., and Nichols, P. L. (1982). A test of the confluence model of intellectual development. *Developmental Psychology, 18*, 192–198.

Braungart, J. M., Fulker, D. W., and Plomin, R. (1992). Genetic mediation of the home environment during infancy: A sibling adoption study of the HOME. *Developmental Psychology, 28*, 1048–1055.

Breland, H. M. (1974). Birth order, family configuration and verbal achievement. *Child Development, 45*, 1011–1019.

Bulmer, M. G. (1970). *The biology of twinning in man*. London: Oxford University Press.

Burlingham, D. (1952). *Twins: A study of three pairs of identical twins*. London: Imago.

Clark, P. M., and Dickman, Z. (1984). Features of interaction in infant twins. *Acta Geneticae Medicae et Gemellologiae, 33*, 165–171.

Cohen, D. J., Dibble, E. D., and Grawe, J. M. (1977). Parental style. *Archives General Psychiatry, 34*, 445–451.

Collins, W. A., Maccoby, E. E., Steinberg, L., Hetherington, E. M., and Bornstein, M. H. (2000). Contemporary research on parenting: The case for nature *and* nurture. *American Psychologist, 55*, 218–232.

Conway, D., Lytton, H., and Pysh, F. (1980). Twin–singleton language differences. *Canadian Journal of Behavioural Sciences, 12*, 264–271.

Coon, H., Fulker, D. W., DeFries, J. C., and Plomin, R. (1990). Home environment and cognitive ability of 7-year-old children in the Colorado Adoption Project: Genetic and environmental etiologies. *Developmental Psychology, 26*, 459–468.

Corter, C., and Stiefel, J. (1983, April). *Sibling interaction and maternal behaviour with young premature twins*. Paper presented at the biennial meeting of the Society for Research in Child Development, Detroit, Mich.

Day, E. (1932). The development of language in twins. *Child Development, 3*, 179–199.

Dibble, E. D., and Cohen, D. J. (1981). Personality development in identical twins: The first decade of life. *Psychoanalytic Study of the Child, 36*, 45–70.

Dunn, J., and Kendrick, C. (1982). *Siblings: Love, envy and understanding*. Cambridge, MA: Harvard University Press.

Gau, J. S., Silberg, J. L., Erickson, M. T., and Hewitt, J. K. (1992). Childhood behavior problems: A comparison of twin and non-twin samples. *Acta Geneticae Medicae et Gemellologiae, 41*, 53–63.

Ge, X., Conger, R. D., Cadoret, R. J., Neiderhiser, J. M., Yates, W., Troughton, E., and Stewart, M. A. (1996). The developmental interface between nature and nurture: A mutual influence model of child antisocial behavior and parent behaviors. *Developmental Psychology, 32*, 574–589.

Geschwind, N., and Behan, P. (1982). Left-handedness: Association with immune disease, migraine, and developmental learning disorder. *Proceedings of the National Academy of Sciences U.S.A., 79*, 5097–5100.

Goldberg, S., Perrotta, M., Minde, K., and Corter, C. (1986). Maternal behavior and attachment in low-birthweight twins and singletons. *Child Development 57*, 34–46.

Goldstein, M. (1988). The family and psychopathology. *Annual Review of Psychology, 39*, 283–299.

Goshen-Gottstein, E. R. (1979). Families of twins: A longitudinal study in coping. *Twins: Newsletter of the International Society for Twin Studies*, Nos. 4–5, p. 2.

Goshen-Gottstein, E. R. (1981). Differential maternal socialization of opposite-sexed twins, triplets, and quadruplets. *Child Development, 52*, 1255–1264.

Hay, D. A., and O'Brien, P. J. (1984). The role of parental attitudes in the development of temperament in twins at home, school and in test situations. *Acta Geneticae Medicae et Gemellologiae, 33,* 191–204.

Hay, D. A., and O'Brien, P. J. (1987). Early influences on the school adjustment of twins. *Acta Geneticae Medicae et Gemellologiae, 36,* 239–248.

Hay, D. A., Prior, M., Collett, S., and Williams, M. (1987). Speech and language development in preschool twins. *Acta Geneticae Medicae et Gemellologiae, 36,* 213–222.

Hur, Y. M., and Bouchard, T. J., Jr. (1995). Genetic influences on perceptions of childhood family environment: A reared-apart twin study. *Child Development, 66,* 330–345.

Inouye, E., and Imaizumi, Y. (1981). Analysis of twinning rates in Japan. In L. Gedda, P. Parisi, and W. E. Nance (Eds.), *Twin research 3, Part A* (pp. 21–33) New York: Liss.

Johnston, C., Prior, M., and Hay, D. A. (1984). Prediction of reading disability in twin boys. *Developmental Medicine and Child Neurology, 26,* 588–595.

Jouanjean-l'Antoene, A. (1997). Reciprocal interactions and the development of communication and language between parents and children. In C. T. Snowdon and M. Hausberger (Eds.), *Social influences on vocal development* (pp. 312–327). Cambridge, England: Cambridge University Press.

Kendler, K. S. (1996). Parenting: A genetic–epidemiologic perspective. *American Journal of Psychiatry, 153,* 11–20.

Kim, C. C., Dales, R. J., Connor, R., Walters, J., and Witherspoon, R. (1969). Social interaction of like-sex twins and singletons in relation to intelligence, language, and physical development. *Journal of Genetic Psychology, 114,* 203–214.

Klaus, M., and Kennell, J. (1982). *Parent–infant bonding.* St. Louis, MO: Mosby.

Koch, H. (1966). *Twins and twin relations.* Chicago: University of Chicago Press.

Kochanska, G. (1991). Socialization and temperament in the development of guilt and conscience. *Child Development, 62,* 1379–1392.

Kopp, C. B. (1983). Risk factors in development. In M. M. Haith and J. J. Campos (Vol. Eds.), *Handbook of Child Psychology: Vol. II. Infancy and developmental psychobiology* (pp. 1081–1188). New York: Wiley.

Levy, F., Hay, D., McLauglin, M., Wood, C., and Waldman, I. (1996). Twin-sibling differences in parental reports of ADHD, speech, reading and behaviour problems. *Journal of Child Psychology and Psychiatry, 37,* 569–578.

Loehlin, J. C., and Nichols, R. C. (1976). *Heredity, environment, and personality.* Austin, TX: University of Texas Press.

Losoya, S. H., Callor, S., Rowe, D. C., and Goldsmith, H. H. (1997). Origins of familial similarity in parenting: A study of twins and adoptive siblings. *Developmental Psychology, 33,* 1012–1023.

Lytton, H. (1980). *Parent child interaction: The socialization process observed in twin and singleton families.* New York: Plenum.

Lytton, H. (1990). Child and parent effects in boys' conduct disorder: A reinterpretation. *Developmental Psychology, 26,* 683–697.

Lytton, H., and Romney, D. M. (1991). Parents' differential socialization of boys and girls: A meta-analysis. *Psychological Bulletin, 109,* 267–296.

Lytton, H., Watts, D., and Dunn, B. E. (1984). *Cognitive and social development from 2 to 9: A twin longitudinal study.* Unpublished Manuscript, University of Calgary, Alberta, Canada.

Lytton, H., Watts, D., and Dunn, B. E. (1987). Twin-singleton differences in verbal ability: Where do they stem from? *Intelligence, 11,* 359–369.

Lytton, H., Watts, D., and Dunn, B. E. (1988). Continuity and change in child characteristics and maternal practices between ages 2 and 9: An analysis of interview responses. *Child Study Journal, 18,* 1–15.

Millar, W. J., Wadhera, S., and Nimrod, C. (1992). Multiple births: Trends and pattern in Canada, 1974–1990. *Health Reports 1992, 4, No. 3,* Statistics Canada.

Minde, K., Corter, C., and Goldberg, S. (1986). The contribution of twinship and health to early interaction and attachment between premature infants and their mothers. In J. D. Call (Ed.), *Frontiers of infant psychiatry* (Vol. 2, pp. 160–175). New York: Basic Books.

Mittler, P. (1971). *The study of twins.* London: Penguin Books.

Moilanen, I., and Pennanen, P. (1997). "Mother's child" and "father's child" among twins: A longitudinal twin study from pregnancy to 21 years of age, with special reference to development and psychiatric disorders. *Acta Medicae et Gemellologiae, 46,* 219–230.

Myrianthopoulos, N. C., Nichols, P. L., and Broman, S. H. (1976). Intellectual development of twins—Comparison with singletons. *Acta Geneticae Medicae et Gemellologiae, 25,* 376–380.

O'Connor, T. G., Hetherington, E. M., Reiss, D., and Plomin, R. (1995). A twin-sibling study of observed parent–adolescent interactions. *Child Development, 66,* 812–829.

O'Connor, T. G., Deater-Deckard, K., Fulker, D., Rutter, M., and Plomin, R. (1998). Genotype–environment correlations in late childhood and early adolescence: Antisocial behavioral problems and coercive parenting. *Developmental Psychology, 34,* 970–981.

Perusse, D., Neale, M. C., Heath, A. C., and Eaves, L. J. (1994). Human parental behavior: Evidence for genetic influence and potential implication for gene-culture transmission. *Behavior Genetics, 24,* 327–335.

Pike, A., McGuire, S., Hetherington, E. M., Reiss, D., and Plomin, R. (1996). Family environment and adolescent depressive symptoms and antisocial behavior: A multivariate genetic analysis. *Developmental Psychology, 32*, 590–603.

Plomin, R. (1995). Genetics and children's experiences in the family. *Journal of Child Psychology and Psychiatry, 36*, 33–68.

Plomin, R., DeFries, J. C., and McClearn, G. E. (1990). *Behavioral Genetics: A primer* (2nd ed.). New York: Freeman.

Plomin, R., Loehlin, J. C., and DeFries, J. C. (1985). Genetic and environmental components of "environmental" influences. *Developmental Psychology, 21*, 391–402.

Plomin, R., McClearn, G. E., Pedersen, N. L., Nesselroade, J. R., and Bergeman, C. S. (1988). Genetic influence on childhood family environment perceived retrospectively from the last half of the life span. *Developmental Psychology, 24*, 738–745.

Plomin, R., Reiss, D., Hetherington, E. M., and Howe, G. W. (1994). Nature and nurture: Genetic contributions to measures of the family environment. *Developmental Psychology, 30*, 32–43.

Plomin, R., and Rowe, D. C. (1979). Genetic and environmental etiology of social behavior in infancy. *Developmental Psychology, 15*, 62–72.

Record, R. G., McKeown, T., and Edwards, J. H. (1970). An investigation of the difference in measured intelligence between twins and single-births. *Annals of Human Genetics, 34*, 11–20.

Rende, R. D., Slomkowski, C. L., Stocker, C., Fulker, D. W., and Plomin, R. (1992). Genetic and environmental influences on maternal and sibling interaction in middle chilhood: A sibling adoption study. *Developmental Psychology, 28*, 484–490.

Rodgers, J. L. (2001). What causes birth order—intelligence patterns? The admixture hypothesis, revised. *American Psychologist, 56*, 505–510.

Rowe, D. C. (1981). Environmental and genetic influence on dimensions of perceived parenting: A twin study. *Developmental Psychology, 17*, 203–208.

Rowe, D. C. (1983). A biometrical analysis of perceptions of family environments: A study of twin and singleton sibling kinships. *Child Development, 54*, 416–423.

Rutter, M., and Redshaw, J. (1991). Growing up as a twin: Twin–singleton differences in psychological development. *Journal of Child Psychology and Psychiatry, 32*, 885–895.

Savic, S. (1980). *How twins learn to talk.* New York: Academic.

Scarr, S., and Carter-Saltzman, L. (1979). Twin method: Defense of a critical assumption. *Behavior Genetics, 9*, 527–542.

Schacter, F. F., Gelutz, G., Shore, E., and Auler, M. (1978). Sibling deidentification judged by mothers. *Child Development, 49*, 543–546.

Scheinfeld, A. (1973). *Twins and supertwins.* London: Pelican Books.

Segal, N. L. (1999). *Entwined lives: Twins and what they tell us about human behavior.* New York: Dutton.

Simonoff, E. (1992). Comparison of twins and singletons with child psychiatric disorders: An item sheet study. *Journal of Child Psychology and Psychiatry, 33*, 1319–1332.

Snow, M. E., Jacklin, C. N., and Maccoby, E. E. (1983). Sex-of-child differences in father–child interaction at one year of age. *Child Development, 54*, 227–232.

Tomasello, M., Mannle, S., and Kruger, A. C. (1986). Linguistic environment of 1- to 2-year-old twins. *Developmental Psychology, 22*, 169–176.

Van den Oord, E. J. C. G., Koot, H. M., Boomsma, D. I., Verhulst, F. C., and Orlebeke, J. F. (1995). A twin–singleton comparison of problem behaviour in 2–3 year-olds. *Journal of Child Psychology and Psychiatry, 36*, 449–458.

Vandell, D. L. (1990). Development in twins. *Annals of Child Development, 7*, 145–174.

Vandell, D. L., Owen, M. T., Wilson, K. S., and Henderson, V. K. (1988). Social development in infant twins: Peer and mother-child relationships. *Child Development, 59*, 168–177.

Volling, B. L., and Belsky, J. (1992). The contribution of mother–child and father–child relationships to the quality of sibling interaction: A longitudinal study. *Child Development, 63*, 1209–1222.

Wilson, K. S. (1987). *Social interaction in twins: Relations between the second and fifth years of life.* Unpublished doctoral dissertation, University of Texas, Dallas.

Zajonc, R. B., and Mullally, P. R. (1997). Birth order: Reconciling conflicting effects. *American Psychologist, 52*, 685–699.

Zazzo, R. (1976). The twin condition and the couple effect on personality development. *Acta Geneticae Medicae et Gemellologiae, 25*, 343–352.

Zazzo, R. (1982). The person: Objective approaches. In W. Hartup (Ed.), *Review of Child Development Research* (Vol. 6, pp. 247–290). Chicago: University of Chicago Press.

# 9

# Child Temperament and Parenting

Samuel P. Putnam
*University of Oregon*
Ann V. Sanson
*University of Melbourne*
Mary K. Rothbart
*University of Oregon*

## INTRODUCTION

Parents often do not become believers in temperament until after the birth of their second child. Before this time, their child's behavior may be seen as a simple result of their upbringing, "a tribute to" or "the fault of" the parents. With the second child, management strategies that worked well with the first child may no longer be effective. Problems experienced with the first child (in feeding, sleeping, coping with strangers) may not exist with the second, but new problems may arise. Such experiences suggest strongly that "nature" as well as "nurture" influence child development, that children differ from each other from early in life, and that these differences have important implications for parent–child interaction. A number of these individual differences fall under the rubric of child temperament, which we define as individual differences in emotional, motor, and attentional reactivity to stimulation, and in patterns of behavioral and attentional self-regulation.

The modern understanding that children make important contributions to their social interactions has two major roots. The first is temperament research initiated by Thomas, Chess, and colleagues in their pioneering New York Longitudinal Study (NYLS; Thomas, Chess, Birch, Hertzig, and Korn, 1963). The second is Bell's (1968) reconceptualization of socialization as a mutually interactive process, with both child and caregiver seeking to redirect, reduce, or augment the behavior of the other. These insights led to the recognition that children differ in such qualities as responsiveness to parental socialization strategies, capacity to control their emotional reactivity, and capacity to bring pleasure or distress to their parents. As Rothbart (1989a, p. 195) put it, "the infant's temperament regulates and is regulated by the actions of others from the earliest hours."

In this chapter, we explore some of the important influences of parenting and temperament on child development. We begin by briefly describing ancient views of individual differences and the NYLS research study by Thomas and Chess begun in the 1950s. In the second section, we briefly review major dimensions of temperament, their stability over childhood, and issues regarding the measurement of temperament in relation to parenting. We then review empirical evidence for relations between temperament and parenting, discussing the role of intervening variables and focusing on combinations of temperament and parenting in the prediction of outcomes. Finally, we discuss future directions for research and implications of temperament theory and research for parenting.

## THE NATURE OF TEMPERAMENT

### Historical Background

Views of temperament as linked to the physiology of the individual are not new. Ancient Chinese philosophies referred to balances among forces of energy, and early Greco-Roman physicians regarded levels of bodily humors as determinants of individual differences in behavior (Diamond, 1974). Although versions of Greco-Roman ideas persisted to the twentieth century in adult temperament concepts (Eysenck and Eysenck, 1985), early research on individual differences in children was dominated by social learning and psychoanalytic approaches. These traditions largely neglected ideas of temperament, focusing instead on the powerful impact of experience. It was not until the 1960s that concepts of temperament began to gain a strong foothold in developmental theory and research.

In some of the earliest research on temperament in childhood, Thomas and Chess (Thomas et al., 1963) took a clinically oriented approach that was strongly related to parenting issues. These researchers reacted against a tradition that saw parents as responsible for their children's problems. Chess and Thomas noted instances of child psychopathology that occurred with healthy and committed parenting and other cases in which children showed a consistently adaptive developmental course despite severe parental disturbance, family disorganization, and social stress (Chess and Thomas, 1989). A major starting point for Thomas and Chess was the idea that the child's temperament must be considered in any discussion of appropriate parenting. In particular, the NYLS concept of *goodness-of-fit* between characteristics of the child and requirements of the child's environment has been influential in guiding later research, including research on parenting–temperament interactions.

### Identifying Basic Dimensions of Temperament

In the early work of the NYLS, Thomas, Chess, and their colleagues analyzed the content of interviews with 22 parents about their infants' reactions to everyday situations (Thomas et al., 1963). This analysis produced a set of nine temperament categories: Activity Level, Rhythmicity, Approach versus Withdrawal, Adaptability, Intensity, Threshold, Mood, Distractibility, and Attention Span/Persistence. They also identified behavioral patterns of "difficult" and "easy" infants.

"*Difficultness*" describes one cluster identified in the NYLS, including negative mood, withdrawal, low adaptability, high intensity, and low rhythmicity (Thomas et al., 1963). The opposite pole to this cluster was described as "*easy*." The "difficult child" construct has had a strong influence on the field, and many studies of temperament and parenting have used measures of child difficultness. In subsequent research in the area, however, measures of dimensions making up this construct have failed to cluster together (Bates, 1989). This has led some researchers to develop their own idiosyncratic difficultness measures, creating problems in understanding and consolidating findings using the construct.

The difficultness construct has also been criticized in the literature for other reasons (Plomin, 1982; Rothbart, 1982). It adds a value-laden connotation to temperament and ignores the fact that any temperament characteristic (e.g., high or low approach, high or low attentional focusing) may be "difficult" or "easy," depending on the age of the child and the requirements of the situation. To label a child as difficult also has the danger of becoming a self-fulfilling prophecy; identification as the "difficult child" may both intensify and maintain the child's expression of these characteristics. Despite our reservations about the usefulness of the construct, many research studies reviewed in this chapter refer to difficultness. When the term does not specifically refer to the cluster of traits identified by Thomas and Chess, we indicate how "difficulty" has been operationalized.

The nine more specific NYLS dimensions have also been widely used in research on childhood temperament. However, concern has arisen about the extent to which scales measuring these dimensions show conceptual overlap with one another or are not internally consistent. Because of these problems, factor analyses of questionnaire items have been carried out on parent-report scales of infant temperament derived from the NYLS categories (Bohlin, Hagekull, and Lindhagen, 1981; Sanson, Prior, Garino, Oberklaid, and Sewell, 1987). A review of results from these analyses, along with analyses of scales derived from other theoretical frameworks, suggests that infant temperamental variability can be accounted for by fewer than nine dimensions (Rothbart and Mauro, 1990). This shorter list of temperament dimensions in infancy includes Fear, Irritability/Anger, Positive Affect (including approach), Activity Level, and Attentional Persistence. A sixth dimension of Rhythmicity has also been reliably extracted, but it tends to account for only a relatively small portion of the variance. Factor analyses of questionnaire items based on the NYLS for older children have revealed similar factors (Prior, Sanson, and Oberklaid, 1989; Sanson, Smart, Prior, Oberklaid, and Pedlow, 1994).

Some consensus about a more limited set of factors to describe childhood temperament is also emerging. Using the Children's Behavior Questionnaire, a parent-report measure of temperament for 3- to 8-year-old children (Ahadi, Rothbart, and Ye, 1993; Rothbart, Ahadi, Hershey, and Fisher, 2000), researchers have consistently found three broad factors. The first, Surgency, is defined primarily by the scales of Approach, High-Intensity Pleasure, and Activity Level, with a negative contribution from Shyness. The second, Negative Affectivity, is defined by the scales of Discomfort, Fear, Anger/Frustration, Sadness, and, loading negatively, Soothability. The third factor, Effortful Control, is defined by the scales of Inhibitory Control, Attentional Focusing, Low-Intensity Pleasure, and Perceptual Sensitivity.

Analysis of temperament questionnaires developed for use with infants, toddlers, and adolescents has revealed both similarities and differences in structure across these age groups (Putnam, Ellis, and Rothbart, in press). Surgency and Negative Affectivity factors were extracted at all ages. In toddlers and adolescents, but not infants, an Effortful Control factor was also obtained. In infants, a factor referred to as Affiliation/Orienting emerged, defined by Duration of Orienting, Cuddliness, Low-Intensity Pleasure, and Soothability scales. A separate Affiliation factor, defined by the scales of Affiliation, Perceptual Sensitivity, and Low-Intensity Pleasure, was also extracted from adolescent data.

The similarity of factors from the Children's Behavior Questionnaire to those arising from item-based analyses of the Childhood Temperament Questionnaire among children in the longitudinal Australian Temperament Project (ATP) is striking. The three major factors emerging from the ATP analysis are labeled Inflexibility, reflecting negative reactivity and lack of adaptability, similar to Negative Affectivity; Approach, encompassing many facets of Surgency; and Persistence, including items concerning attentional control. The fourth ATP factor is Rhythmicity (Sanson, Prior, Oberklaid, and Smart, 1998). McClowry's School Age Temperament Inventory similarly shows a stable factor structure among children aged 8 to 11 years (McClowry, 1995).

The three most common temperament factors additionally show strong similarities with three of the "Big Five" factors that have emerged from analyses of personality in adults (e.g., Goldberg, 1990; McCrae and Costa, 1987). Results of a recent investigation to conceptually and empirically map temperament dimensions onto Big Five personality factors suggest that the Negative Affectivity factor maps on the adult dimension of Neuroticism or Negative Emotionality, Surgency is related to Extraversion, and Effortful Control is related to Control/Constraint. In addition, temperamental Orienting is related to the Big Five Openness factor (Rothbart, Ahadi, and Evans, 2000). Similar findings have recently emerged from the ATP: Across children aged 11 to 12 and 13 to 14 years, Extraversion was predicted by Approach and Activity; Conscientiousness by Persistence; Agreeableness by Reactivity; Neuroticism by Reactivity; and Intellect/Openness (weakly) by Approach and Reactivity (Sanson, 2000).

## Stability of Temperament

It generally has been assumed that, to be meaningful or important, temperament must show substantial stability across time. Typically, however, only modest to moderate stability across age has been found, with correlations ranging from .20 to .40 (see Rothbart, 1989b; Slabach, Morrow, and Wachs, 1991). How might we interpret these levels of stability? It should be noted that even genetic underpinnings do not imply immutability over time (Hinde, 1989) and that some temperamental characteristics show considerable development (Rothbart, 1989b). In addition, later-developing capacities of fear or effortful control may serve to modulate other temperamental reactions (Rothbart and Bates, 1998; Rothbart and Derryberry, in press). Finally, conceptual and methodological problems may lead to lower stability. When these issues are corrected, higher levels of stability are found.

Given major changes in a child's behavioral repertoire, it is necessary to establish continuity in the temperament constructs studied across time (Pedlow, Sanson, Prior, and Oberklaid, 1993). Early work did not attend to this issue with rigor. Apparent instability may therefore have been due to discontinuity in the underlying constructs. Another possible source of instability is likely to be error of measurement, also rarely taken into account. A study by Pedlow et al. (1993) on the ATP sample of children from infancy to 8 years of age used structural equation modeling to estimate stability of factors that applied either across the whole age range (Approach/Sociability, Rhythmicity) or across three or more time intervals (Irritability, Persistence, Cooperation–Manageability, and Inflexibility). The model, which corrects for attenuation of correlations that is due to error of measurement, yielded estimates that were considerably higher than those previously reported, mostly in the range of .70 to .80. Even with these levels of stability, however, there is considerable room for individuals to change in their relative characteristics. When children in the ATP were placed in four categories from lowest to highest on the basis of their temperament scores at each age, few remained in the same category over all years from infancy to 8 years (Sanson, Prior, and Oberklaid, 1991). On the other hand, very few changed from one extreme category to the other.

# RESEARCH ON TEMPERAMENT AND PARENTING

## Conceptual and Methodological Issues

The expectation that child temperament and parenting would be associated, with temperament influencing parenting, parenting influencing temperament, or both, has been addressed by a number of studies in the field. Nevertheless, it has proved difficult to predict on theoretical grounds what the nature of the associations should be and to obtain fully persuasive empirical evidence of such links. Methodological issues are one important basis for this difficulty.

A frequent critique of research relating parenting to child behavior is that apparent effects of parenting on the child may be related to the genetic similarity of parent and child (Scarr, 1992). This observation is particularly salient with regard to temperament, which is assumed to have a genetic basis. Studies reporting direct associations between temperament and parenting are therefore ambiguous, since they may reflect underlying biological factors that influence the behavior of both parents and children.

Compounding this problem, parent report is the most frequent source of data on infant temperament. If parent report is also used to assess parenting, there is clear potential for nonindependence of measures, because characteristics of the parent may affect their reports of both their parenting practices and their child's temperament. Because the child's temperament is likely to be affected by prior parenting, any association between concurrent parenting and child temperament may also be the result of childrearing history. The correlational nature of the majority of such work further clouds interpretation. Clearly, temperament is not open to experimental manipulation, and few studies (e.g., van den Boom, 1994, 1995) have attempted to manipulate parental factors in investigations of parent–temperament relations. Finally, the generalizability of this research is restricted by the lack of research on fathering. Virtually all of the work reviewed in this chapter has investigated only parenting by mothers. The generalizability of findings to fathers or to other primary caregivers awaits further research.

Given these caveats, it is not surprising that relatively few studies of parenting and temperament allow unambiguous interpretation of results. Some general relations between parenting and temperament have been expected; for example, that the more adaptable, easy-to-soothe, or sociable child would elicit warm and responsive parenting, whereas the more irritable, demanding, or withdrawing child would elicit parental irritation and withdrawal of contact or stimulation. Conversely, warm and responsive parenting may decrease the expression of negative emotionality in the child, and distant or inconsistent parenting may increase it. There is some evidence in support of these expectations. Most of the relevant studies have focused on distress-related temperament attributes (e.g., irritability, "difficultness," negative mood), which tend to covary with poor parenting and general unresponsiveness (e.g., Hemphill and Sanson, 2000; Hinde, 1989; Linn and Horowitz, 1983). Others have noted associations between the child's positive affect and self-regulation and parental responsiveness, social interaction, and use of rewards (e.g., Hinde, 1989; Kyrios and Prior, 1990).

It is also possible to argue for another association between parenting and child temperament. If we assume most parents to be highly invested in their children, we might expect parents with more irritable or difficult children to exert more positive efforts with them than with less irritable children, and empirical support has been found for this position. Crockenberg (1986) cited seven studies that found greater parent involvement with greater infant irritability. For example, Fish and Crockenberg (1986) found that amount of crying and time to calm infants at 1 and 3 months of age were associated with more caregiving and social interaction with the mothers at 9 months of age, and Caron and Miller (1981) found that African mothers were more responsive to highly irritable babies. It should also be noted that temperamental "difficulty" may be adaptive in some contexts: When famine struck a Masai community in southern Kenya, the infants most likely to survive were those considered difficult, presumably because of the high levels of attention they demanded from their caregivers (deVries, 1984).

More recent studies have found both "positive" and "negative" parenting correlates of difficult temperament. Rubin, Hastings, Chen, Stewart, and McNichol (1998) found higher levels of both maternal warmth and negative dominance to be associated with male toddlers' dysregulated temperament. Similarly, Gauvain and Fagot (1995) found that difficult 2-year-old toddlers received more cognitive assistance and more disapproval from their mothers during a joint problem-solving task than did temperamentally easy children. Thus difficult temperament may be related to widely divergent parenting behaviors.

## Intervening Variables

Although several studies have found direct associations between parenting and temperament, there are also several published accounts of no association between temperament and parenting (Daniels, Plomin, and Greenhalgh, 1984; Rothbart, 1986; Vaughn, Taraldson, Crichton, and Egeland, 1981; Wachs and Gandour, 1983) and, given the difficulty in getting such null results published, these may be an underestimate. Null findings and evidence for mixed effects in the relation between temperament and parenting lead to the conjecture that third factors may also be involved. It is notable that, whereas the majority of the null findings have been obtained from large-sample studies, most studies that have found associations (both positive and negative) used relatively small samples. The latter findings may be spurious, or it may be that, in large samples, the influence of competing third variables "cancels out" effects found with smaller and more homogeneous samples.

Intervening third variables can operate in one of two ways: as moderators or mediators (Baron and Kenny, 1986). When functioning as a moderator, a third variable alters the strength and/or direction of the relation between two variables. For example, in the subsection on a child's gender, we review evidence suggesting that gender moderates the relation between difficult temperament and father involvement, with difficulty associated with low levels of father involvement with girls, but with higher levels of father involvement with boys. Mediators are third variables seen as mechanisms connecting independent variables to dependent variables. An example discussed in the subsection on parental characteristics considers self-efficacy as a mediator of the relation between infant difficulty and low maternal competence. In this model, difficult infants contribute to lower levels of self-efficacy in mothers; in turn, compromised self-efficacy leads some mothers to become less sensitive to the needs of their infants. In the subsequent review, we consider several third variables, both moderators and mediators, in relation to temperament and parenting.

*The child's age.* Crockenberg (1986) has suggested that age moderates associations between parenting and child temperament. For example, parents may begin by investing greater amounts of time and energy in their distress-prone child, but may not be able to sustain this effort over time. Consistent with this notion are the findings of Peters-Martin and Wachs (1984): When infants were 6 months old, infant withdrawal, as assessed by mothers' report, was related to more maternal emotional and verbal responsiveness and to less restriction and punishment. By the time the infants were 12 months old, intensity (another aspect of negative affect) was related to less maternal involvement and more restriction and punishment. Similarly, in an observational study by Maccoby, Snow, and Jacklin (1984), mothers of boys who were difficult (fussy, intense, hard to soothe) at 12 months of age showed a reduction in their teaching efforts in a joint teaching–learning task when the boys were 18 months of age. Among easygoing boys, mothers' teaching efforts increased over this time. Greater teaching effort when the boys were 12 months of age also predicted a decline in boys' difficultness, suggesting bidirectional effects.

Bates and colleagues (Bates, Olson, Pettit, and Bayles, 1982; Lee and Bates, 1985; Pettit and Bates, 1984) also found a reversal of relations over time. At both 6 and 13 months of age, babies with high ratings on a fussy–difficult measure derived from maternal report and direct observation received more affectionate contact and object stimulation from their mothers. At 24 months of age, however, more difficult children resisted their mothers' efforts at control and received more negative control from their mothers. Although this result may partially reflect changes in underlying definitions of "difficult," these findings suggest that some mothers respond to their harder-to-parent infants with greater efforts, but cannot—or do not—maintain this over time.

*The child's gender.* A meta-analysis by Lytton and Romney (1991) found little difference in parenting of girls and boys overall, but the authors did not consider potential gender-by-temperament interactions. The role of child gender as a moderator of associations between temperament and parenting has, in fact, been documented. Gordon (1983) observed 2- to 4-year-old children interacting with their mothers and found that mothers gave more commands to difficult than to easy girls and fewer commands to difficult than to easy boys. Klein (1984) found that girls and boys who showed intense reactions to stimulation differed in the types of maternal contact they received; highly intense girls received high levels of distal vocal stimulation and intense boys more physical contact. Rubin et al. (1998) found children's temperamental emotion dysregulation to be unrelated to maternal warmth toward girls, but positively correlated with maternal warmth toward boys. Two studies of fathers' parenting also reported gender differences: Lamb, Frodi, Hwang, Forstromm, and Corry (1982) found fathers to be less involved with difficult (high negative affect, low positive affect, low soothability) daughters and easy sons, and Rendina and Dickerscheid (1976) found fathers to be less involved in social activities with difficult girls and more with difficult boys.

The majority of the research has found less parental acceptance of irritability and negative affect in girls than in boys. There have, however, been findings contrary to this pattern. Crockenberg (1986) found mothers to be more responsive to the crying of irritable girls than that of boys. Maccoby et al. (1984) observed greater amounts of teaching effort by mothers to difficult (resistant, hard-to-soothe) than easy girls and less to difficult than to easy boys. Suggesting that the kind of negative affect expressed by the child may be important, Simpson and Stevenson-Hinde (1985) documented better relationships with mothers for shy (socially fearful) than for nonshy girls, but the opposite for boys.

Differential beliefs about the acceptability and the desirability of temperamental attributes for girls and boys might help explain these patterns of parent responses, with more parental acceptance of shyness in girls and of irritability in boys. To the degree that patterns of parenting–temperament relations differ according to children's gender, failing to differentiate between girls and boys is likely to have resulted in some of the inconsistencies in parenting and temperament findings.

*Parental characteristics.* In addition to child attributes, relations between parenting and temperament may be influenced by parents' psychological characteristics. Escalona (1968) noted that more anxious mothers tended to lose confidence when their soothing techniques failed to work with their infants, whereas the confidence of other mothers was relatively unaffected. She suggested that a sense of maternal incompetence might have far-reaching consequences for mother and child. This hypothesis was supported by Teti and Gelfand (1991), who concluded that maternal self–efficacy mediated a link between "fussy–difficult" ratings for infants and their mothers' lower competence (sensitivity, warmth, engagement) (see also Teti and Condeleria, in Vol. 4 of this *Handbook*).

Maternal depression also appears to be implicated in the relation between infant temperament and self-efficacy. Gowen, Johnson-Martin, Goldman, and Appelbaum (1989) found that infant irritability predicted both depression and a sense of parenting incompetence, and Cutrona and Troutman (1986) found infant difficultness (measured with a composite of maternal ratings, cry diaries, and duration of crying observed in the home) to be strongly related to postpartum depression, both directly and mediated through maternal feelings of self-efficacy. Because depressed and nondepressed mothers vary in their parenting (Cummings and Davies, 1994; Goodman and Gotlib, 1999; Zahn-Waxler, Duggal, and Gruber, in Vol. 4 of this *Handbook*), temperamental difficultness may have an indirect impact on parenting.

Mothers' personality characteristics have also been examined as predictors of parenting style. Clark, Kochanska, and Ready (2000) cite several studies showing links between mothers' high levels of negative affectivity–neuroticism and a number of parenting variables, including low responsivity and sensitivity, and high power assertion. In addition to finding the expected link between maternal neuroticism and high power assertion in parenting, Clark et al. (2000) found that child temperament was unrelated to the use of power-assertive techniques among mothers low in extraversion or high in perspective taking (empathy). However, negative temperament was associated with a higher use of power assertion among mothers high in extraversion or low in perspective taking. Whereas neuroticism appears to place mothers "at risk" for the use of power-based parenting techniques regardless of child characteristics, other personality traits may be most predictive of parenting when considered in conjunction with child temperament.

*Social and cultural factors.* In studies of socioeconomic status (SES), Bates et al. (1982) and Bates, Maslin, and Frankel (1985) found no consistent SES interactions with temperament in parent–child relationships. However, Prior, Sanson, Carroll, and Oberklaid (1989) found almost twice as many significant correlations between temperament factors and parenting dimensions in a high-SES group than in a low-SES group in the ATP. The authors interpreted this result as evidence of possible greater sensitivity to the individuality of their children among high-SES mothers.

A second environmental variable of interest in parenting (although one that may be influenced by characteristics of the parent) is low social support, which may have a particularly strong effect on the parenting of irritable children: Crockenberg and McCluskey (1985) found that when mothers had low social support and their babies were more irritable as neonates, the mothers showed less sensitivity to their babies at 12 months of age. In addition to relieving the burden placed on a mother by an irritable child, social support may benefit the child by providing additional sources of caregiving and affection.

Numerous studies have found mean differences on temperament scales among children in different cultures (e.g., Ahadi et al., 1993; Kohnstamm, 1989; Kyrios, Prior, Oberklaid, and Demetriou, 1989), and accounts of cultural differences in parenting practices are frequently reported (Kagitcibasi, 1996; Whiting and Whiting, 1973). Thus research on temperament, parenting, and culture may prove to be an important direction for the future. One possibility for this research involves taking advantage of our knowledge about basic temperamental dimensions to investigate variations across cultures in the value assigned to the same temperamental characteristic. This approach is similar to research on differential values placed on temperament characteristics of girls and boys.

Chen and his colleagues have followed this direction in their study of cultural variation in parental attitudes and practices regarding children's behavioral inhibition in Canada and China (e.g., Chen et al., 1998). They noted that behavioral inhibition (anxiety and inhibition to novelty, reserve) is generally devalued among North Americans, whereas it is valued in Chinese culture. They observed, consistent with this difference, higher levels of behavioral inhibition in Chinese than in Canadian 2-year-old children. In addition, relations among behavioral inhibition and parent attitudes and behaviors differed between the two samples. In the Canadian sample, mothers of highly inhibited children were less accepting and encouraging of achievement and scored higher on measures of punishment orientation and protection and concern than did mothers of less inhibited toddlers. In the Chinese sample, however, high levels of inhibition were associated with high maternal acceptance and encouragement of achievement and independence and with lower rejection and punishment orientation.

These differences are congruent with the idea that cultural values influence parenting. Chinese toddlers who did not display the reticence that is highly valued in their society were more likely to be rejected and punished by their mothers. Conversely, although Canadian mothers were highly protective of their inhibited children, their lower levels of acceptance were in keeping with the less favorable views of shyness held in Western culture.

Another study suggests the involvement of effortful control in the socialization of temperament. Ahadi et al. (1993) found a negative association between Effortful Control and Extraversion/Surgency factors in Chinese 6- to 7-year-old children, but no relation between them in an American sample. In the United States, however, Effortful Control was negatively associated with Negative Affectivity, with no relation in the Chinese sample. These findings require replication, but it would be very interesting if children's effortful or attentional control might be used to promote characteristics that are most valued in a culture and/or to minimize characteristics considered worthy of change.

As previously noted, the search for simple direct associations between parenting and temperament is somewhat unsatisfactory in comparison with more contemporary, process-oriented approaches. In the next subsection, we review recent work that addresses cumulative and interactive effects between temperament and parenting.

## Parent and Child Factors in the Development of Attachment

Debate continues regarding the relation of temperament to attachment. Although it has been argued that parents' sensitivity to infant behavior is the crucial antecedent to security of attachment (e.g., Sroufe, 1985), there is substantial empirical support for the notion that the child's temperament is related to how the child reacts during separation and reunion with the parent in the Strange Situation procedure, influencing the child's attachment classification as securely or insecurely attached (see Goldsmith and Alansky, 1987). Some researchers have failed to find direct relations between temperament and attachment security (e.g., Bates et al., 1985; Sroufe, 1985). However, Calkins and Fox (1992) observed that this null result most frequently occurs in studies in which parent reports of temperament, rather than observational measures, are used.

Several temperament attributes in infancy have been found to relate to later attachment security, including sociability to strangers and mother ratings as "easy" (Frodi, 1983), proneness to distress (Belsky and Rovine, 1987), neonatal distress reactivity (Calkins and Fox, 1992), and "object orientation" versus "person orientation" (Lewis and Feiring, 1989). Temperament characteristics of fear

(Thompson, Connell, and Bridges, 1988) and difficultness (Weber, Levitt, and Clarke, 1986) have also been found to relate to the infant's negative reactions in the Strange Situation.

An example of the dynamic relation among temperament, mother–child interaction, and attachment is found in a series of studies conducted by van den Boom (1989, 1994, 1995); van den Boom (1989) used a neonatal behavior scale to select an extremely irritable group of infants representing the top 17% of the low-SES sample tested and a group of nonirritable infants drawn from the remaining 83% of the sample. She observed the selected infants with their mothers twice a month until the infants were 6 months old, measuring mother sensitivity (looking, affective, stimulating, and soothing behaviors) and infant behavior (positive and negative social signals). A rating scale of maternal sensitivity including general attitude, availability, and physical and social contact was also used. Both mothers and observers completed temperament scales when the infants were 6 and 12 months old, and attachment security was assessed when the infants were 12 months old.

Mother and child behaviors differed in relation to newborn temperament. Irritable neonates expressed less positive, and more negative, affect with their mothers during the first months, but by the time the infans were 6 months old, the two groups were highly similar in their emotional expression. The experience of caring for an irritable infant, however, appeared to have a lasting effect on maternal behavior. Irritability was associated with maternal perceptions of the infant as difficult at the ages of 6 and 12 months, and this difficultness was associated with less maternal involvement with increasing age, with these mothers being particularly unresponsive to the positive signals of their infants. Maternal sensitivity was not related to attachment status when the infants were 12 months old, but temperamentally irritable newborns were more likely to be later rated as insecure, with predominant classification in the avoidant category.

Perhaps the most persuasive part of van den Boom's study is its intervention component (van den Boom, 1994, 1995). Here, 50 low-SES mothers of 6-month-old infants assessed as irritable during the early days of life received specific training in soothing and playing with their babies and were compared with a matched, untreated control group of irritable infants and their mothers. When the infants were 9 months old, intervention group mothers were more responsive, visually attentive, and stimulating. Their babies were more sociable and exploratory, cried less, and were more cognitively sophisticated in their exploratory behavior. Secure attachment, assessed when the infants were 12 months old, was significantly more common in the intervention group (68% versus 28% of the control group; van den Boom, 1994). A follow-up of these groups (van den Boom, 1995) demonstrated enduring effects of the intervention, with the treatment group continuing to contain higher proportions of secure attachments when the infants were 18 months old (72% versus 26% of the control group). When the children 24 and 42 months old, mothers of intervention children were rated as more accepting, accessible, and responsive than control mothers, intervention children were more cooperative than control children, and mother–child interactions in these dyads were more likely to be characterized by observers as secure (van den Boom, 1995).

Suggesting far-reaching intervention effects, children's secure attachments to their mothers appeared to be related to other relationships as well. When their children were 3 years old, fathers in the intervention group were more responsive toward their children than control fathers were. In addition, when viewed during interaction with a same-age peer, intervention group children were more cooperative and more likely to be sought out as a play partner (van den Boom, 1995). Thus changes in mothers' behavior appear to have led to changes in mother–child interactions, facilitating changes in child behavior, which then influenced the children's relationships with others.

This study highlights the importance of tracking both temperament and parenting in detail to unravel the bidirectional processes involved. An irritable infant is predisposed to insecure attachment, which is likely due, at least in part, to the mother's coming to ignore the infant. Intervention prevents this maternal component from further leading the child to develop avoidant coping strategies. This transactional nature of attachment development was suggested by Rothbart and Derryberry (1981, p. 86) two decades ago:

As important as the mother's sensitivity and flexibility may be, the role of the child's constitutional capacities and limitations in shaping her behavior should not be underestimated. Nor should the sensitivity and flexibility of the infant be neglected, for infants vary greatly in their capacity to augment or reduce their own reactivity, and to bring distress or pleasure to their care-givers. It seems essential that the mother–infant interaction and the resulting attachment process be viewed as a function of two intricate and flexible interactional systems, which can achieve a "balance" in a number of ways.

## Temperament and Parenting as Cumulative Influences on Adjustment

Additive effects of temperament and parenting have been found by several researchers. By combining first- and third-year temperament, maternal positive involvement (affection, teaching) and behavior problems of 3-year-old children, Bates and Bayles (1988) were able to strongly predict internalizing and externalizing behavior problems when the children were 6 years old. Similarly, Cameron (1978) had found that an index of difficultness and persistence when the children were 1 year old, along with poorer parenting when the children were 3 years old, predicted later behavior problems. Additive effects were also found by Fisher and Fagot (1992); here, toddler temperament and parental discipline practices were independently related to children's antisocial and coercive behavior when they were 5 to 7 years old.

Temperament and parenting have also been conceptualized as cumulative risk factors for behavioral outcome. For example, in the prediction of 4- to 5-year-old children's externalizing (hostile–aggressive and hyperactive–distractible) and internalizing (anxious–fearful) behavior problems for 1500 children from the ATP, infant difficult temperament on its own had little impact on outcome, but when it occurred in a context reflecting poor mother–child relationship and presumably poorer parenting style, the level of risk for behavioral problems increased substantially (Sanson, Oberklaid, Pedlow, and Prior, 1991). Other biological and environmental factors also contributed to cumulative risk, but the combination of difficult temperament and poor mother–infant relationship was the most reliable risk indicator. This combination was also characteristic of children described as hostile-aggressive at the age 7 to 8 years (Sanson, Smart, Prior, and Oberklaid, 1993).

In other studies, temperament has been conceptualized as a resilience factor when there is a high level of psychosocial stress and parenting is poor (e.g., Werner and Smith 1982). In these situations, the sociable or adaptable child may be able to elicit more care and concern from parents and significant others, who can help protect the child from adverse outcomes. Temperament has also been seen as an important factor in the divorce literature; Lengua, Wolchik, Sandler, and West (2000) found both temperament (low negative emotionality and impulsivity, high positive emotionality) and parenting (low rejection and inconsistency) to be independently predictive of children's successful adjustment following divorce. Interactive effects were also found, with rejection most strongly associated with behavior problems among children low in positive affect and inconsistent discipline most strongly associated with dysfunction for highly impulsive children.

## Temperament–Parenting Interactions and Adjustment

An important development in research on temperament and parenting involves an increased examination of multiplicative combinations of temperament and parent variables in the prediction of outcomes. We subsequently review the examinations of such interactions. We do not attempt an exhaustive review, but focus primarily on findings that have been conceptually replicated in independent samples.

Bates (1989) commented that, in the interests of parsimony, the independent contributions of temperament and parenting to outcome (additive effects) should be assessed before any interactive (multiplicative) effects are addressed. Nevertheless, researchers, having found additive effects, have often not gone on to investigate potential multiplicative ones. It is these more complex interactions that are likely to further our understanding of the processes by which temperament and parenting mutually affect the developmental process. When multiplicative effects have been reported, researchers also differ in their interpretation of the results. A distinction can be made between research in which temperament is seen to moderate the effect of parenting and research that considers parent behavior as a moderator of temperament in the production of outcomes. This distinction is both conceptually important and potentially directive of intervention efforts. Views of temperament as a moderator of parenting may be usefully applied to prevention programs that promote parental sensitivity to children's temperament in the choice of socialization techniques. Views of parenting as a moderator of temperament focus more specifically on how parent behaviors may act as risk or protective factors in child development. Research results in this area are likely to be applied to more selective interventions involving children at risk for, or currently displaying, psychological dysfunction related to their temperament profile.

*Activity level and stimulation.* One of the more robust findings of a multiplicative relation between temperament and parenting concerns activity level as a moderator of parenting in the development of cognitive competencies. Gandour (1989) found high levels of maternal attention focusing to be associated with high exploration scores among inactive 15-month-old children. Among more active toddlers, however, attention focusing was negatively related to exploration competence. Similarly, Wachs (1987) found that, for highly active 12-month-old toddlers, parents' naming of objects was related to less mastery behavior; for low-active children, parents' naming was related to higher mastery. Comparable findings have since been reported by Miceli, Whitman, Borkowski, Braungart-Rieker, and Mitchell (1998). In this study, 4-month-old infants who were high in experimenter-rated responsiveness (a composite of task engagement and activity level scores) showed higher preference for novelty (a characteristic related to later intelligence) when their mothers were less involved during a free-play situation. In contrast, the novelty preference of infants low in responsiveness was not affected by maternal involvement. As suggested by Escalona (1968), children low in activity level may benefit from parental stimulation that helps to guide their explorations, whereas the exploratory behavior of active children, more internally driven, may be interrupted by additional stimulation.

*Parent protectiveness and behavioral inhibition.* A second set of replicated findings investigates parental sensitivity as it is related to the development of behavioral inhibition. Arcus, Gardner, and Anderson (1992) and Park, Belsky, Putnam, and Crnic (1997) measured negative reactivity during infancy. Arcus et al. (1992) measured mothers' responsiveness to fretting and crying and their tendencies to be indirect, rather than controlling, when setting limits on child behavior, whereas Park et al. (1997) used more general indices of parental intrusiveness and sensitivity. In both studies, negative infants who received more sensitive parenting were likely to be behaviorally inhibited as toddlers, whereas parental sensitivity was not associated with inhibition in children who were less negative during infancy.

Conceptually similar are the results of Rubin, Hastings, Stewart, Henderson, and Chen (1997), who found a strong correlation between maternal ratings of child fearfulness and children's observed inhibition toward peers when mothers were oversolicitous (a composite of behaviors including exaggerated positive affect and affection, unsolicited assistance and a lack of attention to child cues). In contrast, when mothers were low in oversolicitousness, there was little association between mother-rated fearfulness and inhibition toward peers. This set of findings suggests that caregivers may inadvertently support the stability of their children's fearful temperament by being overprotective, thus not allowing children to develop regulatory strategies to overcome uncertainty on their own (Kagan, 1994). Another possibility is that parents may be more responsive in the early months to the kind of negative affect that is predictive of later behavioral inhibition.

*Fear, conscience, and aggression.* Recent research has also revealed interactions between fearful temperament and parenting in the development of conscience. Kochanska (1991, 1995) found that parenting characterized as low in power assertion predicted conscience development among fearful (inhibited), but not fearless (uninhibited), children. In contrast, the moral behavior of uninhibited children was higher when mothers were highly responsive and when the mother–child attachment was secure. Responsivity and attachment did not contribute to the conscience development of fearful children (Kochanska, 1995, 1997). Related findings were reported by Colder, Lochman, and Wells (1997); 9- to 11-year-old boys who were highly or moderately fearful were more likely to be aggressive if reared by parents high in self-reported use of harsh punishment, whereas for boys low in fear, harsh punishment and aggression were not significantly related.

These studies strongly suggest different developmental pathways for temperamentally dissimilar children. Gentle discipline that deemphasizes power appears to fit well with fearful children's intrinsically high levels of arousal, allowing the child to more effectively internalize parental messages, whereas high power-assertive techniques may raise these children's arousal to levels that may interfere with encoding of parent agendas. Low power-assertive strategies do not, however, promote morality in fearless children, possibly because gentle discipline does not provoke sufficient levels of arousal. Fearless children appear to be more attuned to the rewarding aspects of responsive parenting and the close relationship with their parent, which may motivate them to endorse parental and societal agendas.

*Negative emotionality, self-regulation, and parenting.* A number of studies have also revealed interactions between more general temperamental negativity and parenting in the development of behavior problems. Crockenberg (1987) found that irritable infants who had angry, punitive mothers were more angry, noncompliant, and less confident as 2-year-old children than were irritable infants with less punitive mothers. Among less irritable infants, however, the links between maternal style and child behavior were attenuated. Belsky, Hsieh, and Crnic (1998) proposed that children with negative temperament are most susceptible to parental influence and found some support for this proposition. Parenting of male infants was more predictive of externalizing behavior problems at 3 years of age for infants high in negativity than it was for infants low in negativity. Stice and Gonzales (1998) also found evidence of temperament moderating the effects of parenting; maternal control and support were more strongly related to antisocial behavior among adolescents who were high on behavioral undercontrol and negative affectivity than among those with less extreme scores. After regressing out main effects for 24-month-old children's externalizing, a three-way interaction among gender, temperament, and parenting in the prediction of 42-month-old children's externalizing disorders was found by Shaw et al. (1998): For boys, noncompliant temperament and maternal rejection held main effects for externalizing. For girls, however, noncompliance was predictive of later behavior problems only when combined with rejection.

The majority of work that views parent behavior as moderating the effects of temperament has concerned aggression and other externalizing difficulties. Maziade et al. (1990), for example, found that children who at 7 years of age had an extremely difficult temperament and came from dysfunctional families (characterized by a lack of rule clarity, consistency, and parental consensus) were highly likely to exhibit oppositional or attention deficit disorders at 12 and 16 years of age. In contrast, few of the children with difficult temperament but good family functioning had behavioral disorders. Finally, few of the extremely easy children exhibited difficulties at the age 12 years, regardless of the level of family functioning.

Three recent studies supplement the findings of Maziade et al. (1990). Calkins and Johnson (1998) measured child frustration, maternal interference, and aggressive behaviors during a battery of tasks designed to elicit frustration in 18-month-old toddlers. Frustration was positively correlated with aggressive behaviors overall, but the relation was stronger when mothers were highly interfering. In a study by Rubin et al. (1998), dysregulated temperament (an aggregate of observed anger expressions and maternal ratings of approach and anger), maternal negative dominance (a composite of negative control and hostile affect), and children's aggression toward peers were measured during separate episodes of two laboratory sessions. When mothers were low in dominance, no relation was found between temperament and aggression. However, dysregulation and aggression were positively correlated among toddlers whose mothers were highly dominant. Finally, in a sample of 5- to 6-year-old children, Paterson and Sanson (1999) found that parental use of physical punishment had little effect on the externalizing behavior of flexible (adaptable, low-reactive) children, but was associated with considerably elevated levels of externalizing behavior among inflexible, reactive children.

In the studies previously discussed, temperament characteristics such as anger, emotion dysregulation, and negativity are most likely to lead to maladaptive outcomes when parents are interfering, negatively dominant, or power assertive. Contrary to these findings are the results of Bates, Pettit, Dodge, and Ridge (1998). In two separate samples, these authors examined temperamental resistance to control as it interacted with maternal restrictive control in predicting externalizing behavior problems. Resistance to control, assessed concurrently when children were 13 and 24 months of age in one sample and retrospectively when children were 5 years of age in the second, referred to children's tendencies to persist in activities when directed to stop by a parent. Restrictive control reflected the frequency with which mothers restrained, scolded, or punished their children when they misbehaved during home observations when the children were 6, 13, and 24 months (sample one) or 5 years (sample two) of age. In both studies, resistance to control was marginally predictive of externalizing difficulties during middle childhood when mothers were high in restrictive control, whereas the relation between resistance to control and externalizing was considerably stronger when maternal control was low. These results were found whether teachers or parents rated externalizing problems.

The inconsistency between the findings of Bates et al. (1998) and the other studies previously summarized is surprising, in that the measures used to index mother behavior were fairly consistent across the studies, typically involving maternal displays of negative affect and control. The key discrepancy between the study by Bates et al. (1998) and the others may be the nature of the temperament variable. In studies finding greater links between temperament and externalizing when parental control was high, the temperament construct of interest was negative affectivity. In contrast, only one of the four questionnaire items indexing resistance to control in the study by Bates et al. (1998) referred to negativity. Bates et al. (1998) contended that resistance to control may reflect a strong attraction to rewards, a weak fear system, and/or low levels of effortful control. Although parental control may lead to coercive cycles of parent–child interaction that result in externalizing problems when children are predisposed to high negativity, children who are resistant, but not particularly negative, may actually benefit from parental intervention by learning to effectively manage their aggressive impulses.

## Summary

Relations between temperament and parenting are complex and affected by a number of additional factors, both internal and external to the family. For example, characteristics such as high negativity appear to be related to parental involvement and concern during early infancy, but to more negative parental reactions in later years. Similarly, some aspects of surgency (e.g., high-intensity pleasure) and negative affect (e.g., anger) may be more accepted in boys, whereas characteristics such as fear and shyness are less discouraged in girls. Values placed on particular expressions of temperament are also set against a backdrop of cultural influence, with more positive reactions to surgency–extraversion in Western societies and greater emphasis on reticence or constraint in Asian cultures. Within a culture, psychological characteristics of parents such as personality and depression also affect parenting behavior. In turn, child temperamental characteristics are likely to influence maternal feelings of self-efficacy and depressive mood.

A recurring theme in research concerning parenting-temperament interactions is the tendency for power-assertive, intrusive parenting to be especially predictive of externalizing disorders for children who are high in negative affect. In comparison, insecure parent–child attachments, combined with low parental responsivity, appear to contribute to compromised moral development among children who are temperamentally high in surgency and/or low in fearfulness or effortful control. On an optimistic note, the intervention component of van den Boom's (1994, 1995) research indicates that training parents to respond to the specific needs of their individual child can successfully lower the incidence of problem behavior.

## Future Directions

Increasing recognition of the importance of temperament for developmental outcomes has led more researchers to insert measures of temperament into their predictive models. Unfortunately, this has sometimes involved a dredging of the available data for temperamentlike constructs, including those retrospectively measured, without due regard for conceptual and measurement issues. Items initially regarded as measures of behavior problems are sometimes reconceptualized as measures of temperament (e.g., Caspi, Henry, McGee, Moffitt, and Silva, 1995; Kendler, Sham, and MacLean, 1997). Given the problem of separating temperament measures from behavior problem measures, even with the best-developed scales (Sanson, Prior, and Kyrios, 1990), such an atheoretical approach to the measurement of temperament is not likely to advance knowledge. In fact, Rothbart and Bates (1998) note that even the best-developed measures of temperament have inadequacies and that an important research task is to try to develop measures with better construct validity. We reiterate this plea.

We previously noted the difficulty of obtaining "clean" measures of both temperament and parenting before they start to influence each other. Some researchers have shown that prenatally measured attitudes are related to postnatal temperament ratings (e.g., Heinecke, in Vol. 3 of this *Handbook*; Vaughn, Bradley, Joffe-Lyle, and Seiffer, 1987). Nevertheless, convergence between maternal and paternal ratings of postnatal temperament is considerably stronger than convergence in prenatal expectations of temperament (Diener, Goldstein, and Manglesdorf, 1995). Other researchers have indicated that beliefs about parenthood remain relatively constant from the prenatal period to 5 months postnatally (Lamb et al., 1982). Differential temperament expectations and attitudes toward parenting may give us hints about what parenting would be like before it is affected by the child's individuality. Parental expectations of the child may influence the socialization strategies used as well as parents' interpretations of their children's actual behavior. In addition to prospectively questioning parents about their expectations of temperament before the birth of their child, we need to follow up by asking questions such as: "You thought X about parenting before your child was born; do you still think so?", "Is this what you do?", "Does it work as you thought it would?". There are little direct data on these questions.

It may be additionally informative to search for particular infant behaviors that contribute to discontinuity in parents' prenatal and postnatal ratings of temperament. A related issue is whether parents modify their parenting attitudes and behavior once the child is born and whether this is systematic for children with different temperament characteristics. Observing several adults interacting with the same group of children, including children differing in their temperament characteristics, may also inform our understanding of the "active" and "evocative" effects of temperament (Scarr and McCartney, 1983).

Given the evidence that temperament is not immutable, it is important to understand conditions in the social environment that promote temperament qualities associated with healthy adjustment, such as self-control–self-regulation, which may lessen problematic qualities such as irritability. To investigate whether and how parenting affects the expression of temperament, we need evidence of changes in temperament when parenting varies or of mutual parenting–temperament changes. In both the observational and the intervention phases of her study, van den Boom (1989, 1994, 1995) provided a good model of the detailed analysis needed to address these issues. Further work following her model of observation and experimental intervention, systematically addressing other aspects of temperament, other facets of parenting, and other child outcome variables among different age groups, would be most beneficial.

The studies reviewed provide a strong case for the importance of third variables for temperament–parenting relations. Parents' underlying beliefs, values, and expectations are likely to significantly affect their responses to children's individual characteristics, including whether parents respond to an irritable and inflexible child with efforts to find effective ways of soothing and managing the child or by labeling the child as "difficult" or "bad." Little research attention has been directed to this issue.

Another area in which additional study is likely to be informative involves relationships with gender. Such research might help to explain the anomaly that, although temperament differences between girls and boys are initially slight (Prior, Smart, Sanson, and Oberklaid, 1993), differences in later social adjustment are marked. We noted that relations between temperament and parenting often differ for girls and boys. Differential beliefs about the desirable characteristics of girls and boys are likely to be part of the story here, but it is also possible that the small differences in temperament between girls and boys may have larger-than-expected effects through their interaction with parenting. In infancy, boys have been found to have higher activity levels (Eaton and Enns, 1986). This, combined with the possibility of earlier language development among girls (Maccoby and Jacklin, 1974), may make girls, on average, more susceptible to early socialization than boys are (Rothbart, 1989a). There is opportunity for careful longitudinal work from infancy to address these questions.

The belief that the developmental process is best explained by a transactional model (involving interactions among temperament, parenting, and other intrinsic and social context variables) appears to be widely endorsed by researchers, and investigations of multiplicative interactions between temperament and parenting have become increasingly prevalent over the past decade. Studies of interaction effects have not always been theory driven, however, so interpretations of findings can be unclear. Future research needs to specify the developmental models being tested and be explicit about expected direct, mediated, and moderated effects. In addition, researchers must replicate existing findings on parent–temperament interactions before these findings can be fully embraced.

Future research will additionally gain from increased specificity, moving from global measures of temperament such as "difficult," which confound several facets of temperament and vary from study to study, to more specific dimensions (self-regulation, irritability, fear or shyness). There is now clear evidence that different aspects of temperament are related in a systematic way to different outcomes (Sanson and Prior, 1999). The research reviewed here further points to differential interactions between facets of temperament and parenting dimensions. Research focusing on basic levels of temperamental variation, along with clearly specified dimensions of parenting, holds great promise for increasing our understanding of temperament and parenting.

One area showing promise for future exploration involves testing of hypotheses concerning particular combinations of temperament traits and parenting. As noted in our review, there are preliminary suggestions that fear can moderate aggressive responses and that self-regulation can moderate reactive tendencies. These suggestions deserve fuller exploration. Observations of parenting in extreme temperament groups may be a useful starting point for this research. We also previously noted that almost all the available research in this area has involved mothers. As the diversity of family structures and parental roles continues to increase, the need to examine these questions among fathers and others in the caregiving role is clear.

Finally, the question of generalizability of results takes us back to issues of parental expectations, beliefs and values. It may be no accident that the current interest in temperament and parenting has arisen in individualistic Western cultures. In more collectivist cultures, in which individuals are more often defined by their relation to the group, temperamental variation among individuals may be of less relevance and salience than in more individualistic Western cultures (Kitayama and Markus, 1994). The applicability of conclusions based on Western samples to other cultural groups thus also needs investigation.

## APPLICATIONS

### Implications for Parenting

One implication of taking children's individuality seriously is that it becomes more difficult to give universal prescriptions for "good parenting." Because children may differ in their responses to similar patterns of parenting, parents need to be attentive to the temperament characteristics of their children and be able to adapt their parenting behaviors to them. This requires attention to the signals of the child concerning their state and needs. A goal of parenting may then be accomplished in one way for one child, and in a different way for another, depending on the child's temperament characteristics.

Another conclusion emerging from the literature is that some temperament characteristics pose more parenting challenges than others, at least in modern Western societies. Although infant crying and irritability may elicit more maternal contact, this contact often does not seem to be sustainable over time, and children's proneness to distress can contribute to the emergence of avoidant or negative, mutually coercive, parent–child interactions. The studies of van den Boom (1994, 1995), however, show that these influences can be countered with extra support and training for mothers of distress-prone infants. The importance of thoughtful socialization is thus enhanced, rather than diminished, when the child's temperament is taken into account.

Temperamental variation is also important when we take a broader perspective on parenting; not only in parents' direct behavior toward the child but also in decisions made about childcare, timing of school entry, size and structure of school, kinds of extracurricular activities, and so forth (Bradley and Sanson, 1992). Some hints of the relation of temperament to childcare come from the findings of Volling and Feagans (1995) that low-quality daycare (characterized by a high child-to-caregiver ratio) was associated with reduced levels of positive peer interactions among fearful, but not fearless, children, and from the observation of Fein, Gariboldi, and Boni (1993) that when children entered childcare, caregivers initially attended most to the distressed children, but after 3 months responded more to children who were cheerful or demanding. Also relevant are the findings of Orth and Martin (1994) that variations in instructional method did not predict off-task behavior of 5- and 6-year-old children who were high in task orientation, whereas children who were lower in task orientation showed lower rates of off-task behavior in a computer-instruction condition than in a teacher-instruction condition. Findings such as these point to the value for parents of taking temperament into account when making decisions about their children's education.

Given culturally based parental beliefs about desired child (or girl versus boy) characteristics, research on individual differences in temperament can help parents and educators avoid a tendency to try to fit all children, all girls, or all boys into a single mold. Temperament research can lead to recognition of the legitimacy and the value of multiple patterns of children's behavior. As has been stressed, whether a particular characteristic is difficult depends on its fit with the environment, whereas the notion of difficult temperament implies that the problem lies in the child.

The notion that the parent's major efforts should be directed toward modifying the child's temperamental expressions is additionally problematic when one considers the initial asymmetry in parent and child contributions to interactions (Rothbart, 1989a). Young infants react to their own internal states and to the immediate situation, including the caregiver's soothing and activating stimulation. Caregivers interpret the infant's emotional reactions as signals of the need for increasing, decreasing, or changing stimulation. Only at later ages can the child be expected to play a more active and anticipatory role in the interaction. Thus the initial responsibility for adaptation lies strongly with the parent.

## Parenting Programs

The literature we have reviewed may be particularly informative for the creation of new parenting programs. Manuals and courses on parenting abound, and community interventions have been directed toward improving parenting skills. How well do these efforts take child temperament into account? Any program giving prescriptions about "the right way to do it" will clearly be deficient if it does not also direct parents' attention to individuality and to the need to be flexible in their approach to childrearing. A number of recent intervention programs have used a temperament-based approach (see McClowry, 1998, and Sheeber and McDevitt, 1998, for reviews). These programs have taken several forms, including educating parents about temperament, providing individualized feedback on children's temperament profiles, giving recommendations for specific parenting strategies to engender goodness-of-fit, and setting up parent support groups for temperamentally difficult children.

Participating parents have consistently reported high levels of satisfaction with these programs, but evaluation of effectiveness has been hampered by a lack of control groups.

One exception is a program directed by Sheeber (Sheeber and McDevitt, 1998). In comparison with mothers in a waiting-list condition, mothers of difficult children who were educated regarding their child's temperament and trained in management techniques reported increased satisfaction with parent–child relationships, greater perceived parenting competence, less depression, and less family disruption. In addition, although ratings of difficult temperament were not lowered by the treatment, mothers in the experimental group reported lower levels of internalizing and externalizing disorders in their children.

In the majority of temperament-based parenting programs, there is a focus on "difficult" temperament. Advice on how to handle particular "difficult" temperament characteristics can be useful, but there may be problems with this approach. We previously identified problems associated with the concept of the difficult child, including the danger of creating a self-fulfilling prophesy by labeling a child as "difficult". The potential for negative outcomes of this type may be particularly high when parents are merely given written material concerning their child's temperament and do not have personal contact with a childcare professional. Cameron, Hansen, and Rosen (1991) found that, compared with mothers of a control group, mothers receiving only written guidance reported higher levels of problematic issues in their children and more difficulty managing these issues, whereas mothers who both met with a temperament counselor and received written feedback showed increases in their ability to manage problem behaviors.

An approach to parenting education that incorporates information about temperament in a more flexible and nonjudgmental way is the *First Three Years* curriculum project developed by Birth to Three in Eugene, Oregon. This program is designed around support groups, in which parents are invited to consider basic individual differences in children's temperament, among other issues (Birth to Three, 2000). Taking into account parental values and goals, as well as the child's developmental stage and temperament, parents are encouraged to consider both the strengths and the challenges of the child's temperament. "For example, if a parent understands that by temperament her child tends to be highly impulsive, that means the child probably will have an easy time with transitions and new experiences (the strength) but will need help with learning self control, focus, and persistence (the challenge). A reserved or 'shy' child may be able to play alone or wait her turn easily (the strength) but will need help with learning to take risks (the challenge). . . . Understanding individual differences helps parents eliminate perceptions of 'bad intent' on the part of the child and, instead, appreciate the challenges their child faces" (J. Rusch, personal communication, August 2000).

In Birth to Three support group sessions, parents develop strategies (games, stories, role playing, songs, and modeling) to give their children a wider range of behaviors from which to choose. Thus a shy child may be given experience in speaking up with an idea or seeking out friendships; a more impulsive child may be trained in slowing down and planning ahead. The idea is not to change the child's temperament, but to work with it to increase the likelihood of positive outcomes. This is a complex view of temperament and development, but one that is both communicable and appropriate to our current understanding. It is also a view that forgoes value judgments about temperamental tendencies, stressing instead the idea that each temperamental characteristic offers both costs and benefits, depending on the child's age, the environmental context, and the specific goals for learning.

## CONCLUSIONS

A child's temperament is apparent from early infancy and is an important influence on development. Variations in temperamental reactivity and self-regulation in children can be assessed in terms of characteristic patterns of positive and negative emotionality, sociability, and attentional persistence. These patterns are moderately stable over time, but are by no means immutable. Temperament contributes to a wide range of child outcomes in behavioral, cognitive, and social domains. The task for parents in thinking about temperament is to take their child's particular characteristics into account when choosing strategies to soothe, control, stimulate, and guide their child and in arranging the overall childrearing environment.

Information for parents can be drawn from analyses of the effects on child outcome of particular combinations of parent behavior and child temperament. Appropriate parenting can lead to positive outcomes even for children extreme in temperament. For instance, van den Boom's (1994, 1995) study has illustrated how maternal training in dealing with irritable infants can lead to improved cognitive, social, and emotional outcomes for these infants. Similarly, studies by Wachs and his colleagues (e.g., Wachs, 1987) reveal how different levels of social and environmental stimulation appear to be appropriate for children with differing temperament profiles.

We have suggested that some of the consequences of taking temperament into account might be to adapt parenting behavior and the child's environment to provide as good a fit to the child's temperament as possible, while at the same time encouraging the child's adaptations to situations; to recognize that, although a child's temperament is not immutable, changes over time are unlikely to be dramatic; and to avoid value judgments about these individual differences. Even though it may be recognized that, in a given social and cultural context, some children take more effort to parent, there is nothing inherently inferior about these children, nor are temperament characteristics the result of "naughtiness."

In sum, the concept of temperament directs our attention to important aspects of child individuality that must be considered in parenting. It has long been recognized that appropriate parenting depends on the age of the child; temperament characteristics also determine what is appropriate. Even if this recognition complicates both the task of the parent and that of the researcher, such complication is unavoidable. The task then for the parent and the practitioner is to foster "respect for the individuality and integrity of each child, and flexibility in creating environments that may lead to positive outcomes for them and for us" (Rothbart, 1989a, p. 236).

## ACKNOWLEDGMENTS

Authors Sanson and Putnam made equivalent contributions to this chapter; they are listed on the opening page in alphabetical order. Preparation of this chapter was supported in part by the U.S. National Institutes of Mental Health grants R01 MH43361 and K05 MH01471 to Mary Rothbart, National Health and Medical Research Council (Australia) grants 980627 and 9937433 to A. Sanson and J. Toumbourou, and by funds allocated to Sam Putnam from the U.S. National Institutes of Mental Health grant 5 T32 MH1893. The authors thank S. Ahadi, M. Prior, and M. Rothbart for their generous help on a previous version of the chapter and J. Bates for directing us to some of the recent research on parent–temperament interactions.

## REFERENCES

Ahadi, S. A., Rothbart, M. K., and Ye, R. M. (1993). Children's temperament in the U.S. and China: Similarities and differences. *European Journal of Personality, 7,* 359–377.

Arcus, D., Gardner, S., and Anderson, C. (1992, April). *Infant reactivity, maternal style, and the development of inhibited and uninhibited behavior profiles.* Paper presented at the Biennial Meeting of the International Society for Infant Studies, Miami, FL.

Baron, R. M., and Kenny, D. A. (1986). The moderator–mediator variable distinction in social psychological research: Conceptual, strategic, and statistical considerations. *Journal of Personality and Social Psychology, 51,* 1173–1182.

Bates, J. E. (1989). Applications of temperament concepts. In G. A. Kohnstamm, J. E. Bates, and M. K. Rothbart (Eds.), *Temperament in childhood* (pp. 321–355). Chichester, England: Wiley.

Bates, J. E., and Bayles, K. (1988). The role of attachment in the development of behavior problems. In J. Belsky and T. Nezworski (Eds.), *Clinical implications of attachment* (pp. 253–299). Hillsdale, NJ: Lawrence Erlbaum Associates.

Bates, J. E., Maslin, C. A., and Frankel, K. A. (1985). Attachment security, mother–child interaction, and temperament as predictors of behavior-problem ratings at age three years. In I. Bretherton and E. Waters (Eds.), *Growing points in attachment theory and research. Society for Child Development Monographs, 50,* (Serial No. 209), 167–193.

Bates, J. E., Olson, S. L., Pettit, G. S., and Bayles, K. (1982). Dimensions of individuality in the mother–infant relationship at 6 months of age. *Child Development, 53,* 446–461.

Bates, J. E., Pettit, G. S., Dodge, K. A., and Ridge, B. (1998). The interaction of temperamental resistance to control and restrictive parenting in the development of externalizing behavior. *Developmental Psychology, 34,* 982–995.

Bell, R. Q. (1968). A reinterpretation of the direction of effects in studies of socialization. *Psychological Review, 75,* 81–95.

Belsky, J., Hsieh, K., and Crnic, K. (1998). Mothering, fathering, and infant negativity as antecedents of boys' externalizing problems and inhibition at age 3 years: Differential susceptibility to rearing experience? *Development and Psychopathology, 10,* 301–319.

Belsky, J., and Rovine, M. (1987). Temperament and attachment security in the Strange Situation: An empirical rapprochement. *Child Development, 58,* 787–795.

Birth to Three (2000). *The first three years curriculum.* Unpublished manuscript. Engene, OR: Birth to Three.

Bohlin, G., Hagekull, B., and Lindhagen, K. (1981). Dimensions of infant behavior. *Infant Behavior and Development, 4,* 83–96.

Bradley, B., and Sanson, A. (1992). Promoting quality in infant day care via research: Conflicting lessons from the day care controversy? *Australian Journal of Early Childhood, 17,* 3–10.

Calkins, S. D., and Fox, N. A. (1992). The relations among infant temperament, security of attachment, and behavioral inhibition at twenty-four months. *Child Development, 63,* 1456–1472.

Calkins, S. D., and Johnson, M. C. (1998). Toddler regulation of distress to frustrating events: Temperamental and maternal correlates. *Infant Behavior and Development, 21,* 379–395.

Cameron, J. R. (1978). Parental treatment, children's temperament, and the risk of childhood behavioral problems: I. Relationships between parental characteristics and changes in children's temperament over time. *Annual Progress in Child Psychiatry and Child Development,* 233–244.

Cameron, J. R., Hansen, R., and Rosen, D. (1991). Preventing behavioral problems in infancy through temperament assessment and parental support programs within health maintenance organizations. In J. H. Johnson and S. B. Johnson (Eds.), *Advances in Child Health Psychology* (pp. 127–139). Gainesville, FL: University Presses of Florida.

Caron, J., and Miller, P. (1981, April). *Effects of infant characteristics on caregiver responsiveness among the Gusii.* Paper presented at the meeting of the Society for Research in Child Development, Boston.

Caspi, A., Henry, B., McGee, R. O., Moffitt, T. E., and Silva, P. A. (1995). Temperamental origins of child and adolescent behavior problems: From age three to fifteen. *Child Development, 66,* 55–68.

Chen, X., Hastings, P. D., Rubin, K. H., Chen, H., Cen, G., and Stewart, S. L. (1998). Childrearing attitudes and behavioral inhibition in Chinese and Canadian toddlers: A cross-cultural study. *Developmental Psychology, 34,* 677–686.

Chess, S., and Thomas, A. (1989). Issues in the clinical application of temperament. In G. A. Kohnstamm, J. E. Bates, and M. K. Rothbart (Eds.), *Temperament in Childhood* (pp. 378–386). Chichester, England: Wiley.

Clark, L. A., Kochanska, G., and Ready, R. (2000). Mothers' personality and its interaction with child temperament as predictors of parenting behavior. *Journal of Personality and Social Psychology, 79,* 274–285.

Colder, C. R., Lochman, J. E., and Wells, K. C. (1997). The moderating effects of children's fear and activity level on relations between parenting practices and childhood symptomatology. *Journal of Abnormal Child Psychology, 25,* 251–263.

Crockenberg, S. B. (1986). Are temperamental differences in babies associated with predictable differences in care giving? In J. V. Lerner and R. M. Lerner (Eds.), *New Directions for Child Development: Vol. 31. Temperament and social interaction during infancy and childhood* (pp. 53–73). San Francisco: Jossey-Bass.

Crockenberg, S. (1987). Predictors and correlates of anger toward and punitive control of toddlers by adolescent mothers. *Child Development, 58,* 964–975.

Crockenberg, S., and McCluskey, K. (1985, April). *Predicting infant attachment from early and current behavior of mothers and infants.* Paper presented at the meeting of the Society for Research in Child Development, Toronto, Ontario, Canada.

Cummings, E. M., and Davies, P. T. (1994). Maternal depression and child development. *Journal of Child Psychology and Psychiatry, 35,* 73–112.

Cutrona, C. E., and Troutman, B. R. (1986). Social support, infant temperament, and parenting self-efficacy: A mediational model of postpartum depression. *Child Development, 57,* 1507–1518.

Daniels, D., Plomin, R., and Greenhalgh, J. (1984). Correlates of difficult temperament in infancy. *Child Development, 55,* 1184–1194.

deVries, M. W. (1984). Temperament and infant mortality among the Masai of East Africa. *American Journal of Psychiatry, 141,* 1189–1194.

Diamond, S. (1974). *The roots of psychology.* New York: Basic Books.

Diener, M. L., Goldstein, L. H., and Mangelsdorf, S. C. (1995). The role of prenatal expectations in parents' reports of infant temperament. *Merrill-Palmer Quarterly, 41*, 172–190.

Eaton, W. O., and Enns, R. (1986). Sex differences in human motor activity level. *Psychological Bulletin, 100*, 19–28.

Escalona, S. A. (1968). *The roots of individuality: Normal patterns of development in infancy.* Chicago: Aldine de Gruyter.

Eysenck, H. J., and Eysenck, M. W. (1985). *Personality and individual differences: A natural science approach.* New York: Plenum.

Fein, G. G., Gariboldi, A., and Boni, R. (1993). The adjustment of infants and toddlers to group care: The first six months. *Early Childhood Research Quarterly, 8*, 1–14.

Fish, M., and Crockenberg, S. (1986). Correlates and antecedents of nine-month infant behavior and mother–infant interaction. *Infant Behavior and Development, 4*, 69–81.

Fisher, P. A., and Fagot, B. I. (1992, April). *Temperament, parental discipline, and child psychopathology: A social-interactional model.* Poster presented at the annual meeting of the Western Psychological Association, Portland, OR.

Frodi, A. M. (1983). Attachment behavior and sociability with strangers in premature and fullterm infants. *Infant Mental Health Journal, 4*, 13–22.

Gandour, M. J. (1989). Activity level as a dimension of temperament in toddlers: Its relevance for the organismic specificity hypothesis. *Child Development, 60*, 1092–1098.

Gauvian, M., and Fagot, B. (1995). Child temperament as mediator of mother–toddler problem solving. *Social Development, 4*, 257–276.

Goldberg, L. R. (1990). An alternative "description of personality": The Big-Five factor structure. *Journal of Personality and Social Psychology, 59*, 1216–1229.

Goldsmith, H. H., and Alansky, J. A. (1987). Maternal and infant predictors of attachment: A meta-analytic review. *Journal of Consulting and Clinical Psychology, 55*, 805–816.

Goodman, S. H., and Gotlib, I. H. (1999). Risk for psychopathology in the children of depressed mothers: A developmental model for understanding mechanisms of transmission. *Psychological Review, 106*, 458–490.

Gordon, B. (1983). Maternal perception of child temperament and observed mother–child interaction. *Child Psychiatry and Human Development, 13*, 153–167.

Gowen, J. W., Johnson-Martin, N., Goldman, B. D., and Appelbaum, M. (1989). Feelings of depression and parenting competence of mothers of handicapped and nonhandicapped infants: A longitudinal study [Special Issue: Research on families]. *American Journal on Mental Retardation, 94*, 259–271.

Hemphill, S., and Sanson, A. (2000, July). *Relations between toddler and preschooler temperament and parenting style in an Australian sample.* Paper presented at the Sixteenth Biennial Meetings of the International Society for the Study of Behavioral Development, Beijing.

Hinde, R. A. (1989). Temperament as an intervening variable. In G. A. Kohnstamm, J. E. Bates, and M. K. Rothbart (Eds.), *Temperament in Childhood* (pp. 27–34). Chichester, England: Wiley.

Kagan, J. (1994). *Galen's Prophecy.* New York: Basic Books.

Kagitcibasi, C. (1996). *Family and human development across cultures.* Mahwah, NJ : Lawrence Erlbaum Associates.

Kendler, K. S., Sham, P. C., and MacLean, C. J. (1997). The determinants of parenting: An epidemiological, multi-informant, retrospective study. *Psychological Medicine, 27*, 549–563.

Kitayama, S., and Markus, H. (1994). *Culture and emotion.* Washington, DC: American Psychological Association.

Klein, P. (1984). The relation of Israeli mothers toward infants in relation to infants' perceived temperament. *Child Development, 55*, 1212–1218.

Kochanska, G. (1991). Socialization and temperament in the development of guilt and conscience. *Child Development, 62*, 1379–1392.

Kochanska, G. (1995). Children's temperament, mothers' discipline, and security of attachment: Multiple pathways to emerging internalization. *Child Development, 66*, 597–615.

Kochanska, G. (1997). Multiple pathways to conscience for children with different temperaments: From toddlerhood to age five. *Developmental Psychology, 33*, 228–240.

Kohnstamm, G. A. (1989). Temperament in childhood: Cross-cultural and sex differences. In G. A. Kohnstamm, J. E. Bates, and M. K. Rothbart (Eds.), *Temperament in Childhood* (pp. 483–508). Chichester, England: Wiley.

Kyrios, M., and Prior, M. (1990). Temperament, stress and family factors in behavioral adjustment of 3–5-year-old children. *International Journal of Behavioral Development, 13*, 67–93.

Kyrios, M., Prior, M., Oberklaid, F., and Demetriou, A. (1989). Cross-cultural studies of temperament: Temperament in Greek infants. *International Journal of Psychology, 24*, 585–603.

Lamb, M. E., Frodi, M., Hwang, C., Forstromm, B., and Corry, T. (1982). Stability and change in parental attitudes following an infant's birth into traditional and nontraditional Swedish families. *Scandinavian Journal of Psychology, 23*, 53–62.

Lee, C. L., and Bates, J. E. (1985). Mother–child interaction at two years and perceived difficult temperament. *Child Development, 56*, 1314–1325.

Lengua, L. J., Wolchik, S. A., Sandler, I. N., and West, S. G. (2000). The additive and interactive effects of parenting and temperament in predicting problems of children of divorce. *Journal of Clinical Child Psychology, 29*, 232–244.

Lewis, M., and Feiring, C. (1989). Infant, mother, and mother–infant interaction behavior and subsequent attachment. *Child Development*, *60*, 831–837.

Linn, P., and Horowitz, F. (1983). The relationship between infant individual differences and mother–infant interaction during the neonatal period. *Infant Behavior and Development*, *6*, 415–427.

Lytton, H., and Romney, D. M. (1991). Parents' differential socialization of boys and girls: A meta-analysis. *Psychological Bulletin*, *109*, 267–296.

Maccoby, E. E., and Jacklin, C. N. (1974). *The psychology of sex differences*. Stanford, CA: Stanford University Press.

Maccoby, E. E., Snow, M. E., and Jacklin, C. N. (1984). Children's dispositions and mother–child interaction at 12 and 18 months: A short-term longitudinal study. *Developmental Psychology*, *20*, 459–472.

Maziade, M., Caron, C., Cote, R., Merette, C., Bernier, H., Laplante, B., Boutin, P., and Thivierge, J. (1990). Psychiatric status of adolescents who had extreme temperaments at age 7. *American Journal of Psychiatry*, *147*, 1531–1536.

McClowry, S. G. (1995). The development of the school-age temperament inventory. *Merrill-Palmer Quarterly*, *41*, 271–285.

McClowry, S. G. (1998). The science and art of using temperament as the basis for intervention. *School Psychology Review*, *27*, 551–563.

McCrae, R. R., and Costa, P. T., Jr. (1987). Validation of the five-factor model of personality across instruments and observers. *Journal of Personality and Social Psychology*, *52*, 81–90.

Miceli, P. J., Whitman, T. L., Borkowski, J. G., Braungart-Rieker, J., and Mitchell, D. W. (1998). Individual differences in infant information processing: The role of temperamental and maternal factors. *Infant Behavior and Development*, *21*, 119–136.

Orth, L. C., and Martin, R. P. (1994). Interactive effects of student temperament and instruction method on classroom behavior and achievement. *Journal of School Psychology*, *32*, 149–166.

Park, S., Belsky, J., Putnam, S., and Crnic, K. (1997). Infant emotionality, parenting, and 3-year inhibition: Exploring stability and lawful discontinuity in a male sample. *Developmental Psychology*, *33*, 218–227.

Paterson, G., and Sanson, A. (1999). The association of behavioural adjustment to temperament, parenting and family characteristics among 5 year old children. *Social Development*, *8*, 293–309.

Pedlow, R., Sanson, A. V., Prior, M., and Oberklaid, F. (1993). The stability of temperament from infancy to eight years. *Developmental Psychology*, *29*, 998–1007.

Peters-Martin, P., and Wachs, T. (1984). A longitudinal study of temperament and its correlates in the first 12 months. *Infant Behavior and Development*, *7*, 285–298.

Pettit, G. S., and Bates, J. E. (1984). Continuity of individual differences in the mother–infant relationship from 6 to 13 months. *Child Development*, *55*, 729–739.

Plomin, R. (1982). Behavioral genetics and temperament. In R. Porter and G. M. Collins (Eds.), *Temperamental Differences in Infants and Young Children* (Ciba Foundation Symposium 89). London: Pitman.

Prior, M., Sanson, A., Carroll, R., and Oberklaid, F. (1989). Social class differences in temperament ratings of pre-school children. *Merrill-Palmer Quarterly*, *35*, 239–248.

Prior, M. R., Sanson, A. V., and Oberklaid, F. (1989). The Australian Temperament Project. In G. A. Kohnstamm, J. E. Bates, and M. K. Rothbart (Eds.), *Temperament in Childhood* (pp. 537–554). Chichester, England: Wiley.

Prior, M., Smart, D. F., Sanson, A. V., and Oberklaid, F. (1993). Sex differences in psychological adjustment from infancy to eight years. *Journal of the American Academy of Child and Adolescent Psychiatry*, *32*, 291–304.

Putnam, S. P., Ellis, L. K., and Rothbart, M. K. (in press). The structure of temperament from infancy through adolescence. To appear in A. Eliasz and A. Angleitner (Eds.), *Advances/proceedings in research on temperament*. Germany: Pabst Scientist.

Rendina, I., and Dickerscheid, J. D. (1976). Father involvement with first-born infants. *Family Coordinator*, *25*, 376–378.

Rothbart, M. K. (1982). The concept of difficult temperament: A critical analysis of Thomas, Chess and Korn. *Merrill-Palmer Quarterly*, *28*, 35–40.

Rothbart, M. K. (1986). Longitudinal observation of infant temperament. *Developmental Psychology*, *22*, 356–365.

Rothbart, M. K. (1989a). Temperament and development. In G. A. Kohnstamm, J. E. Bates, and M. K. Rothbart (Eds.), *Temperament in Childhood* (pp. 187–247). Chichester, England: Wiley.

Rothbart, M. K. (1989b). Biological processes of temperament. In G. Kohnstamm, J. Bates, and M. K. Rothbart, (Eds.), *Temperament in Childhood* (pp. 77–110). Chichester, England: Wiley.

Rothbart, M. K., Ahadi, S. A., and Evans, D. E. (2000). Temperament and personality: Origins and outcomes. *Journal of Personality and Social Psychology*, *78*, 122–135.

Rothbart, M. K., Ahadi, S. A., Hershey, K., and Fisher, P. (in Press). Investigations of Temperament at 3–7 Years: The Children's Behavior Questionnaire. *Child Development*.

Rothbart, M. K., and Bates, J. E. (1998). Temperament. In W. Damon (Series Ed.) and N. Eisenberg (Vol. Ed.), *Handbook of Child Psychology: Vol. 3. Social, Emotional and Personality Development* (5th ed., pp. 105–176). New York: Wiley.

Rothbart, M. K., and Derryberry, D. (1981). Development of individual differences in temperament. In M. E. Lamb and A. L. Brown (Eds.), *Advances in Developmental Psychology* (Vol. 1, pp. 37–86). Hillsdale, NJ: Lawrence Erlbaum Associates.

Rothbart, M. K., and Derryberry, D. (in press). Temperament in children. In C. von Hofsten and L. Backman (Eds.), *Proceedings of the Twenty-Seventh International Congress of Psychology*. Uppsala, Sweden: Psychology Press.

Rothbart, M. K., and Mauro, J. A. (1990). Questionnaire measures of infant temperament. In J. W. Fagen and J. Colombo (Eds.), *Individual Differences in Infancy: Reliability, Stability and Prediction* (pp. 411–429). Hillsdale, NJ: Lawrence Erlbaum Associates.

Rubin, K. H., Hastings, P., Chen, X., Stewart, S., and McNichol, K. (1998). Intrapersonal and maternal correlates of aggression, conflict, and externalizing problems in toddlers. *Child Development, 69*, 1614–1629.

Rubin, K. H., Hastings, P. D., Stewart, S. L., Henderson, H. A., and Chen, X. (1997). The consistency and concomitants of inhibition: Some of the children, all of the time. *Child Development, 68*, 467–483.

Sanson, A. (2000, July) *Temperament and social development.* Keynote address to International Society for the Study of Behavioral Development, Beijing.

Sanson, A., and Prior, M. (1999) Temperamental and behavioral precursors to Oppositional Defiant Disorder and Conduct Disorder. In H. C. Quay and A.E. Hogan (Eds.), *Handbook of Disruptive Behavior Disorders* (pp. 397–417). New York: Kluwer Academic/Plenum.

Sanson, A., Prior, M., Garino, E., Oberklaid, F., and Sewell, J. (1987). The structure of infant temperament: Factor analysis of the Revised Infant Temperament Questionnaire. *Infant Behavior and Development, 10*, 97–104.

Sanson, A., Prior, M., and Kyrios, M. (1990). Contamination of measures in temperament research. *Merrill-Palmer Quarterly, 36*, 179–192.

Sanson, A., Prior, M., and Oberklaid, F. (1991, April). *Structure and stability of temperament in the Australian Temperament Project.* Paper presented at the biennial meeting of the Society for Research in Child Development, Seattle, WA.

Sanson, A., Prior, M., Oberklaid, F., and Smart, D. (1998) Temperamental influences on psychosocial adjustment: From infancy to adolescence. *Australian Educational and Developmental Psychologist, 15*, 7–18.

Sanson, A. V., Oberklaid, F., Pedlow, R., and Prior, M. (1991). Risk indicators: Assessment of infancy predictors of preschool behavioural maladjustment. *Journal of Child Psychology and Psychiatry, 32*, 609–626.

Sanson, A. V., Smart, D. F., Prior, M., and Oberklaid, F. (1993). Precursors of hyperactivity and aggression. *Journal of the American Academy of Child and Adolescent Psychiatry, 32*, 1207–1216.

Sanson, A. V., Smart, D. F., Prior, Oberklaid, F., and Pedlow, R. (1994). The structure of temperament from three to seven years: Age, sex and sociodemographic influences. *Merrill-Palmer Quarterly, 40*, 233–252.

Scarr, S. (1992). Developmental theories for the 1990s: Development and individual differences. *Child Development, 63*, 1–19.

Scarr, S., and McCartney, K. (1983). How people make their own environments: A theory of genotype–environmental effects. *Child Development, 54*, 424–435.

Shaw, D. S., Winslow, E. B., Owens, E. B., Vondra, J. I., Cohn, J. F., and Bell, R. Q. (1998). The development of early externalizing problems among children from low-income families: A transformational perspective. *Journal of Abnormal Child Psychology, 26*, 95–107.

Sheeber, L. B., and McDevitt, S. C. (1998). Temperament-focused parent training. In J. M. Briesmeister and C. E. Schaefer (Eds.) *Handbook of parent training* (pp. 479–507). New York: Wiley.

Simpson, A. E., and Stevenson-Hinde, J. (1985). Temperamental characteristics of three- to four-year-old boys and girls and child-family interactions. *Journal of Child Psychology and Psychiatry, 26*, 43–53.

Slabach, E. H., Morrow, J., and Wachs, T. D. (1991). Questionnaire measurement of infant and child temperament: Current status and future directions. In J. Strelau and A. Angleitner (Eds.), *Explorations in temperament: International perspectives on theory and measurement* (pp. 205–234). New York: Plenum.

Sroufe, L. A. (1985). Attachment classification from the perspective of infant–caregiver relationships and infant temperament. *Child Development, 56*, 1–14.

Stice, E., and Gonzales, N. (1998). Adolescent temperament moderates the relation of parenting to antisocial behavior and substance use. *Journal of Adolescent Research, 13*, 5–31.

Teti, D. M., and Gelfand, D. M. (1991). Behavioral competence among mothers of infants in the first year: The mediational role of maternal self-efficacy. *Child Development, 62*, 918–929.

Thomas, A., Chess, S., Birch, H. G., Hertzig, M. E., and Korn, S. (1963). *Behavioral individuality in early childhood.* New York: New York University Press.

Thompson, R. A., Connell, J. P., and Bridges, L. J. (1988). Temperament, emotional, and social interactive behavior in the Strange Situation: A component process analysis of attachment system functioning. *Child Development, 59*, 1102–1110.

van den Boom, D. C. (1989). Neonatal irritability and the development of attachment. In G. A. Kohnstamm, J. E. Bates, and M. K. Rothbart (Eds.), *Temperament in Childhood* (pp. 299–318). Chichester, England: Wiley.

van den Boom, D. C. (1994). The influence of temperament and mothering on attachment and exploration: An experimental manipulation of sensitive responsiveness among lower-class mothers with irritable infants. *Child Development, 65*, 1457–1477.

van den Boom, D. C. (1995). Do first-year intervention effects endure? Follow-up during toddlerhood of a sample of Dutch irritable infants. *Child Development, 66*, 1798–1816.

Vaughn, B. E., Taraldson, B. J., Crichton, L., and Egeland, B. (1981). The assessment of infant temperament: A critique of the Carey Infant Temperament Questionnaire. *Infant Behavior and Development, 4*, 1–17.

Vaughn, B. E., Bradley, C. F., Joffe-Lyle, S., and Seiffer, R. (1987). Maternal characteristics measured prenatally are predictive of ratings of temperamental "difficulty" on the Carey Infant Temperament Questionnaire. *Developmental Psychology, 23,* 152–161.

Volling, B. L., and Feagans, L. V. (1995) Infant day care and children's social competence. *Infant Behavior and Development, 18,* 177–188.

Wachs, T. D. (1987). Specificity of environmental action as manifest in environmental correlates of infants' mastery motivation. *Developmental Psychology, 23,* 782–790.

Wachs, T. D., and Gandour, M. J. (1983). Temperament, environment, and six-month cognitive-intellectual development: A test of the organismic specificity hypothesis. *International Journal of Behavioral Development, 6,* 135–152.

Weber, R. A., Levitt, M. J., and Clarke, M. C. (1986). Individual variation in attachment security and social interactive behavior in the Strange Situation: The role of maternal and infant temperament. *Child Development, 57,* 56–65.

Werner, E. E., and Smith, R. S. (1982). *Vulnerable, but invincible: A longitudinal study of resilient children and youth.* New York: McGraw-Hill.

Whiting, B., and Whiting, J. (1973). *Children of six cultures: A psychocultural analysis.* Cambridge, MA: Harvard University Press.

# 10

# Parenting and Child Development in Adoptive Families

David M. Brodzinsky
*Rutgers University*
Ellen Pinderhughes
*Vanderbilt University*

## INTRODUCTION

With the rise in family diversity over the past few decades, interest in nontraditional family life has increased significantly among social science researchers (Lamb, 1999). Of particular importance are questions concerning the way in which family diversity has an impact on the developing child, as well as questions concerning the unique parenting experiences encountered by adults who are part of a nontraditional family system. In this chapter, we explore one particular form of nontraditional family life that is becoming increasingly more common—namely, growing up in an adoptive home. Our goals are to examine the unique challenges faced by adoptive parents in rearing their children, as well as to understand how adoption influences children's development and adjustment.

We begin with an examination of historical and contemporary trends in adoption practice, briefly outlining changes in adoption policy and law from the midnineteenth century to the present. We then review research on two different perspectives on adoption—one focusing on adoption as a risk factor in the life of the child and the other focusing on the benefits associated with growing up in an adoptive home. Following this literature review, we discuss family life-cycle issues in rearing infant-placed adopted children, with an emphasis on delineating both the unique developmental issues in the adjustment of these youngsters, as well as the unique childrearing tasks faced by adoptive parents. In the final sections of the chapter, we explore the adjustment outcomes and unique parenting issues associated with adoptions of children with special needs, transracial and intercountry adoptions, and open adoptions. Because this chapter focuses on *parenting* adopted children, a detailed examination of research and theory on adoption adjustment is not presented. Readers interested in this topic are referred to Brodzinsky, Smith, and Brodzinsky (1998) and Groze and Rosenberg (1998).

## HISTORICAL AND CONTEMPORARY PERSPECTIVES
## ON ADOPTION PRACTICE

### Historical Perspectives on Adoption

Historically, the practice of adoption served quite different purposes than it does today (Sokoloff, 1993). Going back as far as antiquity and continuing until the late nineteenth century, adoption was viewed primarily as a means of meeting the needs of adults (e.g., to ensure inheritance lines; for religious purposes; to meet requirements for holding public office; to secure additional labor for the family; to ensure maintenance and care in later years), as well as societal needs (e.g., to strengthen alliances between separate, and potentially rival, social groups) rather than the needs of children (French, in Vol. 2 of this *Handbook*). In the United States, before the 1850s, adoption existed only as an informal affair, without legal recognition of the transfer of care and custody of children from one individual to another (Sokoloff, 1993). Beginning in colonial times, children who were orphaned or abandoned were often placed with relatives or indentured to families to live, work, and learn a skill or craft. In the early 1800s, overcrowded conditions and growing poverty in large eastern cities resulted in the rise of orphan asylums, which typically were cold, inhumane institutions in which children's emotional needs were inadequately met. As a response to the conditions in these orphanages, Charles Loring Brace, the founder of the New York Children's Aid Society, began sending children westward on "orphan trains," where unfortunately they often were exploited as cheap labor by families who were inadequately screened for their motives and suitability to rear these children. In 1851 Massachusetts passed the first adoption statute that set forth the conditions for adopting a child. Thereafter, many states passed similar legislation, although it was not until 1929 that all states had statutes providing some form of judicial supervision regarding adoption. The development of adoption law (Bussiere, 1998) and the rise of the modern adoption agency system beginning in the early 1900s led to a gradual and important shift in the philosphy of adoption practice. The new focus centered on the "best interests of the child" (Goldstein, Freud, and Solnit, 1973).

### Current Trends in Adoption

Each year, tens of thousands of children are adopted in the United States (Stolley, 1993). The majority of these youngsters are placed in their families through public child welfare agencies and licensed private adoption agencies. The remaining children are adopted independently, usually with the assistance of attorneys who serve as intermediaries between birth parents and adoptive parents.

Although the federal government does not maintain accurate statistics on the prevalence of adoption in the United States, it is believed that approximately 2% to 4% of children in this country are adopted (Stolley, 1993). Of these, a slight majority are kinship adoptions with biological family members or stepparents. The remaining children are adopted by individuals with whom they share no biological connection. It is this latter group of adoptees, and their families, that has received most of the attention in the psychological literature and that is the focus of this chapter.

The demographics of children being placed for adoption have changed significantly over the past few decades (Stolley, 1993). Traditionally, most children were healthy, European American infants, adopted within a few days or weeks of birth. However, beginning in the 1960s, changes in social and sexual mores gave rise to greater acceptance of single parenthood, which, coupled with the increase of family support programs, led to a growing number of unmarried mothers deciding to keep their babies (Miller and Coyl, 2000; Weinraub, Horvath, and Gringlas, in Vol. 3 of this *Handbook*). These changes, along with the legalization of abortion and the ready availability of contraception, resulted in a dramatic decrease in the number of healthy, European American infants available for adoption. For example, whereas nearly 20% of infants born to never-married, European American women were relinquished for adoption from the mid-1950s to the early 1970s, by 1995, the corresponding rate was less than 2% (Chandra, Abma, Maza, and Bachrach, 1999). In contrast, rates of adoption placement during this same time period for never-married women of color were quite low, ranging from approximately 1.5% before the 1970s to under 1% in the mid-1990s.

With fewer healthy, European American babies available for adoption in the United States, many prospective adoptive parents have explored other options. One option is transracial adoption—that is, adopting a child of a different race. Typically this practice has involved European American parents' adopting children of color. Although fairly common in the 1960s and early 1970s, domestic transracial adoption declined after 1972 because of opposition from the African American and Native American communities. The passage of the Multi-Ethnic Placement Act of 1994 and the Inter-Ethnic Placement Act of 1996 has opened the door for increases in transracial placements, particularly of children from foster care (Haugaard and Hazan, in Vol. 1 of this *Handbook*).

Prospective adoptive parents also have turned to other countries in their efforts to adopt children. Although beginning after World War II, intercountry adoption escalated dramatically following the Korean and the Vietnam Wars. These placements typically involved adoption of children from countries that were unable to find suitable homes for their orphaned and abandoned children within their own borders (e.g., Russia, China, Korea, Guatamala) by couples from Western, industrialized countries (e.g., United States, Canada, England, Netherlands). In 1993, the Hague Convention on Protection of Children and Cooperation in Respect of Intercountry Adoption was issued, establishing a uniform set of principles and safeguards regarding the international transfer of children for adoption. Recently, with the passage of the Intercountry Adoption Act of 2000, the United States became one of 40 countries to ratify the Hague treaty. The number of intercountry adoptions is growing rapidly in the United States, with over 16,000 such placements occuring in 1999 (National Adoption Information Clearinghouse, 2000). In many cases, these adoptions cross racial lines.

Still other prospective parents began considering adopting foster children whose history and personal characteristics (e.g., older age at placement, minority racial status, exposure to neglect and/or abuse, chronic medical problems, mental and/or psychological disturbance) were once thought to be barriers to adoption. Interest in adopting these so-called *special needs* children grew quickly with the passage of the Adoption Assistance and Child Welfare Act of 1980, which emphasized the need to create nurturing permanent homes for children lingering in foster care. The passage of the Adoption and Safe Families Act of 1997 reaffirmed this commitment to permanency planning for foster children through reunification with the birth family or through the creation of alternative permanency plans, including adoption (Gendell, 2001).

In addition to the changes in characteristics of adopted children, dramatic changes also have taken place in the characteristics of adoptive parents. In the past, most adoptive parents were of middle-socioeconomic to upper-middle-socioeconomic status, married, infertile, European American couples, usually in their 30s or 40s, and free of any form of disability. Adoption agencies routinely *screened out* individuals and couples who did not meet these criteria. Even foster parents were seldom approved to adopt the children in their care. Today, however, adoption agency policy and practice have moved in the direction of *screening in* as many different types of adoption applicants as possible. For example, public agencies now have no income criteria for adoptive parents and offer financial and medical subsidies for children with special needs, which in turn has supported the efforts of blue-collar and low-income families to adopt children, especially those youngsters who otherwise might not find permanent homes. Many agencies also now permit older individuals and single adults to adopt children. A growing number of agencies are also placing children with gay male and lesbian individuals (Brodzinsky, Patterson, and Vaziri, 2001; Patterson, in Vol. 3 of this *Handbook*). Finally, changes in previous policy guidelines regarding adoptions by foster parents have dramatically increased their numbers (Derdeyn, 1990; Haugaard and Hazan, in Vol. 1 of this *Handbook*).

Another significant change in adoption that is radically affecting the way adopted children are being parented is the emergence of open adoption (Baran and Pannor, 1993; Berry, 1993; Grotevant and McRoy, 1998). With the creation of the adoption agency system in the early part of the twentieth century, emphasis was placed on maintaining confidentiality in the adoption process. Adoption records were sealed by law, and birth parents and adoptive parents were prevented from sharing identifying information with one another. As a result, adopted individuals grew up knowing little about their background, having little or no contact with birth family members, and having no access to their original birth certificate. In the 1970s, however, some agencies began to offer the option of open placements, in which birth parents and adoptive parents could meet and share information. In some cases identities are fully disclosed and plans are made for ongoing contact after the adoption placement. Today, there is a discernible trend toward increased openness in adoption, not only in the nature of the adoption placement plan, but also in the laws governing access to adoption records, including the adoptee's original birth certificate (Silverman, 2001).

In summary, adoption today has changed dramatically from its earlier focus. Recent developments in adoption policy, practice, and law highlight the growing complexity in this social service field. This fact alone makes it difficult to generalize about the challenges of parenting adopted children, as well as the possible outcome for these youngsters.

## ADOPTION: RISK OR BENEFIT FOR CHILDREN

Over the past 40 years, considerable attention has been focused on adoption by child welfare professionals and mental health professionals. The perspectives of these two groups, however, have often differed. On the one hand, child welfare professionals generally have viewed adoption as a solution to a variety of societal problems. As such, these individuals have emphasized the benefits associated with being adopted. In contrast, mental health professionals have been more concerned with the psychological risks associated with being adopted. Although they may appear contradictory, these two faces of adoption actually represent "two sides of the same coin." Moreover, both perspectives appear valid. In an attempt to clear up some of the confusion and misrepresentation that exists in the field, a brief overview of the research underlying each perspective is offered.

### Adoption as a Risk Factor in Children's Development

Within the social sciences, interest in the problems associated with adoption can be traced to the work of Schechter (1960) and Kirk (1964), who were among the first researchers to point out that adoption, although a reasonable option for children in need of out-of-home placement is itself linked to increased risk for adjustment difficulties. Three sources of data address this issue: (1) epidemiological studies on the incidence and prevalence of adoptees in mental health settings; (2) presenting symptomatology of clinical samples of adopted and nonadopted children; and (3) psychological characteristics and adjustment patterns of adopted and nonadopted children in nonclinical, community-based settings.

*Epidemiological studies.* One of the most frequently cited research findings is that adopted children and adolescents are significantly overrepresented in both outpatient and inpatient mental health settings (Ingersoll, 1997; Wierzbicki, 1993). For example, although nonkinship adopted youth represent only ~2% of the population of children, their proportion in outpatient clinical settings has been reported to be between 3% and 13% (Goldberg and Wolkind, 1992; Kotsopoulos et al., 1988; Schechter, 1960). In inpatient mental health settings, adopted children and adolescents constitute between 9% and 21% of this population (Dickson, Heffron, and Parker, 1990; Kim, Davenport, Joseph, Zrull, and Woolford, 1988; Rogeness, Hoppe, Macedo, Fischer, and Harris, 1988). Although these data are usually interpreted as indicating more psychological problems among adopted individuals, it has also been noted that adoptive parents may be more willing to refer their children to counseling than nonadoptive parents are (Brodzinsky et al., 1998; Ingersoll, 1997; Warren, 1992). For example, adoptive parents may utilize mental health services more readily than the average parent because of their higher levels of education and income, as well as their familiarity in working with social service professionals and mental health professionals during the preadoption period. Some adoptive parents also may have a negative attributional bias, in which they associate adoption with increased problems (Bugental and Happaney, in Vol. 3 of this *Handbook*). Because their children are adopted, these parents may be primed to identify problems and to utilize mental health services at the first sign of unusual behavior. In addition, parents might seek clinical services because they view the child's problems as a more serious threat to the integrity of the family system. In other words, more tenuous family relationships, coupled with the social stigma associated with adoption, could lead parents to be more reactive to their children's problems, resulting in quicker use of counseling services. Two studies have addressed the question of whether the overrepresentation in mental health counseling among adopted youth reflects greater problem severity among this population or a referral bias on the part of adoptive parents. Drawing on data from different national health surveys of adolescent adjustment, both Warren (1992) and Miller, Fan, Grotevant et al. (2000) found that even when there were no group differences in level of psychological problems, adopted children were more likely than nonadopted children to be referred for counseling by their parents. On the other hand, both groups of researchers reported that serious psychological problems, which were found more often among adopted children, also resulted in greater use of mental health services. In short, these researchers concluded that the overrepresentation of adoptees in outpatient and inpatient clinical settings results both from a greater degree of psychological problems as well as from a greater propensity on the part of adoptive parents to utilize counseling services.

*Clinical studies.*   When seen in clinical settings, are adopted children more likely to manifest specific types of adjustment difficulties compared with those of nonadopted children or are these groups similar in their presenting symptomatology? This question has been the focus of considerable research.

Adopted children are at increased risk for academic problems and learning disabilities (Silver, 1989) and are more likely to be classified for educational purposes as neurologically impaired, perceptually impaired, or emotionally disturbed (Brodzinsky and Steiger, 1991). Adopted children also are overrepresented among those youngsters diagnosed with externalizing symptoms, including attention deficit hyperactivity disorder (Deutsch et al., 1982), oppositionalism and disruptive conduct problems (Fullerton, Goodrich, and Berman, 1986; Kotsopoulos et al., 1988; Kotsopoulos, Walker, Copping, Cote, and Stavrakaki, 1993; Weiss, 1985), and substance abuse (Marshall, Marshall, and Heer, 1994). In contrast, there are few differences among these groups in internalizing disorders such as depresson and anxiety (Kotsopoulos et al., 1988, 1993; Rogeness et al., 1988) or psychotic disorders (Fullerton et al., 1986; Goldberg and Wolkind, 1992; Rogeness et al., 1988).

Other factors also differentiate adopted and nonadopted children who are seen in clinical settings. First, relative to nonadoptees, adopted youth tend to be younger on first admission to a psychiatric facility and are more likely to have had a previous hospitalization for mental health problems (Dickson et al., 1990; Weiss, 1985). They also tend to have longer stays in the hospital (Dickson et al., 1990) and to run away more often from an inpatient facility (Fullerton et al., 1986). As noted previously, adoptive parents are quicker to refer their children for clinical services than nonadoptive parents are (Miller, Fan, Grotevant et al., 2000; Warren, 1992). Furthermore, Cohen, Coyne, and Duvall (1993) reported that the problems of adopted children were less likely to be associated with general marital and family dysfunction than were the problems of nonadopted children and that adoptive parents were more likely to endorse biological and early experience factors as explanations for their children's problems. They also were more likely to consider removing the child from the home as a solution to problems. From a clinical perspective, these latter findings raise concerns about how adoptive parents view their parental role in the emergence of their children's adjustment difficulties. If reliable, these findings suggest that, when adopted children develop adjustment difficulties, parents may be more prone to make the child and others in the child's past scapegoats than to see their own role in the child's and the family's problems.

*Community-based studies.*   Because of the small sample sizes typically associated with clini-cal studies, as well as the inherent difficulty in generalizing the findings from clinical research to the broader population of adopted children and their families, a growing number of researchers have begun to examine the behavioral and personality characteristics and adjustment patterns of adopted and nonadopted children in nonclinical, community settings. These studies have yielded less con-sistent findings than those of the clinic-based data regarding psychological risk associated with adoption.

Regarding infant-placed children, few, if any, significant differences have been found between adopted and nonadopted infants, toddlers, and preschoolers in such areas as temperament (Carey, Lipton, and Myers, 1974), mother–infant attachment (Singer, Brodzinsky, Ramsey, Steir, and Waters, 1985), mental and motor functioning (Plomin and DeFries, 1985), and communication develop-ment (Thompson and Plomin, 1988). Other studies with older participants also have failed to find differences between adopted and nonadopted children and adolescents (Benson, Sharma, and Roehlkepartain, 1994; Borders, Black, and Pasley, 1998; Stein and Hoopes, 1985), and in two cases, adoptees have even been found to be doing better than their nonadopted agemates in terms of more internal locus of control and more positive views of their parenting (Marquis and Detweiler, 1985), as well as higher ratings for prosocial behavior (adopted girls only) and lower ratings for social problems and withdrawn behavior (Sharma, McGue, and Benson, 1996a).

In contrast to these studies, a growing body of nonclinical, community-based research, in which both cross-sectional and longitudinal designs are used, has found adopted children and teenagers to manifest a higher level of academic, behavioral, and psychological problems compared with nonadopted children (Bohman, 1970; Braungart-Rieker, Rende, Plomin, DeFries, and Fulker, 1995; Brodzinsky, Hitt, and Smith, 1993; Brodzinsky, Radice, Huffman, and Merkler, 1987; Brodzinsky, Schechter, Braff, and Singer, 1984; Coon, Carey, Corley, and Fulker, 1992; Deater-Deckard and Plomin, 1999; Fergusson, Lynskey, and Horwood, 1995; Miller, Fan, Christensen, Grotevant, and van Dulmen, 2000; Sharma et al., 1996a; Sharma, McGue, and Benson, 1998). In most cases, the problems were greatest in areas measuring school adjustment and externalizing symptoms such as impulsive and hyperactive behavior, conduct problems, and substance use. Furthermore, age at placement, preplacement history, and gender have often been found to be moderator variables in relation to adjustment outcome—that is, they influence the direction or the strength of the relationship between adoption and adjustment. Being of an older age at the time of placement (Pinderhughes, 1998; Sharma, McGue, and Benson, 1996b), having more adverse preplacement experiences, such as multiple changes in caregiving environment, as well as being neglected or abused (Barth and Berry, 1988; Pinderhughes, 1998; Verhulst, Althaus, and Versluis-den Bieman, 1992), and being a boy (Brodzinsky et al., 1993; Miller, Fan, Christensen et al., 2000; Seglow, Pringle, and Wedge, 1972) have been associated with greater adjustment problems.

Although the bulk of the research supports the view that adopted children and youth have greater adjustment problems than their nonadopted counterparts do, it is important to emphasize that the vast majority of adoptees are well within the normal range. Moreover, even when signficant group differences do emerge, the effect size, which measures the extent of difference between the groups on outcome variables, typically is only small to moderate in magnitude (Miller, Fan, Christensen et al., 2000). In an attempt to reconcile the discrepancy between the large group differences in utilization of clinical services and the small, but signficant, group differences in various measures of academic and psychological adjustment, Haugaard (1998) suggested that adopted and nonadopted youth show different patterns of adjustment on outcome variables primarily near the tails of the score distribution. In other words, he speculated that there was little difference between the groups in the middle range of scores, but as one moved further toward the tails of the score distribution, group differences should become more pronounced. Two studies have supported Haugaard's theoretical analysis. In a comparison of adopted teenagers with their nonadopted siblings, Sharma et al. (1996a) found that in the midrange of the distribution for total problems and illicit drug use, there was a 1:1 ratio for the two groups, whereas in the upper tails of these distributions, the ratio of adopted to birth siblings was more than 3:1. Similarly, Miller, Fan, Christensen et al. (2000) found that the more extreme the percentile examined, the greater the proportion of adopted to nonadopted adolescents for the negative outcome measures studied. In some cases (e.g., drinking alcohol, getting drunk, skipping school), the ratio of adopted to nonadopted teenagers was 10:1.

In summary, the research literature generally suggests that, although most adopted children do quite well, as a group they manifest a higher level of adjustment problems than their nonadopted peers do. But who are these peers? This question brings us back to some of the confusion regarding the issue of whether adoption is a benefit or a risk factor in children's lives.

## Adoption as a Protective Factor in Children's Development

In almost all adoption research, the comparison group comprises children from the same type of community or socioeconomic level that currently characterizes the adoptive family. Yet is this the most appropriate comparison? It is, if the question of interest is whether adoptees are adjusting as well as their current peers—that is, the children with whom the adoptee goes to school, plays with, competes against, and the like. However, this is not the appropriate comparison group if the question of interest is whether adoption, as a social service practice, protects children from the type of physical, social, emotional, and economic trauma that often characterizes their early life and the life of the birth family.

Two important considerations must be kept in mind when the question of adoption as a protective factor is addressed: First, most children move up the socioeconomic ladder when they are adopted. In other words, adoptive parents, on average, are at a more financial and material advantage than are the birth parents of adopted children. In turn, these advantages may well provide opportunities for adopted children that they are unlikely to experience if they continue to live with their biological family. Second, most children who are adopted move from a home setting characterized by insecurity, instability, and a lack of adequate stimulation and nurturance to an environment more often characterized by greater security, stability, stimulation, and nurturance. Therefore, in examining whether adoption is a protective factor, one must compare long-term outcome for adoptees with youngsters from backgrounds similar to those characterized by the adoptees' birth families, as well as to youngsters who remain in foster care or grow up in institutional environments.

A number of studies from the United States, England, Scotland, France, Sweden, and India have compared the adjustment of adopted children with that of several other groups of youngsters living under more adverse social conditions, including children residing in long-term foster care, children in institutional environments, or children living with biological parents who come from disadvantaged backgrounds similar to that of the birth families of the adoptees (Bharat, 1997; Bohman, 1970; Bohman and Sigvardsson, 1990; Dumaret, 1985; Hodges and Tizard, 1989; Maughan and Pickles, 1990; Scarr and Weinberg, 1983; Triseliotis and Hill, 1990; Weinberg, Scarr, and Waldman, 1992). Bohman and his colleagues (Bohman, 1970; Bohman and Sigvardsson, 1990) were also able to compare the adjustment of adopted children with that of youngsters whose biological parents originally had registered them for adoption, but subsequently changed their minds and reared the children themselves. The results of these studies are consistent and telling. First, in each of the studies in which the appropriate comparison was made, adopted children fared significantly better than children who resided in long-term foster care or in institutional-type environments. This result is not surprising and forms the rationale for the emphasis on permanency planning within the child welfare system. Adopted children also fared significantly better than children who were reared by biological parents who either did not want them or showed ambivalence about keeping them. In addition, adopted children were found to display better adjustment than those youngsters living with biological parents whose disadvantaged socioeconomic status was similar to that of the adoptees' own birth families. Although the latter finding should not be interpreted as suggesting that children be removed from their birth families simply because they are living in conditions of poverty, it does suggest that one benefit of adoption is that it can, when appropriate, provide a more advantageous environment for children, which in turn, may well have positive effects on development and adjust-ment (see Hoksbergen, 1999, for a review of the literature on the protective function of adoption).

Finally, research on the adoption of children who are prenatally exposed to drugs and/or alcohol also points to the benefits associated with this form of substitute family life (Barth, Freundlich, and Brodzinsky, 2000). Although past research suggested that infants who are exposed prenatally to various types of illicit drugs suffer devastating, long-term neurobehavioral deficits affecting cognitive, social, and emotional areas of functioning (Chasnoff, Anson, and Moss Iaukea, 1998; Freundlich, 2000; Lester, LaGasse, and Seifer, 1998), Barth and his colleagues (Barth and Brooks, 2000; Barth and Needell, 1996) have shown that placement of these youngsters in a stable and nurturing adoptive home often can significantly reduce the adverse effects of prenatal substance exposure.

Taken as a whole, these research studies provide clear and convincing evidence that adoption can, and usually does, serve as a protective factor in the life of the child whose biological parents cannot or will not provide an appropriate childrearing environment.

## ADOPTIVE FAMILY LIFE CYCLE

Adoptive families, like all other families, progress through various life cyle stages characterized by specific patterns of family structure and age-specific functional tasks that serve as the focal point for family interaction, contributing to the growth and the development of all family members (Brodzinsky 1987; Brodzinsky, Lang, and Smith, 1995; Rosenberg, 1992). Although most of the tasks experienced by adoptive families are similar to those encountered by nonadoptive families, there are unique issues confronting adoptive parents and their children at each stage of the family life cycle. Among the many adoption-related tasks experienced by parents during the course of rearing their children are those associated with the decision to adopt and the initial adjustment to adoptive parenthood, discussing adoption with their child, supporting the child's curiosity about the birth family, helping their child cope with adoption-related loss, supporting a positive view of the child's origins, fostering a positive self-image and identity in their child in relation to adoption, and, in some cases, especially as the adoptee moves into adolescence and adulthood, supporting the decision to search for the birth family.

### The Decision to Adopt a Child

Approximately 95% of newly married couples want and expect to have a child biologically (Glick, 1977). Yet nearly one in six couples will experience a fertility problem (Mosher and Pratt, 1990). When faced with the challenge of infertility, which often is experienced as a major personal and relationship crisis (Leiblum, 1997), couples are forced to confront the meaning and the value of becoming a parent, as well as the steps they are willing to take to achieve the goal of having a child. Many individuals will pursue lengthy, expensive, and, at times, intrusive medical interventions, and ultimately will be successful in conceiving a child biologically. Yet for others, with the passage of time and the continuing failure of infertility treatments, there will be a growing recognition that biological parenthood will not be achieved. For those individuals who continue to want to be parents, other options are considered, including adoption.

Daly (1988, 1990) pointed out that many couples need to "let go" of the biological parenthood identity before they can begin to identify themselves as adoptive parents, whereas other couples are able to pursue both goals simultaneously. For the latter individuals, the primary concern is becoming a parent—the means by which this goal is achieved is less important. Although traditional social casework philosophy suggests that the decision to adopt a child, as well as the success of the adoption placement, rests largely on the extent to which the couple has resolved their feelings about infertility, research and clinical work has found that infertility resolution is not necessarily a prerequisite for a couple's readiness to adopt (Brodzinsky, 1997; Lorber and Greenfield, 1989). In fact, Brodzinsky

(1997, p. 259) suggested that it is "unrealistic to assume that infertility is ever *completely* resolved . . . Instead, the goal of griefwork in dealing with infertility is best understood to be the achievement of a reasonably comfortable way of incorporating this painful loss into a healthy and functional sense of self." Still, although the ability to commit to adopt a child may not require a full resolution of one's feelings about infertility, failure to adequately confront this issue openly and honestly has been linked by numerous adoption theorists and clinicians to postplacement parenting issues and family conflicts (Blum, 1983; Brinich, 1990; Kirk, 1964; Schechter, 1970), including problems associated with compromised feelings of entitlement and attachment to the child, unrealistic expectations regarding the child, difficulty in discussing adoption and coping with the child's curiosity about the birth family, and difficulty in handling adolescent separation and individuation (Brodzinsky, 1997).

## Becoming an Adoptive Parent

Although the transition to parenthood, even for biological parents, has often been viewed as a period of normative crisis, requiring considerable adjustment to increased daily stress (Heinicke, in Vol. 3 of this *Handbook*), becoming an adoptive parent involves even more demands on the individual and the couple (Brodzinsky, 1987; Brodzinsky and Huffman, 1988; Kirk, 1964). To begin with, only adoptive parents require the approval of others before they are able to achieve their goal of parenthood. In most cases, they must submit an application to an adoption agency and undergo an in-depth evaluation—called a homestudy—in order to prove their fitness to be parents. Although the homestudy is intended to educate people and support them in the adoption process, many prospective adoptive parents continue to experience the historical *evaluative* legacy of this practice, which often results in increased anxiety and diminished self-confidence. Furthermore, the fact that there is a probationary period—usually no less than 6 months—that precedes legal finalization of the parent–child relationship serves only to heighten the anxiety of many adoptive parents. Depending on state law and the way in which the infant relinquishment has occurred—that is, through an adoption agency or privately through an intermediary—the child's birth parents may have the right to revoke their consent for adoption during this period, as seen in a number of highly publicized court cases over the past two decades. The knowledge that a placement can be disrupted by circumstances beyond their control prevents some adoptive parents from forming emotional connections to their child as quickly or deeply as they otherwise might.

Another complication in the transition to adoptive parenthood is the uncertain time line that characterizes this process. Unlike pregnancy, the duration of the adoption process is highly variable, ranging from a few months, for a few fortunate individuals, to one or more years for most adoption applicants. The uncertainty of the waiting period often fosters distress, confusion, and feelings of helplessness among prospective adoptive couples. In addition, many agencies are now following the practice of providing birth parents with packets of information about prospective adoptive families and allowing them to choose the individuals who will receive their child. Although this practice is thought to empower the birth parent, leading to fewer postplacement adjustment problems, it may well disempower those prospective adoptive applicants who remain on the agency's waiting list for some time without being chosen by a birth mother.

Adoption also is characterized by social stigma in our society (Kirk, 1964; Miall, 1987), with most people, including many adoption applicants, believing that it is a "second-best" route to parenthood. Consequently, when announcing their intention to adopt a child, prospective adoptive individuals are less likely to receive unqualified support from their extended family, especially when their decision involves adopting across racial lines (Singer et al., 1985) or a child with special needs. In turn, this experience can increase parental resentment, decrease self-confidence and a sense of entitlement to the child, and accentuate parental feelings of "differentness." Furthermore, because adoption is a relatively uncommon way of achieving parenthood, adoptive parents also have fewer readily available role models to turn to when they have questions concerning childrearing issues, especially those related to adoption. Without adequate information and feedback from others, adoptive parents may develop unrealistic expectations concerning their children's behavior and initial adjustment to the family, which can make this process even more stressful than it need be.

Once the child has been placed in the family, parents begin the process of creating a caregiving environment that promotes a healthy and stable parent–child bond. Security in attachment is facilitated when parents are emotionally attuned to the needs of their child and when there is a good match between parental expectations and the child's characteristics and behavior. Although research generally has found little difference in the quality of attachment between infant-placed adopted children and their mothers compared with nonadopted mother–infant dyads (Singer et al., 1985), for some families, the attachment process can be compromised when parents have difficulty claiming the child as their own, either because of unresolved infertility issues, lack of support from family and friends, and/or when their expectations about the child have not been met (Butler, 1989; Rosenberg, 1992). That adopted children are more likely to be born to adults who manifest biologically based psychological problems (Cadoret, 1990; Loehlin, Willerman, and Horn, 1985) and are more likely to experience problems prenatally (Bohman, 1970; McRoy, Grotevant, and Zurcher, 1988) further increases the chances of attachment-related difficulties through a poor match between parental expectations and child characteristics. Finally, risk for attachment problems also increases when children are placed for adoption beyond the early infancy period, experience multiple caregivers, or live in neglectful or abusive conditions before adoption placement (Chisolm, Carter, Ames, and Morison, 1995; Fisher, Ames, Chisolm, and Savoie, 1997; Johnson and Fein, 1991; Yarrow and Goodwin, 1973).

Although the challenges faced by adoptive parents in the early period of the family life cycle are greater, on average, compared with those faced by nonadoptive parents, there are also a number of factors that help buffer the adoptive couple from these unique stressors, leading to quite positive outcomes in postplacement child, parent, and family adjustment (Brodzinsky and Huffman, 1988). To begin with, adoptive couples usually are older than nonadoptive couples when they first become parents, and they are more likely to be settled into their careers and to be more financially secure. They also have been married longer before becoming parents than nonadoptive couples, which may be associated with greater marital sensitivity, communication, and stress management. In addition, in response to the extended period of frustration and emotional pain associated with infertility, the adoptive couple is likely to feel a powerful sense of fulfillment with the arrival of a child, which in turn, may serve as a protective factor in handling the unique stresses associated with the early phase of adoptive family life. Finally, the need to work with adoption agencies in order to become parents, while fostering some resentment and reinforcing a feeling of being different among some couples, also has a beneficial impact on adoptive parents in that they often have more formal preparation for the transition to parenthood than nonadoptive couples. This education and support is particularly beneficial in facilitating more realistic parental expectations, especially in situations in which the child presents with special needs (Glidden, 1991).

In one of the few empirical studies comparing the transition to parenthood for adoptive and nonadoptive couples, Levy-Shiff and her colleagues confirmed that, despite the added stresses associated with adoption, most adoptive parents do quite well in this early phase of family life and, in some areas, fare even better than biological parents (Levy-Shiff, Bar, and Har-Even, 1990; Levy-Shiff, Goldschmidt, and Har-Even, 1991). For example, before the arrival of the child, no differences were found between the groups of parents on measures of ego strength or coping style. On the other hand, prospective adoptive mothers reported less depression and higher scores on some measures of self-concept than pregnant mothers did. Prospective adoptive parents also expressed greater marital satisfaction and perceived greater social support from community resources (i.e., social service agencies) than did biological parents-to-be. Furthermore, they had more positive expectations about the effects of having a child in their lives, which in turn was associated with greater perceived loss that was due to infertility. Finally, 4 months after the arrival of the child, adoptive parents reported better coping with the physical demands of parenthood and more satisfaction with their parental role compared with those of biological parents. Although these results suggest that most individuals who adopt infants make the transition to adoptive family life quite well, Levy-Shiff and her colleagues cautioned that this pattern of positive adjustment may reflect a "honeymoon" period (Schechter, 1970) before the onset of more serious challenges at later stages of the family life cycle.

## Parenting the Preschool Adopted Child

The advent of language and symbolic thought during the toddler and the preschool years paves the way for adoptive parents to begin the process of sharing adoption information with their child (Edwards and Liu, in Vol. 1 of this *Handbook*). Unfortunately, there is often a great deal of confusion and anxiety among adoptive parents as they begin this process. Whereas previously the primary foci of the couple were on *integrating* the child into the family and fostering a strong and secure parent–child bond, there is now a growing recognition that they will have to begin a process of *family differentiation*. This is the developmental period in which most parents begin to talk to their children about adoption (Brodzinsky, Schechter, and Henig, 1992). Children are told of their connection to two families—one that is familiar and the source of their emotional security; the other that is unknown, but the source of their biological origins. Questions concerning what information to share, when to share it, and how the telling process will have an impact on the child abound during this phase of family life. Although not as common today as in the past, some parents consciously decide not to tell their children about the adoption, which is believed to increase the psychological risk for these youngsters should they find out at some later date that their parents lied about the nature of family relationships (Sorosky, Baran, and Pannor, 1978). Other parents, fearing how their child will react to the information, procrastinate and delay the adoption revelation process. Furthermore, when they do begin discussing adoption with the child, these same parents often appear very unsure of themselves, seek to "get through" the telling process as quickly as possible, and minimize any differences between adoptive and nonadoptive family life (Kirk, 1964). In many cases, these parents have not adequately coped with the reality of their infertility or its meaning in their lives, which makes it difficult for them to accept the lack of a biological connection between themselves and their child (Brodzinsky, 1997).

Although disclosing adoption information during the preschool years does not appear to undermine children's psychological adjustment or to disrupt parent–child attachments (Brodzinsky et al., 1998), as some parents fear, it also does not lead to much genuine understanding about adoption, which can be quite confusing to parents who often overestimate their child's adoption knowledge (Brodzinsky, 1983). Once the telling process begins, parents typically report a growing curiosity on the part of children about birth and reproduction, as well as the source of their origins. During this period, children usually begin to label themselves as adopted and quickly learn their "adoption story," at least in some rudimentary form. These accomplishments very often lead parents to assume that their children have at least a basic understanding about adoption. Yet Brodzinsky and his colleagues (Brodzinsky, Schechter, and Brodzinsky, 1986; Brodzinsky, Singer, and Braff, 1984) have shown that this early adoption knowledge is quite superficial and that it is not until 5 to 7 years of age that most children even begin to clearly differentiate between birth and adoption as alternative ways of entering a family. It is this growing awareness of the meaning and the implications of being adopted that sets the stage for the emergence of adoption-related adjustment problems (Brodzinsky et al., 1992, 1998).

## Parenting the School-Age Adopted Child

During middle childhood, roughly when children are between 6 and 12 years of age, a number of important achievements occur in the development of logical reasoning, social cognition, social problem solving, and self-reflection that set the stage for profound changes in the way children understand, and adjust to, adoption (Brodzinsky, 1990, 1993; Brodzinsky et al., 1986, 1998; Brodzinsky, Singer, and Braff, 1984; Collins, Madsen, and Susman-Stillman, in Vol. 1 of this *Handbook*). Based, in part, on their greater comprehension of birth and reproduction (Bernstein and Cowan, 1975) as well as on their developing understanding of what constitutes a family (Newman, Roberts, and Syre, 1993), children now begin to express much more curiosity about their origins: *Where did I come from? What did my birthmother and birthfather look like? Why didn't they keep me? Where are they now? Do I have any brothers and sisters? Can I meet them?* These are some of the questions that emerge when children begin to have a deeper understanding of adoption. School-age children also begin to examine the dilemma faced by birth parents regarding the relinquishment decision and question whether other options might have been chosen. They may ask the following kinds of questions: *If she didn't know how to care for me, why didn't someone help her? If she was poor and didn't have any money, why didn't she get a job?* For some children, the explanations offered by adoptive parents regarding the basis for the relinquishment are no longer as easily accepted as they once were.

The growth of logical thinking also sensitizes children to the inherent loss associated with adoption. For example, to be adopted, one first must be relinquished. As children become more attuned to the nature of logically reciprocal relationships, they begin to appreciate that adoption means not only *gaining* a family, but *losing* one as well. Furthermore, with time, adoption-related loss can become quite profound and include not only the loss of birth parents, birth siblings, and extended birth family, but also status loss associated with adoption-related stigma. In addition, as children get older, they may begin to experience loss of cultural, ethnic, and/or racial heritage, loss of genealogical connections, and loss of identity. Children who have been adopted transracially also experience loss of privacy because of their inability to keep the fact of their adoption from others. According to Brodzinsky (1987, 1990, 1993; Smith and Brodzinsky, 1994), it is the experience of loss that ultimately leads to a sense of ambivalence about being adopted, as well as to the emergence of adoption adjustment problems.

The many changes that children are going through during this period regarding adoption can be quite confusing and pose significant challenges for parents. To begin with, parents must recognize that the child's growing ambivalence about being adopted is perfectly normal. It represents neither a failure of parenting nor an indication of psychopathology on the part of the child. Rather, the child's sense of ambivalence reflects a grief reaction that emerges when the child begins to focus on the inherent loss associated with adoption. Part of the problem for parents is that, in many cases, adoption-related loss is quite subtle. In such situations, unless the child is open with parents about her or his thoughts and feelings, the confusion and/or distress the youngster experiences in relation to adoption may be overlooked or diminished in importance. If this happens, the ability of the child to cope with adoption-related grief may be compromised.

During this stage of the family life cycle, parents must be able to create a caregiving environment that supports their children's growing curiosity regarding their origins, reinforces a respectful view of the birth family and their heritage, maintains open communication about adoption issues, and supports their children's grief work in relation to adoption. In research on the adoptive family system, Kirk (1964) argued that success in achieving these goals is based on the parents' ability to accept an "acknowledgment-of-difference" perspective in understanding adoptive family relationships. In other words, creating an open, nondefensive approach to adoption is facilitated when parents recognize and accept that their child is inextricably linked to two families and that the nature of adoptive family life, for all the similarities it shares with nonadoptive family life, has many unique aspects to it that will color the nature of individual patterns of adjustment and family relationships. In contrast, assuming a "rejection-of-difference" perspective on the part of adoptive parents is thought to create barriers in the family system for discussing adoption openly, honestly, and in a nondefensive way. In such cases, children will have more difficulty expressing their curiosity about their origins and parents will experience their children's questions about adoption as more of a threat to the integrity of the family system. The outcome, according to Kirk, is a breakdown in communication about adoption and an increase in risk for adjustment problems among family members. Although Kirk's views on the dynamics of the adoptive family system have been widely accepted, there actually has been little effort to validate his theory empirically. Furthermore, several groups of researchers (Brodzinsky, 1987; Kaye, 1990; Talen, Pinderhughes, and Groze, 1995) have offered a modification to Kirk's theory, suggesting that family maladjustment is more often associated with extreme communication patterns at either end of the acknowledgment continuum. In other words, adoptive parents who strongly deny differences or who overemphasize differences (called insistence-of-difference by Brodzinsky, 1987) in family discussions about adoption are more likely to create an atmosphere conducive to family dysfunction than are parents who are more moderate in their acknowledgment of family differences.

In summary, the middle childhood phase of the family life cycle presents parents with a number of challenges in relation to coping with adoption. Of greatest importance at this time is the need to facilitate openness in communication within the family and to guard against creating a rigid, impermeable psychological barrier between the biological and the adoptive families, which can present the child with a dilemma of divided loyalties (Butler, 1989). Although most parents appear quite successful in handling these parenting tasks, some are not. It is in the latter case that we begin to see more serious problems in children's adoption adjustment.

## Parenting the Adopted Adolescent

Adolescence brings with it a host of developmental changes that have important implications for all family members as teenagers and their parents continue to cope with issues related to adoption (Steinberg and Silk, in Vol. 1 of this *Handbook*). The emergence of abstract thinking allows adoptees to understand their unique family status in more complex ways, including the biological, sexual, relational, sociocultural, and legal implications of adoption (Brodzinsky, Singer, and Braff, 1984). This new awareness not only reaffirms the biological connection to individuals other than the adoptive parents, but for many adoptees raises questions, perhaps for the first time, about the biological origins of various physical and psychological characteristics that differentiate them from adoptive family members (Brodzinsky et al., 1992). Many adopted teenagers become preoccupied with the lack of physical resemblance between themselves and others in the family. For these youngsters, the inability to look into the faces of their adoptive parents and siblings and see reflections of themselves—something that is typically taken for granted in biological families—is often experienced as disconcerting. In fact, Raynor (1980) reported that both adoptees and their parents were more satisfied with their adoptive experience when they were able to perceive, or imagine, physical resemblance between them.

Perhaps the most significant issue confronting adopted adolescents is the development of a stable and secure ego identity (Brodzinsky, 1987; Brodzinsky et al., 1992; Grotevant, 1997; Grotevant, Dunbar, Kohler, and Esau, 2000; Hoopes, 1990; Sorosky, Baran, and Pannor, 1975; Stein and Hoopes, 1985). According to Grotevant et al. (2000), the adoptive identity is composed of three parts. The first is the intrapsychic component that involves the cognitive and affective processes associated with the self-constructed meaning and salience of adoption in the life of the person. Whereas some individuals find little or no meaning in the fact that they are adopted and are uninterested in exploring this aspect of their identity, others display an intense curiosity about their adoption and view it as one of the core features of who they are. For the majority of individuals, however, adoption, although quite meaningful to them, occupies a more balanced place in their emerging identity. The second component of adoptive identity involves its meaning in the context of family memberships. As noted previously, some families create open communicative systems in which questions and information about adoption flow easily back and forth among family members, whereas in other families, there are attitudinal, emotional, relational and informational barriers that impede communication about adoption. The extent of openness about adoption among family members influences the individual and co-constructed meaning and salience attributed to adoption in the identity of each family member. The third component of adoptive identity involves the internalization of meaning within the context of sociocultural forces. The feedback that adopted individuals receive about their unique family status from peers, teachers, and society in general greatly influences self-perception and identity development during this period of life. The experience of being accepted by others as an adopted person and fitting into the community is likely to enhance self-esteem and foster a more secure sense of self. Conversely, negative feedback about adoption or feeling out of place in the community, as is often the case for a transracially adopted minority member living in a predominantly European American neighborhood, may well undermine the construction of a stable and secure ego identity.

Integrating the past into the present and imagining oneself in the future is another component of identity that may be more complicated for adopted adolescents. According to Sants (1964), because adoptees have been cut off from their origins and are often prevented from gaining relevant information about themselves, they frequently experience confusion and uncertainty about their place within a genealogical line—a condition known as genealogical bewilderment. Sants suggested that the lack of "biological mutuality" among adoptive family members—that is, shared biologically based characteristics, including appearance, intellectual skills, talents, personality traits, and so forth—impedes the teenager's ability to identify with adoptive parents.

In rearing adopted youth, parents must be aware of these many complexities and provide their teenagers with the support they need to cope with these adoption-related tasks. They must recognize that the search for origins, which began earlier in the form of questions about the birth family and the reasons for the relinquishment, is likely to continue in one form or another in the adolescent years. For some adolescents, the search may include developing plans for gaining more information about their origins, visiting their place of birth, or even making contact with birth parents and birth siblings. The need for information and/or contact with the birth family is highly variable among adopted adolescents and adults (Schechter and Bertocci, 1990). What is important for parents to recognize is that such an interest is a normal part of the adoption adjustment process. It does not reflect psychopathology. On the other hand, whether adoptive parents decide to support an active search for additional information and/or birth family during this period of life must be a decision based on a thoughtful consideration of their child's motivation to search, emotional maturity, outcome expectations, and any existing knowledge of the birth family's life circumstances. Although clinical and casework experience suggests that a growing number of adopted adolescents are being supported by their parents as well as by adoption agencies in a search for their origins, relatively little has been written about the process of searching by minors (Brodzinsky et al., 1998). Furthermore, there are no published studies on the outcome of searching during the teenage years, although the data suggest generally favorable outcomes—in terms of feelings of satisfaction—among adopted adults who have been reunited with their birth family (Schechter and Bertocci, 1990).

Although individuals and couples who adopt children in infancy face many different challenges in rearing their youngsters at each stage of the family life cycle, the issues faced by parents who adopt children with special needs, youngsters of a different race, and/or children from other countries are even more complex. Furthermore, many adoption professionals have suggested that the movement toward open adoption may pose added challenges for rearing adopted children. In the following sections, we examine the unique parenting challenges and outcomes for children in relation to adoption of children with special needs, transracial adoption, intercountry adoption, and open adoption.

## SPECIAL NEEDS ADOPTION

In the 1960s and 1970s, increases in teenage pregnancy, illicit drug use, and a growing problem with urban poverty, coupled with the passage of mandatory child abuse reporting laws, resulted in substantially greater numbers of children entering the child welfare system (Downs, Moore, McFadden, and Costin, 2000). Although foster care was historically conceptualized as a temporary placement for children who could not live at home because of parental inadequacy or maltreatment, by the end of the 1970s, there were over 500,000 children in the foster care system, many of whom had been lingering in foster homes for years (Haugaard and Hazan, in Vol. 1 of this *Handbook*). In an effort to remedy this problem, Congress passed the Adoption Assistance and Child Welfare Act of 1980. This legislation was based on the principle of "permanency planning" and mandated public child welfare agencies to take prompt and decisive action to maintain or reunify children with their biological families or place them permanently with other families. As a result of this Act, the number of children in foster care was significantly reduced and there was a dramatic increase in the number of special needs adoptions, that is, adoptions involving children manifesting characteristics that, in the past, delayed or impeded adoptive placement. These characteristics include older age (usually over the age of 4 years), serious emotional and behavioral problems, developmental disabilities and serious medical conditions, minority group status, sibling group membership, and foster care status. Unfortunately, the initial success of the permanency planning programs could not be sustained, and from the mid-1980s to the mid-1990s, the number of children in foster care once again began to rise, culminating in over 500,000 children in care. In response to this social problem, the Clinton administration initiated two new policy directives—the Adoption and Safe Families Act of 1997 and the Adoption 2002 Initiative. Both of these legislative efforts served to refocus the child welfare system on moving children out of foster care and into adoptive homes. In 1998, approximately 36,000 children were adopted from foster care in the United States (Department of Health and Human Services, 2000). With the growth of these types of adoptions has come increased concern about child and family adjustment. In this section, we examine placement outcomes in special needs adoptions and the unique parenting challenges arising in these families.

## Placement Outcomes

Special needs adoptions can be classified into two groups—those involving children with disabilities that have reasonably predictable manifestions (i.e., physical and developmental disabilities, mental retardation, and chronic medical conditions) and those involving children with disabilities that have unpredictable manifestions (i.e., emotional or behavior problems). Generally, adoptions of children with disabilities that have more predictable manifestions tend to be quite successful, as indicated by relatively low rates of placement disruption, whereby the child is removed from the home before to the legal finalization of the parent–child relationship (Rosenthal, 1993). In addition, among intact placements of children with developmental or physical disabilities, parents' satisfaction is usually high and family adjustment is positive (Glidden, 1991, 2000; Rosenthal, 1993). In fact, when compared with a group of birth families of children with developmental disabilities, adoptive parents of children who are developmentally disabled reported significantly less stress in parent, family, and child functioning (Glidden, 1991).

Of greater concern regarding placement outcome are adoptions of children who manifest serious emotional and behavioral problems. Placement disruption rates for these children range from 10% to 20% (Rosenthal, 1993). Older age at the time of placement and/or the presence of severe problems such as chronic stealing, aggressiveness, fire setting, sexual acting out, and suicidal behavior are the most frequent correlates of adoption disruption (Barth and Berry, 1988; Festinger, 1986; Partridge, Hornby, and McDonald, 1986; Rosenthal, 1993). Other factors commonly associated with adoption disruption, as well as postplacement adjustment difficulties, include early environmental adversity such as neglect, physical abuse, sexual abuse, and multiple foster placements (Festinger, 1990; Pinderhughes, 1998). Yet, despite the higher disruption rates and adjustment problems than infant adoptions, the large majority of special needs placements are successful, as measured by family intactness, by parents' and children's reports of satisfaction with the adoption, and by caseworker evaluations of placements (Groze, 1996; Pinderhughes, 1998).

## Parenting the Adopted Child with Special Needs

As adoption agencies began to assume the challenge of finding permanent homes for children lingering in foster care, they were forced to reconsider their assumptions about what constituted an appropriate adoptive parent. Although the selection criteria utilized by adoption agencies in the past eliminated many potential adoptive parents, over the past two decades, these same agencies have become much more inclusive in the adoption recruitment process. Today, parents who adopt children with special needs are quite diverse in their ages, marital status, gender, sexual orientation, financial status, educational level, and ethnicity. Moreover, nontraditional adoptive parents have, on balance, demonstrated quite positive outcomes (Rosenthal, 1993). Minority status, lower income and education levels, older age of parents, and single-parent status, in general, do not increase the risk for disruption. In fact, some of these characteristics may be associated with more favorable outcomes in special needs adoptions (Rosenthal, 1993). For example, it has been suggested that lower-income adoptive parents may have more realistic expectations and greater tolerance than their middle-income and upper-middle-income counterparts do concerning the future adjustment of their children with special needs—especially in relation to school success and job path—which in turn, are likely to lead to less family conflict. In the cases of single and older parents, the lack of difference in placement outcome compared with that of two-parent families and younger parents is all the more remarkable because the former groups are more likely to adopt older, more troubled children (Barth and Berry, 1988; Groze, 1991; Shireman, 1996). Furthermore, despite initial concerns about the lack of adequate screening of foster parents, as well as the inherent conflict between the child's goal of reunification with birth family and the foster parents' hopes of adoption, it is clear that foster parent adoption has been especially successful, even more so than adoptions in which a child is removed from a foster home and placed for adoption with another family (Barth and Berry, 1988).

*Preparation for special needs adoptive parenthood.* Although a majority of families who adopt through licensed agencies receive some formal preparation and education before the placement of the child in the family, this process generally is more involved and more crucial when families decide to take on the responsibility of adopting a child with special needs (Sar, 2000). Preadoption preparation usually begins with the homestudy, which among other things is likely to involve an exploration of the prospective adoptive parents' motivation for adopting a child with special needs, along with their expectations regarding what life with the child will be like. Attendance at group meetings, along with others who are planning special needs adoptions, is also typically part of the preparation process and can be quite useful for discussing common issues associated with these types of placements, including separation and loss, attachment, family communication issues, reaction of others to the adoption, behavior problems and discipline strategies, utilization of supports, and so forth. The final component of preparation occurs when a specific child has been identified for adoption placement with the family and the agency shares the *unique* history of the youngster with the prospective parents, in anticipation of initial visitations and the beginning of integrating the child into the family.

The importance of preparation and education for special needs adoptions cannot be overemphasized. Research has found that the more thorough the preparation, the more realistic the parents' expectations are regarding the adoption, which in turn, is likely to reduce the chances of placement disruption and to increase the chances of positive adjustment among family members (Barth and Berry, 1988; Partridge et al., 1986; Sar, 2000). Preplacement education and support also prepare prospective parents for the many unique parenting challenges they will encounter in rearing their child with special needs.

*Integrating the child into the family.* Any time a child enters a family, the family system must modify its patterns of functioning in order to integrate the new member. Parents assume new roles and responsibilities, children's roles are transformed as their ordinal positions in the family change, dyadic relationships are newly created or altered, and family interactions and routines are disrupted or revised. Although a similar transition occurs when infants are born or adopted into a family, these processes are less predictable and more intense among families who adopt children with special needs. In describing the dilemma faced by parents adopting an older child, Katz (1986, p. 572) noted the following: "Most children placed in middle childhood are neither gratifying to care for nor do they know how to enter into the intense mutuality that comes naturally to the newborn. Instead of a cycle of gratifying the child and feeling gratified themselves, the parents suffer the narcissistic blow of seeing the child's pain and being unable to be the ones who can relieve it."

Even among successful special needs adoptions, the initial integration of the child into the family is often characterized by uncertainty and conflict. Pinderhughes (1996) described four stages through which the family commonly moves as members cope with the inclusion of a youngster with special needs into their midst. The first stage involves *anticipation*, which is concerned with the family's and the child's expectations and fantasies before the child's actual placement in the home. Next comes *accommodation*, which occurs soon after the child's placement and involves the testing of limits by the child, as well as an exploration of the fit between expectations and reality by all family members. For some, but not all, families, a stage of *resistance* follows, especially when family members become ambivalent about the placement and try to maintain preadoption attitudes and behavior, despite evidence that they are dysfunctional. The final stage, *restabilization*, occurs when the family achieves a new equilibrium in the way members interact with one another. At this point, there is a better fit between expectations and reality for all family members.

Most adopted children with special needs have a history of living in family systems that did not work and consequently may be skeptical of attempts to build family cohesion and connection. Families facilitate integration by helping the child identify the daily routines, family traditions, and family patterns from former placements that give her or him comfort, and by incorporating those into the life of the new family. In addition, parents can help children by focusing on similarities between the child and family members and by modifying nuclear and extended family traditions and rituals to include the child. Finally, new family rituals that focus on adoption, such as celebrating the day the child entered the family, can be created. These efforts can be useful, not only in helping the child to feel integrated into the family, but in facilitating emotional bonds between the child and other family members.

*Forming attachments and supporting the grief process.* The development of an attachment bond between parents and their adopted child with special needs is often complicated by the impact of disrupted relationships from earlier periods in the child's life as well as by heightened parental anxiety or a mismatch between parental expectations and the child's characteristics and behavior. Whereas children adopted within the first 6 months of life tend to show normative patterns of secure attachment with adoptive parents (Juffer and Rosenboom, 1997; Singer et al., 1985), those youngsters placed when they are beyond the age 6 to12 months may be at risk for attachment problems and developmental difficulties (Bowlby, 1973; Yarrow and Goodwin, 1973).

Although most adoption professionals emphasize the importance of attachment in the emotional well-being of adopted children with special needs (Johnson and Fein, 1991; Milan and Pinderhughes, 2000), there is still little research on this issue. In one study of special needs adoptions, Barth and Berry (1988) collected ratings of parent and child behaviors associated with relationship dimensions of reciprocity, exploration, and secure attachment. Their data indicated that adoption disruption was more likely to occur when children were less able to have their needs for attention met by parents, manifested less spontaneous affection with family members, displayed less caring about parents' approval, and manifested less curiosity in family interactions. Yet, despite their previous experience with dysfunctional families, most adoptees with special needs hold positive images of families as sources of love and support (Sherrill and Pinderhughes, 1999). Furthermore, older-placed adopted children also tend to improve their views of their parents as trustworthy and reliable sources of safety as they become more integrated into the family, especially when the parents have been successful in gaining a good understanding of them before the child's actual placement (Pinderhughes, 1999). Finally, although adopted children with special needs may be at greater risk for attachment problems than children placed in infancy or nonadopted children from similar socioeconomic backgrounds, at least one study showed that, in some circumstances, adoptive placement can provide a *protective* environment for the youngster, leading to a more secure parent–child relationship (Hodges and Tizard, 1989). In this study, children who had lived for the first few years of their life in an institution were more successful in forming close relationships with parenting figures when they were placed in adoptive homes as opposed to being returned to their birth families. The researchers attributed this finding to the adoptive parents' greater involvement with their child, as well as their greater tolerance of the child's dependent behavior. Birth parents, in contrast, expected more independence from the child, spent less time in shared activities, felt ambivalent toward the child, and guilty about the time the youngster spent in care.

Related to the issue of attachment is the experience of separation and loss, which usually is more acute and obvious in special needs adoptions compared with infant adoptions (Nickman, 1985). Parents of adoptees with special needs must help their children grieve the loss of earlier attachment relationships with birth parents, birth siblings, extended birth family, previous foster family members, and so forth. It is believed by many adoption professionals that learning to cope with these losses is critical for the development of healthy attachments in the adoptive family. Yet, for many adoptive parents, the child's emotional connections to previous birth family and foster family members are experienced as a threat to the integrity and the stability of the family. Consequently adoptive parents tend to minimize the importance of these figures in the child's life and provide little opportunity for the youngster to discuss her or his feelings about being separated from these individuals. In such cases, the chances of coping effectively with adopted-related loss is compromised, leading to increased risk for problems in the adoptive family (Brodzinsky, 1987, 1990; Brodzinsky et al., 1992, 1998; Nickman, 1985; Reitz and Watson, 1992). As children grieve the loss of former relationships and begin to test out new attachments in the adoptive family, their behavior, at times, may become quite unpredictable and confusing and present considerable difficulty for adoptive parents.

*Managing troublesome behaviors.*   Children who currently are available for adoption within the public child welfare system have been described as coming from more problematic families, displaying more troublesome behaviors, and being more difficult to place for adoption than children in the past (Simmons, Allphin, and Barth, 2000). As a result, families adopting older children need to have a good understanding of their youngster's history and current pattern of adjustment, as well as a realistic assessment of the process involved in helping the child become increasingly compliant with parental expectations.

Even if a child with special needs is able to form attachments to new parents, difficulties in interpersonal functioning may persist for several years after placement (Groze, 1996). Behavioral problems, such as hyperactivity, aggression, stealing, fire setting, and sexual acting out, can be particularly detrimental to placements. In fact, these types of problems have been described as the "single largest source of stress for families who adopt older and special needs children" (Rosenthal, 1993, p. 84). Because of their histories with dangerous, unpredictable family situations, older children often enter new adoptive placements with expectations that relationships may be unsafe. As a result, they may manifest behaviors that, while adaptive in previously unsafe situations, differ substantially from the adoptive family's style and expectations. They may withdraw from relationships because they have learned that it is not safe to interact with adults. They may be aggressive as a defense against the belief that the world is a place where adults hurt children. They may constantly "test" their new parents with acting-out behavior—in effect asking *Do you really love me?*, *Will you leave me, too?*. They may display inappropriate sexual behavior because that is how they received attention from adults in the past. They may demonstrate excessive self-reliant behavior, rejecting attempts by parents to nurture them because they have learned to take care of themselves in previous neglectful environments.

Parenting a child with these often entrenched "survival behaviors" requires special skills. Caregivers often find that parenting techniques that were effective with other children may not work with these youngsters. Among the characteristics of adoptive parents often cited as contributing to successful special needs placements are tolerance for ambivalent and negative feelings, a sense of entitlement to care for the child, ability to find happiness in small increments of improvement, flexible expectations, good coping skills, tolerance for rejection, ability to delay parental gratification, good listening skills, a sense of humor, flexible family roles, strong support network, and availability of postplacement social and mental health services (Katz, 1986; Rosenthal, 1993; Smith and Howard, 1999).

Research supports the importance of a number of these characteristics for successful special needs placements. Realistic parental expectations have been linked consistently to more positive adoption outcomes (Barth, 1988; Glidden, 1991; McRoy, 1999). Satisfaction with special needs adoption also has been tied to the parents' capacity to handle troublesome child behavior, including emotional withdrawal and lack of responsivity, as well as acting-out behavior (Rosenthal, Schmidt, and Connor, 1988). In addition, flexible parenting styles and less rigid role models have been associated with lower rates of placement disruption (Festinger, 1986). Flexibility of adoptive fathers, in particular, as assessed by their sense of humor and creative discipline strategies, has been linked to more stable placement outcomes. Indeed, the role of the adoptive father seems to be an especially critical component of special needs placements. When both parents can maintain high levels of parent commitment to their adopted child and the placement, special needs adoptions are more likely to succeed (McRoy, 1999; Partridge et al., 1986). In contrast, negative power-assertive strategies such as scolding, highly controlling behavior, threats and physical punishment (McRoy, 1999), as well as parental inability to maintain warmth and sensitive attitudes in the face of child opposition and/or withdrawal (Rushton, Dance, and Quinton, 2000) are related to less stable placements.

*Maintaining realistic expectations.*   Parents' ability to develop and maintain realistic expectations about the child's current functioning and potential, their own ability to help the child overcome previous problems, and the time frame for integrating the child into the family is one of the most important factors in successfully parenting adopted children with special needs. Expectations formed during the preplacement preparation process are crucial and reflect a level of understanding of the child attained by parents before the youngster's actual arrival (Sar, 2000). Research indicates that adoptions are more likely to disrupt if a child is considerably different from what parents had expected (Barth, 1988; Nelson, 1985) and are more likely to remain intact if parents are able to choose a child based on preferred child characteristics (Partridge et al., 1986) or come to understand the child well before the placement is made (Barth, 1988; Pinderhughes, 1999).

The importance of realistic expectations and understanding the child is underscored by research on adoption of children with developmental disabilities or chronic medical conditions. With predictable manifestations of the disability, parents who are fully informed about their adopted child's condition are able to more realistically anticipate problems and tend to report more satisfaction and more positive family adjustment (Glidden, 1991, 2000). Adoptive parents also reported less stress in parent, family, and child functioning than did a comparison group of birth parents of children with developmental disabilities (Glidden, 1991). One explanation for such results is that adoptive parents of children who are developmentally disabled are likely to have more realistic expectations and a greater sense of control in their transition to parenthood than nonadoptive parents. The former *chose* to adopt a child who was developmentally disabled and were able to prepare for the entrance of the youngster into the family with the assistance of a readily available resource—the adoption agency. In contrast, when a developmentally disabled child is born into a family, there is often shock among family members, followed by efforts to readjust expectations regarding the child and the parenting experience (Hodapp, in Vol. 1 of this *Handbook*). Parents must also grieve the loss of their "ideal" child and begin to learn about the special caregiving needs of their youngster and the resources available to assist them. In this regard, adoptive parents of developmentally disabled children are often a step ahead of their nonadoptive counterparts.

For parents to enter into an adoption with realistic expectations, they must be provided with accurate child-specific background information before placement (Sar, 2000). Unfortunately, many parents do not feel sufficiently prepared by adoption agencies to rear their child with special needs (Nelson, 1985; Rosenthal, Groze, and Morgan, 1996). In a follow-up study of 927 older child adoptions, it was found that provision of insufficient or inaccurate (usually overly optimistic) information about a child was associated with "low-risk" placements that disrupted, whereas placements considered "high risk" were less likely to disrupt when parents were given a complete and realistic assessment of the child's history and current behavior (Barth and Berry, 1988).

Even when parents have unrealistic expectations at the time their child first joins the family, parents' flexibility in changing expectations can facilitate placement success. Modifying initial expectations, however, can be quite challenging for parents (Pinderhughes, 1996). For example, parents must appreciate that their perceptions of a child's need for close and nurturing family ties may not match the child's readiness to accept such closeness. In such situations, parents who are looking to satisfy their own needs through close parent–child ties may feel thwarted by the lack of reciprocity in the relationship as well as by the behavior problems manifested by the child. In their qualitative, longitudinal study of families adopting children from foster care, Eheart and Power (1995) observed that parents' failure to change expectations to be more consonant with the child's actual functioning increased the chances of the adoption placement's disrupting.

*Maintaining preexisting relationships.*   Successful parenting of an adopted child with special needs is closely intertwined with maintenance of positive relationships among other dyads in the family, as well as with the integrity of the family itself. Maintaining a harmonious marital relationship is critical, particularly during the early phases of adoption when little gratification is coming from the adoptee. Both parents need to communicate effectively and to be able to offer support and respite for each other. When the adoptive mother takes on the primary responsibility for day-to-day care of the child, and thus becomes the primary target for the adoptee's unpredictable behavior, the role of the adoptive father in supporting the mother is extremely important. Westhues and Cohen (1990) found that the affective, supportive, and active involvement of the adoptive father was associated with lower adoption placement disruption rates. In contrast, insufficient marital communication has been linked to higher disruption rates (McRoy, 1999).

The impact of a special needs adoptive placement on children already in the home is likely to be substantial (Phillips, 1999). In the course of integrating an older adopted child into their family, parents face the challenge of providing support, and in some cases, protection from physical or sexual abuse by the adoptee, to their other children. It is not unusual for biological, foster, or adoptive children already in the home to be affected negatively by the entrance of a new adopted youngster with special needs into the family system. Emotions such as jealousy, resentment, anger, and fear can persist for months, and even years, after placement (Groze, 1996; McRoy, 1999; Smith and Howard, 1999). To reduce family conflict and support the well-being of the other children in the home, adoption professionals encourage parents to include siblings in the preparation process and to maintain open and clear communication among all family members.

*Managing external stressors and utilizing supports.*   Parents in special needs adoptions also face the challenge of helping their youngster negotiate new relationships with peers and cope with new school settings. Although there are few empirical data on the dynamics involved in friendship formation and maintenance among adopted children with special needs, with their histories of harsh and inconsistent parenting and multiple losses, these children are very likely to have difficulties with peers. Indeed, special needs adoptive parents often report peer problems among their children as a major source of concern (Smith and Howard, 1999). Furthermore, Barth and Berry (1988) noted that involvement with deviant friends and peer problems was linked with adoption disruption. Ironically, the task of facilitating developmentally appropriate peer relations, a normal component of the process of individuation from parents (Ladd and Pettit, in Vol. 5 of this *Handbook*), may run counter to the initial goals of the adoptive parents, who are often preoccupied in the first few years following placement with facilitating strong and secure attachments among themselves and their children (Pinderhughes, 1996).

Adoptees are disproportionately represented among children who receive special education services (Brodzinsky and Steiger, 1991). This is especially the case for older-placed adoptees, whose emotional and behavioral problems may compound learning difficulties. How school personnel respond to adoptees with multiple needs is critical. Yet parents often note that school personnel are poorly informed about the needs of children adopted at older ages and frequently view them in negative and stereotyped ways (Groze, 1996).

To contend successfully with the stressors associated with special needs adoptions, parents need to rely on informal and formal supports such as extended family, friends, neighbors, other adoptive families, former foster families, birth families, therapists, and previous caseworkers. Barth and Berry (1988) found that families whose adoption placements disrupted have fewer relatives within visiting distance and less contact with them compared with families that remained intact. Similarly, other researchers have found that various positive indices of placement outcome are associated with greater approval and support from family and friends and greater involvement with other adoptive families (Groze, 1996; Groze and Rosenthal, 1991; Rosenthal and Groze, 1990). The benefits of such contact include normalization of feelings; alleviation of a sense of isolation and alienation; fostering a sense of belonging in the adopted child; empowerment of adoptive parents; sharing of advice, information, and skills; and increasing the likelihood of seeking professional help when needed.

Financial and medical subsidies are another critical factor in special needs adoptions. In fact, families view these supports as essential for coping with the stress of rearing their troubled children (Rosenthal et al., 1996). Moreover, financial and medical subsidies have been credited with making adoption accessible to minority, low-income, and foster families—groups that typically adopt older children and children with special needs. Without these subsidies, many youngsters with special needs, rather than being adopted, would linger in foster care or end up in institutional placements (Barth and Berry, 1988).

Other service needs that have been identified as being important for successful special needs placements include advocacy for specialized and individualized educational services; individual, group, and family therapy; specialized training of mental health professionals regarding the dynamics of special needs adoptions; parenting skills classes emphasizing behavior management and working with traumatized and attachment-disordered children; identification of community resources; respite care; life planning for youth who are developmentally disabled; intensive family preservation services; and availability of services over the life of the family (Kramer and Houston, 1998; Rosenthal et al., 1996; Smith and Howard, 1999).

In summary, rearing adopted children with special needs presents individuals and couples with several interrelated parenting challenges. Unlike the challenges associated with infant adoptions or rearing birth children, these challenges are linked to the adoptee's previous history in other families and present both internal and external pressures on the family concurrently. When families decide to adopt children of a different race, the challenges can be magnified.

## DOMESTIC TRANSRACIAL ADOPTION

As placements of European American infants declined in the 1960s and 1970s, individuals and couples in the United States began to adopt babies from other racial and ethnic groups—usually African American, Native American, and Latin American children. Between 1960 and 1976, more than 12,000 such placements were made (Silverman and Weitzman, 1986). However, opposition to transracial adoption soon emerged, particularly in the African American and the Native American communities. Critics of transracial adoption argued that such placements increased the risk for psychological problems in children, undermined their development of positive racial attitudes and identity, and ultimately resulted in "cultural genocide" (Chestang, 1972; Chimezie, 1975). As a result of this opposition, transracial placements of infants declined precipitously over the past few decades in the United States (Silverman and Feigelman, 1990). At the same time, however, transracial placements of foster children, often leading to permanent adoptions, continued. In fact, in recent years, approximately 5,000 children adopted from foster care have entered transracial or transcultural placements (National Adoption Information Clearinghouse, 2000). These adoptions were facilitated by the Multi-Ethnic Placement Act of 1994 and the Inter-Ethnic Placement Act of 1996, both of which mandated that race not be a barrier for adoptive placements.

Despite the ongoing concerns about the psychological well-being of children placed for adoption across racial lines (Park and Green, 2000), research generally has found that the vast majority of these youngsters are well adjusted, have positive relationships with parents, and do not suffer from psychological or behavioral problems or low self-esteem (Bagley, 1993; Brooks and Barth, 1999; Feigelman and Silverman, 1983; McRoy and Zurcher, 1983; Silverman, 1993; Simon, Altstein, and Melli, 1994; Vroegh, 1997).

Studies of racial attitudes and racial identity in transracially adopted children and youth have produced more equivocal results, however. Whereas some studies have found that transracial adoptees have reasonably positive racial identities (Brooks and Barth, 1999; Feigelman and Silverman, 1983; Vroegh, 1997), other studies have indicated confused, ambivalent, or negative racial identity among youngsters and adults placed across racial lines (McRoy and Zurcher, 1983; Shireman and Johnson, 1986). DeBerry, Scarr, and Weinberg (1996) examined the impact of families' racial socialization practices on adolescent transracial adoptees' psychological adjustment, racial group preference, and racial identity. Results indicated that parents' racial socialization practices decreased over time. Whereas 43% of parents reported actively incorporating racial and cultural issues into the life of the family when children were 7 years old (the remaining 57% gave little or inconsistent attention to race and culture), only 23% did so when the adoptees were adolescents. Furthermore, adoptee identification with Eurocentric values increased from childhood to adolescence, whereas identification with Afrocentric values decreased. Of importance, parents who more actively promoted discussion and exploration of race and culture in the family had children who reported greater Afrocentric reference group orientation, which in turn, predicted more positive psychological adjustment.

Taken as a whole, research on the effects of transracial adoption on racial identity remains inconclusive, although in a recent meta-analysis of studies in this area, Hollingsworth (1997) concluded that this may be one aspect of the adoptee's life that is negatively affected by placement across racial lines. The lack of consensus among researchers on this issue is partly due to different definitions of racial identity, use of different measures to assess this construct (Brodzinsky et al., 1998), and even different interpretations of data derived from the same measure (Haugaard, 2000). Recent developments in measurement of racial identity point to multiple dimensions of racial socialization (e.g., Hughes and Chen, 1997; Stevenson, 1997) and racial identity (e.g., Phinney, Cantu, and Kurtz, 1997; Smith and Brookins, 1997). This research has the potential to help identify specific parenting behaviors associated with racial socialization that may be differentially related to racial identity among transracial adoptees.

Although transracial placements quite often yield successful outcomes, the challenges experienced by adoptive parents in these families and the impact of family life on children's adjustment and identity are very complicated. Recent interviews with adults who were adopted transracially reveal just how complicated the individual and family dynamics can be (Pindehughes, 1997; Simon and Roorda, 2000). Before adopting across racial lines, prospective adoptive parents need to examine their own views about race, ethnicity, and culture—something they may not have consciously done previously. They must recognize that once they assume the responsibilitiy of rearing a child of another race, they must begin to create a new identity for the family along multiracial and multicultural lines. In addition, they must learn about the child's racial and ethnic heritage in preparation for fostering a positive self-image and secure racial identity in their youngster. They must also prepare their child for, and become effective advocates against, the bigotry and the prejudice that is part of our society. Opponents of transracial adoption fear that many of these tasks are impossible to accomplish for nonminority parents (Park and Green, 2000).

Despite these challenges, many transracially placed children and their families appear to adjust to their unique circumstances quite well and continue to show positive adjustment throughout the family life cycle (Silverman, 1993). The adjustment process appears easier, however, when adoptive families not only are sensitive to the complexities associated with living as a person of color or rearing a person of color in our society, but also act on their sensitivity. Specifically, adoptive parents are more likely to optimize their children's emotional well-being when they promote a strong sense of ethnic and racial pride in their youngsters, participate in experiences in schools and communities that provide a connection to others of the same racial or ethnic background, validate their youngster's efforts to cope with difficult experiences associated with being different, and when necessary, assertively advocate for their children. More specific delineation of the unique parenting behaviors that are linked to variations in outcome among transracial adoptees awaits future research.

## INTERCOUNTRY ADOPTION

Intercountry adoption began as a means of providing orphaned and abandoned children from war-torn countries with safe, nurturing, and permanent homes. Following World War II, the Korean War, and the Vietnam War, thousands of children entered the United States for purposes of adoption. In the past decade, with the fall the Ceaucescu regime in Romania, the breakup of the Soviet Union, and national policy changes in China related to family planning, the number of abandoned children available for intercountry adoption has risen substantially.

Although proponents of intercountry adoption have emphasized the humanitarian benefits of providing loving and permanent homes to orphaned and needy children, there have been many criticisms of this practice (Rios-Kohn, 1998). Opponents of intercountry adoption argue that children have a right to a national identity and that "placing" countries must do more to find permanent homes for children within their own borders. There are also concerns about depriving children of the experience of being reared within their own race and ethnic group. In addition, others worry that intercountry adoption is rife with corruption and baby selling and that there is often a real question as to the legitimacy of a child's status as orphaned or abandoned. Despite these concerns, the practice of intercountry adoption continues to grow, not only in the United States, but also in other Western countries (e.g., Canada, Great Britain, France, Netherlands, Sweden). In fiscal year 1999, for example, over 16,000 foreign-born children were placed for adoption in the United States (National Adoption Information Clearinghouse, 2000). Currently the most common national sources for these children for prospective parents in the United States include Russia, China, South Korea, and Guatamala.

Research on the adjustment and well-being of children placed internationally has yielded inconsistent findings. Although most studies have suggested that these youngsters have adapted well to their home, show positive peers relationships and self-esteem, and do well in school (Altstein and Simon, 1991; Bagley and Young, 1980; Feigelman and Silverman, 1983; Levy-Schiff, Zoran, and Shulman, 1997; Westhues and Cohen, 1997), other studies have reported that intercountry adoptees display a higher level of emotional, psychological, and behavioral problems than their nonadopted agemates do (Hoksbergen, Juffer, and Waardenburg, 1987; Stams, Juffer, Rispens, and Hoksbergen, 2000; Verhulst et al., 1992). The discrepant findings reflect, in part, differences between studies in the children's age at the time of placement, their age at assessment, the nature of their preplacement experiences (e.g., neglect, abuse, orphanage life), their racial/ethnic match to adoptive parents, and the degree of racial/ethnic diversity of the countries into which the children are adopted (e.g., United States versus Sweden, Norway, or the Netherlands).

When children are adopted from other countries, adoptive families face a number of parenting challenges. To begin with, these youngsters often arrive with infectious diseases, malnutrition, digestive problems, intestinal parasites, and growth delay (Gyorkos and MacLean, 1992; Miller, Kiernan, Mathers, and Klein-Gitelman, 1995), as well as preadoptive neurologic diagnoses, some of which are obscure and not always confirmed in postplacement medical evaluations (Albers, Johnson, Hostetter, Iverson, and Miller, 1997). These conditions often are not identified before placement, which can increase the stress associated with the transition to adoptive parenthood. Fortunately, most of the medical problems found in intercountry adoptees are treatable or manageable and do not cause prolonged hardship for the child or family (Smith-Garcia and Brown, 1989).

Parents who adopt children internationally typically do not speak the language of their child's country of origin, and the children, who are old enough to talk, rarely speak English. The frustration of not being able to communicate with others is a common experience in these families. For young children who have been abruptly removed from all that is familiar in their country of origin and placed in a strange environment, not being able to communicate can be quite overwhelming. Fortunately, most young children become fluent in English or the language of their adopted country very quickly.

One of the more serious problems facing parents who adopt internationally is the impact of earlier institutional life on their children. Although rare in the United States, orphanages are quite prevalent throughout the world and are generally associated with low-quality childcare. Moreover, children who are adopted internationally often spend months, and even years, living in these types of facilities. Naturally parents worry about the long-term effects of institutional rearing on their children. Research has documented that, compared with nonadopted children and adopted children with no early adversity, children who have been institutionalized before adoption are more likely to suffer high rates of cognitive and socioemotional impairments (Castle et al., 1999; Tizard and Hodges, 1978; Tizard and Rees, 1975), as well as behavior problems and attachment difficulties (Chisholm, 1998; Chisholms et al., 1995; Fisher et al., 1997). Furththermore, the longer the duration of institutional care, the greater the chances of adjustment problems. The relatively common pattern of insecure and disordered attachments in these youngsters is especially troubling for adoptive parents, who are often unprepared for the stress that is associated with this aspect of family life and lack the parenting skills to handle it effectively. These families usually require intensive postplacement supports, including specialized clinical services for the child and themselves (Hart and Thomas, 2000; Hughes 1997). Despite the bleak picture that some of this research suggests, the prognosis for these youngsters is better than was once thought. With ongoing stimulation and nurturance by adoptive parents, as well as the support offered by medical, mental health, and child welfare professionals, children who have experienced early institutional rearing typically show substantial improvement over time (Fisher et al., 1997).

Because many intercountry adoptions involve transracial placements, adoptive parents also face the challenge of supporting their children's development of positive racial and ethnic attitudes and identity. As in domestic transracial placements, parental attitudes about the child's race and birth culture, as well as efforts to expose children to information about their heritage, play an important role in the child's racial and ethnic identification (Feigelman and Silverman, 1983, Huh and Reid, 2000). It is unclear, however, whether a bicultural identification is necessary for healthy adjustment among these children (Friedlander, 1999). For some individuals it seems to be important; for others it is not. Westhues and Cohen (1998) reported that, although most of the transracially placed, intercountry adopted adolescents and young adults they studied were comfortable with both their racial and ethnic background, few developed a bicultural identity. Furthermore, Friedlander et al. (2000) pointed out the importance of differentiating between ethnic identification and cultural identification. In their qualitative study of a small group of intercountry adopted children and teenagers, virtually all the youngsters labeled themselves ethnically, but were more identified with European American culture than with their native culture. The authors also noted that, although the children and teenagers displayed good psychological adjustment and strong family attachments, many struggled with a sense of "being different."

For parents of intercountry adoptees, the responsibility of helping their children cope with racial and ethnic issues, as well as understand the circumstances of their birth history and the loss of the birth family, is often complicated by an absence of information about the child's origins. Moreover, what little information is available is often of questionable veracity. Consequently, even when they want to be open and honest with their children about the circumstances of the adoption, parents of children placed from other countries frequently are confronted with informational barriers that are difficult to overcome. This is less often the case in domestic adoption, at least for those individuals who are motivated to create openness in the adoptive family system.

## OPEN ADOPTION

When adoption laws were first enacted in the United States in the late nineteenth century and early twentieth century, there was great concern about protecting birth parents and adoptive parents from the unwelcomed curiosity of others, as well as protecting children from the social stigma of illegitimacy. Consequently state adoption statutes emphasized the need for confidentiality in the adoption process, including sealing the child's original birth certificate and identifying adoption records (Bussiere, 1998).

The practice of confidential adoption continued unchallenged until the early 1970s, when members of the adoption triad, as well as some adoption professionals, began to speak out about the problems associated with traditional adoption practice (Baran, Sorosky, and Pannor, 1974; Sorosky, Baran, and Pannor, 1976), and advocated the unsealing of adoption records (Sorosky et al., 1978). As a result, agencies began to explore placement options involving sharing of information between the birth family and adoptive family, including the possibility of postplacement contact. Henney, Onken, McRoy, and Grotevant (1998) reported that, from the mid-1980s to the mid-1990s, most adoption agencies offered a growing range of placement options that included some degree of openness. Moreover, agencies often served as an intermediary between birth families and adoptive families, facilitating the sharing of information and addressing relationship problems between the two families. The shift toward greater openness by the agencies was fueled primarily by three influences: (1) client demand—birth parents, in particular, wanted more information about who was adopting their child; (2) changes in agency philosophy toward embracing the concept of openness; and (3) competition from other agencies that were also offering a greater range of placement options.

Although the concept of open adoption means different things to different people, Grotevant and McRoy (1998) have argued that it is best understood as a continuum of mutual knowledge, communication, and contact that varies greatly from family to family and can change over time. At one end of the continuum are adoption plans in which birth parents and adoptive parents not only know one another's name and location, but also include ongoing, direct contact among the parties, including the children. At the other end of the continuum is the traditional, confidential placement plan in which there is minimal information shared, and certainly no contact, between the two families. In between these two extremes is a range of information sharing and contact that differs from one adoption to another.

Open adoption has certainly been one of the most controversial changes in the adoption field over the past few decades (Berry, 1993; Grotevant and McRoy, 1998). Critics worry that this type of arrangement will undermine the adoptive family system, produce confusion and adjustment problems in the children, and prolong the grief of birth parents. In contast, supporters of open adoption suggest that the elimination of secrecy, which is inherent in traditional adoption practice, is likely to enable adoptive parents to have a more realistic and empathetic view of the birth family, increase the sense of control and security for both sets of parents, reduce postplacement grief for birth parents, and facilitate a deeper understanding of adoption for children, as well as reduce their sense of abandonment, rejection, and loss.

To date, research on open adoption has failed to support the concerns and dire warnings of open adoption critics. Adoptive parents who are involved in open placement arrangements feel more entitled to their child, have a more secure parent–child relationship, communicate more with the child about adoption, have a more understanding and empathetic view of the child's birth parents, and worry less about the birth parents' attempting to reclaim their child (Belbas, 1987; Berry, 1991; Grotevant and McRoy, 1998; Siegel, 1993). In addition, birth parents in open adoptions show better post-placement adjustment than those in confidential adoptions, including an increased sense of control, as well as diminished feelings of depression, grief, guilt, and regret (Brodzinsky 1992; Christian, McRoy, Grotevant, and Bryant, 1997; Grotevant and McRoy, 1998). There is also some evidence that open adoption is associated with fewer parent reported behavior problems in children than closed adoption (Berry, 1991). Moreover, Wrobel, Ayers-Lopez, Grotevant, McRoy, and Friedrick

(1996) found somewhat greater understanding of adoption among children in fully disclosed adoption placements. Nevertheless, the research to date has not found a consistently measurable, beneficial effect for children residing in this type placement arrangement (Berry, Cavazos Dylla, Barth, and Needell, 1998; Grotevant and McRoy, 1998). Importantly, though, the research also has found no significant adverse consequences for children in open adoptions (Grotevant, 2000; Grotevant and McRoy, 1998).

Clearly, open adoption can and does work well, especially when the parties freely choose this type of arrangement. However, when pressured to accept an open adoption, eventual dissatisfacton may well emerge with time for one or both parties. In fact, in their longitudinal study of 764 adoptions involving children who, at the time of placement, ranged in age from infancy to early childhood, Berry et al. (1998) reported that the level of openness between the adoptive and the birth families generally decreased over the first four years of the adoption. Furthermore, for those adoptive families who initially chose an open adoption because they feared they would not otherwise be offered a child, 50% reduced the frequency of contact with the birth family following the placement and another 21% ceased contact altogether.

No firm conclusions concerning the outcomes associated with open adoption can be drawn as yet, especially in relation to the impact on children. Certainly this form of adoption creates many challenges and complexities for families. As Grotevant (2000) has noted, open adoption is a *dynamic* process, with shifting needs and expectations between both sets of parents, as well as the children. Managing family boundaries and maintaining a commitment to the open relationship requires good communication, flexibility, mutual respect, and, above all else, a clear focus on meeting the child's needs. Although open adoption probably is not for everyone, it clearly offers a feasible option for all parties involved in adoption. Questions for the future involve understanding when and under what circumstances different members of the adoption triad are best served by creating greater openness in the placement arrangement, as well as how to support the parties when the needs and the expectations of one party (e.g., adoptive parents) do not match those of another (e.g., birth parents or the adopted child).

## CONCLUSIONS

Adoption is a complex process—legally, socially, and psychologically—and is associated with a highly varied form of nontraditional family life. As noted in the preceding sections, the changes in adoption practice over the past few decades make it difficult to generalize about the average adopted child or the average adoptive family. Although adoption is associated with increased academic and psychological difficulties, the vast majority of children, including those adopted at older ages, transracially, and across national borders, adjust quite well, and their parents report considerable satisfaction with their adoption decision. Furthermore, adoption has been shown to actually benefit children whose biological parents could not or would not provide proper care for them.

The keys to successful parenting of adopted children include good preparation, realistic expectations, effective behavior management skills, good communication, and adequate supports—all of which are common to other families as well. Yet parenting adopted children is a different experience from rearing a biological child and is associated with unique adoption-related tasks (Brodzinsky, 1987; Brodzinsky et al., 1992; Kirk, 1964; Reitz and Watson, 1992). Acknowledging the inherent differences of adoptive family life, creating a rearing environment that is conducive to open and supportive dialogue about these differences, maintaining a respectful and empathetic view of the child's birth family and heritage, and supporting the child's search for self (Brodzinsky et al., 1992) are critical tasks faced by adoptive parents. When adoptive parents are successful in meeting these challenges, as most are, they find the experience of rearing adopted children to be personally rewarding and successful in terms of their children's adjustment.

# REFERENCES

Albers, L. H., Johnson, D. E., Hostetter, M. K., Iverson, S., and Miller, L. C. (1997). Health of the children adopted from the former Soviet Union and Eastern Europe. *Journal of the American Medical Association, 278,* 922–924.

Altstein, H., and Simon, R. J. (Eds.). (1991). *Intercountry adoption: A multinational perspective.* New York: Praeger.

Bagley, C. (1993). Transracial adoption in Britain: A follow-up study, with policy considerations. *Child Welfare, 72,* 285–299.

Bagley, C., and Young, L. (1980). The long-term adjustment and identity of a sample of intercountry adopted children. *International Social Work, 23,* 16–22.

Baran, A., and Pannor, R. (1993). Perspective on open adoption. *The Future of Children, 3,* 119–124.

Baran, S., Sorosky, A. D., and Pannor, R. (1974). Adoptive parents and the sealed records controversy. *Social Casework, 55,* 531–536.

Barth, R. P. (1988). Disruption in older child adoptions. *Public Welfare, 46,* 23–29.

Barth, R. P., and Berry, M. (1988). *Adopton and disruption.* New York: Aldine de Gruyter.

Barth, R. P., and Brooks, D. (2000). Outcomes for drug-exposed children eight years postadoption. In R. Barth, M. Freundlich, and D. Brodzinsky (Eds.), *Adoption and prenatal alcohol and drug exposure: Research, policy, and practice* (pp. 23–58). Washington, DC: Child Welfare League of America.

Barth, R. P., Freundlich, M., and Brodzinsky, D. M. (Eds.). (2000). *Adoption and prenatal alcohol and drug exposure: Research, policy and practice.* Washington, DC: Child Welfare League of America.

Barth, R. P., and Needell, B. (1996). Outcomes for drug-exposed children four years after adoption. *Children and Youth Services Review, 18,* 37–55.

Belbas, N. (1987). Staying in touch: Empathy in open adoption. *Smith College Studies in Social Work, 57,* 184–198.

Benson, P. L., Sharma, A. R., and Roehlkepartain, E. C. (1994). *Growing up adopted: A portrait of adolescents and their families.* Minneapolis, MN: Search Institute.

Bernstein, A. C., and Cowan, P. A. (1975). Children's concepts of how people get babies. *Child Development, 46,* 77–91.

Berry, M. (1991). The practice of open adoption: Findings from a study of 1,396 families. *Children and Youth Services Review, 13,* 379–395.

Berry, M. (1993). Risks and benefits of open adoption. *The Future of Children, 3,* 125–138.

Berry, M., Cavazos Dylla, D. J., Barth, R. P, and Needell, B. (1998). The role of open adoption in the adjustment of adopted children and their families. *Children and Youth Services Review, 20,* 151–171.

Bharat, S. (1997). *Intellectual and psychosocial development of adopted children.* Mumbai, India: Tata Institute of Social Services.

Blum, H. P. (1983). Adoptive parents: Generative conflict and generational continuity. *Psychoanalytic Study of the Child, 38,* 141–163.

Bohman, M. (1970). *Adopted children and their families: A follow-up of adopted children, their background environment, and adjustment.* Stockholm: Proprius.

Bohman, M., and Sigvardsson, S. (1990). Outcome in adoption: Lessons from longitudinal studies. In D. Brodzinsky and M. Schechter, M. (Eds.), *The psychology of adoption* (pp. 93–106). New York: Oxford University Press.

Borders, D. L., Black, L. K., and Pasley, K. B. (1998). Are adopted children and their parents at greater risk for negative outcomes? *Family Relations, 47,* 237–241.

Bowlby, J. (1973). *Attachment and loss: Vol. 2. Separation.* New York: Basic Books.

Braungart-Rieker, J., Rende, R. D., Plomin, R., DeFries, J. C., and Fulker, D. W. (1995). Genetic mediation of longitudinal associations between family environment and childhood behavior problems. *Development and Psychopathology, 7,* 233–245.

Brinich, P. M. (1990). Adoption from the inside out: A psychoanalytic perspective. In D. Brodzinsky and M. Schechter (Eds.), *The psychology of adoption* (pp. 42–61). New York: Oxford University Press.

Brodzinsky, A. B. (1992). *The relation of learned helplessness, social support and avoidance to grief and depression in women who have placed an infant for adoption.* Unpublished doctoral dissertation, New York University.

Brodzinsky, D. M. (1983). *Adjustment factors in adoption* (Rep. No. MH34549). Washington, DC: National Institute of Mental Health.

Brodzinsky, D. M. (1987). Adjustment to adoption: A psychosocial perspective. *Clinical Psychology Review, 7,* 25–47.

Brodzinsky, D. M. (1990). A stress and coping model of adoption adjustment. In D. Brodzinsky and M. Schechter (Eds.), *The psychology of adoption* (pp. 3–24). New York: Oxford University Press.

Brodzinsky, D. M. (1993). Long-term outcome in adoption. *The Future of Children, 3,* 153–166.

Brodzinsky, D. M. (1997). Infertility and adoption adjustment: Considerations and clinical issues. In S. Leiblum (Ed.), *Infertility: Psychological issues and counseling strategies* (pp. 246–262). New York: Wiley.

Brodzinsky, D. M., Hitt, J. C., and Smith, D. W. (1993). Impact of parental separation and divorce on adopted and nonadopted children. *American Journal of Orthopsychiatry, 63,* 451–461.

Brodzinsky, D. M., and Huffman, L. (1988). Transition to adoptive parenthood. *Marriage and Family Review, 12,* 267–286.

Brodzinsky, D. M., Lang, R., and Smith, D. W. (1995). Parenting adopted children. In M. Bornstein (Ed.), *Handbook of parenting: Vol. 3. Status and Social Conditions of Parenting* (pp. 209–232). Mahwah, NJ: Lawrence Erlbaum Associates.

Brodzinsky, D. M., Patterson, C. J., and Vaziri, M. (2001). Adoption agency perspectives on lesbian and gay prospective parents: A national study. Manuscript submitted for publication.

Brodzinsky, D. M., Radice, C., Huffman, L., and Merkler, K. (1987). Prevalence of clinically significant symptomatology in a nonclinical sample of adopted and nonadopted children. *Journal of Clinical Child Psychology, 16*, 350–356.

Brodzinsky, D. M., Schechter, D., Braff, A. M., and Singer, L. (1984). Psychological and academic adjustment in adopted and nonadopted children. *Journal of Consulting and Clinical Psychology, 52*, 582–590.

Brodzinsky, D. M., Schechter, D., and Brodzinsky, A. B. (1986). Children's knowledge of adoption: Developmental changes and implications for adjustment. In R. Ashmore and D. Brodzinsky (Eds.), *Thinking about the family: Views of parents and children* (pp. 205–232). Hillsdale, NJ: Lawrence Erlbaum Associates.

Brodzinsky, D. M., Schechter, M. D., and Henig, R. M. (1992). *Being adopted: The lifelong search for self*. New York: Doubleday.

Brodzinsky, D. M., Singer, L. M., and Braff, A. M. (1984). Children's understanding of adoption. *Child Development, 55*, 869–878.

Brodzinsky, D. M., Smith, D. W., and Brodzinsky, A. B. (1998). *Children's adjustment to adoption: Developmental and clinical issues*. Thousand Oaks, CA: Sage.

Brodzinsky, D. M., and Steiger, C. (1991). Prevalence of adoptees in special education populations. *Journal of Learning Disabilities, 24*, 484–489.

Brooks, D., and Barth, R. P. (1999). Adult transracial and inracial adoptees: Effects of race, gender, adoptive family structure, and placement history on adjustment outcomes. *American Journal of Orthopsychiatry, 69*, 87–99.

Bussiere, A. (1998). The development of adoption law. *Adoption Quarterly, 1*, 3–26.

Butler, I. C. (1989). Adopted children, adoptive families: Recognizing differences. In L. Combrinck-Graham (Eds.), *Children in family contexts* (pp. 161–186). New York: Guilford.

Cadoret, R. J. (1990). Biologic perspectives of adoptee adjustment. In D. Brodzinsky and M. Schechter (Eds.), *The psychology of adoption* (pp. 25–41). New York: Oxford University Press.

Carey, W. B., Lipton, W. L., and Myers, R. A. (1974). Temperament in adopted and foster babies. *Child Welfare, 53*, 352–359.

Castle, J., Groothues, C., Bredenkamp, D., Beckett, C., O'Connor, T., Rutter, M., and the E.R.A. Study Team (1999). Effects of qualities of early institutional care on cognitive attainment. *American Journal of Orthopsychiatry, 69*, 424–437.

Chandra, A., Abma, J., Maza, P., and Bachrach, C. (1999). *Adoption, adoption seeking, and relinquishment for adoption in the United States* (Advance data from vital and health statistics, No. 306). Hyattsville, MD: National Center for Health Statistics.

Chasnoff, I. J., Anson, A. R., and Moss Iaukea, K. A. (1998). *Understanding the drug-exposed child: Approaches to behavior and learning*. Chicago: Imprint.

Chestang, L. (1972). The dilemma of bi-racial adoption. *Social Work, 17*, 100–105.

Chimezie, A. (1975). Transracial adopiton of black children. *Social Work, 20*, 296–301.

Chisholm, K. (1998). A three year follow-up of attachment and indiscriminate friendliness in children adopted from Romanian orphanages. *Child Development, 69*, 1092–1106.

Chisholm, K., Carter, M., Ames, E. W., and Morison, S. J. (1995). Attachment security and indiscriminately friendly behavior in children adopted from Romanian orphanages. *Development and Psychopathology, 7*, 283–294.

Christian, C. L., McRoy, R. G., Grotevant, H. D., and Bryant, C. (1997). Grief resolution of birthmothers in confidential, time-limited mediated, ongoing mediated, and fully disclosed adoptions. *Adoption Quarterly, 1*, 35–58.

Cohen, N. J., Coyne, J., and Duvall, J. (1993). Adopted and biological children in the clinic: Family, parental, and child characteristics. *Journal of Child Psychology and Psychiatry, 34*, 545–562.

Coon, H., Carey, G., Corley, R., and Fulker, D. W. (1992). Identifying children in the Colorado Adoption Project at risk for conduct disorder. *Journal of the American Academy of Child and Adolescent Psychiatry, 31*, 503–511.

Daly, K. (1988). Reshaped parenthood identity: The transition to adoptive parenthood. *Journal of Contemporary Ethnography, 17*, 40–66.

Daly, K. (1990). Infertility resolution and adoption readiness. *Families in Society: The Journal of Contemporary Human Services, 71*, 483–492.

Deater-Deckard, K., and Plomin, R. (1999). An adoption study of etiology of teacher and parent reports of externalizing behavior problems in middle childhood. *Child Development, 70*, 144–154.

DeBerry, K. M., Scarr, S., and Weinberg, R. (1996). Family racial socialization and ecological competence: Longitudinal assessments of African-American transracial adoptees. *Child Development, 67*, 2375–2399.

Department of Health and Human Services, Administration for Children and Families, Administration on Children, Youth and Families, Children's Bureau, AFCARS Rep. No. 2 (Current estimates published January, 2000). [On-line] Available: www.acf.dhhs.gov/programs/cb/dis/afcars/cwstats.html.

Derdeyn, A. P. (1990). Foster parent adoption. In D. Brodzinsky and M. Schechter (Eds.), *The psychology of adoption* (pp. 332–347). New York: Oxford University Press.

Deutsch, D. K., Swanson, J. M., Bruell, J. H., Cantwell, D. P., Weinberg, F., and Baren, M. (1982). Overrepresentation of adoptees in children with the attention deficit disorder. *Behavior Genetics, 12,* 231–238.

Dickson, L. R., Heffron, W. M., and Parker, C. (1990). Children from disrupted and adoptive homes on an inpatient unit. *American Journal of Orthopsychiatry, 60,* 594–602.

Downs, S. W., Moore, E., McFadden, E. J., and Costin, L. B. (2000). *Child welfare and family services: Policies and practice* (6th ed.). Boston: Allyn and Bacon.

Dumaret, A. (1985). IQ, scholarship performance, and behavior of siblings raised in contrasting environments. *Child Psychology, 26,* 553–580.

Eheart, B. K., and Power, M. B. (1995). Adoption: Understanding the past, present, and future through stories. *Sociological Quarterly, 36,* 197–216.

Feigelman, W., and Silverman, A. R. (1983). *Chosen children: New patterns of adoptive relationships.* New York: Praeger.

Fergusson, D. M., Lynskey, M., and Horwood, L. J. (1995). The adolescent outcomes of adoption: A 16-year longitudinal study. *Journal of Child Psychology and Psychiatry, 36,* 597–615.

Festinger, T. (1986). *Necessary risk: A study of adoptions and disrupted adoptive placements.* Washington, DC: Child Welfare League of America.

Festinger, T. (1990). Adoption disruption: Rates and correlates. In D. Brodzinsky and M. Schechter (Eds.), *The psychology of adoption* (pp. 201–220), New York: Oxford University press.

Fisher, L., Ames, E. W., Chisolm, K., and Savoie, L. (1997). Problems reported by parents of Romanian orphans adopted to British Columbia. *International Journal of Behavioral Development, 20,* 67–82.

Freundlich, M. (2000). The impact of prenatal substance exposure: Research findings and their implications for adoption. In R. Barth, M. Freundlich, and D. Brodzinsky (Eds.), *Adoption and prenatal alcohol and drug exposure: Research, policy and practice* (pp. 1–21). Washington, DC: Child Welfare League of America.

Friedlander, M. L. (1999). Ethnic identity development among internationally adopted children: Implications for family therapists. *Journal of Marital and Family Therapy, 25,* 43–60.

Friedlander, M. L., Larney, L. C., Skau, M., Hotaling, M., Cutting, M. L., and Schwam, M. (2000). Bicultural identification: Experiences of internationally adopted children and their parents. *Journal of Counseling Psychology, 47,* 187–198.

Fullerton, C. S., Goodrich, W., and Burman, L. B. (1986). Adoption predicts psychiatric treatment resistances in hospitalized adolescents. *Journal of the American Academy of Child Psychiatry, 25,* 542–551.

Gendell, S. J. (2001). In search of permanency: A reflection on the first 3 years of the Adoption and Safe Families Act implementation. *Family Court Review, 39,* 25–42.

Glick, P. C. (1977). Updating the life cycle of the family. *Journal of Marriage and the Family, 39,* 5–13.

Glidden, L. M. (1991). Adopted children with developmental disabilities: Post-adoptive family functioning. *Child and Youth Services Review, 13,* 363–378.

Glidden, L. M. (2000). Adopting children with developmental disabilities: A long-term perspective. *Family Relations, 49,* 397–405.

Goldberg, D., and Wolkind, S. M. (1992). Patterns of psychiatric disorder in adopted girls: A research note. *Journal of Child Psychology and Psychiatry, 33,* 935–940.

Goldstein, J., Freud, A., and Solnit, A. (1973). *Beyond the best interests of the child.* New York: Free Press.

Grotevant, H. D. (1997). Coming to terms with adoption: The construction of identity from adolescence to adulthood. *Adoption Quarterly, 1,* 3–27.

Grotevant, H. D. (2000). Openness in adoption: Research with the adoption kinship network. *Adoption Quarterly, 4,* 45–66.

Grotevant, H. D., Dunbar, N., Kohler, J. K., and Esau, A. M. L. (2000). Adoptive identity: How contexts within and beyond the family shape developmental pathways. *Family Relations, 49,* 379–387.

Grotevant, H. D., and McRoy, R. G. (1998). *Openness in adoption: Connecting families of birth and adoption.* Thousand Oaks, CA: Sage.

Groze, V. (1991). Adoption and single parents: A review. *Child Welfare, 70,* 321–332.

Groze, V. (1996). *Successful adoptive families: A longitudinal study of special needs adoption.* London: Praeger.

Groze, V., and Rosenberg, K. F. (1998). *Clinical and practice issues in adoption: Bridging the gap between adopees placed as infants and as older children.* Westport, CN: Praeger.

Groze, V., and Rosenthal, J. (1991). A structural analysis of families adopting children with special needs. *Families in Society, 72,* 469–481.

Gyorkos, T. W., and MacLean, J. D. (1992). Medical evaluation of children adopted from abroad. *Journal of the American Medical Association, 268,* 410.

Hart, A., and Thomas, H. (2000). Controversial attachments: The indirect treatment of fostered and adopted children via parent co-therapy. *Attachment and Human Development, 2,* 306–327.

Haugaard, J. J. (1998). Is adoption a risk factor for the development of adjustment problems? *Clinical Psychology Review, 18,* 47–69.

Haugaard, J. J. (2000). Research and policy on transracial adoption: Comments on Park and Green. *Adoption Quarterly, 3,* 35–42.

Henney, S. M., Onken, S., McRoy, R. G., and Grotevant, H. D. (1998). Changing agency practices toward openness in adoption. *Adoption Quarterly, 1*, 45–76.

Hodges, J., and Tizard, B. (1989). Social and family relationships of ex-institutional adolescents. *Journal of Child Psychology and Psychiatry and Allied Disciplines, 30*, 77–97.

Hoksbergen, R. A. C. (1999). The importance of adoption for nurturing and enhancing the emotional and intellectual potential of children. *Adoption Quarterly, 3*, 29–42.

Hoksbergen, R. A. C., Juffer, F., and Waardenburg, B. C. (1987). *Adoptive children at home and at school. The adjustment after eight years of 116 Thai children in the Dutch community.* Lisse, The Netherlands: Swets and Zeitlinger.

Hollingsworth, L. D. (1997). Effect of transracial/transethnic adoption on children's racial and ethnic identity and self-esteem: A meta-analytic review. *Marriage and Family Review, 25*, 99–130.

Hoopes, J. L. (1990). Adoption and identity formation. In D. Brodzinsky and M. Schechter (Eds.), *The psychology of adoption.* (pp. 144–166). New York: Oxford University Press.

Hughes, D. (1997). *Facilitating developmental attachment.* Northvale, NJ: Aronson.

Hughes, D., and Chen, L. (1997). When and what parents tell children about race: An examination of race-related socialization among African American families. *Applied Developmental Science, 1*, 200–214.

Huh, N. S., and Reid, W. J. (2000). Intercountry, transracial adoption and ethnic identity: A Korean example. *International Social Work, 43*, 75–87.

Ingersoll, B. D. (1997). Psychiatric disorders among adopted children: A review and commentary. *Adoption Quarterly, 1*, 57–73.

Johnson, F., And Fein, E. (1991). The concept of attachment: Applications to adoption. *Child and Youth Services Review, 13*, 397–412.

Juffer, F., and Rosenboom, L. (1997). Infant–mother attachment of internationally adopted children in the Netherlands. *International Journal of Behavioral Development, 20*, 93–107.

Kagan, R. M., and Reid, W. J. (1986). Critical factors in the adoption of emotionally disturbed youth. *Child Welfare, 65*, 63–74.

Katz, L. (1986). Parental stress and factors for success in older child adoption. *Child Welfare, 65*, 569–578.

Kaye, K. (1990). Acknowledgment or rejection of differences? In D. Brodzinsky and M. Schechter (Eds.), *The psychology of adoption* (pp. 121–143). New York: Oxford University Press.

Kim, W. J., Davenport, C., Joseph, J., Zrull, J., and Woolford, E. (1988). Psychiatric disorder and juvenile delinquency in adopted children and adolescents. *Journal of the American Academy of Child and Adolescent Psychiatry, 27*, 111–115.

Kirk, H. D. (1964). *Shared fate.* New York: Free Press.

Kotsopoulos, S., Cote, A., Joseph, L., Pentland, N., Chryssoula, S., Sheahan, P., and Oke, L. (1988). Psychiatric disorders in adopted children. *American Journal of Orthopsychiatry, 58*, 608–612.

Kotspoulos, S., Walker, S., Copping, W., Cote, A., and Stavrakaki, C. (1993). A psychiatric follow-up study of adoptees. *Canadian Journal of Psychiatry, 38*, 391–396.

Kramer, L., and Houston, D. (1998). Supporting families as they adopt children with special needs. *Family Relations, 47*, 423–432.

Lamb, M. E. (Ed.). (1999). *Parenting and child development in nontraditional families.* Mahwah, NJ: Lawrence Erlbaum Associates.

Leiblum, S. R. (Ed.). (1997). *Infertility: Psychogical issues and counseling strategies.* New York: Wiley.

Lester, B. M., LaGasse, L. L., and Seifer, R. (1998). Cocaine exposure and children: The meaning of subtle effects. *Science, 282*, 633–634.

Levy-Shiff, R., Bar, O., and Har-Even, D. (1990). Psychological adjustment of adoptive parents-to-be. *American Journal of Orthopsychiatry, 60*, 258–267.

Levy-Shiff, R., Goldschmidt, I., and Har-Even, D. (1991). Transition to parenthood in adoptive families. *Developmental Psychology, 27*, 131–140.

Levy-Shiff, R., Zoran, N., and Shulman, S. (1997). International and domestic adoption: Child, parents, and family adjustment. *International Journal of Behavioral Development, 20*, 109–129.

Loehlin, J. C., Willerman, L., and Horn, J. M. (1985). Personality resemblances in adoptive families when the child are late-adolescent or adult. *Journal of Personality and Social Psychology, 48*, 376–392.

Lorber, J., and Greenfield, D. (1989). Couples' experiences with in vitro fertilization: A phenomenological approach. In Z. Ben-Rafael (Ed.), *Proceedings of the Sixth World Congress on In Vitro Fertilization and Alternative Assisted Reproduction* (pp. 965–971). New York: Plenum.

Marquis, K. S., and Detweiler, R. A. (1985). Does adoption mean different? An attributional analysis. *Journal of Personality and Social Psychology, 48*, 1054–1066.

Marshall, M. J., Marshall, S., and Heer, M. J. (1994). Characteristics of abstinent substance abusers who first sought treatment in adolescence. *Journal of Drug Education, 24*, 151–162.

Maughan, B., and Pickles, A. (1990). Adopted and illegitimate children growing up. In L. Robins and M. Rutter (Eds.), *Straight and devious pathways from childhood to adulthood* (pp. 36–61). New York: Cambridge University Press.

McRoy, R. G. (1999). *Special needs adoption: Practice issues*. New York: Garland.

McRoy, R. G., Grotevant, H. D., and Zurcher, L. A. (1988). *The development of emotional disturbance in adopted adolescents*. New York: Praeger.

McRoy, R. G., and Zurcher, L. A. (1983). *Transracial and inracial adoptees*. Springfield, IL: Thomas.

Miall, C. (1987). The stigma of adoptive parent status: Perceptions of community attitudes toward adoption and the experience of informal social sanctioning. *Journal of Applied Family and Child Studies, 36,* 34–39.

Milan, S. E., and Pinderhughes, E. E. (2000). Factors influencing maltreated children's early adjustment to foster care. *Development and Psychopathology, 12,* 63–81.

Miller, B. C., and Coyl, D. D. (2000). Adolescent pregnancy anad childbearing in relation to infant adoption in the United States. *Adoption Quarterly, 4,* 3–25.

Miller, B. C., Fan, X., Christensen, M., Grotevant, H. D., and van Dulmen, M. (2000). Comparisons of adopted and nonadopted adolescents in a large, nationally representative sample. *Child Development, 71,* 1458–1473.

Miller, B. C., Fan, X., Grotevant, H. D., Christensen, M., Coyl, D., and van Dulmen, M. (2000). Adopted adolescents' over representation in mental health counseling: Adoptees' problems or parents' lower threshold for referral? *Journal of the American Academy of Child and Adolescent Psychiatry, 39,* 1504–1511.

Miller, L. C., Kiernan, M. T., Mathers, M. I., and Klein-Gitelman, M. (1995). Developmental and nutritional status of internationally adopted children. *Archives of Pediatric and Adolescent Medicine, 149,* 40–44.

Mosher, W. D., and Pratt, W. F. (1990). Fecundity and infertility in the United States, 1965–1988. *Advance Data, 192,* 1–9.

National Adoption Information Clearinghouse. (2000). *Transracial adoption*. [On-line]. Available: www.calib.com/naic/pubs/s_trans.htm.

Nelson, K. (1985). *On the frontier of adoption: A study of special needs adoptive families*. New York: Child Welfare League of America.

Newman, J. L., Roberts, L. R., and Syre, C. R. (1993). Concepts of family among children and adolescents: Effects of cognitive level, gender, and family structure. *Developmental Psychology, 29,* 951–962.

Nickman, S. L. (1985). Losses in adoption. The need for dialogue. *Psychoanalytic Study of the Child, 40,* 365–398.

Park, S. M., and Green, C. E. (2000). Is transracial adoption in the best interests of ethnic minority children?: Questions concerning legal and scientific interpretations of a child's best interests. *Adoption Quarterly, 3,* 5–34.

Partridge, S., Hornby, H., and McDonald, T. (1986). *Legacies of loss—visions of gain: An inside look at adoption disruption*. Portland, ME: University of Southern Maine Press.

Phillips, N. K. (1999). Adoption of a sibling: Reactions of biological children at different stages of development. *American Journal of Orthopsychiatry, 69,* 122–126.

Phinney, J. S., Cantu, C. L., and Kurtz, D. A. (1997). Ethnic and American identity as predictors of self-esteem among African American, Latino and White adolescents. *Journal of Youth and Adolescence, 26,* 165–185.

Pinderhughes, E. E. (1996). Toward understanding family readjustment following older child adoptions: The interplay between theory generation and empirical research. *Children and Youth Services Review, 18,* 115–138.

Pinderhughes, E. E. (1998). Short-term placement outcomes for children adopted after age five. *Children and Youth Services Review, 20,* 223–249.

Pinderhughes, E. E. (1999, August). *Child and family readjustment to older child adoption*. Invited paper presented at the international conference on adoption research, Minneapolis, MN.

Pinderhughes, R. B. (1997). *The experience of racial identity development for transracial adoptees*. Unpublished doctoral dissertation, Massachusetts School of Professional Psychology, Boston, MA.

Plomin, R., and DeFries, J. (1985). *Origins of individual differences in infancy: The Colorado Adoption Project*. Orlando, FL: Academic.

Raynor, L. (1980). *The adopted child comes of age*. London: Allen and Unwin.

Reitz, M., and Watson, K. W. (1992). *Adoption and the family system*. New York: Guilford.

Rios-Kohn, R. (1998). Intercountry adoption: An international perspective on the practice and standards. *Adoption Quarterly, 1,* 3–32.

Rogeness, G. A., Hoppe, S. K., Macedo, C. A., Fischer, C., and Harris, W. R. (1988). Psychopathology in hospitalized adopted children. *Journal of the American Academy of Child and Adolescent Psychiatry, 27,* 628–631.

Rosenberg, E. B. (1992). *The adoption life cycle: The children and their families through the years*. New York: Free Press.

Rosenthal, J. A. (1993). Outcomes of adoption of children with special needs. *The Future of Children, 3,* 77–88.

Rosenthal, J. A., and Groze, V. (1990). Special needs adoptions: A study of intact families. *Social Service Review, 64,* 475–505.

Rosenthal, J. A., Groze, V., and Morgan, J. (1996). Services for families adopting children via public child welfare agencies: Use, helpfulness, and need. *Children and Youth Services Review, 18,* 163–182.

Rosenthal, J. A., Schmidt, D., and Connor, J. (1988). Predictors of special needs adoption disruption: An exploratory study. *Children and Youth Services Review, 10,* 101–117.

Rushton, A., Dance, C., and Quinton, D. (2000). Findings from a UK-based study of late permanent placements. *Adoption Quarterly, 3,* 51–71.

Sants, H. J. (1964). Genealogical bewilderment in children with substitute parents. *British Journal of Medical Psychology*, *37*, 133–141.

Sar, B. K. (2000). Preparation for adoptive parenthood with a special-needs child: Role of agency preparation tasks. *Adoption Quarterly*, *3*, 63–80.

Scarr, S., and Weinberg, R. A. (1983). The Minnesota Adoption Studies: Genetic differences and malleability. *Child Development*, *54*, 260–267.

Schechter, M. D. (1960). Observations on adopted children. *Archives of General Psychiatry*, *3*, 21–32.

Schechter, M. D. (1970). About adoptive parents. In E. J. Anthony and T. Benedek (Eds.), *Parenthood: Its psychology and psychopathology*. Boston: Little, Brown.

Schechter, M. D., and Bertocci, D. (1990). The meaning of the search. In D. Brodzinsky and M. Schechter (Eds.), *The psychology of adoption* (pp. 62–92). New York: Oxford University Press.

Seglow, I., Pringle, M. K., and Wedge, P. (1972). *Growing up adopted*. Winsor, UK: National Foundation for Educational Research in England and Wales.

Sharma, A. R., McGue, M. K., and Benson, P. L. (1996a). The emotional and behavioral adjustment of adopted adolescents, Part 1: An overview. *Children and Youth Services Review*, *18*, 83–100.

Sharma, A. R., McGue, M. K., and Benson, P. L. (1996b). The emotional and behavioral adjustment of adopted adolescents, Part 2: Age at adoption. *Children and Youth Services Review*, *18*, 101–114.

Sharma, A. R., McGue, M. K., and Benson, P. L. (1998). The psychological adjustment of United States adopted adolescents and their nonadopted siblings. *Child Development*, *69*, 791–802.

Sherrill, C. L., and Pinderhughes, E. E. (1999). Conceptions of family and adoption among older adoptees. *Adoption Quarterly*, *2*, 21–48.

Shireman, J. F. (1996). Single parent adoptive homes. *Children and Youth Services Review*, *18*, 23–36.

Shireman, J. F., and Johnson, P. R. (1986). A longitudinal study of black adoptions: Single parent, transracial, and traditional. *Social Work*, *31*, 172–176.

Siegel, D. H. (1993). Open adoption of infants: Adoptive parents' perceptions of advantages and disadvantages. *Social Work*, *38*, 15–23.

Silver, L. B. (1989). Frequency of adoption in children and adolescents with learning disabilities. *Journal of Learning Disabilities*, *22*, 325–328.

Silverman, A. R. (1993). Outcomes of transracial adoption. *The Future of Children*, *3*, 104–118.

Silverman, A. R., and Feigelman, W. (1990). Adjustment in interracial adoptees: An overview. In D. Brodzinsky and M. Schechter (Eds.), *The psychology of adoption* (pp. 187–200). New York: Oxford University Press.

Silverman, A. R., and Weitzman, D. (1986). Non-relative adoption in the United States. In R. A. C. Hoksbergen (Ed.), *Adoption in world wide perspective: A view of programs, policies, and legislation in 14 countries*. Royesford, PA: Swets and Zeitlinger.

Silverman, B. S. (2001). The winds of change in adoption laws: Should adoptees have access to adoption records? *Family Court Review*, *39*, 85–103.

Simmons, B., Allphin, S., and Barth, R. P. (2000). The changing face of public adoption practice. *Adoption Quarterly*, *3*, 43–62.

Simon, R. J., Altstein, H., and Melli, M. S. (1994). *The case for transracial adoption*. Washington, DC: American University Press.

Simon, R. J., and Roorda, R. M. (2000). *In their own voices: Transracial adoptees tell their stories*. New York: Columbia University Press.

Singer, L., Brodzinsky, D. M., Ramsay, D., Steir, M., and Waters, E. (1985). Mother–infant attachment in adoptive families. *Child Development*, *56*, 1543–1551.

Smith, D. W., and Brodzinsky, D. M. (1994). Stress and coping in adoption: A developmental study. *Journal of Clinical Child Psychology*, *23*, 91–99.

Smith, E. P., and Brookins, C. C. (1997). Toward the development of an ethnic identity measure for African American youth. *Journal of Black Psychology*, *23*, 359–377.

Smith S. L., and Howard, J. A. (1999). *Promoting successful adoptions: Practice with troubled families*. Thousand Oaks, CA: Sage.

Smith-Garcia, R., and Brown, J. S. (1989). The health of children adopted from India. *Journal of Community Health*, *14*, 227–241.

Sokoloff, B. Z. (1993). Antecedents of American adoption. *The Future of Children*, *3*, 17–25.

Sorosky, A. D., Baran, A., and Pannor, R. (1975). Identity conflicts in adoptees. *American Journal of Orthopsychiatry*, *45*, 18–27.

Sorosky, A. D., Baran, A., and Pannor, R. (1976). The effects of the sealed record in adoption. *American Journal of Psychiatry*, *133*, 900–904.

Sorosky, A. D., Baran, A., and Pannor, R. (1978). *The adoption triangle*. New York: Doubleday.

Stams, G. J. M., Juffer, F., Rispens, J., and Hoksbergen, R. A. C. (2000). The development and adjustment of 7-year-old children adopted in infancy. *Journal of Child Psychology and Psychiatry, 41,* 1025–1037.

Stein, L. M., and Hoopes, J. L. (1985). *Identity formation in the adopted adolescent.* New York: Child Welfare League of America.

Stevenson, H. C. (1997). Managing anger: Protective, proactive, or adaptive racial socialization identity profiles and African-American manhood development. *Journal of Prevention and Intervention in the Community, 16,* 35–61.

Stolley, K. S. (1993). Statistics on adoption in the United States. *The Future of Children, 3,* 26–42.

Talen, M., Pinderhughes, E. E., and Groze, V. (1995, March). Acknowledging differences in adoptive families: Helpful or harmful for adoptive family functioning? Paper presented at the meeting on cognitions and adjustment among children and families united through special needs adoptions, symposium at the Biennial Meeting of the Society for Research in Child Development, Indianapolis, IN.

Thompson, L. A., and Plomin, R. (1988). The sequenced inventory of communication development: An adoption study of two- and three-year-olds. *International Journal of Behavioral Development, 11,* 219–231.

Tizard, B., and Hodges, J. (1978). The effect of early institutional rearing on the development of eight-year-old children. *Journal of Child Psychology and Psychiatry, 19,* 99–118.

Tizard, B., and Rees, J. (1975). The effect of early institutional rearing on the behavior problems and affectional relationships of four-year-old children. *Journal of Child Psychology and Psychiatry, 16,* 61–74.

Triseliotis, J., and Hill, M. (1990). Contrasting adoption, foster care, and residential rearing. In D. Brodzinsky and M. Schechter (Eds.), *The psychology of adoption* (pp.107–120). New York: Oxford University Press.

Verhulst, F. C., Althaus, M., and Versluis-den Bieman, H. J. M. (1992). Damaging backgrounds: Later adjustment of international adoptees. *Journal of the American Academy of Child and Adolescent Psychiatry, 31,* 518–524.

Vroegh, K. S. (1997). Transracial adoptees: Developmental status after 17 years. *American Journal of Orthopsychiatry, 67,* 568–575.

Warren, S. B. (1992). Lower threshold for referral for psychiatric treatment for adopted adolescents. *Journal of the American Academy of Child and Adolescent Psychiatry, 31,* 512–527.

Weinberg, R. A., Scarr, S., and Waldman, I. D. (1992). The Minnesota Transracial Adoption Study: A follow-up of IQ test performance at adolescence. *Intelligence, 16,* 117–135.

Weiss, A. (1985). Symptomatology of adopted and nonadopted adolescents in a psychiatric hospital. *Adolescence, 19,* 77–88.

Westhues, A., and Cohen, J. S. (1990). Preventing disruption of special needs adoptions. *Child Welfare, 69,* 141–156.

Westhues, A., and Cohen, J. S. (1997). A comparison of the adjustment of adolescent and young adult inter-country adoptees and their siblings. *International Journal of Behavioral Development, 20,* 47–65.

Westhues, A., and Cohen, J. S. (1998). The adjustment of intercountry adoptees in Canada. *Children and Youth Services Review, 20,* 115–134.

Wierzbicki, M. (1993). Psychological adjustment of adoptees: A meta-analysis. *Journal of Clinical Child Psychology, 22,* 447–454.

Wrobel, G. M., Ayers-Lopez, S., Grotevant, H. D., McRoy, R. G., and Friedrick, M. (1996). Openness in adoption and the level of child participation. *Child Development, 67,* 2358–2374.

Yarrow, L. J., and Goodwin, M. S. (1973). The immediate impact of separation: Reactions of infants to a change in mother figure. In L. Stone, H. Smith, and L. Murphy (Eds.), *The competent infant.* New York: Basic Books.

# 11

# Foster Parenting

Jeffrey Haugaard
Cindy Hazan
*Cornell University*

## INTRODUCTION

Foster parents provide care to children who cannot remain with their families by bringing these children into their homes. Although this care is meant to be short term and temporary, many children remain with their foster parents for several years and become important members of their foster families. Foster parents are recruited, trained, and supervised by public departments of social services or by private agencies that contract with departments of social services to provide foster care. The characteristics of foster parents in the United States tend to reflect the characteristics of parents throughout the United States. Fifty to sixty years ago, foster parents were primarily middle-income couples, with a mother who often did not work outside the home. Today, foster families are much more structurally and culturally diverse (McFadden, 1996). Although most foster parents today are married, many single women and some single men are foster parents. Foster families come from a wide range of cultural groups and incomes. Many have both birth children and foster children in their families, although others have become foster parents in order to have children in their home.

Adults interested in becoming foster parents usually get in contact with local agencies or may respond to recruiting drives. They often must receive legally mandated training, and their backgrounds, current living situations, and parenting practices are investigated. Agencies then decide whom to accept as foster parents, although, as subsequently described, the current shortage of foster homes encourages many agencies to accept all those who are qualified. Foster parents receive stipends to defray the costs of providing foster care, but these stipends often do not cover the costs of raising a child and many foster parents must subsidize the cost of providing care to the foster children in their home (Chamberlain, Moreland, and Reid, 1992).

Foster parenting is a unique and, even as we write, changing form of parenting. Foster parents provide parenting to very challenging children. They parent infants with drug addictions or AIDS and children and adolescents who have been severely abused or neglected. Many children and adolescents in foster care have experienced little parenting continuity, and some have been moved from home to home repeatedly. Many foster children have significant behavioral or emotional problems, are medically fragile, or have physical or developmental disabilities.

The principal difference between foster parenting and other forms of parenting is that the foster parent–foster child relationship is expected to be temporary. Foster parents are expected to be warm and nurturing and to form a growth-promoting relationship with their foster children, but not to be too warm and nurturing or to create a relationship that is so close that it makes it difficult for the children to return to their birth parents.[1] Another difference is that foster families are open to supervision by child-welfare agencies and possibly to involvement with the birth parents. Thus a primary right of parents in the United States—to rear children without interference from the state—is missing for foster parents (Mnookin, 1978). Negotiating the extent to which foster families, child welfare agencies, and birth families are to work together while parenting a foster child can be difficult.

Despite the challenges faced by foster parents, most express satisfaction with their roles. Dando and Minty (1987) found that 75% of a sample of foster parents in England rated their experiences as *completely* or *mostly* rewarding, whereas only 7% rated their experiences as unhappy or disastrous. Similarly, Denby, Rindfleisch, and Bean (1999) found that 84% of a group of 539 foster parents stated that they had a high level of satisfaction with their experiences.

In this chapter, we explore the experiences of foster parents. We start with a description of the foster care system—exploring the system's history and its current state and describing what we know about the characteristics of foster parents today. We then explore the issues that make foster parenting unique. We do this by exploring three types of relationships that foster parents must negotiate: relationships with the placement agency, with the foster child's birth parents, and with the foster child. We pay particular attention to the role of attachment in the relationship between the foster parent and foster child. We then explore issues related to factors that promote successful foster parenting.

Unfortunately, the research on foster parenting is minimal. Although research on the experiences of foster children has increased over the past two decades, a similar increase of research on foster parents has not occurred. Some existing research involves reviews of agency records, and these records are often incomplete and may contain little specific information about the foster parents. Much of the other research involves surveys mailed to foster parents, with the typical low response rates associated with mailed surveys and subsequent concerns about the representativeness of the data. Consequently, although we do know something about the experiences of foster parents, additional research will need to be conducted before we have more than a rudimentary knowledge about them and their families.

## THE FOSTER CARE SYSTEM

To understand the changing roles of foster parents, it is helpful to know some about the history of foster care in the United States. It is interesting to note the fluctuations of public policy regarding the importance of maintaining children with their birth families and the influence that these policies have had on the number of children in foster care and the role that foster parents play within the child welfare system.

### A Brief History of Foster Care in the United States

Laws concerning dependent children in colonial America were based on the Elizabethan Poor Law of 1601 (Trattner, 1979). Care was provided mainly through indentured servitude, in which dependent

---

[1]The term birth parent or birth family is currently used to describe the parents to whom the child is biologically related. Other terms such as natural parent or biological parent have been used in the past but are seldom used today because they can be seen as implying that a child's foster or adoptive parent are not natural or biological.

children were legally bound to another adult as an apprentice or other worker (Bremner, 1970). Some communities used *vendue*, or the procedure of obtaining publicly funded care for a child by auctioning the child to the person willing to provide the care for the least amount of money (Bremner, 1970).

In the early 1800s, the needs of many children in large cities were met through almshouses—which also housed destitute or ill adults. Conditions in most almshouses were deplorable. For example, of the 1,527 children received at New York City's Foundling Hospital in 1868, only 80 survived their first year (Geiser, 1973). In reaction to these conditions, many charitable groups began sponsoring asylums for orphans, abandoned children, and children with destitute parents. There was general opposition to providing support directly to parents; consequently children had to be taken from their parents to receive any aid. Parents had no legal rights to their children once they had been removed (Rothman, 1971).

Efforts to find substantial numbers of foster families to care for dependent children were started by Charles Loring Brace in the late 1800s, who organized efforts to place children from New York City with families on Western farms. Brace's ideas were not generally accepted, and there was considerable opposition from Catholic and Jewish groups about placing Catholic and Jewish children in primarily Protestant Western families (Bremner, 1970). In addition, several scandals developed when the exploitation of some children was reported, and it became clear that there was little supervision to ensure that the children were not being mistreated (Hollinger, 1991).

The Settlement House movement of the late 1800s promoted the importance of maintaining children in their families whenever possible. Charities developed Settlement Houses in tenement areas to provide education and support directly to parents. The importance of supporting families was reinforced by the White House Conference on Children in 1909, which instigated the development of the federal Children's Bureau and the private Child Welfare League of America. The focus on families also reinvigorated Brace's message of caring for children in foster families. Efforts were made to increase the number of foster families available for children and to increase their funding through local governments and private foundations (Cox and Cox, 1985).

There was little federal financing for foster care until 1961, when the federal government began providing some foster care funds for children who qualified for the federal Aid to Families with Dependent Children (AFDC). Most of the funds were earmarked for out-of-home placements for children rather than for services for families. Thus the federal government created a financial incentive to remove children from troubled families rather than to work with the families (Cox and Cox, 1985).

Partly in response to the large increase in the numbers of children in foster care during the 1960s and 1970s, the Adoption Assistance and Child Welfare Act (AACWA) became federal law in 1980. The law mandated the primary importance of family preservation: the provision of services to families to avoid removal of children or the speedy return of children to their birth families whenever possible if the children had to be removed to foster care. The AACWA had a significant influence on the number, quality, and intensity of services to families that were at risk for having their children removed into foster care. The number of foster children declined dramatically—from approximately 500,000 in the mid-1970s to approximately 250,000 in the early 1980s (e.g., National Commission on Child Welfare and Family Preservation, 1990).

The number of children in foster care began to increase in the mid-1980s. From 1982 to 1992 there was a 69% increase in children in foster care, and, by 1993, 460,000 children were in out-of-home care (Pasztor and Wynne, 1995). The increase was due to dramatic increases in substantiated reports of child abuse and neglect (National Center on Child Abuse and Neglect, 1995), pregnant and parenting women with significant substance abuse problems (Barth, Courtney, Berrick, and Albert, 1994; Steverson, 1994), and family homelessness (Children's Defense Fund, 1987). The greatest growth in children entering care occurred with infants and very young children (Barth et al., 1994).

Because of the apparent failure of the AACWA to reduce the number of children in foster care, and because of concerns that children were being returned to unsafe birth homes where they often suffered repeated maltreatment resulting in their return to foster care, Congress passed the Adoption and Safe Families Act (ASFA) in 1997. Rather than family preservation being of primary importance, the health and safety of children became the paramount concern (Savage, 1999). While retaining an emphasis on providing services to families to avoid removal of their children into foster care, the ASFA provided for easier termination of birth parents' rights so that some children in foster care would be eligible for adoption more quickly.

## The Current Foster Care System

The number of children in the foster care system, the inability of the system to return them home or place them in an adoptive home quickly, the growing lack of foster families, and the ever-increasing caseload of most caseworkers have created a foster care system that many have described as "in crisis" (Goodman, Emery, and Haugaard, 1998). A recent estimate put the number of children in foster care in the U.S. at 480,000 (Child Welfare League, 1997). This is more than double the number of children in foster care in 1985 (U.S. General Accounting Office, 1995). The average out-of-home stay for foster children is approximately 22 months, and 20% to 25% of foster children will not return to their birth home to live (Inch, 1999). Although the number of children needing foster placements has risen, the number of foster families available for these children has dropped considerably (Sanchirico, Lau, Jablonka, and Russell, 1998). Pasztor and Wynne (1995) estimated that the number of foster homes declined from 147,000 in 1985 to 100,000 in 1990. This decline has been attributed to changes in many families in the United States, such as an increase in the number of married women in the workforce (Sanchirico et al., 1998).

The decline in the number of foster homes has been intensified by issues that have made the role of foster parent more difficult and that have increased dissatisfaction among foster parents (e.g., Brown and Calder, 1999; Fees et al., 1998; Jones and Morrissette, 1999; Zima et al., 2000). The severity of the problems presented by foster children has increased dramatically. Efforts to keep children in their birth homes whenever possible mean that children from only the most troubled families, or children with only the most difficult behavioral problems, enter foster care. For example, many foster children have a history of severe abuse, and they may physically or sexually abuse other children in their foster home. Some foster parents feel a lack of recognition and respect from professionals and the community: People who cannot imagine themselves bringing troubled children into their homes may assume that foster parents are doing it for the money they receive as stipends. Many foster parents have concerns about the safety of their birth children and the effect that bringing troubled children into their home will have on their family (Poland and Groze, 1993; Twigg, 1994). The need to deal periodically with the loss of a foster child who is returned home or the death of a medically fragile foster child can be difficult for many families and may discourage some families from continuing as foster families (Inch, 1999; McFadden, 1996).

Foster families can be categorized in several ways, although the labels for these categories may vary from state to state. *Emergency* foster families are those willing to take a child on very short notice, for a short period, while another placement is sought. For example, a child removed from an abusive home by the police might be taken to an emergency until another foster home is found for him. *Short-term* foster homes, which constitute the large majority of foster homes, are those providing care to children who are expected to be able to return to their birth homes at some point. *Long-term* foster homes are for children who will not be returning to their birth homes and for whom adoption is not contemplated (e.g., an older child who does not want to be adopted) (McFadden, 1996).

Over the past two decades there has been a movement toward some short-term and long-term foster homes becoming more specialized. *Specialized* foster homes are those giving care to children with certain characteristics. For example, some homes might specialize in infants with HIV or girls who have been sexually abused. Foster parents in these homes may have special interests in certain types of children and often receive specific training for dealing with the medical, psychological, and social needs of these children. *Treatment* foster homes provide care to children showing high levels of behavioral or emotional disorders—children who are at risk of being placed in a residential treatment center or psychiatric hospital. Foster parents in these homes often work for an agency providing treatment foster care, and they receive training, support, and respite from the agency (McFadden, 1996).

*Kinship* foster care refers to care provided by a relative of a child in care—typically a grandparent, aunt, or uncle. The number of kinship foster care homes has risen dramatically over the past two decades. In 1990, approximately half of all foster children in New York were in homes with kin (Meyers and Link, 1990). The increase in kinship foster care has been driven by several factors, including the increase in children needing placement and the decrease in the number of family foster care homes. In addition, the emphasis on family preservation has encouraged the search for caregivers within dependent children's extended family (Berrick and Barth, 1994). Finally, finding a foster home for a child is likely to be easier among the child's relatives than among strangers, as there are likely to be people who would be willing to provide care to a relative but unwilling to provide care to an unfamiliar child.

## Characteristics of Foster Parents

Adults become foster parents for many reasons. The most common of these are the desire to help a child in need, a wish to do something for one's community or society, or an interest in having children (or more children) (Dando and Minty, 1987; Inch, 1999). Some adults become foster parents because of their interest in eventually adopting one of the children to whom they provide foster care (James Bell Associates, 1993).

No national information about the characteristics of foster parents is available, because no national reporting system about foster care exists. However, four recent studies of fairly large samples of foster parents provide some information about those currently providing foster care. Le Prohn (1994) examined surveys from 180 foster families from across the United States involved with the Casey Family Program (an agency providing long-term foster care). Of the families, 63% were two-parent families, 34% were headed by single mothers, and 3% were headed by single fathers; 41% had yearly incomes of more than $30,000, and 17% had incomes of less than $10,000; 77% owned their home, and 8% were living in subsidized housing.

Seaberg and Harrigan (1997) surveyed 124 families providing nonkinship foster care in a mid-Atlantic state in 1993. All of the families had a foster mother. Of the mothers, 55% were European American, 44% were African American, and 1% were classified as "other"; their average age was 46; 13% had not received a high school diploma or a GED, 52% had finished high school or had a GED, 18% had an associates degree, and 17% had completed college or earned an advanced degree; 43% were employed full time, 19% were employed half time, 8% were retired, and 29% were not employed outside the home; 88% attended religious services at least weekly. Seventy-five percent of the foster families also included a father. The fathers' average age was 48. Of the fathers, 20% did not have a high school diploma or GED, 56% had completed high school or had a GED, 7% had an associates degree, and 17% had a bachelors or advanced degree; 81% were employed full time, 3% were employed part time, 11% were retired, and 5% did not work outside the home; 79% attended religious services at least weekly.

Sanchirico et al. (1998) analyzed questionnaires from 616 foster parents (the gender of the foster parents was not specified) in New York (approximately half from New York City and half from upstate New York). Their average age was 45. Eleven percent had not completed high school, 63% had completed high school, 8% had an associates degree, and 18% had a bachelors degree or advanced degree. The average number of years they had been a foster parent was 4.3, and 40% of them had birth children living with them as well as foster children.

Denby, Rindfleisch, and Bean (1999) received 539 questionnaires from foster parents in Ohio. Approximately 57% of the homes included two parents, 11% were headed by unmarried mothers, and 32% were headed by a mother who was separated, divorced, or widowed. Approximately half of the mothers were European American and half were African American; 48% were from 41 to 60 years old, 36% were younger than 41 years, and 10% were over 60 years old; 17% had not completed high school, 66% were high school graduates, and 17% had a college degree. The average income of 30% of the families was $30,000 to $50,000, with 14% earning more than $50,000 and 46% earning less than $30,000.

The picture of foster parents that emerges from this limited number of studies is one in which approximately 60% of foster homes are headed by two parents, and most of the others are headed by single mothers. The parents' ages tend to be between 35 and 55 years. Most foster parents have obtained a high school degree or have attended some college, but a sizable percentage do not have a high school diploma or GED. Based on family income, approximately half of the families would be considered of middle socioeconomic status (SES), 15% would be considered upper-middle SES, and approximately 35% would be considered blue-collar or low-income families. Religion appears to play an important role in many foster families.

## UNIQUE ROLES OF FOSTER PARENTS

Parents play many roles in their nuclear families, extended families, and communities. Foster parents engage in all of these roles and also in many roles unique to foster parents. Whereas parents in the United States have constitutionally guaranteed rights to privacy within their families and, within certain broad limits, have the right to rear their children as they see fit (Mnookin, 1978), foster parents share their parenting authority with the agency that placed the child with them and with the child's birth parents (Eastman, 1982). The ways in which foster parenting responsibilities are to be shared are often not well defined, and they may change with each foster placement, as the expectations and involvement of the agency caseworkers and the birth parents vary. This can lead to ambiguity in the parenting role and to confusion about how foster parents are expected to parent their foster children (Eastman, 1982). This can, in turn, influence the role that a foster parent has with the foster child.

In this section, we explore the relationships that foster parents have with the agencies that place children in their home, the birth parents of these children, and their foster children. These relationships can have a substantial influence on foster parents' ability to successfully parent their children, on their willingness to continue as foster parents, and on their own mental and physical health.

### Relationship With Placement Agency

When a child is removed from his or her birth home and placed in foster care, the local department of social services must find a suitable foster placement for the child, ensure that the child is well cared for, and, in most cases, create a program of services for the child and the child's birth family that will allow for the child's return. Foster parents must regularly interact with an agency about their parenting and about the children in their care. When foster parents feel connected to and supported by the placement agency, they have higher levels of satisfaction (Chamberlain et al., 1992; Denby et al., 1999; Rodwell and Biggerstaff, 1993). When disagreements between the agency and the foster parent arise, the foster parent may come to see the agency as an opponent, and the agency may come to see the foster parent in the same way. Disagreements may arise about the foster parents' parenting practices (especially if the child's behavior worsens or continues to be very problematic) and about the role that the foster parents should have in making decisions about the child and the child's placement. This may make it difficult for them to work together and may diminish the usefulness of the placement for the child. Mietus and Fimmen (1987, p. 33) asked, "Are foster parents professionals or are they paraprofessionals? Are they employees or are they clients? The ambiguity surrounding the role of foster parents has been a persistent theme in the foster care literature for almost two decades." Fourteen years later, answers to these questions about foster parents' roles and their relationships with the agency placing children in their home are still unclear.

Until the 1970s or so, foster parents were seen largely as caregivers. They were expected to provide a healthy home life and a good parenting example for children who were generally stable, but whose parents were temporarily unable to care for them (Sanchirico and Jablonka, 2000). If specific educational or psychological services were needed by a child, they were supplied by other professionals. Children with significant medical, behavioral, or emotional problems were often cared for in an institution. Over the past three decades, the role of many foster parents has changed to that of an active member of the team delivering services to the foster child and to the child's birth family. Foster parents are expected to be knowledgeable participants in behavioral therapy or psychotherapy received by the child, to actively participate in remedial or other educational programs in which the child is enrolled, to help the child's birth parents create a home environment to which the child can be returned, and to facilitate the continuation or improvement of the relationship between the child and the birth parents (e.g., Warsh, Pine, and Maluccio, 1996; Sanchirico and Jablonka, 2000). Of primary importance, foster parents are now often seen as partners when decisions about the child are made.

These new roles create conflicts between the interests of the agencies and the foster parents in some cases. For example, the agency is charged with supervising the foster placement and removing children from inadequate foster homes, yet the agency depends on the families that it must supervise to provide needed (and sometimes, desperately needed) homes (Dando and Minty, 1987). Consequently agencies may modify what they believe would be best for a child in order to avoid angering the foster parents and thus risking disruption of the placement. For example, some caseworkers have felt pressure to reduce contact between the child and the child's birth family because the foster family found the contact to be troubling (Hess, 1988). Another potential conflict occurs when foster parents are asked to work as partners with the placement agency in promoting the development of the child's birth family and in making decisions about the child and the child's placement, because the foster parents' positive or negative feelings about the child may influence these decisions. Some foster parents who have developed a warm relationship with their child may be hesitant to recommend reunification with the child's birth parents, and foster parents who have developed a conflicted relationship with a child may be eager to have the child returned to the birth parents before it is appropriate to do so. Negotiating these conflicts can be tricky, and when they are not confronted in a forthright manner, they can have a significantly negative influence on the care given to a child.

A particularly nettlesome conflict can arise between foster parents and agencies when a complaint of child maltreatment has been lodged against the foster parents. Although children in foster care are more likely to experience maltreatment than children in the general population, a smaller percentage of child maltreatment complaints against foster parents are determined to be substantiated than are complaints against birth parents and others (Benedict, Zuravin, Brandt, and Abbey, 1994; Runyan and Gould, 1985; for review, see Goodman, Emery, and Haugaard, 1998). Agencies may be caught between their desire to discover child maltreatment and remove children from maltreating parents and their desire to defend the families that have been their partners in providing foster care. This may make it difficult for agencies to adequately judge whether abuse has occurred in a foster home. Foster parents may feel betrayed by the child or by the agency, and this may negatively affect their willingness or ability to provide good foster care. Foster parents may feel particularly vulnerable because they have fewer legal safeguards against agency actions than do birth parents (e.g., having foster children removed from their home) (Carbino, 1991a, 1991b, 1992).

## Relationship Between Foster Parent and Birth Parent

In their role as partners in the delivery of services to foster children, foster parents are often called on to help their foster children maintain or improve their relationships with their birth parents and other relatives, act as advocates and role models for the birth parents, and involve the birth parents in an appropriate level of decision making about their child (Sanchirico and Jablonka, 2000). To accomplish these tasks, foster parents need to have civil relationships with birth parents, and there may be advantages to relationships that are characterized by cooperation, positive regard, and possibly even friendliness. However, several circumstances may work to keep relationships between foster parents and birth parents strained, unfriendly, or perhaps hostile.

Birth parents may see foster parents as part of the system that has taken their children from them. Animosity that might be more appropriately aimed at child protective services, a department of social services, or a family court may instead be directed toward foster parents. Birth parents may be envious of foster parents who can stay at home during the day and care for a child rather than working outside the home, the material goods that they can afford to give to the foster child, or the lifestyle that they can provide their family. Birth parents may be suspicious that the foster parents will try to turn their children against them or may fear that the foster parents will try to adopt their children.

Alternatively, foster parents, many of whom became foster parents because of their concern for children, can feel angry and hostile toward the birth parents who maltreated their children (Sanchirico and Jablonka, 2000; Seaberg and Harrigan, 1999). Differences in lifestyles, SES, or culture may result in foster parents not understanding or agreeing with many of the birth parents' values or actions (McFadden, 1996). Foster parents who form an emotional bond with a foster child may come to see the birth parents as rivals for the child's affections or loyalty (Erera, 1996).

Research has shown that many foster parents have difficult relationships with birth parents, although some have positive relationships from which they both appear to benefit. Seaberg and Harrigan (1999) surveyed 118 foster mothers about their attitudes toward the birth parents with whom they had dealt. On a 6-point scale from positive to negative, the average rating was 3. However, only 13% of the foster mothers felt that their foster child could be returned to their birth parents and do well, with approximately 56% believing that the children should not be returned to their birth parents. In a study of foster families in Israel, Erera (1996) found that only 16% of foster parents had discussed the birth parent's problems with parenting with them, that 20% of the foster parents had ever visited the birth parents, that 14% of the foster parents had initiated contact between their foster children and the childrens' birth parents, and that birth parents had had contact with their children in only 30% of the cases. Sanchirico and Jablonka (2000) obtained results in contrast to those of Erera (1996). They found that 77% of a large group of foster parents had taken their foster children to visits with their birth families, that 63% encouraged their foster children to telephone birth parents and other relatives, and that 48% included birth parents in celebrations for the foster child (e.g., birthdays). The differences between the findings of Erera and those of Sanchirico and Jablonka may reflect different foster care expectations between Israel and New York state, changes in policy occurring between the time of the two studies, or both.

Two interventions specifically designed to increase contact between foster parents and birth parents resulted in closer working relationships between them. Sanchirico and Jablonka (2000) found that specialized training on relationships with birth parents increased visitation between the foster child and the birth parents. Simms and Bolden (1991) found that facilitating structured visits among foster parents, children, and birth parents led to better relationships between the foster parents and the birth parents.

## Relationship Between Foster Parent and Foster Child

Consideration of the relationships between foster parents and foster children naturally raises issues of attachment. Foster parents are, by definition, temporary caregivers. Ideally, they serve as a short-term respite from whatever harmful circumstances resulted in the children's being placed in foster care. Their main task is to provide interim care until the children can be safely reunited with the birth parents. Thus one could argue that it is in the best interests of the children that they not become "too" attached to foster parents. Foster parents, social work agencies, and the courts have struggled for years with the question about the appropriate level of emotional involvement between foster parents and foster children. Before the past two decades, foster parents were expected to be warm parents who provided for their foster children and set a good example for them, but who did not become emotionally involved with them. A court in New York went so far as to remove a child from a foster home because the foster parents had become too attached to the child (*In re* Jewish Child Care Association, 1959; Savage, 1999). In a Supreme Court decision regarding foster parents' rights, a concurring opinion stated that "any case where the foster parents had assumed the emotional role of the child's natural parents would represent not a triumph of the system to be constitutionally safeguarded from state intrusions, but a failure" (Smith v. Organization of Foster Families for Equality and Reform, 1977, p. 861).

Despite the expectation that foster care is only short term, a child's stay in foster care is often extended well beyond the expected period of time. As previously noted, the average stay in foster care is approximately 22 months, and approximately one in four foster children remains in foster care for 4 or more years (American Civil Liberties Union, 1993; Inch, 1999). What is the effect on an older child of the development of a close relationship with a foster parent when the child returns to the birth parent? A related, and perhaps more important, concern relates to the increasing number of infants placed in foster care—many of whom are placed in foster care immediately after birth (National Center for Policy Analysis, 1997). How does one provide adequate care to an infant without satisfying her or his needs for emotional connection? What is the consequence to an infant of forming an attachment with a foster parent and then being returned to live with a birth parent? Unfortunately, insufficient research exists to address these questions. However, attachment theory and related research provides some guidance for addressing them.

*An overview of attachment theory.*  In 1950, British psychiatrist John Bowlby was asked by the World Health Organization to investigate the mental health of the many London children who had been orphaned by the war. His report asserted that separation from primary caregivers, especially during the first few years of life, put children at increased risk for mental illness and behavior problems. Two decades of further observation, research, and thought led to attachment theory (Bowlby, 1951, 1969, 1973, 1980). Attachment theory is rooted in evolutionary thinking: Because human infants cannot survive without the protection and care of adults, humans have evolved a behavioral system to form strong bonds with the adults who protect and care for them. Although this attachment system is innate, an attachment bond takes time to form. During the first 2 months of life, babies care little about who responds to their cries. By the age of 3 or 4 months, they are more selective and direct their bids for contact and comfort to a few preferred individuals. At approximately 6 months of age, infants show wariness toward strangers and are upset by separations from primary caregivers. This separation distress is the accepted marker that an attachment bond has been established.

Ainsworth and her colleagues (Ainsworth, Blehar, Waters, and Wall, 1978) later revealed the effects of intact but poorly functioning infant–caregiver relationships. The laboratory procedure that Ainsworth developed for assessing attachment quality—the Strange Situation—was designed to activate and assess an infant's attachment system. Three distinct patterns of infant attachment were identified through this procedure, and each was linked to specific features of caregiver responsiveness. Caregivers who respond consistently, promptly, and effectively to their infants' signals of distress are likely to have infants who develop a secure attachment. Caregivers who are inconsistent and unpredictable—sometimes warmly responsive but more often angry or unresponsive—are likely to have infants with an insecure–resistant attachment. Caregivers who are consistently rejecting when their infants seek contact are likely to have infants with an insecure–avoidant attachment.

Through repeated interactions with their caregivers, infants learn what to expect in future interactions—what Bowlby called internal working models or mental representations of the self in relation to the caregiver—and adjust their behavior accordingly. Securely attached infants expect to be soothed when distressed because that has been their experience. Insecure–avoidant infants expect rejection so they withdraw when they are distressed and most in need of comfort. Insecure–resistant infants do not know what to expect, and this makes them both anxious and angry. As a result, they tend to be clingy, demanding, and difficult to soothe. Neither of the insecure patterns is optimal but each represents a reasonable strategy for dealing with a caregiver who is inconsistent or rejecting. (For a more in-depth review of attachment theory and research, see Cassidy and Shaver, 1999; Cummings and Cummings, in Vol. 5 of this *Handbook*.)

*Maltreatment and attachment.* Most studies on attachment have used nonclinical samples, in which the rates of maltreatment are assumed to be low. However, recent research has examined patterns of attachment exhibited by abused or neglected children. Secure attachment is relatively rare in children who have been maltreated; estimates range from 0% to 25%, compared with an average of 60% of children who were not maltreated (e.g., Carlson, Cicchetti, Barnett, and Braunwald, 1989; Crittenden, 1985, 1988; Schneider-Rosen and Cicchetti, 1984).

Attachment research with maltreated children was often confounded by the difficulty that many researchers had in classifying maltreated infants into the three traditional attachment categories described by Ainsworth and her colleagues. In response, Main and Solomon (1990) developed criteria for a new *disorganized attachment* pattern. Unlike the insecure patterns, which are coherent coping strategies, disorganized attachment represents a breakdown in organized behavior. In one study of mother–infant dyads from families receiving protective services because of maltreatment, 82% of the infants showed the disorganized pattern of attachment (Carlson et al., 1989). This was viewed as a strong indication that maltreatment has powerful negative effects on infant–caregiver attachment.

*Attachment and foster parenting.* All children who are placed in foster care have, by definition, experienced separation from their primary caregivers. Based on Bowlby's observations and the well-documented sequelae of attachment disruption, it is reasonable to expect that foster children are experiencing some effects of separation. Consequently, foster parents are often presented with a situation in which they have to parent a child who may not be ready for or welcome it. To further complicate matters, most children in foster care have had the kind of care that results in insecure or disorganized attachment or they may have developed a pathological attachment style, such as Reactive Attachment Disorder (American Psychiatric Association, 1994).

Some foster parents may believe that children's attachment problems can be solved with a strong dose of love and devotion. However, altruism and exceptional parenting skills may not be enough to work successfully with a child's attachment problems. An infant or a child with an insecure–resistant pattern of attachment may be almost impossible to soothe or reassure. Their demands could overwhelm even the most dedicated foster parents. An infant or a child with an insecure–avoidant pattern of attachment may be nearly impossible to connect with. Their distancing and aloofness could leave foster parents feeling unneeded and unwanted. Caring for an infant or a child with a disorganized pattern of attachment could be quite baffling.

More worrisome and potentially problematic is the fact that foster parents could inadvertently be drawn into a dysfunctional pattern of interaction. The internal working models that develop as a result of nonoptimal care or maltreatment can influence child behavior in a manner that elicits model-confirming behavior from others. In one of the few studies on this topic, it was found that foster parents tended to complement their foster children's attachment behavior, for example by responding to insecure behavior with rejection (Stovall and Dozier, 2000). Thus even the most sensitive and determined foster parents could unwittingly behave in a way that confirms the negative expectations of their foster child.

The timing of an infant or a child's placement in foster care also has potentially important implications. Recall that it is when the infant is approximately 6 or 7 months of age that the marker of attachment emerges. This suggests that the effects of being moved to foster care in the first few months of life may be qualitatively different from those of being placed at later ages. In fact, studies of infants in foster care consistently show that babies under the age of 7 months adjust easily to a new caregiving environment without problems, whereas babies placed after 7 months generally do not (Colin, 1996). Foster parents obviously have no control over when youngsters are removed from their birth homes, but caseworkers do have some say in deciding when such action is warranted. The relevant research findings clearly support earlier rather than later intervention.

As previously noted, an important policy issue is the extent to which attachments between foster children and foster parents should be encouraged, allowed, or discouraged. The research literature suggests that it is neither advisable nor possible to avoid attachments between foster children and foster parents. Although it may be difficult for infants in foster care to attach to their foster parent and then to have to separate from their foster parent, not encouraging a child to attach to someone during their first 2 years may have more far-reaching consequences. Similarly, although it may be difficult for an older child to develop a close attachment to a foster parent and then be separated from the foster parent, there is compelling evidence that even children suffering from attachment-related pathologies can benefit from a single warm and stable relationship. It does not seem to matter whether this person is a parent, teacher, family friend, or community volunteer (e.g., Main, Kaplan, and Cassidy, 1985). What does matter is that the individual is consistently available to and supportive of the child during the time that the child is with the adult. In this way, foster care may offer an opportunity for a "corrective" attachment experience.

## Summary

As seen throughout this section, foster parents must struggle with roles and relationships that most parents do not encounter. In some cases, these roles and relationships may provide support to the foster parents as they parent the troubled children who have been placed with them. In other cases, these roles and relationships may make the parenting process even more difficult. Foster parents need to be aware of these additional roles and relationships before they take on the challenge of foster parenting.

Although the literature is limited, it does point to the value of education and training to help foster parents, birth parents, and agency caseworkers meet the challenges of their roles. As shown by Sanchirico and Jablonka (2000) and Simms and Bolden (1991), education and training can enhance the relationships between foster and birth parents. Regarding foster parents' attachments to their foster children, Tyrrell and Dozier (1999, p. 62) made these observations: "Without specific attachment-related training, foster parents are at risk for being alienated by foster children's attachment-related difficulties. They are likely to interpret the children's difficult behavior at face value instead of recognizing the children's underlying needs for nurturance.... If this occurs, foster children's attachment-related difficulties are likely to persist and may lead to later social, emotional, and behavioral problems." Educating foster parents so that they have reasonable expectations as well as the requisite skills to cope with the aftermath of separation and insecure or disordered attachment will allow them to work with foster children more effectively.

## SUCCESS AS A FOSTER PARENT

Despite the importance that foster parents can play in the life of a child, few studies have focused on discovering which factors predict successful or effective foster parenting (Seaberg and Harrigan, 1999). Two issues have influenced the lack of research in this area. First, the shortage of foster parents and the reluctance of almost all adults to take on the responsibilities of foster parenting means that recruiting and maintaining an adequate number of adequate foster parents is of primary importance to most agencies. Although all agencies would like to see their children provided with high-quality foster care, identifying parents who can provide high-quality care is often less important than finding parents willing to provide care that is at least adequate. The second issue is that there is no general agreement on how to measure success or effectiveness as a foster parent. How does one operationalize *success* for parents who take a stream of children into their homes who have been badly mistreated and who are likely to have several behavioral or emotional problems? Some studies of foster care have used changes in the children's IQs or changes in the number of reported behavior problems as a way of measuring the value of foster placement (e.g., Fanshel and

Shinn, 1978). However, none of these studies has correlated these changes with characteristics of the foster parents. Interestingly, most measures of foster parent success relate to their ability to maintain foster children in their homes (Guerney and Gavigan, 1981). For example, success has been measured by the percentage of children that foster parents are able to keep in their home until the child is returned to their birth home or placed in an adoptive home or by foster parents' willingness to continue taking foster children into their homes (Chamberlain et al., 1992; Denby et al., 1999). Finally, some studies have used caseworkers' assessments of the foster parents, although the factors on which these assessments are made are seldom specified (e.g., Dando and Minty, 1987).

Positive connections between a placement agency and foster parents has been associated with increased likelihood of parents being willing to continue as foster parents. Higher levels of training have also been associated with continuing as foster parents. Both these associations suggest that treating foster parents as valued partners and providing them with skills to meet challenges increase their satisfaction (Chamberlain et al., 1992; Denby et al., 1999; Rodwell and Biggerstaff, 1993).

The association between foster parents' motivations for their role and their success as foster parents has also been explored. Using fostering as a way of having children for childless couples, as a way of being altruistic, and as an identification with deprived children because of personal experiences were all associated with higher ratings by caseworkers. "Wanting to nurture children" was associated with poor ratings, possibly because of the difficulty that foster children have accepting nurturing and the subsequent disappointment that many foster parents may feel in these relationships (Dando and Minty, 1987). Smith (1994) hypothesized that foster parents who express greater pleasure in their parenting role and have authoritative parenting attitudes would have foster children exhibit fewer behavioral problems, but her study of 38 foster mothers and their children failed to support the hypotheses.

Smith (1994) found that foster parents of 3- to 5-year-old children who provided more language and educational stimulation to the children had foster children who exhibited fewer internalizing and externalizing behavior problems than did foster parents who provided less stimulation. She suggested that this stimulation may have kept the children occupied and thus reduced the time during which they might have misbehaved. It may also have been due to the feelings of competence that the children may have experienced or because the stimulations allowed for more positive interactions between the foster parent and the foster child.

Dando and Minty (1987) found that 57% of foster mothers who stated that they had had an unhappy childhood were rated as excellent foster parents by their caseworkers compared with 24% of those who stated that they had had a happy childhood. They suggested that parents with unhappy childhoods had high motivation to provide a more positive childhood for their foster children than they had experienced.

High levels of stress have been associated with many indications of poor foster parenting, such as increased rate of reported child maltreatment in the foster home and high attrition rates for foster parents (Benedict et al., 1994; Jones and Morrissette, 1999; Spencer and Knudsen, 1992). Alternatively, increased training focused on how to handle child behavior problems successfully resulted in fewer foster placement failures (Smith and Gutheil, 1988).

The relation between demographic variables and foster parent success has also received some attention. The variable most investigated has been the foster family's SES. Several studies have found that foster families from the blue-collar or low-middle-income levels are the most successful (Eastman, 1982). Delgado (1978) found that it was the similarity between the SES of the child and that of the foster family, rather than the SES of the foster family, that predicted success. It may be that the child is more likely to feel comfortable in a family with SES similar to his or her birth family and that moving to a family with similar SES requires fewer accommodations on the part of the foster child.

## CONCLUSIONS

Foster parenting is perhaps one of the most difficult forms of parenting. Foster parents are asked to provide good care to children who are often quite troubled and who probably will live with them for only several months or a few years, but who might live with them longer. They are often asked to mentor the birth families that may have severely maltreated the children in their care. They must often do this with insufficient funds provided by a placement agency, and their motives are often questioned ("Why would anyone want to bring children like that into their home?") To consider the difficulties faced by foster parents, readers might reflect on whether they or any of their friends are foster parents and the issues that have stopped them from taking foster children into their home.

Some of the struggles faced by foster parents are the unique roles and relationships that they must face. Foster parents have an ongoing relationship with the agency placing children in their home. This relationship can be strained because the agency is eager to have a foster parent continue to provide foster care, but at the same time the agency must monitor the parent to ensure that she or he is providing adequate care. Foster parents may feel appreciated by the agency at times and scrutinized and criticized at others. Foster parents are expected to be partners with an agency that decides whether or not the foster parents are able to remain foster parents. Foster parents often must struggle with relationships with their foster children's birth parents. Foster parents often feel angry toward the birth parents whose care of their child has been poor, and the social and cultural differences that exist between many foster parents and birth parents can make it difficult to develop a relationship. Finally, foster parents must develop relationships with a series of troubled children who may be in their home for an unknown period of time, perhaps ranging from a few weeks to several years. The child's early attachment history will have an important influence on the development of this relationship, as it is likely to constrain the ways in which the child can accommodate the new parenting that he or she receives.

The current state of society in the United States suggests that the number of foster parents needed to care for children will not be declining soon and is likely to increase. An understanding of the challenges faced by foster parents and the willingness of society to provide adequate training, support, and monetary compensation is essential for foster parents to continue providing needed service to society.

## REFERENCES

Ainsworth, M. D. S., Blehar, M. C., Waters, E., and Wall, S. (1978). *Patterns of attachment: A psychological study of the Strange Situation*. Hillsdale, NJ: Lawrence Erlbaum Associates.

American Civil Liberties Union. (1993). *A force for change. Children's rights project*. New York: Author.

American Psychiatric Association. (1994). *Diagnostic and statistical manual of mental disorders* (4th ed.). Washington, DC: Author.

Barth, R. P., Courtney, M., Berrick J. D., and Albert, V. (1994). *From child abuse to permanency planning*. New York: Aldine de Gruyter.

Benedict, M., Zuravin, S., Brandt, D., and Abbey, H. (1994). Types and frequency of child maltreatment by family foster care providers in an urban population. *Child Abuse and Neglect, 18*, 577–585.

Berrick, J., and Barth, R. (1994). Research on kinship foster care. *Children and Youth Services Review, 16*, 1–5.

Bowlby, J. (1951). *Maternal care and mental health*. Geneva: World Health Organization.

Bowlby, J. (1969). *Attachment and loss: Vol. 1. Attachment*. New York: Basic Books.

Bowlby, J. (1973). *Attachment and loss: Vol. 2. Separation: Anxiety and Anger*. New York: Basic Books.

Bowlby, J. (1980). *Attachment and loss: Vol. 3. Loss: Sadness and depression*. New York: Basic Books.

Bremner, R. H. (1970). *Children and youth in America* (Vol. 1). Cambridge, MA: Harvard University Press.

Brown, J., and Calder, P. (1999). Concept-mapping the challenges faced by foster parents. *Children and Youth Services Review, 21*, 481–495.

Carbino, R. (1991a). Child abuse and neglect reports in foster care: The issue for foster families of "false' allegations. *Child and Youth Services*, *15*, 233–247.

Carbino, R. (1991b). Advocacy for foster families in the United States facing child abuse allegations: How social agencies and foster parents are responding to the problem. *Child Welfare*, *70*, 131–149.

Carbino, R. (1992). Policy and practice for response to foster families when child abuse or neglect is reported. *Child Welfare*, *71*, 497–509.

Carlson, V., Cicchetti, D., Barnett, D., and Braunwald, K. (1989). Disorganized/disoriented attachment relationships in maltreated infants. *Developmental Psychology*, *25*, 525–531.

Cassidy, J., and Shaver, P. R. (Eds.). (1999). *Handbook of attachment: Theory, research, and clinical implications*. New York: Guilford.

Chamberlain, P., Moreland, S., and Reid, K. (1992). Enhanced services and stipends for foster parents: Effects on retention rates and outcomes for children. *Child Welfare*, *81*, 387–401.

Child Welfare League. (1997). *Children '97: Facts and figures* [On-line]. Available: http://www.cwla.org/.

Children's Defense Fund. (1987). *A children's defense budget*. Washington, DC: Author.

Colin, V. L. (1996). *Human attachment*. New York: McGraw-Hill.

Cox, M. J., and Cox, R. D. (1985). A brief history of policy for dependent and neglected children. In M. J. Cox and R. D. Cox (Eds.), *Foster care: Current issues, policies, and practices* (pp. 1–25). Norwood, NJ: Ablex.

Crittenden, P. M. (1985). Maltreated infants: Vulnerability and resilience. *Journal of Child Psychology and Psychiatry*, *26*, 85–96.

Crittenden, P. M. (1988). Distorted patterns of relationship in maltreating families: The role of internal representational models. *Journal of Reproductive and Infant Psychology*, *6*, 183–199.

Dando, I., and Minty, B. (1987). What makes good foster parents? *British Journal of Social Work*, *17*, 383–400.

Delgado, M. (1978). A Hispanic foster parent program. *Child Welfare*, *57*, 427–431.

Denby, R., Rindfleisch, N., and Bean, G. (1999). Predictors of foster parents' satisfaction and intent to continue to foster. *Child Abuse and Neglect*, *23*, 287–303.

Eastman, K. S. (1982). Foster parenthood: A nonnormative parenting arrangement. *Marriage and Family Review*, *5*, 95–120.

Erera, P. I. (1996). Foster parents' attitudes toward birth parents and caseworkers: Implications for visitations. *Families in Society: The Journal of Contemporary Human Services*, *77*, 511–519.

Fanshel, D., and Shinn, E. B. (1978). *Children in foster care: A longitudinal investigation*. New York: Columbia University Press.

Fees, B. S., Stockdale, D. F., Crase, S. J., Riggins-Caspers, K., Yates, A. M., Lekies, K. S., and Gillis-Arnold, R. (1998). Satisfaction with foster parenting: Assessment one year after training. *Children and Youth Services Review*, *20*, 347–363.

Geiser, R. L. (1973). *The illusion of caring*. Boston: Beacon.

Gillis-Arnold, R., Crase, S. J., Stockdale, D. F., and Shelley, M. C. (1998). Parenting attitudes, foster parenting attitudes, and motivations of adoptive and nonadoptive foster parent trainees. *Children and Youth Services Review*, *20*, 715–732.

Goodman, G., Emery, R., and Haugaard, J. (1998). Developmental psychology and the law: Divorce child maltreatment, foster care, and adoption. In I. Sigel and A. Renninger (Eds.), *Handbook of child psychology* (Vol. 4) (pp. 775–876). New York: Wiley.

Guerney, L. F., and Gavigan, M. A. (1981). Parental acceptance and foster parents. *Journal of Clinical Child Psychology*, *10*, 27–32.

Hess, P. M. (1988). Case and context: Determinants of planned visit frequency in foster family care. *Child Welfare*, *67*, 311–326.

Hollinger, J. H. (Ed.). (1991). *Adoption law and practice*. New York: West Publishing.

Inch, L. J. (1999). Aspect of foster fathering. *Child and Adolescent Social Work Journal*, *16*, 393–412.

James Bell Associates (1993). *The national survey of current and former foster parents*. Washington, DC: U.S. Department of Health and Human Services.

Jones, G., and Morrissette, P. J. (1999). Foster parent stress. *Canadian Journal of Counseling*, *33*, 13–27.

Le Prohn, N. S. (1994). The role of the kinship foster parent: A comparison of the role conceptions of relative and non-relative foster parents. *Children and Youth Services Review*, *16*, 65–84.

Main, M., Kaplan, N., and Cassidy, J. (1985). Security in infancy, childhood, and adulthood: A move to the level of representation. *Monographs of the Society for Research in Child Development*, *50* (1–2, pp. 66–104).

Main, M., and Solomon, J. (1990). Procedures for identifying infants as disorganized/disoriented during the Ainsworth Strange Situation. In M. Greenberg, D. Cicchetti, and M. Cummings (Eds.) *Attachment in the preschool years: Theory, research, and intervention* (pp. 121–160). Chicago: University of Chicago Press.

McFadden, E. J. (1996). Family centered practice with foster-parent families. *Families in Society: The Journal of Contemporary Human Services*, *77*, 545–557.

Meyers, B., and Link, H. (1990). *Kinship foster care: The double edged dilemma*. New York: Task Force for Permanency Planning for Foster Children.

Mietus, K. J., and Fimmen, M. (1987). Role ambiguity among foster parents: Semi-professionals in professionalizing organizations. *Journal of Sociology and Social Welfare, 14*, 33–41.

Mnookin, R. H. (1978). *Child, family, and state*. Boston: Little, Brown.

National Center for Policy Analysis. (1997, August). *The state of the children: An examination of government-run foster care* (Rep. No. 210). Washington, DC: Author.

National Center on Child Abuse and Neglect. (1995). *Child maltreatment in 1993: Reports from the states to the National Center on Child Abuse and Neglect*. Washington, DC: Department of Health and Human Services.

National Commission on Child Welfare and Family Preservation. (1990). *A commitment to change: Interim report*. Washington, DC: American Public Welfare Association.

Pasztor, E. M., and Wynne, S. F. (1995). *Foster parent retention and recruitment*. Washington, DC: Child Welfare League of America.

Poland, D. C., and Groze, V. (1993). Effects of foster care placement on biological children in the home. *Children and Adolescent Social Work Journal, 10*, 153–163.

Rodwell, M., and Biggerstaff, M. (1993). Strategies for recruitment and retention of foster families. *Children and Youth Services Review, 15*, 403–419.

Rothman, D. J. (1971). *The discovery of the asylum*. Boston: Little, Brown.

Runyon, D. K., and Gould, C. L. (1985). Foster care for child maltreatment: Impact on delinquent behavior. *Pediatrics, 75*, 562–568.

Sanchirico, A., and Jablonka, K. (2000). Keeping foster children connected to their biological parents: The impact of foster parent training and support. *Child and Adolescent Social Work Journal, 17*, 185–203.

Sanchirico, A., Lau, W. J., Jablonka, K., and Russell, S. J. (1998). Foster parent involvement in service planning: Does it increase job satisfaction? *Children and Youth Services Review, 20*, 325–346.

Savage, M. F. (1999). The ties that bind. *Cardozo Women's Law Journal, 6*, 129–154.

Schneider-Rosen, K., and Cicchetti, D. (1984). The relationship between affect and cognition in maltreated infants: Quality of attachment and the development of visual self-recognition. *Child Development, 55*, 648–658.

Seaberg, J. R., Harrigan, M. P. (1997). Family functioning in foster care. *Families in Society: The Journal of Contemporary Human Services, 78*, 463–470.

Seaberg, J. R., and Harrigan, M. P. (1999). Foster families' functioning, experiences and views: Variations by race. *Children and Youth Services Review, 21*, 31–55.

Simms, M. D., and Bolden, B. J. (1991). The family reunification project: Facilitating regular contact among foster children, biological families, and foster families. *Child Welfare, 70*, 679–690.

Smith, E., and Gutheil, R. (1988). Successful foster parent recruiting: A voluntary agency effort. *Child Welfare, 67*, 137–146.

Smith, M. C. (1994). Child-rearing practices associated with better developmental outcomes in preschool-age foster children. *Child Study Journal, 24*, 299–326.

Smith V. Orginazation of Foster Families for Equality and Reform, 431 U.S. 816, (1977).

Spencer, W., and Knudsen, D. (1992). Out-of-home maltreatment: An analysis of risk in various settings for children. *Children and Youth Services Review, 14*, 485–492.

Steverson, J. W. (1994). Stopping fetal abuse with no-pregnancy and drug treatment probation conditions. *Santa Clara Law Review, 34*, 295–372.

Stovall, K. C., and Dozier, M. (2000). The development of attachment in new relationships: Single subject analyses for 10 foster infants. *Development and Psychopathology, 12*, 133–156.

Trattner, W. I. (1979). *From poor law to welfare state*. New York: Free Press.

Twigg, R. C. (1994). The unknown soldiers of foster care: Foster care as loss for the foster parents' own children. *Smith College Studies in Social Work, 64*, 297–312.

Tyrrell, C., and Dozier, M. (1999). Foster parents' understanding of children's problematic attachment strategies: The need for therapeutic responsiveness. *Adoption Quarterly, 2*, 49–64.

U.S. General Accounting Office. (1995). *Child welfare: Complex needs strain capacity to provide services*. Washington DC: Author.

Warsh, R., Pine, B. A., and Maluccio, A. (1996). *Reconnecting families: A guide to strengthening family reunification services*. Washington, DC: Child Welfare League of America.

Zima, B. T., Bussing, R., Freeman, S., Yang, X., Belin, T. R., and Forness, S. (2000). Behavior problems, academic skill delays and school failure among school-aged children in placement characteristics. *Journal of Child and Family Studies, 9*, 87–103.

# 12

# Parenting Children Born Preterm

Susan Goldberg
*The Hospital for Sick Children, Toronto*
*University of Toronto*
Barbara DiVitto
*North Shore Children's Hospital, Salem, Massachusetts*

## INTRODUCTION

Each year, from 2% to 9% of newborn babies require specialized care in a neonatal intensive care unit (NICU). The majority of these are babies born prematurely (before 37 weeks of age) and weigh less than 2,500 g (5 lb) at birth. Modern medical technology has doggedly pushed back the frontiers of viability so that as we enter the twenty-first century an increasing number of babies as young as 23 to 24 weeks gestation with weights as low as 500 g are surviving. Parents of all preterm babies confront unique problems engendered by the timing of the birth, a prolonged hospital stay, and distinctive patterns of behavior and development in the infant's early years. In this chapter we review these problems and their effects on parents. In doing so, we focus on parent–infant interactions and relationships in these early years, but include some information on later development. In part, this emphasis reflects the fact that the infancy years have been the most intensively studied. Infancy is the time when these children are most different from others and most challenging to their parents. This review is selective rather than comprehensive and, aside from background history, concentrates on general themes of recent interest.

The chapter includes five main sections. It begins with a history of changes in care of preterm infants and the resulting effects on parents. The second section outlines the conditions that are unique to preterm infants and their parents: the timing of birth, the nature of the hospital experience, and behavioral characteristics of preterm behavior and development. The third part outlines theories of parent–child relationships and their respective interpretations of prematurity. The fourth reviews research on parent–infant relationships, and the fifth considers interventions designed to improve parent–child relationships in this group. Throughout the chapter we use the terms *preterm* and *premature* interchangeably. Quotes from parents of prematurely born infants are interspersed throughout the text to convey firsthand experience of some of the phenomena we discuss.

## HISTORY OF PRETERM CARE: EFFECTS ON PARENTING

Initially, preterm infants, like all other infants, were born at home. If they survived, they were cared for by their parents with help from midwives and physicians. In the late 1800s, Pierre Budin, a Parisian physician, pioneered research on prematurity as a special disorder of the newborn and authored the first text on neonatology (the study of diseases of the newborn; Budin, 1907). He also invented the forerunner of our modern incubators that control temperature, oxygen, and humidity to provide life support for vulnerable infants. In this period, others in Berlin and Helsinki were also investigating solutions for the problems of preterm infants such as poor temperature control, feeding difficulties, and vulnerability to disease (Avery and Litwack, 1983). These innovations all required separation of preterm infants from their parents.

An extreme example of this separation was the exhibition of preterm infants in incubators as a commercial venture that toured fairs and expositions in both the United States and Europe by Martin Cooney, a student of Budin. These infants were not expected to live, and parents often had to be coaxed into taking "survivors" home after they had been on tour. However inhumane this practice appears to us today, it demonstrated the effectiveness of incubators and led to their adoption in North American hospitals.

From the time when hospital care began, parents were considered potential carriers of the germs thought to cause respiratory problems in preterm infants, and early care stressed cleanliness and sterility. Parental contact was considered dangerous for the infant. Even after 1949, when hyaline membrane disease (functional immaturity of the lungs) was recognized as the main cause of these respiratory problems, policies on parental visiting remained largely unchanged (Colon and Colon, 2000).

Major changes in the care of preterms began in the 1960s when neonatology became a recognized medical specialty. New techniques for assisting breathing, equipment and laboratory tests to detect physiological problems, new surgical techniques, and drugs began to reduce the incidence and severity of problems associated with prematurity, enabling smaller and more vulnerable babies to survive. The specially trained staff and equipment were expensive and needed for only a small proportion of newborns, so they were located in regional medical centers rather than local hospitals. The immediate result of this change was to further separate infants and parents. Babies were transported by specially equipped vans or helicopters after delivery, while their mothers remained in the birthing hospital. Depending on the distance between hospitals and between hospital and home, fathers could be torn between visiting the baby or visiting the mother, or both parents might be unable to visit their infant. For those parents able to visit, the "high-tech" environment of the NICU was intimidating and could leave parents feeling overwhelmed, isolated, and unimportant to their baby's care. Furthermore, handling was considered stressful for these vulnerable babies, so affectionate handling was kept to a minimum by both parents and staff; invasive medical procedures were infants' primary human contacts.

In the early 1970s a daring experiment was reported from Stanford University Medical Center. Mothers had been allowed into the NICU to handle and care for their babies. When time periods with parent handling were compared with those without it, the expected increase in infection rates did not occur (Barnett, Leiderman, Grobstein, and Klaus, 1970). A duplication at Case Western Reserve Medical Center confirmed these results (Kennell, Trause, and Klaus, 1975). These data, which showed convincingly that parent contact was not dangerous for preterm babies, led caregivers to question the traditional policy of separation and to studies of the effects of increased contact between mothers and babies. As a result of this work, hospitals began to allow and encourage parents to enter the NICU to handle and care for their infants. However, even in the most supportive nurseries, parent visits to preterms are experiences that differ markedly from taking a term infant home soon after birth.

In recognition of the psychological barriers parents encounter in the NICU, hospitals included spaces where parents could have more privacy with their infants. In addition, they provided opportunities to participate in educational and support groups while their infants were in isolettes in the nursery (Minde, Shosenberg, Thompson, and Marton, 1983; Paludetto, Faggiano-Perfetto, Asprea, De Curtis, and Margara-Paludetto, 1981).

Studies focused on the NICU as an environment for development suggest that affectionate handling such as holding, cuddling, massage, and skin-to-skin contact does not compromise infant well-being (e.g., Bauer, Pyper, Sperling, Uhrig, and Versmold, 1998) and actually has benefits, even for very small fragile babies (e.g., Daga, Ahuja, and Lunkad, 1998). In light of this information, some hospitals have expanded the role of parents by instituting unrestricted visiting and encouraging parent participation in baby care.

The most startling innovation in parent care of preterm infants evolved out of necessity in developing countries like Columbia, where economic constraints on equipment and staff forced parents to take over care of their infants. Regardless of size and weight, those in satisfactory condition 2 to 3 hr after birth would go directly to their mothers, be breast-fed, and carried in an upright position in slings on the mother's chest; hence the name kangaroo care. Infants doing well would go home with their parents as early as 12 hr after birth. These practices produced dramatic reductions in mortality, morbidity, and parent abandonment (Anderson, Marks, and Wahlberg, 1986). As a result, hospitals in more privileged settings, where even relatively healthy preterm infants traditionally spent long periods in incubators, began to adopt kangaroo care.

In short, practices have come full circle from a time when preterm infants, if they survived, were cared for entirely by their parents, through a period of increasing isolation during development of the technology that improved survival, followed by gradual return to greater parent involvement. Our modern challenge is to provide the benefits of the best medical technology while simultaneously supporting the development of parent–infant relationships.

## UNIQUE FEATURES OF PRETERM BIRTH

Three aspects of parental experience are unique to prematurity: the timing of birth, the quality of the initial hospital experience, and the unique nature of the preterm infant as a social partner. In this section we consider how each of these can affect infants, parents, and their relationship.

### Timing of Birth

In the normal course of development, 38–42 weeks from conception is the optimal time for birth. Were the infant to stay in the womb longer, growth would be hampered by lack of space: The infant could become too large to pass through the birth canal, and the mother's body might be unable to meet increased needs for nourishment. However, the fetus requires the support and protection of the uterine environment while major organs and organ systems (e.g., heart, lung, nervous system) are being formed and until capable of functioning outside. Early births produce infants who are well adapted for life in the womb but not prepared for the external environment. The earlier a baby is born, the more physiological functions are compromised and require artificial support and management. At one time, even with artificial support, infants born less than 28 weeks from conception were not considered viable. Modern technology has continued to extend the limits of viability so that more aggressive interventions and long hospital stays of small fragile babies are now routine. However, these babies do not necessarily survive without lingering problems (Lorenz, Wooliever, Jetton, and Paneth, 1998; Volpe, 1998; Wolke, 1998). Many infants born at 27 weeks gestational age or less continue to require special care from parents and professionals as they develop. In this chapter we do not focus on persistent problems in rearing a child born preterm because these issues are covered in other chapters (e.g., Melamed, in Vol. 5 of this *Handbook*).

Parents also undergo a developmental process during pregnancy. For the mother, this includes the physical changes associated with support of a developing life. Both parents experience complex psychological changes as they form expectations for their new infant, engage in preparation for infantcare, and prepare for new roles (Zeanah and McDonough, 1989; Demick, in Vol. 3 of this *Handbook*). When birth occurs prematurely, parents have parenthood thrust on them before these processes are completed. They may have missed childbirth classes, not yet acquired a crib or baby clothes, or arranged space in their home. The crisis aspect of preterm birth and its psychological impact have long been recognized (Caplan, 1960). Parents' expectations for a normal delivery and a healthy infant are violated, and they must come to terms with disappointment and loss (Pederson, Bento, Chance, Evans, and Fox, 1987; Zeanah, Canger, and Jones, 1984) as well as fears for the infant's health and future. The normal joy and rituals surrounding birth are absent, and the discomfort of family and friends can isolate new parents from needed social support. At this time, high levels of depression and anxiety are common among both fathers and mothers (Meyer et al., 1995; Miles, Funk, and Kasper, 1992), as stated by a mother who was interviewed 10 days postdischarge (Goldberg and DiVitto, 1983, p. 111):

> At first, I was afraid to go to the nursery and see him . . . I didn't know what I would find. They practically had to drag me all the way the first time.

A second issue for parents is the realization that they cannot care for their baby on their own, a feeling that is reinforced if the infant is transported to special facilities in another hospital. Instead of looking forward to bringing their baby home in a few days, parents face a hospital stay of unknown length, the possibility of life-threatening complications, compromised development, and the continuing need for professional assistance for their child. The resulting sense of failure may be particularly strong for mothers (Jeffcoate, Humphrey, and Lloyd, 1979), as demonotrated by this mother of a premature infant (Herzog, 1980, cited in Goldberg and DiVitto, 1983, p. 111):

> Ingrid wept as she saw her tiny premature daughter. "My third miscarriage," she said, just loud enough for those close to her to hear.

The mother of Caitlin, born at 33 weeks, had this to say (M. Ladd, personal communication, Nov. 10, 2000):

> I had a lot of experience with children and was not anticipating motherhood would be difficult. But breastfeeding did not progress smoothly since she was too young to latch well. The nurses seemed so much more competent in handling and bathing my baby. Seeing that a stranger could do a better job than me with my baby, I went home from the NICU each night feeling like a failure as a mother.

Although having a small, immature, and sick infant depresses mothers' perceptions of their ability to care for their baby, this effect may diminish over time (Redshaw, 1997).

Third, preterm births occur disproportionately in families with limited resources. Mothers who are very young, have had little or inadequate prenatal care, and endure poverty and social disadvantage have a higher rate of premature birth than those in more advantaged circumstances. These families are more easily overwhelmed and lack resources to cope with the crisis of preterm birth. Even for advantaged families who have insurance or universal health care to cover basic costs, there are unexpected financial burdens associated with preterm birth (e.g., costs of travel, food, and possibly lodging for trips to the hospital).

## The Hospital Environment

Given the precarious ability of the preterm infant to maintain normal body functions, the primary focus of neonatal intensive care is maintaining and enhancing the physical well-being of the infant by artificial means—surgical, chemical, or mechanical. Other considerations, such as psychological development and social relationships, must be secondary. Studies of the ecology of the NICU concur in indicating high noise levels, high illumination, large numbers of caregivers and caregiving interventions, and lack of relation between infant behavior and environmental events (Graven et al., 1992). The extent to which these conditions directly affect infant development is unknown because it is impossible to disentangle specific features of care from the medical conditions that require them. Although considerable thought and effort have been given to humanizing this environment (e.g., Als, Duffy, and McAnulty, 1996; Minde, 2000), the NICU is neither a good approximation of the womb nor a normal home environment. It was never designed to be either of these things but rather to deal with life-threatening medical crises. Parents cope with the confusion and the uncertainty this environment represents to themselves as well as concerns about what this environment means to their infant.

From the point of view of parent–infant relationships, the most salient feature of prolonged hospital care is that it limits shared social experiences for parents and infants. Of course, if the infant were still *in utero*, these experiences would not be available, but once the baby is born, parents have the expectation of establishing a social relationship with their baby and want to do so, as this statement from the father of Caitlin, born at 33 weeks, indicates (T. Ladd, personal communication, Nov. 10, 2000):

> She was in an incubator and looked so tiny and fragile. I felt so hopeless that I couldn't touch her, that she might break. Then the nurse said, "Do you want to hold her?" And I was so relieved, I said, "Yes . . . for the next twenty years or so."

As infants grow older, they become more alert and responsive and are moved to hospital rooms with less intimidating equipment and less intense nursing coverage and thus become more available to parents.

When parents reflect on the salient aspects of their infant's hospitalization during the hospital stay or at the time of discharge, they report that the appearance of the baby and fears about the infant's health and survival provoke the most stress (Miles, 1989; Pederson et al., 1987) followed by alterations in the parental role (Miles, 1989). When looking back at the hospital experience, parents whose infants are healthy at 1 year of age may minimize the stresses of the early experience (Jackson and Gorman, 1988). However, under less positive conditions, mothers recall their responses to their infants' hospitalization and the stresses of NICU care 3 years later (Werceszczak, Miles, and Holditch-Davis, 1997). Mothers and fathers agree on which experiences are stressful but often use different coping strategies (Affleck, Tennen, and Rowe, 1990). Mothers seek social support and use escape strategies, whereas fathers minimize and use instrumental approaches. These different strategies may contribute to marital conflict but may also bring couples closer together if they recognize their strategies as complementary (Affleck et al., 1990).

In recognition of the difficulties faced by parents during the period of intensive care, there have been efforts to enhance confidence and parenting skills (see Patteson and Barnard, 1990, for a review) and to train and support professionals who work with parents (e.g., Marshall, Kasman, and Cape, 1982). An increasing number of hospitals offer support groups run by "veteran" parents with the help of professionals. With few exceptions (e.g., Minde, Shosenberg et al., 1983) the effects of these groups have not been assessed in a systematic way. Nevertheless, they fill important needs of parents during the hospitalization and following discharge (Boukydis, 1982).

## Going Home: Premature Infant Behavior and Development

The transition from hospital to home, much as it is eagerly anticipated as a mark of success and progress toward normalcy, brings new stresses. If their baby is transferred from a regional unit to a local hospital as part of this process, parents encounter new staff, new routines, and new policies. Whether babies go home directly from a regional unit or from a community hospital, parents who have spent weeks and months watching professionals care for their baby may feel overwhelmed by the new responsibility and isolated from the support system they had developed with hospital staff and other parents (Miles and Holditch-Davis, 1997), as stated by the father of Tyler, born at 33 weeks (Tracy and Maroney, 1999, p. 62):

Tyler seemed so tiny and helpless in the hospital. The surroundings were so intimidating, and I just wanted him to come home. Once he came home, I realized I had underestimated what it would really be like. I found myself checking on him at night while my wife pumped breast milk.

The age of preterm infants at birth and discharge varies. Of course, term infants are also born at different ages and return home at different ages from conception, but these variations are small. The best evidence suggests that many aspects of development proceed on a timetable that is not altered by the time of birth (Hunt and Rhodes, 1977). Thus parents of term infants look for developmental milestones on the basis of age from birth, but parents of preterm infants have to wait that much longer to see the expected accomplishments. For example, babies born at term usually begin social smiling at 6 to 8 weeks of age. Preterm infants show social smiles in the second month *past term* (Anisfeld, 1982). Thus a preterm born 10 weeks early may be 16 to 18 weeks past birth before engaging in social smiles. If we remember that the care of any newborn is exhausting and demands parent sacrifices, delay in reaching rewarding milestones can be seen as a frustration for parents, particularly when the potential for permanent handicaps is a concern, as evidenced by the mother of Adam, born at 27 weeks (Tracy and Maroney, 1999, p. 214):

My premie didn't do anything in normal sequence. I couldn't follow the books on typical child development. The doctors kept telling me he'd catch up. It took years, but eventually he did.

Several studies indicate that early parenting by both mothers and fathers influences the long-term outcome for preterm infants just as it does for term infants (e.g., Magill-Evans and Harrison, 1999; McGrath, Sullivan, and Seifer, 1998; Moore, Saylor, and Boyce, 1998; Yogman, Kindlon, and Earls, 1995). Parents may be particularly sensitive to this responsibility in a context of uncertain outcome. As one mother remarked (Biddle-Bruckman, 1999):

Looking back, once Grace was born, I never remember thinking that she would not survive; however, I do remember feeling paralyzed by the fear of the unknown.

In addition to doing things later than term infants, preterm infants' appearance and behavior differ qualitatively from those of term peers. The normal physical features of infants are unique in ways that appeal to adults: a flattened nose, broad cheeks, large head, and relatively large eyes characterize infants of many species. Preterm infants lack these features (Maier, Holmes, Slaymaker, and Reich, 1984) and are judged less attractive than term infants, although experience caring for a preterm baby modifies these judgments (Corter et al., 1978). The cries of babies who experienced stressful medical conditions differ acoustically from those of healthy infants, differences recognizable by naive adults (Friedman, Zahn-Waxler, and Radke-Yarrow, 1982; Lester and Zeskind, 1979). Although initially preterm infants may cry very little, particularly if they have respiratory complications (Molitor and Eckerman, 1992), their cries are more physiologically arousing to adults than those of term infants (Frodi et al., 1978). In the first years, they engage in fewer broad smiles (Segal et al., 1995), are relatively fussy and irritable (e.g., Eckerman, Hsu, Molitor, Leung, and Goldstein, 1999), more difficult to soothe (Friedman, Jacobs, and Werthman, 1982), show more mixed behavioral cues (Eckerman et al., 1999), and are described by parents as showing more sensory-defensive behaviors (Case-Smith, Butcher, and Reed, 1998) and being temperamentally more difficult (Langkamp, Kim, and Pascoe, 1998) than term peers. Research on preterm behavior and development is extensive and detailed review of this material is beyond the scope of this chapter. Rather, we provide this brief synopsis to underscore the different nature of the preterm infant as a social partner and the resulting adjustments demanded of parents. Many parents continue to experience the care of a preterm infant as stressful throughout the infancy and preschool years (Robson, 1997), as the mother of Eric, born at 30 weeks, states (Tracy and Maroney, 1999, p. 214):

I knew I should be grateful to even have my child, but I kept wondering if there would be any developmental problems ahead. There were all those follow-up appointments and therapy sessions. It seemed as though he'd make progress in one area, then slow down in another. I had to do exercises with him every day. I kept wondering when it all would end and I could finally enjoy my family.

Parental behavior may also be influenced by awareness of the infant's status, aside from behaviors and characteristics of preterm infants. Adults who viewed videotapes of infants labeled premature rated them less developed, sociable, active, competent, and liked than when the same infant was labeled full term (Stern and Karraker, 1990). Furthermore, mothers behaved differently toward a baby labeled premature by touching less and offering more immature toys. This suggests that a "prematurity stereotype" of lowered expectations may influence parent behavior toward their premature infants.

Others suggest that parents whose children have experienced a life-threatening medical condition may continue to fear for the child's life even after the danger has passed and become inappropriately overprotective. This idea first appeared in Green and Solnit (1964) as the "vulnerable child syndrome." Empirical data now demonstrate that child vulnerability and parental overprotection are distinct clinical phenomena: Prior life-threatening illness is related to perception of the child as vulnerable but not necessarily to overprotection (Thomasgard, Shonkoff, Metz, and Edelbrock, 1995). Nevertheless, there is evidence that parents of preterm infants are subject to both influences: the perception of the child as vulnerable (Estroff, Yando, Burke, and Snyder, 1994; Thomasgard and Metz, 1996) and the tendency to protect the child more than is necessary (Miles, Holditch-Davis, and Shepherd, 1998).

In summary, parents of preterm infants face a daunting task. They take on the role of parent before they or their baby are ready for it. They do so under highly stressful conditions with limited opportunities for normal interaction, and many find their babies difficult to manage. What are the implications of these circumstances for the formation of parent–child relationships?

## THEORETICAL PERSPECTIVES

Most theoretical approaches to the study of parent–infant relationships emphasize the influence of parents on infants. The explosion of research on infant capacities that began in the 1960s changed our conception of the infant as a passive and helpless being into one of a competent although immature human, influencing surrounding adults, and playing an active role in his or her own development. One line of thinking emphasizes ways in which the behavior and the appearance of preterm infants elicit unique responses from parents. For example, one model of parent–infant interaction emphasized clarity and consistency of infant cues and infant responsiveness as determinants of parent feelings of competence. Within this framework, preterm infants were conceptualized as providing less clarity and consistency of behavior than their term counterparts and would therefore be more challenging for parents (Goldberg, 1977).

A related approach conceptualizes the preterm infant as having a low tolerance for stimulation coupled with a high threshold for active response (Field, 1982). Consequently, to maintain social interactions with a preterm infant, adult caregivers must maintain behavior within the narrow intensity range that elicits infant response without exceeding infant tolerance. Term infants are more flexible and able to tolerate and respond to a wider range of adult behavior. They are therefore less challenging for adult social partners.

A different approach to parent–infant relationships was spearheaded by Klaus and Kennell (1976, 1982) under the rubric of "bonding." Bonding is the process by which parents come to feel an emotional investment in individual offspring. Although this is a lifelong process (Klaus and Kennell, 1982), early work focused on the effects of initial contacts between parents (particularly mothers) and infants. It was suggested that optimal mother–infant relationships were fostered by close contact during a period immediately after birth considered "critical" or "sensitive" for bonding. Many studies of this phenomenon were conducted, and the findings provoked much controversy. Although most of the numerous reviews of this literature concluded that the evidence was unconvincing (e.g., Myers, 1984), this view of bonding achieved such popularity that parents and professionals pressed hospitals for opportunities for early contact. A side effect of this movement was that it left parents who could not experience early contact with feelings of failure, parents of preterm infants among them. When applied to preterm infants, this approach emphasizes the detrimental effects of early separation.

A third approach to parent–infant relationships that has come to dominate the field of social development is that of attachment theory, originally advanced by Bowlby (1969). Bowlby emphasized the protective function of the caregiver as the foundation for formation of infants' emotional ties to parents. Because the human infant cannot survive without intensive adult care, Bowlby argued, our evolutionary history biases infants to behave in ways that elicit care. Over the first year of life, these behaviors become organized into a goal-corrected system focused on a specific caregiver, usually, but not necessarily, the mother. Ainsworth, Blehar, Waters, and Wall (1978) elaborated the concept of the caregiver as protector to emphasize the importance of providing a "secure base" for exploration, and they developed a standard laboratory observation in which infants reveal their confidence in the caregiver as a haven of safety. This procedure, called the Strange Situation, provides a measure of the quality of the infant–parent relationship as perceived by the infant.

Within this framework, the effects of preterm birth can be approached in several ways. First, because Bowlby emphasized an evolutionary history that selected infants for ability to engage adults in caregiving, the survival of infants who would not have been viable in "the environment of evolutionary adaptedness" clearly poses problems for ensuing parent–child relationships. Second, current attachment theory emphasizes the importance of consistent and responsive care for normal social development. Although theoretically the experience of being parented is considered the primary influence on parental caregiving abilities, unexpected burdens, limited opportunity for early contact, and poor social support, coupled with the limited signaling capability of the preterm infant, might also disrupt parental responsiveness (Goldberg, 1977).

The development of the Strange Situation procedure had an important methodological effect on the study of preterm infants and their parents. Ainsworth et al. (1978) demonstrated that 1-year-old infants' reactions to parent returns after separation were systematically related to the type of care infants had experienced at home in the previous year. Many researchers who did not subscribe to attachment theory used the Strange Situation as an outcome measure in studies of preterm infants because it is one of the few well standardized measures of early social development. As a result, there is information on behavior of preterm infants in the Strange Situation as well as extensive normative term data for comparison. Because infant behavior in the Strange Situation is used to make inferences about the caregiver's prior responsiveness, we can think of it as revealing infants' perspectives on relationships with particular caregivers.

These theoretical approaches do not differ in predicted outcomes. All agree that preterm infants and the circumstances that surround their birth present parents with unique challenges. All agree that parent–preterm infant relationships will be more vulnerable to problems than those of term infants. They differ primarily in attributions about the reasons for this vulnerability—which aspects of the preterm experience are most likely to create subsequent problems. Social interaction approaches emphasize limitations of the infant per se; bonding theory emphasizes effects of early and prolonged separations; and attachment theory emphasizes parent ability to provide appropriate care. These are not mutually exclusive approaches, and there have been no studies designed to discriminate among them.

Contemporary research is also influenced by an integrative approach that espouses "transactional" models of development (Sameroff and Chandler, 1975). The transactional approach emphasizes dynamic aspects of development whereby the outcome at any stage (whether for parent, infant, or in the relationship) is the input or shapes response to input in the subsequent stage. No single feature is expected to influence a prolonged developmental period without itself reflecting the effects of the developmental process. From this perspective, we can consider the above theories to emphasize different aspects of a complex process.

## OBSERVATIONS OF PARENT–PRETERM INFANT INTERACTIONS

Empirical research on preterm infants and their parents is a relatively recent phenomenon. The first studies of preterm infants were concerned with survival and health. Although these early themes continued, global measures of psychological outcomes were soon introduced: IQ, school performance, and use of special services. Aside from occasional reports concerning child social functioning, temperament, and behavior problems, parent experience was largely ignored until advances in neonatology brought large numbers of parents of preterm infants into prolonged contact with health professionals. This development increased awareness of the experiences impinging on parents in the NICU.

Earlier, we referred to the innovative experiments that first brought parents into NICUs. With convincing evidence that parent visiting did not compromise infant health and concern about early bonding opportunities, more and more facilities allowed and encouraged parent visiting. Thus, for the first time, there were opportunities to observe and talk with parents whose infants were in incubators. Evaluation of these changes led to general interest in parent–child interactions and parent experiences after hospital discharge. The formation of parent support groups created organized "consumers" eager for practical information and scientific research about parents and preterm infants.

These were practical developments that drew researchers toward studying early social experiences of preterm infants and their families. There were also scientific issues that created the impetus for these studies. Premature birth was increasingly recognized as a "natural experiment" in the study of parent–infant relationships, providing conditions that could not ethically be manipulated (e.g., separation during a hypothesized critical period) for large numbers of families with ready access through hospital units. In the next subsection we summarize research on preterm infants and their parents with an emphasis on observational studies concerned with early parent–child interactions and relationships.

### Parents and Infants in the Hospital

Two kinds of studies provide information about parent–infant relationships during hospitalization. The first focuses on the ecology of the NICU and includes information about parent visiting patterns. These studies report frequency and length of visits and may include information about types of interactions (e.g., caregiving, social interaction, adult conversation). They do not attempt detailed analysis of parent–infant interactions. The second type of study is concerned primarily with parent–infant interactions and focuses on detailed observations of what parents and infants do during hospital visits. We consider information from both study types.

Reports of visiting patterns were common when parent visiting was first introduced. The studies that introduced parents into the NICU (Fanaroff, Kennell, and Klaus, 1972; Leifer, Leiderman, Barnett, and Williams, 1972) reported "low" rates of visiting (once every 6 days and less than twice in 3 weeks, respectively). Later, when such visiting was routine, similar rates were reported at the start of one study (Rosenfield, 1980), whereas in another most parents visited daily (DiVitto and Goldberg, 1979). Thus, even with permission to enter the NICU, there are vast differences in amount of parent visiting. What accounts for these differences?

The most detailed study of NICU visiting patterns was undertaken in the 1970s in Exeter, England (Hawthorne, Richards, and Callon, 1978). In the first week that the infant was in the hospital, the primary determinant of visiting was whether the mother was in the same hospital. If she was, she usually visited at least daily and after discharge visited less often. Mother visiting was more consistent than father visiting. Fathers were likely to visit more often if they were of middle-socioeconomic status and had been present at the birth. "Long-stay" babies (those staying more than 2 weeks) were primarily low-birthweight (mostly premature) babies transferred from other hospitals and were visited less often than babies with shorter stays. For these babies, distance from home, presence of other children at home, and social status affected visiting patterns.

It is also clear that overt and covert messages from unit staff can affect parent visiting. In one effort to increase maternal visiting, NICU staff scheduled weekly "appointments" during which mothers visited their hospitalized babies along with a supportive staff member. Mothers in the appointment group made more spontaneous visits than did those in the control group (Zeskind and Iacino, 1984). Although increased visiting was associated with less positive initial perceptions of the baby, it was associated with more positive long-term expectations.

One of the most intriguing findings regarding visiting patterns is the incidental observation of increased visiting among mothers of babies receiving supplemental stimulation (Rosenfeld, 1980). Two possible reasons were suggested: First, increases in alertness in the experimental group babies may have made visits more pleasurable for mothers and increased their interest in visiting. Second, knowledge that their babies had been singled out for "special treatment" may have motivated mothers to visit more often.

Comparison of neonatal units over the decade of the 1980s noted that social interactions with infants in intensive care had increased, with parents contributing some of that increase (Eyler, Woods, Behnke, and Conlon, 1992). Nevertheless, parents accounted for only 14% of human contacts experienced by an infant in NICU (Gottfried and Gaiter, 1985). There continues to be a general lack of information about parent experiences in NICU.

Much of the existing information reflects interviews or surveys with parents who have experienced the NICU environment. Few efforts have been made to observe what happens when parents visit their infants in hospital. Even with the recent interest in kangaroo care, there are few observations of contact periods (but see the section on clinical interventions for this limited material). One exception is a series of studies conducted by Minde and his colleagues. In these studies, observations recorded on an electronic event recorder provided a continuous record of parent and infant behavior during two visits for each week of hospitalization. Over the course of the hospital stay, mothers increased both the duration of visits and the proportion of time they were actively engaged with the infant. Furthermore, some mothers were consistently more active than others. These mothers called and visited more and were also more actively involved with their infants at subsequent home observations. This was not related to the infants' medical condition. Rather, mothers who reported better relationships with their family of origin and spouses and had fewer social risk factors in their histories were more likely to be in the active group (Minde, Marton, Manning, and Hines, 1980). However, when detailed behavior sequences were analyzed, maternal behavior was related to infant behavior, particularly in the high activity group. In a subsequent study, a detailed medical index assessed the daily medical condition of 184 low-birthweight preterm infants. Infants who were seriously ill were less active than their healthier counterparts, and maternal activity was related to the infant's medical course. Infants with a short hospital course became more active, and their mothers correspondingly increased their vocalization, touching, and looking, whereas infants with a long hospital stay remained inactive, and their mothers maintained lower activity rates. These differences persisted even after infants had been at home for several months (Minde, Whitelaw, Brown, and Fitzhardinge, 1983). A related study demonstrated that mothers of preterm twins were more active with the healthier of the twins (Minde, Perrotta, and Corter, 1982; Lytton with Gallagher, in Vol. 1 of this *Handbook*).

Two studies observed both fathers and mothers during nursery visits. In the first, a small study of 12 infants and their parents, there were few differences between mothers and fathers (Marton, Minde, and Perrotta, 1981). The second (Levy-Shiff, Sharir, and Mogilner, 1989) observed 38 families with preterm infants in which duration of visits and amount of activity increased from the initial observation (when the infant left intensive care) to the time of discharge. The observed differences were consistent with reports of general mother–father differences in behavior with infants. Because the second study observed older and healthier infants no longer in intensive care and the first focused on visits to the NICU, it may be that gender differences in parental behavior develop over time.

In summary, many factors affect the extent to which parents visit and become actively engaged with their preterm babies. There is evidence that active engagement is related to subsequent parent involvement and that hospital policies and practices play a role in encouraging parent involvement.

## Parents and Infants at Home

In contrast to the limited study of parent–infant interactions in the hospital, studies of parents and infants after discharge are numerous. Although most studies focus on mothers, there have also been some studies of fathers. In addition, most studies entail comparisons with term dyads. The earliest studies were strongly influenced by ideas underlying the bonding concept. Animal studies had shown that maternal behavior can be extinguished by even brief separation of infants and mothers shortly after birth (Klaus and Kennell, 1976). The inference from this work is that if a mother is not exposed to the appropriate initiating stimuli (i.e., the infant) during an early critical or sensitive period, maternal behavior is depressed or difficult to establish. The related human studies at first ignored infant behavior and focused on separation effects on maternal behavior. Later reports included infant behavior, and it was consistently noted that preterm infants were less alert and responsive than their term peers and that preterm babies with more medical problems were less active than their healthier peers (DiVitto and Goldberg, 1979; Minde, Whitelaw et al., 1983). Maternal behavior paralleled that of infants. Preterm babies were afforded less body contact, touch and vocalization and those who were more seriously ill had less active mothers (DiVitto and Goldberg, 1979; Minde, Whitelaw et al., 1983). In contrast, Beckwith and Cohen (1978) found that in a large heterogeneous sample of preterm dyads, babies who had experienced more neonatal complications received *more* rather than *less* caregiving from mothers at 1 month corrected age. Subsequent studies showed that this pattern is common in studies of premature infants beyond the first month, whereas the pattern of reduced responsiveness is more typical in studies of newly born preterm infants.

Studies of infants over 3 months (corrected age) indicate that where there are differences between preterm and term infants, preterm infants are described as less attentive (e.g., Malatesta, Grigoyev, Lamb, Albin, and Culver, 1986), less initiating, (e.g., Brown and Bakeman, 1979), less responsive (e.g., Alfasi et al., 1985), showing fewer and less intense smiles (e.g., Segal et al., 1995), and being more irritable (e.g., Stevenson, Roach, Ver Haeve, and Leavitt, 1990). Mothers stay closer to preterm infants (e.g., Greene, Fox, and Lewis, 1983), hold and touch more, and provide more tactile and kinesthetic stimulation (e.g., Crnic, Greenberg, Ragozin, Robinson, and Basham, 1983), direct attention more (e.g., Barnard, Bee, and Hammond, 1984), and are judged to be less sensitive to their infants' cues (e.g., Zarling, Hirsch, and Landry, 1988). We have described this pattern by saying that being the parent of a preterm infant is "more work and less fun" than being the parent of a term infant (Goldberg and DiVitto, 1983).

Data on fathers and preterm infants are sparse. Some studies suggest that, initially, fathers of preterm infants are more engaged with their infants than are fathers of term infants (Brown, Rustia, and Schappert, 1991; Harrison, 1990). This may reflect effects of the early responsibility thrust upon fathers when their preterm infants are in intensive care and mothers are still in hospital, as stated by the father of Mackenzie, born at 26 weeks (Tracy and Maroney, 1999, p. 61):

> When Mackenzie was in the hospital, the role that came most naturally for me was to be the protector. I always had to be there and watch over the difficult or painful procedures.

It may also reflect the recognition that the mother alone cannot carry the heavy burden that care of a preterm infant imposes (Parke and Anderson, 1987). Observations of fathers and older preterm infants are also limited. Whereas two studies of 4- to 5-month-old infants parallel those of younger infants (Field, 1981; Yogman, 1987), one longitudinal study found that fathers with both their 3- and 12-month-old preterm and term infants are less interactive than mothers. This pattern was exaggerated among mothers and fathers of preterm infants (Harrison and Magill-Evans, 1996). These differences could not be explained by differences in infant behavior, parental stress, marital support, or level of parent involvement with the target child. However, as the infants got older, they became more active and parents became less so. These limited data do not establish a clear pattern for father interactions with preterm infants.

Numerous studies substantiate differences in patterns of interaction in preterm and full-term dyads as well as efforts to understand the reasons for these differences. Mothers of preterm infants are sometimes described as overstimulating their babies (e.g., Field, 1977b). Others argue that these differences reflect different needs of preterm and full-term babies and mothers are, in fact, responding to each group in a developmentally appropriate fashion. Thus mothers of preterms are viewed as engaging in compensatory efforts (e.g., Miles and Holditch-Davis, 1995). In the next three subsections, we examine explanations for these differences in interaction patterns and consider how such differences are best interpreted.

## Prematurity, Immaturity, and Illness

One explanation focuses on differences in infant behavior and factors that influence infant capacity for social interaction. The way in which research designs match preterm and term dyads for age has been controversial, although the majority of studies match on "time from conception." However, this means that matches are confounded by interactive experience—in general, at the same postconception age, term dyads have had more time in "normal" interactive environments. Other studies therefore match dyads for "time from discharge" so that all dyads had the same amount of home experience (e.g., Brown and Bakeman, 1979), although infants are not matched for either age from conception or age from birth. Still others matched on "chronological age" (e.g., DiVitto and Goldberg, 1979) to match amount of experience, although type of experience then varies (a larger proportion of the preterm experience takes place in hospital rather than home), and some studies have used more than one strategy (e.g., Crawford, 1982). It is these latter studies that provide information on the relative effects of prematurity (timing of the birth) and immaturity (the infant's developmental status) on dyadic interactions.

When data are compared for chronological versus postconception-matched groups, postconception matches yield fewer preterm–term differences in dyadic interactions (e.g., Alfasi et al., 1985; Roe, 1995). This reduction in differences represents the contribution of immaturity. However, some differences remain, and the majority of studies that used postconception matching are consistent with the description of preterm dyads as having less socially competent infants and more active mothers. Therefore infant immaturity does not account for all differences in either infant or maternal behavior.

Although severity of neonatal medical complications is usually related to gestational age and birthweight, examination of preterm groups that differ in illness status but are matched in gestational age and birthweight can assess the contribution of severity of illness to early dyadic interactions. Such matches are extremely difficult to make, and very few studies have been conducted with such designs. One such effort (Jarvis, Myers, and Creasy, 1989) compared three groups of preterms: those who were healthy (HP), those with respiratory distress syndrome (RDS), and those whose early respiratory problems led to lasting problems with breathing, bronchopulmonary dysplasia (BPD). These three groups were relatively well matched for gestational age (31 to 32 weeks average) and birthweight (1,200 to 1,600 g). Mothers and infants were videotaped in teaching tasks when the infants were 4 and 8 months old. There were no observed differences in infant behaviors, but mothers in the BPD group were scored lower than the others in sensitivity, response to distress, and growth-fostering activities, suggesting that severity of illness contributes to observed differences.

An alternative approach is illustrated in a study that included four groups of infants: term and preterm, with subgroups of healthy and sick infants within birth status (Greene et al., 1983). Although the preterm subgroups differed in the expected direction ("sick" infants were smaller and younger at birth than the healthy ones), the term groups did not. In the newborn period, differences in infant behavior as measured on Brazelton's Neonatal Behavioral Assessment Scales (1973) revealed effects of both maturity and health status. Similarly, maternal behavior in free play when infants were 3 months old showed effects of both maturity and health status. Furthermore, scores on the neonatal assessment predicted maternal responsiveness when infants were 3 months old. Thus this study suggests that early infant behavior is affected by both health and birth status, and maternal behavior is responsive to these early differences.

With a similar design, 278 mother–infant pairs were observed in changing and face-to-face activities when the infants were 2, 4, and 6 months old (corrected age; Schermann-Eizirik, Hagekull, Bohlin, Persson, and Sedin, 1997). As in the previous study (Greene et al., 1983), dyads were divided into four groups according to gestational age and need for intensive care. In contrast to the findings of Greene et al. (1983), in the study of Scherman-Eizirik et al., interactive behavior in the two preterm groups did not differ from that in the healthy term group. This may reflect the fact that most of the observations were done when infants were older than those in the earlier study. However, term infants who required intensive care showed instability of behavior across age and their mothers were scored lower on sensitivity and involvement. These data suggest that illness in a term newborn may have even stronger effects on adult–infant interactions than has been previously reported for preterm dyads.

Thus there is evidence that prematurity, immaturity, and illness affect interactions of preterm infants and their parents, particularly in the early months. In addition to direct effects on infant behavior, there are sometimes indirect effects on parent behavior because differences in parent behavior can be observed after infant differences have diminished. These indirect effects may be the residue of earlier adjustments to infant behavior, or they may reflect psychological effects such as a prematurity stereotype (Stern and Karraker, 1990).

## Overstimulation or Compensation?

This statement was made by the mother of an 8-month-old premature infant (Goldberg and DiVitto, 1983, p. 123):

> I think he needs a lot of stimulation. I know I sometimes overdo it, but if I don't keep him going, he'll just lie there and do nothing. I figure it's better to give him too much than too little.

A second explanation for observed differences between preterm and term dyads is concerned with the appropriateness of maternal behavior to the infant's behavior or developmental needs. "Appropriateness" clearly incorporates value judgments about what is and is not "good" for infants and preterm infants in particular. A pattern of behavior that is "good" for one purpose may compromise other potential parental goals. For example, we often assume that young infants should be held close during feedings and that affectionate social interaction during feedings is beneficial for social development. However, experimental studies of preterm babies indicate that this "normal" amount of physical contact and social exchange overwhelms preterm babies (Field, 1977a; McGehee and Eckerman, 1983) and disrupts feeding. Thus a parent feeding a preterm baby has to weigh the relative importance of nutrition and social development, a decision that is not salient for parents of healthy term babies.

How then are we to decide what is appropriate behavior? Two general approaches have been taken. The first relies on objective scoring schemes that reflect widely accepted judgments of appropriate behavior or interactive goals. The second relies on infant outcomes, either behavior during observation or later developmental achievements. These approaches are by no means "value free." Rather they are "value explicit" in that they provide a clear operational measure that incorporates known values. These approaches do not always concur in arriving at definitions of appropriate behavior. Earlier we noted reports that described mothers of preterm infants as less sensitive or more intrusive than mothers of term infants (e.g., Alfasi et al., 1985; Field 1977a; Zarling et al., 1988) or that mothers of sicker babies were less sensitive (Jarvis et al., 1989). All of these studies reflect reliable scoring procedures. However, in some cases, a different observational approach yields a different interpretation.

One example of this is seen in a study by Field (1977b) regarding feeding behavior of 3- to 4-month-old infants. Field reported that mothers of both preterm and term infants restricted activity with their infant to periods when the nipple was out of the infants' mouth. This is similar to earlier reports that the typical pattern during feedings is for mothers to confine stimulation to times when the infant is not sucking on the nipple. Field (1977b) found that mothers in the preterm group were more likely than those in the term group to be active during "nipple-in" periods. Later, DiVitto and Goldberg (1983) expanded on these findings. They observed four groups of infants (three preterm groups with different levels of health and neonatal complications and one term group) over four occasions: in hospital, 10 days postdischarge, and at home and in the laboratory at 4 months. In examining infant patterns of sucking, they found that, as infants got older, they spent more of the nipple-in time sucking and less time pausing. Preterm infants did more pausing during nipple-in times than terms. As the infant matured, all mothers gradually decreased their stimulation during infant sucking, but this occurred most rapidly in the term group. Thus preterm and term dyads achieved similar organization of maternal behavior around infant sucking patterns, but it developed more slowly in preterm dyads.

Studies focusing on organization of behavior highlight similarities of preterm and term dyads rather than differences and indicate that preterm and term dyads may achieve the same goals in different ways. For example, mothers of 3-month-old preterm infants scored lower on responsiveness and preterm dyads were less positive and had fewer episodes of repeated turn taking. However, there were no group differences in mutual responsiveness (Censullo, 1992). This finding is reinforced by the work of Mann and Plunkett (1992) with a more compromised preterm group (birthweights under 1,250 g). Preterm and term groups did not differ in the amount of mutual gaze at 4 months of age but differed in the context in which it occurred. Preterm infants engaged in more mutual gaze than their term counterparts did when they were held, and they were also held more than infants in the term group. Thus, by holding infants more, mothers in the preterm group succeeded in obtaining as much mutual gaze as mothers in term dyads. These differences in strategy were no longer evident at 8 months, when preterm dyads engaged in more mutual gaze than term dyads. In fact, mutual gaze in the preterm dyads at 8 months was similar to that in the term group at 4 months, again suggesting that different strategies may reflect accommodation to the developmental needs of preterm infants. Thus, although the low-birthweight babies were less responsive than the term infants, the two groups did not differ in amount of mutual engagement, nor were there any differences in infant negative behaviors such as fussing, crying, and squirming. The investigators concluded that this pattern was more consistent with the "compensation" than with the "overstimulation" view.

## Parent–Infant Relationships: Infant Attachment

The appropriateness of maternal behavior may also be evaluated by examination of the subsequent developmental outcome. In this section, we confine ourselves to the quality of the relationship that develops between infants and their parents. For this purpose, we examine studies which used Ainsworth's Strange Situation to assess quality of attachment. In this procedure, criteria developed by Ainsworth and her colleagues are used to classify adult–infant pairs who experience two laboratory separations and reunions into three or sometimes four patterns; one considered optimal (secure), the remaining categories representing different forms of less optimal (insecure) attachment. As noted earlier, infant behavior in this context is considered to reflect the infant's expectation that the caregiver will respond to attachment needs. The validity of this assumption is based on studies showing that patterns of reunion behavior reflect the consistency of maternal response to infant needs over the first year of life (Ainsworth et al., 1978).

Secure infants have experienced consistent and responsive care and are confident that the caregiver will meet their needs. Insecure infants have experienced different forms of inconsistent or unresponsive care and have developed strategies for behaving accordingly, either to "hide" needs for the caregiver by engaging in other activities (avoidant group), or to exaggerate needs for attention by escalating expressions of distress and/or helplessness (ambivalent–resistant group). Some infants have been unable to develop a strategy and show odd inexplicable behaviors (disorganized–disoriented group).

All of the theoretical approaches we reviewed would predict that preterm infants are less likely than term infants to be securely attached. It is well established that, in low-stress samples in North America, as well as a substantial number of samples from other continents, approximately 65% of infants are secure (van IJzendoorn and Kroonenberg, 1988). Early studies comparing preterm and term infants generally did not find differences in the proportion of securely attached infants (e.g., Easterbrooks, 1989; Goldberg, Perrotta, Minde, and Corter, 1986; Rodning, Beckwith, and Howard, 1989).

Two studies diverged from this pattern. In a study of socially disadvantaged families, Wille (1991) found no differences in attachment between healthy and sick preterm infants, but only 44% of the preterms were securely attached compared with 83% of term infants. This finding reflects both a decrease in security in the preterm group (although not below levels typically reported for disadvantaged samples) and an increase in the term group. Indeed, an analysis of attachment data aggregated from clinical samples noted that normative comparison groups typically include substantially more secure babies than expected (van IJzendoorn, Goldberg, Kroonenberg, and Frenkel, 1992). The second discordant study (Plunkett, Meisels, Stiefel, Pasick, and Roloff, 1986) reported that, within the preterm sample, those with more serious medical complications were more likely to be in the ambivalent–resistant group than were their healthier peers. This difference was not a difference in the rate of secure attachment but a difference in relative frequency of different forms of insecurity.

In 1992, van IJzendoorn and his colleagues conducted a meta-analysis of attachment studies that included clinical samples. Meta-analysis is a statistical method of combining data from similar studies to provide a quantitative summary. In this meta-analysis, six studies of preterm infants were aggregated and compared with aggregated data from normative samples. The results showed that, although the data of Plunkett et al. (1986) do deviate from the normative samples, the deviation is not statistically significant. Analyses that included the two preterm studies that used the disorganized category (Goldberg, Lojkasek, Gartner, and Corter, 1989; Rodning et al., 1989) showed some shift in the preterm group toward including more disorganized cases than expected. However, these shifts were not statistically significant.

The preterm infants included in most of these studies were, by current standards, relatively healthy. Two subsequent studies suggest that differences in attachment distributions between preterm and term samples increase when the preterm infants are very small and fragile at birth. Pederson and Moran (1996) found no effect of birth status on attachment when the preterm sample was selected from those infants weighing under 2,000 g. However, a second study (Mangelsdorf et al., 1996) with preterms whose average birthweight was under 1,000 g had different findings. These preterms were compared with term infants at 14 and 19 months of age. Although there was no difference in attachment in the Strange Situation for the preterm and term groups at 14 months of age, by 19 months of age the preterm infants were less likely to be securely attached (47% versus 75%). However, preterm infants were judged to be less secure than term infants in home observations at 14 months when rated with a Q-sort technique designed by Waters (1995).

Although these studies suggest that conclusions about attachment in preterm infants must be considered in the context of birthweight and/or medical complications, we do not yet have the benefit of a meta-analysis that includes the most recent data. Single studies can reflect unique sample characteristics or chance findings. The advantage of a meta-analysis is that it weights such studies in the context of all available information. A meta-analysis of existing samples with birthweight and/or medical complications as a predictor is needed to draw firm conclusions.

In summary, the bulk of the data suggests that, although this may not be the case for the smallest and most fragile preterm infants, by the end of the first 12 to 18 months of life, most preterm infants and their parents have developed a relationship that, with respect to attachment, is not markedly different from that of term infants and their parents. If we consider the formation of a secure attachment to indicate appropriate care in the first year of life, these data suggest that, in spite of observed differences in interaction patterns, preterm and term infants are both most likely to form secure attachments to parents (i.e., to perceive their parents as providing responsive care). Thus we can infer that the observed differences are adaptive. Mothers generally treat their preterm babies in ways that are appropriate to their needs and support normal development.

In addition to reserving judgment about the very smallest and sickest preterm infants, we also note that attachment is only one aspect of parent–child relationships, although a very important one. The finding that term and preterm groups do not differ in attachment patterns does not mean that there are no differences in parent–child relationships, only that there are no differences in attachment.

## Subsequent Development

Some reports indicate that observed interactive differences between preterm and term dyads diminish with age (e.g., Brown et al., 1991; DiVitto and Goldberg, 1983), whereas others find differences continue through the preschool years (e.g., Barnard et al., 1984; Donohue and Pearl, 1995). Although observational studies of older children born preterm are limited, those that focus on parent experience indicate that differences in maternal attitudes toward term and preterm children persist into the preschool years. Mothers of preschoolers born preterm viewed their child as weaker, more vulnerable, and difficult and themselves as more protective and indulgent than did mothers of children born at term (Miles and Holditch-Davis, 1997).

One of the rare studies of later parent–child interactions was conducted as part of a longitudinal study at UCLA Hospital (Beckwith, Rodning, and Cohen, 1992). The initial sample included 62 mother–child dyads with preterm infants. There were multiple assessments during infancy with follow-up assessments at 5, 8, and 12 years. When the infants were, 1, 8, and 24 months of age, interactive observations were made in the home. Frequency of selected behaviors was coded and then aggregated to yield global scores for characteristics of maternal behavior. At 12 years of age, 44 of the original pairs were observed interacting in two laboratory tasks that required cooperation. Observers used the Family Interaction Q-sort (Gjerde, 1986) to arrive at a measure of maternal responsiveness. There was no evidence that mothers who were highly responsive during infancy were also highly responsive to their 12-year-old children. However, the more critical and controlling mothers had been with their toddlers at 24 months of age, the less responsive they were with their 12-year-old children. This is one of the few studies that suggests some long-term continuities in the interactive style of mothers with children born prematurely.

More typically, prospective longitudinal studies focus on relating early parent–infant interaction to later cognitive and social outcomes in the preschool years (e.g., Harrison and Magill-Evans, 1996; Landry, Smith, Miller-Loncar, and Swank, 1998; McGrath et al., 1998), and as late as adolescence (e.g., Beckwith et al., 1992; Cohen, 1995). In the preschool years, children in high-risk categories who performed most competently in language, cognitive, and problem-solving abilities had mothers who demonstrated higher maternal responsivity, involvement, and more appropriate control than children who were less competent (Landry et al., 1998; McGrath et al., 1998).

Relationships between parents and children born prematurely, which are marked by high parent responsiveness through the years, are associated with greater academic and intellectual competence at the age of 12 years, as well as with fewer behavioral and emotional problems, more self-esteem, and more positive perception of the home (Beckwith et al., 1992). In a study of low-risk preterms followed to the age of 18 years, the important predictors of intellectual abilities, school achievement, and social competence were neonatal neurobehavioral organization and early social stimulation (Cohen, 1995). Thus patterns of early social interaction and maternal responsivity in infancy may have effects that persist for years. Hence efforts to improve these early interactions have the potential for long-term benefits.

## CLINICAL CARE AND INTERVENTIONS

In the past, interventions have been implemented both in the hospital and at home to facilitate the development of preterm infants. Some aimed to reduce the developmental difficulties that many preterm infants encounter; others to reduce the parental burden of caring for a preterm infant. Some interventions focus on both parent and infant in an attempt to improve responsivity and relationships. In this section we briefly review some of the earlier interventions and present information on some of the more recent research.

### Formal Interventions

*Infant focused.* Early interventions carried out in the NICU had the goal of providing experiences that resembled those of the fetus *in utero*. These were based on the premise that the preterm baby was an extrauterine fetus and needed a developmentally appropriate "womblike" environment in order to become ready for independent life. A variety of approaches was used to simulate maternal movement including motorized hammocks (Neal, 1968), rockers (Barnard, 1972), and waterbeds (Korner, Kraemer, Faffeur, and Casper, 1975). Tape recordings of heartbeats and the maternal voice (Kraemer and Pierpont, 1976) were introduced to simulate the fetal auditory experience.

Another approach viewed the preterm infant as an immature newborn and assumed that the most appropriate environment should approximate the home. In these studies, infants were exposed to extra handling, stroking, and massaging (e.g., Hasselmeyer, 1964; Solkoff and Matusak, 1975; Solkoff, Yaffe, Weintraub, and Blase, 1969), toys and play (Scarr-Salapatek and Williams, 1973), and stimulation and exercise programs (Rosenfield, 1980), usually carried out by the nursing staff. It is interesting to note that when mothers, who saw their infants less frequently than nurses did, stimulated their infants, the "handled" infants also regained their birthweights faster than control infants. Thus mothers "accomplished" as much as the nurses in fewer contacts (Powell, 1974).

More recently, efforts have been made to tailor caregiving and medical procedures to the individual needs, states, and responses of each infant. One innovative application of this type of intervention involved placing a breathing teddy bear, set to match the infant's breathing rate, in the isolette and allowing the infants to regulate their interactions with it. Preterm infants (32–34 weeks of age) spent more time in contact with the breathing bear than with a nonbreathing bear and showed more neurobehavioral maturation in the form of quiet sleep both in the hospital and at 5 weeks later at home (Thoman and Ingersoll, 1989). Similar benefits have been attributed to kangaroo care, in which the infant's physical closeness to the parent facilitates regular breathing and heart rate, as well as improved tone and less disorganized sleep patterns. One protocol developed to provide kangaroo care to very small or intubated infants involves monitoring individual infants' responses closely while providing opportunities for parents and infants to experience physical closeness (Gale and VandenBerg, 1998).

The work of Als et al. (1986) also emphasized recognition of the characteristics of the infant before intervention and showed that this individualized care resulted in improved medical and developmental outcomes. Such results indicate that an appropriate goal in intervention is to make it more appropriate to each infant's special needs and to "listen to the baby."

*Parent focused.* Systematic intervention directed explicitly to parents is less common than interventions directed toward infants. The early work at Stanford encouraged parents to touch and care for their preterm infants in the NICU (Barnett et al., 1970). Opportunities to handle and care for their infants were shown to increase parental feelings of self-confidence and competence as well as to lead to more positive and affectionate social interactions (Kennell et al., 1975; Klaus et al., 1972; Leiderman and Seashore, 1975; Seashore, Leifer, Barnett, and Leiderman, 1973). Caregiving opportunities help parents to feel that the baby belongs to them rather than to the hospital staff. When parents feel more invested in the relationship, the infant receives better care both before and after discharge, which, in turn, facilitates infant development.

Most hospitals offer opportunities such as rooming-in to enable parents to practice infant care while still having the support of professional staff available. Hospitals have also increasingly realized the need to provide emotional support to parents during the NICU experience and after discharge. Social service and translator services are usually available to assist parents with concrete needs such as housing, transportation, and financial assistance.

Contact with veteran parents who share experiences with new parents in small group meetings or individual sessions may be offered in hospital and often continues after discharge. In one study of these parent support groups, mothers who attended the group sessions visited their infants more often and were more active during visits than was a comparison group of mothers. These mothers also reported more satisfaction with medical and nursing care that their child received. The group experience provided mothers with a better understanding of their child's problems, more confidence in their ability to provide care, and more knowledge of community resources. A year later, the group mothers were found to be more socially stimulating and promoted more independence in their children than did mothers in the comparison group (Minde, Shosenberg et al., 1983). The opportunity to meet and talk with veteran parents reduces stress, offers support, and fosters more positive parenting attitudes in new parents of preterm infants, as shown by the statement of the mother of Carley, born at 28 weeks (Tracy and Maroney, 1999, p. 280):

> Talking with others taught me that things aren't always my fault. I am attempting to close what I consider to be a very unpleasant chapter in my life.

The mother of Kristin, born at 28 weeks, had this to say (Tracy and Maroney, 1999, p. 286):

> It was another mom of a premie who kept me going. We talked on the phone every day. When our babies were healthy, we visited in each other's homes. I felt she was the only person who really understood what I was experiencing.

*Parent–infant focused.*   In recent years, there has been much public interest in a technique called kangaroo care that engages parents and infants together. As was noted earlier, kangaroo care originated in Columbia in the 1970s, where it effectively counteracted health problems caused by poor hospital conditions (Gale and VandenBerg, 1998).

The model of kangaroo care was brought to the United States in the late 1980s and has been used in NICUs in over one third of U.S. hospitals (Gale and VandenBerg, 1998) with increased use expected in the future. Research over the past 15 years has focused primarily on the promotion of physiological stability in preterm infants by use of the kangaroo care position. A number of studies indicate that such positioning promotes stable heart rate, respiratory rate, oxygen saturation, and temperature regulation in infants (Acolet, Sleath, and Whitelaw, 1989; de Leeuw, Colin, Dunnebier, and Mirmiran, 1991; Gale, Franck, and Lund, 1993; Legault and Goulet, 1995; Ludington-Hoe, Hadeed, and Anderson, 1991; Whitelaw, Heisterkamp, Sleath, Acolet, and Richards, 1988). Other benefits include better weight gain and earlier discharge (Affonso, Wahlberg, and Persson, 1989) and less crying at 6 months of age (Whitelaw et al., 1988).

However, this procedure involves and affects parents as well as infants. For instance, the vertical position and physiological benefits of kangaroo care often led to infants' attempts to find the parent's face and make eye contact, resulting in the growth of emotional bonds within the dyad (Gale and VandenBerg, 1998). The increased intimacy of skin-to-skin contact has been shown to help parents feel more connected to their babies and to increase self-confidence and self-esteem (Affonso et al., 1989; Gale et al., 1993). This may reflect parents' greater involvement in the baby's care or pride in the infant's successful growth and development as the physiological benefits of kangaroo care such as improved lactation outcomes (Affonso et al., 1989; Anderson et al., 1986; Gale et al., 1993; Whitelaw et al., 1988) become evident.

More recent studies of kangaroo care consider the parents' well-being and the parent–child relationship during the stressful time of being in the NICU. When compared with mothers whose preterm infants received traditional care, mothers of infants in kangaroo care reported that they felt more competent. Starting kangaroo care earlier rather than later was more effective in boosting maternal confidence (Tessier et al., 1998). However, kangaroo care was associated with feelings of isolation in mothers whose infants spent a longer time in the NICU because of illness or poor weight gain. In these cases, researchers speculated, mothers may have felt overburdened with responsibility for a sick preterm infant and were not getting enough help from hospital staff or family. Nevertheless, mothers in the kangaroo care condition reported feeling less stressed than mothers in the traditional care condition when infants were sicker and had longer hospital stays. This was attributed to a sense of resiliency in the kangaroo care mothers who felt they had more control of their infants' health than did the mothers in the traditional care group.

Finally, mothers in both groups showed behaviors that were adapted to the child's health status. In other words, they were more sensitive and more responsive toward an at-risk infant whose development had been threatened by a longer hospital stay. This, in turn, was associated with a more responsive infant. These effects were stronger in the kangaroo care group. Such findings are consistent with prior work concerning the importance of opportunities for parents to handle and care for their preterm infants in the NICU. When parents feel more invested in the relationship with the infant, the infant receives enhanced care both before and after discharge which, in turn, facilitates later development. Kangaroo care is also appropriate for fathers because they too can position the baby close to the chest and feed with a bottle.

Another general intervention strategy has been to provide parents with skills that compensate for the infant's interactive limitations. Examples of this type of intervention include rocking and massage procedures (Rice, 1977), developmentally stimulating activities and toys (Scarr-Salapatek and Williams, 1973), and efforts to facilitate interactions that match infant skills and temperament (Bromwich and Paremlee, 1979). Such programs have longer-term benefits when they include on-going support to parents after discharge (Barnard and Bee, 1983; Field, Widmayer, Stringer, and Ignatoff, 1980; Patteson and Barnard, 1990; Scarr-Salapatek and Williams, 1973).

Specialized programs that offered home-based teaching in the first year were later evaluated by direct outcome measures (e.g., health and development, length of hospitalization, parent–child interaction and quality of home environment). Despite differences in methodology, most studies showed some positive outcomes, with the common factor being repeated contact with a consistent, supportive figure over time.

*Summary.* Although varied in their approaches, most intervention studies report benefits of early stimulation to infants for both parents and infants. One speculation is that stimulated infants become more alert, responsive, and thus more rewarding for parents. Parent-focused interventions are fewer in number and have been less systematically evaluated. The method of kangaroo care, although originally implemented to improve infant outcome, is now recognized as an intervention focused on parent-infant relationships. Thus, interventions focused on infants alone, parents alone, and those that focus on parent and infant together have all been shown to affect parents of preterm infants. However, the actual implementation of these interventions as part of routine care varies among hospital settings.

## Media Resources

Parents have long relied on books and educational material to become more informed about child development and care. In this respect, parents of preterm infants are no different. However, for a long time, there were few books in print that provided relevant information. In the 1980s, few books or articles actually dealt with the special concerns of preterm infants (Brooten et al., 1986; Field et al., 1980; Goldberg and DiVitto, 1983; Harrison, 1983; Nurcombe et al., 1983; Ross, 1984).

Since that time there has been a substantial increase in reading materials for parents of premature infants. They offer information on a range of topics from a comprehensive view of medical complications and treatments, supporting parents as active participants in their baby's care, coping with the emotions that accompany early birth, to practical information about taking the baby home, insurance issues, and managing ongoing care. The trend has been to provide a "how-to" manual that combines medical and practical facts of premature infant care with support for parents (e.g., Klein and Gannon, 1998). In addition to medical experts, contributors often include parents "who have been there" and can provide invaluable information from their own experiences.

Printed resources such as magazines, newsletters, and books are only a few of many information sources. Parents of preterm infants now find many topics covered in video format, including basic information such as first aid and cardiopulmonary resuscitation, nutrition, and breast-feeding, as well as more specific topics such as how to massage an infant (Rice, Loving Touch Infant Massage) and how to provide kangaroo care at home (Rice, Kangaroo Care Video). The videotape format is compelling, explicit, instructive, and illustrative, and provides a way for busy parents to actually see techniques demonstrated while they are involved in caregiving. Videotapes are also a valuable source of information for those who are not readers or those who find that infant care severely limits reading time.

The most recently developed source of information for parents of preterm infants is the Internet. Parents who "surf the net" will find newsletters, references to recent research, sources for preterm infant clothing and diapers, and websites for both parent support groups and national organizations along with first hand accounts of parent experiences. Although a wealth of information exists in this form, there are limitations to relying entirely on popular sources for education and guidance. Parents are cautioned to check technical information from websites, either through discussion with health care professionals or by seeking out the original references for quoted research findings. Unlike interventions initiated by professionals, informational support by means of media resources, whether in print, video, or on the Internet, is not systematically applied. Some parents have ready access to these resources; others do not. Of those who could potentially use these materials, some will choose to do so and others will ignore them. We know virtually nothing about who uses specific media resources and how effective or ineffective they are. Nevertheless, they are a part of the support system for many parents rearing children born preterm.

## CONCLUSIONS

Significant medical and technical advances in neonatal intensive care have markedly increased the survival rates of low-birthweight preterm infants. As techniques for reducing incidence and severity of problems associated with prematurity developed, isolation of parents from infants increased. However, since the early 1970s hospitals have moved toward allowing and encouraging parents to handle and care for their infants in hospital. Nevertheless, the experience remains stressful and markedly different from that of parents who have term infants. Recent changes in the care of preterm infants acknowledge the need to support not only the infant's well-being but the emotional functioning of the family. For both infant and parent, unique features associated with preterm birth (its timing, the NICU experience, and the unique behavior of the infant) affect parent–child relationships. We have focused on how the effects of these factors can persist, particularly in the first year. Infants are dependent on adults for survival, and preterm infants are more vulnerable to the effects of inadequate care than are their term peers. Because preterm infants are qualitatively different from term infants in physical appearance and behavior, and take longer to attain milestones (such as smiling and reaching for a toy), parents are confronted with the need to adjust their expectations and behavior.

Studies of preterm infants and their parents in hospital indicate a variety of factors that affect the extent to which parents are able to visit and to become actively engaged. Active engagement is positively related to subsequent parent involvement and can be facilitated by supportive hospital policies and practices. The numerous studies of preterm infants and their parents in the first year following hospital discharge focus primarily on mothers, but more limited father studies suggest that father behavior is similar to that of mothers and equally important in influencing long-term outcomes. Reports comparing preterm and term dyads provide conflicting evidence as to the nature and extent of interactional differences. Studies in which the birth and the health status of infant participants are systematically varied indicate that both birth status (preterm versus term) and health status (healthy versus sick) influence infant behavior, and maternal behavior reflects these effects, even after infant behavior differences have disappeared. These differences are best interpreted as the adaptation of parents to the developmental skills and needs of the infant. This is confirmed by the evidence that the majority of preterm infants are securely attached to their mothers by 12 to18 months corrected age.

New developments in hospital and home care for preterm infants are moving to include parents as involved partners from the early days and to individualize care for infants and parents. Research has played a major role in changing patterns of care for preterm infants. Conversely, changes in clinical practice (e.g., the introduction of kangaroo care) have raised new questions for research. Although the developments in medical technology that enabled these infants to survive originally did so with a loss of parent–infant contact, the current wave of innovations includes efforts to make early care more humane for both infants and parents. The evidence suggests that these innovations are not at the expense of physical health and growth but also enhance physical well-being.

## REFERENCES

Acolet, D., Sleath, K., and Whitelaw, A. (1989). Oxygenation, heart rate, and temperature in very low birth weight infants during skin-to-skin contact with their mothers. *Acta Paediatrica Scandinavica, 78*, 189–193.

Affleck, G., Tennen, H., and Rowe, J. (1990). Mothers, fathers, and the crisis of newborn intensive care. *Infant Mental Health Journal, 11*, 12–25.

Affonso, D., Wahlberg, G., and Persson, B. (1989). Mothers' reactions to kangaroo method of care. *Neonatal Network, 7*, 43–51.

Ainsworth, M. D. S., Blehar, M. C., Waters, E., and Wall, S. (1978). *Patterns of Attachment*. Hillsdale, NJ: Lawrence Erlbaum Associates.

Alfasi, A., Schwartz, F. A., Brake, S., Fifer, W. P., Fleishman, A. R., and Hofer, M. (1985). Mother–infant feeding interactions in preterm and full term infants. *Infant Behavior and Development, 8*, 167–180.

Als, H., Duffy, F. H., and McAnulty, G. B. (1996). Effectiveness of individualized neurodevelopmental care in the newborn intensive care unit (NICU). *Acta Pediatrica, 416*, 21–30.

Als, H., Lawhorn, G., Brown, E., Gibes, R., Duffy, F., McAnulty, G., and Blickman, J. (1986). Individualized behavioral and environmental care for the very low birthweight preterm infant at high risk for bronchopulmonary dysplasia: Neonatal intensive care unit and developmental outcome. *Pediatrics, 78*, 1123–1131.

Anderson, G., Marks, E. A., and Wahlberg, V. (1986). Kangaroo care for premature infants. *American Journal of Nursing, 86*, 807–809.

Anisfeld, E. (1982). The onset of social smiling in preterm and full term infants from two ethnic backgrounds. *Infant Behavior and Development, 5*, 387–395.

Avery, M., and Litwack, G. (1983). *The story of a premature baby*. Boston: Little, Brown.

Barnard, K. E. (1972). *The effect of stimulation on the development and amount of sleep and wakefulness in the preterm infant*. Unpublished doctoral dissertation, University of Washington, Seattle.

Barnard, K. E., and Bee, H. L. (1983). The impact of temporally patterned stimulation on the development of the preterm infant. *Child Development, 54*, 1156–1167.

Barnard, K. E., Bee, H. L., and Hammond, M. A. (1984). Development of changes in maternal interaction with term and preterm infants. *Infant Behavior and Development, 7*, 101–113.

Barnett, C., Liederman, P. H., Grobstein, R., and Klaus, M. (1970). Neonatal separation: The maternal side of interactional deprivation. *Pediatrics, 45*, 197–205.

Bauer, K., Pyper, A., Sperling, P., Uhrig, C., and Versmold, H. (1998). Effects of gestational and postnatal age on body temperature, oxygen consumption and activity during early skin-to-skin contact between infants of 25–30 week gestation and their mothers. *Pediatric Research, 44*, 247–251.

Beckwith, L., and Cohen, S. (1978). Preterm birth: Hazardous obstetrical and postnatal events as related to caregiver-infant behavior. *Infant Behavior and Development, 1*, 403–411.

Beckwith, L., Rodning, C., and Cohen, S. (1992). Preterm children at early adolescence and continuity and discontinuity in maternal responsiveness from infancy. *Child Development, 63,* 1198–1208.

Biddle-Bruckman, L. (1999). *What a difference a year makes.* Web page on The Premie Channel (www.geocities.com/Heartland/Valley/7553/index.html). Dr. Robert White, "From the Heart—Poems by and for Parents and Staff of the Newborn ICU."

Boukydis, C. F. Z. (1982). Support groups for parents with premature infants in NICUs. In R. E. Marshall, C. Kasman, and L. S. Cape (Eds.), *Coping with caring for sick newborns* (pp. 215–238). Philadelphia: Saunders.

Bowlby, J. (1969). *Attachment and loss: Vol. 1. Attachment.* New York: Basic Books.

Brazetton, T. B. (1973). Neonatal Behavioral Assessment Scale. *Clinics in Developmental Medicine,* No. 50. London: William Heikeman Medical Books Ltd.

Bromwich, R., and Parmelee, A. H. (1979). An intervention program for preterm infants. In T. M. Field, A. M. Shostek, S. Goldberg, and H. H. Shuman (Eds.) *Infants born at risk* (pp. 389–412). Jamaica, NY: Spectrum.

Brooten, S., Kumar, S., Brown, L., Butts, P., Finkler, S., Bakewell-Sachs, S., Gibbons, A., and Delworia-Papsdopoulos, M. (1986). A randomized clinical trial of early hospital discharge and home follow-up of very low birth weight infants. *New England Journal of Medicine, 315,* 934–939.

Brown, J. V., and Bakeman, R. (1979). Relationships with human mothers with their infants in the first year of life: effects of prematurity. In R. W. Bell and W. P. Smotherman (Eds.), *Maternal influences and early behavior* (pp. 353–374). Jamaica, NY: Spectrum.

Brown, P., Rustia, J., and Schappert, P. (1991). A comparison of fathers of high-risk newborns and fathers of healthy newborns. *Journal of Pediatric Nursing, 6,* 269–273.

Budin, P. (1907). *The nursling.* London: Caxton.

Caplan, G. (1960). Patterns of parental response to the crisis of premature birth. *Psychiatry, 23,* 365–374.

Case-Smith, J., Butcher L., and Reed, D. (1998). Parents' report of sensory responsiveness and temperament in preterm infants. *American Journal of Occupational Therapy, 52,* 547–555.

Censullo, M. (1992, May). Relationship of early responsiveness to one-year outcomes in preterm and full term infants. Paper presented at the International Conference on Infant Studies. Miami, FL.

Cohen, S. E. (1995). Biosocial factors in early infancy as predictors of competence in adolescents who were born prematurely. *Journal of Developmental and Behavioral Pediatrics, 16,* 36–41.

Colon, A. R., and Colon, P. A. ( 2000). *Nurturing children: A history of pediatrics.* Westport, CT: Greenwood.

Corter, C., Trehub, S., Boukydis, C. F. Z., Ford, L., Celhoffer, L., and Minde, K. (1978). Nurses' judgments of the attractiveness of preterm infants. *Infant Behavior and Development, 1,* 373–380.

Crawford, J. W. (1982). Mother–infant interaction in premature and full term infants. *Child Development, 53,* 957–962.

Crnic, K. A., Greenberg, M. T., Ragozin, A. S., Robinson, N. M., and Basham, R. B. (1983). Effects of stress and social support on mothers of preterm and full-term infants. *Child Development, 54,* 209–217.

Daga, S. R., Ahuja, V. K., and Lunkad, N. G. (1998). A warm touch improves oxygenation in newborn babies. *Journal of Tropical Pediatrics, 44,* 170–172.

de Leeuw, R., Colin, E. M., Dunnebier, E. A., and Mirmiran, M. (1991). Physiologic effects of kangaroo care in very small preterm infants. *Biology of the Neonate, 59,* 149–155.

DiVitto, B., and Goldberg, S. (1979). The development of early parent-infant interaction as a function of newborn medical status. In T. M. Field, A. M. Sostek, S. Goldberg, and H. H. Shuman (Eds.), *Infants born at risk* (pp. 311–332). Jamaica, NY: Spectrum.

DiVitto, B., and Goldberg, S. (1983). Talking and sucking: Infant feeding behavior and parent stimulation in dyads with different medical histories. *Infant Behavior and Development, 6,* 157–165.

Donohue, M. L., and Pearl, R. (1995). Conversational interactions of mothers and their preschool children who had been born preterm. *Journal of Speech and Hearing Research, 38,* 1117–1125.

Easterbrooks, M. A. (1989). Quality of attachment to mother and father: Effects of perinatal risk status. *Child Development, 60,* 825–831.

Eckerman, C. O., Hsu, H., Molitor, A., Leung, E. H. L., and Goldstein, R. F. (1999). Infant arousal in an en face exchange with a new partner: Effects of prematurity and perinatal biological risk. *Developmental Psychology, 35,* 282–293.

Estroff, D. B., Yando, R., Burke, K., and Snyder, D. (1994). Perceptions of preschoolers' tvulnerability by mothers who had delivered preterm. *Journal of Pediatric Psychology, 19,* 709–721.

Eyler, F. D., Woods, N. S., Behnke, M., and Conlon, M. (1992, May). Changes over a decade: Adult–infant interaction in the NICU. Paper presented at the International Conference on Infant Studies, Miami, FL.

Fanaroff, A. A., Kennell, J. H., and Klaus, M. H. (1972). Follow-up of low birthweight infants—the predictive value of maternal visiting patterns. *Pediatrics, 49,* 287–290.

Field, T. M. (1977a). The effects of early separation, interactive deficits and experimental manipulations on infant–mother face-to-face interaction. *Child Development, 48,* 763–771.

Field, T. M. (1977b). Maternal stimulation during infant feeding. *Developmental Psychology, 13,* 539–540.

Field, T. M. (1981). Fathers' interactions with their high risk infants. *Infant Mental Health Journal, 2,* 249–256.

Field, T. M. (1982). Affective displays of high risk infants during early interactions. In T. M. Field and A. Fogel (Eds.), *Emotion and early interaction* (pp. 101–126). Hillsdale, NJ: Lawrence Erlbaum Associates.

Field, T. M. Widmayer, S., Stringer, S., and Ignatoff, E. (1980). Teenage lower class mothers and their preterm infants: An intervention and developmental follow-up. *Child Development, 51*, 426–436.

Friedman, S. L., Jacobs, B. S., and Werthman, M. W. (1982). Preterms of low medical risk: Spontaneous behaviors and soothability at expected date of birth. *Infant Behavior and Development, 5*, 3–10.

Friedman, S. L., Zahn-Waxler, C., and Radke-Yarrow, M. (1982). Perception of cries of preterm and full term infants. *Infant Behavior and Development, 5*, 161–174.

Frodi, A., Lamb, M., Leavitt, L., Donovan, W., Neff, C., and Sherry, D. (1978). Father's and mother's response to the faces and cries of normal and premature infants. *Developmental Psychology, 14*, 490–498.

Gale, G., Franck, L., and Lund, C. (1993). Skin-to-skin (kangaroo) holding of the intubated premature infant. *Neonatal Network, 12*(6), 49–57.

Gale, G., and VandenBerg, K. (1998). Kangaroo care. *Neonatal Network, 17*(5), 69–71.

Gjerde, P. F. (1986). The interpersonal structure of family interaction settings: Parent–adolescent relations in dyads and triads. *Developmental Psychology, 22*, 297–304.

Goldberg, S. (1977). Social competence in infancy: A model of parent–infant interaction. *Merrill-Palmer Quarterly, 23*, 163–178.

Goldberg, S., and DiVitto (1983). *Born too soon: Preterm birth and early development.* San Francisco: Freeman.

Goldberg, S., Lojkasek, M., Gartner, G., and Corter, C. (1989). Maternal responsiveness and social development in preterm infants. In M. Bornstein (Ed.), *Maternal responsiveness: characteristics and consequences* (pp. 89–103). San Francisco: Jossey-Bass.

Goldberg, S., Perrotta, M., Minde, K., and Corter, C. (1986). Maternal behavior and attachment in low birthweight twins and singletons. *Child Development, 57*, 34–46.

Gottfried, A. W., and Gaiter, J. (1985). *Infant stress under intensive care.* Baltimore: University Park Press.

Graven, S. N., Bowen, F. W. Jr., Brooten, D., Eaton, A., Graven, M. N., Hack, M., Hall, L. A., Hansen, N., Hurt, H., and Kavalhuna, R. (1992). The high risk infant environment. Part 2. The role of caregiving and the social environment. *Journal of Perinatology, 12*, 267–275.

Green, M., and Solnit, A. J. (1964). Reactions to the threatened loss of a child: A vulnerable child syndrome. *Pediatrics, 34*, 58–66.

Greene, J. G., Fox, N. A., and Lewis, M. (1983). The relationship between neonatal characteristics and three-month mother infant interaction in high risk infants. *Child Development, 54*, 1286–1296.

Harrison, H. (1983). *The premature baby book: A parent's guide to coping and caring in the first years.* New York: St. Martin's.

Harrison, L., and Twardosz, S. (1986). Teaching mothers about their preterm babies. *Journal of Obstetric and Gynecological Nursing, 15*, 165–172.

Harrison, M. J. (1990). A comparison of parental interactions with term and preterm infants. *Research in Nursing and Health, 13*, 173–179.

Harrison, M. J., and Magill-Evans, J. (1996). Mother and father interactions over the first year with term and preterm infants. *Research in Nursing and Health, 19*, 451–459.

Hasselmeyer, E. (1964). The premature infant's response to handling. *American Nurses Journal, 11*, 15–24.

Hawthorne, J. T., Richards, M. P. M., and Callon, M. (1978). A study of parental visiting of babies in a special care unit. In F. S. W. Brimblecombe, M. P. M. Richards, and N. R. C. Roberton (Eds.), *Separation and special care baby units* (pp. 33–54). London: Heinemann Medical Books.

Herzog, J. (1980). A neonatal care syndrome: A plain complex involving neuroplasticity and psychic trauma. Paper presented at the International Conference on Infant Psychiatry, Lisbon. Cited in S. Goldberg and B. DiVitto (1983), *Born too soon: Preterm birth and early development.* San Francisco: Freeman.

Hunt, J. V., and Rhodes, L. (1977). Mental development in preterm infants during the first year. *Child Development, 48*, 204–210.

Jackson, A., and Gorman, W. A. (1988). Maternal attitudes to preterm birth. *Journal of Psychosomatic Obstetrics and Gynecology, 8*, 119–126.

Jarvis, P. A., Myers, B. J., and Creasy, G. L. (1989). The effect of infants' illness on mothers' interaction with prematures at 4 and 8 months. *Infant Behavior and Development, 12*, 25–35.

Jeffcoate, J., Humphrey, M., and Lloyd, J. (1979). The effects of infant' illness on mothers' interaction with prematures at 4 and 8 months. *Developmental Medicine and Child Neurology, 21*, 344–352.

Kennell, J. H., Trause, M. A., and Klaus, M. H. (1975). Evidence for a sensitive period in the human mother. In *Parent-infant interaction*. CIBA Foundation Symposium (No. 33). Amsterdam: Elsevier.

Klaus, M. H., Jerauld, R., Kreger, N., McAlpine, W., Steffa, M., and Kennell, J. H. (1972). Maternal attachment: Importance of the first postpartum days. *New England Journal of Medicine, 286*, 460–463.

Klaus, M. H., and Kennell, J. H. (1976). *Maternal–infant bonding.* St. Louis, MO: Mosby.

Klaus, M. H., and Kennell, J. H. (1982). *Parent–infant bonding.* St. Louis, MO: Mosby.

Klein, A., and Gannon, J. (1998). *Caring for your premature baby: A complete resource for parents*. New York: Harper Perennial.

Korner, A., Kraemer, M., Faffeur, M., and Casper, L. (1975). Effects of waterbed flotation on premature infants: A pilot study. *Pediatrics, 56*, 361–367.

Kraemer, H. C., and Pierpont, M. E. (1976). Rocking, waterbeds, and auditory stimuli to enhance growth of preterm infants. *Journal of Pediatrics, 88*, 297–299.

Landry, S. H., Smith, K. E., Miller-Loncar, C. L., and Swank, P. R. (1998). The relation of change in maternal interactive styles to the developing social competence of full-term and preterm children. *Child Development, 69*, 105–123.

Langkamp, D. L., Kim, Y., and Pascoe, J. M. (1998). Temperament of preterm infants at 4 months of age: Maternal ratings and perceptions. *Journal of Developmental and Behavioral Pediatrics, 19*, 391–396.

Legault, M., and Goulet, C. (1995). Comparison of kangaroo and traditional methods of removing preterm infants from incubators. *Journal of Obstetric, Gynecologic, and Neonatal Nursing, 24*, 502–506.

Leiderman, P. H., and Seashore, M. (1975). Mother-infant separation: some delayed consequences. In *Parent-infant interaction*. CIBA Foundation Symposium (No. 33, pp. 213–239). Amsterdam: Elsevier.

Leifer, A. D., Leiderman, P. H., Barnett, C. R., and Williams, J. A. (1972). Effects of mother–infant separation on maternal attachment behavior. *Child Development, 43*, 1303–1318.

Lester, B. M., and Zeskind, P. S. (1979). The organization and assessment of crying in the infant at risk. In T. M. Field, A. M. Sostek, S. Goldberg, and H. H. Shuman (Eds.), *Infants born at risk* (pp. 121–144). Jamaica, NY: Spectrum.

Levy-Shiff, R., Sharir, H., and Mogilner, M. B. (1989). Mother– and father–preterm relationship in the hospital preterm nursery. *Child Development, 60*, 93–102.

Lorenz, J. M., Wooliever, D. E., Jetton, J. R., and Paneth, N. (1998). A quantitative review of mortality and developmental disability in extremely premature newborns. *Archives of Pediatrics and Adolescent Medicine, 152*, 425–435.

Ludington-Hoe, S., Hadeed, A. J., and Anderson, G. C. (1991). Physiologic responses to skin-to-skin holding contact in hospitalized premature infants. *Journal of Perinatology, 11*(1), 19–24.

Magill-Evans, J., and Harrison, M. J. (1999). Parent–child interactions and development of toddlers born preterm. *Western Journal of Nursing Research, 21*, 292–307.

Maier, R. A., Holmes, D. L., Slaymaker, F. L., and Reich, J. N. (1984). The perceived attractiveness of preterm infants. *Infant Behavior and Development, 7*, 403–414.

Malatesta, C. Z., Grigoyev, P., Lamb, C., Albin, M., and Culver, C. (1986). Emotion socialization and expressive development in preterm and full term infants. *Child Development, 57*, 316–330.

Mangelsdorf, S., Plunkett, J., Dedrick, C., Berlin, M., Meisels, S., McHale, J., and Dichtellmiller, M. (1996). Attachment security in very low birth weight infants. *Developmental Psychology, 32*, 914–920.

Mann, J., and Plunkett, J. (1992, May). Home observations of extremely low birthweight infants: Maternal compensation or overstimulation. Paper presented at the International Conference on Infant Studies, Miami, FL.

Marshall, R. E., Kasman, C., and Cape, L. S. (1982). *Coping with caring for sick newborns*. Philadelphia: Saunders.

Marton, P., Minde, K., and Perrotta, M. (1981). The role of the father for the infant at risk. *American Journal of Orthopsychiatry, 51*, 672–678.

McGehee, L. J., and Eckerman, C. O. (1983). The preterm infant as social partner: Responsive but unreadable. *Infant Behavior and Development, 6*, 461–470.

McGrath, M. M., Sullivan, M. C., and Seifer, R. (1998). Maternal interaction patterns and preschool competence in high-risk children. *Nursing Research, 47*, 309–317.

Meyer, E. C., Coll, C. T. G., Seifer, R., Ramos, A., Kilis, E., and Oh, W. (1995). Psychological distress in mothers of preterm infants. *Developmental and Behavioral Pediatrics, 16*, 412–417.

Miles, M. S. (1989). Parenting needs with preterm infants: Sources of stress. *Critical Care Nursing Quarterly, 12*, 69–74.

Miles, M. S., Funk, S. G., and Kaspar M. A. (1992). The stress response of mothers and fathers of preterm infants. *Research in Nursing and Health, 15*, 261–269.

Miles, M. S., and Holditch-Davis, D. (1995). Compensatory parenting: how mothers describe parenting their 3 year old prematurely born children. *Journal of Pediatric Nursing, 10*, 243–253.

Miles, M. S., and Holditch-Davis, D. (1997). Parenting the prematurely born child: Pathways of influence. *Seminars in Perinatology, 21*, 254–266.

Miles, M. S., Holditch-Davis, D., and Shepherd, H. (1998). Maternal concerns about parenting prematurely born children. *MCN American Journal of Maternal and Child Nursing, 23*, 70–75.

Minde, K. (2000). Prematurity and serious mental conditions in infancy: Implications for development, behavior and intervention. In C. H. Zeanah Jr. (Ed.), *Handbook of infant mental health* (2nd ed., pp. 176–194). New York: Guilford.

Minde, K., Marton, P., Manning, D., and Hines, B. (1980). Some determinants of mother–infant interaction in the premature nursery. *Journal of the American Academy of Child Psychiatry, 19*, 1–21.

Minde, K., Perrotta, M., and Corter, C. (1982). The effect of neonatal complications in premature twins on their mother's preference. *Journal of the American Academy of Child Psychiatry, 21*, 446–452.

Minde, K., Shosenberg, N., Thompson, J., and Marton, P. (1983). Self-help groups in a premature nursery—follow-up at one year. In J. Call, E. Galenson, and R. Tyson (Eds.), *Frontiers of infant psychiatry* (pp. 264–272). New York: Basic Books.

Minde, K., Whitelaw, A., Brown, J., and Fitzhardinge, P. (1983). Effect of neonatal complications in premature infants on early parent–infant interactions. *Developmental Medicine and Child Neurology, 25*, 763–777.

Molitor, A. E., and Eckerman, C. O. (1992, May). Behavioral cues of distress/avoidance in preterm infants. Paper presented at the International Conference on Infant Studies, Miami, FL.

Moore, J. B., Saylor, C. F., and Boyce, G. C. (1998). Parent child interaction and developmental outcomes in medically fragile high-risk children. *Children's Health Care, 27*, 97–112.

Myers, B. J. (1984). Mother-infant bonding: The status of the critical-period hypothesis. *Developmental Review, 4*, 240–274.

Neal, M. (1968). Vestibular stimulation and developmental behavior of the small preterm infant. *Nursing Research Reports, 3*, 2–5.

Nurcombe, B., Rauh, V., Howell, D., Teti, D., Rudoff, P., Murphy, B., and Brennan, J. (1983). An intervention program for mothers of low birthweight infants: Outcomes at 6 and 12 months. In J. Call, E. Galenson, and R. Tyson (Eds.), *Frontiers of infant psychiatry* (pp. 201–210). New York: Basic Books.

Paludetto, R., Faggiano-Perfetto, M., Asprea, A., De Curtis, M., and Margara-Paludetto, P. (1981). Reactions of 60 parents allowed unrestricted contact with infants in the NICU. *Early Human Development, 5*, 401–409.

Parke, R. D., and Anderson, E. R. (1987). Fathers and their at-risk infants: Conceptual and empirical analysis. In P. W. Berman and P. A. Pederson (Eds.), *Men's transitions to parenthood: Longitudinal studies of early family experience* (pp. 197–215). Hillsdale, NJ: Lawrence Erlbaum Associates.

Patteson, D. M., and Barnard, K. E. (1990). Parenting of low birthweight infants. *Infant Mental Health Journal, 11*, 37–56.

Pederson, D. R., Bento, S., Chance, G. W., Evans, B., and Fox, A. M. (1987). Maternal responses to preterm birth. *American Journal of Orthopsychiatry, 57*, 15–21.

Pederson, D. R., and Moran, G. (1996). Expressions of attachment outside of the strange situation. *Child Development, 67*, 915–927.

Plunkett, J., Meisels, S., Stiefel, G., Pasick, P., and Roloff, D. (1986). Patterns of attachment among infants of varying biological risk. *Journal of the American Academy of Child Psychiatry, 25*, 794–800.

Powell, L. (1974). The effect of extra stimulation and maternal involvement on the development of low birthweight infants and on maternal behavior. *Child Development, 45*, 106–113.

Redshaw, M. E. (1997). Mothers of babies requiring special care: Attitudes and experiences. *Journal of Reproductive and Infant Psychology, 15*, 109–120.

Rice, R. (1977). Neurophysiological development in premature infants following stimulation. *Developmental Psychology, 13*, 69–76.

Rice, R. Kangaroo Care Video. Available from Cradle Care, 2909 Florence St Berkeley, CA 94705.

Rice, R. Loving Touch Infant Massage (Video, chart, and Audiotape). Available from Cradle Care, 2909 Florence St Berkeley, CA 94705.

Robson, A. L. (1997). Low birth weight and parenting stress during early childhood. *Journal of Pediatric Psychology, 22*, 297–311.

Rodning, C., Beckwith, L., and Howard, J. (1989). Characteristics of attachment organization in prenatally drug exposed toddlers. *Development and Psychopathology, 1*, 277–289.

Roe, K. V. (1995). Differential gazing and vocal response to mother and stranger of full term and preterm infants across age. *Perceptual and Motor Skills, 81*, 929–930.

Rosenfield, A. G. (1980). Visiting in the intensive care nursery. *Child Development, 51*, 939–941.

Ross, G. (1984). Home intervention for premature infants of low-income families. *American Journal of Orthopsychiatry, 54*, 263–270.

Sameroff, A. K., and Chandler, M. J. (1975). Reproductive risk and the continuum of caretaking casualty. In F. D. Horowitz, E. M. Hetherington, S. Scarr-Salapatek, and G. Siegel (Eds.), *Review of child development research* (Vol. 4, pp. 187–244). Chicago: University of Chicago Press.

Scarr-Salapatek, S., and Williams, M. (1973). The effects of early stimulation on low birthweight infants. *Child Development, 44*, 94–101.

Schermann-Eizirik, L., Hagekull, B., Bohlin, G., Perrson, K., and Sedin, G. (1997). Interaction between mothers and infants born at risk during the first six months of corrected age. *Acta Pediatrica, 86*, 864–872.

Seashore, M., Leifer, A., Barnett, C., and Leiderman, P. (1973). The effects of denial of mother–infant interaction on maternal self–confidence. *Journal of Personality and Social Development, 26*, 369–373.

Segal, L., Oster, H., Cohen, M., Caspi, B., Meyers, M., and Brown, D. (1995). Smiling and fussing in 7-month-old preterm and full-term Black infants in still face. *Child Development, 66*, 1829–1873.

Solkoff, N., and Matusak, D. (1975). Tactile stimulation and behavioral development in low birthweight infants. *Child Psychiatry and Human Development, 6*, 33–37.

Solkoff, N., Yaffe, S., Weintraub, D., and Blase, B. (1969). Effects of handling on the subsequent development of premature infants. *Developmental Psychology, 1*, 765–768.

Stern, M., and Karraker, K. H. (1990). The prematurity stereotype: Empirical evidence and implications for practice. *Infant Mental Health Journal, 1*, 3–11.

Stevenson, M. B., Roach, M. A., Ver Haeve, J. N., and Leavitt, L. A. (1990). Rhythms in the dialog of infant feeding: Preterm and term infants. *Infant Behavior and Development, 13*, 51–70.

Tessier, R., Cristo, M., Velez, S., Giron, M., Figueroa de Calume, Z., Ruiz-Palaez, J., Charpak, Y., and Charpak, N. (1998). Kangaroo mother care and the bonding hypothesis. *Pediatrics, 102*, 1–13.

Thoman, E. B., and Ingersoll, E. W. (1989). The human nature of the youngest humans: Prematurely born babies. *Seminars in Perinatology, 13*, 482–494.

Thomasgard, M., and Metz, W. P. (1996). The 2-year stability of child vulnerability and parental overprotection. Journal of *Developmental and Behavioral Pediatrics, 17*, 222–228.

Thomasgard, M., Shonkoff, J. P., Metz, W. P., and Edelbrock. C. (1995). Parent–child relationship disorders. Part II. The vulnerable child syndrome and its relation to parental overprotection. *Journal of Developmental and Behavioral Pediatrics, 16*, 251–256.

Tracy, A. E., and Maroney, D. (1999). *Your premature baby and child*, New York: Berkeley Books.

van IJzendoorn, M. H., Goldberg, S., Kroonenberg, P., and Frenkel, O. (1992). The relative effects of maternal and child problems on the quality of attachment: A meta-analysis of attachment in clinical samples. *Child Development, 63*, 840–858.

van IJzendoorn, M. H., and Kroonenberg, P. (1988). Cross cultural patterns of attachment: A meta-analysis of the Strange Situation. *Child Development, 59*, 147–156.

Volpe, J. J. (1998). Neurologic outcomes of prematurity. *Archives of Neurology, 55*, 297–300.

Waters, E. (1995). The attachment Q-set. In E. Waters, B. E. Vaughn, G. Posada and K. Kondo-Ikemura (Eds.), Caregiving, cultural and cognitive perspectives on secure-base behavior and working models: New growing points of attachment theory and research. *Monographs of the Society for Research in Child Development, 60* (2–3, Serial No. 244).

Werceszczak, J. K., Miles, M. S., and Holditch-Davis, D. (1997). Maternal recall of the neonatal intensive care. *Neonatal Networks, 16*, 1–8.

Whitelaw, A., Heisterkamp, G., Sleath, K., Acolet, D., and Richards, M. (1988). Skin-to-Skin contact for very low birth weight infants and their mothers. *Archives of Disease in Childhood, 63*, 1377–1381.

Wille, D. E. (1991). Relation of preterm birth with quality of infant–mother attachment at one year. *Infant Behavior and Development, 14*, 227–240.

Wolke, D. (1998). Psychological development of prematurely born infants. *Archives of Diseases of Childhood, 78*, 567–570.

Yogman, M. W. (1987). Father–infant caregiving and play with preterm and full-term infants. In P. W. Berman and P. A. Pederson (Eds.), *Men's transitions to parenthood: Longitudinal studies of early family experience* (pp. 175–195). Hillsdale, NJ: Lawrence Erlbaum Associates.

Yogman, M. W., Kindlon, D., and Earls, F. (1995). Father involvement and cognitive/behavioral outcomes of preterm infants. *Journal of the Academy of Child and Adolescent Psychiatry, 34*, 58–66.

Zarling, C. L., Hirsch, B., and Landry, S. (1988). Maternal social networks and mother-infant interactions in full term and very low birthweight preterm infants. *Child Development, 59*, 178–185.

Zeanah, C., Canger, C., and Jones, J. (1984). Clinical approaches to traumatized parents. Psychotherapy in the intensive care nursery. *Child Psychiatry and Human Development, 14*, 158–169.

Zeanah, C., and McDonough, S. (1989). Clinical approaches to families in early intervention, *Seminars in Perinatology, 13*, 513–522.

Zeskind, P. S., and Iacino, R. (1984). Effects of maternal visitation to preterm infants in the neonatal intensive care unit. *Child Development, 55*, 1887–1893.

# 13

# Parenting Children
# with Mental Retardation

Robert M. Hodapp
*University of California, Los Angeles*

## INTRODUCTION

Rearing a child with mental retardation challenges any parent. Besides the child's cognitive difficulties, children with mental retardation often have associated motor, medical, psychopathological, and other disabilities. So too must one consider the parents' emotional reactions and concerns. Parents of children with mental retardation must cope with having produced a "defective" child, a child who looks and acts differently from agemates. Such parental concerns reoccur throughout the child's life, culminating in the issue of how the adult with mental retardation will live when parents can no longer provide in-home care. And yet, difficult as such parenting issues are, many parents cope successfully with rearing a child with mental retardation. Different families vary in their styles of coping, specific child characteristics influence parental and familial reactions, and many formal and informal supports protect parents from depression and hopelessness.

Before the issues involved in parenting a child with mental retardation are reviewed, three preliminary concerns must be addressed. First, it is necessary to note the area's connections to the parenting of children without mental retardation. Theories of parenting derive from those used to conceptualize parenting of nonretarded children, and most studies compare parents of children with mental retardation with parents of nonretarded children. But many perspectives recently used to understand parenting typical children have only gradually been adopted within studies of parents of children with mental retardation. Complex models of how to think about parenting effects have only rarely appeared within the mental retardation literature; similarly, few mental retardation studies have examined complicated nature–nurture questions or parenting within a network of larger ecological systems (Collins, Maccoby, Steinberg, Hetherington, and Bornstein, 2000). In short, parenting studies within mental retardation, although related to the larger parenting literature, have yet to be influenced by some of the newest ideas from typical parenting and development.

A second related issue concerns the nature of the studies themselves. Many studies—particularly those of the 1960s and 1970s—examined parents and families of children who were "disabled" or "mentally retarded." The prevailing view was that parents react in a similar way to a child with any disability. Only recently have studies more often examined parents of children with specific disability conditions to examine whether parents of children with mental retardation differ from those with motor, visual, hearing, or emotional impairments. Even in studies examining parents of children with mental retardation, most studies continue to examine parents of children who are more versus less severely retarded, as opposed to children with one or another genetic cause of mental retardation (Hodapp and Dykens, 1994). As a result, the subjects of parenting studies vary widely: Some studies examine parents of children with disabilities, others of children with mental retardation, still others of children with Down syndrome or other genetic mental retardation syndromes.

Third, one must address issues of etiology. Over the past 10 to 15 years, researchers have begun to appreciate the effects on behavior of many different genetic mental retardation disorders (Dykens, Hodapp, and Finucane, 2000; O'Brien and Yule, 1995, in press). To note but a few examples, Down syndrome, the most common genetic (chromosomal) cause of mental retardation, seems to predispose children to several etiology-related behaviors. Compared with others with mental retardation, those with Down syndrome generally show greater-than-expected delays in language (especially expressive language and grammar; Fowler, 1990; Miller, 1999), lower prevalence rates of certain psychopathologies (Dykens and Kasari, 1997), and, possibly, more cheerful, sociable personalities (Hodapp, 1996). Prader-Willi syndrome, a less common genetic disorder of mental retardation, predisposes individuals to extreme (often life-threatening) obesity, hyperphagia (i.e., extreme overeating), and food and nonfood obsessions and compulsions (Dykens, 1999; Dykens, Leckman, and Cassidy, 1996).

But if children themselves are prone to exhibit particular etiology-related behaviors, might not parents and others in the child's environment also respond in predictable ways? Studies have only begun to examine these possibilities. In addition, it remains unclear which etiology-related aspects of behavior might constitute the operative mechanisms underlying such child effects on others.

This chapter touches on many of these issues while examining both old and new work in parenting children with mental retardation. The chapter begins with the history of studies on parental reactions to rearing children with mental retardation, the nature of interactions between mothers and these children, and characteristics of such families. Following this discussion, the chapter tackles such theoretical and methodological issues as how one conceptualizes the family of a child with mental retardation, the child's meaning to parents, between-group versus within-group studies, and the role of the child's cause of mental retardation on family functioning. Examining more recent studies, we then return to maternal and paternal reactions, mother–child interactions, and the effects of preexisting parent and family characteristics on parent–family functioning. The chapter ends by providing more practical information and directions for future research.

## HISTORY OF PARENTING STUDIES

### Parents of Children with Mental Retardation

Parents of children with any type of disability have traditionally been considered as prime candidates for emotional disorders. Comparing parents of children with mental retardation, with emotional disorders, and with no impairments, Cummings, Bayley, and Rie (1966) found that mothers of 4- to 13-year-old children with mental retardation were more depressed, more preoccupied with their children, and had greater difficulty in handling their anger toward their children than did mothers of nonretarded children. Fathers, too, have been considered prone to suffer from emotional problems. Cummings (1976) found that, compared with fathers of nonretarded children, fathers of children with mental retardation were more likely to show increased rates of depression; these fathers also scored lower in dominance, self-esteem, and enjoyment of their (mentally retarded) children (see also Erickson, 1969; Friedrich and Friedrich, 1981). Cummings (1976) characterized this constellation of fathers' increased depression and lower dominance, self-esteem, and enjoyment of their children as "neuroticlike constriction."

The marital couple may also be adversely affected by the presence of a child with disabilities. Families of children with mental retardation or other disabilities have generally been thought to follow a "classic" pattern: Mothers become overinvolved with the child with mental retardation, whereas fathers withdraw from the situation, either emotionally or physically (Levy, 1970). In some families, this pattern escalates until marital difficulties predominate: Not all studies show increased levels of divorce in families with children who have mental retardation, but many do. In both the studies by Gath (1977) of children with Down syndrome and the study by Tew, Payne, and Lawrence (1974) of children with cerebral palsy, families of children with disabilities were less likely to be intact than were families with same-aged nonretarded children. Presumably difficulties in dealing with the birth and increased demands of the child with disabilities lead to an increased prevalence of parental breakup (Hagamen, 1980).

Studies of parental pathology and marital breakups form one strand in the history of research on parents of children with mental retardation. A second strand more specifically examines why parents are affected and which psychological mechanisms are involved in their reactions. The orientation of most such studies involves the so-called maternal mourning reaction. Drawing on Freud's work on mourning and melancholia, Solnit and Stark (1961) proposed that mothers mourn the birth of any type of defective infant. This mourning was thought to be akin to the grieving that occurs in response to a death, with the "death" being the loss of the mother's fantasy of the idealized, perfect infant. Solnit and Stark (1961) believed that maternal mourning occurs in response to the birth of a child with any cognitive, motor, social, or physical defect. These researchers were aware that their application of the grief–mourning model was not perfect, in that maternal mourning (as opposed to the actual death of the baby) is contradicted by the presence of an actual, live child. This model did, however, imply the time-bound nature of the mourning process, the idea that one "works through" one's mourning reaction over the first few years of the child's life.

Influenced by Solnit and Stark's model, later workers examined mothers of children with various types of disabilities to determine the nature and course of maternal mourning. Although the number and the names of stages have varied with the author, most workers hypothesized that there are essentially three stages of maternal mourning (see Blacher, 1984, for a review). Directly after birth (or diagnosis), mothers experience shock, involving the dissociation of their knowledge from their feelings about having given birth to a child with disabilities. Mothers say things like "I found myself repeating 'It's not real' over and over again" (Drotar, Baskiewicz, Irvin, Kennell, and Klaus, 1975, p. 712). The second stage involves "emotional disorganization." This disorganization predominantly manifests itself as either anger toward others or depression (that is, anger toward oneself). During this stage, mothers blame doctors, God, or themselves for their child's disability. This period of emotional disorganization may last from months to years, and differs from the first period in that mothers are more in touch with their emotions and have begun to integrate their intellectual and emotional reactions toward rearing the child with mental retardation. The third and final stage involves "emotional reorganization." Having worked through their initial feelings of shock and anger–depression, mothers come to realistically appreciate and love their child with disabilities. Parents now realize that the birth of the child with disabilities was "nothing I had done" and that their child is "very special" (Drotar et al., 1975, p. 713). Parents set about to act in the child's best interests, as they increasingly accept the child's strengths and limitations.

In both the original Solnit and Stark (1961) article and in later studies, no specific time constraints were placed on maternal mourning. Researchers noted only that mothers proceed in order from dissociation to emotional disorganization to emotional reorganization over the early childhood years. For the most part, though, emotional reactions to having a child with disabilities were thought to be worked through during the early childhood years.

Olshansky (1962, 1966) noted that, in contrast to this stage model of mourning, the metaphor of working through a grief reaction is inadequate, that parents continue having strong emotional reactions as the child gets older. He noted that "Most parents of a mentally defective child suffer chronic sorrow throughout their lives.... The intensity of this sorrow varies from time to time for the same person, from situation to situation, and from one family to the next" (Olshansky, 1962, pp. 190–191). Olshansky asked that mental retardation workers change their clinical practices to accommodate long-term reactions that can occur at various points over the child's lifetime. He noted that the view of Solnit and Stark (1961) "appears to be an attempt to define the afflicted parents as neurotic" (Olshansky, 1966, p. 22), when the problem of parenting a child with mental retardation "is clearly both in and outside of the [parents'] psyche" (Olshansky, 1966, p. 21).

Two additional themes are also implicit within the views of Solnit and Stark (and even of Olshansky) of parental reactions (Hodapp, 1998). The first is that the "parent" in almost every case was the mother. Given an essentially Freudian perspective (and the lower percentages of working women overall at that time), Solnit and Stark, Olshansky, and most parenting researchers considered the mother as the main—almost the sole—parent of children with mental retardation. In addition, both the mourning model and Olshansky's chronic sorrow view spoke little of variations among different parents of children with mental retardation. Whether considered neurotic or normal, little attention was paid to which external or internal factors might influence—even change—reactions from one mother to another.

## Parent–Child Dyads

Given this background of either stagelike or recurrent maternal mourning by mothers of children with mental retardation, interactional researchers during the 1970s searched for differences in various parental behaviors between dyads with children who did and did not have mental retardation. As a rule, the earliest studies found such differences. Buium, Rynders, and Turnure (1974) and Marshall, Hegrenes, and Goldstein (1973) found that mothers of children with Down syndrome provided less complex verbal input and were more controlling in their interactive styles than were mothers of same-aged nonretarded children. Although these authors noted only that the two groups of mothers differed in their behaviors, later workers citing these studies referred to the "verbal deprivation" (Mahoney, 1975) encountered by children with mental retardation.

But not all studies found such differences in maternal input. Rondal (1977) and Buckhalt, Rutherford, and Goldberg (1978), for example, observed that mothers of children with mental retardation behaved similarly to mothers of nonretarded children. Rondal (1977, p. 242) noted that, when children with Down syndrome and nonretarded children were matched on the child's mean length of utterance (MLU), "None of the comparisons of mothers' speech to normal and to Down Syndrome children led to differences that were significant or close to significant" between the two groups. Additionally, both groups of mothers adjusted their language upward (i.e., longer MLUs, type–token ratios) as the children's language levels increased. Rondal (1977, p. 242) concluded that "... the maternal linguistic environment of DS children between MLU 1 and 3 is an appropriate one...."

What could lead to such divergent findings from one study to another? Most differences were undoubtedly caused by methodological differences across studies. In general, when the child with mental retardation has been matched to the nonretarded child on chronological age (CA), mothers of children with mental retardation have been found to interact differently. But children with mental retardation are, by definition, functioning below nonretarded agemates; CA matching may thus be inappropriate. A more appropriate strategy might be to match mother-child dyads on the child's mental age (MA) or the child's level of language (MLU). The issue of what constitutes an appropriate matching variable continues to be debated.

## Family Characteristics

A final area of investigation has been the characteristics of families of children with disabilities, the ways in which these families are similar to or different from families of children without mental retardation. In a classic work, Farber (1959) identified several differences between families with and without retarded children. He noted, for example, that the child with mental retardation increasingly violates the family's "rules" concerning appropriate family roles. Whereas the infant with mental retardation plays the "infant role," at later ages the child with mental retardation continues always being "a little kid." The rights and responsibilities typical of middle childhood or the teen years are generally not passed on to the child with mental retardation.

Several implications arise from this lack of movement in the roles undertaken by these children. First, typically developing siblings assume different roles than would normally be expected. Farber (1959) identified the "role tensions" experienced by nonretarded siblings, particularly by the oldest daughter. As older girls are the traditional caregivers in Western society, oldest daughters more often perform household jobs and supervise younger children, thereby freeing their mothers to care for the child with mental retardation (Zukow-Goldring, in Vol. 3 of this *Handbook*). Probably because of their inability to enjoy their childhood years, these oldest daughters more often display depression and other psychopathology (see Lobato, 1983).

The social-role stagnation of the child with mental retardation also does not allow these families to move through a normal family life cycle. Like individual children, families also "develop." They undergo changes in dynamics from the couple's early years of marriage, to the three-, four-, or more-person family rearing young children, to dealing with one or more child's growing independence. In later years, families must deal with their child's "breaking away" and parental negotiation of the "empty nest syndrome," to grandparenthood for the parents and a new family cycle for the now-married children (Carter and McGoldrick, 1988; Combrinck-Graham, 1985; Duvall, 1957; Demick, in Vol. 3 of this *Handbook*). But Farber (1959) noted that, when rearing children with more severe levels of mental retardation (i.e., IQs below 50), parents are never allowed to "grow up" along with their children, thus forcing parents to become stuck in issues of parenting younger children.

Alongside Farber's work on family roles, early (and subsequent) studies delineated basic demographic differences between families with and without children who were retarded. The differences, while expectable, are nonetheless interesting. Families who are more affluent cope better with rearing a child with disabilities than do those making less money (Farber, 1970; Hoff, Laursen, and Tardif, in Vol. 2 of this *Handbook*); two-parent families cope better than one-parent families (Beckman, 1983; Weinraub, Horvath, and Gringlas, in Vol. 3 of this *Handbook*); and women in better marriages cope better than those in troubled marriages (Beckman, 1983; Friedrich, 1979; Wilson and Gottman, in Vol. 4 of this *Handbook*). In addition, families are less likely to use social supports when children are older (Suelzle and Keenan, 1981), even as the childcare needs of such children increase because of the child's becoming taller, heavier, and (oftentimes) more difficult to manage.

As the initial work of a new field, studies of parents, interactions, and familial integration set the stage for the explosion of parenting work over the past two decades. These earlier studies provided basic information about how parents react emotionally and how they interact with their children, as well as how families respond both dynamically and demographically to the child with mental retardation. More importantly, this early work provided the themes that continue to organize parenting research.

## THEORETICAL AND METHODOLOGICAL ISSUES IN PARENTING THE CHILD WITH MENTAL RETARDATION

Five interrelated themes cut across both earlier and later work on parents, interactions, and the larger family unit. These issues include a move from pathology to stress-coping perspectives, the influences of familial meaning systems on parental and familial adaptation, group- versus individual-differences approaches, etiology and indirect effects, and the entire issue of how one best studies parenting children with Down syndrome and other types of mental retardation.

## From Pathology to Stress-Coping: Examining the Models Used to Conceptualize Parenting

The earliest work on families of children with mental retardation considered parents, interactions, and families as a whole in terms of psychopathology. Parents were examined for psychiatric problems and for expressed or latent anger and other negative emotions (e.g., as on the Minnesota Multiphasic Personality Inventory; Erickson, 1969). Interactions between parents and children with mental retardation were examined to determine how such interactions differed from interactions between mothers and nonretarded children, and differences were considered as evidence of deficient interactions. Divorce, role tensions, stuck family cycles for families as a whole—all reflect the dominant "pathology focus" of parenting research during the 1960s and 1970s.

Gradually, however, researchers shifted from considering the child as a cause of psychopathology to a stressor on the family system (Crnic, Friedrich, and Greenberg, 1983). This change in perspective is important, for although stressors can be detrimental, they are not always so. In some situations, stressors can strengthen mothers and fathers—as individuals or couples—and families as groups. This perspective allows for a more positive, albeit realistic, orientation toward the problems and the strengths of these families.

The stress-coping perspective has also led to borrowing models from other areas. Specifically, McCubbin and Patterson's (1983) "ABCX model" has been adapted by family researchers to help explain potential variations among families of children with mental retardation. This model, which McCubbin and Patterson modified (from Hill, 1949) to explain the effects of father absence on families during the Vietnam war, has been further adapted for children with mental retardation into a "Double ABCX model." Briefly stated, the Double ABCX model hypothesizes that the effects of the "crisis" of having a child with mental retardation (X in the model) is due to specific characteristics of the child (the "stressor event," or A), mediated by the family's internal and external resources (B) and by the family's perceptions of the child (C). But compared with father absence or other relatively unchanging situations, children with mental retardation and their effects on families change over time: Characteristics of the child change as the child gets older, the family's internal and external resources may change, and so too may the family's perceptions of the child. Hence the "Double" in the Double ABCX model.

Although an overly broad framework, the Double ABCX model has nevertheless served researchers well. Most important, the model helps explain both negative and positive consequences of rearing a child with mental retardation (Minnes, 1988). For all families, children displaying fewer emotional problems and requiring less physical caregiving may help parents and families to adjust more positively. In the same way, families with few internal or external resources are more likely to be negatively affected by the child with mental retardation; families with more resources should do better.

## The Child's Meaning to the Parents

As scientists in many fields are discovering, human beings are "meaning-makers," creatures obsessed with deriving meaningful understandings of human events (e.g., Bruner, 1990). Yet, until recently, the role of meaning—of what the child with mental retardation means to the parents—has rarely been examined. This recent focus on meaning can best be seen in examinations of interactions between children with mental retardation and their parents. A common finding is that such interactions are both "the same and different" from interactions between nonretarded child–mother dyads (see next subsection). Many interactive differences appear to be due to the different meanings of the child with mental retardation to the mother.

Consider the following vignette from Jones's (1980, p. 221) study of mothers of children with Down syndrome:

There was a strong tendency for the mothers of the Down's syndrome children to refer repeatedly to "teaching" their children when in verbal interaction with them. This was in contrast to the descriptions given by the mothers of the normal children, who felt that although their children probably learned from these "chats" together, it was the children's company they appreciated most at these times. . . . As one mother of a Down's syndrome child explained, "It's sit him on your knee and talk to him, that's the main object. Play with him, speak to the child, teach him something."

In addition to the role of meaning in mother–child interactions, families have complex meaning systems for both the family overall and for each individual member. Using an ecological perspective on the family, Gallimore, Weisner, Kaufman, and Bernheimer (1989) have described the different "social constructions" held by families of children with mental retardation. They note that some families feel that the child with mental retardation needs intensive intervention, whereas others feel that nonretarded children should receive more time and attention. Families then change their day-to-day lifestyles to accommodate their prevailing values. To Gallimore et al., the meaning of the child with mental retardation—and how this child fits within the overall family's meaning system—is the most important influence on the family's behaviors and on how these behaviors are interpreted by each family member.

## Group- Versus Individual-Differences Approaches

All families of children with mental retardation are not alike. Individual mothers and fathers, siblings, families as a unit, and children with mental retardation themselves all display individual characteristics that may affect parenting. Yet partly as a side effect of the Solnit and Stark (1961) formulation, most research on parenting children with mental retardation has contrasted parents, interactions, and families of children with mental retardation to parents, interactions, and families of nonretarded children. Such studies have sought to determine if behaviors are the same or different relative to behaviors occurring in response to nonretarded children. Although such a group-differences approach has been useful in many areas, it needs to be complemented by studies examining intragroup variation among families of children with retardation.

A complementary focus on individual differences has begun to affect the parenting literature, somewhat as a result of the Double ABCX and other stress-coping models. If any one family's reaction is due to a combination of child characteristics and the family's internal and external resources and perceptions, then individual differences—in the child with mental retardation, the parents, and the entire family system—become important foci of research and intervention. Indeed, families differ on a host of factors: in the degree to which they are warm or cold, open or closed, harmonious or unharmonious. Personal characteristics of—and relationships among—mothers, fathers, sisters, brothers, and extended family members all vary from one family to another, and all potentially influence parenting. In the same way, many characteristics of children themselves affect parental and familial reactions. The child's CA, MA, IQ, degree and types of associated disability, personality, and interests might all be important. Most of these characteristics have so far received little attention.

## Etiology and "Indirect Effects"

Another important influence on parental reactions and behaviors may be the child's type of mental retardation. Over the past 10 years, a revolution has occurred in behavioral research in mental retardation. Previously, most behavioral researchers studied children with mental retardation who had similar degrees of impairment: the mild, moderate, severe, and profound levels of mental retardation found in DSM-IV and other classification manuals (Hodapp and Dykens, 1994). Over the past 10 years, however, behavioral studies have proliferated in such disorders as Williams syndrome,

Prader-Willi syndrome, and fragile X syndrome (Dykens, 1995; Dykens and Hodapp, 2001). Even in Down syndrome, the sole etiology to receive research attention over many decades, the number of behavioral studies almost doubled from the 1980s to the 1990s.

To date, most of this work has focused on delineating behavior of the children themselves. Many of these syndromes show etiology-related maladaptive behaviors, cognitive–linguistic profiles, trajectories of development, and (possibly) personalities or perceived personalities (Dykens et al., 2000). Several disorders have even become the battleground for larger issues; children with Williams syndrome—with their higher-than-expected levels of linguistic versus visuospatial skills—have been used to shed light on whether different human abilities are indeed "modular" (Bellugi, Mills, Jernigan, Hickok, and Galaburda, 1999; Mervis, Morris, Bertrand, and Robinson, 1999).

Less well studied have been genetic disorders' indirect effects, or parental (and others') reactions to etiology-related child behaviors (Hodapp, 1997, 1999). The background for indirect effects arises from Bell's classic notion of interaction (Bell, 1968; Bell and Harper, 1977), the idea that, just as parents affect children, so too do children affect their parents. To give but one example, the resilience literature shows that even children reared in the least nourishing, chaotic environments are sometimes able to attract the help they need from surrounding adults (Werner, 1993). Even as toddlers, resilient children are more likely to exhibit a positive social orientation and to be alert and autonomous. Such behaviors, in turn, serve to elicit adult help at various ages, thereby allowing this subset of at-risk children to develop a positive self-concept and internal locus of control (Werner, 1993). In essence, then, through their behaviors, children affect surrounding adults.

In the case of mental retardation, children with a specific syndrome are predisposed to exhibit certain etiology-related behaviors, which in turn may elicit particular behaviors from parents. If parents of nonretarded children react in certain ways to their children's hyperactivity, then might not parents of children with either 5p- or fragile X syndromes—two disorders with particularly high rates of hyperactivity—respond similarly? Although only recently begun, this type of analysis holds great promise for a better understanding of parenting behaviors toward children with mental retardation.

Two final issues concern the indirect effects of genetic mental retardation disorders. The first involves direction of causality. Are children affecting parents or are parents affecting children? Although traditional socialization theory holds that parents affect their children, most studies of parents of children with different syndromes—and indeed, of parents of children with mental retardation in general—often assume the opposite. Moreover, recent longitudinal studies show that the direction of effects often goes from the child's behavior to the parents' or the family's functioning (Keogh, Garnier, Bernheimer, and Gallimore, 2000). Still to be addressed are more complicated questions such as how ongoing parent–child transactions serve to foster, buffer, or negate children's already existing tendencies across a wide variety of behavioral domains.

But even if children affect parents, what is the "active ingredient" about the child that affects parents? In considering this issue, most researchers have taken their lead from the parent–child literature of either typically developing children or children with one or another psychiatric disorder. The idea has been that those behaviors that elicit specific reactions in parents of typically developing (or psychiatrically impaired) children should bring about similar responses when exhibited by a child with a particular type of mental retardation. The particular genetic disorder, then, becomes a proxy for one or a small number of that disorder's characteristic behaviors. Although examples of this approach are provided in the next subsection, suffice it to say here that the nature and the operation of indirect effects remain underexamined.

## Methodological Issues

Since the late 1960s, workers in mental retardation have debated how best to conceptualize behavior in children with mental retardation. One side has included the many defect theorists, researchers who believe that mental retardation is caused by one or another specific defect (for a review, see Zigler and Balla, 1982). On the other have been developmental workers who propose that children with certain types of mental retardation—particularly those demonstrating no specific organic cause—show more general delays across many domains of functioning (Zigler and Hodapp, 1986).

One key aspect of this debate concerns CA versus MA matching, whether it is better to compare children with mental retardation with nonretarded children of the same CA (CA matching) or MA (MA matching). Defect theorists have long advocated CA matching, arguing that CA matching directly demonstrates a child's deficiencies in a particular area. Defect theorists also note that MA is a composite measure, allowing different children to achieve the identical MA in different ways (Baumeister, 1967). Developmentalists respond that, in order to show that a child is "deficient" in a particular area, delayed performance below overall MA must be established. Performance that is deficient to CA matches shows only that a particular task is one of many performed poorly by the child with mental retardation (Cicchetti and Pogge-Hesse, 1982). In addition, with recent debates about the degree to which functioning is "spared" in several genetic disorders (e.g., is language spared in Williams syndrome?), both MA and CA matches may be necessary (Hodapp and Dykens, 2001).

Whatever one's views concerning CA versus MA matching, this debate has revolved around the child with mental retardation's own behavior. How should one study parental reactions, or maternal behaviors within interactions, or the family systems of children with mental retardation? It would seem that research strategies need to be tailored to the question of interest. For example, studies of maternal language input should use children with and without mental retardation who are of the same language age (e.g., Conti-Ramsden, 1989). Because language is the issue, equating the two groups of children on overall levels of linguistic functioning would seem most sensible.

But even this strategy is problematic, in that oftentimes children with Down syndrome or other specific syndromes do not show "flat" or "across-the-board" functioning levels, even within a single domain like language. Children with Down syndrome demonstrate relatively poor grammatical versus pragmatic abilities (Beeghly and Cicchetti, 1987) and poor expressive as opposed to receptive language (Miller, 1992). Furthermore, in several etiological groups, areas of cognitive–linguistic strength or weakness become more pronounced as the child gets older. With increasing chronological age, boys with fragile X syndrome show more pronounced patterns of simultaneous over sequential processing skills (Hodapp, Dykens, Ort, Zelinsky, and Leckman, 1991), children with Williams syndrome show increasingly large discrepancies in linguistic versus nonlinguistic skills (Bellugi et al., 1999), and children with Down syndrome show increasingly salient expressive language deficits compared with their receptive language or with their overall MAs (Miller, 1992, 1999). Even comparisons involving "level-of-ability" measures are proving surprisingly complicated.

In contrast to examinations of input language, CA matching might be more appropriate for studies of family functioning. As Stoneman (1989) notes, families with 10-year-old children are in a particular family stage, even if the child functions at a 5-year-old level. To examine issues such as divorce rates, quality of marriage, sibling reactions, and other family dynamics, CA matching may be the most appropriate strategy. In line with this reasoning, most family studies have compared families of children with and without mental retardation when the children are matched on CA.

At the same time, however, not every family question may be best addressed with a CA match. Specifically, many of the changes of family dynamics involve reactions based on the child's immaturity, on the idea that the child with mental retardation—although she or he may be 10 years old–in fact acts like a much younger child. If families of a child with mental retardation are indeed "stuck" in their development (Farber and Rowitz, 1986), then a match to a group of families of nonretarded children of the same MA might be indicated. Better yet, both CA and MA matching might be useful to address such questions. Such a dual-matching strategy would reveal not only the ways in which these families differ from others at similar "family stages" (i.e., when children are of particular ages), but it would also show the degree to which such families actually are stuck in development because of parenting a child of a particular developmental level. Until now, few parenting studies have used such dual-matching procedures.

The discussion so far concerns group differences, but an additional methodological issue relates to individual differences, the idea that there are wide individual differences from one family to another.

Here, too, many important variables have not yet been examined. We know little, for example, about the family development of families who are more versus less successful in parenting the child with mental retardation, and only generally why some marriages break up whereas others become stronger. How familial adaptation might differ based on the family's socioeconomic status (SES), ethnicity, and parental education levels also remains underexplored. Even those variables that have been studied are usually examined in a piecemeal fashion, making more difficult the determination of each variable's contribution to individual differences among families. Change may be occurring, however, as more researchers use larger, family-systems frameworks to conceptualize their findings. More attention is needed to how to do research from the group-differences versus the individual-differences perspective and what each implies.

## MODERN RESEARCH ON PARENTING THE CHILD
## WITH MENTAL RETARDATION

The five issues discussed in the previous section can be found within much of the modern research in maternal and paternal reactions, mother–child interactions, and the reactions of the family as a whole to rearing the child with mental retardation. Much of this research combines recent theories and methodologies with the perspectives and findings of the 1960s and early 1970s.

### Factors Affecting Maternal and Paternal Reactions

Much modern research has examined the perspectives of both Solnit and Stark and Olshansky to delineate further when and how parents react to the child with mental retardation. When closer, more fine-grained examinations have been performed, researchers have found that several factors affect parental emotional reactions.

*Factors intrinsic to parents themselves.*   To date, *maternal coping styles* have been implicated as a major factor influencing parental reactions. Following from the work of Folkman, Schaefer, and Lazarus (1979), mothers can be identified as predominantly using either "problem-focused" or "emotion-focused" coping strategies (for a review, see Turnbull et al., 1993). In the first, mothers essentially address their child's mental retardation as a practical, concrete problem to be dealt with. These mothers make plans to address everyday problems, work hard to alleviate those problems, and feel that they have learned from their experiences. In contrast, in another group, mothers either totally deny their feelings about their child and the disability, or instead become overconcerned, almost obsessed, with their own feelings of depression and grief. Across a range of studies, active, problem-focused copers seem much better adjusted than emotion-based copers. Although in some sense obvious, a mother's style of social problem solving does seem important for successful adaptation to rearing a child with mental retardation.

So too may differences in the *mothers' genetic status* sometimes lead to different maternal reactions. For example, mothers who carry the fragile X gene have been found to more often be shy, anxious, and withdrawn compared with mothers of children with other types of disabilities (see Dykens, Hodapp, and Leckman, 1994). Such personality characteristics—which appear specific to female carriers of the fragile X gene—contribute to difficulties that professionals often experience in interacting with these women and in the problems these women have in making use of clinical, educational, and other supportive services (Dykens and Leckman, 1990).

An additional difference involves the *ethnicity* of the mother. Although an underresearched area, mothers of different ethnicities do seem to react differently to raising a child with mental retardation. Hispanic mothers, for example, report more problems than do non-Hispanic mothers in finding out information about their child and in participating in parent programs (Heller, Markwardt, Rowitz, and Farber, 1994). Other studies find that many Hispanic mothers are depressed, with levels of depression best predicted by the absence of a spouse or partner, low family cohesion, and poor maternal health (Blacher, Lopez, Shapiro, and Fusco, 1997).

For at least certain ethnic groups, one important—and often overlooked variable—involves religiosity. Although a topic in disability family research for many years (Zuk, Miller, Bertram, and Kling, 1961), the degree to which mothers consider themselves religious may be especially important among Hispanic and African American populations. In Heller et al. (1994), Hispanic (versus non-Hispanic) mothers considered raising a child with mental retardation as a religious duty. In the African American community, mothers benefited both from their personal religious feelings and from the support they received from other church members (Rogers-Dulan, 1998). Mothers thus mentioned how church members ". . . are especially good in helping my daughter's self-confidence," ". . . prayed for Tim the whole time he was in the hospital," and "brought us groceries and things for Kevin like clothes and diapers" (Rogers-Dulan, 1998, p. 98).

Just as the reactions of mothers may differ due to several factors, so too may different reactions occur in *mothers versus fathers*. Few studies have examined paternal compared with maternal reactions, but mothers and fathers do appear to vary. Damrosch and Perry (1989) asked mothers and fathers to retrospectively describe their emotional reactions since the birth of their children with Down syndrome. Two graphs were provided. The first graph, consistent with the mourning model of Solnit and Stark, showed strong emotional reactions early and then gradual acceptance of the child with disabilities. The second graph featured a series of wide emotional swings that was more consistent with the repeated "up-and-down" pattern of Olshansky's recurrent reactions model. Mothers and fathers differed in their reactions: Mothers more often described their feelings as repeatedly up and down (i.e., the recurrent reactions pattern), whereas fathers reported early emotional reactions then later acceptance (i.e., the maternal mourning model).

Mothers and fathers may also differ in how they conceptualize the child and the child's problems. Many studies have found that mothers experience more stress and feel themselves less in control of the situation than do fathers (Bristol, Gallagher, and Shopler, 1988; Damrosch and Perry, 1989; Goldberg, Marcovitch, MacGregor, and Lojkasek, 1986). Mothers may also react more to specific stressors than fathers: For example, mothers much more than fathers express needs for more social and familial support, information to explain the child's disability to others, and help with childcare (Bailey, Blasco, and Simeonsson, 1992).

In contrast, fathers seem more affected by the instrumental and pragmatic aspects of the child with mental retardation, as well as by specific aspects of the child's disability. Fathers are particularly concerned about the costs of caring for a child with disabilities and what the child will mean to the family as a whole (Price-Bonham and Addison, 1978). Comparing factors affecting mothers versus fathers of young children with mental retardation, Krauss (1993, p. 401) noted that "mothers reported more difficulty than did fathers in adjusting to the personal aspects of parenting and parenthood (parental health, restrictions in role, and relations with spouse). . . . fathers reported more stress related to the child's temperament (e.g., child's mood and adaptability) and their relationship to the child (such as feelings of attachment and of being reinforced by the child)."

Given these differences, factors that support mothers may not support fathers. Frey, Greenberg, and Fewell (1989) found that the presence of supportive social networks promotes better coping on the part of mothers of children with mental retardation, whereas fathers cope better when there is a minimal amount of criticism from extended families. Both mothers and fathers cope best if the other spouse is coping well and if each feels a strong measure of personal control in rearing the child with mental retardation.

*Factors related to child characteristics.*  In addition to variables related to parents, several characteristics of the children themselves seem to influence parental reactions. The first of these factors concerns the *age of the offspring with mental retardation*. Several researchers have attempted to determine when emotional reactions and concerns are most likely to occur for mothers of children with disabilities. For example, Emde and Brown (1978) noted that parents of children with Down syndrome undergo several waves of depression over the child's first year of life (Zahn-Waxler, Duggal, and Gruber, in Vol. 4 of this *Handbook*). After experiencing strong feelings of depression at the baby's birth and diagnosis, parents generally do better until the baby is approximately 4 months of age, when feelings of sadness reappear. This second wave of depression occurs as parents realize the behavioral implications of Down syndrome, as their infants show more dampened affect and less consistent social smiles than do same-aged nonretarded children. If the preschool period is considered as a whole, mothers are generally most concerned about milestones appearing during the earliest years (e.g., walking, talking), although certain later-occurring milestones (e.g., toilet training, writing) also bring about high levels of maternal concern (Hodapp, Dykens, Evans, and Merighi, 1992).

Such recurrent emotional reactions continue throughout the childhood years. Wikler (1986) noted that parents experience stress during puberty (ages 11 to 15 years) and during the onset of adulthood (ages 20 to 21 years). Compared with responses from these same mothers 2 years before or after these periods, lesser amounts of stress were reported (Wikler, 1986). In a more general sense, Minnes (1988) described a "pileup" of stressors on mothers as their children get older, even as mothers less often use formal and informal social supports (Suelzle and Keenan, 1981). In evaluating the formulation of Solnit and Stark, it seems that, although parental emotions may be most intense directly after the birth of their children, later events and milestones also evoke strong reactions. As Wikler (1981, p. 284) noted, "The accepted view that a crisis occurs following the diagnosis because of the general disruption of expectancies is probably correct; but the conclusion that the gradually gained equilibrium is permanent is probably incorrect."

In recent years, researchers have also examined parental reactions to their children during a different period of life, when the child with mental retardation becomes an adult. Two contrasting viewpoints have been featured in this work. In the first, wear-and-tear hypothesis, parents of adults with mental retardation are thought, over time, to get beaten down by the day-to-day struggle to parent their now-adult offspring. In the second adaptational hypothesis, parents and their adult offspring come to coexist peacefully, with the caregiver developing new coping strategies and growing psychologically (Townsend, Noelker, Deimling, and Bass, 1989).

For the most part, studies support the second, more hopeful perspective for mothers of adults with mental retardation. In a study of 450 mothers aged 55 to 85 years, Seltzer and Krauss (1989) found that most (78%) reported that their health was good or excellent; compared with other samples of family caregivers, the samples of these mothers showed that they were substantially more satisfied with their lives and reported slightly less caregiving stress and feelings of burden. A high level of involvement by the other (nonretarded) siblings was also helpful, as were the mothers' own constructive coping strategies (Seltzer and Ryff, 1994).

Before too rosy a picture is painted, however, it should also be noted that these families do have their problems. Specifically, approximately half of these older mothers reported experiencing a stressful life event (death of family member or close friend, illness, or the like) over the prior 18 months, and individual mothers showed higher levels of depressive symptoms after experiencing such events (Krauss and Seltzer, 1998). As during their offspring's childhood years, mothers who used more constructive coping styles did better. On balance, though, these mothers and their families were doing relatively well. In some studies, parents even reported that they themselves received support from their adult offspring with mental retardation and that such support was important in mothers reporting greater satisfaction and less caregiving burden (Heller, Miller, and Factor, 1997).

A second factor concerns the *etiology* of the child's mental retardation. Across all but a very few studies, families of children with Down syndrome appear to do better than families of children with other forms of mental retardation, autism, or psychiatric disorders. To give a few examples, when compared with parents of children with autism and of children with unidentified mental retardation, parents of children with Down syndrome exhibit significantly lower amounts of stress (Holroyd and MacArthur, 1976; Kasari and Sigman, 1997; Sanders and Morgan, 1997; Seltzer, Krauss, and Tsunematsu, 1993). Compared with mothers of children with other disabilities, mothers of children with Down syndrome even report experiencing greater support from friends and the greater community (Erikson and Upshure, 1989).

This advantage to families of children with Down syndrome occurs across a range of ages and relative to a variety of contrast groups; it is also found in most, but not all (e.g., Cahill and Glidden, 1996), studies. The previously mentioned studies examined families of persons with mental retardation who ranged from below 2 years (Erikson and Upshure, 1989) through 25 years of age (Seltzer et al., 1993). Some studies compared individuals with Down syndrome with other groups with mental retardation, and some with groups of children with autism. In one study (Thomas and Olsen, 1993), researchers began by considering families of adolescents with Down syndrome as "problem families," akin to two groups of families of adolescents with emotional disturbance. As the study progressed, however, these researchers—finding no group differences—combined their "normal" and Down syndrome families into a single control group, concluding that families of children with Down syndrome were not really problem families after all. A few additional studies have also found no differences between parents and families of typically developing children versus of children with Down syndrome (e.g., Van Riper, Ryff, and Pridham, 1992), although others show that, compared with parents of such typical children, the parents in the Down syndrome group do show higher levels of stress (Roach, Orsmond, and Barratt, 1999). At the very least, parents and families of children with Down syndrome appear to cope better compared with families of children with other types of disabilities.

Several potential explanations might account for this "Down syndrome advantage." First, as a common and widely known disorder, Down syndrome is understandable to parents and families, and to extended family, schools, doctors, and the wider community as well. The syndrome also has many parent groups, often with active local chapters. Second, because of the higher prevalence rates of Down syndrome to mothers of more advanced age, mothers may be more mature and more experienced in the parenting role. Given more years in the workforce, such parents and families might even be more well off than parents of (non-Down syndrome) children with mental retardation. Indeed, the few studies not finding this Down syndrome advantage have suggested that these parents' age and SES may account for differences earlier attributed to the etiology itself (Cahill and Glidden, 1996).

At the same time, however, these children themselves possess several characteristics that may differ from those of others with mental retardation (Hodapp, 1999). Children with Down syndrome may have more upbeat, sociable personalities, particularly during the early years. Such personalities have now been noted from both questionnaire measures (Hodapp, Ly, Fidler, and Ricci, 2001) and in parents' descriptions of their children's personalities (Carr, 1995; Hornby, 1995). Such sociable personalities are evident even from the toddler years, when, compared with other children with mental retardation, toddlers with Down syndrome more often look to their mothers than to surrounding objects (Kasari, Freeman, Mundy, and Sigman, 1995). Such looking to adults continues into the middle childhood years, at times even interfering with these children's completion of intellectual tasks (Kasari and Freeman, 2001).

A second behavioral difference concerns the relative lack of psychopathology—especially severe psychopathology—in the Down syndrome population. Although percentages of children with Down syndrome with significant behavior problems range from 15% to 38% (Hodapp, 1996), such percentages are generally lower than those found in same-aged children with mixed etiologies (Dykens and Kasari, 1997; Meyers and Pueschel, 1991).

Conversely, examined either within or across different etiological groups, the child's maladaptive behavior seems the single best predictor of parental stress. Such studies have ranged across families of children with such different syndromes as 5p- syndrome (Hodapp, Wijma, and Masino, 1997), Prader-Willi syndrome (Hodapp, Dykens, and Masino, 1997), and Smith-Magenis syndrome (Hodapp, Fidler, and Smith, 1998). Similar findings occur when one compares stress levels of parents of children with three etiologies that differed on "sociability" (loosely defined) and on maladaptive behaviors. Thus Fidler, Hodapp, and Dykens (2000) have recently compared parents of children with Down syndrome (high sociability, low maladaptive behavior), Williams syndrome (high sociability, high maladaptive behavior), and Smith-Magenis syndrome (moderate sociability, high maladaptive behavior). Parents of 3- to 10-year-old children with Down syndrome showed less parental pessimism than did the other two groups and less parent and family problems than parents of children with Smith-Magenis syndrome. In both the Williams and the Smith-Magenis groups, the child's degree of maladaptive behavior was the strongest predictor of parental stress (in the Down syndrome group, parents showed slightly decreasing stress levels as the child got older). In essence, then, adults react differently to children with different genetic mental retardation syndromes, and the most important predictor of parental stress reactions is the child's amount of maladaptive behavior.

In addition to the child's behaviors per se, other, more physical, characteristics may also elicit parental reactions. Specifically, children with Down syndrome generally have more infantile or babylike faces, that is, faces that are rounder and with smaller, lower-set features (Allanson, O'Hara, Farkas, and Nair, 1993). More importantly than the faces themselves, however, is the strong tendency of adults to attribute infantile personality characteristics to persons whose faces appear more babylike (Berry and McArthur, 1985). This "babyface overgeneralization" (Zebrowitz, 1997) results in adults rating photographs of more versus less babyfaced individuals (children or adults) as being warmer, friendlier, and more honest, compliant, and sociable.

In a recent study, Fidler and Hodapp (1999) set out to determine if the babyface personality overgeneralization might occur as well in response to faces of children with Down syndrome. They first examined naive adults' reactions to pictures of 8-, 10-, and 12-year-old children with Down syndrome, another genetic mental retardation disorder (5p- syndrome), and same-aged typically developing children. As predicted, respondents rated the children with Down syndrome as more honest, naive, warm, compliant, and sociable. In a second within-group study, those children with Down syndrome who objectively possessed more versus less babyfaced faces were rated higher on these personality characteristics. Although the link has yet to be made among the child's face, parental personality judgment, and parental stress or other reaction, the face may ultimately join behavior as a child characteristic to which adults respond.

In considering the research on parental emotional reactions, then, much progress has occurred since the original formulations of Solnit–Stark and Olshansky. Increasingly, researchers are developing a taxonomy of parent and child characteristics that affect parental reactions, a taxonomy that should promote more effective parental coping strategies throughout the childhood years.

## Mother–Child Interactions

Starting with Rondal's (1977) study showing that mothers of children with Down syndrome provide similar levels of language input as mothers of nonretarded children of the same level of language (i.e., MLU), many studies have examined interactions between mothers and children with a variety of disability conditions. These studies converge on a basic theme: Maternal interactive (mainly linguistic) behaviors with their children with disabilities appear both the same as and different from maternal behaviors with nondisabled children of the same level of language.

With few exceptions, the similarities have occurred when one examines what might be called the structural properties of input language. Mothers provide language that is of the same grammatical complexity, has the same amount of information per sentence, and appears much like the language provided by mothers of nonretarded children of the same language age or MA. As in Rondal's (1977) study, mothers of children who are higher in language provide higher-level input, thereby providing the child with the "developmental scaffold" or Language Assistance Support System (Bruner, 1983) considered important by developmental psycholinguists.

Yet at the same time, these mothers appear very different in their styles of interaction. Even when children with versus without mental retardation are equated on overall mental or linguistic age, mothers of children with Down syndrome and other types of mental retardation are often more didactic, directive, and intrusive compared with mothers of nonretarded children (see Marfo, 1990). Such stylistic differences between mothers of children with and without mental retardation are seen on a number of levels. Tannock (1988) found that, compared with mothers of nonretarded children, mothers of children with Down syndrome took interactive turns that were longer and more frequent; in addition, these mothers more often "clashed" with—or spoke at the same time as—their children (see also Vietze, Abernathy, Ashe, and Faulstich, 1978). Mothers of children with Down syndrome also switched the topic of conversation more often and less often silently responded to the child's utterance. Children with Down syndrome thus participated in "asymmetrical" conversations, conversations in which mothers more often controlled the topic, the child's response, and the nature of the back-and-forth conversation.

Although many studies have now found this stylistic difference, why mothers in the two groups differ remains unclear. The most common explanation is that mothers of children with mental retardation inject their parenting concerns into the interactive session. Greater numbers of mothers of children with mental retardation consider interactions as "teaching sessions," as moments not to be squandered in the nonstop effort to intervene effectively (Cardoso-Martins and Mervis, 1984; Jones, 1980). In contrast, mothers of nonretarded children display fewer fears and concerns; they may simply desire to play—in a more spontaneous and less directive manner—with their nonretarded children.

Complicating things further is the entire issue of infant cues and readability. As they are often more lethargic and more hypotonic, infants and young children with Down syndrome may provide fewer and less clear interactive cues, at least in the months directly before intentional communication (Hyche, Bakeman, and Adamson, 1992). These infants may therefore be less "readable" (Goldberg, 1977; Walden, 1996) to the mother, even as mothers gradually learn to interpret their child's vague or slight communicative behaviors (Sorce and Emde, 1982; Yoder, 1986). To date, it remains unclear why interactions between mothers and children with Down syndrome differ in style (but not in structure) from interactions between mothers and same-level nonretarded children; most likely, some combination of maternal and child factors seems implicated.

A third issue concerns the goals of mother–child interaction. As noted earlier, mothers of children with Down syndrome may feel a greater need to teach as opposed to play with their children, whereas mothers of nonretarded children may often merely play with and enjoy their young offspring (Cardoso-Martins and Mervis, 1984; Jones, 1980). This sense comes from maternal reports of interaction, but also from observations of these mothers' styles of interaction. Mothers of children with mental retardation are much more likely to request higher-level behavior from their children than are mothers of nonretarded children. Mahoney, Fors, and Wood (1990) found that mothers of children with Down syndrome (CA = 30 months; MA = 17 months) requested behavior at approximately the 15-month level, whereas mothers of MA-matched nonretarded children requested behavior at an average level of 10 months. In Vygotskian terms, requesting the highest level behavior should aid the child's development, but such optimally demanding requests fit with the more didactic, directive, and intrusive style of interactions often noted for mothers of children with disabilities.

In line with most work in this area, the preceding review focuses on studies examining differences between maternal behaviors of children with and without mental retardation. But several studies have now examined variation in maternal behaviors *within* samples with mental retardation (usually Down syndrome). The main findings are that not all mothers behave identically and that certain maternal styles of interaction may be more helpful than others for language development in children with Down syndrome.

In the first direct examination of this issue, Crawley and Spiker (1983) rated maternal sensitivity and directiveness of mothers in their interactions with their 2-year-old children with Down syndrome. They found wide individual differences from one mother to another. Some mothers were highly directive, whereas others followed the child's lead; similarly, mothers varied widely in their rated degrees of sensitivity to their children. Because the two dimensions of sensitivity and directiveness were somewhat orthogonal, mothers could be high or low on either sensitivity or directiveness. All four combinations were demonstrated in this study. Just as mothers of nonretarded children vary widely on both directiveness and sensitivity, so too do mothers of children with Down syndrome.

In a similar way, Mahoney et al. (1990) described two groups of mother–child dyads in children with Down syndrome: those who were "turn balanced" versus "turn imbalanced." Turn-balanced mothers produced 52% of turns, whereas the child with Down syndrome produced 48% of turns (i.e., one or more interactive behaviors with less than a 1-second pause). In contrast, turn-imbalanced mothers produced 60% of turns in the interactive session, allowing children only 40% of turns. Although turn-balanced and turn-imbalanced mothers were similar on some measures (e.g., asking for high-level behaviors from their children), many differences between the two groups were also noted. Turn-imbalanced mothers requested actions more often from their children, and their requested actions often differed from the child's focus of attention. The Mahoney et al. (1990) study highlights the ways that mothers of children with Down syndrome differ one from another.

A final issue concerns the effects of different maternal behaviors on children's development. In the sole study of this issue, Harris, Kasari, and Sigman (1996) examined the effects of maternal interactive behaviors on children with Down syndrome's expressive and receptive language behaviors. Examining children when they were 2 and again at 3 years of age, Harris et al. (1996) found that the mean length of time in which mothers and children were engaged in joint attention (i.e., focusing on the same object) was correlated to the child's degree of receptive language gain over the 1-year interval. In addition, the child's receptive language gains were also correlated with the amount of time that mothers maintained the child's attention to child-selected toys, and (negatively) to instances of redirecting the child's focus of attention and of engaging in greater numbers of separate joint-attention episodes. Such findings parallel those found for interactions between mothers and typically developing infants, in which maternal sensitivity (Baumwell, Tamis-LeMonda, and Bornstein, 1997) and joint-attention episodes (Tomasello and Farrar, 1986) also promote young children's early language abilities. For both typically developing children and children with Down syndrome, then, mothers who follow the child's lead, respond to the child's interests and behaviors, and prolong episodes of mother–child joint attention help to facilitate children's processing of maternal input language. The child's receptive abilities increase accordingly.

Mother–child interactions, then, are interesting from the perspective of both group differences and intragroup variation. As a group, mothers of children with mental retardation are the same but different in their interactions from mothers of nonretarded children at similar MAs. They are the same in the structural aspects of their input—such things as MLU, type–token ratio, and other measures of communicative complexity. At the same time, these mothers appear more intrusive, didactic, and "pushy." It remains unclear whether such stylistic differences are due to maternal emotional reactions or to child factors; preliminary evidence, however, indicates that such mother-directed, intrusive interactions are less effective. More effective for the development of children with mental retardation are maternal behaviors that follow the child's lead and that foster periods of mothers and children attending and talking about the same object or event.

## Family Characteristics

Modern research on families continues the historic tradition of delineating the characteristics of families of children with mental retardation. In recent years, however, the conceptual frameworks have shifted from family pathology to family stress and coping. As with parents and mother–child interaction, research emphasizes both differences of these families from families with nonretarded children and intragroup variation across families with a member with mental retardation.

A good example of the change to a stress-coping perspective comes from work on family support. Earlier research noted that families of children with mental retardation were often isolated, with few formal and informal supports. Wikler, Wasow, and Hatfield (1981) even noted a divergence of perception on the part of the families themselves and the social service workers who aid them. Whereas parents were concerned about child milestones occurring both earlier and later (e.g., child reaches adulthood) during the child's life, social service personnel identified the early years as the period of most difficulty for parents and other family members. Such professional perspectives may exacerbate the "front-loading" of services for families of children with mental retardation, the tendency of services to more often be provided during the earliest years, even as these families may require more help—and become less connected to formal support services—as the child gets older (Suelzle and Keenan, 1981).

Yet, although these families may receive less formal support later on, they are not quite as isolated as earlier hypothesized. In work with families of children with mental retardation and with chronic illness, Kazak and Marvin (1984; also Kazak, 1987) noted that families of children with both conditions possess strong informal social networks, but that these networks differ from those of families without a disabled member (Cochran and Niego, in Vol. 4 of this *Handbook*). Specifically, Kazak and Marvin (1984) found that parents of children with disabilities have smaller social networks, but networks that are more dense. These mothers thus receive a fair amount of informal support, but the support comes from the mother's own mother, sister, or a few close family friends. Such networks are denser in that each member of the network interacts with every other member.

As Byrne and Cunningham (1985) noted, the presence of smaller but denser social networks is both good and bad. These families are not isolated, in that they often receive support, encouragement, and respite from day-to-day responsibilities from a small circle of loving friends and relatives. But as the networks are smaller, parents of children with disabilities have fewer contacts with a wider, more diffuse network of friends and associates. Families are often enmeshed in a tightly organized, intimate circle of social support that can at times feel suffocating.

In addition to such group-differences research, sporadic research has also appeared on how families of children with mental retardation differ one from another. Through cluster analysis, Mink, Nihira, and Meyers (1983) identified five types of families of children with severe retardation: (1) cohesive, harmonious families, (2) control-oriented, somewhat unharmonious families, (3) low-disclosure, unharmonious families, (4) child-oriented, expressive families, and (5) disadvantaged, low-morale families. Similar, although not identical, family clusters have been found for families of children with mild and borderline mental retardation (Mink, Nihira, and Meyers, 1984). More and more, then, variation among different families is being characterized.

Such work helps explain which child, individual member, or family variables lead to different family styles. As with parental reactions, the child's type of mental retardation may contribute to different family styles. In Mink et al. (1983), almost two thirds of "cohesive harmonious" families were of children with Down syndrome, a much higher percentage than might be expected by chance. In another study as well, Beavers, Hampson, Hulgus, and Beavers (1986) noted that 7 of the 11 families considered to be functioning "optimally" were families of children with Down syndrome (although it was unclear how many of their 40 study families had children with this syndrome).

As previously noted, we do not yet know why families of children with Down syndrome seem to be doing better. Seltzer et al. (1993) emphasize that, although the reasons for such differences remain unknown, Down syndrome features readily accessible support groups and a more researched, more understood clinical syndrome. Or it may be that, as Mink et al. (1983, p. 495) noted, "Taking into consideration the effects of children on their caretakers, we may speculate that Down syndrome children [or adults] will have a positive effect on the climate of the home."

Recent family work, then, shows a change in emphasis from pathology to stress and coping. Such research also shows the complexity of familial reactions and the strong influences of factors associated with both the child (age, type of mental retardation) and the family (size and nature of family network).

## PRACTICAL INFORMATION

Like the larger field of child development (Sears, 1975), the field of parenting children with mental retardation is not purely a scientific enterprise. Instead, the field has strong and enduring practical concerns. Many family researchers consult with or direct intervention services, others write practical books and manuals for parents of children with various types of mental retardation. This chapter therefore discusses the practical implications of classical and modern research for parents, interactions, and families overall.

## Mothers and Fathers

Compared with parents of only two decades ago, parents of children with mental retardation are now much more visible, playing the role of active decision makers in their children's services. These parents are simultaneously members of parent organizations, advocates for their individual children and for children with disabilities in general, and recipients of professional services (Turnbull and Turnbull, 1986). Professional services themselves have also increased dramatically. Only 40 years ago, many children with mental retardation were institutionalized; nowadays, children and families are served through a variety of services, ranging all the way from services supporting parents in performing in-home care to part- or full-time residential services for children with the most severe and multiple disabilities. This "continuum of services" for individuals with mental retardation gives parents both more rights and more responsibilities.

Many of these expanded rights and responsibilities concern schools, the most important service provided throughout the childhood years. Federal laws such as Public Law (PL) 94-142 (the Education for All Handicapped Children Act of 1975) and the Individuals with Disabilities Education Act, or IDEA (passed in 1990; amended in 1997) now provide as a right a free, appropriate public school education for all children with mental retardation (Yell and Drasgow, 2000). The hallmark of this legislation is that all children be educated in the "least restrictive environment" (LRE). This term, often equated with education within a mainstreamed classroom, actually entails a host of alternatives. LRE allows for full-time integration with nondisabled children, integration for part of the day (the remainder with a resource room or specialist), special classes within a public school, and even special classes or special residential schools when necessary to meet the child's educational needs. Integral to decisions concerning the best educational alternative are the child's Individualized Educational Plan and the series of legal hearings and appeals that are the right of all parents of children with disabilities. Compared with the days when school systems refused to educate children with mental retardation, the years since PL 94-142 and IDEA feature major societal advances for children with mental retardation and their families.

Residential services have also changed enormously over the past 40 years. As recently as the 1960s, parents had two choices: to provide in-home care or to institutionalize their child with mental retardation. In contrast, families now enjoy a continuum of residential alternatives. In-home care is the option of most parents, and many are aided in this choice by parent training programs and part-time childcare aid. Respite care, summer camps and other services allow parents and other family members a break from their parenting duties. Group home and residential care services are also available, particularly for parents of children with profound mental retardation, multiple disabilities, or severe behavior problems. Moreover, in contrast to earlier thinking, families are in reasonably close contact with children who live in residential facilities; in one study, 65% of families of children and adults with mental retardation called their offspring at the residential facility once per week or more (Baker, Blacher, and Pfeiffer, 1996).

Although the range of educational and residential services has expanded tremendously over the past decade, more services are needed. The numbers of respite care homes and other parental supports remain distressingly small in many communities. In addition, these services need to be flexible to the needs of particular parents and families. Furthermore, such services are not always first-rate; an overconcern with the setting of services needs to be replaced with more attention to what occurs *within* the different service settings (Zigler, Hodapp, and Edison, 1990).

In addition to formal educational and residential services, parents also benefit from the many parent support groups that have become prominent over the past several decades. These run the gamut from large to small, from emphases on all disabilities to a focus on a single disability, and from national organizations (often with local chapters) to local groups. The largest and most well-known of the national organizations is the National Association for Retarded Citizens (NARC). Founded in 1950, NARC is a nationwide parent organization with high visibility. Besides providing supportive and informational services, NARC was instrumental in passing PL 94-142, IDEA, the Americans with Disabilities Act, and other federal disability legislation.

Besides organizations concerned with all children with mental retardation, numerous groups also exist for parents of children with different types of mental retardation. The National Down Syndrome Society, National Fragile X Foundation, Prader-Willi Syndrome Association, and other organizations are particularly good sources of support and information for parents of children with each type of mental retardation (for a listing, see Dykens et al., 2000). Most of these groups organize national conferences annually. Parents, researchers, and service providers all attend these conferences, providing interchanges of needs, experiences, and information rarely available in other contexts. If parents, researchers, and service providers are to be linked in a common partnership, more such forums are necessary.

## Mother–Child Interactions

In addition to the many behavior modification and training programs available to help caregivers to parent their children with mental retardation (Baker, 1989), several programs have focused on mother–child interactions. Two deserve notice, one focused on early parenting in general, the second on improving specific behaviors within the mother–child interaction.

The first program, the Parent–Infant Interaction Model, was developed by Bromwich (1976, 1990) in the late 1970s. Designed for mothers of children with a variety of disabilities, this program involves 10 general steps that are individualized to the specific needs of each child, caregiver, and family. The preliminary steps focus on enhancing the quality of parent–infant interaction by improving the caregiver's (usually the mother's) self-esteem, making her feel more comfortable with the child, and teaching her to become a sensitive observer of, and interactor with, her baby. Later steps involve strategies to understand each family's stresses and supports and to help each member of the family deal with rearing a child with mental retardation.

Although not specific to mothers of children with mental retardation, Bromwich's program provides a good general model for mother–child interactions. The hope is that such programs can help to foster productive mother–child interactions, maternal perceptions, and familial responses—all of which can be started, enhanced, and then continue as the child with mental retardation grows older. Bromwich (1990) acknowledges that her program works best with mothers who suffer only from the special strains and emotional reactions felt by any mother of a child with disabilities. She cautions that mothers who have psychiatric disorders or mental retardation might have trouble benefiting from the Parent–Infant Interaction Model and that more intensive therapy for the caregiver might be necessary (as described by Fraiberg, 1980). Even considering these limitations, Bromwich's model provides intervention strategies that seem helpful to most parents of children with mental retardation.

A second intervention approach is more specific, focusing on the behaviors of mothers of children with mental retardation within the interaction setting. Based on studies showing that mothers of children with mental retardation are often more didactic and controlling in their interactive styles, Mahoney (1988) has advocated the Transactional Intervention Program (TRIP). This model features instructions to help mothers become more balanced in their turn taking and to imitate the child's behavior. While reaching these two goals, mothers observe the infant and allow the child opportunities to initiate interactions. Preliminary findings show that infants with Down syndrome develop faster in cognition and in language when provided these "low-directive" as opposed to "high-directive" maternal interactive behaviors (see also Harris et al., 1996). Although focused on only one aspect of parenting, Mahoney's (1988) model may help to produce better, more productive interactions. As one of the few intervention programs specifically tied to the growing literature on mother–child interactions, the TRIP and other such models help to improve mother–child interactions with children with Down syndrome and other forms of mental retardation.

## Families

As service-delivery systems change and the prevalence of in-home care increases, families of children with mental retardation are increasingly the object of attention. This attention has even begun to infiltrate federal legislation. Specifically, PL 99-457 expands educational and support services to the 0- to 3-year-old group, allowing a bridging of services from birth until adulthood. A major component of PL 99-457 is its provision of an individualized family plan, thereby recognizing that the family, more than the child alone, needs services during these early years (Krauss and Hauser-Cram, 1992).

But even as some federal laws are including families, many issues remain unresolved. For example, families of children with severe–profound mental retardation or who have multiple disabilities face severe financial hardships. In addition to documenting the medical costs of caring for such children, Barenbaum and Cohen (1993) noted how simple changes in health care coverage could benefit these families enormously. They suggested that changes can be as easy as considering as a medical-habilitative service the costs of babysitting a child with a shunt or of remodeling a home to make it wheelchair accessible. Such health-habilitation issues have become even more complicated in recent years, as most children and adults with disabilities have started to receive their health care services through Health Management Organizations (often paid for by Medicaid waivers; Kastner, Walsh, and Criscione, 1997).

Other concerns relate to when and how services are provided. As noted by Suelzle and Keenan (1981), families of children with mental retardation receive most services early on, even as they often need more services as the child gets older. Other difficult issues revolve around how care is provided for children with multiple impairments or for those who are "dually diagnosed"—that is, who have both mental retardation and psychiatric impairments. How fathers are reached is another major issue, as is the question of how the needs of mothers and fathers can be addressed as families change (to the extent that they do) as the child with disabilities gets older.

## FUTURE DIRECTIONS IN STUDYING FAMILIES OF CHILDREN WITH MENTAL RETARDATION

With both a research and interventionist bent, research on parenting children with mental retardation has advanced rapidly over the past few decades. Yet a few major areas and problems remain to be addressed in future research.

### Research with Better Theoretical Grounding

The three subareas of parenting children with mental retardation feature a wide, some might say bewildering, array of theoretical orientations. Studies of maternal and paternal emotional reactions often show a psychoanalytic—or at least a clinical—perspective, focusing on the loss of the idealized child and maternal and paternal depression and psychopathology. Mother–child interaction studies use Bell's (1968) interactional theory, and comparisons of dyads with and without retarded children usually focus on MA or other level-of-functioning matching (e.g., MLU) as used in the developmental approach to mental retardation (Zigler and Hodapp, 1986). Family work has used sociological role theory (Farber and Rowitz, 1986), models such as the Double ABCX (Minnes, 1988), and, at times, little or no theories, as when delineating basic family characteristics of families of a child with mental retardation. Yet, to this day, few studies have joined these different perspectives and different bodies of knowledge.

Part of the problem involves the "ownership" of different research questions by researchers in different disciplines or research traditions. For the most part, maternal and paternal reactions have been the province of child psychiatry and child clinical psychology; mother–child interactions, the focus of developmental scientists and special educators; and families, the work of family researchers and social workers. Each research community works in relative isolation, with little attempt to join these different, but mutually influential, levels.

An additional, related problem concerns the difficulties inherent in joining different levels of analyses in behavioral work. Recently, for example, family and interactional researchers have noted that, although their two perspectives should be complementary, few studies join the two perspectives. As a result, interactional research—with its microanalytic coding of individual behaviors—rarely connects with the measurement of family types and other more molar analyses favored by family researchers (Lollis and Kuczynski, 1997). Although such connections are undoubtedly difficult to achieve, they seem necessary if we want a more useful, integrated picture of parental and familial functioning.

In addition to the gaps and lack of coordination in the areas of parental reactions, interactions, and familial adaptation, other areas also require attention. Five areas in particular deserve note.

*Individual differences.* With the exception of the few studies cited earlier, little research has been devoted to the issue of individual differences in the parenting field. There is also a need to simultaneously examine group differences—whether parenting is the same or different when parenting children with and without mental retardation—and individual differences—how and why parents of children with mental retardation differ one from another.

*Etiology.* As we are beginning to appreciate, the child's particular type of mental retardation—and the behaviors and/or physical characteristics generally caused by that etiology—would seem to affect parents and families. Although more studies are now appearing on parent and family functioning of children with specific etiologies (e.g., Van Lieshout, deMeyer, Curfs, and Fryns, 1998), many more such studies are needed. Given that different disorders predispose children to one or another set of behaviors, we may also ultimately gain information about the effects of different, specific behaviors on parental and familial functioning.

*Ethnicity.* Although some sporadic studies exist on certain ethnic groups, we generally know little about family functioning in most ethnic groups. As Sue (1999) notes, the issue may relate to psychology's emphasis—some might even say overemphasis—on issues of internal validity, often to the exclusion of external validity or generalization. More ethnically informed work may be occurring as the United States population itself changes, but such progress is occurring only gradually.

*Lifespan.* Apart from the work of Krauss, Seltzer, and their colleagues (e.g., Seltzer, Krauss, and Tsunematsu, 1993), few researchers have systematically examined the family functioning of older individuals with mental retardation. Indeed, reviews of family work (e.g., Stoneman, 1989) show that the large majority of studies on parental emotional reactions, mother–child interaction, and family reactions focus on children, often during the preschool years. Fewer studies have examined the families of older children with mental retardation, fewer still of adults.

*Methodologies.* In addition to the many gaps in our information about parenting, more attention needs to be paid to how one performs family research in mental retardation. The issue of matching—of whether MA or CA matches are best (previously described)—is one unresolved methodological issue, but there are many others. For example, it remains unresolved whether parenting studies should examine parents of children who are disabled, have mental retardation, or have a particular form of mental retardation. Who, exactly, should be the control or contrast group is also unresolved, particularly when families of children with different types of mental retardation are examined (Hodapp and Dykens, 2001).

## Ties to the Practice of Intervention and to Policy

Even though many family researchers are interested in practical issues, research on parenting in mental retardation connects only marginally with the common practice of intervention or policy. Only a few research findings have been integrated within the majority of intervention programs, and even some obvious concepts rarely become incorporated in intervention work. For example, Olshansky's (1962, 1966; Wikler, 1986) recurrent maternal reactions model continues to be ignored in most service systems; to this day, many services continue to be front-loaded, with fewer services for parents and families of older individuals with mental retardation. In the same way, few concerted efforts have been made to link family research to public policy. Barenbaum and Cohen (1993) highlight just how minor such changes need to be to help parents and families, but rarely are such changes made. One can only hope that the ties between research and practice—on both intervention and policy levels—will soon become stronger.

## CONCLUSIONS

In summarizing the work on parenting children with Down syndrome and other forms of mental retardation, one can envision the glass as either half empty or half full. If judged by the amount of unknown information, the glass is half empty. Even after a decade or more of intense work, we still do not know how parents, interactions, and families "go together," how each level changes over time, how each is affected by many child characteristics, and other interesting issues. The parenting field also continues to be dominated by research on European American, middle-income families, leaving understudied essential questions relating to SES and ethnicity.

Yet, compared with what was known only 40 years ago, the glass is more than half full. From the early days of Farber, of Solnit and Stark, and of Olshansky, we now know much more about these families, their interactions with their children, and the child's effects on siblings and the family as a whole. More important, what we know has been fit into more interesting, less detrimental frameworks, as parents, interactions, and families are now seen as coping under stressful circumstances. Such stress may help or hinder adaptation, but these stress-coping perspectives seem both more accurate and more humane.

In effect, research on parenting children with mental retardation seems a discipline that is beginning to reach its stride. Indeed, probably more has been learned about parenting children with mental retardation in the past 15 years than was known in all the years up until this time. The next 15 years promise continued, near-exponential growth. With an increased joining of different perspectives and more fully considered research paradigms, it is hoped that such work will be more integrated and more useful to service providers and policymakers. This knowledge should also, ultimately, help parents face the many difficult challenges in parenting the child with mental retardation.

## ACKNOWLEDGMENTS

I thank Marc Bornstein and Elisabeth Dykens for comments on earlier versions of this chapter.

## REFERENCES

Allanson, J. E., O'Hara, P., Farkas, G., and Nair, R. C. (1993). Anthropometric craniofacial pattern profiles in Down syndrome. *American Journal of Medical Genetics, 47*, 748–52.

Bailey, D., Blasco, P., and Simeonsson, R. (1992). Needs expressed by mothers and fathers of young children with disabilities. *American Journal on Mental Retardation, 97*, 1–10.

Baker, B. (1989). Parent training and developmental disabilities. *Monograph of the AAMR 13.* Washington, DC: American Association on Mental Retardation.

Baker, B. L., Blacher, J., and Pfeiffer, S. I. (1996). Family involvement in residential treatment. *American Journal on Mental Retardation, 101,* 1–14.

Barenbaum, A., and Cohen, H. J. (1993). On the importance of helping families: Policy implications from a national study. *Mental Retardation, 31,* 67–74.

Baumeister, A. (1967). Problems in comparative studies of mental retardates and normals. *American Journal of Mental Deficiency, 71,* 869–875.

Baumwell, L., Tamis-LeMonda, C. S., and Bornstein, M. H. (1997). Maternal verbal sensitivity and child language comprehension. *Infant Behavior and Development, 20,* 247–258.

Beavers, J., Hampson, R. B., Hulgus, Y. F., and Beavers, W. R. (1986). Coping in families with a retarded child. *Family Process, 25,* 365–378.

Beckman, P. (1983). Influence of selected child characteristics on stress in families of handicapped children. *American Journal of Mental Deficiency, 88,* 150–156.

Beeghly, M., and Cicchetti, D. (1987). An organizational approach to symbolic development in children with Down Syndrome. In D. Cicchetti and M. Beeghly (Eds.), *Symbolic development in atypical children. New Directions for Child Development* (No. 36, pp. 5–29). San Francisco: Jossey-Bass.

Bell, R. Q. (1968). A reinterpretation of the direction of effects in studies of socialization. *Psychological Review, 75,* 81–95.

Bell, R. Q., and Harper, L. V. (1977). *Child effects on adults.* Hillsdale, NJ: Lawrence Erlbaum Associates.

Bellugi, U., Mills, D., Jernigan, T., Hickok, G., and Galaburda, A. (1999). Linking cognition, brain structure, and brain function in Williams syndrome. In H. Tager-Flusberg (Ed.), *Neurodevelopmental disorders* (pp. 111–136). Cambridge: MIT Press.

Berry, D. S., and McArthur, L. Z. (1985) Some components and consequences of a babyface. *Journal of Personality and Social Psychology, 48,* 312–323.

Blacher, J. (1984). Sequential stages of parental adjustment to the birth of the child with handicaps: Fact or artifact? *Mental Retardation, 22,* 55–68.

Blacher, J., Lopez, S., Shapiro, J., and Fusco, J. (1997). Contributions to depression in Latina mothers with and without children with retardation: Implications for caregiving. *Family Relations, 46,* 325–334.

Bristol, M., Gallagher, J., and Shopler, E. (1988). Mothers and fathers of young developmentally disabled and nondisabled boys: Adaptation and spousal support. *Developmental Psychology, 24,* 441–451.

Bromwich, R. (1976). Focus on maternal behavior in infant interaction. *American Journal of Orthopsychiatry, 46,* 439–446.

Bromwich, R. (1990). The interaction approach to early intervention. *Infant Mental Health Journal, 11,* 66–79.

Bruner, J. (1983). *Child's talk.* New York: Norton.

Bruner, J. (1990). *Acts of meaning.* Cambridge, MA: Harvard University Press.

Buckhalt, J. A., Rutherford, R., and Goldberg, K. (1978). Verbal and nonverbal interactions of mothers with their Down Syndrome and nonretarded infants. *American Journal of Mental Deficiency, 82,* 337–343.

Buium, N., Rynders, J., and Turnure, J. (1974). Early maternal linguistic environment of normal and Down syndrome language learning children. *American Journal of Mental Deficiency, 79,* 52–58.

Byrne, E., and Cunningham, C. (1985). The effects of mentally handicapped children on families: A conceptual review. *Journal of Child Psychology and Psychiatry, 26,* 847–864.

Cahill, B. M., and Glidden, L. M. (1996). Influence of child diagnosis on family and parent functioning: Down syndrome versus other disabilities. *American Journal on Mental Retardation, 101,* 149–160.

Cardoso-Martins, C., and Mervis, C. (1984). Maternal speech to prelinguistic children with Down Syndrome. *American Journal of Mental Deficiency, 89,* 451–458.

Carr, J. (1995). *Down's syndrome: Children growing up.* Cambridge: Cambridge University Press.

Carter, B., and McGoldrick, M. (Eds.). (1988). *The changing family life cycle: A framework for family therapy* (2nd ed.). New York: Gardner.

Cicchetti, D., and Pogge-Hesse, P. (1982). Possible contributions of the study of organically retarded persons to developmental theory. In E. Zigler and D. Balla (Eds.), *Mental retardation: The developmental-difference controversy* (pp. 277–318). Hillsdale, NJ: Lawrence Erlbaum Associates.

Collins, W. A., Maccoby, E. E., Steinberg, L., Hetherington, E. M., and Bornstein, M. H. (2000). Contemporary research on parenting: The case for nature and nurture. *American Psychologist, 55,* 218–232.

Combrinck-Graham, L. (1985). A developmental model for family systems. *Family Process, 24,* 139–150.

Conti-Ramsden, G. (1989). Parent–child interaction in mental handicap: An evaluation. In M. Beveridge, G. Conti-Ramsden, and I. Levdar (Eds.), *Language and communication in mentally handicapped people* (pp. 218–225). London: Chapman and Hall.

Crawley, S., and Spiker, D. (1983). Mother–child interactions involving two-year olds with Down syndrome: A look at individual differences. *Child Development, 54,* 1312–1323.

Crnic, K., Friedrich, W., and Greenberg, M. (1983). Adaptation of families with mentally handicapped children: A model of stress, coping, and family ecology. *American Journal of Mental Deficiency, 88,* 125–138.

Cummings, S. (1976). The impact of the child's deficiency on the father: A study of fathers of mentally retarded and chronically ill children. *American Journal of Orthopsychiatry, 46,* 246–255.

Cummings, S., Bayley, H., and Rie, H. (1966). Effects of the child's deficiency on the mother: A study of mentally retarded, chronically ill, and neurotic children. *American Journal of Orthopsychiatry, 36,* 595–608.

Damrosch, S., and Perry, L. (1989). Self-reported adjustment, chronic sorrow, and coping of parents of children with Down Syndrome. *Nursing Research, 38,* 25–30.

Drotar, D., Baskiewicz, A., Irvin, N., Kennell, J., and Klaus, M. (1975). The adaptation of parents to the birth of an infant with congenital malformation: A hypothetical model. *Pediatrics, 56,* 710–717.

Duvall, E. (1957). *Family development.* Philadelphia: Lippincott.

Dykens, E. (1995). Measuring behavioral phenotypes: Provocations from the "new genetics." *American Journal on Mental Retardation, 99,* 522–532.

Dykens, E. M. (1999). Prader-Willi syndrome: Toward a behavioral phenotype. In H. Tager-Flusberg (Ed.), *Neurodevelopmental disorders* (pp. 137–154). Cambridge, MA: MIT Press.

Dykens, E. M., and Hodapp, R. M. (2001). Research in mental retardation: Toward an etiologic approach. *Journal of Child Psychology and Psychiatry, 42,* 49–71.

Dykens, E. M., Hodapp, R. M., and Finucane, B. (2000). *Genetics and mental retardation syndromes: A new look at behavior and treatment.* Baltimore: Brookes.

Dykens, E. M., Hodapp, R. M., and Leckman, J. F. (1994). *Behavior and development in fragile X syndrome.* Newbury Park, CA: Sage.

Dykens, E. M., and Kasari, C. (1997). Maladaptive behavior in children with Prader-Willi syndrome, Down syndrome, and nonspecific mental retardation. *American Journal on Mental Retardation, 102,* 228–237.

Dykens, E. M., and Leckman, J. F. (1990). Developmental issues in fragile X syndrome. In R. M. Hodapp, J. A. Burack, and E. Zigler (Eds.), *Issues in the developmental approach to mental retardation* (pp. 226–245). New York: Cambridge University Press.

Dykens, E. M., Leckman, J. F., and Cassidy, S. B. (1996). Obsessions and compulsions in Prader-Willi syndrome. *Journal of Child Psychology and Psychiatry, 37,* 995–1002.

Emde, R., and Brown, C. (1978). Adaptation to the birth of a Down's syndrome infant: Grieving and maternal attachment. *Journal of the American Academy of Child Psychiatry, 17,* 299–323.

Erickson, M. (1969). MMPI profiles of parents of young retarded children. *American Journal of Mental Deficiency, 73,* 727–732.

Erikson, M., and Upshure, C. C. (1989). Caretaking burden and social support: Comparison of mothers of infants with and without disabilities. *American Journal on Mental Retardation, 94,* 250–258.

Farber, B. (1959). The effects of the severely retarded child on the family system. *Monographs of the Society for Research in Child Development, 24* (No. 2).

Farber, B. (1970). Notes on sociological knowledge about families with mentally retarded children. In M. Schreiber (Ed.), *Social work and mental retardation* (pp. 118–124). New York: Day.

Farber, B., and Rowitz, L. (1986). Families with a mentally retarded child. *International Journal of Research in Mental Retardation, 14,* 201–224.

Fidler, D. J., and Hodapp, R. M. (1999). Craniofacial maturity and perceived personality in children with Down syndrome. *American Journal on Mental Retardation, 104,* 410–421.

Fidler, D. J., Hodapp, R. M., and Dykens, E. M. (2000). Stress in families of young children with Down syndrome, Williams syndrome, and Smith-Magenis syndrome. *Early Education and Development, 11,* 395–406.

Folkman, S., Schaefer, C., and Lazarus, R. S. (1979). Cognitive processes as mediators of stress and coping. In V. Hamilton and D. S. Warburton (Eds.), *Human stress and cognition* (pp. 265–298). New York: Wiley.

Fowler, A. (1990). Language abilities in children with Down syndrome: Evidence for a specific syntactic delay. In D. Cicchetti and M. Beeghly (Eds.), *Children with Down syndrome: A developmental perspective* (pp. 302–328). Cambridge, England: Cambridge University Press.

Fraiberg, S. (Ed.). (1980). *Clinical studies of infant mental health: The first year of life.* New York: Basic Books.

Frey, K., Greenberg, M., and Fewell, R. (1989). Stress and coping among parents of handicapped children: A multidimensional perspective. *American Journal on Mental Retardation, 94,* 240–249.

Friedrich, W. L., and Freidrich, W. N. (1981). Psychosocial assets of parents of handicapped and nonhandicapped children. *American Journal of Mental Deficiency, 85,* 551–553.

Friedrich, W. N. (1979). Predictors of coping behavior of mothers of handicapped children. *Journal of Consulting and Clinical Psychology, 47,* 1140–1141.

Gallimore, R., Weisner, T., Kaufman, S., and Bernheimer, L. (1989). The social construction of ecocultural niches: Family accomodation of developmentally delayed children. *American Journal on Mental Retardation, 94,* 216–230.

Gath, A. (1977). The impact of an abnormal child upon the parents. *British Journal of Psychiatry, 130,* 405–410.

Goldberg, S. (1977). Social competence in infancy: A model of parent–infant interaction. *Merrill-Palmer Quarterly, 23,* 163–177.

Goldberg, S., Marcovitch, S., MacGregor, D., and Lojkasek, M. (1986). Family responses to developmentally delayed preschoolers: Etiology and the father's role. *American Journal on Mental Retardation, 90,* 610–617.

Hagamen, M. B. (1980). Family adaptation to the diagnosis of mental retardation in a child and strategies of intervention. In L. S. Syzmanski and P. E. Tanguay (Eds.), *Emotional disorders of mentally retarded persons* (pp. 149–171). Baltimore: University Park Press.

Harris, S., Kasari, C., and Sigman, M. (1996). Joint attention and language gains in children with Down syndrome. *American Journal on Mental Retardation, 100,* 608–619.

Heller, T., Markwardt, R., Rowitz, L., and Farber, B. (1994). Adaptation of Hispanic families to a member with mental retardation. *American Journal of Mental Retardation, 99,* 289–300.

Heller, T., Miller, A. B., and Factor, A. (1997). Adults with mental retardation as supports to their parents: Effects on parental caregiving appraisal. *Mental Retardation, 35,* 338–346.

Hill, R. (1949). *Families under stress.* New York: Harper & Row.

Hodapp, R. M. (1996). Down syndrome: Developmental, psychiatric, and management issues. *Child and Adolescent Psychiatric Clinics of North America, 5,* 881–894.

Hodapp, R. M. (1997). Direct and indirect behavioral effects of different genetic disorders of mental retardation. *American Journal on Mental Retardation, 102,* 67–79.

Hodapp, R. M. (1998). *Development and disabilities: Intellectual, sensory, and motor impairments.* Cambridge: Cambridge University Press.

Hodapp, R. M. (1999). Indirect effects of genetic mental retardation disorders: Theoretical and methodological issues. *International Review of Research in Mental Retardation, 22,* 27–50.

Hodapp, R. M., and Dykens, E. M. (1994). The two cultures of behavioral research in mental retardation. *American Journal on Mental Retardation, 98,* 675–687.

Hodapp, R. M., and Dykens, E. M. (2001). Strengthening behavioral research on genetic mental retardation syndromes. *American Journal on Mental Retardation, 106,* 4–15.

Hodapp, R. M., Dykens, E. M., Evans, D. W., and Merighi, J. R. (1992). Maternal emotional reactions to young children with different types of handicaps. *Journal of Developmental and Behavioral Pediatrics, 13,* 118–123.

Hodapp, R. M., Dykens, E. M., and Masino, L. L. (1997). Families of children with Prader-Willi syndrome: Stress-support and relations to child characteristics. *Journal of Autism and Developmental Disorders, 27,* 11–24.

Hodapp, R. M., Dykens, E. M., Ort, S. I., Zelinsky, D. G., and Leckman, J. F. (1991). Changing patterns of intellectual strengths and weaknesses in males with fragile X syndrome. *Journal of Autism and Developmental Disorders, 21,* 503–516.

Hodapp, R. M., Fidler, D. J., and Smith, A. C. M. (1998). Stress and coping in families of children with Smith-Magenis syndrome. *Journal of Intellectual Disability Research, 42,* 331–340.

Hodapp, R. M., Ly, T. M., Fidler, D. J., and Ricci, L. A. (2001). *Is there a Down syndrome personality? Group and age effects.* Manuscript submitted for publication.

Hodapp, R. M., Wijma, C. A., and Masino, L. L. (1997). Families of children with 5p- (*cri du chat*) syndrome: Familial stress and sibling reactions. *Developmental Medicine and Child Neurology, 39,* 757–761.

Holroyd, J., and MacArthur, D. (1976). Mental retardation and stress on parents: A contrast between Down's syndrome and childhood autism. *American Journal of Mental Deficiency, 80,* 431–436.

Hornby, G. (1995). Fathers' views of the effects on their families of children with Down syndrome. *Journal of Child and Family Studies, 4,* 103–117.

Hyche, J., Bakeman, R., and Adamson, L. (1992). Understanding communicative cues of infants with Down syndrome: Effects of mothers' experience and infants' age. *Journal of Applied Developmental Psychology, 13,* 1–16.

Jones, O. (1980). Prelinguistic communication skills in Down's Syndrome and normal infants. In T. Field, S. Goldberg, D. Stern, and A. Sostek (Eds.), *High-risk infants and children: Adult and peer interaction* (pp. 205–225). New York: Academic.

Kasari, C., and Freeman, S. F. N. (2001). Task-related social behavior in children with Down syndrome. *American Journal on Mental Retardation, 106,* 253–264.

Kasari, C., Freeman, S. F. N., Mundy, P., and Sigman, M. (1995). Attention regulation by children with Down syndrome: Coordinated joint attention and social referencing. *American Journal on Mental Retardation, 100,* 128–136.

Kasari, C., and Sigman, M. (1997). Linking parental perceptions to interactions in young children with autism. *Journal of Autism and Developmental Disorders, 27,* 39–57.

Kastner, T., Walsh, K. K., and Criscione, T. (1997). Overview and implications of Medicaid managed care for people with developmental disabilities. *Mental Retardation, 35,* 257–269.

Kazak, A. (1987). Families with disabled children: Stress and social networks in three samples. *Journal of Abnormal Child Psychology, 15,* 137–146.

Kazak, A., and Marvin, R. (1984). Differences, difficulties, and adaptation: Stress and social networks in families with a handicapped child. *Family Relations, 33,* 67–77.

Keogh, B. K., Garnier, H. E., Bernheimer, L. P., and Gallimore, R. (2000). Models of child-family interactions for children with developmental delays: Child-driven or transactional? *American Journal on Mental Retardation, 105*, 32–46.

Krauss, M. (1993). Child-related and parenting stress: Similarities and differences between mothers and fathers of children with disabilities. *American Journal on Mental Retardation, 97*, 393–404.

Krauss, M. W., and Hauser-Kram, P. (1992). Policy and program development for infants and toddlers with disabilities. In L. Rowitz (Ed.), *Mental retardation in the year 2000* (pp. 184–196). New York: Springer-Verlag.

Krauss, M. W., and Seltzer, M. (1998). Life-course perspectives in mental retardation research: The case of family caregiving. In J. A. Burack, R. M. Hodapp, and E. Zigler (Eds.), *Handbook of mental retardation and development* (pp. 504–520). Cambridge, England: Cambridge University Press.

Levy, D. (1970). The concept of maternal overprotection. In E. J. Anthony and T. Benedek (Eds.), *Parenthood* (pp. 387–409). Boston: Little, Brown.

Lobato, D. (1983). Siblings of handicapped children: A review. *Journal of Autism and Developmental Disorders, 13*, 347–364.

Lollis, S., and Kuczynski, L. (1997). Beyond one hand clapping: Seeing bidirectionality in parent–child relations. *Journal of Social and Personal Relationships, 14*, 441–461.

Mahoney, G. (1975). Ethological approach to delayed language acquisition. *American Journal of Mental Deficiency, 80*, 139–148.

Mahoney, G. (1988). Enhancing the developmental competence of handicapped infants. In K. Marfo (Ed.), *Parent–child interaction and developmental disabilities* (pp. 203–219). New York: Praeger.

Mahoney, G., Fors, S., and Wood, S. (1990). Maternal directive behavior revisited. *American Journal on Mental Retardation, 94*, 398–406.

Marfo, K. (1990). Maternal directiveness in interactions with mentally handicapped children: An analytical commentary. *Journal of Child Psychology and Psychiatry, 31*, 531–549.

Marshall, N., Hegrenes, J., and Goldstein, S. (1973). Verbal interactions: Mothers and their retarded children versus mothers and their nonretarded children. *American Journal of Mental Deficiency, 77*, 415–419.

McCubbin, H., and Patterson, J. (1983). Family transitions: Adaptations to stress. In H. McCubbin and C. Figley (Eds.), *Stress and the family. Vol. 1. Coping with normative transitions* (pp. 5–25). New York: Brunner/Mazel.

Mervis, C. B., Morris, C. A., Bertrand, J., and Robinson, B. F. (1999). Williams syndrome: Findings from an integrated program of research. In H. Tager-Flusberg (Ed.), *Neurodevelopmental disorders* (pp. 65–110). Cambridge, MA: MIT Press.

Meyers, B. A., and Pueschel, S. M. (1991). Psychiatric disorders in persons with Down syndrome. *Journal of Nervous and Mental Disease, 179*, 609–613.

Miller, J. F. (1992). Lexical development in young children with Down syndrome. In R. Chapman (Ed.), *Processes in language acquisition and disorders* (pp. 202–216). St. Louis, MO: Mosby.

Miller, J. F. (1999). Profiles of language development in children with Down syndrome. In J. F. Miller, M. Leddy, and L. A. Leavitt (Eds.), *Improving the communication of people with Down syndrome* (pp. 11–39). Baltimore: Brookes.

Mink, I., Nihira, C., and Meyers, C. (1983). Taxonomy of family life styles: I. Homes with TMR children. *American Journal of Mental Deficiency, 87*, 484–497.

Mink, I., Nihira, C., and Meyers, C. (1984). Taxonomy of family life styles: II. Homes with slow-learning children. *American Journal of Mental Deficiency, 89*, 111–123.

Minnes, P. (1988). Family stress associated with a developmentally handicapped child. *International Review of Research on Mental Retardation, 15*, 195–226.

O'Brien, G., and Yule, W. (Eds.). (1995). *Behavioural phenotypes*. London: MacKeith.

O'Brien, G., and Udwin, O. (Eds.) (in press). *Behavioural phenotypes in clinical practice*. London: MacKeith.

Olshansky, S. (1962). Chronic sorrow: A response to having a mentally defective child. *Social Casework, 43*, 190–193.

Olshansky, S. (1966). Parent responses to a mentally defective child. *Mental Retardation, 4*, 21–23.

Price-Bonham, S., and Addison, S. (1978). Families and mentally retarded children: Emphasis on the father. *The Family Coordinator, 27*, 221–230.

Roach, M. A., Orsmond, G. I., and Barratt, M. S. (1999). Mothers and fathers of children with Down syndrome: Parental stress and involvement in childcare. *American Journal on Mental Retardation, 104*, 422–436.

Rogers-Dulan, J. (1998). Religious connectedness among urban African American families who have a child with disabilities. *Mental Retardation, 36*, 91–103.

Rondal, J. (1977). Maternal speech in normal and Down's syndrome children. In P. Mittler (Ed.), *Research to practice in mental retardation: Vol. 3. Education and training* (pp. 239–243). Baltimore: University Park Press.

Sanders, J. L., and Morgan, S. B. (1997). Family stress and adjustment as perceived by parents of children with autism or Down syndrome: Implications for intervention. *Child and Family Behavior Therapy, 19*, 15–32.

Sears, R. R. (1975). *Your ancients revisited: A history of child development*. Chicago: University of Chicago Press.

Seltzer, M., and Krauss, M. W. (1989). Aging parents with mentally retarded children: Family risk factors and sources of support. *American Journal on Mental Retardation, 94*, 303–312.

Seltzer, M., Krauss, M. W., and Tsunematsu, N. (1993). Adults with Down syndrome and their aging mothers: Diagnostic group differences. *American Journal on Mental Retardation, 97*, 496–508.

Seltzer, M., and Ryff, C. (1994). Parenting across the lifespan: The normative and nonnormative cases. *Life-Span Development and Behavior, 12,* 1–40.

Solnit, A., and Stark, M. (1961). Mourning and the birth of a defective child. *The Psychoanalytic Study of the Child, 16,* 523–537.

Sorce, J. F., and Emde, R. (1982). The meaning of infant emotional expression: Regularities in caregiving responses in normal and Down's syndrome infants. *Journal of Child Psychology and Psychiatry, 23,* 145–158.

Stoneman, Z. (1989). Comparison groups in research on families with mentally retarded members: A methodological and conceptual review. *American Journal on Mental Retardation, 94,* 195–215.

Sue, S. (1999). Science, ethnicity, and bias: Where have we gone wrong? *American Psychologist, 54,* 1070–1077.

Suelzle, M., and Keenan, V. (1981). Changes in family support networks over the life cycle of mentally retarded persons. *American Journal of Mental Deficiency, 86,* 267–274.

Tannock, R. (1988). Mothers' directiveness in their interactions with children with and without Down syndrome. *American Journal on Mental Retardation, 93,* 154–165.

Tew, B., Payne, H., and Lawrence, K. (1974). Must a family with a handicapped child be a handicapped family? *Developmental Medicine and Child Neurology, 16,* Supplement 32, 95–98.

Thomas, V., and Olsen, D. H. (1993). Problem families and the circumplex model: Observational assessment using the clinical rating scale (CRS). *Journal of Marital and Family Therapy, 19,* 159–175.

Tomasello, M., and Farrar, M. J. (1986). Joint attention and early language. *Child Development, 57,* 1454–1463.

Townsend, A., Noelker, L., Deimling, G., and Bass, D. (1989). Longitudinal impact of interhousehold caregiving on adult children's mental health. *Psychology and Aging, 4,* 393–401.

Turnbull, A. P., and Turnbull, H. R. (1986). *Families, professionals, and exceptionality: A special partnership.* Columbus, OH: Merrill.

Turnbull, A. P., Patterson, J. M., Behr, S. K., Murphy, D. L., Marquis, J. G., and Blue-Banning, M. J. (Eds.). (1993). *Cognitive coping, families, and disability.* Baltimore: Brookes.

Van Lieshout, C. F. M., de Meyer, R. E., Curfs, L. M. G., and Fryns, J. P. (1998). Family contexts, parental behaviour, and personality profiles of children and adolescents with Prader-Willi, fragile X, or Williams syndrome. *Journal of Child Psychology and Psychiatry, 39,* 699–710.

Van Riper, M., Ryff, C., and Pridham, K. (1992). Parental and family well-being in families of children with Down syndrome: A comparative study. *Research in Nursing and Health, 15,* 227–235.

Vietze, P., Abernathy, S., Ashe, M., Faulstich, G. (1978). Contingency interaction between mothers and their developmentally delayed infants. In G. P. Sackett (Ed.), *Observing behavior.* (Vol. 1). Baltimore: University Park Press.

Walden, T. A. (1996). Social responsivity: Judging signals of young children with and without developmental delays. *Child Development, 67,* 2074–2085.

Werner, E. (1993). Risk, resilience, and recovery: Perspectives from the Kauai Longitudinal Study. *Development and Psychopathology, 5,* 503–515.

Wikler, L. (1981). Chronic stresses in families of mentally retarded children. *Family Relations, 30,* 281–288.

Wikler, L. (1986). Periodic stresses in families of mentally retarded children: An exploratory study. *American Journal of Mental Deficiency, 90,* 703–706.

Wikler, L., Wasow, M., and Hatfield, E. (1981). Chronic sorrow revisited: Attitudes of parents and professionals about adjustment to mental retardation. *American Journal of Orthopsychiatry, 51,* 63–70.

Yell, M. L., and Drasgow, E. (2000). Reauthorization of the Individuals with Disabilities Education Act: Analysis and implications for practice—Introduction. *Journal of Special Education, 33,* 194.

Yoder, P. (1986). Clarifying the relation between degree of infant handicap and maternal responsivity to infant communicative cues: Measurement issues. *Infant Mental Health Journal, 7,* 281–293.

Zebrowitz, L. A. (1997). *Reading Faces: Window to the Soul?* Boulder, CO: Westview.

Zigler, E., and Balla, D. (Eds.). (1982). *Mental retardation: The developmental-difference controversy.* Hillsdale, NJ: Lawrence Erlbaum Associates.

Zigler, E., and Hodapp, R. M. (1986). *Understanding mental retardation.* New York: Cambridge University Press.

Zigler, E., Hodapp, R. M., and Edison, M. (1990). From theory to practice in the care and education of retarded individuals. *American Journal on Mental Retardation, 95,* 1–12.

Zuk, G. H., Miller, R. L., Bertram, J. B., and Kling, F. (1961). Maternal acceptance of retarded children: A questionnaire study of attitudes and religious background. *Child Development, 32,* 525–540.

# 14

# Parents of Aggressive
# and Withdrawn Children

Kenneth H. Rubin
Kim B. Burgess
*University of Maryland at College Park*

*All children are essentially criminal.*

—*Diderot*, 1713–1784

*A child is a curly, dimpled lunatic.*

—*Ralph Waldo Emerson*, 1803–1882

*Having children is like having a bowling ball installed in your brain.*

—*Martin Mull*, 1978

## INTRODUCTION

A glance at the quotations offered above would lead one to assume that parenting is not a simple matter. For hundreds of years, writers of philosophy, fiction, and comedy have portrayed the child as a significantly stressful addition to the family unit. Nevertheless, it is also the case that the arrival of an infant usually brings a great deal of joy and enthusiastic anticipation. Or to offer yet another observation: "My mother had a great deal of trouble with me, but I think she enjoyed it" (Mark Twain, in Byrne, 1988, p. 301).

Most people would agree that children represent a challenge to their parents. Yet parents often meet the challenges with acceptance, warmth, responsiveness, and sensitivity. At times, however, parents meet the challenge of childrearing in unaccepting, unresponsive, insensitive, neglectful, and/or hostile ways. It may be that ecologically based stressors produce such negative childrearing behaviors (e.g., lack of financial resources, parental separation and divorce, lack of social support); or perhaps infant and child characteristics evoke negative parenting beliefs, affect, and behaviors. Also, perhaps parents themselves have experienced particularly negative childrearing histories and model the behaviors of their own parents and family culture or norms in rearing their own children (Covell, Grusec, and King, 1995; Main, Kaplan, and Cassidy, 1985). It is our belief that when parents think about childrearing and child developmental trends in ways that deviate from cultural norms and/or when they interact with and respond to their children in psychologically inappropriate ways, they will develop negative relationships with their children. We also believe that when parent–child relationships and parent–child interactions within the family are negative, it does not auger well for normal child development.

Thus in our chapter we focus on the parent–child relationships and the interactions of two types of children who deviate from their agemates vis-à-vis their social, emotional, and behavioral profiles. Typically these children have been referred to as (1) aggressive and interpersonally hostile, or (2) socially withdrawn, socially anxious, shy, or behaviorally inhibited. Our focus is on childhood aggression and withdrawal because these behaviors reflect the two most commonly described behavioral disorders in childhood—*externalizing* and *internalizing* problems (Mash and Barkley, 1996).

## Aggression in Childhood

Aggression is a behavioral reflection of psychological *undercontrol*; it is also one of the major reasons for treatment referral in childhood. This is the case not only because the child's behavior is "out of control," but also because it is interpersonally destructive and longitudinally stable (e.g., Tremblay, Pihl, Vitaro, and Dobkin, 1994). Furthermore, aggression in childhood forecasts later maladaptive outcomes such as delinquency and criminality (see Coie and Dodge, 1998, for a recent overview). Finally, aggression and other behavioral markers of undercontrol are associated with a plethora of other difficulties. For example, children who have conflicts with the environment (heretofore referred to as children with externalizing disorders) have deficits in understanding the perspectives, feelings, and intentions of others (Crick and Dodge, 1994; Rubin, Bream, and Rose-Krasnor, 1991). Sometimes they bully their classmates and quickly establish negative reputations amongst their peers (e.g., Coie and Kupersmidt, 1983). Given the potential danger of hostile, unthinking aggressive behavior for victims, it is not surprising that the phenomenon of aggression in childhood has attracted voluminous and compelling conceptual and empirical treatments (Coie and Dodge, 1998).

There is growing evidence that the quality of children's relationships with parents and the experience of particular forms of parenting practices contribute significantly to the development of undercontrolled, aggressive behavioral profiles. One of our purposes in this chapter, therefore, is to review the relevant literature concerning the associations among parenting, parent–child relationships, and childhood aggression.

## Social Withdrawal in Childhood

The study of childhood aggression has a broader, richer conceptual and empirical history than that of psychological *overcontrol* and its behavioral manifestations, which include social withdrawal. The predominant interest in externalizing disorders, and specifically aggression, stems from a variety of significant factors. First, from the earliest years of childhood, aggression is more salient and likely to evoke some form of negative affect (e.g., anger) in the perceiver than is social withdrawal (Mills and Rubin, 1990; Younger, Gentile, and Burgess, 1993). Second, children in Western cultures are attending group care and educational settings at earlier ages for longer periods of the lifespan than in earlier generations. Consequently, control in these group settings is necessary for caregivers and educators; children who are undercontrolled are viewed as serious challenges to the delivery of appropriate group care and/or education. Children who demonstrate aggressive, impulsive, or overactive symptoms are targeted early and often for ameliorative attention (e.g., Coie and Dodge, 1998). Quiet, affectively overcontrolled young children, on the other hand, often represent veritable models of proper school decorum. As a result, they are less likely to be disruptive, and their difficulties may go undetected or ignored by the typically harried caregiver or educator.

Nevertheless, it *is* the case that professionals have persisted in regarding psychological overcontrol and its behavioral manifestations in childhood as comprising a major category of disorder (e.g., Mash and Barkley, 1996) and as warranting intervention (e.g., Dadds, Spence, Holland, Barrett, and Laurens, 1997). Moreover, the primary behavioral manifestation of overcontrol—social withdrawal—becomes increasingly salient to caregivers and peers with increasing age (e.g., Bugental and Cortez, 1988; Bugental and Shennun, 1984; Younger et al., 1993). As such, the social reticence of withdrawn children makes interaction effortful for others and contributes to the development of distant and sometimes difficult relationships (Hymel, Rubin, Rowden, and LeMare, 1990). Further, from a developmental perspective, it has been proposed that peer interaction represents a social context within which children learn to consider the perspectives of others and to coordinate others' perspectives with their own (e.g., Rubin, Bukowski, and Parker, 1998). Thus children who consistently demonstrate behaviors that are paradigmatically "driven by" problems within the self (heretofore referred to as internalizing problems) may be at major risk for failing to develop those social and social–cognitive skills that purportedly result from peer interactive experiences. Not only are socially withdrawn children lacking in social–cognitive and social competence (Adalbjarnardottir, 1995; LeMare and Rubin, 1987), but with increasing age they come to recognize their shortcomings and express strong feelings of loneliness and negative self-regard (Boivin and Hymel, 1997). Moreover, social withdrawal in childhood is both developmentally stable (Olweus, 1984; Rubin, Hymel, and Mills, 1989) and predictive of internalizing difficulties in adolescence (e.g., Renshaw and Brown, 1993; Rubin, Chen, McDougall, Bowker, and McKinnon, 1995).

As is the case with aggression, researchers now ask whether the quality of parent–child relationships and the experience of particular parenting styles contribute to the development of social withdrawal in childhood. Unlike the extensive parenting literature concerning childhood aggression, studies of the parent–child relationships and the socialization experiences of children who are described as psychologically overcontrolled are relatively scarce. What is known, however, is addressed in this review.

In summary, it is our intention to examine the extant literature concerning the parents of children who suffer from two of the most serious impediments to a normal, happy, and adaptive life—aggression and social withdrawal. We begin by defining and contrasting the constructs of social competence and incompetence; as one might expect, aggression and withdrawal are viewed as manifestations of social incompetence. Then we briefly describe a number of theories that have drawn parents into the developmental equation in which pathways to children's behavioral undercontrol and overcontrol are predicted. Thereafter we describe research in which (1) the quality of the parent–child relationship, (2) parental beliefs or ideas about the development of social competence, aggression, and withdrawal, and (3) parenting practices are associated with the expression of childhood aggression and social withdrawal. In the final section, we examine factors that may influence the types of parent–child relationships, parental beliefs, and parenting behaviors associated with the development of aggression and social withdrawal.

## DEFINITIONS AND THEORY OF SOCIAL COMPETENCE AND INCOMPETENCE

### Social Competence

Given that the expressions of both aggression and social withdrawal have been considered clear manifestations of a lack of social competence, this chapter begins with some working definitions. It is highly probable that there are as many definitions of social competence as there are students of it; as such, the definitions offered must be taken as reflecting the personal biases of the authors. We begin by making three assumptions. First, it seems reasonable to assume that social competence is both desirable and adaptive. Second, an equally reasonable assumption is that both aggressive and socially wary or withdrawn children are lacking in social skills. Third, drawing on the first two assumptions, we believe that the demonstration of childhood aggression and/or social withdrawal is maladaptive and not conducive to normal social and emotional growth and well-being.

At least two themes can be recognized in approaches to the study of social competence (Rose-Krasnor, Rubin, Booth, and Coplan, 1996). One theme is focused on *social effectiveness*. This functional approach emphasizes the child's ability to meet her or his needs during social interaction. A second theme emphasizes the extent to which the child's interactions with adults and peers are *positive* and appropriately supportive and responsive. Taken together, these themes have led us to define social competence as the ability to achieve personal goals in social interaction while simultaneously maintaining positive relationships with others over time and across settings (Rubin and Rose-Krasnor, 1992). Thus the consistent demonstration of friendly, cooperative, altruistic, successful, and socially acceptable behavior over time and across settings is likely to lead one to judge the actor as socially competent. Furthermore, the display of socially competent behavior in childhood results in peer acceptance and in successful adolescent and adult outcomes. Empirical research supports these contentions (e.g., Masten et al., 1995).

On the other hand, the demonstration of unfriendly, agonistic, hostile behavior, even if directed to very few individuals within a limited number of settings, and even if the behavior results in personally successful outcomes, is likely to be unacceptable and judged as incompetent (e.g., Coie, Dodge, and Kupersmidt, 1990). Moreover, the reasonably consistent demonstration of social reticence, of unassertive social strategies to meet social goals, and of relatively high rates of unsuccessful social outcomes has been judged as incompetent (Stewart and Rubin, 1995). Thus, children who have been identified by peers, teachers, and/or parents as aggressive or socially withdrawn cannot be characterized as socially competent.

If one believes that the attainment of social competence is adaptive, then aggressive or withdrawn children display behaviors, emotions, and probably cognitions that could be considered maladaptive, thereby placing these children at risk for the development of psychological difficulties. Childhood aggression predicts the expression of externalizing disorders, school dropout, and criminality in adolescence (Bierman and Wargo, 1995; Coie, Terry, Lenox, Lochman, and Hyman, 1995), whereas social withdrawal in childhood predicts adolescent problems of an internalizing nature (Rubin, Chen et al., 1995).

Having reached these three conclusions, we can ask "How do children acquire social competence, or in the case of aggression and withdrawal, social incompetence?" Two potential sources of social competence are the parent–child relationship and the child's parenting experiences.

## Parents and Social Competence: Developmental Theory

According to Hartup (1985), parents serve at least three functions in the child's development of social competence. First, parent–child interaction is a context within which many competencies necessary for social interaction develop. This relationship furnishes the child with many of the skills required for initiating and maintaining positive relationships with others, such as language skills, the ability to control impulses, and so forth. Second, the parent–child relationship constitutes emotional and cognitive resources that allow the child to explore the social and nonsocial environments. It is a safety net that permits the child the freedom to examine features of the social universe, thereby enhancing the development of problem-solving skills. Third, the early parent–child relationship is a forerunner of all subsequently formed extrafamilial relationships. It is within this relationship that the child begins to develop expectations and assumptions about interactions with other people and to develop strategies for attaining personal and social goals.

In keeping with these functions, both classical theorists and contemporary researchers have implicated parents and the quality of parent–child relationships in the development of adaptive and maladaptive social behaviors. Early *psychoanalytic theorists* (e.g., Cohler and Paul, in Vol. 3 of this *Handbook*; Freud, 1973/1938) noted that parents were both directly and indirectly responsible for the resolution of the Oedipus complex (Hetherington and Martin, 1986). Of particular relevance, the ego defense mechanisms were thought to underlie the display of undercontrolled behaviors. For example, for those of the psychoanalytic persuasion, resolution of the Oedipus complex partly resulted from identification with the aggressor. To avoid the threat of castration (or, for girls, the threat of whatever the Freudians believed to be worse than castration), the child identified with the parent who posed the perceived threat. If the parent with whom the child identified was hostile and authoritarian, the child would be predicted to exhibit angry, aggressive behaviors in both familial and extrafamilial contexts. Similarly relevant was the ego defense mechanism of displacement; in this case, the child displaced affect onto a person other than the appropriate one. Thus, if the child's anger was parent driven, hostility was directed toward less threatening targets, such as siblings or peers. Also relevant was the development of the superego, which was viewed by psychoanalysts as yet another offshoot of Oedipus complex resolution. Thus, in classic psychoanalytic theory, identification with a given parent allowed the child to internalize the social and the moral standards of the parent. Accordingly, the development of the superego was thought to provide children with the ability to control aggressive impulses and with the motivation to perform altruistic acts that would benefit others.

*Ethological* adaptations of psychoanalytic models also have provided a rationale for a strong association between parenting and both adaptive and maladaptive child functioning (Ainsworth, 1973). The connection between attachment theory and the production of undercontrolled and overcontrolled behaviors is best understood by reference to Bowlby's (1973) construct of "internal working models." For example, Bowlby proposed that the early mother–child relationship lays the groundwork for the development of internalized models of familial and extrafamilial relationships. These internal working models were thought to be the product of parental behavior—specifically, parental sensitivity and responsivity (Spieker and Booth, 1988). Given an internal working model that the parent is available and responsive, it was proposed that the young child would feel confident, secure, and self-assured when introduced to novel settings. Thus *felt security* has been viewed as a highly significant developmental phenomenon that provides the child with sufficient emotional and cognitive sustenance to allow the active exploration of the social environment. *Exploration* purportedly results in play (LaFreniere and Sroufe, 1985), which leads to the development of problem-solving skills and competence in both the impersonal and the interpersonal realms (Rubin and Rose-Krasnor, 1992). From this perspective, then, the association between security of attachment in infancy and the quality of children's social skills is attributed, indirectly, to maternal sources (Sroufe, 1988).

Alternatively, the development of an insecure infant–parent attachment relationship has been posited to result in the child's developing an internal working model that interpersonal relationships are rejecting or neglectful. In turn, the social world is perceived as a battleground that must either be attacked or escaped from (Bowlby, 1973). Thus, for the insecure and angry child, opportunities for peer play and interaction are nullified by displays of hostility and aggression in the peer group. Such behavior, in turn, results in the child's forced (by the peer group) lack of opportunities to benefit from the communication, negotiation, and perspective-taking experiences that will typically lead to the development of a normal and adaptive childhood. For insecure and wary or anxious children, opportunities for peer play and interaction are nullified by the children themselves. Consequently, social and emotional fearfulness prevail to the point at which the benefits of peer interaction are practically impossible to obtain. Empirical support for connections between security of attachment and the display of aggressive or socially fearful and withdrawn behavior is described below.

Finally, *behaviorists* have suggested that parents shape children's social behaviors through processes of conditioning and modeling (Grusec, in Vol. 5 of this *Handbook*). Children's tendencies to directly imitate adult communicative, prosocial, aggressive, and even socially anxious and withdrawn behaviors have been reported consistently in the literature; in addition, social behaviors have been described as responsive to reinforcement principles (Radke-Yarrow and Zahn-Waxler, 1986). A strong link between parental socialization techniques and the display of child behavior in nonfamilial settings has been central to proponents of social learning theory (Sears, 1961).

In summary, almost all major psychological theories that deal with the development of children's social and emotional development in general, and more specifically with the development of competent and adaptive behaviors versus incompetent and maladaptive behaviors (aggression and social withdrawal), place a primary responsibility on parental attributes and behaviors, as well as on the quality of the parent–child relationship. Historically, these theories have provided the undercarriage for a quickly growing corpus of data concerning the nexus of parent–child relationships, parenting behaviors, and child "outcomes." We review the literature in the next section as it pertains to the parents of children who exhibit overcontrolled and undercontrolled emotions and social behaviors.

## ATTACHMENT RELATIONSHIPS, SOCIAL COMPETENCE, AND AGGRESSION AND SOCIAL WITHDRAWAL

One theoretically driven research stream is focused on the purported effects of the *quality of the parent–child relationship*. This focus derives primarily from ethological theory and the constructs of secure and insecure attachments and internal working models of the self in relation to others (Cummings and Cummings, in Vol. 5 of this *Handbook*). The methodologies used are drawn mainly from the classic "Strange Situation" (Ainsworth, Blehar, Waters, and Wall, 1978), which allows distinctions to be made between parent–child partners who have secure or insecure attachment relationships. Concurrent and predictive associations between varying attachment classifications and the expression of competent, aggressive, and withdrawn behaviors are subsequently examined.

### Social Competence and Security of Attachment

The inability to regulate one's emotions and, relatedly, to control one's behavioral impulses places the child "at risk" for psychological dysfunction. Given the risk status of children who have emotion- and behavior-regulation difficulties, researchers have raised questions about the etiology of these phenomena. As it happens, it has been common for researchers, parents, and childcare professionals to turn to the quality of the child's relationships with primary caregivers as possible explanatory starting points.

During infancy, parenting that is warm, responsive, and sensitive leads to the development of a secure internal working model of relationships (Cummings and Cummings, in Vol. 5 of this *Handbook*). Thus the sensitive and responsive parent is able and willing to recognize the infant's or the toddler's emotional signals, to consider the child's perspective, and to respond promptly and appropriately according to the child's needs. In turn, the child develops a working belief system that incorporates the parent as one who can be relied on for protection, nurturance, comfort, and security; a sense of trust in relationships results from the secure infant–parent or toddler–parent bond. Furthermore, the child forms a belief that the self is competent and worthy of positive response from others.

Thus attachment theory predicts at least three influences on children's internal working models that bear on their developing social competencies (Elicker, Englund, and Sroufe, 1992). First, a secure attachment relationship with the primary caregiver promotes *positive social expectations*. Children are disposed to engage other children and expect peer interaction to be rewarding. Second, their experience with a responsive and empathic caregiver builds the rudiments of a social understanding of *reciprocity*. Finally, responsive and supportive parental care lays the foundation for the development of a sense of *self-worth and efficacy*. This internal outlook is thought to be important for promoting curiosity, enthusiasm, and positive affect, characteristics that other children find attractive.

The internal working model of the securely attached child allows her or him to feel confident and self-assured when introduced to novel settings, and this sense of felt security fosters the child's active exploration of the social environment (Sroufe, 1983). In turn, exploration of the social milieu allows the child to address a number of significant "other-directed" questions such as "What are the properties of this other person?", "What is she or he like?", and "What can and does she or he do?". Once these exploratory questions are answered, the child can begin to address "self-directed" questions such as "What can *I* do with this person?" This is the question that defines peer *play*.

It is during play with peers that children experience the interpersonal exchange of ideas, perspectives, roles, and actions. From social negotiation, discussion, and conflict with peers, children learn to understand others' thoughts, emotions, motives, and intentions (e.g., Rogoff, 1990). In turn, armed with these new social understandings, children are able to think about the consequences of their social behaviors, not only for themselves but also for others. The development of these social–cognitive abilities has long been thought to result in the production of socially competent behaviors (e.g., Selman, 1985).

Support for these conjectures emanates from research in which it has been demonstrated that securely attached infants are likely to be well adjusted, socially competent, and well accepted by their peers during the early and the middle years of childhood (Cummings and Cummings, in Vol. 5 of this *Handbook*). Also, securely attached preschoolers are more likely to demonstrate socially competent responses to provocative events than are their insecure counterparts (Cassidy, Kirsh, Scolton, and Parke, 1996). Further, contemporaneous associations exist between the security of parent–child attachment and peer popularity (Cohn, 1990) and the ability to regulate negative emotions as assessed in middle childhood (Contreras, Kerns, Weimer, Gentzler, and Tomich, 2000).

## Aggression, Withdrawal, and Insecurity of Attachment

According to Bowlby, attachment behavior that is not met with comfort or support arouses anger and anxiety. A baby whose parent has been inaccessible and unresponsive is frequently angry because the parent's unresponsiveness is painful and frustrating. At the same time, because of uncertainty about the parent's responsiveness, the infant is apprehensive and readily upset by stressful situations. To protect against these intolerable emotions, it is postulated that the infant develops ego defense strategies. These strategies involve excluding from conscious processing any information that aroused anger and anxiety in the past (Bowlby, 1980; Case, 1991). In situations that could arouse these emotions, the infant blocks conscious awareness and the processing of thoughts, feelings, and desires associated with her or his need of the parent. This information-processing blockage causes the behavioral expression of attachment-related thoughts and emotions to be inhibited.

When stressful situations arouse the infant's need for contact with the parent, different coping strategies are activated that depend on the nature of the infant's expectations and assumptions about the parent (Bowlby, 1973). Thus, in their subsequent peer relationships, insecure–avoidant infants ("A" babies) are guided by previously reinforced expectations of parental rejection and authoritarian control; hence, they are believed to perceive peers as potentially hostile and tend to strike out proactively and aggressively (Troy and Sroufe, 1987). Indeed, researchers have reported that insecure–avoidant A babies exhibit more hostility, anger, and aggressive behavior in preschool and school settings than their secure counterparts do (Egeland, Pianta, and O'Brien, 1993; Sroufe, 1983, 1988; Troy and Sroufe, 1987). Significantly, however, this connection between insecure–avoidant status in infancy and the demonstration of aggressive behaviors thereafter appears significant only for children reared in high-risk homes; A babies from middle-income homes do not appear to demonstrate aggression in preschool and school settings (Bates, Maslin, and Frankel, 1985; Fagot and Kavanaugh, 1990).

There is now evidence that those infants categorized as having a disorganized–disoriented attachment relationship with parents are also at risk for developing aggressive and externalizing symptoms. These "D" babies typically demonstrate a lack of a consistent strategy for coping with the stresses of separation and the need for comfort. Unlike A babies, they do not manage stress by avoidance of the primary caregiver, nor do they appear distressed on separation as the insecure–ambivalent ("C") babies do. Instead, their responses to separations and reunions are extremely idiosyncratic and can include behavioral stereotypes, expressions of depression, freezing, disoriented wandering in the presence of the parent, and sequential displays of attachment and avoidance behaviors (Main and Soloman, 1990).

Ofttimes, D status is reported for insecure infants whose parents are depressed or otherwise psychologically impaired or who are abusive (Lyons-Ruth, Repacholi, McLeod, and Silva, 1991). Interactions between mothers and their D babies have been characterized as communicatively confusing and inappropriate and mutually rejecting (Lyons-Ruth et al., 1991). Evidence that disorganized–disoriented attachment status in infancy predicts the subsequent display of aggression amongst preschool and elementary school children derives from several sources (Greenberg, Speltz, DeKlyen, and Endriga, 1991; Lyons-Ruth, 1996; Lyons-Ruth, Easterbrooks, and Cibelli, 1997; Lyons-Ruth, Easterbrooks, and Davidson, 1995).

Insecure–ambivalent infants (C babies) are thought to be guided by a fear of rejection; consequently, in their extrafamilial peer relationships they are postulated to attempt to avoid rejection through passive, adult-dependent behavior and withdrawal from the prospects of peer interaction (Renken, Egeland, Marvinney, Sroufe, and Mangelsdorf, 1989). Researchers have indicated that C babies are more whiney, easily frustrated, and socially inhibited at 2 years of age than their secure agemates (Fox and Calkins, 1993; Matas, Arend, and Sroufe, 1978). At 4 years of age, children who had been classified at 1 year of age as C babies have been described as lacking in confidence and assertiveness (Erickson, Sroufe, and Egeland, 1985) and at 7 years of age as passively withdrawn (Renken et al., 1989).

Spangler and Schieche (1998) reported that, of the 16 C babies they identified in their research, 15 were rated by their mothers as behaviorally inhibited. Importantly, it has been suggested that inhibition in infancy and toddlerhood is a precursor of social withdrawal in early and middle childhood. Spangler and Schieche found that when behaviorally inhibited toddlers were faced with novelty or social unfamiliarity, they became emotionally dysregulated; it was this dysregulation that appeared to lead them to retreat from unfamiliar adults and peers. That these youngsters became unsettled was supported by findings that confrontation with unfamiliarity brings with it increases in hypothalamic–pituitary–adrenocortical (HPA) activity (Spangler and Schieche, 1998).

Interestingly, this relation between confrontation with unfamiliarity and increases in HPA activation have been reported, in the Strange Situation, for insecurely attached children (e.g., Gunnar, Mangelsdorf, Larson, and Hertsgaard, 1989; Nachmias, Gunnar, Mangelsdorf, Parritz, and Buss, 1996). More to the point, C babies experienced this increased HPA activity (Spangler and Schieche, 1998). Thus it appears that both insecure attachment status and behavioral inhibition serve as the early impetuses for the development of socially fearful and withdrawn behaviors in childhood.

In summary, it would appear that a secure attachment relationship sets the stage for the development of social competence and positive peer relationships. Conversely, insecure attachment relationships in infancy seem to set in motion developmental processes that have been shown to predict the expression of undercontrolled, aggressive behavior or overcontrolled, wary, inhibited, and passively withdrawn behavior in childhood. Thus early developing internal working models that apply to issues of interpersonal trust and security, empathy, reciprocity, self-worth, and self-assuredness (van IJzendoorn, 1997) and that result from the development of attachment relationships with parents appear to guide the subsequent expression of emotion and behavior in children.

The internal working models, which were previously described as guiding the expression of competent and incompetent, adaptive and maladaptive emotional and behavioral expressions, are generally construed as residing within the minds of children. It is important, however, to note that parents also have internal working models of relationships. These models have been framed recently within the constructs of parental beliefs, ideas, and cognitions about the development, maintenance, and dissolution of relationships and about the behaviors that might contribute to the quality of relationships. Next we review this literature as it pertains to social competence, withdrawal, and aggression.

## PARENTS' BELIEFS ABOUT ADAPTIVE AND MALADAPTIVE BEHAVIORS

A second major research stream linking parent and child domains consists of studies concerning parents' cognitions or ideas about development and the socialization goals and strategies they believe to be most appropriate for promoting child development. Studies in this stream have focused, for example, on how parents' attributions about their children's behaviors influence their strategic and affective responses to those behaviors (e.g., Baden and Howe, 1992; Miller, 1995). Reviews of parental beliefs and ideas (e.g., Bugental and Happaney, in Vol. 3 of this *Handbook*) have highlighted the significance of this domain for understanding the socialization process; and these authors have emphasized collectively the need to clarify relations among parental belief structures, parenting behaviors, and child outcomes.

There is emerging evidence that parents' ideas, beliefs, and perceptions concerning child development, in general, and the development and maintenance of adaptive and maladaptive behavioral and emotional styles, in particular, predict and partially explain the development of socially competent and incompetent behaviors in childhood. The conceptual underpinnings of this research are drawn from researchers' beliefs that parents' childrearing practices represent a behavioral expression of parental notions about how children become socially competent, how family contexts should be structured to shape children's behaviors, and how and when children should be taught to initiate and maintain relationships with others (Bugental and Happaney, in Vol. 3 of this *Handbook*; Sigel and Kim, 1996).

To this end, research concerned with parents' ideas about children's socioemotional development represents an examination of their own inner working models of the relations among social skills, emotion regulation, and social relationships. Thus many researchers believe that parenting behaviors are cognitively driven (Gretarsson and Gelfand, 1988; Johnston and Patenaude, 1994) and that these cognitions are themselves influenced by such factors as parents' educational status, socioeconomic status, and ethnicity, as well as a child's gender, age, developmental level, and temperament (Putnam, Sanson, and Rothbart, in Vol. 1 of this *Handbook*); and parents' own history of parent–child relationships (Bacon and Ashmore, 1985; Dix, Ruble, and Zambarano, 1989; Hastings and Rubin, 1999). In this section, therefore, we consider whether parenting attitudes and beliefs are associated with children's social competencies and behavioral disturbances—specifically, aggression and social withdrawal.

## Parents' Beliefs About Social Competence

It seems reasonable to conclude that the more parents think it is important for their children to be socially competent, the more likely it is for them to be involved in promoting it. For example, Cohen (1989) reported that the more mothers valued and felt responsible for their children's sociability, the more they tended to be involved in promoting their children's peer relationships. Further, Rubin et al. (1989) found that mothers who considered the development of social skills to be very important had children who were observed to demonstrate social competence in their preschools. These children more frequently initiated peer play, used appropriate kinds of requests to attain their social goals, were more prosocial, and were more successful at gaining peer compliance than their agemates whose mothers did not place a high priority on the development of social competence. In general, parents tend to view their children optimistically and forecast healthy developmental outcomes for them. Parents of socially competent children believe that, in early childhood, they should play an active role in the socialization of social skills by means of teaching and providing peer-interaction opportunities (see Parke and Buriel, 1998, for a review). They also believe that when their children display maladaptive behaviors, it is due to transitory and situationally caused circumstances (Dix and Grusec, 1985; Goodnow, Knight, and Cashmore, 1985).

Parents whose preschoolers display socially incompetent behaviors (such as social reticence, hostility, aggression) are less likely to endorse strong beliefs in the acquisition of social skills (Rubin et al., 1989). Furthermore, they are more likely to attribute the development of social competence to internal factors ("Children are born that way"), to believe that incompetent behavior, once attained, is difficult to alter, and to believe that interpersonal skills are best taught through direct instructional means (Rubin et al., 1989).

These findings give insights about how parents' ideas about social development may influence their socialization behaviors. Thus external attributions for the development of social competence may be conducive to the use of constructive means to teach social skills. Internal attributions about how children develop competent and incompetent social skills may lead to one of two potential child-rearing styles (Rubin, Rose-Krasnor, Bigras, Mills, and Booth, 1996). On the one hand, the belief that social behavior is "internally" caused can lead to parental feelings of hopelessness and helplessness; in this case parental neglect may ensue, whereby parents adopt a "laissez-faire" permissive approach to socializing social skills or to dealing with maladaptive social behavior. On the other hand, parents may adopt a "spare the rod, spoil the child" rearing style. In this case, parents may try harder to counter the influence of factors perceived as being internally caused, thereby adopting an authoritarian, highly power-assertive socialization belief system. These speculations have received initial support (see Rubin and Mills, 1992; Rubin et al., 1996).

One conclusion that may derive from these findings is that parental involvement in the promotion of social competence is mediated by strong beliefs in the importance of social skills. When a socially competent child demonstrates poor social performance, parents who place a relatively high value on social competence are likely to be the most involved and responsive. Over time, such involvement may be positively reinforced by the child's acquisition of social skills. At the same time, parents are likely to value social skills displayed by their children, and these children will be perceived as interpersonally competent and capable of autonomous learning. Hence parental beliefs and child characteristics will influence each other in a reciprocal manner (Mills and Rubin, 1993a).

## Parents' Beliefs About Aggression and Withdrawal

Recently researchers have begun to explore how parents feel about, think about, and consequently deal with children's aggression and social wariness and withdrawal. To a large extent, this research is guided by information-processing approaches to the study of parenting problems (Bugental and Happaney, in Vol. 3 of this *Handbook*).

According to Bugental (1992), parenting may be a source of considerable stress, especially if the child is viewed as a "problem." The *problematic* child who demonstrates difficult behaviors at a given point in time may evoke rather different parental emotions and cognitions from the *normal* child who rarely demonstrates the identical maladaptive behaviors. In the case of normal children, the production of aggression or social withdrawal and wariness may activate parental feelings of concern, puzzlement, and, in the case of aggression, anger. These affects are regulated by the parent's attempts to understand, rationalize, or justify the child's behavior and by the parent's knowledge of the child's social skills history and the known quality of the child's social relationships at home, at school, and in the neighborhood. Thus, in the case of nonproblematic children, the evocative stimulus produces adaptive, solution-focused parental ideation that results in the parent's choice of a reasoned, sensitive, and responsive approach to dealing with the problem behavior (Bugental and Happaney, in Vol. 3 of this *Handbook*). In turn, the child views the parent as supportive and learns to better understand how to behave and feel in similar situations as they occur in the future. As such, a reciprocal connection develops between the ways and means of adult and child social information processing.

In the case of aggressive children, any hostile behavior, whether directed at peers, siblings, or parents, may evoke strong parental feelings of anger and frustration. Such emotions are often difficult to regulate given that they are accompanied by significant physiological responses (e.g., increases in heart rate and electrodermal activity; Obrist, 1982). As a consequence, parents may be unable to control their expressive behaviors, and the socialization strategy provoked is one that may be best regarded as undercontrolled, power assertive, and coercive (Bugental, 1992). Needless to say, this parental response, mediated by affect and beliefs or cognitions about the intentionality of the child behavior (Strassburg, 1995), the historical precedence of child aggression, and the best means to control child aggression, is likely to evoke negative affect and cognitions in the child (MacKinnon-Lewis et al., 1994). The result of this interplay between parent and child beliefs, affect, and behavior may be the reinforcement and extension of family cycles of hostility (Patterson, Capaldi, and Bank, 1991; Patterson and Fisher, in Vol. 5 of this *Handbook*).

In the case of socially wary and withdrawn children, any expression of social fearfulness in the peer group may evoke parental feelings of concern, sympathy, and perhaps, with increasing child age, a growing sense of frustration. The parent may be overcome by a strong belief that the child is vulnerable and must be helped in some way (Burgess, Rubin, Cheah, and Nelson, in press). Such a "read" of the situation and of the child may be guided by a developing belief system that social withdrawal is dispositionally based, that it is accompanied by strong and debilitating child feelings of fear and social anxiety, and by child behaviors that evoke, in peers, attempts to be socially dominant. The resultant parental behavior, guided by the processing of affect and historically and situationally based information, may be of a "quick-fix" variety for parent and child. That is, to release the child from social discomfort, the parent may simply "take over" by telling the child what to do and how to do it (Rubin, Nelson, Hastings, and Asendorpf, 1999). Alternatively, the parent may simply solve the child's social dilemmas by asking other children for information desired by the child, obtaining objects desired by the child, or requesting that peers allow the child to join them in play. Needless to say, these direct parenting activities are likely to reinforce the child's feelings of insecurity, resulting in the maintenance of a systemic cycle of child hopelessness or helplessness and parent overcontrol or overprotection (see Mills and Rubin, 1993a, for an elaboration of this latter case).

## Parents' Beliefs About Aggression and Withdrawal: Normative Studies

Students of developmental psychopathology generally agree that an understanding of normalcy and normal development is prerequisite to understanding deviations from the norm (Cicchetti and Toth, 1998). Thus, knowing how parents of normal and competent children respond to questions concerning their feelings about, attributions for, and preferred means of dealing with their children's displays of aggression and/or social withdrawal is a starting point. These beliefs are examined also insofar as they are related to the age of the child. This latter perspective provides the reader with an appreciation of the significance of child-based factors (such as age) on the parental belief system. Following this review, we contrast the beliefs of parents of aggressive, withdrawn, and competent children.

Not surprisingly, parents have very different ideas about the derivation of aggression and withdrawal and how they might react to them. For example, parents of preschoolers (4 years old) and elementary schoolers (6 and 7 years old) express great concern when asked how they would feel if they were to observe their own child consistently behaving in an aggressive or withdrawn fashion (e.g., Schneider, Attili, Vermigly, and Younger, 1997). However, parents report that aggressive behavior elicits anger and disappointment, whereas withdrawal is more inclined to evoke surprise and puzzlement (Grusec, Dix, and Mills, 1982; Mills and Rubin, 1990). Given these reported affective reactions, it is not surprising that parents are more likely to suggest the use of high power-assertive strategies to deal with their children's aggression than with their social withdrawal (Dodge, Pettit, and Bates, 1994; Mills and Rubin, 1990). These parental reactions to hostility with hostility aptly point to the importance of accepting a bidirectional influence vis-à-vis the development and maintenance of childhood aggression (Patterson, 1982). It is also of interest to note that parents of preschoolers report that children's expressions of hostile aggression and wary withdrawal may be attributed to transient states such as a passing developmental stage (Mills and Rubin, 1990).

The preceding findings apply to parents of relatively young children. Obviously, parents' beliefs, perceptions, and attitudes change as their children grow older (McNally, Eisenberg, and Harris, 1991; Mills and Rubin, 1992). Parents recognize that advances in social skill occur with age, and therefore they think that older children must be held more responsible than younger children for their negative behaviors. For example, mothers tend to react to socially inappropriate behaviors with increasing negative affect with increasing child age (Dix, 1991; Dix et al., 1989). Dix and Grusec (1985) proposed that changes in disciplinary beliefs are associated with changes in parental attributions about the causes of specific child behaviors as children grow older.

In accordance with principles of attribution theory, behaviors that are very discrepant from normative standards tend to be attributed to stable traits or internal dispositions. These attributions, in turn, influence parental perceptions (Miller, 1995). Mothers consider negative behaviors as more intentional and dispositional in older than in younger children, which is consistent with this analysis. Furthermore, the more intentional and/or dispositional parents believe negative behaviors to be, the more upset they get when these behaviors are expressed (Dix, Ruble, Grusec, and Nixon, 1986; Dix et al., 1989). These affective reactions may lead some parents to respond with anger to their children's behaviors and others to respond by "moving away" from, or neglecting, the producer of these negative behaviors.

In support of these arguments, Mills and Rubin (1992) found a number of changes in the ways that mothers appraised displays of aggression and withdrawal, in the strategies they chose to deal with these behaviors, and in the beliefs that they had about how children learn social skills. For example, in children from the ages of 4 to 6 years, displays of aggression and withdrawal became less easily excused as reflecting immaturity or as being caused by sources external to the children (e.g., "other children began the fight"; "other children would not allow my child to join them in play"). Instead, there was an increase in the extent to which mothers attributed these behaviors to internal dispositional characteristics. For withdrawal, these trait attributions were associated with an increase, on the part of mothers, not to respond to the behavior. These findings suggest that, during their child's early years, the parent may make active efforts to deal with the child's social wariness and withdrawal; however, over time, if the parent judges that her or his efforts have fallen short, she or he may choose to ignore or avoid the problem.

Interestingly, no such developmental change in behavioral response was obtained for aggression; despite being attributed to dispositional causes, aggression seemed more difficult to excuse than the continued expression of withdrawal. Perhaps this finding resulted from the salience of aggression and from its clear negative consequences for children, their parents, their teachers, and their peers.

In summary, it seems likely that parents' feelings about, attributions for, and behavioral reactions to the expression of aggression and withdrawal change with child age. The extant data are descriptive of parental beliefs for children who are of preschool and early elementary school age; thus further developmental data are currently required. Moreover, there have been few, if any, studies in which the beliefs of mothers about the development of social competence have been compared with the beliefs of fathers; and mother versus father beliefs for sons versus daughters have rarely been compared. Consequently, it would appear that this area requires further investigation.

## Parents of Aggressive and Withdrawn Children: Parental Beliefs

The research previously reviewed concerning parental beliefs about the development of social skills and of aggression and withdrawal derived from parents who had children who were socially and emotionally normal. Researchers who have followed a social information-processing model in their studies of parental beliefs have posited a number of ways in which parents of socially "different" children might think about social and emotional development (Bugental, 1992; Mills and Rubin, 1993a, 1993b).

*Parents of aggressive children.* Mothers of aggressive children appear to hold beliefs about social development that vary from those of nonaggressive, normal children (Rubin and Mills, 1990, 1992). For example, when asked to indicate how a variety of social skills (e.g., making friends, sharing with peers) might best be learned by their preschoolers, they were more likely than mothers of nonaggressive children to suggest that they would take a highly directive approach. In short, they would tell their children what to do and how to behave, leaving few degrees of freedom for the child. Parents of aggressive preschoolers believe more strongly than mothers of nonaggressive children in the use of "low-distancing" teaching styles (Sigel, 1982) that provide children with minimal opportunities to think about alternative perspectives, consequences of interactive behaviors for themselves and for others, and social planning. Given that low-distancing strategies have been associated with incompetent performance vis-à-vis the development of impersonal problem-solving skills (McGillicuddy-DeLisi, 1982), it would not be a stretch to suggest a nonoptimal social outcome for children whose parents believe that social skills can be taught through direct instruction.

Although their children are highly aggressive and they indicate that aggression makes them angry, mothers of young aggressive children are nevertheless more inclined than mothers of nonaggressive children to choose very indirect strategies or no strategies at all to deal with their children's aggressive behavior. Thus for mothers of aggressive children there seems to be some disparity between their proactive beliefs, which suggest a preference for highly directive parenting styles (Campbell, Pierce, Moore, Markovitz, and Newby, 1996; Dodge et al., 1994), and their choice of reactive strategies, which indicate a preference for a laissez-faire style (Rubin and Mills, 1990, 1992). This disparity may stem from their attribution of aggressive behavioral displays to age-related dispositional factors.

Mothers who advocate authoritarian childrearing beliefs and attitudes tend to respond to aggression with high control and anger, blame their children for aggression, and focus on child compliance instead of teaching skills (Hastings and Rubin, 1999). However, it may be that these mothers' attempts to teach social skills in a direct manner are unsuccessful; moreover, they may be somewhat intimidated by their child's aggressiveness. Perhaps they attribute child behavior and their own lack of success to short-lived age-related factors and choose less direct strategies in order to lessen their anxiety, avoid confrontation, and wait out what they hope will be a passing phase. Consequently, it may be that these mothers attempt to normalize their children's behavior despite the fact that it makes them feel angry. Such conflicting emotions and attributions could perpetuate a high level of aggression in the child in precisely the way Patterson and his colleagues (Patterson and Fisher, in Vol. 5 of this *Handbook*) have found; that is, by initiating an erratic pattern of behavioral interchanges in which undesirable behavior is sometimes rewarded or ignored as the parent attempts to avoid confrontation, and desirable behavior is sometimes, out of frustration, dealt with in an authoritarian fashion.

Interestingly, the mothers of aggressive elementary school children attribute the attainment of social skills and the consistent expression of aggressive behavior to internal, dispositional sources (Rubin et al., 1996). Given the stability of aggressive behavior in childhood (Farrington, 1995), this finding is hardly surprising. Furthermore, with increasing age, mothers of aggressive children report not only that their children's hostility causes them to feel angry, but they also express less surprise and puzzlement than mothers of nonaggressive children when their children demonstrate aggressive behavior. In short, these mothers appear to be getting used to their children's maladaptive behavioral styles. Acceptance of the causes of aggression and the lack of surprise for its occurrence do *not* engender a laissez-faire attitude in reaction to elementary school-age children's aggressive behavior. Rather, mothers of aggressive children are more inclined than mothers of nonaggressive children to suggest the use of high-powered, punitive strategies to deal with aggression. Thus it is likely that with increasing age parents find it increasingly difficult to accept the hostile behavior of their children, despite believing that their behavior is dispositionally based. Perhaps the belief in a dispositional basis for aggressive behavior is merely defensive and expressive of parental frustration. Perhaps, too, the child's behavior results in negative reports to parents by teachers, schoolmates, and neighborhood parents. Such information may not prove to be surprising, and the parent may attempt to explain the behavior by implicating biology in the development of aggression. However, the end result is that the behavior must be brought under control. As a consequence, power-assertive techniques become highly favored.

Among older children, particularly adolescents, several authors have noted that parents of antisocial youths often have the attitude that certain antisocial behaviors are normal (Lahey, Waldman, and McBurnett, 1999). Lahey et al. (1999) give examples such as parents thinking it is appropriate, at certain ages, for their children to hit other children or for their adolescents to shoplift. Consequently, as Lahey et al. (1999) point out, these parents would not discourage their children from engaging in such behaviors even if they were adequately supervising and aware of it.

*Parents of socially withdrawn children.* Like mothers of aggressive children, mothers of extremely withdrawn preschoolers tend to think about children's social development in ways that differ considerably from those of mothers of average children. For example, when asked to indicate how a variety of social skills might best be learned by their preschoolers, mothers of withdrawn children were more likely to suggest that they would *tell* their child directly how to behave and they were less likely to believe that their children learn best by being active participants in and processors of their social environments (Rubin and Mills, 1990, 1992). This pattern of parental beliefs appears to be a direct response to their perceptions of their child's social wariness and fearfulness. For example, it has recently been shown that mothers and fathers who view their toddlers as socially wary and shy are less likely to encourage their child's independence at age 4 years (Rubin et al., 1999). Furthermore, mothers of behaviorally inhibited toddlers endorse overly protective childrearing strategies (Chen et al., 1998). Last, if mothers of inhibited toddlers do endorse overprotective strategies, then when their children are preschool age, they react to cases in which their children demonstrate withdrawal by suggesting that they would deal with their child's problematic behavior through direct, authoritarian means (Hastings and Rubin, 1999). Taken together, the lack of encouragement of independence combined with attitudes pertaining to overprotectiveness will undoubtedly minimize children's opportunities to explore the environment, as well as stultify thoughts about alternative perspectives, social planning, and consequences of behaviors for themselves and others. Social incompetence in withdrawn children, as in aggressive children, may partly result from parental use of low-distancing socialization strategies (McGillicuddy-DeLisi, 1982).

Although the mothers of socially withdrawn preschoolers believe more strongly than the mothers of average children that social skills can be taught directly, mothers of elementary school-age withdrawn children believe more strongly than do mothers of average children that it would be difficult to alter social skill deficiencies (Mills and Rubin, 1993b). On the one hand, these parents express a strong belief in low-distancing strategies to aid in the initial development of social skills; on the other hand, they do not think strongly of a positive prognosis for parental intervention when skills fail to develop.

Insofar as *reactive* parental beliefs are concerned, it has been shown that when mothers of socially withdrawn preschoolers were asked about their reactions to hypothetical incidents of their child's expression of peer-directed aggression and withdrawal, they indicated that: (1) they would feel more guilty and embarrassed; (2) they would more likely attribute such behaviors to internal, dispositional sources; and (3) they would react to such displays of maladaptive behavior more often in coercive, highly power-assertive ways than did mothers of average or competent preschoolers (Rubin and Mills, 1990). The finding that mothers have strong negative reactions to social withdrawal has recently been replicated by Schneider et al. (1997).

In summary, we have painted a portrait of mothers (and fathers; Rubin et al., 1999) of socially withdrawn preschoolers as having beliefs that endorse overprotective parenting strategies. If such an endorsement is realized in parental behavior, it would assuredly be detrimental to the child's developing senses of autonomy and social efficacy in the peer milieu; moreover, such parenting beliefs, if instantiated in parental behavior, are not conducive to the healthy development of social competence or positive self-regard. Indeed, early research has shown that an overprotective, overly concerned parenting style is associated with submissiveness, dependency, and timidity in early childhood (see below); and these characteristics are descriptive of children who are socially withdrawn in the peer culture (Olweus, 1993).

The causal attributions and reported emotional reactions of these mothers were also indicative of overdirection. Mothers of socially withdrawn preschoolers not only express more anger, disappointment, guilt, and embarrassment about their children's maladaptive social behaviors than do other mothers, but they are also more inclined to blame such behaviors on traits in their child (e.g., Hastings and Rubin, 1999). This constellation of emotions and attributions suggests that these mothers may be somewhat unable to moderate their affective reactions to problematic behaviors. Perhaps in an attempt to regulate their own emotions about their children's behaviors, these mothers choose to "keep their house in order" by overregulating their children's activities. In summary, the extant data provide an initial empirical hint that socially withdrawn preschoolers are exposed to a rather complex mix of conflicting maternal emotions and attributions and that their mothers may overidentify with them (Parker, 1983).

Interestingly, these observations appear to change with the increasing age of the withdrawn child. For example, during elementary school (5 to 9 years old), mothers of withdrawn children described their affective reactions to social withdrawal as involving less surprise and puzzlement than did those of mothers of normal children. These data are themselves unsurprising, given the stability of withdrawal from the early to the middle years of childhood (e.g., Asendorpf, 1993). Furthermore, although mothers of withdrawn elementary schoolers also attributed withdrawal to internal, personality traits in their children, they no longer suggested that they would react to displays of withdrawal in a power-assertive manner (Mills and Rubin, 1993b).

In summary, parents of aggressive and withdrawn children appear to differ from those of nonaggressive and nonwithdrawn children in the ways in which they think about socializing social skills and in the ways that they reportedly react to their children's displays of social withdrawal or aggression. It is plausible that these parental beliefs have some bearing on the ways in which parents actually behave with their children.

## PARENTING BEHAVIORS AND CHILDREN'S AGGRESSION AND SOCIAL WITHDRAWAL

If parents' cognitions about the development of social competence, aggression, and withdrawal are implicated in the expression of parental behavioral "styles," then the socialization practices of parents whose children are aggressive or withdrawn ought to differ from those of parents whose children are socially competent and normal. One means by which such parenting differences have been examined has involved the conceptualization of two basic dimensions of parenting—*warmth–responsiveness* and *control–demandingness* (Baumrind, 1971; Parke and Buriel, 1998). The first dimension concerns the *affective* continuum of parenting; it ranges from warm and sensitive behavior on the one hand to cold or hostile behavior on the other hand. The second dimension deals with issues of *power assertion*. At one end of the continuum is the frequent use of restrictive demands and high control; but at the opposite end of the continuum is frequent lack of supervision and low control. The interaction of the two continua constitutes an oft-mentioned fourfold scheme that includes (1) *authoritative* parenting (high warmth, high control), (2) *authoritarian* parenting (low warmth, high control), (3) *indulgent–permissive* parenting (high warmth, low control), and (4) *indifferent–uninvolved* parenting (low warmth, low control) (see Baumrind, 1971).

These different parenting classifications may mesh well with notions concerning the development of social competence, aggression, and social withdrawal in childhood. Both contemporaneously and longitudinally, researchers have shown that the children of authoritative parents tend to be socially responsible and competent, friendly and cooperative with peers, and generally happy (Baumrind, 1967, 1971, 1991). The authoritative and democratic parenting (child-centered) style is both concurrently and predictively associated with the development of mature moral reasoning and prosocial behavior (Hoffman, 1970; Yarrow, Waxler, and Scott, 1971), high self-esteem (Loeb, Horst, and Horton, 1980), and academic achievement (Lamborn, Mounts, Steinberg, and Dornbusch, 1991; Steinberg, Lamborn, Dornbusch, and Darling, 1992). It is also the case that parents who can best be described as child centered in their interactions and who provide appropriate levels and styles of guidance and support have children who are socially competent (Mize and Pettit, 1997; Rose-Krasnor et al., 1996; Russell and Finnie, 1990).

In contrast, parents who provide insufficient or imbalanced responsiveness and control (authoritarian, permissive, and uninvolved) are likely to have children who are socially incompetent, aggressive and/or socially withdrawn (Baumrind, 1967, 1971; Dishion, 1990; Lamborn et al., 1991). The subsections that follow document in greater detail the particular forms of parenting behavior that distinguish among parents of aggressive, withdrawn, and socially competent children.

## Parenting Behavior and Childhood Aggression

With respect to the affective dimension of parenting, the types of behaviors and emotions parents display during interactions with their children are linked with child behavior. Specifically, both parental hostility and warmth are associated with childhood aggression. Parents who are hostile or rejecting may also be high on the control or power-assertiveness dimension of parenting; indeed, rejecting parents frequently and inappropriately apply power-assertive techniques and punishment. Parental rejection or hostility, and closely related constructs (e.g., harsh discipline, coercive parenting), predict aggressiveness in children (Campbell et al., 1996; Dishion, 1990; Dodge et al., 1994), as well as other externalizing problems (e.g., misconduct). Even as early as the toddler stage, maternal displays of hostile affect (e.g., insults, criticism, yelling) and negative control (e.g., verbal intrusion, dominating free play) are associated with aggression and externalizing problems (Rubin, Hastings, Chen, Stewart, and McNichol, 1998). Indeed, parental hostility is regarded as the single most significant risk factor in the prediction of childhood aggression (Rutter and Quinton, 1984). Thus, in a recent study Denham et al. (2000) reported that maternal and paternal anger predicted continuity in externalizing behavior problems from early to middle childhood, particularly for children whose problems were in the clinical range.

It is not only the presence of parental negativity that bodes poorly for children, but also the *absence* of parental positive affect and positive behavior. A lack of parental warmth has been linked not only with aggression, but also with other kinds of psychological and school adjustment problems in childhood (McFayden-Ketchum, Bates, Dodge, and Pettit, 1996; Mize and Pettit, 1997). Contrasted with the impact of parental hostility or rejection, maternal warmth has been shown to buffer children from adjustment problems (MacDonald, 1992; Patterson, Cohn, and Kao, 1989). Thus, rather than being considered a risk factor implicated in child aggression, parental warmth has been considered a protective factor for subsequent adjustment outcomes.

Furthermore, maternal and paternal displays of positive regard for the child and setting clear limits or expectations have been shown to predict *less* externalizing behavior over time. With this research, initial levels of externalizing difficulties are controlled, thereby demonstrating the significant influence of parental behavior (Collins, Maccoby, Steinberg, Hetherington, and Bornstein, 2000). More generally, it has been found that parents who are cold and rejecting, physically punitive, and who discipline their children in an inconsistent fashion have aggressive children (e.g., Conger et al., 1992, 1993; Dishion, 1990; Eron, Huesmann, and Zelli, 1991; Mills and Rubin, 1998; Olweus, 1980; Weiss, Dodge, Bates, and Pettit, 1992). For example, Olweus (1980) found that childhood aggression could be predicted by mothers' negative affect toward their sons and by their use of high power-assertive techniques when disciplining them. These maternal variables continued to predict aggressive behavior even after child temperament and mothers' permissiveness for aggression were controlled for. Similarly, Weiss et al. (1992) found that harsh parental discipline predicted child aggression in school. This relation remained significant after child temperament, SES, and marital violence had been controlled for.

The process by which parental hostility, rejection, punitiveness, and lack of warmth lead to childhood aggression is not difficult to understand. First, such a parenting style creates a familial environment that elicits feelings of frustration among its members. Frustration, in turn, may result in feelings of anger and hostility; these feelings, if left unchecked or unregulated, likely produce hostile and aggressive interchanges between children and their parents (Dollard, Doob, Miller, Mowrer, and Sears, 1939). Second, parental rejection and punishment serve as a model of hostility and inappropriate forcefulness for the child (Bandura, 1977). Third, as noted earlier, it is also possible that parental hostility, rejection, and lack of warmth constitute a basis for the child to develop an internal working model of the self as unworthy and of the social world as cold, distrustful, and hostile (Bowlby, 1969, 1973). These negative perceptions and feelings about the world may contribute to the child's lack of expressed consideration of others in social interactions and to the development of an unfriendly and hostile behavioral repertoire.

It is important to note that parents of aggressive children are not always cold and punitive; rather, it appears that they apply power-assertive techniques and punishments in an inconsistent fashion (Loeber and Stouthamer-Loeber, 1986; Patterson et al., 1991). Inconsistent discipline interferes with the child's ability to identify rules and expectations, and inadvertently reinforces noncompliant behavior (Katz, 1971; Martin, 1975). As a result, the child is inadequately socialized and behaves impulsively, aggressively, and irresponsibly. For example, parents may punish and discourage deviant, hostile behavior in the home, but may actually encourage their child's hostility and aggression in the peer group. Moreover, parents of aggressive children have been found to use power-assertive techniques proactively when or where it is actually inappropriate to do so (e.g., during parent–child free play), but fail to provide appropriate control and support as necessary (e.g., in a highly structured situation, such as helping the child solve a "homework-type" problem). Finally, some researchers have reported that parents of aggressive children actually respond *positively* to deviant child behavior, but *aversively* to nondeviant behavior (Lobitz and Johnson, 1975; Patterson, 1982; Snyder, 1977). Parents' encouragement of a child's aggressive behavior may result from an aspiration for the child to be dominant in the peer group. It is also possible that these parents actually believe that aggression and violence are appropriate means by which to solve interpersonal problems. Thus it can be safely concluded that relatively frequent but inconsistent use of parental high power assertion fosters aggressive behavior in childhood.

In addition to parental rejection and high power-assertive strategies, parental permissiveness, indulgence, and lack of supervision have often been found to correlate with children's aggressive behavior. For example, in Baumrind's original studies (1967, 1971), permissive parents who failed to exercise necessary control and to make demands for mature behavior tended to have impulsive, acting-out, and immature children. Olweus (1980) also found that maternal permissiveness of aggression was the *best* predictor of child aggression. Importantly, it has been shown that low control by fathers predicts preschool children's externalizing difficulties (Miller, Cowan, Cowan, Hetherington, and Clingempeel, 1993). Parental neglect and lack of monitoring and supervision have also been related to truancy, drinking problems, precocious sexuality, and delinquency in adolescence and adulthood (Lamborn et al., 1991; Patterson, 1982; Pulkkinen, 1982). Poor supervision has a stronger relation to antisocial behavior in later childhood than in earlier childhood (Reid and Patterson, 1989). Thus some aspects of parenting may be less or more pertinent at different developmental periods. Last, it may not be difficult to understand these associations of lax supervision and permissiveness with a child's externalizing behavior, given that parental tolerance and neglect of this behavior may actually legitimize and encourage aggression.

Although an overview of the extant literature would paint a picture of the parent of an aggressive child as being a harsh disciplinarian, as using punitive measures inconsistently, as not monitoring or providing necessary supervision in situations that require it, and as behaving in a cold rejecting manner, it is nevertheless the case that not all data are supportive of this portrait. From time to time, researchers fail to report a contemporaneous association between "negative" parenting and children's aggression (see Hart, DeWolf, Wozniak, and Burts, 1992). Furthermore, even if one were to argue that the corpus of data is largely supportive of the associations previously noted, one could not argue with much conviction that negative indices of parenting "caused" childhood aggression. For example, in several longitudinal studies (e.g., Eron, Huesmann, Dubow, Romanoff, and Yarmel, 1987; Vuchinich, Bank, and Patterson, 1992), predictive relations between parental discipline and child antisocial behavior were found to be nonsignificant, although contemporaneous reciprocal relations between them were statistically significant. Researchers who have aggregated scores of parenting skills, including parental nurturance and rejection, monitoring, and inconsistent parenting, have demonstrated reliable results in predicting childhood aggression (e.g., Conger et al., 1992, 1993; Dishion, 1990).

In summary, much research exists in which parental hostility, rejection, and lack of warmth have been associated with the expression of children's aggressive behavior. However, parenting practices do not represent the best long-term predictors of aggression, delinquency, and criminality.

For example, Eron and colleagues (Eron et al., 1987; Lefkowitz, Eron, Walder, and Huesmann, 1977) reported that, whereas parental behavior could reliably predict aggression in childhood, it was childhood aggression, not parental behavior, that best predicted aggression and criminality in adolescence and adulthood. Moreover, other parental factors also figure into the parent behavior–child aggression relation. For instance, if a biological parent engages in chronic antisocial behavior, then the offspring is more likely than other adolescents to engage in antisocial behavior (Farrington, 1995; Lahey et al., 1999).

The long-term effects of parental variables on later aggression and criminality, through the mediation of childhood aggression, have also been documented in other research programs (e.g., Farrington, 1983). Thus it would appear that negative parental behavior helps establish and maintain a pattern of *childhood* aggression, which itself provides a strong foundation for the development of undercontrolled, externalizing problems in later life.

## Parenting Behavior and Social Withdrawal in Childhood

Compared with the literature concerning the parents of aggressive children, what is known about the parents of socially withdrawn children is negligible. The general lack of information in this regard may stem from several factors. Until recently, the phenomenon of social withdrawal was viewed neither as a "risk variable" nor as a "marker" of psychological maladaptation. To the extent that these beliefs dominated the clinical literature, there was little reason to study the etiology of the phenomenon (see Rubin and Burgess, 2001). Furthermore, the study of behavioral inhibition, shyness, and social withdrawal has been dominated by literature pertaining to putative biological origins. Somewhat in support of this biological perspective has been the consistent report that these phenomena are stable (Caspi and Silva, 1995; Kagan, Reznick, and Snidman, 1987, 1989; Rubin, Coplan, Fox, and Calkins, 1995; Rubin et al., 1995)—inhibited, shy or withdrawn children appear to remain so from one year to the next. Also, stable patterns of right frontal EEG asymmetries in infancy predict temperamental fearfulness and behavioral inhibition in early childhood (Fox and Calkins, 1993), and right frontal EEG asymmetries are associated with the demonstration of socially reticent and withdrawn behavior during the preschool period (Fox, Schmidt, Calkins, Rubin, and Coplan, 1996).

Thus both the documented stability and the physiological correlates of socially inhibited and reticent behavior may have given rise to the belief that inhibition and social withdrawal were relatively unaffected by parents' socialization beliefs and behaviors. Yet, in truth, the stability data reported thus far have been rather imperfect. Children do change, and some more than others. With this in mind, a significant question to ask is "What factors are associated with, or predict, both stability and change in behavioral inhibition and social withdrawal?"

It bears noting that there has now emerged a literature in which behavioral inhibition and social withdrawal have been shown to reflect psychological maladaptation and to predict internalizing difficulties (e.g., Fox et al., 1996; Rubin, Chen, and Hymel, 1993; Rubin, Chen et al., 1995). This literature, and that which demonstrates that some, if not most, behaviorally inhibited and socially withdrawn children do change over time, has led to the search for parenting associations and predictors (see Burgess et al., in press, for a review).

The construct of social withdrawal includes the demonstration of social wariness and anxiety, the virtual nonexistence of exploration in novel social situations, social deference, submissiveness, sad affect during encounters with peers, and negative self-regard concerning one's own social skills and relationships (Boivin, Hymel, and Bukowski, 1995; see Rubin and Burgess, 2001, for an extensive review). With these defining properties in mind, it is noteworthy that Baumrind (1967) found that the parents of socially anxious, unhappy children who were insecure in the company of peers were more likely to demonstrate authoritarian socialization behaviors than the parents of more socially competent children. Other researchers have reported that children whose parents use authoritarian childrearing practices tend to have low self-esteem and lack spontaneity and confidence (Coopersmith, 1967; Lamborn et al., 1991; Lempers, Clark-Lempers, and Simons, 1989). Furthermore, MacDonald and Parke (1984) found that boys perceived by teachers as socially withdrawn, hesitant, and as spectators in the company of peers tend to have fathers who are highly directive and less engaging and physically playful in their interactions with their sons. Their mothers were described as being less likely than mothers of nonwithdrawn sons to engage them in verbal exchange and interaction. The findings were less clear-cut for socially withdrawn daughters. In general, however, the parents of socially withdrawn children are less spontaneous, playful, and affectively positive than are parents of more sociable children.

Children's social timidity, withdrawal, and adult dependency are associated with parental *overprotection* (Eisenberg, 1958; Kagan and Moss, 1962; Martin, 1975; Parker, 1983), a practice that is conceptually related to the constructs of power assertion and intrusion. Overprotective parents tend to restrict their child's behavior and actively encourage dependency. For instance, overprotective parents encourage their children to maintain close proximity to them, and they do not reinforce risk taking and active exploration in unfamiliar situations. Parents of socially wary or fearful children may sense their children's difficulties and perceived helplessness, and then might try to support their children directly either by manipulating their children's behaviors in a power-assertive, highly directive fashion (e.g., telling the children how to act or what to do) or by actually intervening and taking over for the children (e.g., inviting a potential playmate to the home; intervening during peer or object disputes).

Parental influence and control can maintain and exacerbate child inhibition and social withdrawal. For example, Rubin, Hastings, Stewart, Henderson, and Chen (1997) observed toddlers interacting with unfamiliar peers and adults in a variety of novel situations in a laboratory; they found that the toddlers who were the most inhibited across contexts were rated by their mothers as being of wary or shy temperament. Furthermore, these mothers were observed to display overly solicitous behaviors (i.e., intrusively controlling, unresponsive, physically affectionate) during free-play, snack-time, and clean-up sessions. When interacting with their inhibited toddlers, then, mothers were highly affectionate and shielding of them when it was neither appropriate nor sensitive to be this way.

In a follow-up of these children and their mothers, Rubin, Burgess, and Hastings (in press) found that child behavioral inhibition at age 2 years predicted socially reticent behavior during the preschool years; however, the data also indicated that, for toddlers whose mothers were highly intrusive, inhibited behavior amongst peers significantly predicted subsequent reticence as well as problems of an internalizing nature (e.g., anxiety, withdrawal). For toddlers whose mothers were *not* intrusively controlling, the relation between toddler inhibition and preschool internalizing problems was nonsignificant.

In a related study, Henderson and Rubin (1997) explored whether emotion-regulatory processes, as measured physiologically, interacted with parental behavior to predict preschoolers' socially reticent behavior among peers. These researchers began with the premise that vagal tone, a marker of the tonic level of functioning of the parasympathetic nervous system, should be associated with the display of social behavior in the peer group. Children with low vagal tone, at the age of 2 years, have been found to be more inhibited in the presence of an adult stranger and more reticent among peers at the age of 4 years. Having examined a possible connection among child physiology, child behaviors, and particular parenting styles, Henderson and Rubin (1997) reported that for preschoolers who showed low resting vagal tone, observed *and* reported maternal directive and critical behaviors were associated with a child's reticent, wary, and anxious behaviors among peers. For children with high resting vagal tone, such maternal direction and criticism were not associated with behavioral reticence.

Park, Belsky, Putnam, and Crnic (1997) conducted naturalistic home observations of parents with their male infants and toddlers, and later assessed boys' inhibition at the age of 3. They found that the parents of inhibited boys were high on sensitivity and positive affect but low on intrusiveness; moreover, parents were actually accepting of their child's inhibition or trouble coping with anxiety. It is difficult to compare these findings with those of the study by Rubin et al. (1997), except to offer a few possible explanations. A high amount of affection under certain conditions could reinforce fearful, wary behavior, especially if provided during situations in which the demonstration of warmth is inappropriate. The contradictory finding of Park et al. (1997) that parents were *not* intrusive could be explained in light of three factors. First, parenting behaviors were assessed before the observation of child inhibition as opposed to concurrently; this may suggest that parents of inhibited children are actually not overcontrolling in the earliest stage of development, and it is only when they recognize their child's wariness or fearfulness (or it becomes more obvious as their child approaches the toddler and the preschool years) that they try to "fix" or change it. Second, Park et al. assessed parents' behaviors in a natural setting with familiar people (i.e., home environment), whereas Rubin et al. assessed parent–child interactions in an unfamiliar laboratory setting with unfamiliar people. Third, Park et al. did not analyze whether parents behaved differently under free play versus demand situations.

Exploring parental behaviors with respect to the related construct of *social reticence*, Rubin, Cheah, and Fox (2001) reported that mothers whose preschoolers frequently displayed reticent behavior among unfamiliar peers were more likely than mothers whose children rarely displayed social reticence to use highly controlling behaviors and statements during a mother–child free-play session. This finding strengthens the contention that children who tend to avoid social interaction have mothers who provide guidance and directives in an otherwise pleasant situation. Directiveness during goal-oriented tasks may be expected of parents (e.g., Kuczynski and Kochanska, 1995), but controlling the child's behavior in a nonstressful free-play environment is unnecessary; at the very least, such maternal behavior precludes the child from freely exploring the environment. The use of a highly directive parenting style during free play could suggest that the parent attempts to protect the child from stress or harm when neither is objectively present.

In a follow-up of this group of children at the age of 7 years, Cheah, Rubin, and Fox (1999) explored the influence of parenting and temperament of preschool-age children on the display of social solitude in middle childhood. Consistent with earlier research on the stability of socially withdrawn behavior, reticence in 4-year-old children significantly predicted reticent, socially anxious behaviors in 7-year-old children. Furthermore, mothers' displays of highly controlling and oversolicitous behaviors during a free-play session with 4-year-old children uniquely predicted behavioral reticence in children at the age of 7 years over and above the initial level of reticence when the children were 4 years old. Again, it appears that reticent children's mothers who are overcontrolling and overinvolved (when it is unnecessary) exacerbate child reticence. Notably, this study revealed that such parenting behaviors make a contribution to reticence that is beyond the contribution of child temperament.

Another way in which parents of socially wary and withdrawn children vary from those of socially competent children is the extent to which affective interchanges are contingently responsive as well as psychologically derisive. LaFreniere and Dumas (1992) found that mothers of anxious–withdrawn children (aged $2\frac{1}{2}$ to 6 years) did not respond contingently to their children's displays of positive behavior and affect, but they did respond aversively to their child's negative behavior and negative affect. Among older, school-aged children, Mills and Rubin (1998) observed that, relative to mothers of normal children, mothers of extremely anxious–withdrawn children (aged 5 to 9 years) directed significantly more behavior control statements to their children. Furthermore, mothers of anxious–withdrawn children used more psychological control statements, defined as devaluation statements or nonresponsiveness to the child.

Taken together, the extant data concerning the parenting behaviors and styles associated with social withdrawal focus clearly on at least two potential socialization contributors—psychological and behavioral control and overprotection. Parents who use high power-assertive strategies and who place many constraints on their children tend to rear shy, dependent children. Thus the issuance of parental commands combined with constraints on exploration and independence may hinder the development of children's competence in the social milieu. Restrictive control might also deprive the child of opportunities to interact with peers.

Importantly, parental overcontrol may be a *response* to children's early displays of behavioral inhibition. Parents may sense their children's anxiety or distress and choose to constrain independent action rather than subject their children to possible psychological or physical risk. That this may be the case has been supported by research in which mothers' and fathers' perceptions of toddler inhibition predicted subsequent beliefs in *not* encouraging child independence two years hence (Rubin et al., 1999).

The findings previously described, however, stem from relatively few databases. Again, this may be the result of the putative understanding that socially wary and withdrawn behavior is mainly a function of biological factors. We hope that our review of the parenting cognitions and practices associated with, and predictive of, socially reticent and withdrawn behavior will encourage researchers to further explore the ways in which parenting matters.

## FACTORS INFLUENCING THE PARENTS OF AGGRESSIVE AND WITHDRAWN CHILDREN

It has long been argued that the development of maladaptive social behavior derives principally from the quality of children's relationships with their parents and from experience with particular parenting practices such as rejection, neglect, overprotection, and/or the inappropriate and incompetent use of harsh disciplinary techniques. Despite these traditional perspectives, it is the case that researchers are now able to demonstrate that parental affect, cognition, and behavior may be a function of *child* characteristics (Bell and Chapman, 1986; Lytton, 1990; Putnam, Sanson, and Rothbart, in Vol. 1 of this *Handbook*; Rubin et al., 1999). That is, parents respond differently to children who are dispositionally easy, wary, or difficult (or are *perceived* by parents to have a particular disposition). Furthermore, researchers have reached the conclusion that parenting emotions, cognitions, and behaviors must be examined within a broad context of background variables, including family resources, positive and negative life experiences, the quality of the spousal relationship (if one exists), and the availability of social support for parents (e.g., Belsky, 1984; Cochran and Niego, in Vol. 4 of this *Handbook*; Grych, in Vol. 4 of this *Handbook*; Minuchin, 1985). In the subsections that follow, we describe these contextual influences on parents and children, keeping in mind child outcomes of social competence, aggression, and social withdrawal.

### Stress, Parenting, and Child Behavior

In recent years, researchers have attempted to understand how the experience of stress, the availability of social and emotional support, and parental psychopathology interact and conspire to influence parenting behaviors known to predict child maladjustment (Belsky, 1984; Conger et al., 1992, 1993; Patterson et al., 1991). For example, *economic stress* that is due to lack of financial resources makes scarce the availability of necessary goods. It also creates feelings of frustration, anger, and helplessness that can be translated into less than optimal childrearing styles (Magnuson and Duncan, in Vol. 4 of this *Handbook*). Stressful economic situations predict parental negativism and inconsistency (Elder, Van Nguyen, and Caspi, 1985; Lempers et al., 1989; Weiss et al., 1992). Thus parents who are financially distressed generally tend to be more irritable and moody than parents who have few financial difficulties (Ackerman, Izard, Schoff, Youngstrom, and Kogos, 1999). They are less nurturant, involved, child centered, and consistent with their children (Conger, McCarty, Young, Lahey, and Kropp, 1984; Elder et al., 1985; Patterson, 1983, 1986). Relatedly, parents of lower SES tend to have a more authoritarian, punitive, disapproving, and controlling style than do higher-SES parents (Hart and Risley, 1995; Kelley, Sanchez-Hucies, and Walker, 1993). As previously noted, these latter parenting behaviors are associated with the development and display of maladaptive child behaviors. Thus it should not be surprising that a positive association has also been reported between economic stress and children's affectively underregulated, aggressive behavior (e.g., Bolger, Patterson, Thompson, and Kupersmidt, 1995; Dooley and Catalano, 1988; Weiss et al., 1992; Windle, 1992). These results mirror those reported earlier for those children whose families experienced the Great Depression (Elder, 1974; Elder et al., 1985).

*Interspousal conflict* or marital discord is another stressor that predicts parenting behaviors associated with child maladjustment (Wilson and Gottman, in Vol. 4 of this *Handbook*). Researchers have reported consistently that spousal discord and marital dissatisfaction predict negative parental attitudes about childrearing as well as insensitive, unresponsive parenting behaviors (Emery, 1982; Jouriles et al., 1991). As previously outlined, these parenting cognitions and behaviors are associated with both aggression and withdrawal in childhood. Spousal hostility can also affect children directly by providing them with models of aggressive behavior; indeed, children observe or witness the marital conflict. Thus it is not surprising to find that child aggression is predicted by spousal conflict (Cummings and Davies, 1994; Dadds and Powell, 1991; Emery, 1982; Jouriles et al., 1991; Katz and Gottman, 1993). It is important to note, however, that marital conflict is more predictive of child aggression in boys than in girls (Block, Block, and Morrison, 1981).

Yet another family-based stressor is *parental psychopathology* (Campbell, 1995; Zahn-Waxler, Duggal, and Gruber, in Vol. 4 of this *Handbook*). For example, maternal depression is associated with a lack of parental involvement, responsivity, spontaneity, and emotional support in childrearing (Downey and Coyne, 1990; Kochanska, Kuczynski, and Maguire, 1989; Zahn-Waxler et al., 1988). Given that depression is associated with maternal feelings of hopelessness and helplessness (Gurland, Yorkston, Frank, and Stone, 1967), the pattern of parenting behaviors previously noted is not surprising. Furthermore, families with one or two depressed parents are found to be less cohesive and emotionally expressive than families in which the parents are psychologically well (Billings and Moos, 1985).

Given the findings previously reported, it should not be surprising that parental depression is associated with social inhibition, wariness, and withdrawal in young children (Kochanska, 1991; Rubin, Both, Zahn-Waxler, Cummings, and Wilkinson, 1991; Welner, Welner, McCrary, and Leonard, 1977). Moreover, given that social withdrawal is viewed as reflecting psychological problems of an internalizing nature, it is likewise unsurprising that parental depression is associated with, and predictive of, depression and anxiety during childhood (McKnew, Cytryn, Efron, Gershon, and Bunney, 1979).

Parental depression, however, is not only associated with parental uninvolvement and withdrawal from childrearing responsibilities. When depressed parents attempt to gain some element of control in their lives, they may resort to highly authoritarian patterns of childrearing (e.g., Gelfand and Teti, 1990; Hammen, 1988; Kochanska and Radke-Yarrow, 1992). This mix of parental uninvolvement and overinvolvement is likely responsible for reports that parental depression is associated not only with social withdrawal in children, but with aggression as well (e.g., see Downey and Coyne, 1990, for a review; Webster-Stratton and Hammond, 1988). How it is that some children of depressed parents develop behavioral patterns of social withdrawal and wariness whereas others become aggressive is not known.

Finally, it is important to note that the effects of stress on parenting behaviors can be moderated, or buffered, by the availability of *social support* (Cochran and Niego, in Vol. 4 of this *Handbook*; Cohen and Wills, 1985). For example, in a study by Jennings, Staff, and Conners (1991), a group of mothers was interviewed extensively about their social networks; also they were observed during a play session with their children. Mothers who were more satisfied with their personal social support networks were more likely to praise their children and less likely to intrusively control them. Social support systems and good marital relationships also serve as protective factors in parenting behavior (Cohen and Wills, 1985; Rutter, 1990). For example, Rutter and Quinton (1984) found that institution-reared women who had supportive spouses were more competent parents than those who had the same childhood experiences but lacked spousal support. It has been argued that supportive social networks may be sources of emotional strength and of information that enhance feelings of competence in coping with stresses, including those concerned with parenting.

## Parenting: A Mediator and Moderator of Family Stress and Resources

Parenting behavior has been conceived as both mediating and moderating the direct effects of stress on the child. *Mediated* (indirect) effects are demonstrated when parenting behavior accounts for the relation between the predictor (e.g., family stress) and the criterion (child adjustment) (see Baron and Kenny, 1986). In most conceptually driven models pertaining to the development of aggression and withdrawal, therefore, variables such as stress and support are viewed as *distal* influences on child behavior. These distal variables are seen as influencing parental beliefs and behavior (Mills and Rubin, 1990), the more proximal influences on child outcomes. To this end, parental behavior has been considered a factor that mediates between distal ecological variables and children's adaptive and maladaptive behaviors (Belsky, 1984).

Parenting behavior as a *moderator* would affect the strength or direction of the relation between family stress and child adjustment (see Baron and Kenny, 1986). One could take as an example supportive versus nonsupportive parenting. As a moderator, one might expect the relation between stress and child behavior to be significant only for those children whose parents are unsupportive.

Recent advances in statistical technology have allowed the examination of the mediator role of parental behaviors and beliefs. For example, a typical procedure in hierarchical regression analysis is to enter first into the equation a given parenting variable (or variables), and then subsequently to enter the conceptually distal, ecological "influences" in the prediction of some child outcome. The significantly reduced power of ecological variables in predicting child behavior after partialing parenting variables allows the implication that parenting behavior plays a mediator role. Path analysis and structural equation modeling also have been applied to obtain a more complete description of the relations among family stresses, resources, parenting, and child behavior (e.g., Conger et al., 1992, 1993). For example, Lempers et al. (1989) found that economic hardship had a significant and negative direct effect on parental nurturance and a positive direct effect on inconsistent discipline. In turn, parental nurturance had a negative direct effect on children's depression and loneliness; inconsistent parenting had a positive direct effect on children's depression–loneliness and delinquency. Finally, economic stress had a positive indirect effect on depression–loneliness and delinquency through the mediation of parenting practices. Conger et al. (1992, 1993) examined relations among economic stress, parental depression, marital conflict, parenting, and adolescent adjustment. Economic stress had a positive direct effect on parental depression; in turn, depression had a negative direct effect on parental nurturance and involvement. Finally, parental nurturance and involvement were found to contribute positively to the prediction of adolescent adjustment and negatively to adolescent maladjustment (antisocial behavior and depression).

Parents can also "buffer" their children from stressful life circumstances. The notion of moderation derives from findings that not all children who are exposed to stress or risk factors exhibit problems associated with abnormal development; some protective factors moderate the negative effects of the risk factors. Simply put, "good parenting" serves the function of protecting the child from the negative influences associated with such factors as family stress (Masten, Morison, Pellegrini, and Tellegen, 1990; Rutter, 1990), or even difficult or inhibited temperament (Rubin et al., 1997; Rubin, Hastings et al., 1998). For example, Masten et al. (1990) found that children who experienced many stressful life events but who had family support and nurturance tended to be less aggressive and disruptive and less disengaged in social situations than those who experienced stress but did not have supportive parents. Last, Rubin, Hastings et al. (1998) found that toddlers with difficult temperament whose mothers were authoritarian in their parenting practices were more aggressive than their difficult agemates whose mothers did not demonstrate authoritarian patterns of parenting.

Thus the extant research suggests that children's interactions and relationships with parents have important implications and ramifications for their psychological and social functioning. Although various theoretical rationales have been proffered for the connection between the parent–child relationship and child outcomes, there generally tends to be agreement about the kinds of relationship and parenting style that are beneficial to children. On the one hand, parent–child relationships that feature warmth, support, emotional security, and responsiveness are associated with positive outcomes. On the other hand, parent–child relationships that are characterized by low warmth, low responsiveness, and overcontrol or undercontrol are associated with poor psychological–behavioral outcomes for children, including aggression and withdrawal.

## FUTURE DIRECTIONS IN THE STUDY OF AGGRESSIVE
## AND SOCIALLY WITHDRAWN CHILDREN

In this chapter we have attempted to describe the family as a complex system that is influenced not only by its constituent members, but also by external, socioecological forces. Interactions between family members are bidirectional and mutually influential (Cowan, Powell, and Cowan, 1998). This conceptualization of the family as a *transactional system* represents an evocative starting point for future studies of the development of childhood aggression and social withdrawal.

What we know about the *parents* of aggressive and withdrawn children fails to capture some of the very simplest tenets of a transactional model of family systems. For instance, it is safe to conclude that virtually nothing is known about *paternal* contributions to problems of psychological undercontrol and overcontrol in children. Although we indicated that an association exists between the quality of the parent–infant or parent–child attachment relationship and the later expression of competent and incompetent social behavior in childhood, the *relative* contributions of the quality of father–son versus father–daughter attachment relationships and mother–son versus mother–daughter attachment relationships to the prediction of internalizing and externalizing behavior problems in boys and girls is unknown. Also unknown are the relative contributions of paternal versus maternal beliefs and parenting behaviors to the prediction of internalizing and externalizing forms of behavior in boys and girls. In short, a plethora of questions remains to be addressed vis-à-vis father/mother–son/daughter relationships and interactive patterns in order for us to understand the etiology of behavioral maladjustment in children.

Another relative unknown is the degree to which parents can influence the development, maintenance, and amelioration of child behavior problems at different points in the span of childhood. Are parents better able to influence child behavior during the early rather than middle to late years of childhood? Parents believe they are more influential in contributing to social developmental outcomes during early than during late childhood (e.g., Mills and Rubin, 1992). Moreover, with increasing child age, parents increasingly attribute child maladjustment to internal, dispositional characteristics of the child (Mills and Rubin, 1993a). These data hint at the possibility that parents think about and interact with their children in different ways at different points in childhood (see also Rubin et al., 1996). A catalogue of beliefs and behaviors within and across situations (e.g., at home or in public; free play or structured activities) for parents of socially competent, aggressive, and withdrawn children during the early, middle, and later years of childhood would be invaluable. This "mapping" within- and across-group, cross-age parental characteristics should be on the agenda of those interested in the developmental course of maladaptive behavior and its prevention or intervention.

We have described the results of many studies, almost all of which were completed in North America and Western Europe. The fact is that we do not know whether the characteristics of the parents of competent, aggressive, and withdrawn children vary from culture to culture or whether the etiologies of behavioral disorders are identical from one culture to another. In fact, we do not even know whether behaviors viewed as abnormal in Western cultures are similarly evaluated in other cultures! One relevant example of these latter issues stems from the research of Chen and colleagues in China. In a series of studies, they reported that aggression, not shyness or withdrawal, is evaluated negatively by peers and teachers. These findings are consistent from the toddler period through the beginning of high school (Chen et al., 1998; Chen, Rubin, and Li, 1995; Chen, Rubin, Li, and Li, 1999; Chen, Rubin, and Sun, 1992). Furthermore, parents of aggressive Chinese children have been found to lack warmth and be authoritarian, just as in Western samples; but parents of withdrawn children were not different behaviorally from parents of socially competent children (Chen, Dong, and Zhou, 1997; Chen and Rubin, 1994; Chen, Rubin, and Li, 1997).

As a counterpoint, in some cultures indices of aggression may be perceived as positive and more valued than in Eastern and Western cultures. For instance, investigators in Sicily reported that peers associated children's aggression with social leadership and sociability (Casiglia, Lo Coco, and Zappulla, 1998). These studies and others like it (Farver, Kim, and Lee, 1995; Schneider et al., 1997; Weisz et al., 1988) raise a large question mark vis-à-vis the universality and generalizability of the findings we have reported herein. Researchers would do well to be aware that cultural values play an enormous role in determining the "meanings" of behavioral adaptation and normalcy; and within cultures parental beliefs and behaviors are likely to be associated with child outcomes in meaningful ways. We face the task of determining the meanings of normalcy and maladaptation in the context of culture.

Last, there are many different forms of aggression and solitude. For example, researchers have described constructs such as proactive versus reactive aggression, direct–hostile versus indirect–relational aggression, and instrumental aggression (see Coie and Dodge, 1998, for a review). Researchers also have described forms of solitude, each of which carries different psychological meanings (e.g., reticence, passive withdrawal; Coplan, Rubin, Fox, Calkins, and Stewart, 1994). Researchers have rarely distinguished among these different forms of aggression and withdrawal in their studies of parenting and parent–child relationships. This lack of research presents a wealth of opportunity to discover the characteristics of the parents of different types of aggressive and withdrawn children.

In summary, many questions remain to be addressed in future studies of the parents of aggressive and socially withdrawn children. We have provided some initial "leads" concerning where we think the immediate research action should be.

## CONCLUSIONS

Although is not easy being a parent, we have attempted to demonstrate that being the child of an insensitive, unresponsive parent is more difficult. Psychologically undercontrolled and overcontrolled behavior problems in childhood derive from a complex mix of ecological factors, child characteristics, parent–child relationships, and parental beliefs and behaviors. In our concluding commentary, we attempt to put the pieces of the developmental puzzle together by suggesting two conceptually based pathways that may serve as models for the future study of the relations among parent–child relationships, parenting, and the development of aggression and withdrawal in childhood.

### A Developmental Pathway to Aggression in Childhood

We begin by positing that babies who are viewed by their parents as difficult and overactive *and* who are born into less than desirable situations may be at risk for the receipt of less than optimal care. Temperamentally difficult infants tend to have mothers who are more aggressive, less nurturant, more anxious, and less responsive than mothers of nondifficult babies (Egeland and Farber, 1984; Spieker and Booth, 1988). Ecological conditions may be critical mediating factors; for example, Crockenberg (1981) reported that mothers of temperamentally difficult babies who have social and financial support are less negative in their interactions with their infants than are "high-risk" mothers. Thus, for some families, the *interaction* between infant dispositional characteristics and stressful setting conditions may promote parental socialization practices that produce qualitatively poor early parent–child relationships that can be characterized as *insecure*, and perhaps hostile, in nature (Engfer, 1986).

As noted earlier, an insecure attachment relationship has been thought to conjure up, in children, an internal working model of a comfortless and unpredictable social universe. These cognitive representations may lead some insecurely attached children to behave in the peer group "by . . . doing battle with it" (Bowlby, 1973, p. 208). Indeed, there is a group of babies who, having established insecure attachment relationships with their primary caregivers by 12 or 18 months of age, direct hostility, anger, and aggression toward their peers during the preschool years (Sroufe, 1983). Once expressed in a relatively consistent manner, aggression is an unforgiving and highly salient, determining cause of peer rejection from early childhood (Rubin, Bukowski, and Parker, 1998). Thus it follows logically (and, indeed, empirically) that children who are rejected by their peers because of their proactive hostility may soon become precluded from the sorts of activities that supposedly aid in the development of social skills—peer interaction, negotiation, and discussion. Furthermore, aggressive children are unlikely to trust their peers; for example, it has been shown that aggressive children usually believe that others intentionally cause negative social experiences (Dodge and Frame, 1982). This mistrust and misattribution of others' intentions suggest that the aggressive child's peer relationships can be characterized as hostile and insecure.

Given the salience of externalizing behaviors, it is not surprising that children's peers and teachers tend to agree about who can be characterized as hostile and aggressive (e.g., Hymel et al., 1990; Ledingham, Younger, Schwartzman, and Bergeron, 1982). Moreover, given that aggression is highly disruptive when produced on school grounds and during school time, it is not surprising that teachers often request meetings with the parents of aggressive perpetrators. These school-based external appraisals are certainly discomforting to parents, especially those parents who have not enjoyed a secure and pleasant relationship with their child or those who have experienced a good deal of stress. One may posit at least two possible outcomes from such school-based teacher–parent "confrontations": (1) Parents may attribute their child's maladaptive behavior to dispositional or biological factors, thereby absolving themselves of the responsibility of dealing with aggressive displays. This type of attribution bias may lead to parental feelings of helplessness in the face of child aggression and thus predict a permissive or laissez-faire response to aggressive behavior; (2) Parents may attribute their child's behaviors to external causes and utilize overly harsh, power-assertive techniques in response to their children's maladaptive behavior. Both the neglect of aggression and the harsh treatment of it, especially in an environment lacking warmth, are likely to create even more problems for children, for parents, and for their relationships (Patterson and Fisher, in Vol. 5 of this *Handbook*).

In summary, social incompetence of an externalizing nature may be the product of difficult temperament, of insecure parent–child relationships, of authoritarian or laissez-faire parenting, of family stress, and most likely of the joint interactions among "all of the above." It is extremely important to note that, despite beginning this first pathway with a description of temperamentally difficult infants, many such children do *not* develop insecure attachment relationships and do *not* behave in an abnormally aggressive fashion during the preschool and elementary school years. Indeed, in most studies of predictive relations between infant difficult temperament and the subsequent development of attachment relationships, no clear predictive picture emerges (e.g., Bates, Bayles, Bennett, Ridge, and Brown, 1991; Putnam, Sanson, and Rothbart, in Vol. 1 of this *Handbook*). Thus it may be posited that skilled parenting, under conditions of limited stress and optimal support, can buffer the effects of potentially negative biology. Basically, this is the classic argument of "goodness of fit" between parental characteristics and infant dispositional characteristics originally offered by Thomas and Chess (1977).

## A Developmental Pathway to Social Withdrawal in Childhood

This pathway begins with newborns who may be biologically predisposed to have a low threshold for arousal when confronted with social (or nonsocial) stimulation and novelty. Studies of temperamental inhibition show that, under conditions of novelty or uncertainty, some babies demonstrate physical and physiological changes that suggest that they are "hyperarousable" (e.g., Fox and Calkins, 1993; Kagan et al., 1987)—a characteristic that may make them extremely difficult to soothe and comfort. Indeed, some parents find infantile hyperarousability aversive and/or worrisome (Kagan, Reznick, Clarke, Snidman, and Garcia-Coll, 1984); consequently, under some circumstances, parents may react to easily aroused and wary babies with insensitivity, a lack of responsivity, or perhaps overprotectiveness. Each of these parental variables also predicts the development of insecure parent–infant attachment relationships and they can be significantly accounted for by environmental and personal stressors. Thus, as with the first pathway, an interplay of endogenous, socialization, and early relationship factors, as they coexist under the "umbrella" of negative setting conditions, will lead to a sense of felt insecurity. In this way, the internal working models of insecurely attached, temperamentally inhibited children may lead them to "shrink from" rather than "do battle with" (Bowlby, 1973, p. 208) their social milieu.

Children who are socially inhibited and who do shrink anxiously away from their peers preclude themselves from the positive outcomes associated with social exploration and peer play. Thus one can predict a developmental sequence in which an inhibited, fearful, insecure child withdraws from the social world of peers, fails to develop those skills derived from peer interaction and, therefore becomes increasingly anxious and isolated from the peer group. With age, social reticence or withdrawal becomes increasingly salient to the peer group (Younger and Boyko, 1987; Younger, Schwartzman, and Ledingham, 1986). This deviation from age-appropriate social norms is associated with the establishment of negative peer reputations. Thus, by the middle to late years of childhood, social withdrawal and anxiety are as strongly correlated with peer rejection and unpopularity as aggression is (see Rubin, Bukowski, and Parker, 1998, for a review).

Unlike their aggressive counterparts, however, anxiously withdrawn children rarely get into trouble by "acting out" at home or school. Given their reticence to explore their environments, these children may demonstrate difficulties in getting social "jobs" done or social problems ameliorated. Sensing the child's difficulties and perceived helplessness, parents may try to aid them very directly by either manipulating their child's social behaviors in a power assertive, highly directive fashion or by actually intervening and carrying out the child's social interchanges themselves. Such overcontrolling, overinvolved socialization strategies have long been associated with social withdrawal in childhood (e.g., Brunk and Henggeler, 1984; Hetherington and Martin, 1986). Parental overdirection is likely to maintain rather than ameliorate postulated problems associated with social inhibition. Being overly directive will not help the child deal firsthand with social interchanges and dilemmas: It probably prevents the development of a belief system of social self-efficacy, and it likely perpetuates feelings of insecurity within and outside of the family.

In summary, social incompetence of an overcontrolled nature may be the product of inhibited temperament, of insecure parent–child relationships, of overly directive, overprotective parenting, of family stress, and most likely of the joint interactions among all of the above. A fearful, wary inhibited temperament may be "deflected" in a pathway toward the development of social competence by responsive and sensitive caregiving and by a low-stress environment. Similarly, inhibited temperament is unnecessary for the development of an internalizing behavior pattern. Parental overcontrol and overinvolvement, especially when accompanied by familial stress and lack of social support, are hypothesized to deflect the temperamentally easygoing infant to a pathway of internalizing difficulties.

The pathways just described represent useful heuristics for studying the etiology of aggression and social withdrawal in childhood. They are also suggestive of the indirect and direct ways that parents may contribute to the development and the maintenance of these phenomena. However, they should certainly not be taken as the only routes to the development of overcontrolled and undercontrolled psychological disorders in childhood. It is also important to note that in other cultures each developmental pathway with its connections between aggressive or withdrawn behavior and parenting, and potential outcomes, might "look" quite different. Thus we welcome the research community's support in providing alternative and international perspectives, as well as empirically derived information at an international level, concerning the relations among parent–child relationships, parenting cognitions and behaviors, and the ontogeny of childhood aggression and social withdrawal.

## REFERENCES

Ackerman, B., Izard, C., Schoff, K., Youngstrom, E., and Kogos, J. (1999). Contextual risk, caregiver emotionality, and the problem behaviors of six- and seven-year-old children from economically disadvantaged families. *Child Development, 70,* 1415–1427.

Adalbjarnardottir, S. (1995). How schoolchildren propose to negotiate: The role of social withdrawal, social anxiety, and locus of control. *Child Development, 66,* 1739–1751.

Ainsworth, M. D. S. (1973). The development of infant–mother attachment. In B. Caldwell and H. Ricciuti (Eds.), *Review of child development research* (Vol. 3, pp. 1–94). Chicago: University of Chicago Press.

Ainsworth, M., Blehar, M., Waters, E., and Wall, S. (1978). *Patterns of attachment*. Hillsdale, NJ: Lawrence Erlbaum Associates.

Asendorpf, J. B. (1993). Beyond temperament: A two-factorial coping model of the development of inhibition during childhood. In K. H. Rubin and J. B. Asendorpf (Eds.), *Social withdrawal, inhibition and shyness in childhood* (pp. 265–289). Hillsdale, NJ: Lawrence Erlbaum Associates.

Bacon, M. K., and Ashmore, R. D. (1985). How mothers and fathers categorize descriptions of social behavior attributed to daughters and sons. *Social Cognition, 3*, 193–217.

Baden, A. D., and Howe, G. W. (1992). Mothers' attributions and expectancies regarding their conduct-disordered children. *Journal of Abnormal Child Psychology, 20*, 467–485.

Bandura, A. (1977). *Social learning theory*. Englewood Cliffs, NJ: Prentice-Hall.

Baron, R. M., and Kenny, D. A. (1986). The moderator–mediator variable distinction in social psychological research: Conceptual, strategic, and statistical considerations. *Journal of Personality and Social Psychology, 51*, 1173–1182.

Bates, J. E., Bayles, K., Bennett, D. S., Ridge, B., and Brown, M. (1991). Origins of externalizing behavior problems at eight years of age. In D. J. Pepler and K. H. Rubin (Eds.), *The development and treatment of childhood aggression*. Hillsdale, NJ: Lawrence Erlbaum Associates.

Bates, J. E., Maslin, C. A., and Frankel, K. A. (1985). Attachment security, mother–child interaction, and temperament as predictors of behavior-problem ratings at three years. In I. Bretherton and E. Waters (Eds.), Growing points of attachment theory and research. *Monographs of the Society for Research in Child Development, 59* (No's. 2 & 3, Serial No. 244, pp. 167–193).

Baumrind, D. (1967). Child care practices anteceding three patterns of preschool behavior. *Genetic Psychology Monographs, 76*, 43–88.

Baumrind, D. (1971). Current patterns of parental authority. *Developmental Psychology Monographs, 4*.

Bell, R. Q., and Chapman, M. (1986). Child effects in studies using experimental or brief longitudinal approaches to socialization. *Developmental Psychology, 22*, 595–603.

Belsky, J. (1984). The determinants of parenting: A process model. *Child Development, 55*, 83–96.

Bierman, K. L., and Wargo, J. B. (1995). Predicting the longitudinal course associated with aggressive-rejected, aggressive (nonrejected), and rejected (nonaggressive) status. *Development and Psychopathology, 7*, 669–682.

Billings, A. G., and Moos, R. H. (1985). Children of parents with unipolar depression: A controlled 1 year follow-up. *Journal of Abnormal Child Psychology, 14*, 149–166.

Block, J. H., Block, J., and Morrison, A. (1981). Parental agreement–disagreement on child-personality correlates in children. *Child Development, 52*, 965–974.

Boivin, M., and Hymel, S. (1997). Peer experiences and social self-perceptions: A sequential model. *Developmental Psychology, 33*, 135–145.

Boivin, M., Hymel, S., and Bukowski, W. M. (1995). The roles of social withdrawal, peer rejection, and victimization by peers in predicting loneliness and depressed mood in childhood. *Development and Psychopathology, 7*, 765–785.

Bolger, K., Patterson, C., Thompson, W., and Kupersmidt, J. (1995). Psychosocial adjustment among children experiencing persistent and intermittent family economic hardship. *Child Development, 66*, 1107–1129.

Bowlby, J. (1969). *Attachment and loss: Vol. 1. Attachment*. New York: Basic Books.

Bowlby, J. (1973). *Attachment and loss: Separation, anxiety, and anger*. New York: Basic Books.

Bowlby, J. (1980). *Attachment and loss: Vol. 2. Loss*. New York: Basic Books.

Brunk, M. A., and Henggeler, S. W. (1984). Child influences on adult controls: An experimental investigation. *Developmental Psychology, 20*, 1074–1081.

Bugental, D. B. (1992). Affective and cognitive processes within threat-oriented family systems. In I. E. Sigel, A. V. McGillicuddy-DeLisi, and J. J. Goodnow (Eds.), *Parental belief systems: The psychological consequences for children* (pp. 219–248). Hillsdale, NJ: Lawrence Erlbaum Associates.

Bugental, D. B., and Cortez, V. (1988). Physiological reactivity to responsive and unresponsive children—as modified by perceived control. *Child Development, 59*, 686–693.

Bugental, D. B., and Shennun, W. A. (1984). "Difficult" children as elicitors and targets of adult communication patterns: An attributional–behavioral transactional analysis. *Monographs of the Society for Research in Child Development, 49* (1, Serial No. 205).

Burgess, K. B., Rubin, K. H., Cheah, C., and Nelson, L. J. (in press). Behavioral inhibition, social withdrawal, and parenting. In R. Crozier and L. Alden (Eds.), *International Handbook of social anxiety: Concepts, research, and interventions relating to the self and shyness*. Sussex, England: Wiley.

Byrne, R. (1988). *1,911 best things anybody ever said*. New York: Ballantine Books.

Campbell, S. B. (1995). Behavior problems in preschool children: A review of recent research. *Journal of Child Psychology and Psychiatry and Allied Disciplines, 36*, 113–149.

Campbell, S. B., Pierce, E. W., Moore, G., Markovitz, S., and Newby, K. (1996). Boys' externalizing problems at elementary school age: Pathways from early behavior problems, maternal control, and family stress. *Development and Psychopathology, 8*, 701–719.

Case, D. (1991). *The mind's staircase*. Hillsdale, NJ: Lawrence Erlbaum Associates.

Casiglia, A. C., Lo Coco, A., and Zappulla, C. (1998). Aspects of social reputation and peer relationships in Italian children: A cross-cultural perspective. *Developmental Psychology, 34*, 723–730.

Caspi, A., and Silva, P. A. (1995). Temperamental qualities at age three predict personality traits in young adulthood: Longitudinal evidence from a birth cohort. *Child Development, 66*, 486–498.

Cassidy, J., Kirsh, S. J., Scolton, K. L., and Parke, R. D. (1996). Attachment and representations of peer relationships. *Developmental Psychology, 32*, 892–904.

Cheah, C. S. L., Rubin, K. H., and Fox, N. A. (1999, April). *Predicting reticence at seven years: The influence of temperament and overprotective parenting at four years*. Poster presentation at the biennial meeting of the Society for Research in Child Development, Albuquerque, NM.

Chen, X., Dong, Q., and Zhou, H. (1997). Authoritative and authoritarian parenting practices and social and school adjustment. *International Journal of Behavioural Development, 20*, 855–873.

Chen, X., Hastings, P. D., Rubin, K. H., Chen, H., Cen, G., and Stewart, S. L. (1998). Childrearing practices and behavioral inhibition in Chinese and Canadian toddlers: A cross-cultural study. *Developmental Psychology, 34*, 677–686.

Chen, X., and Rubin, K. H. (1994). Family conditions, parental acceptance, and social competence and aggression in Chinese children. *Social Development, 3*, 269–290.

Chen, X., Rubin, K. H., and Li, B. (1995). Social and school adjustment of shy and aggressive children in China. *Development and Psychopathology, 7*, 337–349.

Chen, X., Rubin, K. H., and Li, D. (1997). Maternal acceptance and social and school adjustment in Chinese children: A longitudinal study. *Merrill-Palmer Quarterly, 53*, 663–681.

Chen, X., Rubin, K. H., Li, D., and Li, Z. (1999). Adolescent outcomes of social functioning in Chinese children. *International Journal of Behavioral Development, 23*, 199–223.

Chen, X., Rubin, K. H., and Sun, Y. (1992). Social reputation and peer relationships in Chinese and Canadian children: A cross-cultural study. *Child Development, 63*, 1336–1343.

Cicchetti, D., and Toth, S. L. (1998). Perspectives on research and practice in developmental psychopathology. In I. E. Sigel and A. E. Renninger (Eds.), *Handbook of child psychology: Vol. 4. Child psychology in practice* (pp. 479–484). New York: Wiley.

Cohen, J. S. (1989). *Maternal involvement in children's peer relationships during middle childhood*. Unpublished doctoral dissertation, University of Waterloo, Waterloo, Ontario, Canada.

Cohen, S., and Wills, T. A. (1985). Stress, social support, and the buffering hypothesis. *Psychological Bulletin, 98*, 310–357.

Cohn, D. A. (1990). Child–mother attachment of six-year-olds and social competence at school. *Child Development, 61*, 152–162.

Coie, J. D., and Dodge, K. A. (1998). Aggression and antisocial behavior. In W. Damon (Series Ed.) and N. Eisenberg (Ed.), *Handbook of child psychology: Vol. 3. Social, emotional, and personality development* (5th ed., pp. 389–462). New York: Wiley.

Coie, J. D., Dodge, K., and Kupersmidt, J. B. (1990). Peer group behavior and social status. In S. R. Asher and J. D. Coie (Eds.), *Peer rejection in childhood*. New York: Cambridge University Press.

Coie, J. D., and Kupersmidt, J. B. (1983). A behavioral analysis of emerging social status in boys' groups. *Child Development, 54*, 1400–1416.

Coie, J. D., Terry, R., Lenox, K., Lochman, J., and Hyman, C. (1995). Childhood peer rejection and aggression as predictors of stable patterns of adolescent disorder. *Development and Psychopathology, 7*, 697–714.

Collins, W. A., Maccoby, E. E., Steinberg, L., Hetherington, E. M., and Bornstein, M. H. (2000). Contemporary research on parenting: The case for nature and nurture. *American Psychologist, 55*, 218–232.

Conger, R. D., Conger, K. J., Elder, G. H., Jr., Lorenz, F., Simons, R., and Whitbeck, L. (1992). A family process model of economic hardship and adjustment of early adolescent boys. *Child Development, 63*, 526–541.

Conger, R. D., Conger, K. J., Elder, G. H., Jr., Lorenz, F., Simons, R., and Whitbeck, L. (1993). Family economic stress and adjustment of early adolescent girls. *Developmental Psychology, 29*, 206–219.

Conger, R. D., McCarty, J. A., Young, R. K., Lahey, B. B., and Kropp, J. P. (1984). Perception of child, childrearing values and emotional distress as mediating links between environmental stressors and observed maternal behavior. *Child Development, 55*, 2234–2247.

Contreras, J. M., Kerns, K. A., Weimer, B. L., Gentzler, A. L., and Tomich, P. L. (2000). Emotion regulation as a mediator of associations between mother–child attachment and peer relationships in middle childhood. *Journal of Family Relationships, 14*, 111–124.

Coopersmith, S. (1967). *The antecedents of self-esteem*. San Francisco: Freeman.

Coplan, R. J., Rubin, K. H., Fox, N. A., Calkins, S. D., and Stewart, S. L. (1994). Being alone, playing alone, and acting alone: Distinguishing among reticence, and passive- and active-solitude in young children. *Child Development, 65*, 129–138.

Covell, K., Grusec, J. E., and King, G. (1995). The intergenerational transmission of maternal discipline and standards for behavior. *Social Development, 4*, 32–43.

Cowan, P. A., Powell, D., and Cowan, C. P. (1998). Parenting interventions: A family systems perspective. In I. E. Sigel and K. A. Renninger (Eds.), *Handbook of Child Psychology: Vol. 4. Child psychology in practice* (5th ed., pp. 3–72). New York: Wiley.

Crick, N. R., and Dodge, K. A. (1994). A review and reformulation of social information-processing mechanisms in children's social adjustment. *Psychological Bulletin, 115*, 74–101.

Crockenberg, S. B. (1981). Infant irritability, mother responsiveness, and social support influences on the security of mother-infant attachment. *Child Development, 52*, 857–865.

Cummings, E. M., and Davies, P. (1994). *Marital conflict.* New York: Guilford.

Dadds, M. R., and Powell, M. B. (1991). The relationship of interparental conflict and global marital adjustment to aggression, anxiety, maturity in aggressive and nonclinic children. *Journal of Abnormal Child Development, 19*, 553–567.

Dadds, M. R., Spence, S. H., Holland, D. E., Barrett, P. M., and Laurens, K. R. (1997). Prevention and early intervention for anxiety disorders: A controlled trial. *Journal of Consulting and Clinical Psychology, 65*, 627–635.

Denham, S. A., Workman, E., Cole, P. M., Weissbrod, C., Kendziora, K. T., and Zahn-Waxler, C. (2000). Prediction of externalizing behavior problems from early to middle childhood: The role of parental socialization and emotion expression. *Development and Psychopathology, 12*, 23–45.

Dishion, T. J. (1990). The family ecology of boys' peer relations in middle childhood. *Child Development, 61*, 874–892.

Dix, T. H. (1991). The affective organization of parenting: Adaptive and maladaptive processes. *Psychological Bulletin, 110*, 3–25.

Dix, T. H., and Grusec, J. E. (1985). Parent attribution processes in the socialization of children. In I. E. Sigel (Ed.), *Parental belief systems: The psychological consequences for children* (pp. 201–233). Hillsdale, NJ: Lawrence Erlbaum Associates.

Dix, T. H., Ruble, D., Grusec, J. E., and Nixon, S. (1986). Social cognition in parents: Inferential and affective reactions to children of three age levels. *Child Development, 57*, 879–894.

Dix, T. H., Ruble, D. N., and Zambarano, R. J. (1989). Mothers' implicit theories of discipline: Child effects and the attribution process. *Child Development, 60*, 1373–1391.

Dodge, K. A., and Frame, C. L. (1982). Social cognitive biases and deficits in aggressive boys. *Child Development, 53*, 620–635.

Dodge, K. A., Pettit, G. A., and Bates, J. E. (1994). Socialization mediators of the relation between socioeconomic status and child conduct problems. *Child Development, 65*, 649–665.

Dollard, J., Doob, L. W., Miller, N. E., Mowrer, O. H., and Sears, R. R. (1939). *Frustration and aggression.* New Haven, CT: Yale University Press.

Dooley, D., and Catalano, R. (1988). Recent research on the psychological effects of unemployment. *Journal of Social Issues, 44*, 1–12.

Downey, G., and Coyne, J. C. (1990). Children of depressed parents: An integrative review. *Psychological Bulletin, 108*, 50–76.

Egeland, B., and Farber, E. A. (1984). Infant–mother attachment: Factors related to its development and changes over time. *Child Development, 55*, 753–771.

Egeland, B., Pianta, R., and O'Brien, M. A. (1993). Maternal intrusiveness in infancy and child maladaptation in early school years. *Development and Psychopathology, 5*, 359–370.

Eisenberg, L. (1958). School phobia: A study in the communication of anxiety. *American Journal of Psychiatry, 114*, 712–718.

Elder, G. H., Jr. (1974). *Children of the Great Depression.* Chicago: University of Chicago Press.

Elder, G. H., Jr., Van Nguyen, T., and Caspi, A. (1985). Linking family hardship to children's lives. *Child Development, 56*, 361–375.

Elicker, J., Englund, M., and Sroufe, L. A. (1992). Predicting peer competence and peer relationships in childhood from early parent–child relationships. In R. Parke and G. Ladd (Eds.), *Family–peer relationships: Model of linkage.* Hillsdale, NJ: Lawrence Erlbaum Associates.

Emery, R. (1982). Interparental conflict and the children of discord and divorce. *Psychological Bulletin, 92*, 310–330.

Engfer, A. (1986). Antecedents of behavior problems in infancy. In G. A. Kohnstamm (Ed.), *Temperament discussed: Temperament and development in infancy and childhood* (pp. 165–180). Lisse, The Netherlands: Swets & Zeitlinger.

Erickson, M. F., Sroufe, L. A., and Egeland, B. (1985). The relationship between quality of attachment and behavior problems in preschool in a high risk sample. In I. Bretherton and E. Waters (Eds.), Growing points of attachment theory and research. *Monographs of the Society for Research in Child Development, 50* (Nos. 1-2, Serial No. 209).

Eron, L. D., Huesmann, L. R., Dubow, E., Romanoff, R., and Yarmel, P. W. (1987). Aggression and its correlates over 22 years. In D. H. Crowell, I. M. Evans, and C. R. O'Donnell (Eds.), *Childhood aggression and violence* (pp. 249–262). New York: Plenum.

Eron, L. D., Huesmann, R., and Zelli, A. (1991). The role of parental variables in the learning of aggression. In D. J. Pepler and K. H. Rubin (Eds.), *The development and treatment of childhood aggression* (pp. 169–188). Hillsdale, NJ: Lawrence Erlbaum Associates.

Fagot, B. I., and Kavanaugh, K. (1990). The prediction of antisocial behavior from avoidant attachment classification. *Child Development, 61,* 864–873.

Farrington, D. P. (1983). Randomized experiments on crime and justice. In M. Ronry and N. Morris (Eds.), *Crime and justice* (Vol. 4, pp. 257–308). Chicago: University of Chicago Press.

Farrington, D. P. (1995). The development of offending and antisocial behavior from childhood: Key findings from the Cambridge Study in delinquency development. *Journal of Child Psychology and Psychiatry, 36,* 929–964.

Farver, J. M., Kim, Y. K., and Lee, Y. (1995). Cultural differences in Korean- and Anglo-American preschoolers' social interaction and play behaviors. *Child Development, 66,* 1088–1099.

Fox, N., and Calkins, S. (1993). Relations between temperament, attachment, and behavioral inhibition: Two possible pathways to extroversion and social withdrawal. In K. H. Rubin and J. Asendorpf (Eds.), *Social withdrawal, inhibition, and shyness in childhood.* Hillsdale, NJ: Lawrence Erlbaum Associates.

Fox, N. A., Schmidt, L. A., Calkins, S. D., Rubin, K. H., and Coplan, R. J. (1996). The role of frontal activation in the regulation and dysregulation of social behavior during the preschool years. *Development and Psychopathology, 8,* 89–102.

Freud, S. (1973). *An outline of psychoanalysis.* London: Hogarth. (Original work published 1938)

Gelfand, D. M., and Teti, D. M. (1990). The effects of maternal depression on children. *Clinical Psychological Review, 10,* 329–353.

Goodnow, J. J., Knight, R., and Cashmore, J. (1985). Adult social cognition: Implications of parents' ideas for approaches to development. In M. Perlmutter (Ed.), *Cognitive perspectives and behavioral development: Vol. 18. The Minnesota symposia on child psychology* (pp. 287–329). Hillsdale, NJ: Lawrence Erlbaum Associates.

Greenberg, M. T., Speltz, M. L., DeKlyen, M., and Endriga, M. C. (1991). Attachment security in preschoolers with and without externalizing problems: A replication. *Development and Psychopathology, 3,* 413–430.

Gretarsson, S. J., and Gelfand, D. M. (1988). Mothers' attributions regarding their children's social behavior and personality characteristics. *Developmental Psychology, 24,* 264–269.

Grusec, J. E., Dix, T. H., and Mills, R. S. L. (1982). The effects of type, severity, and victim of children's transgressions on maternal discipline. *Canadian Journal of Behavioural Science, 14,* 276–289.

Gunnar, M., Mangelsdorf, S., Larson, M., and Hertsgaard, L. (1989). Attachment, temperament, and adreno-cortical activity in infancy: A study of psychondocrine regulation. *Developmental Psychology, 25,* 355–363.

Gurland, B., Yorkston, N., Frank, L., and Stone, A. (1967). *The structured and scaled interview to assess maladjustment.* Mimeographed booklet, Biometric Research, Department of Mental Hygiene, New York.

Hammen, C. (1988). Self-cognitions, stressful events and the prediction of depression in children of depressed mothers. *Journal of Abnormal Child Psychology, 16,* 347–360.

Hart, G. H., DeWolf, D. M., Wozniak, P., and Burts, D. C. (1992). Maternal and paternal disciplinary styles: Relations with preschoolers' playground behavioral orientations and peer status. *Child Development, 63,* 879–892.

Hart, B., and Risley, T. R. (1995). *Meaningful differences in the everyday experience of young American children.* Baltimore: Brookes.

Hartup, W. W. (1985). Relationships and their significance in cognitive development. In R. A. Hinde, A. Perret-Clermont, and J. Stevenson-Hinde (Eds.), *Social relationships and cognitive development* (pp. 66–82). Oxford, England: Clarendon.

Hastings, P. D., and Rubin, K. H. (1999). Predicting mothers' beliefs about preschool-aged children's social behavior: Evidence for maternal attitudes moderating child effects. *Child Development, 70,* 722–741.

Henderson, H. A., and Rubin, K. H. (1997, April). *Internal and external correlates of self-regulation in preschool aged children.* Poster presented at the biennial meeting of the Society for Research in Child Development, Washington, DC.

Hetherington, E. M., and Martin, B. (1986). Family factors and psychopathology in children. In H. C. Quay and J. S. Werry (Eds.), *Psychopathological disorders of childhood* (3rd ed., pp. 332–390). New York: Wiley.

Hoffman, M. L. (1970). Moral development. In P. H. Mussen (Ed.), *Handbook of Child Psychology* (Vol. 2, pp. 211–236). New York: Wiley.

Hymel, S., Rubin, K. H., Rowden, L., and LeMare, L. (1990). Children's peer relationships: Longitudinal predictions of internalizing and externalizing problems from middle to late childhood. *Child Development, 61,* 2004–2021.

Jennings, K. D., Staff, V., and Conners, R. E. (1991). Social networks and mothers' interactions with their preschool children. *Child Development, 62,* 966–978.

Johnston, C., and Patenaude, R. (1994). Parent attributions of inattentive-overactive and oppositional–defiant child behaviors. *Cognitive Therapy and Research, 18,* 261–275.

Jouriles, E. N., Murphy, C. M., Farris, A. M., Smith, D. A., Richlers, J. E., and Waters, E. (1991). Marital adjustment, parental disagreements about child rearing and behavior problems in boys: Increasing the specificity of the marital assessment. *Child Development, 62,* 1424–2433.

Kagan, J., and Moss, H. A. (1962). *Birth to maturity: A study in psychological development.* New York: Wiley.

Kagan, J., Reznick, J. S., Clarke, C., Snidman, N., and Garcia-Coll, C. (1984). Behavioral inhibition to the unfamiliar. *Child Development, 55,* 2212–2225.

Kagan, J., Reznick, J. S., and Snidman, N. (1987). The physiology and psychology of behavioral inhibition in children. *Child Development, 58,* 1459–1473.

Kagan, J., Reznick, J. S., and Snidman, N. (1989). Issues in the study of temperament. In G. A. Kohnstamm, J. E. Bates, and M. K. Rothbart (Eds.), *Temperament in childhood* (pp. 133–144). London: Wiley.

Katz, R. C. (1971). Interactions between the facilitative and inhibitory effects of a punishing stimulus in the control of children's hitting behavior. *Child Development, 42,* 1433–1446.

Katz, L. F., and Gottman, J. M. (1993). Patterns of marital conflict predict children's internalizing and externalizing behaviors. *Developmental Psychology, 29,* 940–950.

Kelley, M. L., Sanchez-Hucies, J., and Walker, R. (1993). Correlates of disciplinary practices in working- to middle-class African-American mothers. *Merrill-Palmer Quarterly, 39,* 252–264.

Kochanska, G. (1991). Patterns of inhibition to the unfamiliar in children of normal and affectively ill mothers. *Child Development, 62,* 250–263.

Kochanska, G., Kuczynski, L., and Maguire, M. (1989). Impact of diagnosed depression and self-reported mood on mothers' control strategies: A longitudinal study. *Journal of Child Psychology, 17,* 493–511.

Kochanska, G., and Radke-Yarrow, M. (1992). Inhibition in toddlerhood and the dynamics of the child's interaction with an unfamiliar peer at age five. *Child Development, 63,* 325–335.

Kuczynski, L., and Kochanska, G. (1995). Function and content of maternal demands: Developmental significance of early demands for competent action. *Child Development, 66,* 616–628.

LaFreniere, P., and Dumas, J. E. (1992). A transactional analysis of early childhood anxiety and social withdrawal. *Development and Psychopathology, 4,* 385–402.

LaFreniere, P., and Sroufe, L. A. (1985). Profiles of peer competence in the preschool: Interrelations between measures, influence of social ecology, and relation to attachment history. *Developmental Psychology, 17,* 289–299.

Lahey, B. B., Waldman, I. D., and McBurnett, K. (1999). Annotation: The development of antisocial behavior: An integrative causal model. *Journal of Child Psychology and Psychiatry, 40,* 669–682.

Lamborn, S. D., Mounts, N. S., Steinberg, L., and Dornbusch, S. M. (1991). Patterns of competence and adjustment among adolescents from authoritative, authoritarian, indulgent and neglectful families. *Child Development, 62,* 1049–1065.

Ledingham, J., Younger, A., Schwartzman, A., and Bergeron, G. (1982). Agreement among teacher, peer and self-ratings of children's aggression, withdrawal and likeability. *Journal of Abnormal Child Psychology, 10,* 363–372.

Lefkowitz, M. M., Eron, L. D., Walder, L. O., and Huesmann, L. R. (1977). *Growing up to be violent: A longitudinal study of the development of aggression.* New York: Pergamon.

LeMare, L., and Rubin, K. H. (1987). Perspective-taking and peer interactions: Structural and developmental analyses. *Child Development, 58,* 306–315.

Lempers, J. D., Clark-Lempers, D., and Simons, R. L. (1989). Economic hardship, parenting and distress in adolescence. *Child Development, 60,* 25–39.

Lobitz, W. C., and Johnson, J. (1975). Normal versus deviant children: A multi-method comparison. *Journal of Abnormal Psychology, 3,* 353–374.

Loeb, R. C., Horst, L., and Horton, P. J. (1980). Family interaction patterns associated with self-esteem in preadolescent girls and boys. *Merrill-Palmer Quarterly, 26,* 205–217.

Loeber, R., and Stouthamer-Loeber, M. (1986). Family factors as correlates and predictors of juvenile conduct problems and delinquency. In M. Tonry and N. Morris (Eds.), *Crime and justice: A review of research* (Vol. 7, pp. 29–149). Chicago: University of Chicago Press.

Lyons-Ruth, K. (1996). Attachment relationships among children with aggressive behavior problems: The role of disorganized early attachment patterns. *Journal of Consulting and Clinical Psychology, 64,* 64–73.

Lyons-Ruth, K., Easterbrooks, M. A., and Cibelli, C. D. (1997). Infant attachment strategies, infant mental lag, and maternal depressive symptoms: Predictors of internalizing and externalizing problems at age seven. *Developmental Psychology, 33,* 681–692.

Lyons-Ruth, K., Easterbrooks, M. A., and Davidson, C. (1995, April). *Disorganized attachment strategies and mental lag in infancy: Prediction of externalizing problems at seven.* Paper presented at the biennial meeting of the Society for Research in Child Development, Indianapolis, IN.

Lyons-Ruth, K., Repacholi, B., McLeod, S., and Silva, E. (1991). Disorganized attachment behavior in infancy: Short-term stability, maternal and infant correlates, and risk-related subtypes. *Development and Psychopathology, 3,* 377–396.

Lytton, H. (1990). Child and parent effects in boys' conduct disorder: A reinterpretation. *Developmental Psychology, 26,* 683–697.

MacDonald, K. (1992). Warmth as a developmental construct: An evolutionary analysis. *Child Development, 63,* 753–773.

MacDonald, K., and Parke, R. D. (1984). Bridging the gap: parent–child play interaction and peer interactive competence. *Child Development, 55,* 1265–1277.

MacKinnon-Lewis, C., Volling, B. L., Lamb, M. E., Dechman, K., Rabiner, D., and Curtner, M. E. (1994). A cross-contextual analysis of boys' social competence: From family to school. *Developmental Psychology, 30,* 325–333.

Main, M., Kaplan, N., and Cassidy, J. (1985). Security in infancy, childhood, and adulthood: A move to the level of representation. In I. Bretherton and E. Waters (Eds.), Growing points of attachment theory and research. *Monographs of the Society for Research in Child Development, 50* (Serial No. 209, pp. 66–104). Chicago: University of Chicago Press.

Main, M., and Soloman, C. (1990). Procedures for identifying infants as disorganized/disoriented during the Ainsworth Strange Situation. In M. Greenberg, D. Cicchetti, and E. M. Cummings (Eds.), *Attachment in the preschool years: Theory, research, and intervention* (pp. 121–160). Chicago: University of Chicago Press.

Martin, B. (1975). Parent–child relations. In F. Horowitz (Ed.), *Review of child development research* (pp. 463–540). Chicago: University of Chicago Press.

Mash, E., and Barkley, R. (Eds.). (1996). *Child Psychopathology*. New York: Guilford.

Masten, A. S., Coatsworth, J. D., Neemann, J., Gest, S. D., Tellegen, A., and Garmezy, N. (1995). The structure and coherence of competence from childhood through adolescence. *Child Development, 66,* 1635–1659.

Masten, A. S., Morison, P., Pellegrini, D., and Tellegen, A. (1990). Competence under stress: Risk and protective factors. In J. Rolf, A. S. Masten, D. Cicchetti, K. H. Nuechterlein, and S. Weintraub (Eds.), *Risk and protective factors in the development of psychopathology* (pp. 236–256). New York: Cambridge University Press.

Matas, L., Arend, R. A., and Sroufe, L. A. (1978). The continuity of adaptation in the second year: Relationship between quality of attachment and later competence. *Child Development, 49,* 547–556.

McFayden-Ketchum, S. A., Bates, J. E., Dodge, K. A., and Pettit, G. S. (1996). Patterns of change in early childhood aggressive-disruptive behavior: Gender differences in predictions from early coercive and affectionate mother–child interactions. *Child Development, 67,* 2417–2433.

McGillicuddy-DeLisi, A. V. (1982). Parental beliefs about developmental processes. *Human Development, 25,* 192–200.

McKnew, D. H., Cytryn, L., Efron, A. M., Gershon, E. S., and Bunney, W. E. (1979). Offspring of parents with affective disorders. *British Journal of Psychiatry, 134,* 148–152.

McNally, S., Eisenberg, N., and Harris, J. D. (1991). Consistency and change in maternal childrearing practices: A longitudinal study. *Child Development, 62,* 190–198.

Miller, S. A. (1995). Parents' attributions for their children's behavior. *Child Development, 66,* 1557–1584.

Miller, N. B., Cowan, P. A., Cowan, C. P., Hetherington, E. M., and Clingempeel, W. G. (1993). Externalizing in preschoolers and early adolescents: A cross-study replication of a family model. *Developmental Psychology, 29,* 3–18.

Mills, R. S. L., and Rubin, K. H. (1990). Parental beliefs about problematic social behaviors in early childhood. *Child Development, 61,* 138–151.

Mills, R. S. L., and Rubin, K. H. (1992). A longitudinal study of maternal beliefs about children's social behavior. *Merrill-Palmer Quarterly, 38,* 494–512.

Mills, R. S. L., and Rubin, K. H. (1993a). Socialization factors in the development of social withdrawal. In K. H. Rubin and J. Asendorpf (Eds.), *Social withdrawal, inhibition and shyness in childhood.* Hillsdale, NJ: Lawrence Erlbaum Associates.

Mills, R. S. L., and Rubin, K. H. (1993b). Parental ideas as influences on children's social competence. In S. Duck (Ed.), *Learning about relationships* (pp. 98–117). Newbury Park, CA: Sage.

Mills, R. S. L., and Rubin, K. H. (1998). Are behavioral control and psychological control both differentially associated with childhood aggression and social withdrawal? *Canadian Journal of Behavioural Sciences, 30,* 132–136.

Minuchin, P. (1985). Families and individual development: Provocations from the field of family therapy. *Child Development, 56,* 289–302.

Mize, J., and Pettit, G. (1997). Mothers' social coaching, mother–child relationship style, and children's peer competence: Is the medium the message? *Child Development, 68,* 312–332.

Nachmias, M., Gunnar, M., Mangelsdorf, S., Parritz, R. H., and Buss, K. (1996). Behavioral inhibition and stress reactivity: The moderating role of attachment security. *Child Development, 67,* 508–522.

Obrist, P. A. (1982). Cardiac–behavioral interactions: A critical appraisal. In J. T. Cacioppo and R. E. Petty (Eds.), *Perspectives in cardiovascular psychophysiology* (pp. 265–291). New York: Guilford.

Olweus, D. (1980). Familial and temperamental determinants of aggressive behavior in adolescent boys: A causal analysis. *Developmental Psychology, 16,* 644–660.

Olweus, D. (1984). Stability in aggressive and withdrawn, inhibited behavior patterns. In R. M. Kaplan, V. J. Konecni, and R. W. Novaco (Eds.), *Aggression in children and youth* (pp. 104–136). The Hague: Nijhoff.

Olweus, D. (1993). Victimization by peers: Antecedents and long-term outcomes. In K. H. Rubin and J. B. Asendorpf (Eds.), *Social withdrawal, inhibition and shyness in childhood* (pp. 315–341). Hillsdale, NJ: Lawrence Erlbaum Associates.

Park, S., Belsky, J., Putnam, S., and Crnic, K. (1997). Infant emotionality, parenting, and 3-year inhibition: Exploring stability and lawful discontinuity in a male sample. *Developmental Psychology, 33,* 218–227.

Parke, R. D., and Buriel, R. (1998). Socialization in the family: Ethnic and ecological perspectives. In N. Eisenberg (Ed.), *Handbook of Child Psychology: Vol. 3. Social, emotional and personality development* (5th ed., pp. 463–522). New York: Wiley.

Parker, G. (1983). *Parental overprotection: A risk factor in psychosocial development.* New York: Grune and Stratton.

Patterson, G. R. (1982). *Coercive family process.* Eugene, OR: Castilia.

Patterson, G. R. (1983). Stress: A change agent for family process. In N. Garmezy and M. Rutter (Eds.), *Stress, coping, and development in children* (pp. 235–264). New York: McGraw-Hill.

Patterson, G. R. (1986). Maternal rejection: Determinant or product for deviant child behavior? In W. Hartup and Z. Rubin (Eds.), *Relationships and development.* Hillsdale, NJ: Lawrence Erlbaum Associates.

Patterson, G. R., Capaldi, D., and Bank, L. (1991). An early starter model for predicting delinquency. In D. J. Pepler and K. H. Rubin (Eds.), *The development and treatment of childhood aggression* (pp. 139–168). Hillsdale, NJ: Lawrence Erlbaum Associates.

Patterson, C., Cohn, D., and Kao, B. (1989). Maternal warmth as a protective factor against risks associated with peer rejection among children. *Development and Psychopathology, 1*, 21–38.

Pulkkinen, L. (1982). Self-control and continuity from childhood to late adolescence. In P. B. Baltes and O. G. Brim, Jr. (Eds.), *Life-span development and behavior* (Vol. 4, pp. 63–105). New York: Academic.

Radke-Yarrow, M., and Zahn-Waxler, C. (1986). The role of familial factors in the development of prosocial behavior: Research findings and questions. In D. Olweus, J. Block, and M. Radke-Yarrow (Eds.), *Development of antisocial and prosocial behavior* (pp. 207–234). Orlando, FL: Academic.

Reid, J. B., and Patterson, G. R. (1989). The development of antisocial behavior patterns in childhood and adolescence. *European Journal of Personality, 3*, 107–119.

Renken, B., Egeland, B., Marvinney, D., Sroufe, L. A., and Mangelsdorf, S. (1989). Early childhood antecedents of aggression and passive-withdrawal in early elementary school. *Journal of Personality, 57*, 257–281.

Renshaw, P. D., and Brown, P. J. (1993). Loneliness in middle childhood: Concurrent and longitudinal predictors. *Child Development, 64*, 1271–1284.

Rogoff, B. (1990). *Apprenticeship in thinking: Cognitive development in social context.* Oxford, England: Oxford University Press.

Rose-Krasnor, L., Rubin, K. H., Booth, C. L., and Coplan, R. J. (1996). Maternal directiveness and child attachment security as predictors of social competence in preschoolers. *International Journal of Behavioral Development, 19*, 309–325.

Rubin, K. H., Both, L., Zahn-Waxler, C., Cummings, M., and Wilkinson, M. (1991). The dyadic play behaviors of children of well and depressed mothers. *Development and Psychopathology, 3*, 243–251.

Rubin, K. H., Bream, L., and Rose-Krasnor, L. (1991). Social problem solving and aggression in childhood. In D. J. Pepler and K. H. Rubin (Eds.), *The development and treatment of childhood aggression* (pp. 219–248). Hillsdale, NJ: Lawrence Erlbaum Associates.

Rubin, K. H., Bukowski, W., and Parker, J. (1998). Peer interactions, relationships, and groups. In N. Eisenberg (Ed.), *Handbook of Child Psychology: Vol. 3. Social, emotional, and personality development* ( 5th ed., pp. 619–700). New York: Wiley.

Rubin, K. H., and Burgess, K. B. (2001). Social withdrawal and anxiety. In M. W. Vasey and M. R. Dadds (Eds.), *The developmental psychopathology of anxiety* (pp. 407–434). Oxford, England: Oxford University Press.

Rubin, K. H., Burgess, K. B., and Hastings, P. D. (in press). Stability and social-behavioral consequences of toddlers' inhibited temperament and parenting. *Child Development.*

Rubin, K. H., Cheah, C. S. L., and Fox, N. A. (in press). Emotion regulation, parenting, and the display of social reticence in preschoolers. *Early Education and Development.*

Rubin, K. H., Chen, X., and Hymel, S. (1993). The socio-emotional characteristics of extremely aggressive and extremely withdrawn children. *Merrill-Palmer Quarterly, 39*, 518–534.

Rubin, K. H., Chen, X., McDougall, P., Bowker, A., and McKinnon, J. (1995). The Waterloo Longitudinal Project: Predicting adolescent internalizing and externalizing problems from early and mid-childhood. *Development and Psychopathology, 7*, 751–764.

Rubin, K. H., Coplan, R. J., Fox, N. A., and Calkins, S. D. (1995). Emotionality, emotion regulation, and preschoolers' social adaptation. *Development and Psychopathology, 7*, 49–52.

Rubin, K. H., Hastings, P. D., Chen, X., Stewart, S. L., and McNichol, K. (1998). Intrapersonal and maternal correlates of aggression, conflict, and externalizing problems in toddlers. *Child Development, 69*, 1614–1629.

Rubin, K. H., Hastings, P. D., Stewart, S. L., Henderson, H. A., and Chen, X. (1997). The consistency and concomitants of inhibition: Some of the children, all of the time. *Child Development, 68*, 467–483.

Rubin, K. H., Hymel, S., and Mills, R. S. L. (1989). Sociability and social withdrawal in childhood: Stability and outcomes. *Journal of Personality, 57*, 237–255.

Rubin, K. H., and Mills, R. S. L. (1990). Maternal beliefs about adaptive and maladaptive social behaviors in normal, aggressive, and withdrawn preschoolers. *Journal of Abnormal Child Psychology, 18*, 419–435.

Rubin, K. H., and Mills, R. S. L. (1992). Parent's thoughts about children's socially adaptive and maladaptive behaviors: Stability, change and individual differences. In I. Sigel, J. Goodnow, and A. McGillicuddy-De Lisi (Eds.), *Parental belief systems* (pp. 41–68). Hillsdale, NJ: Lawrence Erlbaum Associates.

Rubin, K. H., Nelson, L. J., Hastings, P. D., and Asendorpf, J. (1999). The transaction between parents' perceptions of their children's shyness and their parenting styles. *International Journal of Behavioral Development, 23*, 937–958.

Rubin, K. H., and Rose-Krasnor, L. (1992). Interpersonal problem-solving and social competence in children. In V. B. van Hasselt and M. Hersen (Eds.), *Handbook of social development: A lifespan perspective.* New York: Plenum.

Rubin, K. H., Rose-Krasnor, L., Bigras, M., Mills, R. S. L., and Booth, C. (1996). Predicting parental behavior: The influences of setting conditions, psychosocial factors and parental beliefs. In G. M. Tarabulsy and R. Tessier (Eds.), La Développement

Emotionnel et Social De l'Enfant [The Emotional and Social Development of an infant] (pp.11–32). Sainte Foy, Québec: Presses de l'Université du Québec.

Russell, A., and Finnie, V. (1990). Preschool children's social status and maternal instructions to assist group entry. *Developmental Psychology*, *26*, 603–611.

Rutter, M. (1990). Psychosocial resilience and protective mechanisms. In J. Rolf, A. S. Masten, D. Cicchetti, K. H. Nuechterlein, and S. Weintraub (Eds.), *Risk and protective factors in the development of psychopathology* (pp. 181–214). New York: Cambridge University Press.

Rutter, M., and Quinton, D. (1984). Parental psychiatric disorder: Effects on children. *Psychological Medicine*, *14*, 853–880.

Schneider, B. H., Attili, G., Vermigly, P., and Younger, A. (1997). A comparison of middle class English-Canadian and Italian mothers' beliefs about children's peer directed aggression and social withdrawal. *International Journal of Behavioral Development*, *21*, 133–154.

Sears, R. R. (1961). Relation of early socialization experiences to aggression in middle childhood. *Journal of Abnormal and Social Psychology*, *63*, 466–492.

Selman, R. L. (1985). The use of interpersonal negotiation strategies and communicative competences: A clinical-developmental exploration in a pair of troubled early adolescents. In R. A. Hinde, A. Perret-Clermont, and J. Stevenson-Hinde (Eds.), *Social relationships and cognitive development* (pp. 208–232). Oxford, England: Clarendon.

Sigel, I. E. (1982). The relationship between parental distancing strategies and the child's cognitive behavior. In L. M. Laosa and I. E. Sigel (Eds.), *Families as learning environments for children* (pp. 47–86). New York: Plenum.

Sigel, I. E., and Kim, M. I. (1996). The answer depends on the question: A conceptual and methodological analysis of a parent belief-behavior interview regarding children's learning. In S. Harkness and C. M. Super (Eds.), *Parents' cultural belief systems: Their origins, expressions, and consequences* (pp. 83–120). New York: Guilford.

Snyder, J. J. (1977). Reinforcement analysis of interaction in problem and non-problem families. *Journal of Abnormal Psychology*, *86*, 528–535.

Spangler, G., and Schieche, M. (1998). Emotional and adrenocortical responses of infants to the Strange Situation: The differential function of emotional expression. *International Journal of Behavioral Development*, *22*, 681–706.

Spieker, S. J., and Booth, C. L. (1988). Maternal antecedents of attachment quality. In J. Belsky and T. Nezworski (Eds.), *Clinical implications of attachment* (pp. 95–135). Hillsdale, NJ: Lawrence Erlbaum Associates.

Sroufe, L. A. (1983). Infant–caregiver attachment and patterns of adaptation in preschool: Roots of maladaptation and competence. In M. Perlmutter (Ed.), *Minnesota symposia on child psychology* (Vol. 16, pp. 41–81). Hillsdale, NJ: Lawrence Erlbaum Associates.

Sroufe, L. A. (1988). The role of infant–caregiver attachment in development. In J. Belsky and T. Nezworski (Eds.), *Clinical implication of attachment* (pp. 18–38). Hillsdale, NJ: Lawrence Erlbaum Associates.

Steinberg, L., Lamborn, S. D., Dornbusch, S. M., and Darling, N. (1992). Impact of parenting practices on adolescent achievement: Authoritative parenting, school involvement and encouragement to succeed. *Child Development*, *63*, 1266–1281.

Stewart, S. L., and Rubin, K. H. (1995). The social problem solving skills of anxious–withdrawn children. *Development and Psychopathology*, *7*, 323–336.

Strassburg, Z. (1995). Social-information processing in compliance situations by mothers of behavior-problem boys. *Child Development*, *66*, 376–389.

Thomas, A., and Chess, S. (1977). *Temperament and development*. New York: Brunner/Mazel.

Tremblay, R., Pihl, R., Vitaro, F., and Dobkin, P. (1994). Predicting early onset of male antisocial behavior from preschool behavior. *Archives of General Psychiatry*, *51*, 732–739.

Troy, M., and Sroufe, L. A. (1987). Victimization among preschoolers: Role of attachment relationship history. *Journal of the American Academy of Child and Adolescent Psychiatry*, *26*, 166–172.

van IJzendoorn, M. H. (1997). Attachment, emergent morality, and aggression: Toward a developmental socioemotional model of antisocial behavior. *International Journal of Behavioral Development*, *21*, 703–727.

Vuchinich, S., Bank, L., and Patterson, G. R. (1992). Parenting, peers and the stability of antisocial behavior in preadolescent boys. *Developmental Psychology*, *28*, 510–521.

Webster-Stratton, C., and Hammond, M. (1988). Maternal depression and its relationship to life stress, perceptions of child behavior problems, parenting behaviors, and child conduct problems. *Journal of Abnormal Child Psychology*, *16*, 299–315.

Weiss, B., Dodge, K. A., Bates, J. E., and Pettit, G. S. (1992). Some consequences of early harsh discipline: Child aggression and maladaptive social information processing study. *Child Development*, *63*, 1321–1335.

Weisz, J. R., Suwanlert, S., Chaiyasit, W., Weiss, B., Walter, B. R., and Anderson, W. W. (1988). Thai and American perspectives on over- and undercontrolled child behavior problems: Exploring the threshold model among parents, teachers, and psychologists. *Journal of Consulting and Clinical Psychology*, *56*, 601–609.

Welner, Z., Welner, A., McCrary, M. D., and Leonard, M. A. (1977). Psychopathology in children with depression: A controlled study. *Journal of Nervous and Mental Disease*, *164*, 408–413.

Windle, M. (1992). A longitudinal study of stress buffering for adolescent problem behaviors. *Developmental Psychology*, *28*, 522–530.

Yarrow, M. R., Waxler, C. Z., and Scott, P. M. (1971). Child effects on adult behavior. *Developmental Psychology, 5,* 300–311.

Younger, A. J., and Boyko, K. A. (1987). Aggression and withdrawal as social schemas underlying children's peer perceptions. *Child Development, 58,* 1094–1100.

Younger, A., Gentile, C., and Burgess, K. B. (1993). Children's perceptions of social withdrawal: Changes accross age. In K. H. Rubin and J. Asendorpf (Eds.), *Social withdrawal, inhibition, and shyness in childhood.* Hillsdale, NJ: Lawrence Erlbaum Associates.

Younger, A. J., Schwartzman, A. E., and Ledingham, J. E. (1986). Age-related differences in children's perceptions of social deviance: Changes in behavior or perspective? *Developmental Psychology, 22,* 531–542.

Zahn-Waxler, C., Mayfield, A., Radke-Yarrow, M., McKnew, D. H., Cytryn, L., and Davenport, D. (1988). A follow-up investigation of offspring of parents with bipolar disorder. *American Journal of Psychiatry, 145,* 506–509.

# Author Index

Clayton, V., **III**, 146, *166*
Clearly, P. A., **V**, 334, *344*
Cleary, P. D., **IV**, 107, *119*; **V**, 451, 452, *457*
Clemens, L. P., **I**, 59, *70*
Clement, C., **IV**, 334, *357*
Clements, D., **V**, 384, *404*
Clements, M., **III**, 79, 89, *104*; **IV**, 207, 210, 215, *225*
Clements, W. A., **III**, 264, 276, *284*
Clewell, B. C., **III**, 179, 200, 201, *203, 206*
Clewes, J. L., **I**, 211, *221*
Clifford, E., **I**, 79, 81, *95*; **III**, 342, 346, *360*
Clifford, M. M., **V**, 183, *192*
Clifford, R., **III**, 232, 235, 240, *245*
Clingempeel, W. G., **I**, 117, 118, *129, 133*, 399, *415*; **III**, 60, *67*, 95, *101*, 132, *140*, 154, *166*, 288, 289, 290, 292, 298, 299, 300, 301, 302, 303, 304, 305, 306, 309, *310, 312*, 345, 347, *358*, 590, 591, *596*; **IV**, 228, *253*
Clogg, C. C., **I**, 142, 144, *158*; **III**, 180, *203*
Cloutier, M. M., **IV**, 15, *19*
Cloutier, P., **V**, *348*
Cluman, R. B., **V**, 64, *84*
Clune, W. H., **V**, 477, *482*
Clure, C., **IV**, 333, 343, *353*
Clutton-Brock, T. H., **II**, 8, 18, *27*
Clyman, R. B., **I**, 58, *67*; **IV**, 162, *176*
Coates, D. L., **III**, 17, *23*; **IV**, 37, *45*, 281, 282, *285*
Coatsworth, J. D., **I**, 386, *415*; **II**, 304, *312*
Cobb, S., **IV**, 126, 129, *147*
Cobbett, P., **II**, 79, *91*
Cochlear Corporation, **IV**, 278, *285*
Cochran, D. L., **IV**, 49, 54, *57*
Cochran, M., **III**, 488, *506*; **IV**, 126, 127, 128, 130, 131, 132, 133, 135, 136, 138, 139, 141, 142, 143, 145, 146, *147*
Cochran, M. M., **III**, 222, 234, *244, 245*; **IV**, 135, 136, *147*; **V**, 287, *302*
Cochran, S. W., **I**, 193, *216*
Cocking, R. R., **II**, 267, 268, 269, *277*; **V**, 352, *370*
Cockshott, C., **II**, 150, *176*
Coddington, R. D., **II**, 292, *308*
Coe, C. L., **II**, 50, *54*, 62, *88*, 120, 127, 128, 130, *134*, 156, *178*; **V**, 69, *84*
Coe, R. D., **IV**, 98, *118*
Coelen, C., **III**, 231, 232, 233, 236, 237, *250*; **V**, 378, 380, 388, 395, *404*
Coffey, R. M., **V**, 449, *461*
Coffman, H., **II**, 104, *133*
Cohan, M., **III**, 44, 45, *69*
Cohen, A., **IV**, 317, *323*
Cohen, D., **I**, 48, 50, *69*; **II**, 359, *375*; **V**, 222, *237*
Cohen, D. J., **I**, 233, 234, 236, 238, *251*; **V**, 46, *55*
Cohen, D. K., **V**, 29, *32*
Cohen, E. E., **III**, 17, *23*
Cohen, E. V., **IV**, 26, *42*
Cohen, H., **V**, 5, 6, 10, *31*
Cohen, H. A., **II**, 70, *95*

Cohen, H. J., **I**, 374, 376, *377*
Cohen, J., **I**, 154, *159*; **II**, 70, *88*; **IV**, 205, *223*
Cohen, J. B., **III**, 187, *206*
Cohen, J. S., **I**, 298, 301, 302, *311*, 391, *411*; **V**, 292, *302*
Cohen, L., **I**, 206, *220*; **V**, 155, *165*
Cohen, L. J., **III**, 6, *25*; **IV**, 276, *285*
Cohen, L. L., **V**, 316, *325*
Cohen, M., **I**, 334, 339, *353*
Cohen, M. B., **III**, 579, *593*
Cohen, N. E., **III**, 89, 93, *102*; **V**, 398, *403*
Cohen, N. J., **I**, 283, *306*
Cohen, O., **III**, 291, *311*
Cohen, P., **IV**, 300, *323*; **V**, 334, *344*
Cohen, P. N., **II**, 207, *226*
Cohen, R., **I**, 86, *97*; **III**, *136*, 590, *593*; **IV**, 54, *56*; **V**, 337, *346*, 363, *371*
Cohen, R. J., **V**, 263, *264*
Cohen, R. S., **IV**, 232, *258*
Cohen, S., **I**, 339, 344, *349, 350*, 404, *411*; **II**, 297, *308*
Cohen, S. E., **I**, 344, *350*
Cohen, Y., **II**, 261, *277*
Cohler, B. J., **I**, 140, *157*; **II**, 240, *252*; **III**, 145, 147, 164, *166*, 539, 557, *559*, 563, 564, 570, 571, 574, 576, 577, 578, 579, 581, 585, 588, 590, 592, *593, 595*; **IV**, 296, 298, *322*
Cohn, D., **I**, 398, *416*; **V**, 273, 277, *302*
Cohn, D. A., **I**, 199, *218*, 389, *411*
Cohn, J., **II**, 39, *54*; **III**, 429, *437*; **IV**, 306, *321*
Cohn, J. E., **I**, 20, *35*, *39*
Cohn, J. F., **I**, 195, *225*, 266, *276*; **IV**, 240, 249, *253*, 264, *285*, 342, *353, 358*; **V**, 49, *54*, 273, *301*
Coie, D., **I**, 386, *411*
Coie, J. D., **I**, 84, *95*, *100*, 384, 386, 407, *410, 411*; **II**, 305, *308*; **III**, 32, *65*; **V**, 128, 130, 132, *135*
Coie, L., **III**, 32, *65*
Coiro, M. J., **III**, 201, *214*, 290, 305, 306, *315*
Coker, G., **IV**, 265, *285*
Colangelo, N., **V**, 201, *215*
Colarusso, C. A., **III**, 567, 570, 571, 578, 588, 592, *594, 597*
Colby, A., **III**, 256, 257, *282*; **V**, 14, *31*, 114, *135*
Colder, C. R., **I**, 266, *273*; **V**, 129, *135*, 159, *164*
Cole, A., **I**, 199, *221*
Cole, A. K., **V**, 272, 273, *305*
Cole, C., **V**, 337, *345*
Cole, M., **I**, 9, *35*; **III**, 256, 276, *280, 284*
Cole, P., **II**, 274, *277*; **IV**, 318, *326*
Cole, P. M., **I**, 398, *412*; **IV**, 314, *321*; **V**, 47, *55*, 130, *136*
Cole, R., **IV**, 111, *120*, 170, 172, *179*
Cole, R. E., **III**, *386*, 443, *459*; **IV**, 158, *174*, 382, *384*, 399, 400, *409*; **V**, 16, 29, 105, *107*, 284, *301*
Cole, S., **IV**, 306, *322*
Cole, S. S., **IV**, 266, *285*

Cole, T. M., **IV**, 266, *285*
Colecchia, N., **III**, 229, *244*
Coleman, C., **V**, 289, *305*
Coleman, C. C., **V**, 277, *305*
Coleman, J. S., **II**, 234, *248*; **IV**, 9, *17*; **V**, 190, *192*
Coleman, M., **III**, 95, *103*, 298, 299, 300, 302, *312*
Coleman, P. K., **III**, 495, *506*, 512, *531*
Coleman, R. W., **III**, 539, *559*
Coleman, S. M., **III**, 550, 557, *561*
Coles, C. D., **II**, 169, *177*; **IV**, 338, 339, 341, *353, 358*
Coles, R., **V**, 200, 213, *215*
Coley, R. L., **II**, 296, *308*; **III**, 41, 44, *64*, 122, *136*, 173, 175, 178, 179, 180, 183, 186, 194, 195, 196, 199, 200, *205, 206*; **IV**, 103, *117*; **V**, 291, *302*
Colin, E. M., **I**, 346, *350*
Colin, V. L., **I**, 322, *326*; **V**, 35, 37, 38, 42, 45, *55*
Coll, C. G., **III**, 189, *206*
Coll, C. T. G., **I**, 332, *352*; **II**, 330, *340*
Collazo, J., **IV**, 262, *292*
Collett, S., **I**, 242, *252*
Colletta, N., **IV**, 130, *147*
Colletta, N. D., **III**, 186, *206*, 292, *311*
Collier, A. F., **III**, 546, *559*
Collier, G. A., **V**, 232, *237*
Collier, J., **III**, 546, *559*
Collins, J., **II**, 70, 72, *92*
Collins, M., **V**, 384, *405*
Collins, M. A., **V**, 179, *192*
Collins, M. H., **V**, 343, *346*
Collins, N. L., **V**, 251, *264*
Collins, P. A., **V**, 356, *369*
Collins, R. L., **III**, 349, *359*
Collins, W. A., **I**, 15, 21, 22, 24, *35*, 76, 79, 80, 82, 85, 88, 93, *95*, 97, 106, 107, 115, 116, 117, 120, 122, 125, *127*, *128, 130*, 199, 212, 214, *218*, 249, *251*, 355, *377*, 398, *411*; **II**, 19, 23, 27, 29, 142, *174*, 232, 235, 242, *248*, 249, 258, 277, 333, 338, *340*; **III**, 28, 32, 61, *66*, 364, 386, *386*, 396, 399, 408, *409*, 430, *435*, 440, 449, *457, 458*, 469, *482*, 485, 487, *506, 532*; **IV**, 182, 183, 188, *198*, 363, *386*; **V**, 61, *84*, 116, *135*, 147, 163, *164*, 270, 296, *302*, 364, *370*
Collinsworth, P., **III**, 162, *171*
Collis, G. M., **II**, 193, 194, *199, 202*; **IV**, 281, *289*
Collishaw, S., **IV**, 187, *199*
Collmer, C. W., **V**, 284, *307*
Collu, M., **II**, 78, *97*
Colon, A. J., **II**, 347, 350, 352, 354, 355, 356, 357, 365, 373, *375*
Colón, A. R., **I**, *35*, 330, *350*
Colón, P. A., **I**, *35*, 330, *350*; **II**, 347, 350, 352, 354, 355, 356, 357, 365, 373, *375*
Colpin, H., **III**, 343, 346, *357*
Colten, M. E., **IV**, 345, *353*

Reger, Z., **II**, 238, 239, *251*
Regeser Lopez, S. R., **IV**, 23, 32, 39, *40*
Register, C., **IV**, 275, *291*
Reglin, G. L., **IV**, 79, 80, *91*
Rehabilitation Act, **IV**, 263, *291*
Rehm, R. S., **IV**, 35, *44*; **V**, 339, *347*
Reich, J., **II**, 153, *178*
Reich, J. N., **I**, 334, *352*
Reich, W., **IV**, 310, *323*
Reichard, T., **II**, 124 *136*
Reichardt, C. S., **I**, 173, *186*
Reichert, D., **V**, 498, *506*
Reichhart-Erickson, M., **III**, 235, 239, *247*
Reichman N., **IV**, 103, *119*
Reichman, N. E., **III**, 201, *211*
Reid, G., **I**, 78, 79, *96*
Reid, J. B., **I**, 399, *416*; **III**, 345, *359*, 464, 472, *483*; **IV**, 169, 171, *176*, *179*, 374, *387*; **V**, 60, 62, 66, 67, 71, 72, 73, 74, 75, 76, 80, *83*, *84*, *85*, *87*, 129, 133, *140*, *141*, 277, 278, *307*
Reid, K., **I**, 313, 318, 324, *326*
Reid, M., **I**, 76, *99*
Reid, P. T., **I**, 193, *223*
Reid, W. J., **I**, 302, *308*
Reifman, A., **I**, 212, *224*
Reimer, M., **I**, 124, *132*
Reimers, T. M., **I**, 91, *96*
Reiner, C. D., **I**, 16, *42*
Reingold, H., **I**, 56, *69*
Reinhold, D. P., **III**, 515, *531*
Reinisch, J. M., **II**, 24, 25, *30*
Reis, S. M., **V**, 170, *193*, 208, 211, *217*
Reisbick, S., **II**, 38, *58*
Reiser, M., **V**, 96, 105, *108*, 116, *136*
Reiser, R. A., **V**, 364, *372*
Reiss, C., **III**, 522, *531*
Reiss, D., **I**, 118, 124, *129*, 167, 181, *187*, 247, *252*, *253*; **II**, 8, *28*, 293, *312*; **III**, 59, 72, 89, *104*, 194, *211*, 288, 289, 290, 298, 300, 304, *313*, *314*, 463, 466, 477, *483*; **IV**, 182, 183, *200*; **V**, 61, *87*, 104, *109*, 270, 300, *308*, 332, 333, 340, *347*
Reiss, I., **III**, 174, *211*
Reite, M., **II**, 48, *54*, 100, 128, *138*
Reiter, S. L., **IV**, 230, *254*
Reitz, M., **I**, 296, 304, *309*
Reivich, K., **III**, 512, *534*
Rende, R. D., **I**, 181, *187*, 247, *253*, 284, *305*
Rendina, I., **I**, 260, *275*
Rendina-Gobioff, G., **IV**, 157, *177*
Rendon, L., **IV**, 82, 84, *89*
Renick, M. J., **III**, 384, *388*
Renken, B., **I**, 199, *223*, 390, *416*
Renne, K., **IV**, 11, *19*
Renou, P., **III**, 353, *358*
Renshaw, P. D., **I**, 385, *416*
Repacholi, B., **I**, 389, 390, *414*
Repetti, R. L., **II**, 209, 223, *228*; **III**, 49, 50, *71*, *72*, 241, *250*, 245, *267*
Report on Preschool Programs, **V**, 385, *404*
Resch, N. L., **I**, 150, 151, 152, *160*

Rescorla, L., **III**, 237, *247*
Resnick, G., **III**, 84, *101*, 118, *136*
Resnick, L., **V**, 212, *217*
Resnick, M., **I**, 120, *132*
Resnick, S., **I**, 23, *41*
Resnik, R., **IV**, 340, *356*
Restmeier, R., **II**, 24, *27*
Restrepo, A., **I**, 118, *132*
Rettenbach, R., **IV**, 269, *291*
Reuter, M. A., **V**, 163, *166*
Revenstorf, D., **IV**, 235, *257*
Reves, R., **V**, 444, *460*
Revilla, L., **IV**, 66, 67, *87*
Reynolds, A. J., **IV**, 36, *44*
Reynolds, H. N., **IV**, 268, 269, *291*
Reynolds, R. A., **V**, 448, 449, *461*
Reynolds, R. J., **IV**, 36, *44*
Reynolds, S., **III**, 516, 518, *533*
Reynolds, V., **II**, 100, *138*
Rezac, S. J., **I**, 117, *127*, 143, *157*
Reznick, J. S., **I**, 12, *38*, 400, 408, *413*; **II**, 236, *249*, *251*; **III**, 384, *388*, 515, 518, 519, 520, *534*
Rhee, E., **IV**, 64, *91*
Rheinberger, M. M., **IV**, 378, *388*
Rheingold, H. L., **I**, 204, *223*; **II**, 100, 126, *138*, 154, 156, *179*, 193, 194, *202*, 298, *312*; **III**, 37, *72*; **V**, 147, *166*
Rheinhold, D. P., **IV**, 374, *385*
Rhinehart v. Nowlin, **V**, 465, *484*
Rhoades, K., **II**, 237, 240, 247, *250*, 330, *342*; **V**, 191, *193*
Rhodes, J. M., **II**, 104, *132*; **III**, 426, *435*
Rhodes, L., **I**, 334, *351*
Ribble, M. A., **III**, 539, *562*
Ricardo, E., **III**, 464, 471, *483*
Ricci, L. A., **I**, 367, *379*
Ricciuti, H. N., **III**, 110, 111, *139*
Rice, E. F., **II**, 292, *312*
Rice, M. E., **V**, 125, 126, *141*
Rice, M. L., **I**, 62, *69*
Rice, R., **I**, 347, 348, *353*
Richard, C., **II**, 274, *279*
Richard, J. V., **III**, 118, *139*
Richard, M., **III**, 160, *167*
Richards, D. P., **IV**, 269, 273, 282, 283, *287*
Richards, E. L., **III**, 538, 557, *562*
Richards, H. C., **IV**, 273, *291*
Richards, J. S., **II**, 35, *55*
Richards, L., **III**, 96, *103*
Richards, M., **I**, 346, *354*; **II**, 152, *177*; **III**, 32, *68*
Richards, M. H., **I**, 91, *98*, 105, 107, 115, 117, *130*, *132*, 211, *223*; **II**, 210, *228*
Richards, M. P. M., **I**, 337, *351*; **II**, 44, *58*, 152, *173*
Richards, P., **III**, 41, *65*
Richards, S., **III**, 349, *359*
Richardson, G. A., **IV**, 340, 342, *357*
Richardson, J., **III**, 463, 470, *483*
Richardson, J. L., **IV**, 75, *91*, 158, *179*, 399, *409*
Richardson, L., **V**, 223, *237*
Richardson, S. A., **IV**, 264, 265, *291*

Richert, E. S., **V**, 208, 209, 210, *217*
Richlers, J. E., **I**, 404, *413*
Richman, A. L., **II**, 234, *251*, 267, 270, 273, 278, 279; **III**, 451, *459*; **IV**, 30, *44*, 398, *409*; **V**, 232, *238*
Richman, E. L., **I**, 208, *223*
Richmond, J. B., **III**, 417, *435*; **V**, 440, *461*
Richter, C. B., **II**, 115, *139*
Richter, K. P., **V**, 311, *327*
Richters, J. E., **I**, 77, 78, *98*, *99*; **II**, 331, *343*; **IV**, 299, *324*; **V**, 158, *166*, 495, *506*
Rickards, W. H., **I**, 108, *130*
Rickert, H., **II**, 215, *225*; **III**, 232, *251*
Ricketts, W., **III**, 319, 320, 330, *338*
Rickman, J., **II**, 259, *277*
Ricon, C., **V**, 296, *303*
Riddle, J. M., **II**, 347, 360, 368, *376*
Riddle, O., **II**, 40, *58*, 64, *95*
Rideout, V. J., **I**, 109, *132*; **IV**, 390, *409*; **V**, 349, 350, 355, 356, 357, 358, 361, 362, 363, 364, *372*
Ridge, B., **I**, 267, *273*, 408, *410*; **IV**, 167, *174*; **V**, 116, *134*, 159, *164*
Ridgeway, D., **IV**, 318, *326*; **V**, 228, *239*
Ridley, C. A., **V**, 245, *265*
Ridley-Johnson, R., **V**, 342, *346*
Rie, H., **I**, 356, *378*
Rieber, M., **II**, 221, *228*
Rieder, R., **IV**, 302, *324*
Riegel, K., **III**, 398, *412*
Rienzi, B. M., **IV**, 273, *291*
Rieser-Danner, L., **III**, 227, *250*
Riggins, R., **I**, 61, *66*
Riggins, R., Jr., **III**, 217, *245*
Riggins-Caspers, K., **I**, 316, *326*
Riggs, E. P., **IV**, 262, 280, *284*
Riggs, M. L., **IV**, 340, *354*
Rigler, D., **III**, 417, *437*
Rijt-Plooij, H. H. C., **II**, 104, 107, 108, 109, 118, 120, *138*
Riksen-Walraven, J. M., **III**, 425, *437*; **V**, 173, 190, *193*
Riley, C., **III**, 320, *338*
Riley, D., **IV**, 128, 130, 132, 135, 136, 141, 146, *147*, *148*; **V**, 287, *302*
Rimm, S., **V**, 208, 209, *217*
Rimmer, M., **III**, 408, *411*
Rinaldi, C. M., **III**, 276, *282*
Rindfleisch, N., **I**, 314, 317, 318, 324, *326*
Rinehart, P., **I**, 107, 126, *127*
Rinholm, J., **I**, 210, *225*
Riniti, J., **IV**, 306, *322*
Rinne, A., **I**, 17, *39*
Riordan, D., **IV**, 301, 302, *324*
Riordan, K., **I**, 23, *41*
Rios, D. I., **IV**, 31, *41*
Rios-Kohn, R., **I**, 301, *309*
Ripp, C., **II**, 80, *96*
Risenhoover, N., **I**, 20, *38*
Risley, T. R., **I**, 22, 29, *37*, 197, *220*, 403, *413*; **II**, 239, *249*, 286, 289, 299, *310*,*312*
Risman, B. J., **I**, 193, *223*
Rispens, J., **I**, 301, *311*

AI-84

Author Index

Wisconsin v. Yoder, **V**, 20, *34*, 470, 476, 477, 481, *485*
Wise, D. A., **II**, 44, *60*
Wise, L., **III**, 43, *64*
Wise, R. A., **II**, 77, 78, *97*
Wise, S., **III**, 17, *23*, 341, *360*
Wissoker, D., **V**, 382, *402*
Witcher-Alagna, S., **V**, 443, 452, *462*
Witherspoon, R., **I**, 241, *252*
Witsberger, C., **V**, 382, *405*
Witt, A., **V**, 323, *326*
Wittig, B. A., **III**, 400, *409*
Wittig, D. S., **II**, 23, *26*
Wittmer, D. S., **V**, 386, *405*
Wohlwill, J. F., **II**, 282, 285, 291, *314*
Wolchik, S., **V**, 127, *137*
Wolchik, S. A., **I**, 204, 205, *218*, 264, *274*; **III**, 293, 294, *310*
Wolf, A., **II**, 273, *278*
Wolf, A. W., **II**, 273, *280*; **IV**, *354*
Wolf, B., **III**, 127, 128, 129, *140*; **V**, 281, *309*
Wolf, B. M., **III**, 127, *140*
Wolf, D. A., **V**, 382, 390, *405*
Wolf, D. L., **IV**, *92*
Wolf, D. P., **III**, 263, *286*
Wolf, E., **III**, 566, 570, 571, 576, 577, 583, 590, *596*, *599*
Wolf, E. R., **IV**, 22, 24, 32, *46*
Wolf, M., **IV**, 63, 65, 72, *92*
Wolfe, B., **III**, 181, *209*, 443, *458*; **IV**, 111, *118*
Wolfe, D. A., **IV**, 361, 370, 379, *384*, *388*; **V**, 25, *32*, 284, 285, *309*, 368, *373*
Wolfer, L. T., **II**, 221, *229*
Wolff, P. H., **II**, 190, 192, *203*
Wolfinger, N. H., **III**, 290, *315*
Wolfsdorf, J. I., **V**, 337, *345*
Wolfshorf, J., **V**, 338, 341, *345*
Wolin, S., **III**, 288, *315*
Wolinsky, F. D., **V**, 450, *462*
Wolke, D., **I**, 331, *354*
Wolkind, S. M., **I**, 282, 283, *307*; **III**, 373, *388*; **IV**, 191, *201*; **V**, 72, *85*
Wolkind, S. N., **IV**, 190, *202*
Wolman, C., **III**, 521, *532*
Wolock, I., **IV**, 335, *359*
Womack, M., **II**, 221, *228*
Wonderlick, M., **V**, 399, *400*
Wong, M. G., **IV**, 80, *92*
Wong, P., **III**, 514, *535*
Wong, P. Y., **II**, 62, 69, *90*, *94*, 148, 150, *175*; **III**, 35, *66*
Wood, B. A., **II**, 11, *30*
Wood, C., **I**, 241, *252*; **III**, 353, *358*, *360*
Wood, D., **I**, 53, *71*, 85, *97*; **II**, 119, *140*; **III**, 257, *286*; **V**, 98, *110*
Wood, J., **II**, 209, 223, *228*; **III**, 241, *250*; **V**, 245, *267*
Wood, J. L., **IV**, 35, *41*
Wood, N., **V**, 451, *461*
Wood, S., **I**, 369, 370, *380*; **II**, 65, *97*
Wood, V., **III**, *172*, 567, *599*
Wooding, C., **II**, 238, *248*; **V**, 225, 229, 234, *237*

Woodruff, D., **II**, 110, *135*
Woods, J. R., **IV**, 340, *359*
Woods, M., **III**, 48, *73*
Woods, N. S., **I**, 338, *350*
Woodside, B., **II**, 52, *60*
Woodward, K., **III**, 143, 149, 152, 154, *169*
Woodworth, S., **II**, 239, *252*; **III**, 428, 432, *434*; **V**, 246, 247, 249, 250, 255, 256, 257, 259, 260, 261, *263*, *264*, *267*
Wooley, H., **IV**, 309, *325*
Woolfolk, R. L., **IV**, 373, *386*
Woolford, E., **I**, 282, *308*
Woolgar, M., **I**, 195, 222; **IV**, 319, *321*
Wooliever, D. E., **I**, 331, *352*
Woollett, A., **III**, 276, 277, 278, *285*, *286*
Woolley, H., **IV**, 309, *325*
Wootton, J. M., **V**, 129, *137*
Worchel, F. F., **II**, 153, *181*
Wordsworth, W., **III**, 581, *599*
Workk, B. A., **III**, 11, *24*
Workman, E., **I**, 398, *412*; **IV**, 314, *321*; **V**, 130, *136*
World Health Organization, **II**, 285, 295, *314*; **V**, 60, *88*
Worsfold, V. L., **V**, 5, 6, *34*
Worthman, C. M., **II**, 146, 149, 155, 156, 160, 166, 167, *176*, *180*, *181*
Worthy, J., **V**, 356, *373*
Wozniak, P., **I**, 399, *413*; **V**, 278, *304*
Wozniak, R. H., **I**, 80, *94*
Wrangham, R. W., **II**, 100, *138*
Wright, A., **IV**, 262, *284*
Wright, B., **III**, 496, *505*, 520, 528, *530*, 545, *559*; **V**, 71, *83*
Wright, D., **IV**, 79, 80, 82, 83, 84, *91*
Wright, D. W., **II**, 221, *229*
Wright, E. J., **II**, 150, *178*
Wright, F. L., **V**, 210, *219*
Wright, J., **V**, 355, 361, 362, 363, *373*
Wright, J. C., **I**, 84, *98*, *101*; **II**, 300, *310*; **V**, 352, 355, 357, 362, 363, 364, 366, *371*, *372*, *373*
Wright, J. D., **II**, 234, 237, 242, *252*; **IV**, 102, *121*
Wright, J. M., **III**, 320, 323, *338*
Wright, M. K., **III**, 184, *203*
Wright, P. C., **II**, 100, 116, 129, 131, *140*
Wright, R., **II**, 108, *140*
Wright, S. A., **IV**, 377, *388*
Wright, S. R., **II**, 234, 237, 242, *252*; **IV**, 102, *121*
Wrightman, J., **V**, 104, *108*
Wrobel, G. M., **I**, 75, *101*, 303, *311*
Wroble, M., **III**, 518, *533*
Wu, C., **IV**, 208, *225*
Wu, C.-I., **I**, 29, *41*; **V**, 73, *88*
Wu, D. Y. H., **IV**, 67, 72, 75, 80, *92*
Wu, M., **V**, 324, *327*
Wulczyn, F. H., **III**, 161, *167*
Wundt, W., **II**, 189, *203*
Wurf, E., **III**, 495, *507*
Wust, S., **II**, 148, *177*
Wyatt, F., **III**, 571, 576, 588, *599*
Wyatt, J., **V**, 21, 22, 23, *34*

Wyckoff, J. L., **III**, 398, 399, 409, *413*
Wyer, M. M., **III**, 308, *312*
Wyler, S. R., **IV**, 269, *293*
Wyllie, A., **III**, 7, *22*
Wynn, G. R., **III**, 29, *68*
Wynn, R. L., **III**, 229, *252*
Wynne, L. C., **IV**, 298, 302, *325*
Wynne, S. F., **I**, 315, 316, *327*
Wynne-Edwards, K. E., **II**, 44, *56*, 164, 165, 166, *177*, *179*, *180*, *181*; **III**, 35, 36, *73*

## X

Xeri, M. L., **I**, 214, *220*
Xia, Y., **III**, 492, *507*
Xie, Q., **IV**, 74, *93*
Xie, Y., **IV**, 82, *88*
Xing, G., **II**, 84, *94*
Xu, X., **III**, 30, *73*

## Y

Yaffe, S., **I**, 345, *353*
Yalom, I., **III**, 579, *599*
Yamamoto, T., **III**, 403, *410*
Yamamura, H. I., **II**, 76, *88*
Yamamura, N., **II**, 164, *181*
Yamasaki, K., **III**, 550, *562*; **V**, 314, *328*
Yamomato, A. E., **II**, 116, *140*
Yando, R., **I**, 335, *350*
Yang, M., **V**, 324, *327*
Yang, Q. Z., **II**, 79, *91*, *97*
Yang, R., **I**, 29, *35*; **III**, 427, *435*
Yang, X., **I**, 316, *327*
Yao, E. L., **IV**, 80, 81, 82, 83, *93*
Yarbrough, C., **III**, 262, *283*
Yarlas, A., **I**, 75, *98*
Yarmel, P. W., **I**, 399, 400, *412*
Yarrow, A. L., **III**, 45, *73*
Yarrow, L. J., **I**, 62, *71*, 288, 295, *311*; **III**, 17, *25*, 185, 187, *212*, 363, 366, *388*, 581, *598*; **V**, 228, *241*
Yarrow, M. R., **I**, 397, *418*; **III**, 585, *599*; **IV**, 343, *359*; **V**, 125, *142*
Yates, A. M., **I**, 316, *326*
Yates, M., **V**, 127, *142*
Yates, W. R., **I**, 245, 248, 249, *251*; **IV**, 184, 191, *198*, 311, *322*, 336, *359*; **V**, 70, *85*
Yau, J., **I**, 106, 118, 119, 123, *132*, *133*
Ybarra, G. L., **II**, 222, *229*; **V**, 318, *328*
Ybarra, V. C., **IV**, 33, *44*
Ye, R. M., **I**, 257, 261, 262, *272*
Yeargin-Allsopp, M., **III**, 398, *410*
Yee, B. W. K., **IV**, 67, 71, *93*
Yee, J. L., **I**, 150, *159*
Yell, M. L., **I**, 372, *381*
Yeo, J. A. G., **II**, 39, *60*
Yerkes, A. W., **II**, 99, *140*
Yerkes, R. M., **II**, 99, 106, 108, 118, 119, 123, *140*
Yeung, W. J., **III**, 30, 31, 32, 33, 48, 49, *73*, 190, *206*; **IV**, 399, *408*
Yi, J., **III**, 492, *507*

# Subject Index

An environmentally friendly book printed and bound in England by www.printondemand-worldwide.com

#0254 - 270515 - C0 - 254/178/33 - PB - 9780415648226